Lecture Notes in Computer Science   11679

More information about this series at http://www.springer.com/series/7412

Mario Vento · Gennaro Percannella (Eds.)

Computer Analysis of Images and Patterns

18th International Conference, CAIP 2019
Salerno, Italy, September 3–5, 2019
Proceedings, Part II

Springer

Editors
Mario Vento ⓘ
Department of Computer and Electrical
Engineering and Applied Mathematics
University of Salerno
Fisciano (SA), Italy

Gennaro Percannella ⓘ
Department of Computer and Electrical
Engineering and Applied Mathematics
University of Salerno
Fisciano (SA), Italy

ISSN 0302-9743   ISSN 1611-3349   (electronic)
Lecture Notes in Computer Science
ISBN 978-3-030-29890-6   ISBN 978-3-030-29891-3   (eBook)
https://doi.org/10.1007/978-3-030-29891-3

LNCS Sublibrary: SL6 – Image Processing, Computer Vision, Pattern Recognition, and Graphics

This Springer imprint is published by the registered company Springer Nature Switzerland AG
The registered company address is: Gewerbestrasse 11, 6330 Cham, Switzerland

Preface

This book is one of two volumes for the proceedings of the 18th international Conference on Computer Analysis of Images and Patterns (CAIP 2019), which was held in Salerno, Italy, during September 3–5, 2019.

CAIP is a series of biennial international conferences devoted to all aspects of computer vision, image analysis and processing, pattern recognition, and related fields. Previous conferences were held in Ystad, Valletta, York, Seville, Münster, Vienna, Paris, Groningen, Warsaw, Ljubljana, Kiel, Prague, Budapest, Dresden, Leipzig, Wismar, and Berlin.

The conference included a main track held during September 3–5 at the Grand Hotel Salerno in the center of the city of Salerno. The conference hosted four keynote talks provided by world-renowned experts: James Ferryman (University of Reading, UK) gave a talk on "Biometrics and Surveillance on the Move: Vision for Border Security," Luc Brun (ENSICAEN, France) on "Graph Classification," Gian Luca Marcialis (University of Cagliari, Italy) on "Fingerprint Presentation Attacks Detection: from the "loss of innocence" to the "International Fingerprint Liveness Detection" competition," and Nicolai Petkov (University of Groningen, The Netherlands) on "Representation learning with trainable COSFIRE filters."

The scientific program of the conference was extended with satellite events held at the University of Salerno on the day before and after the main event. In particular, two tutorials on "Contemporary Deep Learning Models and their Applications," by Aditya Nigam and Arnav Bhavsar (Indian Institute of Technology Mandi) and on "Active Object Recognition: a survey of a (re-)emerging domain," by Francesco Setti (University of Verona, Italy) were given on September 2; while on September 6 we had a contest entitled "Which is Which? - Evaluation of local descriptors for image matching in real-world scenarios," organized by Fabio Bellavia and Carlo Colombo (University of Florence, Italy), together with two workshops, namely "Deep-learning based computer vision for UAV," by Hamideh Kerdegari and Manzoor Razaak (Kingston University, UK) and Matthew Broadbent (Lancaster University, UK), and "Visual Computing and Machine Learning for Biomedical Applications," by Sara Colantonio and Daniela Giorgi (ISTI-CNR, Italy) and Bogdan J. Matuszewski (UCLan, UK).

The program covered high-quality scientific contributions in deep learning, 3D vision, biomedical image and pattern analysis, biometrics, brain-inspired methods, document analysis, face and gestures, feature extraction, graph-based methods, high-dimensional topology methods, human pose estimation, image/video indexing and retrieval, image restoration, keypoint detection, machine learning for image and pattern analysis, mobile multimedia, model-based vision, motion and tracking, object recognition, segmentation, shape representation and analysis, and vision for robotics.

The contributions for CAIP 2019 were selected based on a minimum of two, but mostly three reviews. Among 183 submissions, 106 were accepted with an acceptance rate of 58%.

We are grateful to the Steering Committee of CAIP for giving us the honor of organizing this reputable conference in Italy. We thank the International Association for Pattern Recognition (IAPR) that endorsed the conference, Springer that offered the best paper award, and the Italian Association for Computer Vision, Pattern Recognition and Machine Learning (CVPL) that offered the CVPL prize assigned to a young researcher, author of the best paper presented the conference. We thank the University of Salerno for the sponsorship and, specifically, its Department of Computer and Electrical Engineering and Applied Mathematics, also SAST Gmbh, A.I. Tech srl, and AI4Health srl as gold sponsors, and Nexsoft spa, Gesan srl, and Hanwha Techwin Europe Ltd. as silver sponsors.

We thank the authors for submitting their valuable works to CAIP; this is of prime importance for the success of the event. However, the success of a conference also depends on a number of volunteers. We would like to thank the reviewers and the Program Committee members for their excellent work. We also thank the local Organizing Committee and all the other volunteers who helped us organize CAIP 2019.

We hope that all participants had a pleasant and fruitful stay in Salerno.

September 2019   Mario Vento
                                                       Gennaro Percannella

Organization

CAIP 2019 was organized by the Intelligent Machines for the recognition of Video, Images and Audio (MIVIA) Laboratory, Department of Computer and Electrical Engineering and Applied Mathematics, University of Salerno, Italy.

Executive Committees

Conference Chairs

Mario Vento   University of Salerno, Italy
Gennaro Percannella   University of Salerno, Italy

Program Chairs

Pasquale Foggia   University of Salerno, Italy
Luca Greco   University of Salerno, Italy
Pierluigi Ritrovato   University of Salerno, Italy
Nicola Strisciuglio   University of Groningen, The Netherlands

Local Organizing Committee

Vincenzo Carletti   University of Salerno, Italy
Antonio Greco   University of Salerno, Italy
Alessia Saggese   University of Salerno, Italy
Vincenzo Vigilante   University of Salerno, Italy

Web and Publicity Chair

Vincenzo Carletti   University of Salerno, Italy

Steering Committee

George Azzopardi   University of Groningen, The Netherlands
Michael Felsberg   Linköping University, Sweden
Edwin Hancock   University of York, UK
Xiaoyi Jiang   University of Münster, Germany
Reinhard Klette   Auckland University of Technology, New Zealand
Walter G. Kropatsch   Vienna University of Technology, Austria
Gennaro Percannella   University of Salerno, Italy
Nicolai Petkov   University of Groningen, The Netherlands
Pedro Real Jurado   University of Seville, Spain
Mario Vento   University of Salerno, Italy

Program Committee

Marco Aiello	University of Stuttgart, Germany
Enrique Alegre	University of Leon, Spain
Muhammad Raza Ali	InfoTech, Pakistan
Furqan Aziz	Institute of Management Sciences, Pakistan
George Azzopardi	University of Groningen, The Netherlands
Andrew Bagdanov	Computer Vision Center, Spain
Donald Bailey	Massey University, New Zealand
Antonio Bandera	University of Malaga, Spain
Ardhendu Behera	Edge Hill University, UK
Abdel Belaid	University of Lorraine, France
Fabio Bellavia	University of Florence, Italy
Michael Biehl	University of Groningen, The Netherlands
Gunilla Borgefors	Uppsala University, Sweden
Kerstin Bunte	University of Groningen, The Netherlands
Kenneth Camilleri	University of Malta, Malta
Vincenzo Carletti	University of Salerno, Italy
Modesto Castrillon Santana	University of Las Palmas de Gran Canaria, Spain
Kwok-Ping Chan	University of Hong Kong, SAR China
Rama Chellappa	University of Maryland, USA
Dmitry Chetverikov	Hungarian Academy of Sciences, Hungary
Danilo Coimbra	Federal University of Bahia, Brazil
Carlo Colombo	University of Florence, Italy
Donatello Conte	University of Tours, France
Carl James Debono	University of Malta, Malta
Santa Di Cataldo	Politecnico di Torino, Italy
Mariella Dimiccoli	Institut de Robòtica i Informàtica Industrial, Spain
Junyu Dong	University of China, China
Alexandre Falcao	University of Campinas (Unicamp), Brazil
Giovanni Maria Farinella	University of Catania, Italy
Reuben A. Farrugia	University of Malta, Malta
Gernot Fink	TU Dortmund University, Germany
Patrizio Frosini	University of Bologna, Italy
Eduardo Garea	Advanced Technologies Applications Center, Cuba
Benoit Gaüzère	Normandie Université, France
Daniela Giorgi	ISTI-CNR, Italy
Rocio Gonzalez-Diaz	University of Seville, Spain
Javier Gonzalez-Jimenez	University of Malaga, Spain
Antonio Greco	University of Salerno, Italy
Cosmin Grigorescu	European Patent Office, EU
Miguel A. Gutiérrez-Naranjo	University of Seville, Spain
Michal Haindl	Czech Academy of Sciences, Czech Republic
Vaclav Hlavac	Czech Technical University in Prague, Czech Republic
Yo-Ping Huang	National Taipei University of Technology, Taiwan

Atsushi Imiya	IMIT Chiba University, Japan
Xiaoyi Jiang	University of Münster, Germany
Maria Jose Jimenez	University of Seville, Spain
Martin Kampel	Vienna University of Technology, Austria
Hamideh Kerdegari	Kingston University of London, UK
Nahum Kiryati	Tel Aviv University, Israel
Reinhard Klette	Auckland University of Technology, New Zealand
Walter G. Kropatsch	Vienna University of Technology, Austria
Wenqi Li	King's College London, UK
Guo-Shiang Lin	China Medical University, Taiwan
Agnieszka Lisowska	University of Silesia, Poland
Josep Llados	Universitat Autònoma de Barcelona, Spain
Rebeca Marfil	University of Malaga, Spain
Manuel J. Marín-Jiménez	University of Cordoba, Spain
Heydi Mendez-Vazquez	Advanced Technologies Applications Center, Cuba
Eckart Michaelsen	Fraunhofer IOSB, Germany
Mariofanna Milanova	University of Arkansas at Little Rock, USA
Adrian Muscat	University of Malta, Malta
Paolo Napoletano	University of Milan Bicocca, Italy
Andreas Neocleous	University of Groningen, The Netherlands
Mark Nixon	University of Southampton, UK
Stavros Ntalampiras	University of Milan, Italy
Darian Onchis	University of Vienna, Austria
Arkadiusz Orłowski	Warsaw University of Life Sciences, Poland
Constantinos Pattichis	University of Cyprus, Cyprus
Marios Pattichis	University of New Mexico, USA
Gennaro Percannella	University of Salerno, Italy
Nicolai Petkov	University of Groningen, The Netherlands
Fiora Pirri	University of Rome Sapienza, Italy
Giovanni Poggi	University of Naples Federico II, Italy
Xianbiao Qi	Shenzhen Research Institute of Big Data, China
Manzoor Razaak	Kingston University, UK
Pedro Real Jurado	University of Seville, Spain
Emanuele Rodolà	University of Rome Sapienza, Italy
Robert Sablatnig	Vienna University of Technology, Austria
Alessia Saggese	University of Salerno, Italy
Hideo Saito	Keio University, Japan
Albert Ali Salah	Utrecht University, Turkey
Angel Sanchez	Rey Juan Carlos University, Spain
Lidia Sánchez-González	University of León, Spain
Antonio-José Sánchez-Salmerón	Universitat Politècnica de València, Spain
Gabriella Sanniti di Baja	ICAR-CNR, Italy
Carlo Sansone	University of Naples Federico II, Italy
Sudeep Sarkar	University of South Florida, USA
Christos Schizas	University of Cyprus, Cyprus

Klamer Schutte	TNO, The Netherlands
Francesc Serratosa	Universitat Rovira i Virgili, Spain
Fabrizio Smeraldi	Queen Mary University of London, UK
Akihiro Sugimoto	National Institute of Informatics, Japan
Bart Ter Haar Romeny	Eindhoven University of Technology, The Netherlands
Bernard Tiddeman	Aberystwyth University, UK
Klaus Toennies	Otto-von-Guericke University, Germany
Javier Toro	Desarrollo para la Ciencia y la Tecnología, Venezuela
Andrea Torsello	University of Venice Ca Foscari, Italy
Francesco Tortorella	University of Salerno, Italy
Carlos M. Travieso-Gonzalez	University of Las Palmas de Gran Canaria, Spain
Radim Tylecek	University of Edinburgh, UK
Herwig Unger	FernUniversität in Hagen, Germany
Ernest Valveny	Universitat Autònoma de Barcelona, Spain
Mario Vento	University of Salerno, Italy
Vincenzo Vigilante	University of Salerno, Italy
Arnold Wiliem	University of Queensland, Australia
Michael H. F. Wilkinson	University of Groningen, The Netherlands
Richard Wilson	University of York, UK
Wei Wi Yan	Auckland University of Technology, New Zealand
Zhao Zhang	Hefei University of Technology, China

Invited Speakers

James Ferryman	University of Reading, UK
Luc Brun	ENSICAEN, France
Gian Luca Marcialis	University of Cagliari, Italy
Nicolai Petkov	University of Groningen, The Netherlands

Tutorials

Aditya Nigam	Indian Institute of Technology Mandi, India
Arnav Bhavsar	Indian Institute of Technology Mandi, India
Francesco Setti	University of Verona, Italy

Workshops

Hamideh Kerdegari	Kingston University, UK
Manzoor Razaak	Kingston University, UK
Matthew Broadbent	Lancaster University, UK
Sara Colantonio	ISTI-CNR, Italy
Daniela Giorgi	ISTI-CNR, Italy
Bogdan J. Matuszewski	UCLan, UK

Contest

Fabio Bellavia	University of Florence, Italy
Carlo Colombo	University of Florence, Italy

Additional Reviewer

W. Al-Nabki	A. Griffin	M. Norouzifard
M. G. Al-Sarayreh	D. Helm	E. Paluzo-Hidalgo
D. Batavia	J. Hladůvka	C. Pramerdorfer
M. G. Bergomi	H. Ho	E. Rusakov
P. Bhowmick	C. Istin	J. R. R. Sarmiento
R. Biswas	A. Joshhi	J. Smith
P. Blanco	D. Kossmann	M. Soriano-Trigueros
M. Callieri	P. Marín-Reyes	E. Talavera
D. Chaves	F. A. Moreno	F. Wolf
D. Freire-Obregón	M. Mortara	D. Zuñiga-Noël
A. Gangwar	F. Moya	

Endorsing Institution

International Association for Pattern Recognition (IAPR)

Sponsoring Institutions

Department of Computer and Electrical Engineering and Applied Mathematics, University of Salerno
Springer Lecture Notes in Computer Science
Italian Association for Computer Vision, Pattern Recognition and Machine Learning (CVPL)

Sponsoring Companies

A.I. Tech srl
SAST Gmbh
AI4Health srl
Gesan srl
Hanwha Techwin Europe Ltd
Nexsoft SpA

Contents – Part II

Contents – Part I

Image and Texture Analysis

Machine Learning for Image and Pattern Analysis

Data Sets and Benchmarks

Structural and Computational Pattern Recognition

Poster Session

Poster Session

3D Color CLUT Compression by Multi-scale Anisotropic Diffusion

David Tschumperlé(✉), Christine Porquet, and Amal Mahboubi

Normandie University, UNICAEN, ENSICAEN, CNRS, GREYC, 14000 Caen, France
david.tschumperle@ensicaen.fr
http://www.greyc.fr

Abstract. *3D CLUT*s (Color Look Up Tables) are popular digital models used in image and video processing for color grading, simulation of analog films, and more generally for the application of various color transformations. The large size of these models leads to data storage issues when trying to distribute them on a large scale. Here, a highly effective lossy compression technique for *3D CLUT*s is proposed. It is based on a multi-scale anisotropic diffusion scheme. Our method exhibits an average compression rate of more than 99%, while ensuring visually indistinguishable differences with the application of the original *CLUT*s.

Keywords: *3D CLUT*s · Generic color transformations · Compression of smooth data · Anisotropic diffusion

1 Introduction

Color calibration and correction tools are generally used in the fields of photograph retouching, video processing and other artistic disciplines, in order to change the color mood of digital images. *CLUT*s (*Color Look Up Tables*) are among the most popular digital models used for color calibration and alteration.

Let RGB be the continuous domain $[0, 255]^3 \subset \mathbb{R}^3$ representing the $3D$ color cube (of discretized resolution 256^3). A *CLUT* is a compact color function on RGB, modelled as a $3D$ associative array encoding the precomputed transform for all existing colors [1].

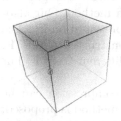

(a) *CLUT*, visualized in 3*D*   (b) Original image   (c) Image after transformation

Fig. 1. Application of a $3D$ *CLUT* to a $2D$ image for a color alteration (here, to simulate vintage color fading). (Color figure online)

© Springer Nature Switzerland AG 2019
M. Vento and G. Percannella (Eds.): CAIP 2019, LNCS 11679, pp. 3–14, 2019.
https://doi.org/10.1007/978-3-030-29891-3_1

Let $\mathbf{F} : RGB \rightarrow RGB$ be a $3D$ $CLUT$.

Applying $\mathbf{F}$ to a color image $\mathbf{I} : \Omega \rightarrow RGB$ is done as follows:

$$\forall \mathbf{p} \in \Omega, \quad \mathbf{I}_{(\mathbf{p})}^{\text{modified}} = \mathbf{F}(I_{R(\mathbf{p})}, I_{G(\mathbf{p})}, I_{B(\mathbf{p})})$$

where I_R, I_G and I_B are the RGB color components of $\mathbf{I}$. It should be noted that, most often, a $CLUT$ is a volumic function that is *continuous* or, at worst, *piecewise continuous* (Fig. 1a).

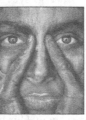

Original image "Color Negative" "60's" "Ilford Delta 3200" "Late Sunset"

Fig. 2. Generic nature of color transformations allowed by $3D$ $CLUT$s. (Color figure online)

Figure 2 exhibits a small set of various colorimetric modifications done with $CLUT$s, taken from [2,10]. It illustrates the large diversity of the effects that $CLUT$s allow, *e.g.* color fading, chromaticity boost, color inversion, hue shift, black-and-white conversion, contrast enhancement, etc.

Usually, a $CLUT$ is stored, either as an $ASCII$ zipped file (with extension file .cube.zip) which maps a color triple $\mathbf{F}_{(\mathbf{X})}$ to each voxel $\mathbf{X}$ of the RGB cube (in float-valued format), or as a .png image corresponding to the set of all colors $\mathbf{F}_{(\mathbf{X})}$ unrolled as a $2D$ image (Fig. 3b). In both cases, the large amount of color voxels composing the RGB cube implies a storage size often larger than a megabyte (Mb) for a single $CLUT$, even when the RGB space is subsampled (typically to sizes $32^3, 48^3, 64^3, \dots$). There arises the issue of storing and delivering $CLUT$s files at a large scale (several hundreds at a time).

Here, this issue is addressed: an efficient technique for $CLUT$ compression is put forward, as well as the corresponding decompression method. Our algorithm takes a $CLUT$ $\mathbf{F}$ as input and generates a smaller representation $\mathbf{F}_c$. The reconstruction algorithm operates on $\mathbf{F}_c$ to generate a reconstructed $CLUT$ $\widetilde{\mathbf{F}}$. Our compression scheme is said to be *lossy* [11], as $\widetilde{\mathbf{F}}$ is different from $\mathbf{F}$, but with an error that remains visually unnoticeable.

Surprisingly, very few references dealing with $CLUT$ compression can be found in the literature. In [4], a *lossless* $CLUT$ compression method is proposed; it is based on two different predictive coding schemes, the former being differential hierarchical coding and the latter cellular interpolative predictive coding. In both cases, a prior preprocessing step for data reorganization is needed. However, experimentations are only made on small-sized $CLUT$s (resolution 17^3),

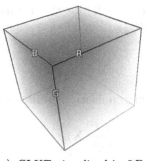

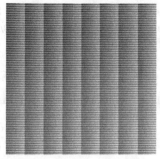

a) *CLUT* visualized in 3*D*   b) Storage as a 2*D* image

Fig. 3. Storage of a *CLUT* as a `.png` file: The 64^3 colors of the *CLUT* are here unrolled as a 2D image of size 512^2. Despite the apparent continuity of the 3*D* function, the 2*D* resulting image exhibits lots of discontinuities, which make its compression harder.

and the *lossless* method leads to compression rates (around 30%) that are much less effective than what we get with our approach.

In essence, our *CLUT* compression technique relies on the storage of a set of color keypoints in *RGB*, associated to a fast interpolation algorithm performing a dense 3*D* reconstruction using anisotropic diffusion *PDEs*. It should be noted that the idea of compressing/decompressing 2*D* image data by diffusion *PDEs* has already been proposed in [8], but the discontinuous aspect of natural images used for their experiments makes it actually harder to achieve high compression rates. In our case, the diffusion model proves to be perfectly suited for interpolating colors in the *RGB* cube, thanks to the clear continuity of the 3*D* dense functions we are trying to compress.

The paper is organized as follows: in Sect. 2, our *CLUT* reconstruction algorithm is described and the corresponding compression scheme is developed in Sect. 3. Our method is evaluated on a large variety of *CLUT*s, and compression/reconstruction results are finally discussed in Sect. 4.

2   Reconstruction of a 3*D CLUT* from a Set of Keypoints

First, let us assume we have a set $\mathcal{K} = \{\mathbf{K}_k \in RGB \times RGB \mid k = 1 \ldots N\}$ of N color keypoints, located in the *RGB* cube, such as $\mathcal{K}$ provides a sparse representation of a *CLUT* $\mathbf{F} : RGB \to RGB$.

The kth keypoint of $\mathcal{K}$ is defined by vector

$$\mathbf{K}_k = (\mathbf{X}_k, \mathbf{C}_k) = (x_k, y_k, z_k, R_k, G_k, B_k),$$

where $\mathbf{X}_k = (x_k, y_k, z_k)$ is the 3*D* keypoint position in the *RGB* cube and $\mathbf{C}_k = (R_k, G_k, B_k)$ its associated color.

Reconstruction Scheme: In order to reconstruct $\mathbf{F}$ from $\mathcal{K}$, we propose to propagate/average the colors $\mathbf{C}_k$ of the keypoints in the whole *RGB* domain through a specific diffusion process. Let $d_{\mathcal{K}} : RGB \to \mathbb{R}^+$ be the distance function, giving for each point $\mathbf{X} = (x, y, z)$ of RGB, the Euclidian distance to the set of keypoints $\mathcal{K}$, $i.e.$

$$\forall \mathbf{X} \in RGB, \qquad d_{\mathcal{K}(\mathbf{X})} = \inf_{k \in 0 \dots N} \|\mathbf{X} - \mathbf{X}_k\|$$

$\mathbf{F}$ is then reconstructed by solving the following anisotropic diffusion PDE:

$$\forall \mathbf{X} \in RGB, \qquad \frac{\partial \mathbf{F}}{\partial t}(\mathbf{X}) = m_{(\mathbf{X})} \frac{\partial^2 \mathbf{F}}{\partial \eta^2}(\mathbf{X}) \tag{1}$$

$$\text{where} \quad \eta = \frac{\nabla d_{\mathcal{K}(\mathbf{X})}}{\|\nabla d_{\mathcal{K}(\mathbf{X})}\|} \quad \text{and} \quad m_{(\mathbf{X})} = \begin{cases} 0 & \text{if } \exists k, \ \mathbf{X} = \mathbf{X}_k \\ 1 & \text{otherwise} \end{cases}$$

From an algorithmic point of view, this PDE can classically be solved by an $Euler$ method, starting from an initial estimate $\mathbf{F}_{t=0}$ as close as possible to a solution of (1). A quite good estimate for $\mathbf{F}_{t=0}$ is actually obtained by propagating the colors $\mathbf{C}_k$ inside the Voronoï cells associated to the set of points $\mathbf{X}_k$ (for instance by $watershed$-like propagation [5]), then by smoothing it by an isotropic $3D$ gaussian filter (Fig. 4b). A more efficient multi-scale scheme for estimating $\mathbf{F}_{t=0}$ is detailed hereafter.

From a geometric point of view, the diffusion PDE (1) can be seen as a local color averaging filter along the lines connecting each point $\mathbf{X}$ of the RGB cube to its nearest keypoint [14]. This filtering is done for all points $\mathbf{X}$ of RGB, except for the keypoints $\mathbf{X}_k$ which keep their initial color $\mathbf{C}_k$ throughout the diffusion process. Figure 4 below shows the reconstruction of a dense $CLUT$ with (1), from a set $\mathcal{K}$ composed of 6 colored keypoints.

Spatial Discretization: Numerically, $d_{\mathcal{K}}$ is efficiently computed (in linear time) by a distance transform, such as the one proposed in [9]. The discretization of the diffusion directions η requires some care, as the gradient $\nabla d_{\mathcal{K}}$ is not formally defined on the whole RGB domain. Actually, $d_{\mathcal{K}}$ is not differentiable at the peaks of the distance function, $i.e.$ at the points that are local maxima. Therefore, the following numerical scheme for the discretization of $\nabla d_{\mathcal{K}}$ is put forward:

$$\nabla d_{\mathcal{K}(\mathbf{X})} = \begin{pmatrix} \text{maxabs}(\partial_x^{\text{for}} d_{\mathcal{K}}, \partial_x^{\text{back}} d_{\mathcal{K}}) \\ \text{maxabs}(\partial_y^{\text{for}} d_{\mathcal{K}}, \partial_y^{\text{back}} d_{\mathcal{K}}) \\ \text{maxabs}(\partial_z^{\text{for}} d_{\mathcal{K}}, \partial_z^{\text{back}} d_{\mathcal{K}}) \end{pmatrix} \tag{2}$$

where

$$\text{maxabs}(a, b) = \begin{cases} a \text{ if } |a| > |b| \\ b \text{ otherwise} \end{cases}$$

and

$$\partial_x^{\text{for}} d_{\mathcal{K}} = d_{\mathcal{K}(x+1,y,z)} - d_{\mathcal{K}(x,y,z)}$$
$$\partial_x^{\text{back}} d_{\mathcal{K}} = d_{\mathcal{K}(x,y,z)} - d_{\mathcal{K}(x-1,y,z)}$$

are the discrete $forward$ and $backward$ first derivative approximations of the continuous function $d_{\mathcal{K}}$ along the x axis. We proceed similarly along y and z.

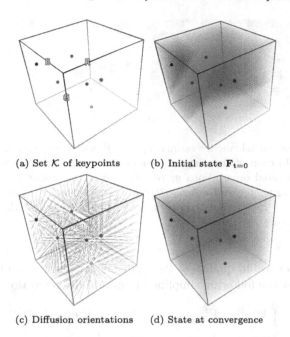

(a) Set $\mathcal{K}$ of keypoints   (b) Initial state $\mathbf{F}_{t=0}$

(c) Diffusion orientations   (d) State at convergence

Fig. 4. Reconstruction of a *3D CLUT* $\mathbf{F}$ from a set of keypoints $\mathcal{K}$ using anisotropic diffusion PDE (1) (here, from 6 keypoints).

By doing so, one avoids locally misdirected estimations of η on the local maxima of $d_{\mathcal{K}}$, which systematically happen with the *centered, forward* or *backward* numerical schemes classically used for estimating the gradient, see Fig. 5.

In practice, complying to our spatial discretization scheme (2) has a great influence, both on the reconstruction quality of the *CLUT* $\mathbf{F}$ (in comparison with usual discretization schemes introducing visible artifacts on reconstructed structures), and on the effective time of convergence towards the solution of (1). A stable state is reached more quickly. This is particularly true with the use of the multi-scale scheme described hereafter, where reconstruction errors may be amplified when switching from a low resolution scale to a more detailed one.

Temporal Discretization: For the sake of algorithmic efficiency, the explicit *Euler* scheme corresponding to the evolution of (1) becomes the following *semi-implicit* scheme:

$$\frac{\mathbf{F}^{t+dt}-\mathbf{F}^t}{dt} = m_{(\mathbf{X})} \left[\mathbf{F}^t_{(\mathbf{X}+\eta)} + \mathbf{F}^t_{(\mathbf{X}-\eta)} - 2\,\mathbf{F}^{t+dt}_{(\mathbf{X})} \right]$$

which leads to:

$$\mathbf{F}^{t+dt}_{(\mathbf{X})} = \frac{\mathbf{F}^t_{(\mathbf{X})} + dt\, m_{(\mathbf{X})} \left[\mathbf{F}^t_{(\mathbf{X}+\eta)} + \mathbf{F}^t_{(\mathbf{X}-\eta)} \right]}{1 + 2\,dt\, m_{(\mathbf{X})}}$$

A major advantage of using such a *semi-implicit* scheme to implement the evolution of (1) is that you can choose dt arbitrarily large, without loss of stability

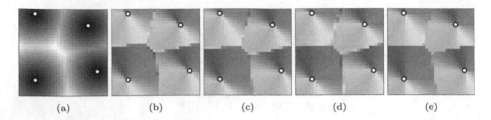

(a)   (b)   (c)   (d)   (e)

Fig. 5. Influence of our scheme for estimating the diffusion orientations η (shown here on a small 40×40 crop of the distance function $d_{\mathcal{K}}$). Hues displayed at each point represent the estimated orientations η: *(a) Keypoints and distance function $d_{\mathcal{K}}$, (b) Estimation of η using forward scheme $\partial^{for} d_{\mathcal{K}}$,(c) Estimation of η using backward scheme $\partial^{back} d_{\mathcal{K}}$, (d) Estimation of η using centered scheme $\frac{1}{2}(\partial^{for} d_{\mathcal{K}} + \partial^{back} d_{\mathcal{K}})$,(e) Estimation of η using our scheme (2).*

or significant decrease in quality of the diffusion process (as studied in [6,15]). Therefore, we get the following simplified temporal discretization scheme:

$$\begin{cases} \mathbf{F}^{t+dt}_{(\mathbf{X})} = \mathbf{F}^t_{(\mathbf{X})} & \text{if } m_{(\mathbf{X})} = 0 \\ \mathbf{F}^{t+dt}_{(\mathbf{X})} = \frac{1}{2}\left[\mathbf{F}^t_{(\mathbf{X}+\eta)} + \mathbf{F}^t_{(\mathbf{X}-\eta)}\right] & \text{otherwise} \end{cases} \tag{3}$$

where $\mathbf{F}^t_{(\mathbf{X}+\eta)}$ and $\mathbf{F}^t_{(\mathbf{X}-\eta)}$ are accurately estimated using tricubic spatial interpolation.

Starting from $\mathbf{F}_{t=0}$, the scheme (3) is iterated until convergence (Fig. 4d). It should be noted that, for each iteration, the computation of (3) can be advantageously parallelized, as the calculations are done independently for each voxel $\mathbf{X}$ of RGB.

Multi-scale Resolution: As with most numerical schemes involving diffusion *PDEs* [14], it can be observed that the number of iterations of (3) required to converge towards a stable solution of (1) increases quadratically with the $3D$ resolution of the $CLUT$ $\mathbf{F}$ to be reconstructed. In order to limit this number of iterations for high resolutions of $CLUT$s, we suggest to solve (1) by a *multi-scale ascending* technique.

Rather than initializing $\mathbf{F}_{t=0}$ by *watershed*-like propagation for computing the diffusion at resolution $(2^s)^3$, $\mathbf{F}_{t=0}$ is estimated as a trilinear upscaling of the $CLUT$ reconstructed at half resolution $(2^{s-1})^3$. The latter is closer to the stable state of the PDE (1) at resolution $(2^s)^3$, and the number of necessary iterations of (3) to reach convergence is considerably reduced. By performing this recursively, it is even possible to start the reconstruction of $\mathbf{F}$ at resolution 1^3 (by simply averaging the colors of all keypoints), then applying the diffusion scheme (3) successively on the upscaled results obtained at resolutions 2^3, 4^3, 8^3 ..., until the desired resolution is reached (Fig. 6).

Comparison with RBF Reconstruction: The reconstruction of a dense function from a set of isolated keypoints is an interpolation problem which has been already well documented in the literature [3,12]. Most traditional solutions to this

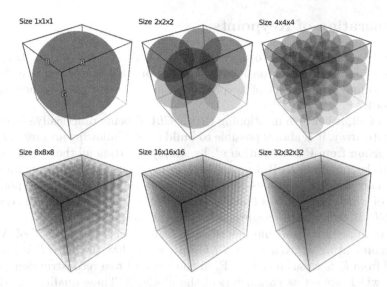

Fig. 6. Multi-scale reconstruction scheme: A reconstructed $CLUT$s at resolution $(2^s)^3$ is linearly upscaled and used as an initialization for applying the diffusion scheme at a higher resolution $(2^{s+1})^3$.

problem propose to model the function to be reconstructed as a weighted sum, whose number of terms is equal to the number of available keypoints. For instance, the popular RBF (*Radial Basis Function*) method applied to $CLUT$ reconstruction estimates each color component $\mathbf{F}^i$ of $\mathbf{F}$ ($i = R, G$ or B) by:

$$\forall \mathbf{X} \in RGB, \quad \mathbf{F}^i_{(\mathbf{X})} = \sum_{k=1}^{N} w^i_k \, \phi(\|\mathbf{X} - \mathbf{X}_k\|),$$

with $\phi : \mathbb{R}^+ \to \mathbb{R}$, a given function (*e.g.* $\phi(r) = r^2 \ln r$, for a *thin plate spline* interpolation [7]). The weights w^i_k are obtained by solving a linear system, involving the known values of the keypoints $\mathbf{C}_k$ and a matrix whose coefficients are $\phi(\|\mathbf{X}_p - \mathbf{X}_q\|)$, calculated for all possible pairs (p, q) of keypoints. This reconstruction technique generates $3D$ interpolations of good quality, and is simple to implement, as it can be calculated directly at full resolution. Unfortunately, its algorithmic complexity is expressed as $O(N^3 + N\,r^3)$ for the reconstruction of a $CLUT$ of resolution r^3, which becomes prohibitive when the number of keypoints increases notably (*e.g.* $N > 300$, which happens frequently in our case, see Fig. 8).

Conversely, the complexity of one single iteration of our diffusion scheme (3) is expressed as $O(r^3)$, regardless of the number of keypoints. Thanks to our multi-scale approach that speeds up convergence towards a stable state, no more than twenty diffusion iterations per reconstruction scale are necessary in practice. This ensures a reconstruction of a decent size $CLUT$ (*e.g.* resolution 64^3) in less than one second on a standard multi-core computer (for several tens of seconds with a RBF approach), and this, with an equally good reconstruction quality.

3   Generation of Keypoints

Now that the reconstruction of a dense CLUT $\mathbf{F}$ from a set of color keypoints $\mathcal{K}$ has been detailed, let us consider the inverse problem, *i.e.* given only $\mathbf{F}$, is it possible to find a sparse set of keypoints $\mathcal{K}$ that allows a good reconstruction quality of $\mathbf{F}$?

First of all, it is worth mentioning that a *CLUT* being practically stored as a $3D$ discrete array, it is always possible to build a set $\mathcal{K}$ allowing an *exact discrete reconstruction* from $\mathbf{F}$ at resolution r^3, by simply inserting all the r^3 color voxels from $\mathbf{F}$ as keypoints in $\mathcal{K}$. But as a *CLUT* is most often a continuous function, it is actually feasible to represent it fairly accurately by a set of keypoints $\mathcal{K}$ the size of which is *much less than the number of voxels* composing the discrete cube RGB. $\mathcal{K}$ then gives a *compressed* representation of $\mathbf{F}$.

The compression algorithm described hereafter generates a set $\mathcal{K}$ of N keypoints representing a given input *CLUT* $\mathbf{F}$, such that the *CLUT* $\widetilde{\mathbf{F}}_N$ reconstructed from $\mathcal{K}$ is close enough to $\mathbf{F}$, in the sense of two reconstruction quality criteria (which are set as parameters of the method). These quality criteria are chosen as: $\Delta_{\max} = 8$, the maximum reconstruction error allowed at one point of RGB, and $\Delta_{\mathrm{avg}} = 2$, the average reconstruction error for the entire *CLUT* $\mathbf{F}$.

The algorithm consists of three distinct steps:

1. Initialization: The set $\mathcal{K}$ is initialized with the 8 keypoints located at the vertices of the RGB cube, with the colors of the *CLUT* to be compressed, *i.e.* $\mathcal{K} = \{(\mathbf{X}_k, \mathbf{F}_{(\mathbf{X}_k)} \mid k = 1 \ldots 8\}$, for all $\mathbf{X}_k$ whose coordinates in x, y and z are either 0 or 255.

2. Adding keypoints: Let $E_N : RGB \rightarrow \mathbb{R}^+$ be the point-to-point error measurement between the original *CLUT* $\mathbf{F}$ and the *CLUT* $\widetilde{\mathbf{F}}_N$ reconstructed from $\mathcal{K}$, using the algorithm described in Sect. 2:

$$E_{N(\mathbf{X})} = \|\mathbf{F}(\mathbf{X}) - \widetilde{\mathbf{F}}_{N(\mathbf{X})}\|$$

where

$$E_{\max} = \max_{\mathbf{X} \in RGB}(E_{N(\mathbf{X})}) \quad \text{and} \quad E_{\mathrm{avg}} = \bar{E_N}$$

respectively denote the maximum error and the average reconstruction error.

As long as $E_{\max} > \Delta_{\max}$ or $E_{\mathrm{avg}} > \Delta_{\mathrm{avg}}$, a new keypoint

$$\mathbf{F}_{N+1} = (\mathbf{X}_{N+1}, \mathbf{F}_{N+1(\mathbf{X}_{N+1})})$$

is added to $\mathcal{K}$, located at coordinates $\mathbf{X}_{N+1} = \mathrm{argmax}_{\mathbf{X}}(E_N)$ of the maximum reconstruction error. In practice, one can observe that these keypoints added iteratively are scattered throughout the entire RGB domain, so as to jointly minimize the two criteria of reconstruction quality $\Delta_{\max}$ and Δ_{avg} (Fig. 7).

3. Deleting keypoints: Sometimes, the addition of the last keypoint at step 2 leads to a *CLUT* reconstructed with an higher quality than expected, *i.e.* with $E_{\max} < \Delta_{\max} - \epsilon$ and $E_{\mathrm{avg}} < \Delta_{\mathrm{avg}} - \epsilon$ and a non negligible $\epsilon > 0$. In this case, there is usually a subset of $\mathcal{K}$ that also verifies the reconstruction quality criteria,

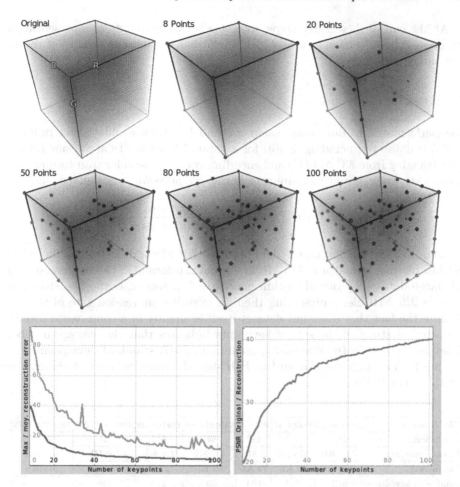

Fig. 7. Overview of the first 100 iterations of our proposed $3D$ $CLUT$s compression algorithm. **Top:** Target $CLUT$ **F** and approximations by iteratively adding keypoints. **Bottom:** Evolution of the maximum error (in green) and average error (in red), and of the $PSNR$ (in blue) of the reconstructed $CLUT$ $\widetilde{\mathbf{F}}_N$ with respect to the target $CLUT$ **F**. (Color figure online)

with an ϵ closer to 0. We can therefore try to increase the compression rate while maintaining the desired quality of reconstruction, by removing a few keypoints from $\mathcal{K}$. This is simply achieved by iteratively going through all the keypoints $\mathbf{K}_k$ of $\mathcal{K}$ (in the order of their insertion, $k = 1 \ldots N$), and checking whether the deletion of the kth keypoint $\mathbf{K}_k$ allows to reconstruct a $CLUT$ $\widetilde{\mathbf{F}}_N$ with quality constraints that still hold. If this is the case, the keypoint $\mathbf{K}_k$ is discarded from $\mathcal{K}$ and the algorithm is resumed from where we left it. According to the degree of continuity of the processed $CLUT$, this third step sometimes allows to withdraw up to 25% of keypoints in $\mathcal{K}$ (it also happens that no keypoint can be removed this way).

At the end of these three steps, we get a set or keypoints $\mathcal{K}$ representing a compressed lossy version of a $CLUT$ **F**, such that a minimum quality of reconstruction is guaranteed.

4   Results

The performance of our compression method has been evaluated on publicly available datasets (including [2,10]) for a total of 552 CLUTs at various resolutions (ranging from 33^3 to 144^3) and encoding very diverse color transformations. In our case, the relevant measurement is the *compression rate*, defined as:

$$\%cRate = 100 \left(1 - \frac{\text{Size of } compressed \text{ data}}{\text{Size of } input \text{ data}} \right)$$

The set of all the original $CLUT$ data occupies 708 Mb of disk storage (including 593 Mb in .png format and 115 Mb in .cube.zip format). The compression of this large dataset by our algorithm generates 552 sets of keypoints, stored in a single **2.5 Mb** file, representing then an overall compression rate of 99.65% (despite the fact that the input dataset itself is already in a compressed form!). A statistical study of the sets of keypoints indicates that the average number of keypoints is 1078 (minimum: 35, maximum: 2047, standard deviation: 587), which is high enough to make our fast PDE-based reconstruction technique more suitable than $RBFs$.

$CLUT$ name	Bourbon 64	Faded 47	Milo 5	Cubicle 99	Fusion 88	Sprocket 231	Paladin 1875
Resolution	16^3	32^3	48^3	64^3	64^3	128^3	144^3
Size in .cube.zip	23.5 Kb	573 Kb	3 Mb	1.2 Mb	1.4 Mb	5.6 Mb	5.4 Mb
Size in .png	3.7 Kb	22 Kb	72 Kb	92 Kb	127 Kb	765 Kb	979 Kb
Number of keypoints	562	294	894	394	210	290	59
$PSNR$	45.8 dB	45.6 dB	45 dB	45.2 dB	46.1 dB	46.4 dB	43.9 dB
Compression time	28 s	92 s	1180 s	561 s	257 s	3003.s	1432 s
Decompression time	67 ms	157 ms	260 ms	437 ms	452 ms	3281 ms	6739 ms
Keypoints in .png	1.9 Kb	1.5 Kb	4.2 Kb	1.9 Kb	1.3 Kb	1.7 Kb	0.44 Kb
$\%cRate$/.cube.zip	92.1%	99.7%	99.8%	99.8%	99.9%	$\approx$ 100%	$\approx$ 100%
$\%cRate$/.png	49.5%	93.3%	94.2%	98%	99%	99.8%	$\approx$ 100%

Fig. 8. Results of our CLUT compression algorithm, on different $CLUTs$ from [2] (with $\Delta_{\max} = 8$ and $\Delta_{\text{avg}} = 2$).

The table in Fig. 8 provides individual compression measurements for a sample of 7 $CLUTs$ taken from [2]. It shows the compression rates we get for various $CLUTs$ at different resolutions (our sets of N keypoints being stored as color .png images at resolution $2 \times N$), with respect to the input $CLUT$ data stored in the usual way, *i.e.* compressed files in .png and .cube.zip formats. It is worth noting that the number of generated keypoints does not depend on the resolution of the *CLUT* to be compressed, but rather on its *degree of continuity* (the keypoints being naturally located on the most discontinuous areas of the *CLUTs*, Fig. 7).

By limiting the average reconstruction error, the quality criterion $\Delta_{avg} = 2$ ensures a minimal value of 42.14 dB for the *PSNR* between an input *CLUT* $\mathbf{F}$ and its compressed reconstruction $\widetilde{\mathbf{F}}$. In theory, this criterion alone is not enough to guarantee visually imperceptible differences. However, this is the case in practice, as our algorithm simultaneously takes into account another quality criterion $\Delta_{max} = 8$ which limits the maximum reconstruction error.

For the purpose of scientific reproducibility, our *CLUT* compression/decompression algorithms have been integrated into *G'MIC*, a full-featured open-source framework for image processing [13].

5   Conclusions

The *CLUT* compression/decompression techniques we presented in this paper are surprisingly effective. This is mainly due to the perfect adequacy of the proposed 3*D* diffusion model (1) to the type of data processed (smooth, volumetric, color-valued). As a result, all the 552 *CLUTs* compressed by our method and integrated into *G'MIC* [13] make it, to the best of our knowledge, the image editing software that offers photographers and illustrators the greatest diversity of color transformations, and this, *for a minimal storage cost*. We are convinced that the integration of these algorithms into other image or video processing software will trigger the distribution of *CLUT*-based color transformations at a much larger magnitude scale than current standards.

References

1. Explanation of what a 3D CLUT is. http://www.quelsolaar.com/technology/clut.html. Accessed 21 Mar 2019
2. RocketStock, 35 Free LUTs for Color Grading. https://www.rocketstock.com/free-after-effects-templates/35-free-luts-for-color-grading-videos/. Accessed 21 Mar 2019
3. Anjyo, K., Lewis, J.P., Pighin, F.: Scattered data interpolation for computer graphics. In: ACM SIGGRAPH 2014 Courses, p. 27. ACM (2014)
4. Balaji, A., Sharma, G., Shaw, M., Guay, R.: Preprocessing methods for improved lossless compression of color look-up tables. J. Imaging Sci. Technol. **52**(4), 040901 (2008). https://doi.org/10.2352/J.ImagingSci.Technol
5. Beucher, S., Meyer, F.: The morphological approach to segmentation: the watershed transformation. Optical Eng.-NY-Marcel Dekker Incorporated **34**, 433–433 (1992)
6. Duarte-Carvajalino, J.M., Castillo, P.E., Velez-Reyes, M.: Comparative study of semi-implicit schemes for nonlinear diffusion in hyperspectral imagery. IEEE Trans. Image Process. **16**(5), 1303–1314 (2007)
7. Duchon, J.: Splines minimizing rotation-invariant semi-norms in sobolev spaces. Constructive Theory of Functions of Several Variables, vol. 571, pp. 85–100. Springer, Berlin (1977). https://doi.org/10.1007/BFb0086566

8. Galić, I., Weickert, J., Welk, M., Bruhn, A., Belyaev, A., Seidel, H.P.: Image compression with anisotropic diffusion. J. Math. Imaging and Vision **31**(2–3), 255–269 (2008)

9. Meijster, A., Roerdink, J.B., Hesselink, W.H.: A general algorithm for computing distance transforms in linear time. Mathematical Morphology and its Applications to Image and Signal Processing, pp. 331–340. Springer, Boston (2002). https://doi.org/10.1007/0-306-47025-X_36

10. RawTherapee: Film Simulation Pack. https://rawpedia.rawtherapee.com/Film_Simulation. Accessed 21 Mar 2019

11. Salomon, D., Motta, G.: Handbook of Data Compression, 5th edn. Springer, London (2009). https://doi.org/10.1007/978-1-84882-903-9

12. Tropp, J.A., Gilbert, A.C.: Signal recovery from random measurements via orthogonal matching pursuit. IEEE Trans. Inf. Theor. **53**(12), 4655–4666 (2007)

13. Tschumperlé, D., Fourey, S.: G'MIC: GREYC's Magic for Image Computing: A Full-Featured Open-Source Framework for Image Processing (2008–2019). https://gmic.eu/

14. Tschumperlé, D., Deriche, R.: Vector-valued Image Regularization with PDE's: a common framework for different applications. IEEE Trans. Pattern Anal. Mach. Intell. **27**(4), 506–517 (2005)

15. Weickert, J., Romeny, B.T.H., Viergever, M.A.: Efficient and reliable schemes for nonlinear diffusion filtering. IEEE Trans. Image Process. **7**(3), 398–410 (1998)

Analysis of Skill Improvement Process Based on Movement of Gaze and Hand in Assembly Task

Yohei Kawase$^{(\boxtimes)}$ and Manabu Hashimoto

Chukyo University,
101-2 Yagoto-Honmachi, Showa-ku, Nagoya, Aichi 466-8666, Japan
{kawase,mana}@isl.sist.chukyo-u.ac.jp

Abstract. In this paper, we propose a method to analyze the characteristics of the movements of the workers at each skill level in an assembly task. First, the method quantizes the positional information of the gaze and hands into eighteen areas and converts the positional information into a code. Second, the method calculates pairs of codes for the gaze and hands in each frame. Third, the method calculates the frequency of those pairs and generates co-occurrence histograms of the codes for the gaze and hands. In this research, we clearly distinguish the dominant hand from non-dominant hand because, the degree of skill improvement differs between the dominant hand and non-dominant hand. Therefore, the method generates co-occurrence histograms for the gaze and the dominant hand, as well as for the gaze and non-dominant hand. These histograms are proposed as feature for analyzing the characteristics of the movements. The results of the analysis of the skill improvement process show that the non-dominant hand at the elementary level stays in two areas, and the non-dominant hand at the intermediate level moves to five areas. This suggests that workers can move their non-dominant hand more efficiently at the intermediate level than at the elementary level. In addition, we found that the gaze at the intermediate level moves to eight areas, and the gaze at the expert level moves to three areas. This indicates that the gaze at the expert level remains at the center of the workbench.

Keywords: Skill improvement process · Assembly task ·
Movement of the gaze · Movement of hands

1 Introduction

In a factory, the skills of the workers affect the quality of the product and productivity. Shortage in expert level workers leads to low productivity and low quality of the products [1]. Therefore, workers need to develop their skills to the expert level fast.

In skill improvement process, workers grow in steps from elementary level to expert level. In order for workers to get to the next skill level fast, it is necessary to close the difference in movements with the next skill level at each

Supported by JSPS KAKENHI Grant Number JP17K06471.

M. Vento and G. Percannella (Eds.): CAIP 2019, LNCS 11679, pp. 15–26, 2019.
https://doi.org/10.1007/978-3-030-29891-3_2

stage of growth. For example, in order to grow elementary level to intermediate level, elementary level should close the difference in the movements with intermediate level. In our research, we clarify the difference in movements between skill levels.

The purpose of this research is to analyze the characteristics of the movements at each skill level in order to find the difference between skill levels. The OWAS method, RULA method, Posture targeting method [2–5] have been proposed for analyzing the skill improvement process. These methods analyze the physical burden during work however, they are based on subjective evaluation.

To overcome the limitations of the conventional methods, we focus on the movements of the gaze and hands and show the characteristics of these movements quantitatively at each skill level. As humans tend to perform actions based on information gleaned from their sense of vision, we think that the relationship between the movements of the gaze and hands depends on the skill level. However, analyzing the movements of the gaze and hands separately cannot be used to determine this relationship. Therefore, we analyze the relationship by designing the features that integrate the positional information of the gaze and hands. Also, the proposed method clearly distinguishes dominant hand from non-dominant hand, because we think that the degree of skill growth is different between the dominant and non-dominant hands.

This research offers two contributions. First, we propose a method to analyze skill improvement process objectively. Second, we confirmed the characteristics of motions for each skill level by analyzing skill improvement process.

Hereafter, Sect. 2 introduces relevant research on analyzing skill improvement process. Section 3 describes the method of analysis, Sect. 4 shows the results, and Sect. 5 concludes the paper.

2   Related Research on Analysis of Skill Improvement Process

The principles of the motion economy were proposed [6]. These principles are the rules for doing work efficiently. Each rule shows the workers the points for improvement. An example rule is 'Two hands should not be idle at the same time except during rest period.' In this research, we set seven points of movement for the hands, gaze, posture, rhythm, placement of the parts, equipment such as lighting, and others as points of improvement. And, all improvement points are points for improving human movement. In this research, we classify each rule into seven improvement points. For example, the rule where 'workers use both hands at the same time' applies to the movement of the hands. Also, the rule where 'there should be a definite and fixed place for all tools and materials' applies to placement of the parts. In this research, we classify these improvement points into 2 types. One is method improve human movement by optimizing the movement of the workers. Other is method improve human movement by optimizing working environment such as placement of the parts. In this research, we analyze human movement than working environment preferentially.

Because, working environment is always different depend on target products. As an example, if the target product is changed, placement of the parts is changed. Thus, it is difficult to generalize working environment. However, in the common motions such as motions for grasping the parts and motions for tightening a screw, we can generalize movement of the workers. Therefore, in this research, we analyze movement of the worker. On the basis of this Fig. 1, we decided that the gaze and the movement of hands are important points of improvement. Therefore, we focus on positional information of the gaze and hands to analyze the skill improvement process.

In another research, the Ovako Working Posture Analyzing System method was proposed [2]. This method evaluates points of improvement for workers by visual analysis of humans. This method evaluates the physical burden of workers from the back of worker, upper body, lower body, and the weight of the products. The OWAS method comprehensively evaluates four items and quantitatively expresses physical burden in four stages. OWAS method has realized the quantitative evaluation of the physical burden. However, the limitation of this method is that the evaluation is subjective.

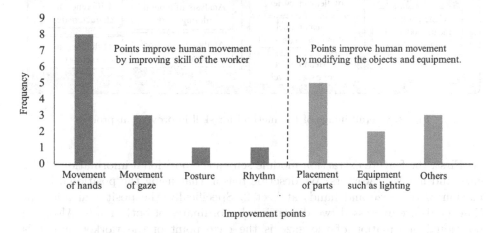

Fig. 1. Classification of the principles of motion economy

3   Analysis of Skill Improvement Process Based on the Movement of the Gaze and Hands

Here, we describe the method of analyzing the skill improvement process. Hereafter, Sect. 3.1 presents the overall image of the analysis of the skill improvement process. Section 3.2 explains the method of symbolizing positional information of the gaze and hands. Section 3.3 explains the method of extracting the gaze/motion integration features.

3.1   Method for Analyzing Skill Improvement Process

Figure 2 shows the overall image of the method for analyzing skill improvement process used in this research. The method consists of a module for extracting feature and a module for analyzing skill improvement process.

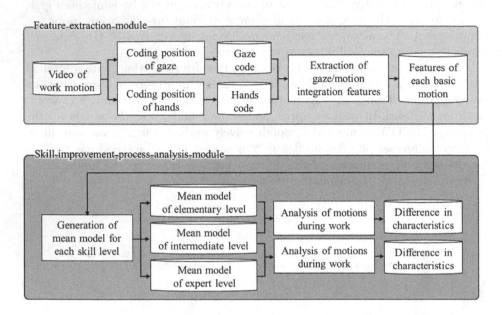

Fig. 2. Overall image of the method for skill improvement process

First, the feature extraction module senses the positional information of the gaze and hands of workers. We describe reason that using the positional information of the gaze and hands at Sect. 2. Specifically, the positional information hands are expressed two dimensional coordinates of both hands. Also, the positional information of the gaze is the gaze point of the worker and it is expressed two dimensional coordinates in egocentric image. Second, it quantizes the positional information and generates a column of the gaze code, a column of the right-hand code, and a column of the left-hand code. Third, it extracts gaze/motion integration features to analyze the skill improvement process from these columns of codes. Our feature expresses the frequency of pairs of the gaze code and the hands code as co-occurrence histograms. In addition, the proposed method generates co-occurrence histograms of the gaze and dominant hand, as well as co-occurrence histograms of the gaze and non-dominant hand.

Next, we explain the skill improvement process analysis module. First, it generates a mean model for each skill level by using the feature. The mean model is generated by using co-occurrence histograms of the gaze and dominant hand, as well as co-occurrence histograms of the gaze and non-dominant hand.

If there are three skill levels, three mean models are generated. Second, it evaluates the characteristics of the movement at each skill level by comparing the mean models of each skill level. Comparison of the mean models is a process that is performed by visual analysis of humans.

3.2   Coding Positional Information of the Gaze and Hands

Figure 3 shows the flow of coding of the positional information. Figure 3c shows a code table, in which we divided the area of a workbench into eighteen areas. The code table is expressed by codes of 18 types from 'a' to 'r', one code shows one area.

First, the coding module senses the position of the gaze and hands in each frame t. Second, it quantizes the position of the gaze and hands by applying the coordinates of the gaze and hands to the code table. For example, in Fig. 3, the gaze is coded as 'p', the right hand is coded as 'q' and the left hand is coded as 'k'. The column of codes is generated by performing this process in each frame.

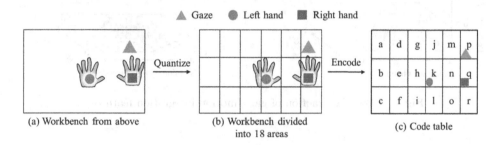

Fig. 3. Flow of coding of the positional information

3.3   Gaze/Motion Integration Features to Analyze Skill Improvement Process

In this section, we explain the method of extracting the gaze/motion integration features to analyze skill improvement process.

First, the method calculates pairs of codes of the gaze and the dominant hand in each frame. It also calculates pairs of codes of the gaze and the non-dominant hand in each frame. The proposed method analyzes skill improvement process by clearly distinguishing the dominant hand from the non-dominant hand. The reason is that the degree of the skill growth differs between the dominant and non-dominant hands. Second, it calculates these pairs in all frames and generates two co-occurrence histograms. These histograms are called gaze/motion integration features. The letters 'a' to 'r' on the axis of the code of the gaze and hands express one area. We presume the motions of a worker by using our feature.

In the co-occurrence histogram of the gaze and the dominant hand in Fig. 4, the frequency of pairs of the same code is high. Therefore, we can conclude from the co-occurrence histogram that the gaze and the dominant hand move to the same area.

The method for generating the mean models is as follows. First, the feature is classified based on skill level. Second, the mean value of each element of the co-occurrence histogram for each skill level is calculated. Finally, the co-occurrence histogram of the gaze and dominant hand, as well as the co-occurrence histogram of the gaze and non-dominant hand are calculated by using the mean value. These histograms are the mean models.

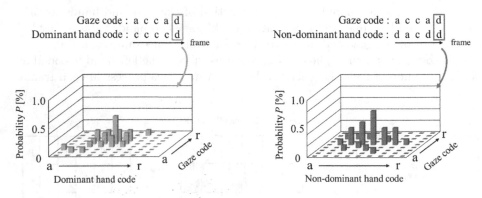

Fig. 4. Flow of extraction of gaze/motion integration features

4   Results of Skill Improvement Process Analysis

In this section, we explain the experimental requirements and results of the analysis of the skill improvement process. First, Sect. 4.1 explains the work motions and the target product in this research. Next, Sect. 4.2 describes the workers and the experimental environment. Finally, Sect. 4.3 shows the results of the analysis of the skill improvement process.

4.1   Target Product and Working Motions

The target product is a toy of airplane type. Figure 5 shows the parts of the target product and their names. It is difficult to differentiate quality of the product by using this plane model. Because, a completed product of the target product is a certain quality if the worker can complete the target product. Therefore, it is difficult to differentiate quality of the product, because evaluation of quality of the target product is 2 types of completed or uncompleted. However, we think that we do not have to consider quality. As a reason, there are two methods of evaluation of quality. First method evaluates quality of the product that are made regardless working time. This method is applied to the products such as traditional craft. Second method evaluates quality of the product made in a fixed working time. This method is applied to assembly products. The former needs to make the product of higher quality. However, the latter does not have to make the product of high quality if it has a certain quality. In assembly tasks of this research, we do not consider the quality of the product.

We use the parts of Fig. 5 in the description of the work process. There are six work processes. Process 1 is a motion that grasps the main wing and attaches it to the lower part of the airplane body. Process 2 is a motion that grasps the tail wing and attaches it to the lower part of the airplane body. Process 3 is a motion that grasps the upper part of the airplane body and attaches it to the lower part of the airplane body. Process 4 is a motion that grasps the propellers and assembles them by tightening the screws. Process 5 is a motion that grasps the tail part and assembles it by tightening the screws. Process 6 is a motion that grasps the part of the upper part of the airplane body and assembles it by tightening the screws. In this research, we classify the work motions into three basic motions. We show an example of basic motions in Fig. 6. The basic motions are motions of grasping the parts, moving the parts to center of the workbench, and assembling the parts. The proposed method extracts the feature of each basic motion and analyzes the characteristics of the movement at each skill level.

Also, some of the sequence are fixed but some of them are not fixed. As an example of the former, there are a process like assembly tasks. In this process, sequence is fixed in all skill levels, because sequence is normalized in advance. In fixed sequence, expert level knows the method for early making the product. Thus, expert level in this process does not optimize the sequence. As an example of the latter, there are a process like a traditional craft. In this process, the sequence is different by the workers, because this process includes many complex motions. Therefore, expert level in this process optimizes the sequence.

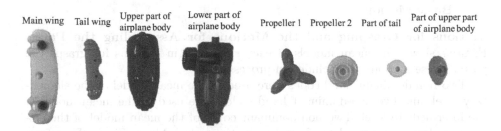

| Main wing | Tail wing | Upper part of airplane body | Lower part of airplane body | Propeller 1 | Propeller 2 | Part of tail | Part of upper part of airplane body |

Fig. 5. Names of the parts

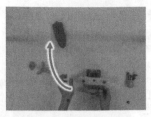

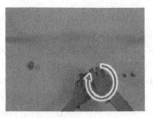

(a) Motions for grasp the parts   (b) Motions for move the parts to   (c) Motions for tighten screws
                                         center of the workbench

Fig. 6. Examples of basic motions

4.2   Workers and Experimental Environment

The workers in this research are four students who have never assembled the target product before. Three of the workers are right handed, and one is left handed. The workers assemble thirty products, and we gather the positional information of the gaze and hands of the workers during that time.

We categorize skill levels into elementary level, intermediate level, and expert level. The skill level of the workers is evaluated from two standpoints work time and quality of the product. Tanimizu [7] and Haraguchi [8] showed that the work time decreases exponentially as the amount of production increases in the assembly task. However, the quality of a product is evaluated at a certain level if the workers can complete the product. Therefore, in this research, we evaluate the skill level based on work time.

We used Tobii Pro Glasses 2, made by Tobii, to measure the positional information of the gaze. In addition, we used Flex 13, made by OptiTrack, to measure the positional information of the hands.

4.3   Results of Analysis of Skill Improvement Process of Each Basic Motions

Motions for Grasping and the Motions for Assembling the Parts. Figure 7 shows the mean models of each skill level in motions for grasps the parts. These motions are included in process 4.

Two non-dominant hand codes were used in the mean model of the elementary level, and five non-dominant hand codes were used in the mean model of the intermediate level. Two non-dominant codes of the mean model of the elementary level correspond to 'f' and 'i' in the code table in Fig. 3. Therefore, the non-dominant hand at elementary level stays in two areas near the initial position of the non-dominant hand like Fig. 8. However, the non-dominant hand at the intermediate level moves to five areas. Therefore, their the non-dominant hand moves to several positions like Fig. 9. Also, many gaze codes were used in the mean models of the elementary and intermediate levels. Therefore, we can assume that the gaze at these levels moves to the positions of the parts like

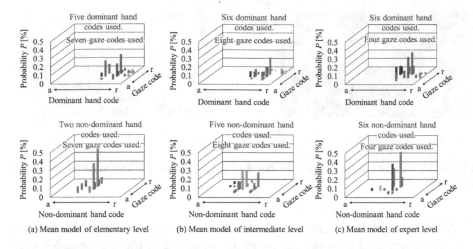

Fig. 7. Mean models of each skill level for grasping motions (right handed).

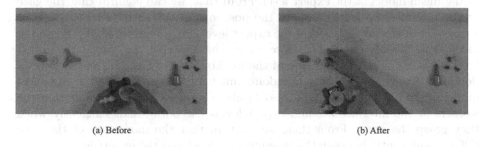

Fig. 8. Movements at non-dominant hand of elementary level in motions for grasp the parts

Fig. 11. The movement of the non-dominant hand differs significantly between the elementary level and intermediate level.

The mean models of elementary level and intermediate level at Fig. 10 when the worker is left-handed. Two non-dominant hand codes were used in the mean model of the elementary level, and five non-dominant hand codes were used in the mean model of the intermediate level. Two non-dominant codes of the mean model of the elementary level correspond to 'l' and 'o' in the code table in Fig. 3. The non-dominant hand stays in two areas near the initial position when the worker is left-handed. This corresponds with the results of the analysis for the right handed workers.

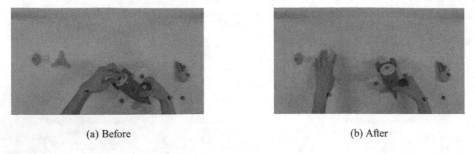

(a) Before   (b) After

Fig. 9. Movements at non-dominant hand of intermediate level in motions for grasp the parts

Next, we explain the difference in movements between the intermediate level and the expert level by using the mean model in Fig. 7. Eight gaze codes were used in the mean model of the intermediate level, and four gaze codes were used in the mean model of the expert level. From that, we can confirm that the gaze at the intermediate level moves to the positions of the parts like Fig. 11. Four gaze codes of the mean model of the expert level correspond to 'h', 'i', 'k', and 'l' in the code table in Fig. 3. Therefore, we can assume that the gaze at the expert level stays in the central position of the workbench like Fig. 12. In addition, six dominant hand codes and five non-dominant hand codes were used in the mean model of the intermediate and expert levels. Therefore, we can assume that the workers at the intermediate and expert levels use both hands efficiently when they grasp the parts. From that, we confirm that the movement of the gaze differs significantly between the intermediate level and the expert level.

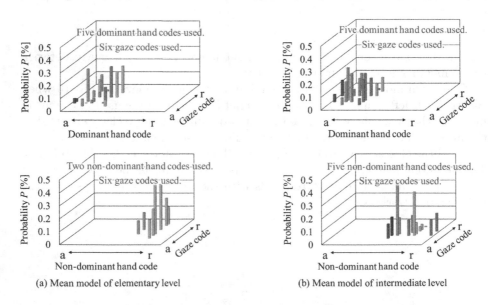

(a) Mean model of elementary level   (b) Mean model of intermediate level

Fig. 10. Mean models of each skill level for grasping motions (left handed).

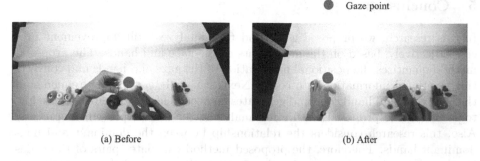

(a) Before   (b) After

Fig. 11. Movements at the gaze of intermediate level in motions for grasp the parts

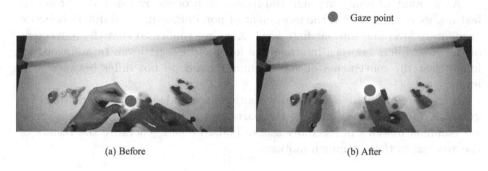

(a) Before   (b) After

Fig. 12. Movements at the gaze of expert level in motions for grasp the parts

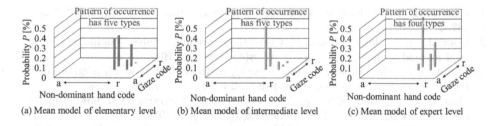

(a) Mean model of elementary level   (b) Mean model of intermediate level   (c) Mean model of expert level

Fig. 13. Mean models of each skill level for screw-tightening motions

Motions for Tightening a Screw. Figure 13 shows the mean models of each skill level in the motions for tighten screws. We can confirm that the shapes of the histograms of each skill level are the same from Fig. 13. These gaze codes correspond to 'h' and 'k' in the code table in Fig. 3. The non-dominant hand codes correspond to 'i' and 'l'. These codes correspond to the central position of the workbench. The positions of the gaze and hands do not shift, because the motions are the motions for turning a tool at the center of the workbench. The results show that the difference in movements between skill levels lies in the motions of grasping the parts.

5   Conclusion

In this research, we proposed a method that analyzes skill improvement process objectively, based on the movements of the gaze and hands. The proposed method quantizes the positional information of the gaze and hands and converts this positional information into codes. Next, it calculates the pair frequency of the gaze code and hand code and generates co-occurrence histograms. These histograms are the proposed feature for analyzing the skill improvement process. Also, this research considers the relationship between the dominant and non-dominant hands. Therefore, the proposed method calculates pairs of the codes for the gaze and the dominant hand, as well as the gaze and the non-dominant hand.

As a result of analyzing skill improvement process by using the proposed feature, we confirmed that the movement of non-dominant hand differs between elementary level and intermediate level. Also, we confirmed that the movement of the gaze differs between intermediate level and expert level. In addition, we found that the movements of the dominant hand do not differ between skill levels.

If the target kits are change, new motions are added. However, motions for grasping, motions for assembling the parts and motions for tightening a screw are common motions in assembly tasks. Thus, we can generalize the results of the analysis in these common motions.

References

1. Nakayama, Y.: Methods for knowledge transfer. J. Jpn. Soc. Artif. Intell. **22**(4), 467–471 (2007)
2. Kuorinka, I., Karhu, O., Kansi, P.: Correcting working postures in industry: a practical method for analysis. Appl. Ergon. **8**(4), 199–201 (1977)
3. Corlett, E.N., McAtamney, L.: Rula: a survey method for the irwestigation of world-related upper limb disorders. Appl. Ergon. **24**(2), 91–99 (1993)
4. Manenica, I., Corlett, E.N., Madeley, S.J.: Posture targeting: a technique for recording working postures. Ergonomics **22**(3), 357–366 (1979)
5. Rohmert, W.: Aet–a new job-analysis method. Ergonomics **28**(1), 245–254 (1985)
6. Barnes, R.M.: Motion and time study : Design and measurement of work (1980)
7. Yokotani, T., Iwamura, K., Sugimura, N., Tanimizu, Y., Ishii, S.: Development of a work instruction system based on analysis of learning processes for cellular manufacturing. Jpn Soc. Mech. Eng. **80**(814), TRANS0142 (2014)
8. Fuji, N., Haraguchi, H., Kaihara, T.: A study on operator allocation aiming at the skill improvement for cell production system. Jpn. Soc. Mech. Eng. **81**(825), 1400–1406 (2014)

Hybrid Function Sparse Representation Towards Image Super Resolution

Junyi Bian[1], Baojun Lin[1,2(✉)], and Ke Zhang[1]

[1] ShanghaiTech University, School of Information Science and Technology,
Shanghai 201210, China
bianjy@shanghaitech.edu.cn
[2] Chinese Academy of Sciences, Shanghai Engineering Center for Microsatellites,
Shanghai 201203, China
linbaojun@aoe.ac.cn

Abstract. Sparse representation with training-based dictionary has been shown successful on super resolution(SR) but still have some limitations. Based on the idea of making the magnification of function curve without losing its fidelity, we proposed a function based dictionary on sparse representation for super resolution, called hybrid function sparse representation (HFSR). The dictionary we designed is directly generated by preset hybrid functions without additional training, which can be scaled to any size as is required due to its scalable property. We mixed approximated Heaviside function (AHF), sine function and DCT function as the dictionary. Multi-scale refinement is then proposed to utilize the scalable property of the dictionary to improve the results. In addition, a reconstruct strategy is adopted to deal with the overlaps. The experiments on 'Set14' SR dataset show that our method has an excellent performance particularly with regards to images containing rich details and contexts compared with non-learning based state-of-the art methods.

Keywords: Super resolution · Sparse representation ·
Multi-scale refinement · Hybrid-function dictionary

1 Introduction

The target of the single image super resolution (SISR) is to produce a high resolution (HR) image from an observed low resolution (LR) image. This is meaningful due to its valuable applications in many real-world scenarios such as remoting sensing, magnetic resonance and surveillance camera. However, SR is an ill-posed issue which is very difficult to obtain the optimal solution. The approaches for SISR can be divided into three categories including interpolation-based methods [3,4,11,16,22], reconstruction-based methods [2,6,7,9,18], and learning-based methods [5,10,12,15,17,20]. Reconstruction-based methods and learning-based methods often yield more accurate results than interpolation-based algorithm, since those methods can acquire more information from statistical prior and external data even though more time-consuming. Algorithm can be integrated from multiple categories mentioned above, which is not strictly independent.

© Springer Nature Switzerland AG 2019
M. Vento and G. Percannella (Eds.): CAIP 2019, LNCS 11679, pp. 27–37, 2019.
https://doi.org/10.1007/978-3-030-29891-3_3

As classic approaches in SR, interpolation-based methods follow a basic strategy to construct the unknown pixel of HR image such as bicubic, bilinear and nearest-neighbor(NN). However, nearest-neighbor interpolation always causes a jag effect. In this aspect, bicubic and bilinear perform better than NN and are widely used as zooming algorithms but easier to generate a blur effect on images.

Reconstruction-based methods usually model an objective function with reconstruction constraints from image priors and regularization terms to lead better solutions for the inverse problem. The image priors for reconstructions include the gradient priors [18], sparsity priors [6,7,14] and edge priors [9]. Those methods usually restore the images with sharp edges and less noises, but will be invalid when the upscaling factor becomes larger.

Learning-based algorithms mainly explore the relationship between LR and HR image patches. In the early time, Freeman et al. [10] predict the HR image from LR input by Markov Random Field trained by belief propagation. Sparse-representation for SISR is firstly proposed by Yang et al. [20] and achieves state-of-the-art performance. Zhang et al. [24] propose a novel classification method based on sparse coding autoextractor. Zeyde et al. [21] improve the algorithm by using K-SVD [1] based dictionary and orthogonal matching pursuit (OMP) optimization method. Recently, deep neural network has been extensively used in super-resolution task. Dong et al. [5] firstly design an end-to-end mapping from LR to HR called SRCNN. Generative adversarial network [13] is introduced to SR by [15,17] to encourage the network to favor solutions that look more like natural images. The learning-based algorithms are not generally promoted, since most of the algorithms only focus on the specific upscaling factor and need to be retrained on external large dataset once the upscaling factor is changed.

In this paper, we propose hybrid function sparse representation (HFSR), which uses function-based dictionary to replace conventional training-based dictionary. The special property of such dictionary are utilized to reinforce the SR algorithm. Primary idea of the proposed method is that the upscaling of the function curve will keep it's fidelity, and to represent the patches from LR image by linear combination of functions. We select approximate Heaviside function (AHF), discrete cosine transformation (DCT) function, and sine function to form the dictionary. Unlike the work of [4], we adopt diverse functions instead of single AHF, and do not mix the sparsity and intensity priors together for representation which needs ADMM to solve the objective loss. As a consequence, approach applying with sparse representation performs much faster than the algorithm in [4]. Different from the conventional sparse representation method, our algorithm requires no additional training for dictionary on high resolution images, and there is no scale constraint since the dictionary can be scaled up to any size. Once being represented by hybrid functions, dictionary can be stored by parameters rather than matrixs with large size. The algorithm we design is related to the interpolation-based method and reconstruction-based method. In view of this, we compare our results with two interpolation-based algorithms and another reconstruction-based algorithm [12].

The remaining part of the paper is organized as follows: Sect. 2 briefly introduces the sparse representation algorithm for single image super resolution. Section 3 describes the proposed HFSR approach from dictionary designing to multi-scale refinement and then to the construction of whole image. Section 4 discusses the results of the proposed method and the paper is concluded in Sect. 5.

2 Super Resolution via Sparse Representation Preliminaries

The goal of single image super resolution is to recover the HR image $\mathbf{x}$ by giving an observed LR image $\mathbf{y}$. Relationship between LR images and HR images is denoted as:

$$\mathbf{y} = D\mathbf{x} + v \tag{1}$$

where D is the degradation matrix combining with down sampling operator and blur operator, and v is the independent Gaussian noise. Sparse representation method processes the image in patch level, which means a LR image is divided into several small patches of the same size. Then each patch is approximately represented as linear combination of the dictionary atoms. A HR patch p_H could be reconstructed by the corresponding HR dictionary with the shared representation α obtained from LR patch p_L.

$$p_L \approx \Phi_1\alpha, \quad p_H = \Phi_s\alpha \tag{2}$$

We denote $\Phi_s \in \mathcal{R}^{m \cdot s^2 \times N}$ as the dictionary, where s is the upscaling factor. If the value of s is 1, Φ_s exactly becomes $\Phi_1 \in \mathcal{R}^{m \times N}$ for the LR patches. N is the size of the whole dictionary, and $m = w \cdot w$ is the vectorization size of square patch with w length. Therefore, the size of p_L is m, while the size of p_H for HR image is $m \cdot s^2$.

The SR task is ill-posed which means there are infinite $\mathbf{x}$ satisfying the Eq. (1). The sparse representation methods provide sparse prior for the representation of patch p_L to regularize the task. Sparse prior assumes $\|\alpha\|_0$, the coefficients of representation, should be as small as possible, while still contains the low reconstruction error. With the constraint above, SR task can be formulated as an optimization problem:

$$\min \|\alpha\|_0 \quad s.t. \quad \|p_L - \Phi_1\alpha\|_2^2 \leq \varepsilon \tag{3}$$

The aforementioned problem is still non-convex and NP-hard. However, work on [8] shows that (3) can be converted by replacing the objective with the l^1-norm:

$$\min \|\alpha\|_1 \quad s.t. \quad \|p_L - \Phi_1\alpha\|_2^2 \leq \varepsilon \tag{4}$$

Applied with Langrange multipliers, (4) becomes a convex problem which can be efficiently solved by LASSO [19].

$$\alpha = \arg \min_{\alpha} \left\{ \|p_L - \Phi_1 \alpha\|_2^2 + \lambda \|\alpha\|_1 \right\} \tag{5}$$

λ denotes sparse regularization to balance the sparsity of the representation and the reconstruction error. In conventional sparse representation method [20], we need external images to train the dictionary Φ_1 and Φ_s. However, since it is not required in the proposed algorithm, the part of describing dictionary from training has been excluded.

3   Hybrid Functions Sparse Representation

3.1   Function-Based Dictionary

It is critically important to choose dictionary for sparse coding. Despite the training-based algorithm, another type of dictionary uses wavelets and curvelets which shares some similarity with proposed function-based dictionary. However, the ability of adapting different types of data for this dictionary is limited and do not perform well under sparse prior [23].

There are some advantages of using the function to generate the dictionary, in which we can leverage the property of the function to fine tune parameters or enlarge the dictionary to any scale as is required. The relation between dictionary and functions is connected as:

$$\Phi_1^k(i, j | \Theta^k) = f^k(i, j, \Theta^k) \tag{6}$$

Here, $\Theta = \{\Theta^1, \Theta^2, ..., \Theta^N\}$ is the set of parameters for the whole dictionary. $\Phi_1^k \in \mathcal{R}^m$ represents the kth element in the LR dictionary, which is the vectorized result from the patch with size $\mathcal{R}^{w \times w}$, so the integer pair (i, j) maps the pixel value by coordinate from the raw patch to the $(i * w + j)^{th}$ position in Φ_1^k, f^k and Θ^k is the kth function in dictionary and its corresponding parameter, respectively.

$$f^k(i, j, \Theta^k) \in \begin{cases} \arctan\left((i \cdot \cos\theta^k + j \cdot \sin\theta^k + b^k)/\xi^k\right)/\pi \\ \sin((i \cdot \cos\theta^k + j \cdot \sin\theta^k + b^k) \cdot a^k) \\ \cos\left(\frac{\pi a^k}{w}(i + \frac{1}{2})\right) \cdot \cos\left(\frac{\pi b^k}{h}(j + \frac{1}{2})\right) \end{cases} \tag{7}$$

As is shown in Eq. (7), three categories of function are combined here. The approximate Heaviside function can be used to fit the edge in patch, where one-dimensional AHF is $\psi(x) = \frac{1}{2} + \frac{1}{\pi} \arctan(\frac{x}{\xi})$, and the parameters ξ control the smoothness of margin between 1 and 0. Then the function is extended to two-dimensional case for our task, thus $f_{AHF}(\mathbf{z}) = \psi(\mathbf{z} \cdot \mathbf{d}^T + b)$, where $\mathbf{d} = (\cos\theta, \sin\theta)$ and $\mathbf{z} = (i, j)$ is the coordinate in patch. Since sine is a simple periodic function and is suitable for representing stripes, we adopt it as one of

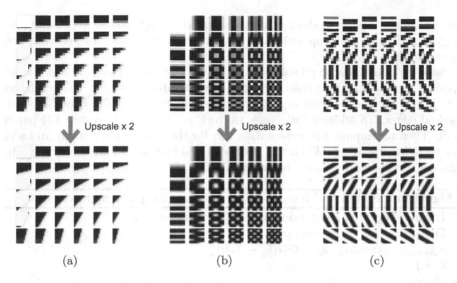

(a)   (b)   (c)

Fig. 1. The visualization of LR patches and corresponding HR patches sampled from the hybrid of (a) AHF, (b) DCT function and (c) Sin function. The first row are the LR patches from Φ_1, the second row are the HR patches from Φ_2.

the basic functions and extend it to two-dimensional case as what we did for AHF. $f_{Sin}(\mathbf{z}) = \sin(a\mathbf{z} \cdot \mathbf{d}^T + b)$, where parameter a and θ for 2D-sine function controls the intensity and direction of the stripes, respectively. The idea of using over-complete discrete cosine transformation (DCT) as one of the functions is inspired by [1], the pixel value in DCT patch is generated by $\cos\left(\frac{\pi a}{w}(i + \frac{1}{2})\right) \cdot \cos\left(\frac{\pi b}{h}(j + \frac{1}{2})\right)$. We have designed several functions and tried various mixed strategies, then we find the hybrid of these three functions work better than single functions or other mixed forms.

$$\Theta^k \in \begin{cases} \{\theta_k, b_k, \xi_k\} \\ \{\theta_k, a_k, b_k\} \\ \{a_k, b_k\} \end{cases} \tag{8}$$

The parameter selections of three functions are listed in the Eq. (8). Figure 1 depict upscaling process using three functions above, respectively. One of the advantages of HFSR approach is that the dictionary for reconstructing the HR image with a specific size could be directly obtained by functions. Generating the HR dictionary and LR Dictionary can be connected in a similar way.

$$\Phi_s(i, j|\Theta) = \Phi_1(i/s, j/s|\Theta) = f(i/s, j/s, \Theta) \tag{9}$$

3.2 Multi-scale Refinement

The patches are sampled in raster-scan order from the raw LR image and processed independently. The full representation for each patch is computed by two processes. Sparse coding is firstly applied to get coarse representation α_{coarse}, and then the proposed multi-scale refinement is used to generate fine representation α_{fine}.

Suppose α is the optimal solution, then the difference of $p_L - D\Phi_s\alpha$ should equal to zero, where D is the downsampling operator. However, the condition is typically unsatisfied with α_{coarse}, and the difference usually contains some residual edges. To address this issue, we pick $p_L - D\Phi_s\alpha$ as a new LR patch to fit. Then recompute a representation $\Delta\alpha$ for the new residual input and add $\Delta\alpha$ to α for updating. When the values in residual image are small enough, refinement ends with a better representation α_{fine}.

Algorithm 1. HFSR with multi-scale refinement for patch approximation

---

Input: $\{p_L : \text{low resolution patch }\} \ \{\Phi : \text{dictionary}\}$
Output: $\{\alpha_{fine}: \text{representation}\}$
1 $\alpha_{coarse} = \arg\min_\alpha \|p_L - \Phi_1\alpha\|_2^2 + \lambda_1\|\alpha\|_1$
2 $k = 1$
3 $p_L^0 = p_L$
4 $\alpha^0 = \alpha_{coarse}$
5 **for** $\bar{s} \in scales$ **do**
6   **for** $iter = 1: iters_{\bar{s}}$ **do**
7      $p_L^k = p_L^{k-1} - D\Phi_{\bar{s}}\alpha^{k-1}$
8      $\alpha^k = \arg\min_\alpha \|p_L^k - \Phi_1\alpha\|_2^2 + \lambda_2\|\alpha\|_1$
9      $k = k + 1$

10 $\alpha_{fine} = \alpha_{coarse} + \sum_{i=1}^k \alpha^i$

Generic refinement method downsample the patch from HR patch with specific upscaling factor s. To utilize the scalable property of our function-based dictionary, we also put forward a new refinement algorithm called multi-scale refinement. Scaling up an image with s by interpolation-based algorithm can be viewed as a process of iteratively expanding an image by multi-steps. During each step, images are enlarged slightly compared with the ones in the previous step. As such, our proposed algorithm could perform this procedure due to the scalable property. Here, it is necessry to make an assumption that during the iterative process of expanding an image, if representation for each patch is well-obtained, the reconstruction could be of high quality at each zooming step rather than perform well only in a certain scale but distort at other optional scaling factors. This assumption can be viewed as a regularization that saves the ill-posed problem from massive solutions. Therefore, we make the refinement for each scale to enforce the stability of its reconstruction results. The difference of kth scale refinement with scaling factor s_k hence becomes $p_L - D\Phi_{s_k}\alpha$. Experiments demonstrate that multi-scale refinement improved the results and is less time consuming.

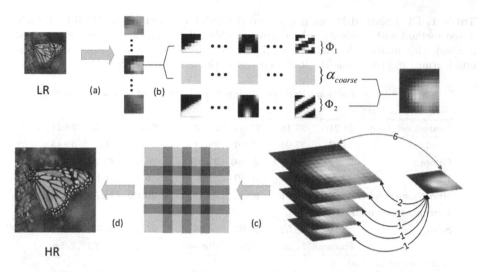

Fig. 2. Overview of the proposed HFSR method. Process (a) sample the patches from the LR image, (b) compute the coarse representation for each patch, (c) apply multi-scale refinement to obtain fine representation, (d) reconstruct the HR image from overlaped patches. The red arrow represents the conventional refinement used for comparison. (Color figure online)

3.3   Image Reconstruction from Patches

The whole image can be reconstructed after calculating the representation for each patch in raster-scan order. However the borders of adjacent patches are not compatible which may cause patchy result. To deal with this issue, the adjacent patches are sampled with overlaps which would assign multiple values to each pixel. General method is to average these pixel values for reconstruction. Based on the aforementioned analysis, objective loss represents the reconstruction quality of the patch and can be involved in reconstruction process for more precise result. Following this idea, we make weighted summation according to the reconstruction objective loss to recover the pixel value.

$$HR(x,y) = \frac{1}{\sum_{j=1}^{|p|} loss^j} \sum_{i}^{|p|} loss^i \cdot p_H^i(x^i, y^i) \tag{10}$$

$HR(x,y)$ represents the pixel in HR image with coordinate (x, y). Suppose the pixel is covered by $|p|$ patches, and $p_H^i(x^i, y^i)$ is the corresponding value in i^{th} constructed patch while $loss^i$ is the objective loss. The strategy works better than generic average approach especially when the objective loss vary dramatically among different patches. Figure 2 demonstrates the concrete procedures of HFSR algorithm.

Table 1. The PSNR (dB) results obtained through the experiments, HFSR is the proposed method with conventional refinement, while HFSR(multi-scale) is the proposed method with multi-scale Refinement. The bold means the highest score among the non-learning method while the italic represents the second best score.

	Baboon	Barbara	Bridge	Coastguard	Comic	Face	Flowers
Non-learning method							
Nearest neighbor	24.21	27.18	27.94	28.19	24.61	33.63	28.41
Bicubic	24.67	27.94	28.96	29.13	26.05	34.88	30.43
Glasner	25.11	**28.54**	**29.66**	**29.80**	26.66	**35.24**	**31.48**
HFSR	*25.12*	28.15	29.50	29.47	*26.88*	34.45	31.27
HFSR(multi-scale)	**25.13**	*28.16*	*29.52*	*29.49*	**26.90**	*34.46*	*31.29*
Learning-based method							
ScSR	25.24	28.52	29.97	30.28	27.66	35.56	32.58
	Foreman	Lenna	Man	Butterfly	Pepper	PPT3	Zebra
Non-learning method							
Nearest neighbor	30.35	32.35	28.01	30.19	31.09	25.05	27.37
Bicubic	32.66	34.74	29.27	32.97	33.08	26.85	30.68
Glasner	**34.15**	**35.78**	**30.32**	**36.22**	**35.08**	**29.65**	31.13
HFSR	33.56	35.07	29.72	33.98	33.67	27.46	*31.56*
HFSR(multi-scale)	*33.57*	*35.10*	*29.74*	*34.00*	*33.68*	*27.47*	**31.59**
Learning-based method							
ScSR	34.45	36.21	30.46	35.92	34.12	28.97	32.99

4   Experimental Results

In this section, the proposed algorithm HFSR is evaluated with two classical interpolation methods and one of the state-of-the art methods proposed by glasner et al. [12]. The hyperparameter and some implementation details are also analyzed and discussed here. ScSR [20] is not compared here because it requires HR images for training. AHF [4] approach is not sparse coding method and needs the inverse of matrix to solve ADMM problem which runs extremely slowly, the comparison is hence excluded either. All experiments are implemented in Python 3.6 on Macbook Pro of 8Gb RAM and 2.3 GHz Intel Core i5.

The performance is measured by peak signal-to-noise ratio (PSNR), and upscaling factor s is set to 2 for all experiments. RGB input images are first converted into YC_BC_R color space with three channels. Y channel represents luma component which is processed in most SR algorithms. Therefore, we upscale it independently by the proposed model. To evaluate the result, we only compared the Y channel by PSNR. The remaining two channels C_B and C_R are enlarged by bicubic interpolation so that YC_BC_R image can be transformed to the original RGB image for visualization. Grayscale input images can be directly applied by the proposed method and evaluation.

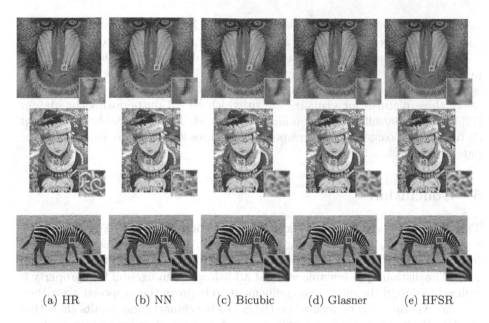

(a) HR   (b) NN   (c) Bicubic   (d) Glasner   (e) HFSR

Fig. 3. Results of images including baboon, comic and zebra with upscaling factor 2 (from top to bottom) and comparison of HR(Ground truth), NN, Bicubic, Glasner [12] and proposed HFSR (from left to right)

The priority is to firstly tune the parameters in dictionary. For AHF, θ is sampled from 16 angles, which are distributed evenly on $[0, 2\pi]$. b is sampled from $[-6, 6]$ with 12 isometric intervals. ξ is sampled from $[0.1, 10^{-4}]$. For Sin function, 6 angles are ranged form $[0, \pi]$ for θ, b is sampled from $[0, 1, 2, 3, 4, 5, 6]$ and a is sampled from $[2.5, 2.25, 2]$. For DCT function, a is average sampled from $[0, 5]$ with 1 distance. b are sampled in the same way as a. Then the dictionary is composed by parameter combinations and excludes those whose norm of its corresponding constructed patch less than 1.0. The total size of the dictionary in our experiment is 334.

The size of patches sampled from the LR image is 6×6 and the overlap of the patch is set as 4. Smaller size of the patch like 5×5 may work better when the image details are more complex but it is more time consuming. In original refinement, all of the 6 iterations are operated on the patch with fixed upscaling factor 2. In multi-scale refinement, patches are enlarged from size 6×6 to 12×12 where the upscaling factors are sampled from $[\frac{7}{6}, \frac{8}{6}, \frac{9}{6}, \frac{10}{6}, \frac{11}{6}, \frac{12}{6}]$, the number of iterations $iters_{\bar{s}}$ in each scale with corresponding upscaling factor, in order, are $[1, 1, 1, 1, 0, 2]$.

Large sparse regularization parameters λ will degrade the quality for α to approximate p_L but lead better upscaling results for what it represents. Small λ usually gets less reconstruct error for p_L, but it is easy to lose the fidelity when recovering the HR image. Hence, it is important to select an optimal value λ so as to balance the two effects above. Ultimately, the sparse regularization λ_1 for coarse sparse representation and λ_2 for refinement are both tuned as 10^{-4}.

The experimental results from Table 1 on the dataset Set14 show that HFSR performs much better than conventional interpolation-based methods, and multi-scale refinement is verified to improve PSNR score. Furthermore, in Fig. 3, we select three pictures for visualization in which HFSR outperforms the glanser [12] and find that all of them contain rich textures. This is probably because our dictionary well contains the corresponding features and therefore can recover the patch robustly.

5   Conclusion

This paper proposed a framework of using function-based dictionary for sparse representation in SR task. In our HFSR model, AHF, DCT function and sine function are combined for patch approximation to form a hybrid function dictionary. The dictionary is scalable without additional training, and this property is utilized to design the multi-scale refinement to improve the proposed algorithm.

The experiment is performed on the Set14 benchmark, and results show that the HFSR algorithm performs well on a certain type of images which contains complex details and contexts. For future improvements, the dictionary comprising more functions can be explored. Many interesting topics are remained, including using the learning-based method to fine tune parameters of the dictionary or apply HFSR to other domain such as image compression or image denoising. To encourage future works of proposed algorithm and discover effects in other applications, we public all the source code and materials on website: https://github.com/Eulring/Hybrid-Function-Sparse-Representation.

References

1. Aharon, M., Elad, M., Bruckstein, A., et al.: K-svd: An algorithm for designing overcomplete dictionaries for sparse representation. IEEE Trans. Signal Process. **54**(11), 4311 (2006)
2. Babacan, S.D., Molina, R., Katsaggelos, A.K.: Variational bayesian super resolution. IEEE Trans. Image Process. **20**(4), 984–999 (2011)
3. Dai, S., Han, M., Xu, W., Wu, Y., Gong, Y.: Soft edge smoothness prior for alpha channel super resolution. In: 2007 IEEE Conference on Computer Vision and Pattern Recognition, pp. 1–8. IEEE (2007)
4. Deng, L.J., Guo, W., Huang, T.Z.: Single image super-resolution by approximated Heaviside functions. Inf. Sci. **348**, 107–123 (2016). https://doi.org/10.1016/j.ins.2016.02.015
5. Dong, C., Loy, C.C., He, K., Tang, X.: Learning a deep convolutional network for image super-resolution. In: Fleet, D., Pajdla, T., Schiele, B., Tuytelaars, T. (eds.) ECCV 2014. LNCS, vol. 8692, pp. 184–199. Springer, Cham (2014). https://doi.org/10.1007/978-3-319-10593-2_13
6. Dong, W., Zhang, L., Shi, G., Li, X.: Nonlocally centralized sparse representation for image restoration. IEEE Trans. Image Process. **22**(4), 1620–1630 (2013)

7. Dong, W., Zhang, L., Shi, G., Wu, X.: Image deblurring and super-resolution by adaptive sparse domain selection and adaptive regularization. IEEE Trans. Image Process. **20**(7), 1838–1857 (2011)

8. Donoho, D.L.: For most large underdetermined systems of linear equations the minimal ℓ1-norm solution is also the sparsest solution. Commun. Pure and Appl. Math.: A J. Issued Courant Inst. Math. Sci. **59**(6), 797–829 (2006)

9. Fattal, R.: Image upsampling via imposed edge statistics. ACM Trans. Graph. (TOG) **26**(3), 95 (2007)

10. Freeman, W.T., Pasztor, E.C., Carmichael, O.T.: Learning low-level vision. Int. J. Comput. Vis. **40**(1), 25–47 (2000)

11. Getreuer, P.: Contour stencils: total variation along curves for adaptive image interpolation. SIAM J. Imag. Sci. **4**(3), 954–979 (2011)

12. Glasner, D., Bagon, S., Irani, M.: Super-resolution from a single image. In: 2009 IEEE 12th International Conference on Computer Vision, pp. 349–356. IEEE, Kyoto September 2009. https://doi.org/10.1109/ICCV.2009.5459271

13. Goodfellow, I., Pouget-Abadie, J., Mirza, M., Xu, B., Warde-Farley, D., Ozair, S., Courville, A., Bengio, Y.: Generative adversarial nets. In: Advances in Neural Information Processing Systems. pp. 2672–2680 (2014)

14. Kim, K.I., Kwon, Y.: Single-image super-resolution using sparse regression and natural image prior. IEEE Trans. Pattern Anal. Mach. Intell. **32**(6), 1127–1133 (2010)

15. Ledig, C., et al.: Photo-realistic single image super-resolution using a generative adversarial network. In: Proceedings of the IEEE Conference on Computer Vision and Pattern Recognition, pp. 4681–4690 (2017)

16. Li, X., Orchard, M.T.: New edge-directed interpolation. IEEE Trans. Image Process. **10**(10), 1521–1527 (2001)

17. Sajjadi, M.S., Scholkopf, B., Hirsch, M.: Enhancenet: single image super-resolution through automated texture synthesis. In: Proceedings of the IEEE International Conference on Computer Vision. pp. 4491–4500 (2017)

18. Sun, J., Xu, Z., Shum, H.Y.: Image super-resolution using gradient profile prior. In: 2008 IEEE Conference on Computer Vision and Pattern Recognition. pp. 1–8. IEEE (2008)

19. Tibshirani, R.: Regression shrinkage and selection via the lasso. J. Roy. Stat. Soc.: Ser. B (Methodological) **58**(1), 267–288 (1996)

20. Yang, J., Wright, J., Huang, T.S., Ma, Y.: Image super-resolution via sparse representation. IEEE Trans. Image Process. **19**(11), 2861–2873 (2010). https://doi.org/10.1109/TIP.2010.2050625

21. Zeyde, R., Elad, M., Protter, M.: On single image scale-up using sparse-representations. In: Boissonnat, J.-D., et al. (eds.) Curves and Surfaces 2010. LNCS, vol. 6920, pp. 711–730. Springer, Heidelberg (2012). https://doi.org/10.1007/978-3-642-27413-8_47

22. Zhang, L., Wu, X.: An edge-guided image interpolation algorithm via directional filtering and data fusion. IEEE Trans. Image Process. **15**(8), 2226–2238 (2006)

23. Zhang, Y., Liu, J., Yang, W., Guo, Z.: Image super-resolution based on structure-modulated sparse representation. IEEE Trans. Image Process. **24**(9), 2797–2810 (2015)

24. Zhang, Z., Li, F., Chow, T.W., Zhang, L., Yan, S.: Sparse codes auto-extractor for classification: a joint embedding and dictionary learning framework for representation. IEEE Trans. Signal Process. **64**(14), 3790–3805 (2016)

Toward New Spherical Harmonic
Shannon Entropy for Surface Modeling

Malika Jallouli[1], Wafa Belhadj Khalifa[1], Anouar Ben Mabrouk[2,3,4],
and Mohamed Ali Mahjoub[1(✉)]

[1] LATIS- Laboratory of Advanced Technology and Intelligent Systems,
Université de Sousse, Ecole Nationale d'Ingénieurs de Sousse, 4023 Sousse, Tunisia
jallouli.malika3@gmail.com, wafa.bhk@gmail.com, medalimahjoub@gmail.com
[2] Department of Mathematics, Faculty of Sciences, Research Unit of Algebra,
Number Theory and Nonlinear Analysis UR11ES50, 5019 Monastir, Tunisia
anouar.benmabrouk@gmail.com
[3] Department of Mathematics, Higher Institute of Applied Mathematics
and Informatics, Street of Assad Ibn Al-Fourat, 3100 Kairouan, Tunisia
[4] Department of Mathematics, Faculty of Sciences,
University of Tabuk, King Faisal Rd, Tabuk, Saudi Arabia

Abstract. Genus zero surfaces are widespread forms in real life. It is
important to have adequate mathematical tools that best represent them.
Spherical harmonics are special bases able to model them in a compact
and a relevant way. The main problem of the spherical harmonics modeling process is how to define the optimal reconstruction order that best
represent the initial surface. This paper proposed a new spherical harmonics shannon-type entropy to optimize reconstruction and to provide
an accurate and efficient evaluation method of the reconstruction order.

Keywords: Spherical harmonics · Image processing · Reconstruction ·
Shannon entropy

1 Introduction

Surface representation and shape modeling play increasingly prominent roles in
many computer vision and image processing applications such as astronomy,
chemistry, medical imaging... Many technics have been developed for surface
reconstruction. The spherical harmonics (SHs) approach has been used essentially for the representation of genus zero surfaces. This particular basis helps
performing functional information analysis or classifying different types of forms.
In fact, SH shape description allows to approximate 3D complex objects efficiently with minimal storage cost. The main challenges arise from two tasks:
The first one is 3D surface modeling using SHs, and the second one is the determination in a precise and accurate way of the optimal reconstruction order that
represents well the initial 3D object. SHs represent genus zero surfaces with a
relevant and a compact way. Whereas, the main problematic remains with the
determination of the optimal reconstruction order mathematically and precisely.

© Springer Nature Switzerland AG 2019
M. Vento and G. Percannella (Eds.): CAIP 2019, LNCS 11679, pp. 38–48, 2019.
https://doi.org/10.1007/978-3-030-29891-3_4

This work is based on 3D SH modeling and proposes a new approach that allows an efficient representation of the spherical model. This approach is based on the concept of Shannon entropy to define in a precise way the optimal reconstruction order.

Entropy has been generalized and investigated in many domains such as computer information theory, topological entropy, metric entropy of Kolmogorov-Sinai and dynamical systems in mathematics. In signal analysis a temporal definition of entropy has been applied in [1,2] to study seismicity in different parts of the earth. In 2D image case, entropy concept remains a new approach. It is introduced recently in segmentation in [3] using maximum entropy thresholding. In [4], algorithms have been proposed to analyze the irregularity on spatial scales, which extends the 1D multi-scale entropy to the 2D case. In [5], the measure of entropy has been applied to derive automatic localization of positions.

In this paper, we propose a new expression of 3D Shannon entropy. A correlation type relation between entropy and SHs modeling is defined. We proposed to apply the new 3D entropy in surface modeling in order to identify in a precise and automatic way the final reconstruction order of SHs models that best represents initial images. In this case, a new entropy based on the SHs decomposition is proposed and applied on 3D surfaces.

This paper is organized as follow: the second section is a fast presentation of SHs analysis. Section 3 will describe the proposed method based on a new set of SH Entropy (SHE). Then, experimental results performed on the modeling of different 3D objects will aim to validate the proposed approach. We finish by the conclusion and the perspectives of this work.

2 Spherical Harmonics

The SHs are the angular parts of the solution of the Laplace equation $\Delta^2 f = 0$ in the spherical coordinates system. For $l \in \mathbb{N}$, $m \in \mathbb{Z}$; $|m| \leq l$

$$Y_{l,m} = K_{l,m} P_{l,m}(cos\theta) e^{im\varphi}, \tag{1}$$

where $K_{l,m}$ is the normalization constant

$$K_{l,m} = (-1)^m \sqrt{\frac{(2l+1)(l-m)!}{4\pi(l+m)!}} \tag{2}$$

and $P_{l,m}$ is the associated Legendre polynomial of degree l and order m

$$P_{l,m}(x) = \frac{(-1)^m}{2^l l!} (1-x^2)^{\frac{m}{2}} \frac{d^{l+m}}{dx^{l+m}} (x^2-1)^l. \tag{3}$$

The basis of SHs $(Y_{l,m})$ has several mathematical properties useful for modeling and pattern recognition.

(1) S^2 being a compact group, the Fourier Transform is therefore represented by the Fourier coefficients with respect to the associated Legendre base.
(2) SHs form a complete set on the surface of the sphere.

These two properties make it possible to deduce the reconstruction formula of the surface to be modeled, and any function $f \in R^2$ can be represented as

$$f(\theta, \varphi) = \sum_{l=0}^{\infty} \sum_{m=-l}^{l} S_{l,m} Y_{l,m}(\theta, \varphi), \tag{4}$$

where $S_{l,m}$ is the harmonic coefficient in the degree l and order m calculated by analogy to the 2D Fourier coefficients as the scalar product of the surface function or the spherical parameterization function with the basis of the SHs,

$$S_{l,m} = \int_0^{2\pi} \int_0^{\pi} f(\theta, \varphi) \overline{Y_{l,m}}(\theta, \varphi) \sin\theta d\theta d\varphi. \tag{5}$$

It's holds that the coefficients that contain the most information are those related to low frequencies. This property is very interesting for the reconstruction since it is possible to have a reconstructed surface very close to the initial one with a limited number of coefficients.

The most common problem in modeling with SHs is how to define the optimal reconstruction order that represents the closest model to the initial surface to be modeled. This information remains until now subjective and is determined always iteratively. At each iteration, the reconstruction order is incremented. The reconstruction is finished when the desired model is obtained.

3   Proposed Method

In this paper, we intend to present the use of the SH modeling in 3D surface modeling. A new approach based on Shannon entropy is proposed to solve the problem of choosing the optimal order of reconstruction. The diagram bellow illustrates the different steps of this work.

The overview of our proposed segmentation method is illustrated in Fig. 1 which highlights the two essential phases of the proposed approach resumed here-after.

– SH modeling process: it is important to note that a spherical parameterization step is necessary to model any genus zero surface. Then, a determination of the SH base $(Y_{l,m})$ given by Eq. (1) and the SH coefficients $S_{l,m}$ in Eq. (5) will allow to define the model reconstruction formula in Eq. (4).
– Shannon-type entropy process: at each iteration and for each order L, the SHE is calculated. In the following paragraph we will prove mathematically that when SHE value is stabilized when the order is increased, we can conclude that the final reconstructed order is reached.

3.1   SH Modeling Process

In this section, we intend to present the characteristics of the SHs and its impact on 3D surface modeling. The basis of SHs has several useful mathematical properties for modeling and pattern recognition.

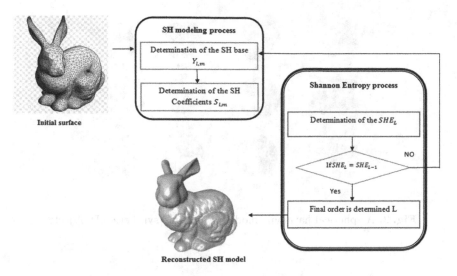

Fig. 1. SH modeling process using the new SHE

These properties permit to deduce make it possible to deduce the reconstruction formula from the surface to model. These mathematical properties can be illustrated by applying them on 3D synthetic images via the formula

$$\begin{pmatrix} X(\theta,\varphi) \\ Y(\theta,\varphi) \\ Z(\theta,\varphi) \end{pmatrix} = A_n^m \begin{pmatrix} \cos(\theta)\cos(\varphi) \\ \cos(\theta)\sin(\varphi) \\ \sin(\theta) \end{pmatrix} \qquad (6)$$

with:

$$A_n^m = \left(\sum_{n \in N} \sum_{m=0}^n (a_n^m \cos(m\varphi) + b_n^m \sin(m\varphi)) P_n^m(\cos(\theta)) \right). \qquad (7)$$

By varying m and n on a suitable grid we obtain a family of synthetic surfaces. Fig. 2 illustrates the relevance of the SH modeling. It is clearly notiaciable that as the order L gets up more details appear. On the other hand, the coefficients number of the reconstructed model remains much smaller than the number of points of the initial surface. This demonstrate the interest of this modeling method which aims to reproduce a 3D surface with a faithful and compact model. The Fig. 2 shows some examples of SHmodeling of synthetic surfaces obtained by Eq. (6).

It is important to note that the final order of reconstruction increases when the initial surface presents many details.

Figure 3 above highlights the compactness of the SHs. In fact, these curves represent the frequency spectrum relative to the HS according to the order of reconstruction. This illustrates that the main information lies around 0.

SH modeling remains an optimal representation of genus zero surfaces because of its pertinence and compactness. Whereas, the main problem remains

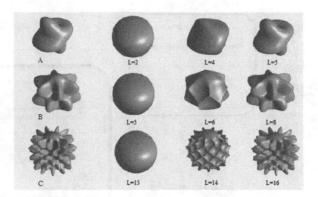

Fig. 2. A spherical harmonic modeling of some synthetic 3D objects

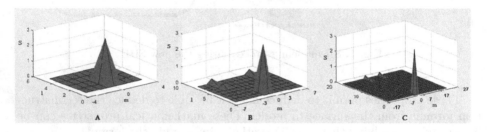

Fig. 3. SH coefficients representation of surfaces of Fig. 2.

on how to define the final reconstruction order. In the following section, we demonstrate how the new SHEs allows to define mathematically and precisely the final reconstruction order.

3.2 Spherical Harmonics Entropy

Shannon's entropy, due to Claude Shannon, is a mathematical function that measures to the amount of information contained or delivered by a source of information.

For a process characterized by a number N of states or classes of events, the Shannon entropy [6] is defined by

$$S = H_1 = -\sum_{i=1}^{N} p_i \log(p_i), \qquad (8)$$

p_i is the probability of occurrence of the events in each ith class.

In the continuous framework the Shannon entropy S is defined by

$$S = -\int_0^\infty p(x) \log(p(x)) dx \qquad (9)$$

x is a point in the space domain and $P(x)$ is the spatial probability density.

In the discrete case, the energy of the signal can be approximated by:

$$SHsE(l, m) = |S_{l,m}|^2 \tag{10}$$

Next, as for the context of wavelet entropy, the l-level energy of f is the sum on the grid $|m| \leq l$

$$SHsE(l) = \frac{1}{N} \sum_{|m| \leq l} SHsE(l, m) \tag{11}$$

The total energy is the sum over all the l-multiresolution levels

$$SHsE = \sum_{l} SHsE(l) = \frac{1}{N} \sum_{l} \sum_{|m| \leq l} SHsE(l, m). \tag{12}$$

In practice, of course, we could not compute all levels l, as these may be infinite, and thus we estimate the energy by means of a finite approximation

$$SHsE_L = \sum_{l=0}^{L} SHsE(l) = \frac{1}{N} \sum_{l=0}^{L} \sum_{|m| \leq l} SHsE(l, m) \tag{13}$$

which we call by the next the L-approximation of SHs' energy.

Next, as for Shannon entropy, we introduce the SHs' distribution or SHs probability density at the level l by

$$SHsP(l) = \frac{SHsE(l)}{SHsE} = \frac{\sum_{|m| \leq l} SHsE(l, m)}{\sum_{l} \sum_{|m| \leq l} SHsE(l, m)} \tag{14}$$

or equivalently

$$SHsP(l) = \frac{\sum_{|m| \leq l} |S_{i,m}|^2}{\sum_{l} \sum_{|m| \leq l} |S_{j,m}|^2}. \tag{15}$$

Finally, the $SHsEnt$ is defined by

$$SHsEnt = -\sum_{l} SHsP(l) \log(SHsP(l)). \tag{16}$$

In practice, as previously, we compute the L-estimation of the SHE

$$SHsEnt_L = -\sum_{l=0}^{L} SHsP(l) \log(SHsP(l)). \tag{17}$$

An overview of our SHE is summarized by the Algorithm 1.

Algorithm 1 : Spherical Harmonic Entropy

Input : $L, S_{l,m}$
Output : $SHEnt$

Begin
   For i=1 **to** L
      $E1 = SHsE(i)$;   (see equation 11)
      $E2 = SHsE$;   (see equation 13)
      $E3 = SHsP(i)$;   (see equation 15)
      $E4 = SHsEnt(i)$; (see equation 17)
     $SHEnt(i) = E4$;
   End for
  Return $SHEnt$;
End

4 Experimentation

In this section, the validation of the proposed method is performed to prove the correlation between SHE, defined in this paper, and the SH modeling process. First, an SH modeling is presented to show the importance of this form representation technique in the 3D domain. Then, we introduce the new SHE to evaluate automatically and effectively the most appropriate reconstruction order for each surface.

Figure 4 illustrates some examples of 3D surfaces with different complexities represented as 3D triangular meshes. The SH modeling process is performed on these surfaces to reconstruct the final models related to these surfaces.

The main problem of the SH reconstruction process is how to define the optimal order which represents the best model which fits the original object. Previous works [7] used Average Square Error (ASE) applied on SH coefficients via the formula

$$D_l^2 = \frac{1}{N} \sum_{i=1}^{N} (R_i(O_l) - R_i(O_{l-1}))^2 \tag{18}$$

where:

- R_i is the ith ray calculated on the ith point of the SH model.
- O_l is the SH model reconstructed at l order.
- O_{l-1} is the SH model reconstructed at $l-1$ order.
- N is the number of points of the initial surface.

This distance measures the difference between two successive SH reconstructed models. This distance should be minimum when the optimal model is reached. In fact, when the optimal order l is reached, reconstructed models at l and $l+1$ orders are almost the same. Equation (18) is based on the difference between rays calculated on two successive reconstructed models. This distance should not be performing in our case especially because rays are information non defining a 3D surfaces especially when we do not consider spherical angles.

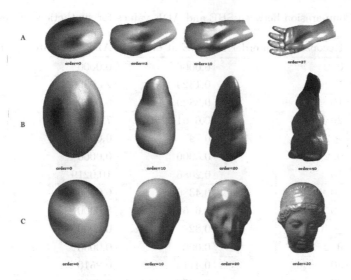

Fig. 4. 3D models reconstructed using SH: A-Hand reconstructed, B-Rabbit reconstructed, C-Venus reconstructed

Now, we demonstrate how the SHE proposed in this paper should be representative for determining the optimal reconstruction order. Although SH modeling has been widely used in different applications, in our knowledge, no method that precisely defines the optimal reconstruction order that defines the closest model to the initial surface has been developed.

This paper proves that SHE can be a good information to resolve this problematic. In fact, it should be a somehow global measure of invariance for the studied systems. Its value should be quietly constant as the multiresolution level increases. This is shown in Fig. 4.

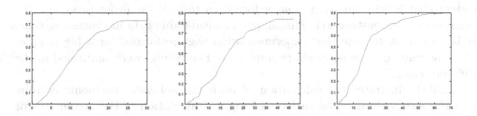

Fig. 5. Variation of SHsEnt of the surfaces A, B and C of Fig. 4.

These different curves show the variation of SHE during the SH modelling process.

Table 1. Comparasion between SHE and ADE values for synthetic surfaces of Fig. 4.

Surface	Reconstruction order L	SHE at order L	ADE calculated on L order
Fig. 4A	0..2	0,0000	0,0000
	5	0,1329	24,9390
	10	0,3829	0,0000
	20	0,6461	7,4459
	≥ 27	0,79	0,0000
Fig. 4B	0..2	0,0000	0,0000
	10	0,2086	10,0219
	20	0,4386	6,0000
	30	0,6960	8,0000
	≥ 40	0,82	0,0000
Fig. 4C	0..2	0,0000	0,0000
	20	0,4115	0,2510
	30	0,6370	3,0000
	40	0,6765	1,0600
	≥ 50	0,79	0,2100
	≥ 51	0,79	0,0000

where:

- L is the order.
- SHE_l is the SHE calculated at the order l.
- D_l is the Average Distance Error (ADE) calculated at the order l.

It is remarkable that for a precise value of l, SHE becomes stationary. Experimentation led us to conclude that this is the value of the optimal reconstruction order. That is why we are no longer forced to test all the order preceding the final order of reconstruction. This allows a considerable gain in processing time. It is important to note that experimentation was performed for a big number of genus zero surfaces of varying complexity. The results were confirmed in the different cases.

Table 1 illustrates the calculation of both the spherical harmonic entropy and the ADEs obtained on surfaces of Fig. 4. Calculation of the distance error on different surfaces shows that its value is null for the first orders, it increases for the following orders and when optimal order is reached.

The variation of the D_l value is especially due to comparison between two successive reconstructed orders. Whereas comparison should be done between the initial surface and reconstructed model. This is why SHE is a better and more precise method to define effectively and automatically the optimal order.

Table 2 shows that for a simple surface i.e., that does not presents many details SHE and ADE give the same results for the extraction of the final order.

Whereas, when the surface is more complicated, SHE detected the final order easier and earlier.

This result is due to the global characteristic of SHE which is the global energy calculated on the 3D signal of the initial surface.

Table 2. Final order dertermination using SHE and ADE methods.

Initial surface	Nb of points	Optimal order with SHE	Optimal order with ADE
Fig. 4A	36619	27	31
Fig. 4B	70658	40	45
Fig. 4C	100759	50	59

Comparison between the reconstructed model and the initial surface with SHE is more pertinent than comparing rays of two successive reconstructed models especially because of the non completeness of the ray information of a 3D surface.

5 Conclusion

In this paper, SHs have been examined and proved to be efficient candidates in the reconstruction of spherical image processing. The stimulating idea is based on the connection between well-known SH coefficients and signal energy. Fast and accurate algorithms have been obtained. Moreover the new definition of 3D entropy based on the SHs coefficients has improved the work, it makes it possible to measure the complexity of models to be reconstructed, easily and quickly to have a perfect reconstruction in real time.

References

1. Telesca, L., Lapenna, V., Lovallo, M.: Information entropy analysis of seismcity of umbria-marche region (Central Italy). Nat. Hazards Earth Syst. Sci. **4**(5/6), 691–695 (2004)
2. Telesca, L., Lovallo, M., Molist, J.M., Moreno, C.L., Mendelez, R.A.: Using the fisher-shannon method to characterize continuous seismic signal during volcanic eruptions: application to 20112012 El Hierro (Canary Islands) eruption. Terra Nova. **26**, 425–429 (2014)
3. Wanga, B., Chena, L.L., Chengc, J.: New result on maximum entropy threshold image segmentation based on P system. Optik **163**, 81–85 (2018)
4. Nicolis, O., Mateu, J.: 2D anisotropic wavelet entropy with an application to earthquakes in Chile. Entropy **17**(6), 4155–4172 (2015)
5. Vazquez, P.-P., Feixas, M., Sebert, M., Heidrich, W.: Viewpoint Selection using Viewpoint Entropy, pp. 21–23. Stuttgart, Germany (2001)
6. Shannon, C.: A mathematical theory of communication. Bell Syst. Tech. J. **27**, 379–423 (2008)

7. Khelifa, W.B., Ben Abdallah, A., Ghorbel, F.: Three dimensional modeling of the left ventricle of the heart using spherical harmonic analysis. In: ISBI, pp. 1275–1278 (2008)

8. Arfaoui S., Rezgui, I., Ben Mabrouk, A.: Wavelet Analysis On The Sphere, Spheroidal Wavelets, Degryuter. Degruyter, ISBN 978-3-11-048188-4 (2017)

9. Jallouli, M., Zemni, M., Ben Mabrouk, A., Mahjoub, M.A.: Toward recursive spherical harmonics-issued bi-filters: Part I: theoretical framework. Soft Computing. Springer, Berlin (2018). https://doi.org/10.1007/s00500-018-3596-9

10. Muller, I.: Entropy and energy, a universal competition. Entropy **10**, 462–476 (2008)

11. Robinson, D.W.: Entropy and uncertainty. Entropy **10**, 493–506 (2008)

12. Muller, I.: Extended thermodynamics: a theory of symmetric hyperbolic field equations. Entropy **10**, 477–492 (2008)

13. Ruggeri, T.: The entropy principle from continuum mechanics to hyperbolic systems of balance laws: the modern theory of extended thermodynamics. Entropy **10**, 319–333 (2008)

14. Fradkov, A.: Speed-gradient entropy principle for nonstationary processes. Entropy **10**, 757–764 (2008)

15. Sello, S.: Wavelet entropy and the multi-peaked structure of solar cycle maximum. New Astron. **8**, 105–117 (2003)

16. Brechbuhler, C., Gerig, G., Kubler, O.: Parametrization of closed surfaces for 3-D shape description. Comput. Vis. Image Underst. **16**, 154–170 (1996)

17. Chen, C., Huang, T.: Left ventricle motion analysis by hierarchical decomposition. ICASSP **3**, 273–376 (1992)

18. Staib, L.H., Duncan, J.S.: Model-based deformable surface finding for medical imaging. IEEE Trans. Med. Imag. **15**, 720–731 (1996)

19. Ibrahim Mahmoud, M.M., Ben Mabrouk, A., Abdallah Hashim, M.H.: Wavelet multifractal models for transmembrane proteins' series. Int. J. Wavelets Multires. Inf. Process. **14**, 1650044 (2016)

20. Makadia, A., Daniilidis, K.: Direct 3D-rotation estimation from spherical images via a generalized shift theorem. In: IEEE Computer Society Conference on Computer Vision and Pattern Recognition, Proceedings, pp. 18–20 (2003)

Over Time RF Fitting for Jitter Free 3D Vertebra Reconstruction from Video Fluoroscopy

Ioannis Ioannidis$^{(\boxtimes)}$ and Hammadi Nait-Charif

Bournemouth University, Poole BH12 5BB, UK
yioannidis@bournemouth.ac.uk

Abstract. Over the past decades, there has been an increasing interest in spine kinematics and various approaches have been proposed on how to analyse spine kinematics. Amongst all, emphasis has been given to both the shape of the individual vertebrae as well as the overall spine curvature as a means of providing accurate and valid spinal condition diagnosis. Traditional invasive methods cannot accurately delineate the intersegmental motion of the spine vertebrae. On the contrary, capturing and measuring spinal motion via the non-invasive fluoroscopy has been a popular technique choice because of its low incurred patient radiation exposure nature. In general, image-based 3D reconstruction methods focus on static spine instances. However, even the ones analysing sequences yield in unstable and jittery animations of the reconstructed spine. In this paper, we address this issue using a novel approach to robustly reconstruct and rigidly derive a shape with no inter-frame variations. This is to produce animations that are jitter free across our sequence based on fluoroscopy video. Our main contributions are (1) retaining the shape of the solid vertebrae across the frame range, (2) helping towards a more accurate image segmentation even when there's a limited training set. We show our pipeline's success by reconstructing and comparing 3D animations of the lumbar spine from a corresponding fluoroscopic video.

1 Introduction

In orthopaedics, identifying and accurately reconstructing 3D spine has always been of a great interest. Accurate shape and motion of the spine is essential to both physicians, medical students and patients. It is important because it is the means of understanding, assessing and providing a spinal condition diagnosis. Spine shape and kinematics reconstruction has been extensively studied [24,25]

Many studies focus on individual vertebrae surface reconstruction or use predefined rigid models (usually from CT scans) for the quantification of in vivo inter-vertebral motion. They are fitted to sequences of images and rotoscoped and registered on the target frames or on each subsequent frame in video sequences [24,25]. From an animation point of view, these approaches are limited in a sense that potential video sequences would be reconstructed statically per frame. Hence the per frame errors would result in jittery and unstable reconstructed animations. These methods lack shape representation as they assume

© Springer Nature Switzerland AG 2019
M. Vento and G. Percannella (Eds.): CAIP 2019, LNCS 11679, pp. 49–61, 2019.
https://doi.org/10.1007/978-3-030-29891-3_5

the vertebrae shapes stay solid throughout the captured image sequence, not accounting for projection noise across a sequence. This is not always the case, even though spine vertebrae are theoretically solid, and it is mostly because of the presence of noise in the target images. To address issues such as incorrect model initialization, segmentation and tracking error accumulation, a number of successful techniques have been developed to minimize the resulting errors for both surface reconstruction and kinematic analysis [2,15]. The majority of them are solving temporal coherency based on some sort of interpolation method as in [24]. Many, such as Prabhu et al. [14], have used Kalman Filtering (KF) to smooth the fitted landmarks after fitting. Others used either the current shape parameters and (KF) to update the view space per frame or even used convolutional neural networks (CNN) to accurately track and reconstruct [8,13].

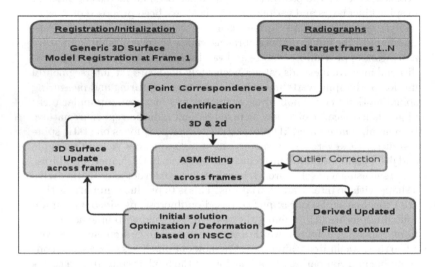

Fig. 1. Animation reconstruction pipeline

Crivellaro et al. [7] estimate the pose in a given frame, and then add it as a component of the pose prior for the next frame using KF for smoothing. Liao et al. [11] apply 3D score maps on a per CT slice basis (for the same frame). Hence leaving out the over time segmentation information whereas [1,16] work on neighbour slices only and consecutive frames. Wand et al. [21] achieve the global smoothness over time by iteratively merging geometry from adjacent frames. The work in [9] is based on as rigid as possible (ARAP) principle presented in [18]. It assumes there's a slight deformation model that is guided from frame to frame. In [23] CNN are employed however as it is obvious from the results, the final tracking is jittery. Salzmann et al. [17] smooth out predictions over a predefined set of frames to alleviate jitter.

Despite the above mentioned methods applied time varying analysis filters to smooth out and improve tracking accuracy, they usually suffer from 2 major problems. At first, they are sensitive to outliers. Secondly, inevitably the smoothing applied amongst the shapes between frames derives slightly different per frame morphologies for the final tracked objects. This is unwanted, as the aim is to rigidly segment from pose to pose and across all frames based on the underlying image information so as to produce a realistic animation with minimal jitter. Our method addresses the above by relying on random forests (RF) for the selection of displacements for all shapes' correction across the frame range simultaneously. More analytically, we used the whole target frame range, such that each next iteration prediction, for each shape of the sequence, is based on a collection of RF predictions across the whole frame range from the previous iteration. This way we can improve segmentation, as wrongly chosen individual landmark displacements obey a global per iteration displacement factor. Thus they can't severely affect the next frame segmentation in case of accumulated errors. Possible shape deviations are corrected as part of a more general drag towards the most significant displacements imposed to the rest of the shapes across the frame range. In our method we applied RF over time across the test frame range to fit the reconstructed 3D surface model to our video sequence. This is a different approach compared to [12] where RF have been used to improve individual image segmentation.

In our method, we used as a basis and extended the traditional active shape model (ASM) [5]. ASM has been extensively used mostly because of its proven robustness especially when dealing with large image inconsistencies and noise variations which is what fluoroscopy produces. The main contributions of this paper are:

- A novel approach which uses ASM allowing it to retain the shape of the supposedly solid vertebrae across the frame range
- A more accurate image segmentation, as a consequence of the first contribution, even when there's a limited training set because of global drag towards the most significant displacements

2   Method Overview

In Fig. 1 we present the pipeline of our method. We start with the input of both target images and a generic 3D surface model for a particular vertebra. These are then fed to the point correspondence step where we identify the 3D model points that correspond to the 2D radiographic landmarks. Then, ASM fitting is performed across the target frame range simultaneously for all frames using RF for the choice displacement predictions and the derived new contours are computed for each frame at this iteration. After having acquired the updated contours, we update our initial surface model solution with the derived contours and deform across all target frames for this iteration based on an adaptation of the non stereo corresponding contour (NSCC) algorithm [10] and the cycle continues.

3   Methods

In this section, we analytically present our method of extending ASM by iteratively fitting over time using RF voting (OTRF).

3.1   Traditional ASM Method

In ASM [5], a statistical shape model (SSM) framework, also named point distribution model (PDM) is used to fit a shape contour to a 2D image by iteratively deforming the initial shape instance according the PDM. Each shape is a vector of 2D landmark points $v_i = \{l_{i_1}..l_{i_n}\}$, where n is the total number of points of the shape. For each shape in the training set a v vector is created and all vectors are the aligned via principle component analysis (PCA) [5]. Shape alignment results in a mean shape $\bar{x} = \frac{1}{n}\sum_{i=1}^{n} v_i$, where n is the total number of training shapes. Now, after PCA we can describe our model with the following:

$$x \approx \bar{x} + Pb \tag{1}$$

where b is a vector of the most significant shape coordinate parameters of the deformable model [5] and P is the covariance matrix of first t eigenvectors calculated during PCA. This matrix contains eigenvectors and their corresponding eigenvalues λ_i. The largest eigenvalue describes the most significant shape variation and only a few t eigenvalues are needed to describe most of the shape's variation [3]. Equation 1 is then re-written to the following:

$$b = P^{-1}(x_i - \bar{x}) \tag{2}$$

By varying the parameters of b within $-3\lambda_i < b_i < 3\lambda_i$, we can vary the mean shape towards the most significant eigenvectors of P matrix when fitting to a target image. So, at first during training, for each of the landmarks of the shape, we create SSM derivative profiles (see Fig. 2) sampled along the normal of each landmark across the frame range of images, $dg_{i_j} = [g_{i_{j_1}} - g_{i_{j_0}}, ..., g_{i_{j_{2k+1}}} - g_{i_{j_{2k}}}]$, where dg_{i_j} is each landmark's derivative profile, k is the number of sampled profile points on either side of the landmark along the normal, i refers to every image of the training set and j to each landmark of the shape across images [3]. Their corresponding covariance matrices C are also computed

$$C_i = \frac{1}{n}\sum_{i=1}^{n}(g_{i_j} - \bar{g}_j)(g_{i_j} - \bar{g}_j)^T \tag{3}$$

and we finally derive the mean normalized derivative profile for each landmark across the frame range.

$$\bar{g}_j = \frac{1}{n}\sum_{i=1}^{n} g_{i_j} \tag{4}$$

where n is the total number of images in the training set. Then during fitting, for each of the landmarks, we create a derivative search profile by sampling small segments of m pixels across n pixels on either side of our landmark along the normal $(m < n)$ and compare to the mean normalized derivative profile using Mahalanobis distance,

$$D = (g_j(d) - \bar{g}_j)S^{-1}(g_j(d) - \bar{g}_j) \tag{5}$$

where g_j is current search profile, $\bar{g}$ is the mean model profile, d is the center pixel of the current profile sample across the normal and S is the mean covariance matrix for this specific landmark. Minimizing D is equal to maximizing the probability of $g(d)$, hence the d that achieves the minimum D is the one towards which this landmark should be moved [3]. We do this for all landmarks to derive their new most likely locations on the image. Finally, at every fitting iteration we update the b model parameters with $g_j(d)$

$$b = P^T(g_j(d) - \bar{x}) \tag{6}$$

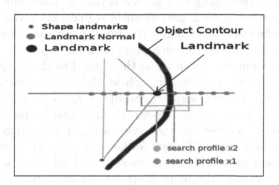

Fig. 2. Search profile along landmark normal

3.2   Proposed Method

In our approach, we extend ASM by iteratively fitting across the test frame range simultaneously using random forests (RF) for the choice displacement predictions. We refer to it as 'over time' prediction as well. The traditionally derived new contour predictions are computed for each frame at each iteration and are used to simultaneously feed each next iteration's shape fitting parameters, across the frame ranges tested. More analytically, at each iteration i we build displacement choice decision trees $T_{j_{i_r}}$ from each test frame range r for each of the landmarks of our shape.

$$T_{j_{i_r}} = \{T_{i_{j_1}}..T_{i_{j_r}}\} \tag{7}$$

where j is the current landmark, i is the current iteration and r total number of frame ranges to simultaneously segment. Consequently, we use Eq. 7 across the shape landmarks

$$S = \{T_1..T_n\} \tag{8}$$

where n is the total number of landmarks and i and j subscripts have been omitted in Eq. 8 for notation simplicity. Once, our trees are built per iteration, we use them to build and train a random forest and then derive a prediction per landmark to represent the most likely best choice for displacement for this landmark across the test frame ranges. From S we derive a vector of our shape predictions, for each landmark separately

$$fp_i = \{fp_{i_1}..fp_{i_j}\} \tag{9}$$

where j represents a single landmark of our shape and i is the current iteration number.

In Fig. 3 we show how we used the different searched frame ranges across the target frames to produce trees, as well as how each of them is fed to the RF so as to finally produce a displacement vector per iteration out of the predictions per landmark across these ranges. The idea is that by searching over time, and not on a per frame basis, each next frame's segmentation doesn't rely solely on static image information. Similarly, the pose across the target frame ranges doesn't depend exclusively on the each previous frame's pose. In the traditional ASM, during search phase we scan along the normal to the point in question or its surrounding area and use a metric such as Mahalanobis distance to express the likelihood of the current searched profile compared to the training set's equivalent profile as shown in Fig. 2, per each individual frame.

In our method, we harvest the underlying image information for both shape and pose over time and across all target frames and compute a refined shape that is insensitive to local noise and takes into account both local and global shape variations. Because of this, the shape keeps its rigidity across the sequence and overcomes the possibly inaccurate smoothing caused by interpolating 2 frames (as KF based approaches [6]). For example, in this paper Cordea et al. [6] used an extended Kalman filtering approach and applied it onto Active appearance models (AAM) [4]. They updated the shape and pose parameters per iteration during fitting. Huang et al. here [8] also used this approach to update shape and pose parameters and refine per frame, along with a temporal matching filter to smooth inter-frame shape differences.

These methods inevitably result in some sort of smoothing because of the nature of Kalman filtering itself. In medical imaging and specifically fluoroscopy, a low-radiation incurring technique, there is a high possibility of increased amounts of variation even between successive frames. Hence, one frame might have been precisely segmented and another not. This would result in an in between displacement for this particular landmark which would deviate from the image feature. The smoothed interpolated position that KF approaches are based on, would then result in successive frames to be clearly different from each other.

In our method, what we are suggesting is that the final shape is as solid as possible (subject to sub pixel inaccuracy), driven by the information of the whole range of target images and any inter-frame shape inconsistencies are only due to sub pixel inaccuracies caused during segmentation. Thus, producing a smooth and overall accurate animation result with no visually distracting jitter. We manage to achieve this using over time RF (OTRF) displacement choices across our frame ranges as described previously.

Most KF based and extended KF (EKF) approaches that update the shape are either updated within each frame [8] using information from previous iterations, between successive frames [13] or across a sequence to reinforce shape

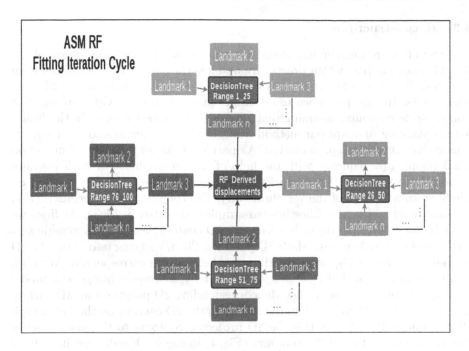

Fig. 3. RF fitting across frame ranges

parameters [6]. In [22] KF is used to correct the global rigid motion after fitting
has converged on each frame. Consequently, the use of KF which is mostly used
to derive a better initial shape for each of the next frames, is not involved in
iterative shape fitting. Additionally, KF is usually accompanied with a smoother
or similar method that smooths the in between observations. This is because KF
methods are generally sensitive to outliers and there is a need for a more robust
outlier detection method to handle tracking inaccuracies. Wadehn et al. show
in [20], a smoother that was put in place to address possible outliers. Others,
such as Ting et al. in [19] followed a weighted least squares approach by applying weights to data observations to tackle outliers and hence improve tracking
robustness.

However, all the above mentioned methods could result in some sort of inter-
frame inaccuracies owed to the nature of KF and consequently shape inconsistencies in an animation reconstruction pipeline. The shape will change and
adapt to inter-frame smoothing and in the presence of outliers successive frame
shapes will vary even more significantly. This is undesirable when our aim is to
robustly reconstruct and rigidly derive a shape with no inter-frame variations
and produce animations that are jitter free across our sequence.

3.3   Reconstruction

The rest of the reconstruction pipeline is mostly based on an adaptation of the NSCC algorithm [10], which practically updates the surface of a 3D model from a contour based on correspondences between associated 3D surface and 2D contour points. In this paper we use a single plane fluorscopy video to segment lumbar spine contours, assuming that there's no in-plane rotation. In the future we are planning to adapt our method using bi-planar sequences so as to achieve a more robust shape representation. As part of ASM we trained our model on a 2D fluoroscopy sequence with the help of a radiographer. For each instance of our shape we used 43 landmarks to represent it. We have only focused on the 3D reconstruction of the vertebral body. The complete Maya reconstruction pipeline described in the following paragraph is depicted in Fig. 4. At first, we identify point correspondence between our 2D contours and our 3D generic surface model within Autodesk Maya 3D package. Then, we bring into Maya the 2D segmented contours C_{2_D} and superimpose them on the corresponding vertebra at a particular frame f (Fig. 4, image 1). Secondly, we import our generic model M_{3_D} and identify in planar view the corresponding 2D points on its 3D surface (Fig. 4, image 2). Then, we align the model on the 2D contour on the radiograph (Fig. 4, image 3) and after this the 3D projected contours to the model (hence the 3D projected to the 2D contour) (Fig. 4, image 4). Finally, we iteratively deform the 3D projected contour C_{3_D} to C_{2_D} on this particular frame (Fig. 4, image 5) and then we deform the rest of the M_{3_D} to reflect the displaced C_{3_D} (Fig. 4, image 6). This way, the 3D model adapts to each new frame segmented with ASM and when this process is over we derive an animation based on the whole sequence segmentation. It is important to highlight that as our method is based on a 'model to images' correspondence to derive the 3D reconstruction, it is evident that the final reconstructed shape will be in immediate relation with the 2D segmentation. This is why it is crucial to derive a 'solid' 2D shape in the first place.

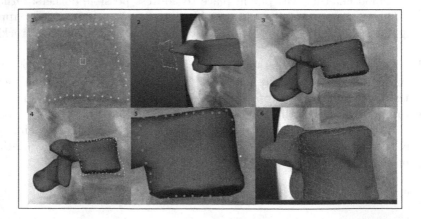

Fig. 4. Maya reconstruction pipeline. From 2D segmented points imported (upper left image), all the way down to final model deformation (bottom right image)

When the reconstruction is completed across the target frame range we can monitor the inter-frame shape differences. By applying our method, we derive an almost rigid (subject to sub pixel inaccuracy) shape across the sequence whilst tracking the vertebra in question. This is owed to the fact that the 3D model shape is driven by and adapted exclusively to the 2D segmented contour. This segmented contour from ASM is iteratively updated based on the most RF voted displacement and it remains solid. In contrast, the commonly used KF with a fixed lag smoother is causing a smoothing effect between observations.

Figure 5 shows the process of RF voting and choosing the most voted displacement. We are doing the same for all shape's landmarks and derive a solid contour across frames. In Fig. 6, the 2D contour drives the 3D shape at each frame of our video sequence and in Fig. 7 we present the final reconstructed frames.

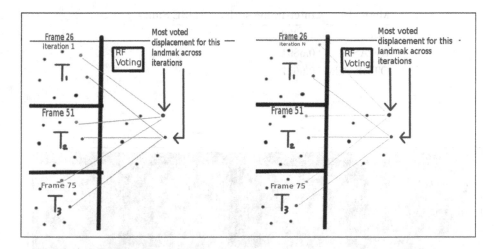

Fig. 5. RF range voting across frames' at every iteration

4   Experiments

Figure 7 shows 2 final reconstructed frames f_1, f_{75}. As seen in both Fig. 6 (bottom right image 8) and Fig. 7, there is no visible inter-frame surface variation amongst the compared frames whilst tracking is correctly achieved.

We implemented the traditional ASM method and a commonly used fixed-lag KF alongside with our over time RF fitting (OTRF) extension. Table 1 shows the quantified results of their mean inter-frame RMSE (root mean squared error). We derive our final RMSE metric f_c.

$$f_c = \frac{1}{n-1} \sum_{i=1}^{n-1} err_{i_{i+1}} \qquad (10)$$

where f_c is the inter-frame error metric across the sequence and i is every frame in our sequence. Finally, we can derive the average RMSE for each method by averaging f_c across the frame range, as shown in Eq. 11.

$$\bar{f}_c = \frac{1}{n} \sum_{i=1}^{n} f_c \qquad (11)$$

As shown in Table 1, our proposed OTRF produces less inter-frame mean error than the traditional ASM and the KF based ASM and thus leading to smoother and more accurate animation reconstructions which becomes more obvious in the presence of outliers or a limited training set.

Table 1. Inter-frame RMSE results across 75 frames.

Method	Inter-frame surface RMSE Sum - $\bar{f}c$
ASM	1.2330
KF ASM	0.6891
OTRF ASM	0.6617

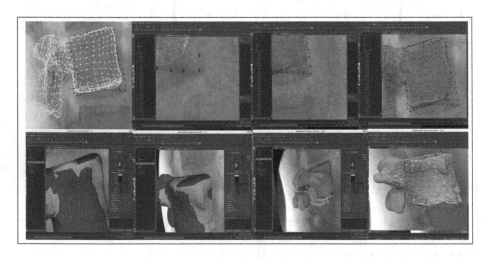

Fig. 6. Reconstruction pipeline and final coloured difference comparison. Images 1 to 4: Individual 3D projected contour fitted to 2D segmented contour. Images 5 and 6: Frame f_{26}, f_{75} after fitting and reconstructed with KF and traditional ASM. Images 7 and 8: f_{26}, f_{51}, f_{75} reconstruction with over time RF voting (OTRF) displacement ASM fitting. Image 8 superimposes OTRF reconstructed f_{26}, f_{51}, f_{75} to highlight the minimal colour differences across the range.

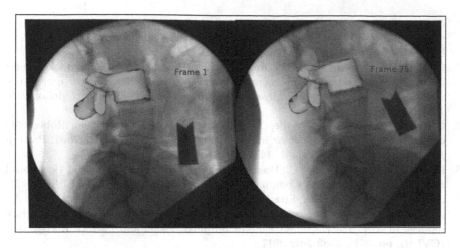

Fig. 7. Final reconstructed frames f_1, f_{75}

5 Conclusion

In this paper, we introduced a novel extension method applied on ASM which addresses the issue of jittery 3D reconstruction animations when reconstructing from 2D images. We trained and segmented using a test fluoroscopy video of a lumbar spine. The reconstructed 3D shape retains its rigidity across the sequence and it doesn't suffer from inaccurate smoothing caused by interpolating adjacent frames. We used random forests as a voting method to select the next iteration's most likely displacements during ASM fitting, simultaneously across all frames. The algorithm outperformed the traditional ASM and KF implementations on the same dataset in terms of rigidity, whilst correctly segmenting the 2D and thus tracking the 3D vertebra in question. Our future plan is to improve the developed pipeline and extend it to incorporate another view so as to reconstruct using a biplane rather than a single plane set up.

References

1. Allan, M., Ourselin, S., Hawkes, D.J., Kelly, J.D., Stoyanov, D.: 3-D pose estimation of articulated instruments in robotic minimally invasive surgery. IEEE Trans. Med. Imag. **37**(5), 1204–1213 (2018)
2. Bassani, T., Ottardi, C., Costa, F., Brayda-Bruno, M., Wilke, H.J., Galbusera, F.: Semiautomated 3D spine reconstruction from biplanar radiographic images: prediction of intervertebral loading in scoliotic subjects. Front. Bioeng. Biotechnol. **5**, 1 (2017). https://doi.org/10.3389/fbioe.2017.00001. https://www.frontiersin.org/article/10.3389/fbioe.2017.00001
3. Chen, Y.W., Jain, L.C.: Subspace Methods for Pattern Recognition in Intelligent Environment. Springer, Berlin (2016). https://doi.org/10.1007/978-3-642-54851-2
4. Cootes, T.F., Edwards, G.J., Taylor, C.J.: Active appearance models. In: Burkhardt, H., Neumann, B. (eds.) Computer Vision, pp. 484–498. Springer, Berlin (1998). https://doi.org/10.1007/BFb0054760

5. Cootes, T.F., Taylor, C.J., Cooper, D.H., Graham, J.: Active shape models — their training and application. Comput. Vis. Image Underst. **61**(1), 38–59 (1995). https://doi.org/10.1006/cviu.1995.1004

6. Cordea, M.D., Petriu, E.M., Petriu, D.C.: Three-dimensional head tracking and facial expression recovery using an anthropometric muscle-based active appearance model. IEEE Trans. Instrum. Meas. **57**(8), 1578–1588 (2008). https://doi.org/10.1109/TIM.2008.923784

7. Crivellaro, A., Rad, M., Verdie, Y., Yi, K.M., Fua, P., Lepetit, V.: Robust 3D object tracking from monocular images using stable parts. IEEE Trans. Pattern Anal. Mach. Intell. **40**(6), 1465–1479 (2018)

8. Huang, C., Ding, X., Fang, C.: Pose robust face tracking by combining view-based aams and temporal filters. Comput. Vis. Image Underst. **116**(7), 777–792 (2012)

9. Jaimez, M., Cashman, T.J., Fitzgibbon, A., Gonzalez-Jimenez, J., Cremers, D.: An efficient background term for 3D reconstruction and tracking with smooth surface models. In: 2017 IEEE Conference on Computer Vision and Pattern Recognition (CVPR). pp. 2575–2583 July 2017

10. Laporte, S., Skalli, W., Guise, J.D., Lavaste, F., Mitton, D.: A biplanar reconstruction method based on 2D and 3D contours: application to the distal femur. Comput. Meth. Biomech. Biomed. Eng. **6**(1), 1–6 (2003). pMID: 12623432

11. Liao, H., Mesfin, A., Luo, J.: Joint vertebrae identification and localization in spinal ct images by combining short- and long-range contextual information. IEEE Trans. Med. Imag. **37**(5), 1266–1275 (2018)

12. Lindner, C., Bromiley, P.A., Ionita, M.C., Cootes, T.F.: Robust and accurate shape model matching using random forest regression-voting. IEEE Trans. Pattern Anal. Mach. Intell. **37**(9), 1862–1874 (2015)

13. Peterfreund, N.: Robust tracking of position and velocity with kalman snakes. IEEE Trans. Pattern Anal. Mach. Intell. **21**(6), 564–569 (1999)

14. Prabhu, U., Seshadri, K., Savvides, M.: Automatic facial landmark tracking in video sequences using kalman filter assisted active shape models. In: Kutulakos, K.N. (ed.) Trends Top. Comput. Vis., pp. 86–99. Springer, Berlin (2012). https://doi.org/10.1007/978-3-642-35749-7_7

15. Rui, Z., Huai-yu, W., Ruo-hong, W.: Facial feature point tracking algorithm based on eyes tracking and active appearance model step fitting. In: 2015 34th Chinese Control Conference (CCC). pp. 3695–3701 July 2015

16. Wang, S.: Regularized shape deformation for image segmentation. In: 2001 IEEE International Conference on Acoustics, Speech, and Signal Processing. Proceedings (Cat. No.01CH37221). vol. 3, pp. 1569–1572 May 2001

17. Salzmann, M., Pilet, J., Ilic, S., Fua, P.: Surface deformation models for nonrigid 3D shape recovery. IEEE Trans. Pattern Anal. Mach. Intell. **29**(8), 1481–1487 (2007)

18. Sorkine, O., Alexa, M.: As-rigid-as-possible surface modeling. In: Proceedings of the Fifth Eurographics Symposium on Geometry Processing. pp. 109–116. SGP 2007, Switzerland (2007)

19. Ting, J.-A., Theodorou, E., Schaal, S.: Learning an outlier-robust kalman filter. In: Kok, J.N., Koronacki, J., Mantaras, R.L., Matwin, S., Mladenič, D., Skowron, A. (eds.) ECML 2007. LNCS (LNAI), vol. 4701, pp. 748–756. Springer, Heidelberg (2007). https://doi.org/10.1007/978-3-540-74958-5_76

20. Wadehn, F., Bruderer, L., Dauwels, J., Sahdeva, V., Yu, H., Loeliger, H.: Outlier-insensitive kalman smoothing and marginal message passing. In: 2016 24th EUSIPCO, pp. 1242–1246, August 2016

21. Wand, M., Jenke, P., Huang, Q., Bokeloh, M., Guibas, L., Schilling, A.: Reconstruction of deforming geometry from time-varying point clouds. In: Proceedings of the Fifth Eurographics Symposium on Geometry Processing, pp. 49–58. SGP 2007, Eurographics Association, Switzerland (2007)
22. Wang, C., Song, X.: Tracking facial feature points with prediction-assisted view-based active shape model. Face and Gesture **2011**, 259–264 (2011)
23. Wang, P., Patel, V.M., Hacihaliloglu, I.: Simultaneous segmentation and classification of bone surfaces from ultrasound using a multi-feature guided CNN. In: Frangi, A.F., Schnabel, J.A., Davatzikos, C., Alberola-López, C., Fichtinger, G. (eds.) MICCAI 2018. LNCS, vol. 11073, pp. 134–142. Springer, Cham (2018). https://doi.org/10.1007/978-3-030-00937-3_16
24. Yu, W., Zheng, G.: Atlas-Based 3D Intensity Volume Reconstruction from 2D Long Leg Standing X-Rays: Application to Hard and Soft Tissues in Lower Extremity, pp. 105–112. Singapore (2018)
25. Zheng, G.: Statistical Shape Models and Atlases: Application to 2D–3D Reconstruction in THA, pp. 183–190. Singapore (2018)

Challenges and Methods of Violence Detection in Surveillance Video: A Survey

Wafa Lejmi[1]([✉])[iD], Anouar Ben Khalifa[2][iD], and Mohamed Ali Mahjoub[2][iD]

[1] University of Sousse, Institut Supérieur d'Informatique et des Techniques de Communication de Hammam Sousse, LATIS - Laboratory of Advanced Technology and Intelligent Systems, 4011 Sousse, Tunisia
Wafa.Lejmi@uc.rnu.tn
[2] University of Sousse, Ecole Nationale d'Ingénieurs de Sousse, LATIS - Laboratory of Advanced Technology and Intelligent Systems, 4023 Sousse, Tunisia
http://www.latis-eniso.org/

Abstract. This article presents a survey of the latest methods of violence detection in video sequences. Although many studies have described the approaches taken to detect violence, there are few surveys providing exhaustive review of the available methods. We expose the main challenges in this area and we classify the methods into five broad categories. We discuss each category and present the main techniques that proposed improvements as well as some performance measures using public datasets to evaluate the different existing techniques of violence detection.

Keywords: Video · Violence · Detection · Challenges · Methods · Classification · Extraction · Features

1 Introduction

The field of video surveillance is becoming a daily necessity to control the behavior of people, to detect their presence in certain places and to study their actions in order to contribute to preventing and reducing crimes. Categorizing video content according to certain human interactions is a task of growing interest in video surveillance, especially after the multiple terrorist attacks around the world in recent years, and the detection of violent scenes receives considerable attention in surveillance systems to better ensure the safety of people in public places. However, the gap is significant between the amount of video data continuously captured by the cameras and the human tendency to efficiently analyze this visual information. In other words, it is possible to miss certain activities and suspicious behavior will not be detected in time to prevent incidents requiring an automatic understanding of human actions. The recognition of human activities is therefore a hard task because of various difficulties and it depends on other several factors. Throughout these last years, various works on the automatic recognition of human action have been proposed [13,21], however the characterization

© Springer Nature Switzerland AG 2019
M. Vento and G. Percannella (Eds.): CAIP 2019, LNCS 11679, pp. 62–73, 2019.
https://doi.org/10.1007/978-3-030-29891-3_6

of violence has been comparatively less explained. The automatic detection of aggressive behavior presents some challenges because of its subjective nature in defining what should be considered as violence [12,16]. Indeed, some human actions can be poorly recognized as aggressive behaviors [15]. Therefore, it is important to resolve these ambiguities so that the system proves more reliability and robustness. The purpose of this paper is to reinforce the few available exhaustive reviews in this field [19] by presenting a wide number of violence detection methods and outlining their general concepts. Actually, the main types of violence actions considered in the literature can be individual actions like hitting each other or collective actions such as violent behaviors in crowded scenes like an assault carried out by a group of persons. These are the basic contributions of this survey: We study the major challenges of the violence detection in video sequences. Then, we classify the violence detection approaches in groups based on the kind of techniques associated with each category and we describe the proposed tools. We present different performances via some public benchmark datasets used in evaluating the approaches. This paper is organized as follows: In the next section, we discuss the various problems encountered in the video violence detection work and the solutions that have been proposed. In Sect. 3, we group violence detection methods into main categories, we describe their general concepts and present the adopted techniques. In Sect. 4, we expose an overview of public datasets used in violence detection and we report our experimental results of the method we intended to improve. This paper is concluded with the future directions to work on in this field.

2 Challenges to Violence Detection in Video

Detecting violent behavior is not easy due to many difficulties encountered while capturing moving persons. Below, the main challenging issues are explored:

2.1 Dynamic Illumination Variations

Tracking becomes difficult when analyzing scenes with changing illumination, a common property of naturalistic environments. Outdoor cameras are subject to natural illumination changes that result in poor contrast when recording footage at night, which can make description of content difficult. Zhou, et al. [43] gave a better tolerance to illumination variation. They used an LHOG descriptor which is extracted from a "block" composed of "cells". The Local Histogram of Oriented Gradient (LHOG) features result from RGB images. To handle illumination variation, they took two strategies: firstly, the block stride by half of itself, i.e., the overlap is half of a block. Then, the normalization is conducted for each LHOG. The Local Histogram of Optical Flow (LHOF) is extracted from the motion magnitude images that captures dynamic information. Also, adaptive background subtraction algorithm [2] yields a reliable method which deals with lighting changes, repetitive and long-term scene changes.

2.2   Presence of a Non-stationary Background

Sometimes videos are of low resolution and may contain background movement caused by camera motion or environmental light change, rendering noise removal a must. In [8] the optical flow approach is adopted for motion analysis, since the magnitude of the optical flow vector is a very strong cue for measuring the amount of motion and the flow direction can provide additional motion information. A background motion-resilient algorithm is applied to compute the optical flow between every two consecutive frames. The camera motion usually induces a relative movement of the background at a uniform speed. Human activities are more likely to move less uniformly. This allowed to filter background movement noise. In [30] different procedures are applied and include a 3*3 Gaussian kernel to reduce noise effect, a histogram equalization to distribute pixel intensities to a larger contrast range and a background subtraction using Mixture of Gaussians (MoG) to avoid objects not related to the actors. The dominating background portions may interfere with the prediction of action recognition models. To mitigate this issue, we need to consider localizing action instances and avoiding the influence of background video at the same time. Wang et al. [34] noticed a remarkable amount of horizontal movement in the background due to the camera motion. Inspired by improved dense trajectories [32], they suggested to add warped optical flow as input modality. They extracted them by estimating homography matrix and compensating camera motion. This removes the background motion and helps to focus on the actor. In [33], new aggregation functions are added to the temporal segment network framework. This is efficient to highlight important snippets while suppressing background noise.

2.3   Motion Blur

This is a challenging problem for the optical flow-based motion estimation: The geometric feature points of a human body, e.g., head, hands, feet, shoulders, and elbows, provide characteristic abstraction of various poses. In [3] Deniz et al. proposed a method that does not involve tracking or optical flow techniques and which is suitable for measuring extreme accelerations. They noted that extreme acceleration implies image blur, which makes tracking less precise or impossible. Indeed, camera motion could cause blur in the image. To remove it, they performed a deconvolution preprocessing step. The phase of correlation technique is first used to infer global motion between each pair of consecutive frames. If global motion is detected, the estimated angle and length of the displacement is used to form a PSF (Point Spread Function) and to perform deconvolution of the second frame (using Lucy-Richardson iterative deconvolution method).

2.4   Occlusion

Occlusion is one of the problems that cannot be avoided in applications of individual tracking process. Many algorithms suffer due to the presence of occluded objects in a scene. The region which is occluded though, depends on the camera viewpoint. A wide range of techniques and algorithms is reported in the review presented in [1] for object detection under occlusions. In some scenarios angle of the camera can define which part is occluded and which one is not, consequently in [14] some techniques were proposed such as minimization approach, temporal selection, graph cut method and sum of squared distance The original idea to predict occlusion in tracking stems from the geometric information. A possible solution is using the fusion of several cameras to know the depth and subsequent estimation of the hidden part. Depth estimation is challenging, therefore a polynocular stereo algorithm helps to handle occlusion. Furthermore, temporary and trajectory prediction is suggested for the same worry. Since geometry of a scene plays a crucial role in handling occlusion, the epipolar lines and disparity map technique are used to obtain the robust solution as well as the suppression trick which uses ordering constraint. The occlusion areas are identified by two occlusion maps, whereas the displacement field between the images is a key part in this proficiency. One of the simplest methods is cross checking and extrapolation. A normalized cross correlation method for handling occlusion was adopted later in addition to a subtraction of the mean and a division of the standard deviation. Image segmentation was used for handling occlusion adopting Mean shift algorithm [5]. It is also possible to use disparity maps obtained with the help of optimization based on modified constant space belief propagation. Wojek et al. [35] focused on reliable multi-object tracking from a moving platform in challenging real world scenes with object-object occlusion using SVM (Support vector machine) and DPM (Deformable Parts Model) that is good in long term occlusion, especially on human detection. In [7] the occluding objects were fully removed from the image in order to look at what is behind them using the canny edge detector function and disparity map generation. Kalman filtering is the classical method widely employed for tracking. Appearance models are used for handling occlusions in each track [25]. Other works resorted to two layers classifiers using Conditional Random Field (CRF) and Deformable Parts Model (DPM) without any knowledge from previous frames [24]. A new

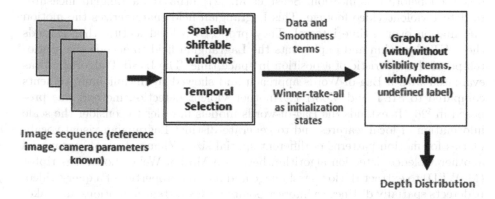

Fig. 1. Proposed techniques for occlusion handling [14].

approach was adopted in [39] based on Kannade-Lucas Tomasi (KLT) method. In [40] an aggregation of Weber Local Descriptor (WLD) histograms of neighboring areas was proposed. Motion Weber Local Descriptor (MoWLD) captures local appearance with an aggregated histogram of gradients from adjacent areas offering better tolerance to partial occlusion. In [18] using visual texture is well suited for the unstructured patterns resulting from occlusions caused by crowding (Fig. 1).

3   Violence Detection Methods

Many feature extraction methods are available for detecting violence in videos. We can broadly classify them in five groups detailed as follows:

3.1   Local Methods Based on Interest Points

Almost all of these methods are based on the standard SIFT algorithm to find visually distinctive interest points in the spatial domain. Then the candidate points with insufficient optical flow around the neighborhood are rejected, leaving only spatio-temporal interest points with strong motion. Nievas et al. [23] worked on assessing the performance of modern action recognition approaches for detecting fights in videos using two of the best methods currently available (STIP and MoSIFT). They implemented a versatile and accurate fight detector using local descriptors approach which reliably detects violence in sports footage, even in the presence of camera motion. Xu et al. [37] proposed an approach based on the MoSIFT algorithm and the sparse coding scheme. MoSIFT was used to capture distinctive local shape and motion patterns of an activity, then Kernel Density Estimation KDE-based feature selection method selected the most representative features of the MoSIFT descriptor, and finally sparse coding method paired with max pooling procedure generated a discriminative high-level video representation from local features. Then, the Bag-of-Words model was used before classification. Senst et al. [27] utilized Lagrangian measures to detect violent video footage. This Lagrangian field characterizes the motion information over a time interval. They proposed a local feature that extends the SIFT algorithm and implements the Lagrangian field to encode the spatio-temporal characteristic of a position in space time. The LaSIFT algorithm was evaluated with a Bag-of-Words approach and showed significant improvements compared to SIFT and MoSIFT. Another violent detection method was proposed in [26]. It extends the Bag-of-words models in order to consider the scale information of local features and to generate distinct Lagrangian-visual vocabularies for motion patterns of different spatial sizes. Zhang et al. [40] proposed another violence detection algorithm based on Motion Weber Local Descriptor (MoWLD) to extract the low-level image and motion properties of a query video. It detects spatially distinctive interest points with substantial motions and takes the advantages of both SIFT in terms of computing the histogram using the magnitude and orientation of gradient and Local Binary Pattern (LBP) in terms of computational efficiency. The second aspect is removing irrelevant features using Kernel Density Estimation (KDE). Sparse coding is adopted to transform the low-level descriptors into compact mid-level features. Max pooling algorithm is used to get more discriminative representation of extracted features.

3.2 Methods Relying on Magnitudes of the Optical Flow Fields

A fast and robust framework for detecting and localizing violence in surveillance scenes was proposed in [41] A Gaussian Model of Optical Flow (GMOF) is suggested to extract candidate violence regions, which are adaptively modelled as a deviation from the normal behavior of crowd observed in the scene. Violence detection is then performed on each video volume constructed by densely sampling the candidate violence regions. The proposed descriptor is called Orientation Histogram of Optical Flow (OHOF) and fed into a linear SVM for classification of violent and non-violent events. GMOF is discriminatorily inefficient, when the background is disordered and dynamic. Other works [8,28] have merged statistical features extracted from spatio-temporal motion spots, such as mean, variance, standard deviation, axis center position, area, and so on. The advantage of these models is their low complexity of computation, but their performances are limited in terms of classification precision. The work proposed in [10] examined statistics on changes in the magnitude of the flow velocity vector for violent behavior of the crowd and described a novel method to real-time detection of breaking violence in crowded scenes. This method considers statistics of how flow-vector magnitudes change over time. These statistics, collected for short frame sequences, are represented using the VIolent Flows (ViF) descriptor which is then classified as either violent or non-violent using linear SVM. The means offered by this method are computationally efficient for crowd violence detection. A feature extraction technique named Oriented VIolent Flows (OViF) based on ViF descriptor in [10] is presented in [9] and takes full advantage of the motion magnitude change information in statistical motion orientations. Huang et al. [11] presented a statistic approach based on optical flow field to detect violent crowd behaviors. It considers the statistical characteristics of optical flow field and extracts a SCOF descriptor from these features to represent the sequences of video frames. Actions are then categorized as either normal or violent using linear SVM. The SCOF descriptor models only motion information and cannot capture appearance characteristics. Zhou et al. [43] presented a method using low-level features. First, they segmented the motion regions according to the distribution of optical flow fields. Then, in the motion regions, they suggested extracting two kinds of low-level features: LHOG descriptor extracted from RGB images and LHOF descriptor from optical flow images. Finally, the features are coded using Bag-of-Words model to remove redundant information and a specific-length vector is obtained for each video clip. A smart video system was developed in [30] to analyze long sequences from a large number of cameras. Here, the use of Census Transform Histogram (CENTRIST) based features helps to identify violence context. In order to detect violent behavior in crowded and non-crowded scenes, Mahmoodi et al. [20] presented a new feature descriptor named Histogram of Optical flow Magnitude and Orientation (HOMO). Input frames are initially converted to the grayscale format and the optical flow between two consequence frames is computed. Then, the optical flow magnitude and orientation of each pixel in each frame are compared separately with its predecessor frame to obtain meaningful changes of magnitude and orientation. Next, threshold values are applied to the magnitude and orientation changes to obtain six histograms. Finally, these histograms are concatenated to achieve a vector named HOMO and the classification is processed by a SVM classifier.

3.3   Methods Based on Acceleration Patterns

Datta et al. [2] tracked and monitored an area for violent actions between people by relying on motion trajectory and orientation information of a person's limbs. They defined an Acceleration Measure Vector (AMV) composed of motion direction and magnitude and defined Jerk to be the temporal derivative of AMV. An adaptive Background Subtraction method is used to model each pixel as a mixture of Gaussian by probabilistic measurements based on the mean and covariance of pixel color history and weight. A new approach was proposed in [3] using Extreme Acceleration Patterns as the main discriminative feature of aggressive behavior. It is efficiently estimated by the application of the Radon transform to the power spectrum of consecutive frames. But, this implies image blur which makes tracking less precise or even impossible. A novel video descriptor is presented in [22] based on substantial derivative, an important concept in fluid mechanics, which captures the rate of change of a fluid property as it travels through a velocity field. This approach exploits the spatio-temporal features of substantial derivative. Indeed, the spatial and temporal motion patterns are captured by computing the convective and local accelerations for each video. Then, the Bag-of-words paradigm is used for each motion pattern separately, and the two resulting histograms are concatenated to form the final descriptor.

3.4   Approaches Using Deep Learning Techniques

The ideal methods would detect violent behavior in overcrowded scenes. Deep convolutional networks have recently shown success for visual recognition in still images. The concepts to design effective ConvNet architectures for action recognition in videos were exposed in [34] via a novel framework for video-based action recognition called Temporal Segment Network (TSN) and based on long-range temporal structure modelling. It combines a sparse temporal sampling strategy and video-level supervision to enable efficient learning using the whole action video. The method used in [6] extracts spatio-temporal features from video sequences. Saliency information (SI) is extracted of video frames as the feature representation in the spatial domain. To extract the accurate motion information, Multi-scale Histogram Optical Flow (MHOF) can be obtained through Optical flow. MHOF and SI were combined into the spatio-temporal features of video frames and a deep learning network PCANet, was adopted to extract high-level features for abnormal event detection. Inspired by the development of convolutional networks on common activity recognition, Zhou et al. [42] set up a FightNet to represent the complicated visual violence interaction. They proposed a new input modality, image acceleration field to better extract the motion attributes. FightNet was trained with three kinds of input modalities, i.e., RGB images for spatial networks, optical flow images and acceleration images for temporal networks. Xu et al. [36] presented an unsupervised deep learning framework for anomalous event detection in complex video scenes named Appearance and Motion DeepNet (AMDN) which uses deep neural networks to automatically learn feature representations. Stacked denoising autoencoders were suggested to learn both appearance and motion features in addition to a joint representation (early fusion). Multiple one-class SVM models were used to foresee the anomaly scores of each input, which are then integrated with a late fusion strategy for final anomaly detection. A framework named Three-Stream Deep Convolutional Neural Networks is proposed in [4] for person-to-person intense violence detection. It adopts the Long Short Term Memory on top of three streams (i.e., spatial, temporal and acceleration streams) to model long-term temporal information. In [31] an end-to-end trainable deep neural network model is presented. It consists of a convolutional neural network (CNN) for frame level feature extraction followed by feature aggregation in the temporal domain using convolutional long short term memory (convLSTM). Overall, deep neural networks for video violence detection are pre-trained on UCF101 [29] to avoid overfitting.

3.5 Methods Using Crowd Texture

Lloyd et al. [18] described violent situations that occur in city center environments using Gray Level Co-occurrence Matrix (GLCM) applied in crowd density estimation and used temporal encoding to describe crowd dynamics. They referred to the method of Violent Crowd Texture (VCT). Real-world surveillance footage of night time environments and the violent flows dataset were tested using a random forest classifier to evaluate the ability of the highly effective VCT method at discriminating between violent and non-violent behavior. To exactly identify violent scenes, Lloyd et al. [17] suggested a linear combination of three measures of motion trajectory to produce a response map that highlights spatio-temporal regions which are suggestive of violent behavior. Motion trajectories are computed using a particle advection process widely used in pedestrian analysis thanks to its robustness to minor occlusions.

4   Experimental Results

The main public benchmark datasets used in all the mentioned works are assembled in the Fig. 2 and the values are reported from the analyzed papers.

Different performances for violence seen within city, street and indoor environments are presented. "Hockey Fight dataset" is the most used (detection performance exceeds 97% with deep learning Convolutional LSTM method).

Violence Detection Methods Performances (%)

Public violence Datasets	Local methods based on Interest Points					Methods based on magnitudes of Optical Flow fields								Acceleration patterns methods		Methods based on Deep Learning algorithms							Methods based on Crowd Textures	
	STIP	MoSIFT +HDE+SC	LaSIFT +BoW	MoWLD +HDESC	MoWLD +BoW	OHOF +SVM	Motion Analysis	K-largest Motion blobs +RF	OViF+VIF +Adaboost +SVM	SCOF +SVM	LHOG+LHOF HOG+SVM +BoW	CENTRIST +SVM	HOMO +SVM	Extreme acceleration patterns +SVM	Derivative Substantial	TSN (3 modalities)	MHOF SI +	PCANet model	FightNet +Softmax	AMDN +SVM	Deep Networks (3 streams)	LSTM (Convolutional)	GLCM Subtraction +RF	Local Trajectory Response +Linear SVM
Works References	[23]	[37]	[27,26]	**[40]**	[41]	[8]	[28]	[9]	[11]	[43]	[30]	[20]	**[3]**	[22]	[34]	**[6]**	[42]	[36]	**[4]**	[31]			[18]	[17]
Hockey Fight	90	94.3	94.42	94.9	91.9		84.5	82.4	87.5	86.9	95.1	92.79	89.3	90.1								93.9	97.1	87.4
Crowd Violence		89.05	93.12	87.17		82.79				83.35	94.31			85.43										
UCF101									79.5							94.2								
Riots 2011			84.00																			98.38		
BEHAVE				94.9		85.29					100				94.8									
CAVIAR						86.75																		
HMDB51																69.4								
VID																			97.06					
UCSD pedestrian																				92.1				
UMN Unusual Crowd																		99.87	99.95				98.45	
Web abnormality																						92.87		
Violent Flows									86			91.46	76.83									94.57	91.34	81.7

Fig. 2. Overview of all the violence detection methods mentioned in this survey with the performances respectively obtained using 12 public datasets.

"Crowd Violence dataset" is less used and shows a good detection performance (it exceeds 94% with LHOG+LHOF+BoW method). Also, "BEHAVE dataset" is less frequently used but shows an excellent detection performance (it reaches 100% with the same method). However, few methods rely on acceleration patterns. In order to improve the approach that relies on the substantial derivative, we resorted to one more public dataset named SBU-Kinect-Interaction [38]. We computed the substantial derivative using the optical flow and extracted features using HOG descriptor, but instead of SVM classifier, we chose k-Nearest Neighbors algorithm (KNN) which is more efficient since its processing time is slightly lower. It showed good recognition rate depending on the value of k. Best results were achieved when its value was exactly 100. The accuracy was near 98% for "Hugging", 90% for "Pushing" and 85% for "Punching" interactions.

5   Conclusion

In this paper, various aspects of violence detection have been studied. First, we provided an extensive review of the challenges encountered and the main techniques proposed to handle them. Then, we divided the existing methods into five broad categories based on the common points of the suggested approaches. We exposed an overview of twelve public datasets used by the violence detection techniques and reported the best values of the experimental results from the analyzed works. We implemented our own test to improve the substantial derivative-based approach by choosing the k-Nearest Neighbors classifier which yielded good performance. We are aware that further improvements are possible for violence detection methods by further analyzing physical interaction forces which dominate the motion of the individuals.

References

1. Chandel, H., Vatta, S.: Occlusion detection and handling: a review. Int. J. Comput. Appl. **120**, 33–38 (2015). https://doi.org/10.5120/21264-3857
2. Datta, A., Shah, M., Da Vitoria Lobo, N.: Person-on-person violence detection in video data. In: Object Recognition Supported by User Interaction for Service Robots. vol. 1, pp. 433–438. August 2002. https://doi.org/10.1109/ICPR.2002.1044748
3. Deniz, O., Serrano, I., Bueno, G., Kim, T.: Fast violence detection in video. In: 2014 International Conference on Computer Vision Theory and Applications (VISAPP), vol. 2, pp. 478–485. January 2014
4. Dong, Z., Qin, J., Wang, Y.: Multi-stream deep networks for person to person violence detection in videos. In: CCPR (2016)
5. Enzweiler, M., Eigenstetter, A., Schiele, B., Gavrila, D.M.: Multi-cue pedestrian classification with partial occlusion handling. In: 2010 IEEE Computer Society Conference on Computer Vision and Pattern Recognition. pp. 990–997. June 2010. https://doi.org/10.1109/CVPR.2010.5540111
6. Fang, Z., et al.: Abnormal event detection in crowded scenes based on deep learning. Multimedia Tools Appl. **75**, 14617–14639 (2016). https://doi.org/10.1007/s11042-016-3316-3
7. Fehrman, B., McGough, J.: Handling occlusion with an inexpensive array of cameras. In: 2014 Southwest Symposium on Image Analysis and Interpretation, pp. 105–108. April 2014. https://doi.org/10.1109/SSIAI.2014.6806040
8. Fu, E.Y., Leong, H.V., Ngai, G., Chan, S.: Automatic fight detection based on motion analysis. In: 2015 IEEE International Symposium on Multimedia (ISM), pp. 57–60. December 2015. https://doi.org/10.1109/ISM.2015.98
9. Gao, Y., Liu, H.W., Sun, X., Wang, C., Liu, Y.: Violence detection using oriented violent flows. Image Vis. Comput. **48–49**, 37–41 (2016)
10. Hassner, T., Itcher, Y., Kliper-Gross, O.: Violent flows: real-time detection of violent crowd behavior. In: 2012 IEEE Computer Society Conference on Computer Vision and Pattern Recognition Workshops, pp. 1–6. June 2012. https://doi.org/10.1109/CVPRW.2012.6239348
11. Huang, J., Chen, S.: Detection of violent crowd behavior based on statistical characteristics of the optical flow. In: 2014 11th International Conference on Fuzzy Systems and Knowledge Discovery (FSKD), pp. 565–569. August 2014. https://doi.org/10.1109/FSKD.2014.6980896
12. Jegham, I., Ben Khalifa, A.: Pedestrian detection in poor weather conditions using moving camera. In: 2017 IEEE/ACS 14th International Conference on Computer Systems and Applications (AICCSA), pp. 358–362. October 2017. https://doi.org/10.1109/AICCSA.2017.35
13. Jegham, I., Ben Khalifa, A., Alouani, I., Mahjoub, M.A.: Safe driving : driver action recognition using surf keypoints. In: 2018 30th International Conference on Microelectronics (ICM), pp. 60–63. December 2018. https://doi.org/10.1109/ICM.2018.8704009
14. Kang, S.B., Szeliski, R., Chai, J.: Handling occlusions in dense multi-view stereo. In: Proceedings of the 2001 IEEE Computer Society Conference on Computer Vision and Pattern Recognition. CVPR 2001. vol. 1, pp. I-I. December 2001. https://doi.org/10.1109/CVPR.2001.990462

15. Lejmi, W., Ben Khalifa, A., Mahjoub, M.A.: Fusion strategies for recognition of violence actions. In: 2017 IEEE/ACS 14th International Conference on Computer Systems and Applications (AICCSA), pp. 178–183. October 2017. https://doi.org/10.1109/AICCSA.2017.193

16. Lejmi, W., Mahjoub, M.A., Ben Khalifa, A.: Event detection in video sequences: challenges and perspectives. In: 2017 13th International Conference on Natural Computation, Fuzzy Systems and Knowledge Discovery (ICNC-FSKD), pp. 682–690. July 2017. https://doi.org/10.1109/FSKD.2017.8393354

17. Lloyd, K., Rosin, P.L., Marshall, A.D., Moore, S.C.: Violent behaviour detection using local trajectory response. In: 7th International Conference on Imaging for Crime Detection and Prevention (ICDP 2016), pp. 1–6. November 2016. https://doi.org/10.1049/ic.2016.0082

18. Lloyd, K., Marshall, A.D., Moore, S.C., Rosin, P.L.: Detecting violent crowds using temporal analysis of glcm texture. CoRR abs/1605.05106 (2016)

19. Mabrouk, A., Zagrouba, E.: Abnormal behavior recognition for intelligent video surveillance systems: a review. Expert Syst. Appl. **91**, 480–491 (2018). https://doi.org/10.1016/j.eswa.2017.09.029

20. Mahmoodi, J., Salajeghe, A.: A classification method based on optical flow for violence detection. Expert Syst. Appl. **127**, 121–127 (2019). https://doi.org/10.1016/j.eswa.2019.02.032

21. Mimouna, A., Khalifa, A.B., Ben Amara, N.E.: Human action recognition using triaxial accelerometer data: selective approach. In: 2018 15th International Multi-Conference on Systems, Signals Devices (SSD). pp. 491–496. March 2018. https://doi.org/10.1109/SSD.2018.8570429

22. Mohammadi, S., Kiani, H., Perina, A., Murino, V.: Violence detection in crowded scenes using substantial derivative. In: 2015 12th IEEE International Conference on Advanced Video and Signal Based Surveillance (AVSS), pp. 1–6. August 2015. https://doi.org/10.1109/AVSS.2015.7301787

23. Nievas, E.B., Déniz-Suárez, O., García, G.B., Sukthankar, R.: Violence detection in video using computer vision techniques. In: CAIP, pp. 332–339 (2011)

24. Niknejad, H.T., Kawano, T., Oishi, Y., Mita, S.: Occlusion handling using discriminative model of trained part templates and conditional random field. In: 2013 IEEE Intelligent Vehicles Symposium (IV), pp. 750–755. June 2013. https://doi.org/10.1109/IVS.2013.6629557

25. Senior, A., Hampapur, A., Li, Y., Brown, L., Pankanti, S., Bolle, R.: Appearance models for occlusion handling. Image Vis. Comput. **24**, 1233–1243 (2006). https://doi.org/10.1016/j.imavis.2005.06.007

26. Senst, T., Eiselein, V., Kuhn, A., Sikora, T.: Crowd violence detection using global motion-compensated lagrangian features and scale-sensitive video-level representation. IEEE Trans. Inf. Forensics Secur. **12**(12), 2945–2956 (2017). https://doi.org/10.1109/TIFS.2017.2725820

27. Senst, T., Eiselein, V., Sikora, T.: A local feature based on lagrangian measures for violent video classification. In: 6th International Conference on Imaging for Crime Prevention and Detection (ICDP-15), pp. 1–6. July 2015. https://doi.org/10.1049/ic.2015.0104

28. Serrano Gracia, I., Deniz, O., Bueno, G., Kim, T.K.: Fast fight detection. PLOS ONE **10**, e0120448 (2015). https://doi.org/10.1371/journal.pone.0120448

29. Soomro, K., Zamir, A.R., Shah, M.: UCF101: A dataset of 101 human actions classes from videos in the wild. CoRR abs/1212.0402 (2012)

30. Souza, F.D., Pedrini, H.: Detection of violent events in video sequences based on census transform histogram. In: 2017 30th SIBGRAPI Conference on Graphics, Patterns and Images (SIBGRAPI). pp. 323–329. October 2017. https://doi.org/10.1109/SIBGRAPI.2017.49

31. Sudhakaran, S., Lanz, O.: Learning to detect violent videos using convolutional long short-term memory. In: 2017 14th IEEE International Conference on Advanced Video and Signal Based Surveillance (AVSS), pp. 1–6. August 2017. https://doi.org/10.1109/AVSS.2017.8078468

32. Wang, H., Schmid, C.: Action recognition with improved trajectories. In: 2013 IEEE International Conference on Computer Vision, pp. 3551–3558. December 2013. https://doi.org/10.1109/ICCV.2013.441

33. Wang, L., et al.: Temporal segment networks for action recognition in videos. In: IEEE Transactions on Pattern Analysis and Machine Intelligence, pp. 1–1 (2018). https://doi.org/10.1109/TPAMI.2018.2868668

34. Wang, L., et al.: Temporal segment networks: towards good practices for deep action recognition. In: Leibe, B., Matas, J., Sebe, N., Welling, M. (eds.) ECCV 2016. LNCS, vol. 9912, pp. 20–36. Springer, Cham (2016). https://doi.org/10.1007/978-3-319-46484-8_2

35. Wojek, C., Walk, S., Roth, S., Schiele, B.: Monocular 3D scene understanding with explicit occlusion reasoning. CVPR **2011**, 1993–2000 (2011). https://doi.org/10.1109/CVPR.2011.5995547

36. Xu, D., Ricci, E., Yan, Y., Song, J., Sebe, N.: Learning deep representations of appearance and motion for anomalous event detection. In: BMVC, September 2015. https://doi.org/10.5244/C.29.8

37. Xu, L., Gong, C., Yang, J., Wu, Q., Yao, L.: Violent video detection based on mosift feature and sparse coding. In: 2014 IEEE International Conference on Acoustics, Speech and Signal Processing (ICASSP), pp. 3538–3542. May 2014. https://doi.org/10.1109/ICASSP.2014.6854259

38. Yun, K., Honorio, J., Chattopadhyay, D., Berg, T.L., Samaras, D.: Two-person interaction detection using body-pose features and multiple instance learning. In: 2012 IEEE Computer Society Conference on Computer Vision and Pattern Recognition Workshops, pp. 28–35. June 2012. https://doi.org/10.1109/CVPRW.2012.6239234

39. Zhang, C., Xu, J., Beaugendre, A., Goto, S.: A klt-based approach for occlusion handling in human tracking. In: 2012 Picture Coding Symposium, pp. 337–340. May 2012. https://doi.org/10.1109/PCS.2012.6213360

40. Zhang, T., Jia, W., Yang, B., Yang, J., He, X., Zheng, Z.: Mowld: a robust motion-image descriptor for violence detection. Multimedia Tools Appl. **76**, 1419–1438 (2015). https://doi.org/10.1007/s11042-015-3133-0

41. Zhang, T., Yang, Z., Jia, W., Yang, B., Yang, J., He, X.: A new method for violence detection in surveillance scenes. Multimedia Tools Appl. **75**, 7327–7349 (2015). https://doi.org/10.1007/s11042-015-2648-8

42. Zhou, P., Ding, Q., Luo, H., Hou, X.: Violent interaction detection in video based on deep learning. J. Phys.: Conf. Ser. **844**, 012044 (2017). https://doi.org/10.1088/1742-6596/844/1/012044

43. Zhou, P., Ding, Q., Luo, H., Hou, X.: Violence detection in surveillance video using low-level features. PLOS ONE **13**(10), 1–15 (2018). https://doi.org/10.1371/journal.pone.0203668

Uncertainty Based Adaptive Projection Selection Strategy for Binary Tomographic Reconstruction

Gábor Lékó$^{(\boxtimes)}$, Szilveszter Domány, and Péter Balázs

Department of Image Processing and Computer Graphics,
University of Szeged, Árpád tér 2, Szeged 6720, Hungary
{leko,pbalazs}@inf.u-szeged.hu, Domany.Szilveszter@stud.u-szeged.hu

Abstract. The goal of binary tomography is to examine the inner structure of homogeneous objects based on their projections. The 2D slices of the objects can be represented by binary matrices and the aim is to recreate these matrices from a collection of their line sums. For cost-effectiveness and speed reasons it is worth to do the reconstruction from as few projections as possible while still maintaining an acceptable image quality. The key is to specify the most informative projection angles. In this paper we propose a reconstruction uncertainty based adaptive (online) projection selection method for binary tomographic reconstruction. We compare our algorithm to other already published methods.

Keywords: Binary tomography · Adaptive projection selection ·
Online projection selection · Uncertainty · Reconstruction

1 Introduction

In Computed Tomography [5], X-ray radiation is used to produce the projections of an object. Gathering these projections from different angles one can reconstruct the interior of the subject of investigation. In general, for a reconstruction with an acceptable quality, $m\pi/2$ projections are needed, where m is the number of detectors. Furthermore, if the size of the image representing the cross-sectional slice is $n \times n$ then $m \geq \lceil \sqrt{2} \cdot n \rceil$ must also hold. However, fewer projections might be sufficient when prior information is also accessible. This could be, e.g., that the examined object consists of a single material with a known attenuation coefficient. In that case the slices can be represented by binary matrices. One pixel in the cross-section image holds the information of the presence or absence of the material.

The task of Binary Tomography (BT) [6,7] is to reconstruct binary matrices from their projections (line sums). BT is well-suited to reconstruct homogeneous objects in a non-destructive way.

Nowadays, with the increasing computational capacity, the Algebraic Reconstruction Techniques are coming more and more into view, which can perform

M. Vento and G. Percannella (Eds.): CAIP 2019, LNCS 11679, pp. 74–84, 2019.
https://doi.org/10.1007/978-3-030-29891-3_7

well even with small number of projections. Previous studies [10,12] showed that the quality of the reconstruction highly depends on the projection angles. The goal of the projection selection is to find the most informative angles. The adaptive projection selection algorithms allow to perform dense sampling in the information-rich and sparse sampling in the information-poor areas [1,2,4]. Two main projection selection strategies are distinguished. While in the case of offline approaches all the sampled angles and the projections taken from them are known in advance (typically, when a blueprint image is available) [8,11], online approaches determine the successive angles during the acquisition, based on the already available projection information. In the latter case the number of projections to produce is not known in advance, although, depending on the projection selection algorithm, an upper bound can be specified. In this paper we present an online projection selection method which uses the reconstruction uncertainty [13] of the available projections to choose the next angle. Compared to the paper [13] the main novelty here is that uncertainty is not directly used to improve the quality of the reconstruction, rather to choose the most informative projection directions.

The structure of the paper is the following. In Sect. 2 we describe the reconstruction problem and an algebraic approach how to solve it, containing the theoretical background of reconstruction uncertainty. In Sect. 3 we present the state-of-the-art methods that we used to compare our method with. In Sect. 4 we describe our proposed uncertainty based projection selection method. In Sect. 5 we present the experimental results. Finally, Sect. 6 is for the conclusions.

2   Reconstruction and Uncertainty

2.1   The Reconstruction Problem

We consider the reconstruction of 2D slices of a homogeneous object using just a few parallel-beam projections. Instead of the analytic reconstruction approaches which need hundreds of projections, this problem is often solved by algebraic methods. The idea is to describe the connections between projections and pixels using equations. Assuming that the size of the image to be reconstructed is $n \times n$, the reconstruction problem can be formalized as a system of linear equations

$$\mathbf{Ax} = \mathbf{b}, \quad \mathbf{A} \in \mathbb{R}^{n^2 \times m}, \quad \mathbf{x} \in \{0,1\}^{n^2}, \quad \mathbf{b} \in \mathbb{R}^m, \tag{1}$$

where $\mathbf{x}$ is the vector of all n^2 unknown image pixels, m is the total number of projection lines, $\mathbf{b}$ is the vector of all m measured projection values and $\mathbf{A}$ describes the projection geometry with all $a_{i,j}$ elements giving the length of the line segment of the ith projection line through the jth pixel (see Fig. 1 for illustration). In applications of binary image reconstruction, the projection data is often perturbed with noise. As a consequence, the reconstruction problem may happen to have no exact solution. In Binary Tomography, an approximate solution of (1) is often found by a thresholded version of the Simultaneous Iterative Reconstruction Technique (TSIRT) [5]. In TSIRT we start out from a given initial image and approximate the correct reconstruction by iteratively back-propagating the projection error of the current image onto the image pixels. Finally, we binarize the image.

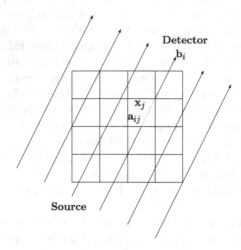

Fig. 1. Equation system-based representation of the parallel-beam projection geometry on a discrete image.

2.2   Reconstruction Uncertainty

We can determine the uncertainty of the reconstruction using the results of [13] that we shortly recall here. Due to the incomplete information in the projection data, there can be several solutions of (1) in which the pixel values may vary. Knowing all the reconstructions we could calculate the probability of x_j ($j = 1, \ldots, n$) taking the value $x_j = 1$, by

$$p_j = \frac{\mathcal{N}_b^A(x_j = 1)}{\mathcal{N}_b^A} \, , \tag{2}$$

where $\mathcal{N}_b^A$ denotes the number of solutions of (1), and $\mathcal{N}_b^A(x_j = 1)$ stands for the number of binary solutions with $x_j = 1$. The probabilities given, we can determine the uncertainty of pixel x_j as

$$\mathcal{H}(x_j) = -(p_j \log_2(p_j) + (\bar{p}_j) \log_2(\bar{p}_j)) \, , \tag{3}$$

where $\bar{p}_j = 1 - p_j$. Taking an image and indicating all the pixels with their uncertainty values, we get the so-called entropy map of the reconstruction (Fig. 2). Furthermore, we can also calculate the global uncertainty of the whole reconstruction by summing the pixel uncertainties as

$$\mathcal{U}(\mathbf{x}) = \frac{\sum_{i=j}^{n^2} \mathcal{H}(x_j)}{\frac{1}{p} \sum_{i=1}^{m} b_i} \, , \tag{4}$$

where p is the number of projections. Of course, reconstruction uncertainty (both on pixel as well as on global level) depends on the reconstruction algorithm and the number of projections applied.

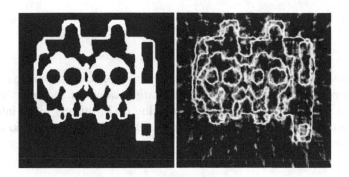

Fig. 2. A binary image (left) and the entropy map of its reconstruction (right).

Calculating (4) needs in practice an unreasonable amount of processing time, since all the reconstructions satisfying the projection set have to be generated. Here, we will use the deterministic method proposed in [13] to approximate pixel uncertainties. This method is based on the SIRT algorithm and forces the range of the pixel intensities of the reconstructed image to be in the [0, 1] interval. As initial guess it uses an image matrix filled with 0.5 values which enables the reconstruction to converge to the most uncertain solution. To produce the entropy map of the solution, we substitute the probability variables in (3) with the pixel values of the reconstructed image. In [13] it was shown that this procedure is a good approximation of the theoretical uncertainty.

3 State-of-the-Art Methods

We now briefly present three state-of-the-art algorithms for online projection selection which we will use for comparing our method to. The first two algorithms are discussed in [4] while the third (naive) approach is from [11].

3.1 Spectral Richness Based Selection

One of the most successfully used adaptive samplings [3] is level crossing sampling scheme (LCSS), where the samples are captured only when the input signal crosses one of the predefined thresholds. Thus, the samples are not uniformly spaced. The major advantage of the LCSS is that lesser number of samples are required to reconstruct the analog signal. The spectral richness varies periodically with time and becomes maximum when the rate of change of the signal is the highest. Therefore, more samples in spectrally rich areas ensure more samples in rapidly varying regions. Spectral richness based selection adaptively selects the projections based on the spatial spectral richness of the image function. We will refer to this algorithm as `Alg1` as the authors did in the original paper [4].

3.2 Reconstruction Error Based Selection

Let $\mathbf{x}^{(k)}$ denote the reconstruction after the kth projection. Then, an error function can be defined by

$$E_k = \log_{10}(\sum_{j=1}^{n^2} |x_j^{(k)} - x_j^{(k-1)}|^2) , \tag{5}$$

which is a measure of how much the most recent reconstructed image is different from the immediate past one. Emphasis on larger values of the error function is compensated by the log function. Larger value of E_k means more informative kth projection and hence smaller step angle is defined. The pseudo code of $\mathtt{Alg2}$ from [4] is the following:

- Step 1
  - Set an initial step size μ_{init}.
  - Take the first two projections at $\beta_0 = \beta_{init}$, $\beta_1 = \beta_0 + \mu_{init}$.
  - Compute E_0 and E_1, associated with these two projections using (5).
  - Calculate the reference error function as $E_{ref} = (E_0 + E_1)/2$.
  - Let $k = 1$.
- Step 2
  - Compute the per unit change as $\nabla E = (E_k - E_{ref})/E_k$.
  - Compute the required change in the step size as $\nabla \mu = \eta_r \bar{\mu} \nabla E$, where $\bar{\mu}$ is the average step size calculated so far, and η_r is a parameter that couples ∇E and $\nabla \mu$.
  - If $\nabla \mu > \nabla \mu_{max}$ then let $\nabla \mu = \nabla \mu_{max}$, where $\nabla \mu_{max}$ is the maximum allowed change in the step size.
- Step 3
  - Update the step size: $\mu = \mu_{init} - \nabla \mu$.
- Step 4
  - Let $k = k + 1$.
  - Calculate the next projection angle by $\beta_k = \beta_{k-1} + \mu$.
  - Terminate if $\beta_k \geq 180°$.
- Step 5
  - Take the projection at β_k and compute E_k by (5).
  - Go to step 2.

3.3 Naive Approach

The $\mathtt{Naive}$ approach, as the authors of [11] refer to, is simply to choose an equiangular angle set $\{i\frac{180°}{p} \mid i = 0, \ldots, p-1\}$, where p denotes the number of projections. In fact, this means that no adaptive projection selection strategy is applied. Therefore, this method can be regarded as a basic standard in comparing projection selection methods.

4   Reconstruction Uncertainty Based Projection Selection

Our key observation is the following. In the case of small number of projections, the linear equation system (1) might be underdetermined, meaning that there can be several feasible reconstructions belonging to the same set of projections. The grade of reconstruction ambiguity can be expressed by the reconstruction uncertainty measure discussed in Subsect. 2.2. While Alg2 takes only one reconstruction into consideration when selecting the consecutive projections angles, we can modify this algorithm to take into account all the possible reconstructions in each iteration. For this purpose we replace the error function (5) with

$$E_k = \log_{10}(\sum_{j=1}^{n^2} |\mathcal{H}(x_j^{(k)}) - \mathcal{H}(x_j^{(k-1)})|^2) \, , \qquad (6)$$

and modify steps 1 and 5 of Alg2 accordingly, to use this measure when evaluating the projection angle candidates. Then, in each iteration, the candidate ensuring the biggest decrease in reconstruction uncertainty is selected. We will refer to this algorithm as Alg2Unc.

We could also follow the strategy of [9] and evaluate the reconstruction ambiguity using global uncertainty (4). However, we want to stay consistent with the original error function (5), which is a pixel-based approach. Therefore, instead of global uncertainty, we use the entropy maps in (6). Another advantage of this approach is that the entropy map holds more information than the value of global uncertainty, being this latter an aggregated form of the former one.

5   Experimental Results

To compare the performance of our novel algorithm with the others presented, we conducted experiments on a set of binary software phantoms. Our image database consisted of 22 phantoms of different structural complexity, each with size 256×256 pixels. Some of them can be seen in Fig. 3.

We used parallel beam geometry. In every projection we set the distance of the beams and detector elements to 1 pixel and used $\lceil 256 \cdot \sqrt{2} \rceil$ of them to cover the whole image. The rotation center was placed into the center of the image.

The reconstructions were performed by the thresholded SIRT algorithm [5] taking 100 iterations. The algorithms were implemented in Matlab R2016b and the tests ran on a machine with 2.20 Ghz Intel(R) Core(TM) i7-3632QM CPU and 8 GB RAM.

We performed several simulations to find the optimal parameter setting. On the basis on this, for all three algorithms we set $\mu_{init} = 10$. In the case of Alg2 and Alg2Unc we set $\eta_r = 0.8$, while in case of Alg1, the coupling constant η_s (having the same role as η_r has in Alg2) was set to $\eta_s = 0.6$. We restarted each algorithm 180 times with the initial integer starting angles $\beta_{init} = 0°, \ldots 179°$.

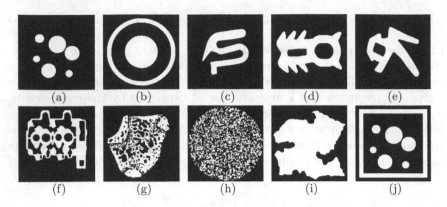

Fig. 3. Some of the software phantoms that were used for testing. Figures from (a) to (j) are in Table 1 P1, P2, P6, P8, P11, P14, P16, P17, P19, and P20, respectively.

Table 1. RME values belonging to phantoms produced by different projection selection methods, when **Alg2Unc**'s best RME values were used for the comparison.

phantoms	nr. of projs	Alg1	Alg2Unc	Alg2	Alg2Unc	Naive	Alg2Unc
P1	18	NaN	0.0086	0.0117	**0.0086**	0.0123	**0.0086**
P2	18	0.0040	**0.0031**	NaN	0.0031	**0.0030**	0.0031
P3	18	0.0084	**0.0079**	NaN	0.0079	0.0126	**0.0079**
P4	17	0.0154	**0.0118**	0.0138	**0.0118**	0.0203	**0.0118**
P5	18	0.0249	**0.0221**	0.0228	**0.0221**	0.0304	**0.0221**
P6	19	0.0112	**0.0103**	NaN	0.0103	0.0185	**0.0103**
P7	19	0.0097	**0.0088**	0.0081	0.0088	0.0156	**0.0088**
P8	19	0.0113	**0.0101**	0.0120	**0.0101**	0.0133	**0.0101**
P9	19	0.0093	**0.0082**	0.0105	**0.0082**	0.0119	**0.0082**
P10	17	0.0091	**0.0068**	0.0075	**0.0068**	0.0135	**0.0068**
P11	19	0.0135	**0.0124**	NaN	0.0124	0.0170	**0.0124**
P12	17	0.0018	**0.0010**	0.0010	**0.0010**	0.0023	**0.0010**
P13	19	**0.0080**	0.0080	NaN	0.0080	0.0098	**0.0080**
P14	19	0.0742	**0.0731**	0.0850	**0.0731**	0.0864	**0.0731**
P15	18	0.2521	**0.2219**	NaN	0.2219	0.2833	**0.2219**
P16	20	0.2328	**0.2070**	NaN	0.2070	0.2356	**0.2070**
P17	19	0.5901	**0.5793**	NaN	0.5793	0.6076	**0.5793**
P18	18	0.0162	**0.0151**	0.0189	**0.0151**	0.0190	**0.0151**
P19	19	**0.0061**	0.0063	NaN	0.0063	0.0077	**0.0063**
P20	20	0.0511	**0.0065**	0.0188	**0.0065**	0.0357	**0.0065**
P21	18	0.0052	**0.0047**	0.0067	**0.0047**	0.0077	**0.0047**
P22	19	**0.0435**	0.0447	NaN	0.0447	0.0560	**0.0447**

To measure the reconstruction quality we applied the formula of Relative Mean Error (RME) which is

$$RME(\mathbf{x}, \mathbf{x}^*) = \frac{\sum_{j=1}^{n^2} |x_j - x_j^*|}{\sum_{j=1}^{n^2} x_j^*} , \tag{7}$$

where $\mathbf{x}^*$ and $\mathbf{x}$ is the original and the reconstructed image, respectively. Informally, RME gives the pixel error proportional to the number of object pixels in the original image.

Table 1 summarizes the results of our experiment. For each test image, we first identified the projection number belonging to the smallest RME provided by algorithm Alg2Unc. The second column of Table 1 shows the number of projections used, while the identical fourth, sixth, and eighth columns show the RME values of Alg2Unc. Then, we selected the best RME values given by Alg1,

Table 2. RME values belonging to phantoms produced by different projection selection methods, when Alg2's best RME values were used for the comparison.

phantoms	nr. of projs.	Alg1	Alg2Unc	Alg2	Alg2Unc	Naive	Alg2Unc
P1	17	0.0104	**0.0092**	**0.0087**	0.0092	0.0157	**0.0092**
P2	17	0.0043	**0.0040**	0.0047	**0.0040**	0.0082	**0.0040**
P3	16	NaN	NaN	0.0084	NaN	0.0126	NaN
P4	19	**0.0113**	0.0145	**0.0126**	0.0145	0.0195	0.0145
P5	17	0.0298	**0.0233**	**0.0223**	0.0233	0.0350	**0.0233**
P6	17	0.0152	**0.0128**	**0.0116**	0.0128	0.0224	**0.0128**
P7	19	0.0097	**0.0088**	**0.0081**	0.0088	0.0139	**0.0088**
P8	19	0.0113	**0.0101**	0.0120	**0.0101**	0.0136	**0.0101**
P9	16	**0.0130**	0.0133	**0.0104**	0.0133	0.0157	0.0133
P10	17	0.0091	**0.0068**	0.0075	**0.0068**	0.0153	**0.0068**
P11	18	0.0140	**0.0133**	0.0138	**0.0133**	0.0169	**0.0133**
P12	17	0.0018	**0.0010**	0.0010	0.0010	0.0023	**0.0010**
P13	17	0.0090	**0.0087**	0.0092	**0.0087**	0.0105	**0.0087**
P14	20	0.0802	NaN	0.0774	NaN	0.0848	NaN
P15	17	0.2625	**0.2594**	**0.2240**	0.2594	0.3010	**0.2594**
P16	19	0.2298	**0.2234**	0.2316	**0.2234**	0.2440	**0.2234**
P17	18	0.6037	**0.5943**	0.5969	**0.5943**	0.6057	**0.5943**
P18	17	NaN	NaN	0.0177	NaN	0.0218	NaN
P19	17	**0.0064**	0.0065	0.0071	**0.0065**	0.0115	**0.0065**
P20	20	0.0511	**0.0065**	0.0188	**0.0065**	0.0427	**0.0065**
P21	18	0.0052	**0.0047**	0.0067	**0.0047**	0.0091	**0.0047**
P22	18	0.0470	**0.0452**	0.0463	**0.0452**	0.0563	**0.0452**

`Alg2`, and `Naive` using the same number of projections (see the third, fifth, and seventh columns of the table, respectively).

Thus, all four algorithms selected the same number of projections, but not necessarily with identical starting angles. The smallest RME values are highlighted in each row. It was important to check all the 180 possible integer starting angles, because the list of the selected angles heavily depends on the orientation of the object.

The NaN entries denote the cases when none of the 180 runs of the certain algorithm finished with the same projection number as `Alg2Unc` did. We observe that, where comparison was possible, in 10 out of 12 cases `Alg2Unc` performed better than `Alg2`. Against `Alg1` in 18 out of 21 cases, and compared to the `Naive` in 21 out of 22 cases, again, `Alg2Unc` gave better results.

We also repeated the experiment such that in the first step the number of projections was fixed by the best result of `Alg2` and `Alg1` instead of `Alg2Unc`. In Tables 2 and 3 we collect the results in a similar way as in Table 1.

Table 3. RME values belonging to phantoms produced by different projection selection methods, when `Alg1`'s best RME values were used for the comparison.

phantoms	nr. of projs	Alg1	Alg2Unc	Alg2	Alg2Unc	Naive	Alg2Unc
P1	20	0.0080	NaN	NaN	NaN	0.0096	NaN
P2	19	0.0039	NaN	NaN	NaN	0.0028	NaN
P3	19	**0.0074**	0.0086	NaN	0.0086	0.0111	**0.0086**
P4	19	**0.0113**	0.0145	**0.0126**	0.0145	0.0178	**0.0145**
P5	20	0.0206	NaN	NaN	NaN	0.0276	NaN
P6	19	0.0112	**0.0103**	NaN	0.0103	0.0172	**0.0103**
P7	20	0.0088	NaN	NaN	NaN	0.0123	NaN
P8	19	0.0113	**0.0101**	0.0120	**0.0101**	0.0125	**0.0101**
P9	18	**0.0090**	0.0092	0.0108	**0.0092**	0.0125	**0.0092**
P10	18	**0.0070**	0.0071	0.0079	**0.0071**	0.0129	**0.0071**
P11	19	0.0135	**0.0124**	NaN	0.0124	0.0160	**0.0124**
P12	19	**0.0008**	0.0010	NaN	0.0010	0.0016	**0.0010**
P13	19	0.0080	0.0080	NaN	0.0080	0.0108	**0.0080**
P14	19	0.0742	**0.0731**	0.0850	**0.0731**	0.0977	**0.0731**
P15	20	0.2208	NaN	NaN	NaN	0.2365	NaN
P16	19	0.2298	**0.2234**	0.2316	**0.2234**	0.2373	**0.2234**
P17	19	0.5901	**0.5793**	NaN	0.5793	0.6041	**0.5793**
P18	19	**0.0151**	0.0163	NaN	0.0163	0.0175	**0.0163**
P19	19	**0.0061**	0.0063	NaN	0.0063	0.0082	**0.0063**
P20	18	**0.0051**	0.0065	0.0272	**0.0065**	0.0424	**0.0065**
P21	18	0.0052	**0.0047**	0.0067	**0.0047**	0.0081	**0.0047**
P22	23	0.0301	NaN	NaN	NaN	0.0387	NaN

Again, NaN entries denote the cases when none of the 180 runs of the certain algorithm finished with the same projection number as the reference algorithm did. We can see that even using the best RMEs of `Alg2` and `Alg1` to identify the number of projections, `Alg2Unc` still performs very well.

When dealing with online methods, running time is another important aspect of analysis. We found that `Alg1` requires less computation than `Alg2` and `Alg2Unc` do. With the presented settings, the average running time for a fix starting angle of algorithm `Alg1`, `Alg2` and `Alg2Unc` was 2.34, 7.81 and 8.83 seconds, respectively, on our test machine. By changing the parameters, e.g., increasing μ_{init}, the algorithms would choose fewer projections, yielding a shorter running time but also a poorer reconstruction quality. Furthermore, by choosing a more effective implementation language (e.g., C++) all three methods could be highly speeded up, even to work on-the-fly, when there was a practical need for it.

6   Conclusions

In this paper, we suggested a modified version of the online projection selection method `Alg2` presented in [4]. The key idea was to use reconstruction uncertainty instead of reconstruction error to select projection angles. We compared our algorithm to already published methods using experimental tests on software phantom images. We showed that our new method `Alg2Unc` can outperform the state-of-the-art algorithms and provides a good alternative solution for selecting projection angles.

Acknowledgements. Gábor Lékó was supported by the UNKP-18-3 New National Excellence Program of the Ministry of Human Capacities. This research was supported by the project "Integrated program for training new generation of scientists in the fields of computer science", no EFOP-3.6.3-VEKOP-16-2017-0002. The project was supported by the European Union and co-funded by the European Social Fund. Ministry of Human Capacities, Hungary grant 20391-3/2018/FEKUSTRAT is acknowledged.

References

1. Batenburg, K.J., Palenstijn, W.J., Balázs, P., Sijbers, J.: Dynamic angle selection in binary tomography. Comput. Vis. Image Underst. **117**(4), 306–318 (2013)
2. Dabravolski, A., Batenburg, K., Sijbers, J.: Dynamic angle selection in x-ray computed tomography. Nucl. Instrum. Meth. Phys. Res. Sect. B: Beam Interact. Mater. Atoms **324**, 17–24 (2014)
3. Ellis, P.: Extension of phase plane analysis to quantized systems. IRE Trans. Autom. Control **4**(2), 43–54 (1959)
4. Haque, M.A., Ahmad, M.O., Swamy, M.N.S., Hasan, M.K., Lee, S.Y.: Adaptive projection selection for computed tomography. IEEE Trans. Image Process. **22**(12), 5085–5095 (2013)
5. Herman, G.T.: Fundamentals of Computerized Tomography: Image Reconstruction from Projections, 2nd edn. Springer Publishing Company, New York (2009). https://doi.org/10.1007/978-1-84628-723-7

6. Herman, G.T., Kuba, A.: Discrete Tomography: Foundations, Algorithms, and Applications. Birkhäuser, Basel (1999)
7. Herman, G.T., Kuba, A.: Advances in Discrete Tomography and Its Applications. Birkhäuser, Basel (2007)
8. Lékó, G., Balázs, P.: Sequential projection selection methods for binary tomography. In: Barneva, R.P., Brimkov, V.E., Kulczycki, P., Tavares, J.M.R.S. (eds.) CompIMAGE 2018. LNCS, vol. 10986, pp. 70–81. Springer, Cham (2019). https://doi.org/10.1007/978-3-030-20805-9_7
9. Lékó, G., Balázs, P., Varga, L.G.: Projection selection for binary tomographic reconstruction using global uncertainty. In: Campilho, A., Karray, F., ter Haar Romeny, B. (eds.) ICIAR 2018. LNCS, vol. 10882, pp. 3–10. Springer, Cham (2018). https://doi.org/10.1007/978-3-319-93000-8_1
10. Nagy, A., Kuba, A.: Reconstruction of binary matrices from fan-beam projections. Acta Cybernetica **17**(2), 359–385 (2005)
11. Varga, L., Balázs, P., Nagy, A.: Projection selection algorithms for discrete tomography. In: Blanc-Talon, J., Bone, D., Philips, W., Popescu, D., Scheunders, P. (eds.) ACIVS 2010. LNCS, vol. 6474, pp. 390–401. Springer, Heidelberg (2010). https://doi.org/10.1007/978-3-642-17688-3_37
12. Varga, L., Balázs, P., Nagy, A.: Direction-dependency of binary tomographic reconstruction algorithms. Graph. Models **73**(6), 365–375 (2011). computational Modeling in Imaging Sciences
13. Varga, L.G., Nyúl, L.G., Nagy, A., Balázs, P.: Local and global uncertainty in binary tomographic reconstruction. Comput. Vis. Image Underst. **129**, 52–62 (2014). special section: Advances in Discrete Geometry for Computer Imagery

Non-contact Heart Rate Monitoring Using Multiple RGB Cameras

Hamideh Ghanadian and Hussein Al Osman[✉]

University of Ottawa, Ottawa, ON, Canada
{hghan053, hussein.alosman}@uottawa.ca

Abstract. Recent advances in computer vision and signal processing are enabling researchers to realize mechanisms for the remote monitoring of vital signs. The remote measurement of vital signs, including heart rate (HR), Heart Rate Variability (HRV), and respiratory rate, presents important advantages for patients. For instance, continuous remote monitoring alleviates the discomfort due to skin irritation and/or mobility limitation associated with contact-based measurement techniques. Recently, several studies presented methods to measure HR and HRV by detecting the Blood Volume Pulse (BVP) from the human skin. They use a single camera to capture a visible segment of the skin such as face, hand, or foot to monitor the BVP. We propose a remote HR measurement algorithm that uses multiple cameras to capture the facial video recordings of still and moving subjects. Using Independent Component Analysis (ICA) as a Blind Source Separation (BSS) method, we isolate the physiological signals from noise in the RGB facial video recordings. With respect to the ECG measurement ground truth, the proposed method decreases the RMSE by 18% compared to the state-of-the-art in the subject movement condition. The proposed method achieves an RMSE of 1.43 bpm and 0.96 bpm in the stationary and movement conditions respectively.

Keywords: Photoplethysmogram · Independent component analysis (ICA) · Remote heart rate measurement · Multiple camera monitoring

1 Introduction

Vital signs, including HR, HRV, and respiration rate, are important indicators of the patient's health [1]. They provide critically needed information to make life-saving decisions. Continuous monitoring of HR and HRV is becoming an important aspect of home-based healthcare. In addition to physical health assessment, HR and HRV measurement can be employed for psychological health monitoring. For instance, mental stress can be effectively assessed using HR and HRV measures [2, 3]. Methods to measure HR are classified into two categories: Contact and Non-Contact based. Contact based measurement involves the use of sensors attached to the patient's skin. There are several limitations in contact based-measurement. These sensors limit the movement of the patient due to their wiring. Moreover, in some cases, connecting the sensor to the skin is not possible due to the patient's condition. For example, monitoring vital signs in the Neonatal Intensive Care Unit (NICU) requires the use of

© Springer Nature Switzerland AG 2019
M. Vento and G. Percannella (Eds.): CAIP 2019, LNCS 11679, pp. 85–95, 2019.
https://doi.org/10.1007/978-3-030-29891-3_8

adhesives to attach sensors to the skin of pre-term infants, which might result in pain and skin irritation [4]. However, non-contact measuring methods address effectively theses issues. Optical non-contact methods estimate a photoplethysmography (PPG) signal without directly being placed on the subject's body. In recent studies, the PPG signals have been acquired using RGB (Red, Green, Blue) image sequences [5]. Furthermore, researchers have extracted HR [5], HRV [6] and respiration rate [7] parameters from the remotely measured PPG signals.

There are many approaches to recover the BVP. One of the most prevalent methods is BSS. Physiological signals are often mixed with other independent noise signals. Independent component analysis (ICA) [8] is a BSS technique that separates multi-variate signals from underlying sources. Poh et al. [5] used ICA to extract the channel containing BVP information from the RGB channels of a facial video.

Ghanadian et al. [9] demonstrated the feasibility of monitoring HR during movement using a single camera. However, such system is limited to the Field of View (FoV) of a single camera. As soon as the subject steps outside of the camera's FoV, the physiological signal measurement is interrupted.

For the proposed method, we use a head pose detection scheme to ensure that we collect the best possible signal from the group of cameras interfacing to the system. The human head pose can be described by pitch, yaw and roll. Head pose detection has many applications in HCI research. For instance, the influence of banner advertisements on attention has been studied using head pose and gaze detection algorithms in [10]. Moreover, Stiefelhagen [11] used head pose detection to track the attention of the audience during meetings; they postulated that if an individual wants to pay attention to an object, he/she typically turns his/her head towards it.

In the proposed method, we prove that the application of multiple cameras in a room can increase the accuracy of remote HR estimation. There are many applications where the use of multiple cameras can refine the performance of remote physiological monitoring. For instance, in elderly care facilities, monitoring vital signs, especially HR, can be achieved more accurately using multiple cameras mounted at each corner of the rooms. Moreover, in some cases, existing surveillance cameras can double as remote physiological monitoring sensors.

2   Background and Related Works

Sun et al. [12] presented the first remote pulse measurement scheme using thermal imaging. They achieved the HR measurement by computing the frequency of pulses obtained from changes in the temperature of the vessels. The temperature is regulated by pulsatile blood flow. However, due to the thermal sensitivity of the sensor, the changes in the room temperature can have an adverse effect on the performance of the system [13]. Moreover, this approach requires the use of a relatively expensive thermal camera compared to RGB cameras.

Takano and Ohta [14] measured the cardiac pulse rate using a digital camera. They calculated the average brightness of time-lapse skin images recorded by a CCD camera. They extracted the HR using auto-regressive spectral analysis on the video frames.

McDuff et al. [15] developed an HR and HRV measurement system that uses a five band camera (Red, Orange, Green, Cyan and Blue) to capture the facial video recording. To find the facial landmark coordinates that allow them to localize the ROI, they utilized the local evidence aggregated regression algorithm. They presented the spatially averaged color spaces to the ICA to separate the source signals from noise. Their results showed that combining the Cyan, Green and Orange channels achieved better results than any other color combination. Similar to thermal cameras, the five band cameras are comparatively expensive.

Poh et al. [5] proposed to recover the HR using RGB cameras. They used the openCv [16] face detection method to locate the face, and a face tracker algorithm to track the head motions of the subjects during measurement. The movements of subjects were restricted to small motions of the head such as nodding, looking up/down, and leaning forward/backward.

Ghanadian et al. [9] investigated the possibility of HR measurement in the presence of movement. They utilized a low cost RGB camera to record facial images. Then, they presented the spatially averaged color channels over the images to the ICA. They proposed a machine-learning algorithm to choose the component generated through ICA that is most reflective of PPG. Moreover, they presented an algorithm to equalize the light effects on the facial images by normalizing the light across the frames of video segments. They posited that 50% of the face of the subjects should be visible to the camera to make accurate measurements.

McDuff [17] estimated the HRV of stationary subjects using multiple cameras. They evaluated their method under various levels of motion while the subjects were seated. Their method still has some limitations. The subjects cannot roam the room freely.

Other works that considered multiple cameras to extract vital signs remotely [18, 19] used an infra-red and an RGB camera to capture two PPG signals at different wavelengths. However, our method uses multiple cameras to increase the FoV resulting from the combination of the images simultaneously captured by all cameras.

3   Method

We base our approach on the system proposed by Ghanadian et al. [9] Fig. 1a depicts the overall processing steps involved in the latter method. They used a single camera to detect the face of still and moving subjects. The movement of the subjects was limited to walking towards and away from the camera. They required the capture of at least 50% of the face as ROI to extract the PPG signal. To reduce the negative effects of light changes as the subject roamed the room, they decomposed the ROI to Hue, Saturation and lightness (HSL) color space and normalized the L value. Then, they decomposed the ROI to extract the RGB signals by averaging the Red, Green and Blue values over the ROI pixels in each frames. They presented the RGB signals to the ICA to separate them to into three independent components. They proposed a machine Learning (ML) algorithm to select the best signal generated through ICA that reflects PPG. They calculated the HR from the PPG signal.

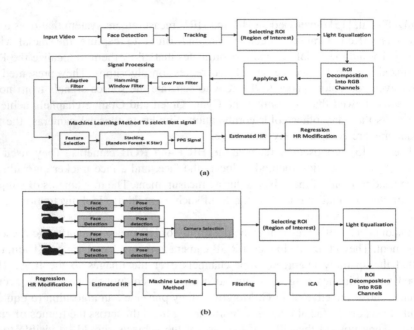

Fig. 1. HR prediction algorithm for the (a) Ghanadian et al. [9] and (b) proposed method

Figure 1b shows the steps necessary to extract HR from video using the multi-camera proposed approach. In the following sub-sections, we describe the new modules added to the method described in [9].

3.1 Face and Head Pose Detection

During movement, the angle of the subject's face with respect to the camera changes frequently. Hence, we utilize multiple cameras to capture the subject's face under a variety of head poses. We use a face detection method to capture the face in a video recorded by a standard RGB camera. We utilize four 24-bit RGB cameras recording at 30-frames per second and 640 × 480 pixels per frame. Each camera operates independently and simultaneously with other cameras. We locate the face in all of the video streams (originating from all the cameras) using a face detection method (OpenFace) [16] and calculate the head pose of the subject with respect to each camera. OpenFace [16] identifies sixty-eight facial landmarks including points on the nose, eyebrows, chin, eye corners and mouth for face detection and pose estimation [20].

3.2 Camera Selection

We assume there are N cameras in the room. Hence, we divide the room into ω non-intersecting partitions, where ω is calculated using Eq. (1). We place the cameras along the perimeter of a circle co-centered with the room. We ensure that the distance between adjacent cameras is equal for all cameras.

$$\omega = \frac{360°}{N} \tag{1}$$

The system continuously selects every time-period t the most appropriate camera to measure the HR. The head pose angle of the subject is calculated with respect to each camera's axis. We refer to this angle as A_i where i is the index of the camera and ranges from 0 to $N - 1$. Hence, the head pose angle of a subject looking directly at the camera is 0 degrees. Figure 2 shows the different head pose degrees with respect to each camera. To calculate HR, for time-period t, we use the frames captured by the camera corresponding to the smallest A_i. Hence, we create a series of images originating from one or more cameras. This series of images is processed in the same way a video captured from a single camera is treated by the algorithm presented in [9]. Hence, the light equalization method of [9] is applied to this series of images, which reduces the effect of light differences between the various frames originating from the camera(s) in an unevenly lit room.

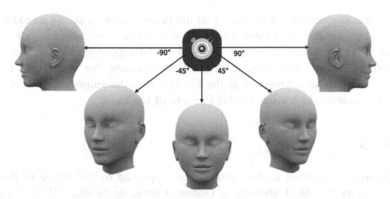

Fig. 2. Head Pose degrees with respect to a camera

For the experimental scenario, we employed four cameras placed at each corner of a square-shaped room. Therefore, video frames depicting a subject's head pose angle between $[-45°, 45°]$ are used to estimate the HR. If we assume an HR monitoring session lasts M measurement time-periods, hence:

$$T = M \times t \tag{2}$$

Where T is the length of the recording session. Therefore, to measure HR during T, we collect M sets of frames from the N available cameras. The M sets of frames are considered the input video to the HR estimation method.

We select the entire face of the subjects as the ROI to increase the amount of information extracted from the face. By increasing the distance of the subjects from the cameras, the ROI becomes smaller, hence choosing the entire face allows us the maximize the useful information. To construct the raw RGB signals, the selected ROI

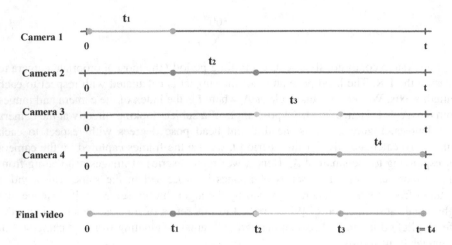

Fig. 3. Face images extraction from multiple camera in stationary mode

in every frame is spatially averaged over all the pixels. Figure 3 shows an example of how the frames are compiled from N cameras to produce a single facial video.

Using multiple camera increases the probability of capturing the face with one of the cameras. However, evidently, there are no guarantees that one of the cameras captures the face at an appropriate angle. For instance, the subject might come very close to the camera which crops her/his face out of the frame.

4   Dataset

The experiments discussed in this section were approved by the Office of Research Ethics and Integrity at the University of Ottawa (Certificate Number: H02-17-13). We collected a dataset with ten volunteering subjects (3 female and 7 male) who signed consent forms to participate in this study. The dataset consists of two subsets: stationary and movement mode subsets.

4.1   Stationary Mode

We asked participants to sit in front of one camera and rotate towards the next camera with a speed of 30°/s. We asked them to stop for 10 s while facing each camera with minimum movement. The subjects wore a physiological sensor (Zephyr Bioharness[1]) that collects an ECG signal at a sampling rate of 250 Hz. The data collected by the sensor is used as ground truth to evaluate the accuracy of our results. Figure 4a shows the experimental setup for the stationary mode using multiple cameras. The videos

---

[1] "Zephyr TM Performance Systems | Performance Monitoring Technology." [Online]. Available: https://www.zephyranywhere.com/. [Accessed: 17-Apr-2018].

were collected by four conventional RGB camera (Logitech Webcam C920) filming at 30-frames per second and 640×480 pixels per frame. The cameras were mounted on the four corners of a 4×4 m square-shaped room and the subject was seated at the center of the room. The lighting in the room was a mixture of natural sunlight coming from windows and fluorescent ceiling light. Table 1 describes the conditions for the stationary mode subset collection with multiple cameras.

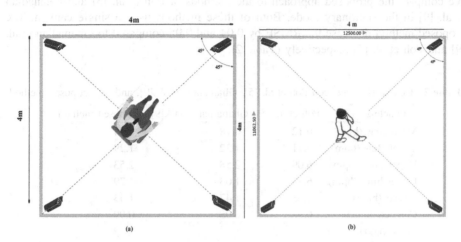

Fig. 4. Experimental setup for (a) Stationary mode, (b) Movement mode

4.2   Movement Mode

For the Movement Mode subset, we asked the subjects to move in the room for 4 min by walking, talking, or lying down (see Fig. 4b). The dimensions of the room are $4 \text{ m} \times 4 \text{ m}$. The subjects could move freely without any constraint. The rest of the experimental conditions, including lighting, camera, and sensor were identical to the ones used for the stationary mode. Table 1 shows the conditions for the movement mode subset collection with multiple cameras.

Table 1. Description of the stationary and movement mode data subsets

Parameters	Movement mode	Stationary mode
Experiment length per subject (second)	240	180
# of participants	10	10
	(3 F, 7 M)	(3 F, 7 M)
Distance from camera (meter)	0–4	2
Recording rate (fps)	30	30
# of 1 min video segments	40	30
# of frames	72000	54000

5 Evaluation

In this section, we present the evaluation of the proposed contributions as detailed in Sect. 3. The dataset used in the experiments is described in Sects. 4.1 and 4.2.

5.1 Stationary Mode

We compare the proposed approach to the methods of Poh et al. [5] and Ghanadian et al. [9] in the stationary mode. Both of these methods used a single camera. The proposed method decrease the RMSE by 0.04 and 0.95 compared to Ghanadian et al. [9] and Poh et al. [5] respectively (Table 2).

Table 2. Comparison between Poh et al. [5], Ghanadian et al. [9], and the proposed method

Parameters	Poh et al. [5]	Ghanadian et al. [9]	Proposed method
Mean Bias (bpm)	−0.12	0.78	0.74
SD of Bias (bpm)	3.11	1.32	1.29
Upper limit (bpm)	6.09	2.58	2.53
Lower limit (bpm)	−6.33	−1.03	−1.79
RMSE (bpm)	2.38	1.47	1.43
Corr. coefficient	0.98*	0.98*	0.99*

*: ($p < 0.004$)

5.2 Movement Mode

Ghanadian et al. [9] utilized a single camera to capture the facial videos. The level of movement in these videos is limited to walking towards and away from the camera. In the proposed method, the subjects can move freely in the room. The proposed method can fail to capture the physiological signal only if none of the cameras can capture the face. We test the Ghanadian et al. [9] method in a scenario where subjects can roam the room without any restrictions (using the dataset described in Sect. 4.2). Table 3 presents a comparison between the proposed method and Ghanadian et al. [9] in the movement mode. The use of multiple cameras drastically decreases the RMSE from 5.08 bpm to 0.96 bpm.

Table 3. Comparison of Ghanadian et al. [9], and proposed method using multiple cameras in movement

Parameters	Ghanadian et al. [9]	Proposed method
Mean Bias (bpm)	6.65	1.08
SD of Bias (bpm)	6.34	1.36
Upper limit (bpm)	12.42	2.66
Lower limit (bpm)	−5.77	−1.58
RMSE (bpm)	5.08	0.96
Corr. coefficient	0.85*	0.98*

*: ($p < 0.004$)

Figure 5 presents the performance of the proposed method and bland Altman plot. Bland-Altman plot in Fig. 5 analyze the agreement between the estimated HR from the proposed algorithm using multiple cameras and the HR extracted from the ground truth (i.e. HR obtained from the Zephyr Bioharness ECG sensor).

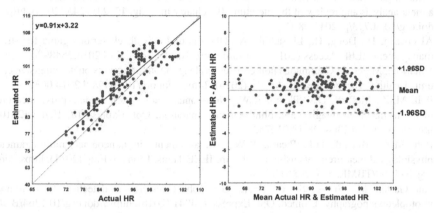

Fig. 5. Statistical results of Bland and Altman plot in multiple camera experiment

6 Discussion

The results show that using multiple cameras can improve the accuracy of remote HR estimation. The combination of multiple cameras creates a larger collective FoV which gives the patient more freedom in the movement during monitoring without risking interruptions. Each frame's ROI is spatially averaged and corresponds to a data point in the remotely measured PPG signal. During movement, the subject's ROI might fall out of the FoV in a single camera solution thus degrading the quality of the PPG signal which in turn adversely affects the accuracy of the HR estimate.

Collecting frames from several cameras produces a series of images taken from various vantage points which results in a variety of lighting conditions. Therefore, equalizing the lightness across the frames stabilizes the lighting condition.

7 Conclusion

Remote monitoring of HR in real-life situations requires a robust technology that can measure continuously with the fewest possible number of interruptions. We realize that using a single camera limits the FoV of the system. Hence, we proposed a remote HR monitoring method that uses multiple cameras to address the latter limitation. The proposed method presents the possibility of continuous measurement of physiological vital signs for still and moving subjects. To realize a multi-camera system, we combine video segments from multiple cameras. We achieved an RMSE of 0.96 bpm for the estimation of HR during subject movement.

Refrences

1. Kranjec, J., Begus, S., Drnovsek, J., Gersak, G.: Novel methods for noncontact heart rate measurement: a feasibility study. IEEE Trans. Instrum. Meas. **63**, 838–847 (2014). https://doi.org/10.1109/TIM.2013.2287118
2. Kim, H.-G., Cheon, E.-J., Bai, D.-S., Lee, Y.H., Koo, B.-H.: Stress and heart rate variability: a meta-analysis and review of the literature. Psychiatry Investig. **15**, 235–245 (2018). https://doi.org/10.30773/pi.2017.08.17
3. Al Osman, H., Dong, H., El Saddik, A.: Ubiquitous biofeedback serious game for stress management. IEEE Access (2016). https://doi.org/10.1109/ACCESS.2016.2548980
4. Villarroel, M., et al.: Continuous non-contact vital sign monitoring in neonatal intensive care unit. Healthc. Technol. Lett. **1**, 87–91 (2014). https://doi.org/10.1049/htl.2014.0077
5. Poh, M.-Z., McDuff, D.J., Picard, R.W.: Non-contact, automated cardiac pulse measurements using video imaging and blind source separation. Opt. Express **18**, 10762 (2010). https://doi.org/10.1364/OE.18.010762
6. Poh, M.Z., McDuff, D.J., Picard, R.W.: Advancements in noncontact, multiparameter physiological measurements using a webcam. IEEE Trans. Biomed. Eng. (2011). https://doi.org/10.1109/TBME.2010.2086456
7. van Gastel, M., Stuijk, S., de Haan, G.: Robust respiration detection from remote photoplethysmography. Biomed. Opt. Express **7**, 4941 (2016). https://doi.org/10.1364/BOE.7.004941
8. Comon, P.: Independent component analysis, a new concept?*. Signal Process. **36**, 28–314 (1994). Comon/Signal Process.
9. Ghanadian, H., Ghodratigohar, M., Al Osman, H.: A machine learning method to improve non-contact heart rate monitoring using an RGB camera. IEEE Access (2018). https://doi.org/10.1109/ACCESS.2018.2872756
10. Sajjacholapunt, P., Ball, L.J.: The influence of banner advertisements on attention and memory: human faces with averted gaze can enhance advertising effectiveness. Front. Psychol. **5**, 166 (2014). https://doi.org/10.3389/fpsyg.2014.00166
11. Stiefelhagen, R.: Tracking focus of attention in meetings. In: 4th IEEE International Conference on Multimodal Interfaces. IEEE Computer Society (2002)
12. Sun, N., Garbey, M., Merla, A., Pavlidis, I.: Imaging the cardiovascular pulse. In: 2005 IEEE Computer Society Conference on Computer Vision and Pattern Recognition (CVPR 2005), pp. 416–421. IEEE (2005). https://doi.org/10.1109/CVPR.2005.184
13. Pereira, C.B., Yu, X., Czaplik, M., Rossaint, R., Blazek, V., Leonhardt, S.: Remote monitoring of breathing dynamics using infrared thermography. Biomed. Opt. Express **6**, 4378–4394 (2015). https://doi.org/10.1364/BOE.6.004378
14. Takano, C., Ohta, Y.: Heart rate measurement based on a time-lapse image. Med. Eng. Phys. **29**, 853–857 (2007). https://doi.org/10.1016/j.medengphy.2006.09.006
15. McDuff, D., Gontarek, S., Picard, R.W.: Improvements in remote cardiopulmonary measurement using a five band digital camera. IEEE Trans. Biomed. Eng. (2014). https://doi.org/10.1109/TBME.2014.2323695
16. Viola, P., Jones, M.: Rapid object detection using a boosted cascade of simple features. In: Proceedings of the 2001 IEEE Computer Society Conference on Computer Vision and Pattern Recognition. CVPR 2001, p. I-511–I-518. IEEE Computer Society (2001). https://doi.org/10.1109/CVPR.2001.990517
17. Mcduff, D.: Fusing partial camera signals for noncontact pulse rate variability measurement. IEEE Trans. Biomed. Eng. **65**, 1725–1739 (2018). https://doi.org/10.1109/TBME.2017.2771518

18. Estepp, J.R., Blackford, E.B., Meier, C.M.: Recovering pulse rate during motion artifact with a multi-imager array for non-contact imaging photoplethysmography. In: 2014 IEEE International Conference on Systems, Man, and Cybernetics (SMC), pp. 1462–1469. IEEE (2014). https://doi.org/10.1109/SMC.2014.6974121
19. Gupta, O., McDuff, D., Raskar, R.: Real-time physiological measurement and visualization using a synchronized multi-camera system. In: 2016 IEEE Conference on Computer Vision and Pattern Recognition Workshops (CVPRW). pp. 312–319. IEEE (2016). https://doi.org/10.1109/CVPRW.2016.46
20. Baltrušaitis, T., Robinson, P., Morency, L.-P.: OpenFace: an open source facial behavior analysis toolkit. In: IEEE Winter Conference on Applications of Computer Vision (WACV). IEEE (2016)

An Efficient Anaglyph 3D Video Watermarking Approach Based on Hybrid Insertion

Dorra Dhaou[1]([✉]), Saoussen Ben Jabra[1,2], and Ezzeddine Zagrouba[1]

[1] Université de Tunis El Manar, Institut Supérieur d'Informatique, LR16ES06
Laboratoire de Recherche en Informatique, Modélisation et Traitement de
l'Information et de la Connaissance (LIMTIC),
2 Rue Abou Raihane Bayrouni, 2080 Ariana, Tunisia
dorradhaou@gmail.com, saoussen.bj@gmail.com, ezzeddine.zagrouba@uvt.tn
[2] Université de Sousse, École Nationale d'Ingénieurs de Sousse (ENISo),
BP 264, 4023 Sousse Erriadh, Tunisia

Abstract. Digital watermarking techniques have been proposed as an efficient solution to protect different media from illegal manipulations. However, for 3D videos, this domain has not been developed enough where only three watermarking methods exist for anaglyph 3D videos. These existing methods suffer from robustness insufficiency, especially against malicious attacks such as video compression. In this paper, a robust hybrid anaglyph 3D video watermarking algorithm, which is based on spatial and frequency domains (Least Significant Bit (LSB), Discrete Wavelet Transform (DWT) and Discrete Cosines Transform (DCT)) is proposed. First, the original anaglyph 3D video is divided into a set of frames, then each frame is split into cyan and red images. A first signature will be inserted in cyan and red images using, respectively, DCT and LSB based techniques. Second, the obtained anaglyph frame is processed by the first level of the DWT, where the second signature is inserted in a low frequency. The inverse of a DWT is performed to obtain the final marked anaglyph frame. The proposed approach is evaluated based on invisibility and robustness criteria and shows a high level of invisibility and robustness against different video compression standards such as MPEG-4 and H264-AVC.

Keywords: Anaglyph 3D video · Watermarking · DWT · DCT · LSB · Robustness · Invisibility

1 Introduction

3D has been a buzzword in the technology sector for recent years. Thus, we have become surrounded by 3D televisions with or without glasses, 3D computer screens, 3D video games, 3D consoles, 3D Web streaming, etc. 3D video

M. Vento and G. Percannella (Eds.): CAIP 2019, LNCS 11679, pp. 96–107, 2019.
https://doi.org/10.1007/978-3-030-29891-3_9

visualization is more attractive since it is more realistic than 2D videos. Actually, there are varied display techniques for 3D images and videos: active shutter 3D systems, polarized 3D systems, anaglyph 3D systems and virtual reality. The anaglyph system is the most economical and easiest way to make 3D images and videos that require only colored glasses viz. red/cyan glasses. Indeed, an anaglyph image is composed of two pairs of stereo images with complementary colors illustrating a similar scene and seen from a hardly noticeable offset points: the right view in cyan and the left one in red. A lot of researchers have been interested in this display way in many areas. Therefore, several anaglyph generation techniques have been proposed in order to improve the perceptual quality of anaglyph 3D images and videos [5].

Seeing that 3D videos have become more and more admired and well-liked by different categories of people, their transmission through the Web networks has increasing daily and is becoming easier. Thus, the protection of 3D videos from malicious manipulations is necessary. Digital watermarking is the most adequate and appropriate technique to secure them since it has grown dramatically and has become a major area in image processing, where the number of publications has risen rapidly from its first appearance to now. 3D video watermarking consists in embedding an invisible mark in an original 3D video to protect its content and in essaying to recover the embedded mark after applying various attacks on the marked 3D video.

Various 2D video watermarking algorithms have been put forward in the literature [1]; but concerning 3D videos, there is a limited number of suggested techniques related especially to anaglyph 3D videos. A video is a succession of images, so any image-based watermarking technique can be used on the whole of video frames, hence protecting the video sequence. Multiple watermarking algorithms based on anaglyph 3D images have been put forward, where the signature is embedded in a specified image, and using a specific insertion domain. In fact, the authors in [8] inserted the mark into only one type of images, either cyan or red. Whereas in [12], the three images composing the anaglyph 3D image (cyan, red and depth images) were marked with a given signature. Actually, the final marked 3D anaglyph image would be obtained by combining either the marked blue or red image to its corresponding unmarked image. In the latter work, the authors selected to insert the signature in the anaglyph cyan images because the human eye was less sensitive to blue color. This embedding technique provided a good invisibility level and decreased robustness against most attacks [7]. On the other hand, the writers chose to embed the mark using a frequency domain such as the Discrete Wavelet Transform (DWT) [3,8,12], the Discrete Cosines Transform (DCT) [6,11], and the Fourier Fractional Transformation (FrFT) [2]. Most of existing 3D anaglyph watermarking methods are principally based on the DWT and the DCT to insert the mark [7,8,11] due to the provided highest invisibility level and the robustness against usual manipulations, as geometric attacks and additional noises. Besides, all existing watermarking methods dedicated for anaglyph 3D video were based on the DWT where the mark was embedded according to the selected embedding frames. Indeed, in [10], the signature was inserted in the cyan images of all frames composing the original anaglyph 3D video. Whereas in [9], the signature was added into all cyan images of the frames where a change of scene was observed. In addition, in [4], the mark was inserted in I, B and R images of each set of Groups Of Pictures (GOP) where cyan, red and depth images were modified. For more details of the proposed anaglyph 3D image and video watermarking approaches, please refer to the survey paper [5].

The remaining of this paper is organized as follows: The suggested approach of anaglyph 3D video watermarking based on hybrid insertion is presented in the next section. Section 3 evaluates the performance of the proposed method by giving the experimental results. Finally, a conclusion and some perspectives are drawn.

2   Proposed Watermarking Approach

Based on the proposed work discussed in the previous section, inserting the mark only when a change in the scene is detected cannot be robust enough if the video sequence has just one scene or a few numbers of scenes. Moreover, the insertion of a mark only in cyan images can cause robustness deficiency because the signature can be easily removed if cyan images are attacked. The suggested watermarking techniques have shown a high level of imperceptibility but a lack of robustness against malicious manipulations such as MPEG-4 and H264-AVC compression.

In order to enhance the robustness especially against MPEG compression, a novel robust and invisible anaglyph 3D video watermarking method is suggested, which is based on hybrid insertion using three embedding domains and where the mark is embedded into both red and cyan images forming each anaglyph frame. Thus, if the cyan images are attacked and the mark is removed, the mark can be extracted from the red ones.

The general flowchart of the suggested scheme is presented in Fig. 1. First, the original 3D anaglyph video is divided into a set of frames, and then each frame is divided into red and cyan images. Second, the first mark is embedded in the least significant bits of each red image, where the LSB of the original red image are replaced by the most significant bits of the first mark and a marked red image is obtained. The LSB technique is applied to red images because of the embedding of marks in the least significant bits does not affect the perceptual quality of the marked red image since the human eye is more sensitive to red color. Third, the same mark is embedded into cyan images using the DCT, where the mark is embedded into the mid-frequency bands of cyan images since these bands allow avoiding the most visual parts of an image rather low and high-frequency bands, where the low-frequency band deforms the visual quality of the image since it contains maximum image data, while the high-frequency band can be eliminated for compression intention. After the two embedding schemes, both marked cyan and red images are combined together to generate the marked anaglyph frame. To enhance the authentication of the anaglyph 3D video, a second embedding is performed to the obtained marked frames with LSB and DCT techniques.

In fact, a second mark with a small size is used. Every obtained marked anaglyph frame and the second mark are decomposed using the first level of DWT, where the low-frequency coefficients of the LL band of the mark are added to those of the obtained marked anaglyph frame using an invisibility factor. Finally, the inverse of the DWT is applied to obtain the final marked anaglyph frames, and then the latter are recombined to reconstruct the marked anaglyph 3D video.

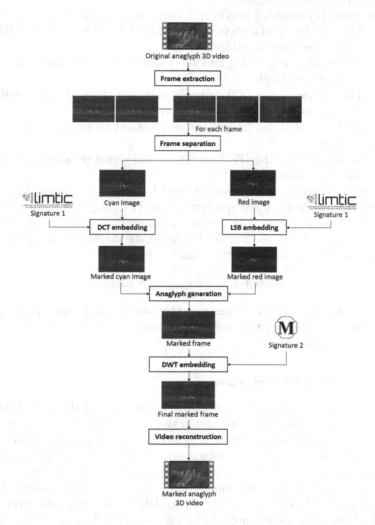

Fig. 1. General architecture of proposed method.

2.1   Proposed Embedding Scheme

Two binary signatures are used for the embedding process. The suggested embedding process is decomposed in several steps as follows:

1. Divide the original 3D anaglyph video into a set of frames.
2. Divide each frame into red and cyan images.
3. Embed the first binary signature into both red and cyan images as follows:
   (a) The least significant bits of each pixel of the original red image is replaced
       by the most significant bits of the mark to obtain the marked red image.
       If the LSB value is '1', then it is replaced by '0'; and if the LSB value is
       '0', it remains unchanged.
   (b) The mark is embedded into cyan images using the DCT as follows:
       i. The cyan image of each frame is divided into 8 * 8 blocks and 2D-DCT
          is performed to every block.
       ii. The mark is embedded into the coefficients in the middle-frequency
           band of each block.
       iii. The inverse of the DCT is performed into the mid-band coefficients
            of each block to obtain the marked cyan image.
4. The marked cyan and red images are recombined to generate each marked
   anaglyph frame.
5. Apply the first level of the DWT to the second signature and each obtained
   marked anaglyph frame.
6. Add the low-frequency coefficients of the LL band of the mark (LL_{mark}) to
   those of the obtained marked anaglyph frame (LL_{frame}) using an invisibility
   factor θ, which was chosen in a way to maintain a good balance between
   invisibility and robustness, in order to obtain the marked low-frequency coefficients ($Marked_{LL}$) following the equation below:

$$Marked_{LL} = LL_{frame} + \theta * LL_{mark} \qquad (1)$$

7. Apply the inverse of DWT to generate the final marked anaglyph frames.
8. Recombine all final marked anaglyph frames to reconstruct the marked
   anaglyph 3D video.

2.2   Proposed Extraction Scheme

The extraction process consists of checking the presence of the embedded mark
in the marked anaglyph 3D video and trying to extract it. The detection of
the signature should be succeeded after applying several attacks on the marked
anaglyph 3D video to prove the robustness of the suggested technique. The
general scheme of the extraction process is composed of different steps. The two
first steps are similar to the embedding process, but instead of the original video,
the marked anaglyph 3D video is utilized to detect the mark. Moreover, in the
proposed scheme, the detection of the second embedded mark proves that the
marked anaglyph 3D video is not altered. Thus, the first signature can be then
extracted. The different extraction steps are as follows:

1. Divide the marked anaglyph 3D video into a set of marked frames.
2. Divide each frame into red and cyan images.
3. Extract the first embedded mark from the marked cyan and red images as
   described below:

(a) Get the least significant bit of each marked red image to obtain the inserted mark.
(b) Divide the marked and original cyan image of each frame into 8*8 blocks and perform a 2D-DCT to each block.
(c) Select only the middle-frequency bands of original and marked cyan images and subtract the embedded coefficients from the marked ones.
(d) Convert the subtracted coefficients to binary to obtain the mark.

4. Extract the second embedded mark by applying the 1st level of DWT to each marked and original anaglyph frame.
5. Subtract the low-frequency coefficients of the LL band of the marked anaglyph frame ($Marked_{LL}$) from those of the original anaglyph frame (LL_{frame}) using the same invisibility factor θ as in the embedding process to obtain the low-frequency coefficients of the inserted mark (LL_{mark}) following the equation below:

$$LL_{mark} = \frac{1}{\theta} * (Marked_{LL} - LL_{frame}) \qquad (2)$$

6. Apply the I-DWT to the extracted coefficients to obtain the recovered mark.

3 Experimentations

The suggested method is developed in a MATLAB 8.6 platform on a PC provided with an Intel Core i7-7500U CPU and 8 GB of memory. The evaluation of the proposed scheme is based on the two main criteria: invisibility and robustness against attacks. In order to prove the performance of the suggested watermarking technique, several experimental tests are applied on various selected anaglyph 3D videos with different characteristics (movement, background texture, resolution and number of frames), using two signatures with multiple sizes.

3.1 Invisibility Evaluation

To evaluate the invisibility level of the suggested technique, we have embedded different sizes of signatures to select the good ones which verify the trade-off between invisibility, capacity, and robustness. Figure 2 shows the impact of the mark size on the invisibility of the proposed scheme. We notice that the visual quality of the marked videos decreases when the size of the first signature is greater than 512×240 and the size of the second one is greater than 256×256. Thus, we evaluate the proposed technique using two signatures with a size of 128×60 and 32×32, respectively.

After embedding the two selected signatures in each test anaglyph 3D video, there is no visual distortion or degradation noticeable with the human eye compared with the original test anaglyph 3D videos, as illustrated in Fig. 3.

To prove this high level of invisibility, the Peak Signal to Noise Ratio (PSNR) is used to calculate the degree of similarity between every marked and original frame forming respectively the marked and original test video. The average of obtained PSNR values confirm the high invisibility level where the maximum value is about 70 dB and the minimum is about 61 dB for most of the used test videos (Table 1).

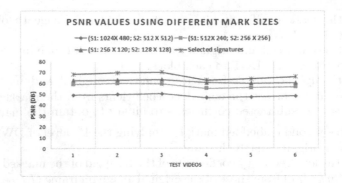

Fig. 2. Impact of mark size on invisibility.

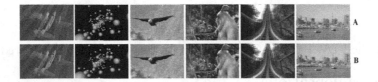

Fig. 3. A. Original frames, B. Corresponding marked frames

Table 1. PSNR values of different test videos.

	Video 1	Video 2	Video 3	Video 4	Video 5	Video 6
PSNR (dB)	68.25	69.49	70.15	62.84	63.93	65.87

3.2   Robustness Evaluation

The robustness of the suggested approach is evaluated using various usual and malicious attacks, which are applied to the marked anaglyph 3D videos in order to remove the embedded mark and to alter the perceptual quality of the video. To confirm that the proposed scheme is robust against any kind of attack, the Normalized Correlation (NC) and the Bit Error Rate (BER) are calculated between the original and extracted marks by quantifying the visual quality of the extracted signature. Indeed, the BER calculates the error rate as a number of error bits and indicates the degree of difference between the extracted and original signatures (Eq. 3). Whereas, the NC measures the correlation between original and extracted signatures S et $\hat{S}$, respectively, as given in Eq. 4. Actually, the BER values are close to 0 if there is a correlation between original and extracted signatures; otherwise, it converges to 1. On the other hand, the NC values are close to 1 if the original and extracted signatures are the same, and it converges to 0 if not.

$$BER = error\ bits\ /total\ bits \qquad (3)$$

$$NC = \frac{\sum_i \sum_j W(i,j).\hat{W}(i,j)}{\sum_i \sum_j [W(i,j)]^2} \tag{4}$$

In the experimentations, geometric attacks are first applied on the marked anaglyph 3D videos in order to remove the embedded marks such as translation, rotation using different angles, scaling, resizing and cropping. In fact, we have tested different rotation angles from 10° to 180° and translations and we have tried to extract the embedded mark. The extraction of the mark has been achieved with an NC value greater than 0.899 and a BER value between 0.003 and 0.002. This is due to the invariance characteristics of DWT facing these attacks. In addition, we have tried to detect the signature after resizing, enlarging, reducing the marked frames forming the video, and cropping some parts from the marked video frames. Due to the duplication of the mark into each frame, the proposed approach will be robust against these applied attacks. The obtained NC and BER values confirm the robustness of the suggested approach, and they are about 0.91 and 0.002, respectively. Figure 4(a) and (b) illustrate, respectively, the obtained NC and BER values after applying the previously mentioned attacks to different test videos.

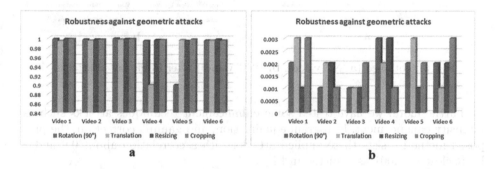

Fig. 4. Obtained (**a.** NC values, **b.** BER values) after geometric attacks.

Second, some additional noises, filtering, and blurring are applied on the marked anaglyph 3D video in order to determine the robustness of the proposed scheme against these manipulations. Actually, the proposed approach resists salt & pepper, Gaussian, Poisson and Speckle noises using different variances due to the embedding of the mark in the middle-frequency bands of the DCT. The obtained results of the NC and the BER are presented, respectively, in Fig. 5(a) and (b).

Third, some frame-based attacks are applied on different test videos such as deleting some frames from the marked video, changing the order of some frame and adding some frames to the marked anaglyph 3D video. The suggested technique withstands frame suppression, swapping and insertion due to the embedding of marks into each frame composing the video and into red and cyan images composing each frame video. To confirm this robustness, Fig. 6 shows the obtained NC and BER values calculated for different test videos.

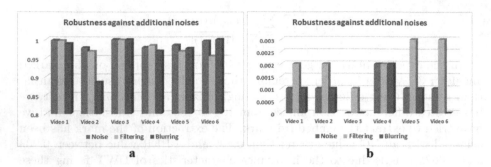

Fig. 5. Obtained (**a.** NC values, **b.** BER values) after additional noises.

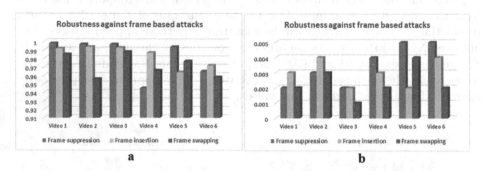

Fig. 6. Obtained (**a.** NC values, **b.** BER values) after frame based attacks.

Furthermore, we have tested some enhancement techniques attacks such as intensity enhancement, histogram equalization, and gamma correction. the proposed method resists these applied attacks with a correlation about 0.9 and a BER close to 0.001 as depicted in Fig. 7.

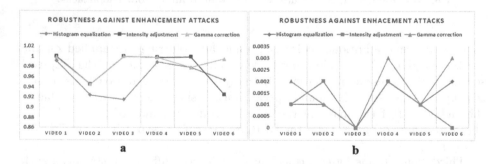

Fig. 7. Obtained (**a.** NC values, **b.** BER values) after enhancement attacks.

Finally, the proposed scheme has been tested against dangerous attacks such as MPEG-4 and H264-AVC compression attacks using variable bit rates from

2 Mbps to 128 Kbps. The compression has been done using the MediaCoder software[1], which is a free universal media transcoder. The retrieved NC and BER values show the robustness of the suggested scheme against compression attacks (Fig. 8). This achievement is due to the mark embedding in the middle frequency bands of the DCT and in the low-frequency bands of the DWT which are robust against compression.

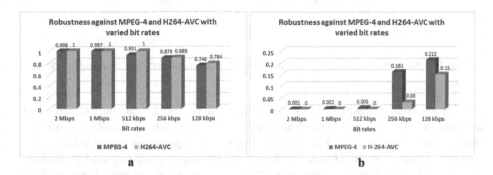

Fig. 8. Obtained (**a.** NC values, **b.** BER values) after compression attacks.

4   Comparative Study

To assess the suggested anaglyph 3D video watermarking technique, the retrieved results are compared with those of related work based on invisibility and robustness factors. The proposed scheme is compared with the three existing watermarking schemes dedicated to anaglyph 3D videos: [4] which is based a DWT embedding in red, cyan and depth channels generated from all images of all the GOP composing the video, [9] which was based on DWT embedding in the cyan images of the frames where a scene change is identified, and [10] which was based on DWT embedding in all cyan images of all the frames.

According to the PSNR values calculated between the marked and the original anaglyph 3D videos, the suggested approach provides a high invisibility level. The PSNR in [4] was about 70 dB. The perceptual quality of marked videos was enhanced compared with the existing work in [9,10] (Fig. 9).

Based on the NC values calculated between the original and extracted marks, a comparison between the proposed scheme and the existing approaches has been performed in order to evaluate the robustness of our proposal against usual and malicious manipulations, as illustrated in Table 2. Firstly, the proposed method and the existing methods [4,9,10] can resist geometric attacks like rotation, translation, scaling, cropping and resizing. Secondly, all the suggested methods are robust against additional noises such as Salt & Pepper, Gaussian noise, Average and Gaussian filtering, and blurring. However, only our proposed approach

---

[1] http://www.mediacoderhq.com.

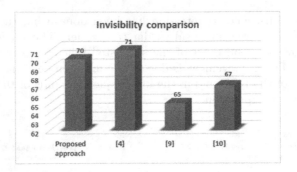

Fig. 9. Obtained PSNR value compared with existing watermarking techniques.

and [4] are robust against Speckle and Poisson noises. Moreover, all proposed techniques resist enhancement manipulations like intensity adjustment and histogram equalization. In addition, the suggested approaches by [9,10] did not withstand frame based attacks as frame suppression, inserting and swapping. Whereas, the put forward scheme by [4] and our proposed approach resist these frame based attacks. Finally, our proposed method is robust against MPEG-4 and H264-AVC compression attacks compared with existing work in [9,10]. In [4], the scheme resisted only MPEG compression.

Table 2. Robustness comparison based on NC values.

Attacks	Geometric attacks	Additional noises	Enhancement attacks	Frame based attacks	Compression	
					MPEG-4	H264-AVC
Proposed approach	0.988	0.989	0.998	0.979	0.995	1
[4]	0.994	0.996	0.997	0.995	0.994	NR[a]
[9]	0.984	0.938	0.996	NR	NR	NR
[10]	0.964	0.889	0.998	NR	NR	NR

[a] Not Robust.

5 Conclusion

To protect anaglyph 3D videos from usual and malicious attacks such as MPEG-4 and H264-AVC compression, a robust and invisible watermarking scheme based on a hybrid insertion has been put forward in this paper. Spatial and frequency embedding domains (LSB, DWT, and DCT) have been used in the proposed approach. First, the original anaglyph 3D video is split into a number of frames, each frame is then re-split into cyan and red images. Second, the latter are processed, respectively, by a DCT and LSB embedding algorithms to insert the first signature, then the obtained marked ones are recombined to create a marked anaglyph frame. After that, the obtained marked anaglyph frame is processed by the 1st level of DWT and a second signature is inserted in its low-frequency band. The inverse of DWT is performed to generate the final marked anaglyph frame. Finally, the marked anaglyph 3D video is obtained by recombining all the marked frames. The experimentations have shown a good imperceptibility level and good robustness against several attacks like geometric attacks, additional noises and filtering, frame-based attacks and different video compression standards. Besides, the suggested scheme has been compared with existing work and has shown the good performance based on the invisibility and the robustness criteria. In future work, the robustness against dangerous attacks like collusion will be considered.

References

1. Bayoudh, I., Jabra, S.B., Zagrouba, E.: A robust video watermarking for real-time application. In: Blanc-Talon, J., Penne, R., Philips, W., Popescu, D., Scheunders, P. (eds.) ACIVS 2017. LNCS, vol. 10617, pp. 493–504. Springer, Cham (2017). https://doi.org/10.1007/978-3-319-70353-4_42
2. Bhatnagar, G., Wu, J., Raman, B.: A robust security framework for 3D images. J. Vis. **14**(1), 85–93 (2011)
3. Devi, H.S., Singh, K.M.: A robust and optimized 3D red-cyan anaglyph blind image watermarking in the dwt domain. Contemp. Eng. Sci. **9**, 1575–1589 (2016). https://doi.org/10.12988/ces.2016.69156
4. Dhaou, D., Ben Jabra, S., Zagrouba, E.: An efficient group of pictures decomposition based watermarking for anaglyph 3D video. In: the 13th International Joint Conference on Computer Vision, Imaging and Computer Graphics Theory and Applications (VISIGRAPP 2018, VISAPP), pp. 501–510 (2018)
5. Dhaou, D., Ben Jabra, S., Zagrouba, E.: A review on anaglyph 3D image and video watermarking. 3D Res. **10**(2), 13 (2019)
6. Munoz-Ramirez, D.O., Reyes-Reyes, R., Ponomaryov, V., Cruz-Ramos, C.: Invisible digital color watermarking technique in anaglyph 3D images. In: 12th International Conference on Electrical Engineering, Computing Science and Automatic Control (CCE), pp. 1–6 (2015)
7. Prathap, I., Anitha, R.: Robust and blind watermarking scheme for three dimensional anaglyph images. Comput. Electr. Eng. **40**(1), 51–58 (2014). https://doi.org/10.1016/j.compeleceng.2013.11.005
8. Ruchika, P., Parth, B.: Robust watermarking for anaglyph 3D images using dwt techniques. Int. J. Eng. Tech. Res. (IJETR) **3**(6), 55–58 (2015)
9. Salih, J.W., Abid, S.H., Hasan, T.M.: Imperceptible 3D video watermarking technique based on scene change detection. Int. J. Adv. Sci. Technol. **82**, 11–22 (2015). https://doi.org/10.14257/ijast.2015.82.02
10. Waleed, J., Jun, H.D., Hameed, S., Hatem, H., Majeed, R.: Integral algorithm to embed imperceptible watermark into anaglyph 3D video. Int. J. Adv. Comput. Technol. **5**(13), 163 (2013)
11. Wang, C., Han, F., Zhuang, X.: Robust digital watermarking scheme of anaglyphic 3D for RGB color images. Int. J. Image Process. (IJIP) **9**(3), 156 (2015)
12. Zadokar, S.R., Raskar, V.B., Shinde, S.V.: A digital watermarking for anaglyph 3D images. In: International Conference on Advances in Computing, Communications and Informatics (ICACCI), pp. 483–488 (2013)

A Computer Vision Pipeline that Uses Thermal and RGB Images for the Recognition of Holstein Cattle

Amey Bhole[1]([⊠]), Owen Falzon[2], Michael Biehl[1],
and George Azzopardi[1]([⊠])

[1] University of Groningen, Groningen, The Netherlands
{a.bhole,m.biehl,g.azzopardi}@rug.nl
[2] University of Malta, Msida, Malta
owen.falzon@um.edu.mt

Abstract. The monitoring of farm animals is important as it allows farmers keeping track of the performance indicators and any signs of health issues, which is useful to improve the production of milk, meat, eggs and others. In Europe, bovine identification is mostly dependent upon the electronic ID/RFID ear tags, as opposed to branding and tattooing. The RFID based ear-tagging approach has been called into question because of implementation and management costs, physical damage and animal welfare concerns. In this paper, we conduct a case study for individual identification of Holstein cattle, characterized by black, brown and white patterns, in collaboration with the Dairy campus in Leeuwarden. We use a FLIR E6 thermal camera to collect an infrared and RGB image of the side view of each cow just after leaving the milking station. We apply a fully automatic pipeline, which consists of image processing, computer vision and machine learning techniques on a data set containing 1237 images and 136 classes (i.e. individual animals). In particular, we use the thermal images to segment the cattle from the background and remove horizontal and vertical pipes that occlude the cattle in the station, followed by filling the blank areas with an inpainting algorithm. We use the segmented image and apply transfer learning to a pre-trained AlexNet convolutional neural network. We apply five-fold cross-validation and achieve an average accuracy rate of 0.9754 ± 0.0097. The results obtained suggest that the proposed non-invasive approach is highly effective in the automatic recognition of Holstein cattle from the side view. In principle, this approach is applicable to any farm animals that are characterized by distinctive coat patterns.

Keywords: Transfer learning · Individual identification ·
Computer vision · Holstein cattle

1 Introduction

Modern agriculture is developing rapidly in different sectors, such as organic farming, agribusiness, animal husbandry and precision agriculture, due to

© Springer Nature Switzerland AG 2019
M. Vento and G. Percannella (Eds.): CAIP 2019, LNCS 11679, pp. 108–119, 2019.
https://doi.org/10.1007/978-3-030-29891-3_10

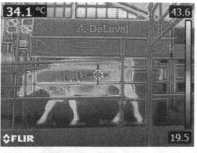 

(a) Thermal image   (b) RGB image

Fig. 1. Examples of thermal and RGB images acquired at the same time by the FLIR E6 thermal camera from a distance of five meters.

technological advancements. In animal husbandry, it is important for the farmer to keep track of the animal's performance and health in order to improve the production of commodities such as milk, cheese, meat and other products. An example where traceability of animals is important is when the cattle are approaching or leaving the milking station. Identification methods based on collar id and ear-tagging are used for individual recognition of cattle. These methods do not provide effective solutions for the identification of cattle due to loss of ear-tags, fading of labels on ear-tags and physical damage [6,9,21]. In Europe, bovine identification is mostly dependant on electronic identification devices, such as radio frequency identification (RFIDs) [26]. It is a technology that uses electromagnetic waves for the identification and tracking of the RFID tags placed on the ears of Holstein cattle. The RFID tags are also used with an ear-tagging approach for cattle identification. That approach, however, has issues related to implementation, cost and management of large scale monitoring of livestock animals [8]. There is, therefore, a need for non-invasive methods for the identification of cattle in farms.

In this paper, we explore the possibility of integrating animal biometric with modern agriculture. We perform a case study to identify individual Holstein cattle based on the unique coat pattern. We propose a solution consisting of a pipeline of image acquisition using a thermal camera, image processing and transfer learning [19] using a pre-trained convolution neural network. We also release a benchmark data set consisting of side-view images of Holstein cattle, as shown in Fig. 1, collected at the Dairy Campus in Leeuwarden, the Netherlands. The proposed solution provides an effective system for the individual identification of Holstein cattle using a non-invasive computer vision approach, which can be set up in a practically relevant environment.

2   Related Work

In this section, we evaluate three different methodologies proposed in the literature for individual identification of cattle. Specifically, for each approach, we describe the classification performance, the ability to automate the process, and the adequacy of using the method in a relevant practical setting.

Almost a century ago it was found that the muzzle patterns of cows exhibit individually unique traits [20]. Such patterns have been investigated and turned out to be, indeed, promising biometric features. Handcrafted feature-description algorithms, such as Scale-Invariant Feature Transform (SIFT) [17], have been used for muzzle prints for individual identification of cattle with classification accuracy of 93% [2]. In more recent work a deep learning framework [15] was used for individual identification of cattle and identification accuracies in the region of 95.98%–98.9% were reported for tests carried out on 500 subjects. That approach, however, can be burdensome to be completely automated and executed in an application where the cattle has to be identified during the milking process. Due to the non-cooperative behaviour of cattle, it is difficult to set up a system for acquiring good quality images of muzzles.

Identification of animals, such as horses or cattle, can also be performed based on iris patterns including arching ligaments, furrows, ridges, crypts, rings and zigzag collarette [4]. A new cattle identification system was proposed based on iris analysis and recognition in [18], and it achieved identification accuracy of 96% for 6 cows. While those results look promising more experiments need to be carried out on a large database to better assess the robustness of that approach. Moreover, the eye image captured by a video camera may lack uniformity making this method difficult to automate.

In recent work, the coat patterns of the Holstein cattle, which exhibit black, brown and white coat patterns, patches, and markings over their bodies were used for individual identification. In particular, an R-CNN [22] adaptation of the VGG CNN M 1024 network was used for individual identification of cattle [1]. That approach achieved a mean average precision of 86.07% over two-fold cross validation for the identification of 89 cows using top-view still RGB images. The promising results demonstrated that individual identification of Holstein cattle is possible based on the coat patterns.

In the method that we propose we also use the coat patterns for individual identification but unlike the work in [1], we leverage the side-view instead of the top-view images to capture maximum information related to the coat patterns of cattle. We also use thermal images to capture the temperature distribution in the scene and use it to segment the cow from the background. Moreover, we use an inpainting technique to replace occluding components with more meaning-ful values related to the coat pattern of the cattle. Finally, we use the AlexNet convolutional neural network [16] with transfer learning to demonstrate the effec-tiveness of the conceptually simple pipeline that we propose. AlexNet [14] made a breakthrough in computer vision by achieving outstanding results in the image classification tasks of the ImageNet Large Scale Visual Recognition Challenge [23]. In recent applications, transfer learning has been employed with pre-trained CNNs to overcome the problem of the restricted availability of data in certain applications, and it has been shown how effective it is in different applications, including health care [7,27], natural language processing [13] and self-driving cars [3].

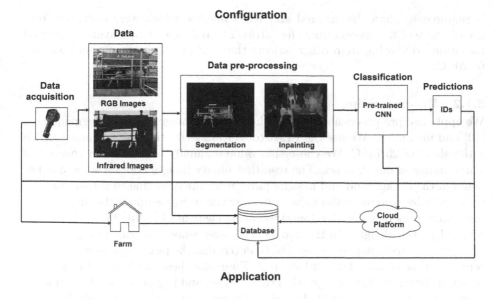

Fig. 2. Schematic overview of the proposed solution

3 Method

In Fig. 2 we illustrate a schematic overview of the proposed solution. It consists of two main components, namely configuration and application. The configuration part includes data acquisition, data pre-processing and determination of the classification model by transfer learning. The data acquisition is used to capture the side-view of the cattle when they are leaving from the milking station. Figure 1 shows an example of a pair of thermal and RGB images captured while the concerned cow was walking out from the milking station. In data pre-processing we use the distinctive body temperature of the cattle to segment it from the background and apply an inpainting algorithm to fill the gaps generated by the occluding rods. The preprocessed images are then used to learn our classification model.

3.1 Configuration

3.1.1 Data Acquisition

The data acquisition process was carried out at the Dairy campus in Leeuwarden over a period of nine days using the FLIR E6 thermal camera, which has a straightforward point and shoot operation. The camera has an image resolution of 640 × 480 pixels and the ability to detect temperature differences as small as 0.06 °C. The camera has three main parameters to be evaluated for collection of images, namely emissivity, distance and reflected temperature. The emissivity of a surface depends not only on the material but also on the nature of the surface. In this case, the emissivity used was 0.98. The distance parameter in the camera is required to align the infrared and RGB images, which were captured from the distance of five meters from the cattle. The reflected temperature is thermal radiation originating from other objects that reflect off the target and was set to 20 °C.

3.1.2   Pre-processing

We apply two pre-processing steps to the acquired images, namely segmentation [10] and inpainting. We use the FLIR tools to binarize the thermal images with a threshold of 25.75 °C. We chose this value manually after visually inspecting some images of our data set. The resulting binary images contain some components in the background and missing parts from the cows due to the presence of rods. In order to remove the gaps caused by the rods, we apply the area closing morphology operation with a line structuring element of radius 18 pixels. In this way, all parts belonging to the cow become one connected component. Finally, we use connected component analysis to determine the largest component, which represents the cow, and discard the rest. Figure 3b shows a binarized image as a result of the segmentation algorithm that we use, and Fig. 3c shows the extracted region of interest after morphological and connected component analysis.

Next, we crop the connected component representing the cow and recover the gaps caused by the rods. In order to ensure that all rods-related pixels are removed we widen slightly the gaps with a dilation operation that uses a disc structuring element of radius 3 pixels. Figure 3d illustrates the widened gaps on the corresponding cropped RGB image. Finally, we apply the inpainting algorithm based on the fast marching method proposed in [25] to replace the gaps with more relevant values determined from the local neighbourhoods, Fig. 3e.

3.1.3   Classification Model

We build a classification model by using transfer learning on a pre-trained model. Transfer learning exploits source knowledge gained from learning one task and applying it to solve another one [11], and it is suitable when there is limited availability of training images per class, such as our data set. We use the AlexNet convolutional neural network, which was pre-trained on the ImageNet Database [5] and fine tuned it with our training data. The architecture of AlexNet consists of five convolutional layers and three fully connected layers where the ReLU activation function is applied after every convolutional and fully connected layers. Dropout regularization [24] of 50% is applied before the first and the second fully connected layer. We changed the last fully connected layer of AlexNet by replacing it from the 1000 classes used for the image classification of ImageNet to 136 classes corresponding to the number of distinct cows in our data set.

3.2   Application

A given query image is evaluated by first applying the pre-processing steps described above and then fed to the AlexNet CNN classifier. The output of the network is the identifier of the cow to which the given query image is assigned.

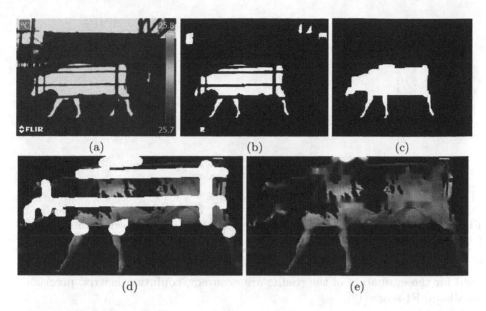

(a)   (b)   (c)

(d)   (e)

Fig. 3. Segmentation of the region of interest. (a) Thermal image with lower and upper limits clipped at 25.7 °C and 25.8 °C, respectively. (b) The binary image obtained after using a threshold of 25.75 °C on the image in (a). (c) The cow mask obtained by dilating the image in (b) and determining the largest connected component. (d) The corresponding cropped RGB image with dilated gaps and (e) the result of the inpainting that we use.

AlexNet CNN classifier can be deployed on various cloud platforms. It can also be updated periodically for new classes.

4   Experiments and Results

Below we provide details about the data set used, the evaluation method, hyper-parameters and the results of our experiments.

4.1   Data Set

In this study we use images with resolution of 640 × 480 pixels before pre-processing. The data set contains 1237 unique pairs of RGB and infrared images of 136 cows. Figure 4 shows the distribution of the number of images per class (i.e. per cow) sorted in ascending order, where the median is 9, the mean is 9.09, and the minimum and maximum number of images per class are 6 and 14, respectively.

4.2   Evaluation Methods

We evaluate the proposed approach by using five-fold cross validation with stratified sampling, and report the average performance measurements. The metrics

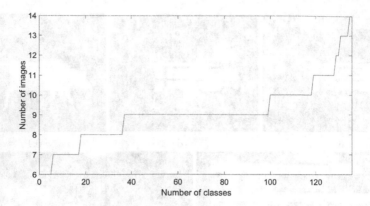

Fig. 4. Distribution of the number of images per class (i.e. per cow), with a mean of 9.09 and standard deviation of 1.49.

used for the evaluation of the results are accuracy, confusion matrix, precision, recall and F1-score [12].

4.3   Training Parameters

According to the requirement of AlexNet we resize the images to 227×227 pixels and normalise them by subtracting the mean. We use the stochastic gradient descent with momentum as the optimizer to re-train the last layer of AlexNet classification model with 50 epochs for each of the five folds. The mini-batch size for training is 32, the global learning rate is set to 0.001 and momentum of 0.9. All experiments, including training and evaluation, were carried out with a computer equipped by NVIDIA GeForce GTX 1050 and Intel Core i7-7700HQ CPU @ 2.80 GHz with 24 GB RAM.

4.4   Results

Table 1 reports the average results obtained over five folds of experiments and Fig. 5 shows the sum of confusion matrices obtained over the five folds. There were a total of 31 images that were misclassified across all folds. For each fold, we fine-tuned a new AlexNet classifier by transfer learning using the training images available in that fold and we calculated the macro F1-score, which is based on the average precision and recall computed for each class in a one-vs-all setup.

Table 1. Mean results obtained for individual identification from five-fold cross validation

Accuracy	Macro precision	Macro recall	Macro F1-score
0.9754 ± 0.0097	0.9808 ± 0.0060	0.9765 ± 0.0082	0.9786 ± 0.0062

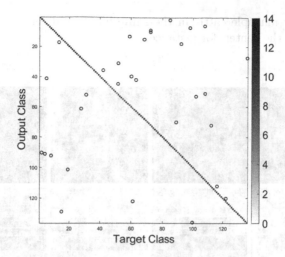

Fig. 5. Sum of the confusion matrices across the five folds. The circles indicate the positions of the false positives, which all have a value of 1.

5   Discussion

The contributions of this work are two-fold. Firstly, we propose an effective pipeline of image acquisition, image processing, computer vision and machine learning components, which can be deployed in farms for the identification of cattle from the side-view in milking stations. To the best of our knowledge, this is the first study that addresses this challenge and proposes an effective solution that can be easily deployed. Secondly, we make available[1] a data set of 1237 pairs of thermal and RGB images of 136 cows, which can be used for benchmarking.

In this work we use the thermal images only for segmentation purposes and then we apply the AlexNet CNN on the corresponding RGB data. This configuration expects all cows to have sufficient amount of coat pattern and, therefore, it lacks robustness to the recognition of cattle in the rare cases where there is no or very little coat pattern, Fig. 6. In order to make the system more robust, in future work we plan to investigate a fusion approach that uses features from both RGB and thermal images for the final classification of a given query image. Furthermore, retraining AlexNet with limited number of images per class may be prone to overfitting. In order to improve the generalization, we plan to implement different data augmentation techniques.

While the aisle in the milking station is restricted to allow one cow at a time, it may happen that two cows appear in the same image. The scope of this study did not consider such situations and, in fact, some of the images were misclassified due to this problem, as shown in the examples given in Fig. 7. In order to overcome this issue, in future work we plan to investigate techniques

---

[1] The data set is available here: http://infosysdemos.cs.rug.nl.

that can identify multiple cattle in the same image and segment only the one that is closest to the center, for instance.

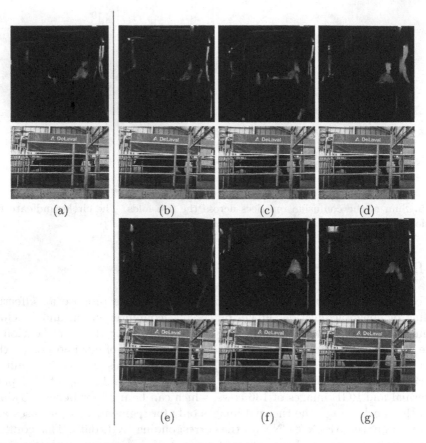

Fig. 6. (a) Example of an incorrectly classified query image due to insufficient coat pattern. In (b–d) and (e–g) there are samples of the training images from the class (ID-0675) with which the query image was supposed to be classified and samples of the training images from the class (ID-7600) with which it was incorrectly classified, respectively. All instances are represented by (top) the preprocessed image and (bottom) the original RGB image.

Another direction for future research is to explore the capturing of multiple images of the same cow while it is walking through aisle. In that case, we may investigate the processing of all images through the classifier and finally aggregate all decisions into a stronger one. Such a solution would circumvent the situations where the occluded part of the cattle contains one or more of the most defining features, which cannot be recovered by the inpainting algorithm. Figure 8 shows one such example. The consideration of multiple images of the same query cow would substantially reduce the risk of such situations.

(a)   (b)   (c)   (d)

Fig. 7. The images in (a–b) are the original RGB and preprocessed images with two cattle, and the images in (c–d) show another instance of the main cow, with ID equals to 9884, alone.

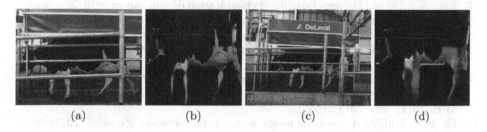

(a)   (b)   (c)   (d)

Fig. 8. Two pairs of RGB and preprocessed images of the cow with ID equals to 0091. In the images in (c–d) the cow has one of the defining coat features occluded, and the inpainting algorithm fails to reconstruct it properly.

6   Conclusions

The proposed pipeline for the recognition of cattle from the side-view in milking stations is very effective. Our approach is completely automatic, non-invasive, and does not require the farms to change anything in their infrastructure or in the way they handle cattle in the milking stations. The pipeline consists of image acquisition with a thermal camera, segmentation, inpainting and the AlexNet CNN with transfer learning. The proposed solution is flexible to be integrated with systems already present in the farms and can be deployed on cloud platforms.

Acknowledgements. We thank the Dairy campus in Leeuwarden for permitting the data collection used in this project and for approving its availability for academic use.

References

1. Andrew, W., Greatwood, C., Burghardt, T.: Visual localisation and individual identification of Holstein Friesian cattle via deep learning. In: Proceedings of the IEEE International Conference on Computer Vision, pp. 2850–2859 (2017)

2. Awad, A.I., Zawbaa, H.M., Mahmoud, H.A., Nabi, E.H.H.A., Fayed, R.H., Hassanien, A.E.: A robust cattle identification scheme using muzzle print images. In: 2013 Federated Conference on Computer Science and Information Systems, pp. 529–534. IEEE (2013)
3. Choi, D., An, T.H., Ahn, K., Choi, J.: Driving experience transfer method for end-to-end control of self-driving cars. arXiv preprint arXiv:1809.01822 (2018)
4. Daugman, J.G.: High confidence visual recognition of persons by a test of statistical independence. IEEE Trans. Pattern Anal. Mach. Intell. **15**(11), 1148–1161 (1993)
5. Deng, J., Dong, W., Socher, R., Li, L.J., Li, K., Fei-Fei, L.: ImageNet: a large-scale hierarchical image database. In: CVPR09 (2009)
6. Edwards, D., Johnston, A., Pfeiffer, D.: A comparison of commonly used ear tags on the ear damage of sheep. Anim. Welf. **10**(2), 141–151 (2001)
7. Esteva, A., et al.: Dermatologist-level classification of skin cancer with deep neural networks. Nature **542**(7639), 115 (2017)
8. Feng, J., Fu, Z., Wang, Z., Xu, M., Zhang, X.: Development and evaluation on a RFID-based traceability system for cattle/beef quality safety in China. Food control **31**(2), 314–325 (2013)
9. Fosgate, G., Adesiyun, A., Hird, D.: Ear-tag retention and identification methods for extensively managed water buffalo (bubalus bubalis) in trinidad. Prev. Vet. Med. **73**(4), 287–296 (2006)
10. Fu, K.S., Mui, J.: A survey on image segmentation. Pattern Recognit. **13**(1), 3–16 (1981)
11. Goodfellow, I., Bengio, Y., Courville, A.: Deep Learning. MIT Press, Cambridge (2016). http://www.deeplearningbook.org
12. Hastie, T., Tibshirani, R., Friedman, J.: The Elements of Statistical Learning. Springer Series in Statistics. Springer, New York (2001). https://doi.org/10.1007/978-0-387-21606-5
13. Howard, J., Ruder, S.: Universal language model fine-tuning for text classification. arXiv preprint arXiv:1801.06146 (2018)
14. Krizhevsky, A., Sutskever, I., Hinton, G.E.: ImageNet classification with deep convolutional neural networks. In: Advances in Neural Information Processing Systems, pp. 1097–1105 (2012)
15. Kumar, S., et al.: Deep learning framework for recognition of cattle using muzzle point image pattern. Measurement **116**, 1–17 (2018)
16. LeCun, Y., et al.: Backpropagation applied to handwritten zip code recognition. Neural Comput. **1**(4), 541–551 (1989)
17. Lowe, D.G., et al.: Object recognition from local scale-invariant features
18. Lu, Y., He, X., Wen, Y., Wang, P.S.: A new cow identification system based on iris analysis and recognition. Int. J. Biom. **6**(1), 18–32 (2014)
19. Pan, S.J., Yang, Q.: A survey on transfer learning. IEEE Trans. Knowl. Data Eng. **22**(10), 1345–1359 (2010)
20. Petersen, W.: The identification of the bovine by means of nose-prints. J. Dairy Sci. **5**(3), 249–258 (1922)
21. Phillips, C.: Cattle Behaviour and Welfare. Wiley, Hoboken (2008)
22. Ren, S., He, K., Girshick, R., Sun, J.: Faster R-CNN: towards real-time object detection with region proposal networks. In: Advances in Neural Information Processing Systems, pp. 91–99 (2015)
23. Russakovsky, O., et al.: Imagenet large scale visual recognition challenge. Int. J. Comput. Vis. **115**(3), 211–252 (2015)

24. Srivastava, N., Hinton, G., Krizhevsky, A., Sutskever, I., Salakhutdinov, R.: Dropout: a simple way to prevent neural networks from overfitting. J. Mach. Learn. Res. **15**, 1929–1958 (2014). http://jmlr.org/papers/v15/srivastava14a.html

25. Telea, A.: An image inpainting technique based on the fast marching method. J. Graph. Tools **9**(1), 23–34 (2004)

26. Wamba, S.F., Anand, A., Carter, L.: RFID applications, issues, methods and theory: a review of the AIS basket of TOP journals. Procedia Technol. **9**, 421–430 (2013)

27. Wieslander, H., et al.: Deep convolutional neural networks for detecting cellular changes due to malignancy. In: Proceedings of the IEEE International Conference on Computer Vision, pp. 82–89 (2017)

DeepNautilus: A Deep Learning Based System for Nautical Engines' Live Vibration Processing

Rosario Carbone, Raffaele Montella$^{(\boxtimes)}$, Fabio Narducci, and Alfredo Petrosino

Department of Science and Technologies, University of Naples "Parthenope",
Naples, Italy
{rosario.carbone,raffaele.montella,fabio.narducci,
alfredo.petrosino}@uniparthenope.it

Abstract. Recent advances in sensor technologies and data analysis techniques allow reliable and efficient systems for the early diagnosis of breakdowns in the production chain of the car industry and, more generally, of engines. The performance of these systems is based fundamentally on the quality of the features extracted and on the learning technique. In this paper, we show our preliminary, but encouraging, results carried out through our research effort in the field of using deep neural network to recognize and eventually predict engine failures. We present the prototypal blueprint of the system DeepNautilius devoted to detect failures in marine engines using deep learning with the ambitious goal of reducing marine pollution. Our envision comprises a distributed sensor data acquisition system based on the fog/edge/cloud computing paradigm, with a consistent part of the computation located on the edge side. While our architectural approach is described as a design oriented issue, in this work we present our experience with the deep neural network (DNN) computational core, using a literature dataset from an air compression engine. We demonstrate that our approach is not only comparable with the one in literature but is even better performing.

Keywords: Deep neural network · Edge computing ·
Internet of Things

1 Introduction

The maintenance phase of the machines is nowadays not just a necessity, but is considered a crucial aspect for most industries. The possible approaches to cope with this aspect are:

- Preventive maintenance;
- Corrective maintenance;
- Maintenance based on conditions or status.

M. Vento and G. Percannella (Eds.): CAIP 2019, LNCS 11679, pp. 120–131, 2019.
https://doi.org/10.1007/978-3-030-29891-3_11

Of the three, the maintenance based on conditions or status has been proved to be the most effective and reliable approach, since it allows for early reporting of any fault and avoiding invasive interventions, analyzing the various acquired parameters indicating the status of an engine, reducing the total cost of ownership and improving the overall security and safeness in the involved operations [9].

In order to apply this paradigm, a naive approach is based on a manual creation of the features' fingerprints framing an engine failure condition or failure premonition. In this scenario, the engineers manually design a system leveraging on statistical parameters and signal processing based analysis [8]. In the sake of deep learning techniques, a more up to date approach has recently emerged, which works by obtaining features representation in those kind of applications [19], as already done with excellent results in the application field of image processing and speech recognition [4].

In this paper, we present some techniques to learn features through Deep Neural Network (DNN) in order to improve their performance.

In a first approach, the features are generated in 3 phases:

1. manual extraction of features using traditional techniques;
2. initialization of the weights using DNN through stacked denoising auto-encoder, with the characteristics extracted by hand in an unsupervised way;
3. application of DNN techniques for the fine tuning phase.

In a second approach, the same data obtained in phase 1 – features extraction, were used to train a Generative Adversarial Network (GAN), focusing the attention on two aspects:

- semi-supervised learning;
- generation of realistic samples.

In the latter case, unlike most of the work on generative models, the goal is not to train a model that assigns a high probability distribution on the test data, but to have a model that can learn correctly without the use of labels.

The experiments of both DNN models were conducted on a dataset composed of compressed air engine recordings. The results obtained, which are in line with those in the reference articles, show that the proposed approach can be reliable and efficient in some application areas.

We motivate the use of the proposed approach as a key component of the Distributed Leisure Yacht-Carried Sensor-Network for Atmosphere and Marine Data Crowdsourcing Applications (DYNAMO) [14], which enforces data crowdsourcing in coastal and marine monitoring [10,12,16] and management due to the challenges of the marine environment. A distributed operational system based on the findings shown in this work could substantially improve the safe of men at sea and the environmental protection.

The rest of this paper is organized as follows: in Sect. 2 we describe the proposed architecture, the literature available dataset used for evaluation (Subsect. 2.1) and the related data acquisition system; the software component tools used in this paper are detailed in the Sect. 3: the Stacked Denoising Auto-encoder (SDAE, see Subsect. 3.1), the Generative Adversarial Network

(GAN, see Subsect. 3.2), and the Semi Supervised Generative Adversarial Network (SSGAN, see Subsect. 3.3); the evaluation and the results are described and discussed in Sect. 4, while the final remarks, the conclusions, and the future directions of this research are pointed out in the final Sect. 5.

2   System Architecture

In the system taken as reference, the acoustic data obtained from the transducers are analyzed in the frequency domain through the application of the FFT (Fast Fourier Transform), carrying out a normalization of the signal power, and passed in input to a deep neural network model called Stacked Denoising Auto Encoder [20], in order to generate features that help us to reduce the intra-class difference of patterns, and at the same time increase the inter-class difference of patterns. Furthermore, this step makes a considerable reduction in the data size, so as to operate the classification phase more quickly, as visualized in Fig. 1.

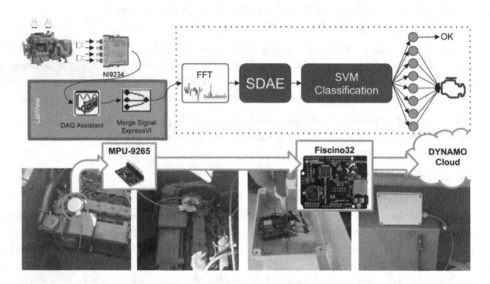

Fig. 1. Fault Diagnosis System. Top: the controlled environment used to deal with data and related methodologies described in this work. Middle: the acquisition system developed in order to perform real world experiments devoted to collect a brand new failure dataset based on marine engine vibrations. Bottom: a real setup of the DeepNautilius system on a small leisure boat engine.

In the real world application use cases we consider in this work, data is collected using accelerometer sensors mounted the engine side. IoT devices, enabling double precision numeric representation, perform local process to compute FFT at the fog computing level. Data is stored on the platform on the edge of the cloud and then finally transferred to the cloud using a fast, secure, reliable, and resilient data transfer protocol [11,17] for the DDN processing on elastic computing resources [3].

2.1   Dataset

In order to validate the proposed system, we used the dataset composed by Verma et al. [21], representing labelled features about an air compression engine behaviour and failures. Data is captured using multiple acoustic sensors. Eight different states are artificially induced, including a healthy state and seven fault states, such as suction valve failure (LIV), drain valve failure (LOV), fault to non-return valve (NRV), piston seal failure, malfunction flywheel, belt failure and bearing failure (Fig. 2).

The recorded data is stored in different files each containing 250000 samples. For each state, 225 recordings were made (for a total of 1800 recordings). The recording files are organized according to a 1800 × 250000 matrix, and a vector containing the 1800 associated labels.

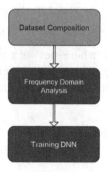

Fig. 2. Dataset composition.

The acquisition system is the one proposed in the literature by Verma et al. [21], where 4 unidirectional microphones have been appropriately positioned on the motor of a compressor. The NI9234 digital analog converter and the Labview software are used to combine the signal acquired from the 4 microphones.

3   DNN Tools

3.1   Stacked Denoising Auto-Encoder - SDAE

An auto-encoder is a three-layer neural network. It was suggested for the realization of associative memories, according to which feeding in part of the information the goal is to have the reconstruction of the whole information in output. In this case, it is used in its version of *denoiser*. This way, the intermediate layer produces a higher level of abstraction useful for regenerating the input.

An example of auto-encoder is shown in Fig. 3, where it tries to learn a function $h_{W,b}(x)$ about equal to the input x vector, where W and b correspond to the input weights and biases respectively. For a given training set, the cost

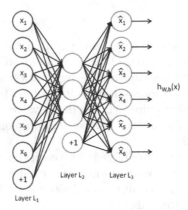

Fig. 3. Typical structure of an auto-encoder, with six nodes in the input level, three nodes in the intermediate level and six nodes in the output level.

function is represented by Eq. 1 where network weights and bias are updated using the back-propagation algorithm. The parameter λ is the regularization parameter used to prevent overfitting on the training data.

$$J(W,b) \quad = \quad \left[\frac{1}{m} \sum_{i=1}^{m} \left(\frac{1}{2} \left\| h_{W,b}(x^{(i)}) - \widehat{x}^{(i)} \right\|^2 \right) \right] \quad + \quad \frac{\lambda}{2} \sum_{i=1}^{S_l} \sum_{j=1}^{S_{l+1}} (W_{ji})^2 \quad (1)$$

The basic algorithm then applies changes to the specific case, especially those here referred to as Stacked Denoising Auto-Encoder [20], which is a special class of auto-encoders where a stochastic noise is added to the input layer, in order to train it to give in output the same input filtered from the noise. This step makes the auto-encoder robust to noise. Another trick we have applied concerns the number of hidden levels. In fact, having fewer nodes in the intermediate levels, the input is transformed so as to be represented with less features, forcing the auto-encoder to give a compact representation of the features with low redundancy. As can be seen from the left side of the image in Fig. 4, our stack consists of intermediate levels of each auto encoder.

3.2   Generative Adversarial Network

On one hand the solution of [21] has some advantages, such as speed of convergence of the method during training. However, at the same time, it also presents some disadvantages, such as a low generalization, due to the fact that is very dependent on the parameters proposed by the authors. To find a solution to these limits, we propose a system using adversarial networks [7], where the generative model is opposed to an "adversary" as presented in Fig. 5. As it can be seen, this is a discriminating model that learns to determine if a sample comes from the distribution of the generative model or from the distribution of data.

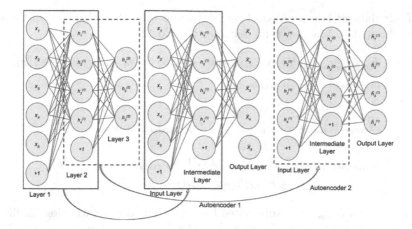

Fig. 4. A stacked auto-encoder trained one layer at a time.

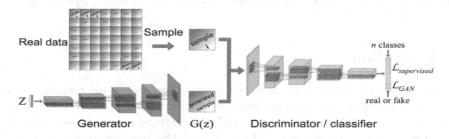

Fig. 5. GAN model scheme.

A model of this type can be seen as analogous to a group of counterfeiters who try to produce fake coins and use them without being detected, while the discriminating model can be seen as analogous to the police, which tries to detect counterfeit coins. The competition in this "game" between the two models pushes them to improve their methods until the counterfeits are not distinguishable from the original samples.

3.3   Semi Supervised Generative Adversarial Network

The training of a GAN network consists in finding a balance of Nash in a non-cooperative two-player game where each of them wants to minimize their cost function. In the semi-supervised approach [18], which is also the one that we are proposing, we try to find a solution to the difficulties in finding a balance of Nash. Considering a standard classifier, this model accepts a sample x as input and generates a k-dimensional logic vector $\{l_1, ..., l_k\}$, which can be transformed into probabilities of belonging to a given class. We can perform semi-supervised learning by simply adding the samples produced by the GAN G generator into our dataset, tagging them with the addition of a new "generated" class and then increasing the output size of our classifier from K to $K+1$. Assuming that half of our dataset is composed of real data and that the other half of them is generated, our loss function then becomes the Eq. 2:

$$L = -E_{x,y \sim p_{data}(x,y)}\left[logp_{model}(y|x)\right] - E_{x \sim G}\left[logp_{model}(y = K + 1|x)\right]$$
$$= L_{supervised} + L_{unsupervised}, \tag{2}$$

where:

$$L_{supervised} = -E_{x,y \sim p_{data}(x,y)} logp_{model}(y|x, y < K + 1) \tag{3}$$

$$L_{unsupervised} = -E_{x \sim p_{data}(x)} log[1 - p_{model}(y = K + 1|x)] \tag{4}$$
$$+ E_{x \sim G} log[p_{model}(y = K + 1|x)], \tag{5}$$

The sum of a $L_{supervised}$ supervised loss function (the negative log-likelihood of the classes, given the actual samples), and a $L_{unsupervised}$ non-supervised loss function that depends on the GAN model. This semi-supervised approach means that we introduce an interaction between G and our classifier, optimizing the generation phase.

4   Evaluation

One of the main phases of the proposed solution foresees in the training phase the generation of samples starting from the distribution of the starting dataset. In particular, the reference works for GANs operate on image dataset, and the accuracy of the samples generated above all from the human perceptual point of view is evaluated. The samples of our dataset are instead, by their nature, not easily recognizable by man, so in order to evaluate the goodness, and to allow us a further comparison of the two methods used, we have reorganized the samples generated by the SSGAN network with the relative class labels and materially added to the "Air Compressor" dataset. The dataset consists of the acquired samples and "generated" samples by the proposed GAN model (Fig. 6). As a consequence, the dataset thus composed is passed into input to the deep SDAE network and subsequently the features extracted are classified with SVM [2].

4.1   Experiments and Results

The results, obtained starting from the evaluation of the SDAE solution, are summarized in Table 1, where the labels from $S1$ to $S5$ correspond to different configurations obtained by varying the number of auto-encoder levels and the number of nodes for each level (Fig. 7: it is remarkable the strong dependence on the configuration proposed by the authors indicated with the label $S1$, while in the other configurations the performances are drastically degraded.

In Table 2 we compare the results obtained using the original dataset on the SDAE model and on the SSGAN model with those obtained using the dataset with the addition of the samples generated in the learning phase of the SSGAN. There is an improvement in performance and we have also found that the samples generated are of good quality.

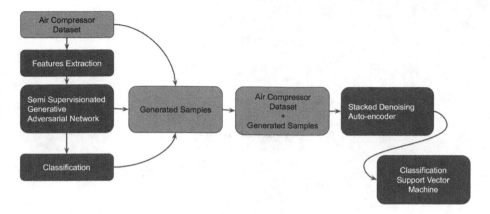

Fig. 6. Workflow of proposed solution.

Table 1. Performance evaluation using SVM Classifier

Dataset/Feature	Deep learning based FFT features					
	SDAE	SDAE with Tensor Flow				
	S1	S1	S2	S3	S4	S5
Air compressor	99.44	**99.65**	85.42	85.84	94.17	92.78

Setup/feature	1024	512	256	125	49	24	8
S1			*	*	*		
S2	*	*	*	*	*		
S3	*		*	*	*		
S4			*	*	*	*	
S5			*	*	*	*	*

Fig. 7. Layer configuration.

Table 2. Accuracy comparison using the SVM Classifier

Datasets/Features	Deep learning based FFT features		
	SDAE	SSGAN	SSGAN+SDAE
Air compressor	**99,65**	**99,72**	**99,67**

In the graphs shown in Fig. 8 we can see the progress of the accuracy during the training phase of the model on the "Air compressor" dataset (a), compared with the accuracy trend using the same SSGAN learning technique on the MNIST dataset (b). It can be seen that they have a comparable appearance. These graphs were generated using Tensorflow's Tensorboard tool.

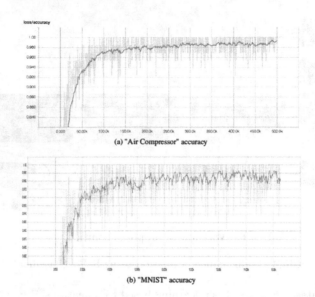

(a) "Air Compressor" accuracy

(b) "MNIST" accuracy

Fig. 8. GAN accuracy comparison on "Air Compressor" and "MNIST".

In Fig. 9 we show the preliminary results form the DeepNautilius data acquisition system based on Fiscino32 miro-controller as computation at the edge resource and the MPI-9225 accelerometer as vibration sensor. In this experiment we compared the signature obtained processing the vibration signal in two engine status: regular running and blocked air filter.

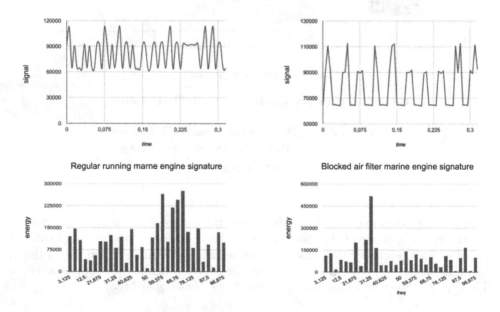

Fig. 9. DeepNautilius data acquisition.

5   Conclusion and Future Directions

The novel contribution of this preliminary research work is expected to be twofold: facing the extreme networking environment experienced in marine applications, we developed a dedicated data transfer framework in a store and forward bundle protocol fashion; in the sake of preventing accidents and enforcing the safe of life at sea we enabled the use of vibration sensors and deep learning in order to recognize engine failures.

We applied the proposed approach on a dataset for the diagnosis of motor failures, demonstrating the potentials of deep networks in the generation of representative features. In tests carried out using the SDAE model, although little improvement was achieved, the fact remains that these results were obtained on features about 5 times smaller. Even more innovative is the execution of experiments using a model of semi-supervised GAN networks, obtaining also in this case satisfactory results from the point of view of the accuracy of the classification. Furthermore, a method has been proposed for the evaluation of the samples generated during the classification phase by the GAN network.

These excellent results have led us to propose as a future application the creation of a dataset for the prediction of failures on combustion engines like those of pleasure boats, using open-hardware technologies, and open-source software and the integration of this failure prediction system into a mobile cloud technology [13] powered with accelerators at the edge [15].

We will continue our experiments in both controlled environment and real world in order to prepare a dataset for further research work. In particular we expect to collect a dataset of labelled processed vibration label performing a laboratory sampling campaign inducing failures in an artificial fashion. As long term research topic, we plan to integrate the proposed system in environmental modelling applications [1,6] in order to perform live assessment of pollutant emissions related with nautical engines [5].

Acknowledgment. This research is partially included in the framework of the project "MOQAP - Maritime Operation Quality Assurance Platform" financed by Italian Ministry of Economic Development. We thank Futura Elettronica (Futura Group srl) for the generous contribute in terms of FishinoMega and Fischino32 IoT devices donation.

References

1. Ascione, I., Giunta, G., Mariani, P., Montella, R., Riccio, A.: A grid computing based virtual laboratory for environmental simulations. In: Nagel, W.E., Walter, W.V., Lehner, W. (eds.) Euro-Par 2006. LNCS, vol. 4128, pp. 1085–1094. Springer, Heidelberg (2006). https://doi.org/10.1007/11823285_114
2. Chang, C.C., Lin, C.J.: LIBSVM: a library for support vector machines. ACM Trans. Intell. Syst. Technol. (TIST) **2**(3), 27 (2011)
3. Chard, R., Chard, K., Bubendorfer, K., Lacinski, L., Madduri, R., Foster, I.: Cost-aware elastic cloud provisioning for scientific workloads. In: 2015 IEEE 8th International Conference on Cloud Computing (CLOUD), pp. 971–974. IEEE (2015)

4. De Marsico, M., Petrosino, A., Ricciardi, S.: Iris recognition through machine learning techniques: a survey. Pattern Recognit. Lett. **82**, 106–115 (2016)
5. Farooqui, Z.M., John, K., Sule, N.: Evaluation of anthropogenic air emissions from marine engines in a coastal urban airshed of texas. J. Environ. Prot. **4**(07), 722 (2013)
6. Giunta, G., Montella, R., Mariani, P., Riccio, A.: Modeling and computational issues for air/water quality problems: a grid computing approach. Nuovo Cimento C Geophys. Space Phys. C **28**, 215 (2005)
7. Goodfellow, I., et al.: Generative adversarial nets. In: Advances in Neural Information Processing Systems, pp. 2672–2680 (2014)
8. Isermann, R.: Model-based fault-detection and diagnosis-status and applications. Annu. Rev. Control. **29**(1), 71–85 (2005)
9. Jardine, A.K., Lin, D., Banjevic, D.: A review on machinery diagnostics and prognostics implementing condition-based maintenance. Mech. Syst. Signal Process. **20**(7), 1483–1510 (2006)
10. Marcellino, L., et al.: Using GPGPU accelerated interpolation algorithms for marine bathymetry processing with on-premises and cloud based computational resources. In: Wyrzykowski, R., Dongarra, J., Deelman, E., Karczewski, K. (eds.) PPAM 2017. LNCS, vol. 10778, pp. 14–24. Springer, Cham (2018). https://doi.org/10.1007/978-3-319-78054-2_2
11. Montella, R., Di Luccio, D., Kosta, S., Giunta, G., Foster, I.: Performance, resilience, and security in moving data from the fog to the cloud: the DYNAMO transfer framework approach. In: Xiang, Y., Sun, J., Fortino, G., Guerrieri, A., Jung, J.J. (eds.) IDCS 2018. LNCS, vol. 11226, pp. 197–208. Springer, Cham (2018). https://doi.org/10.1007/978-3-030-02738-4_17
12. Montella, R., et al.: Processing of crowd-sourced data from an internet of floating things. In: Proceedings of the 12th Workshop on Workflows in Support of Large-Scale Science, p. 8. ACM (2017)
13. Montella, R., Ferraro, C., Kosta, S., Pelliccia, V., Giunta, G.: Enabling android-based devices to high-end GPGPUs. In: Carretero, J., Garcia-Blas, J., Ko, R.K.L., Mueller, P., Nakano, K. (eds.) ICA3PP 2016. LNCS, vol. 10048, pp. 118–125. Springer, Cham (2016). https://doi.org/10.1007/978-3-319-49583-5_9
14. Montella, R., Kosta, S., Foster, I.: Dynamo: distributed leisure yacht-carried sensor-network for atmosphere and marine data crowdsourcing applications. In: 2018 IEEE International Conference on Cloud Engineering (IC2E), pp. 333–339. IEEE (2018)
15. Montella, R., et al.: Accelerating linux and android applications on low-power devices through remote GPGPU offloading. Concurr. Comput. Pract. Exp. **29**(24), e4286 (2017)
16. Montella, R., et al.: Marine bathymetry processing through GPGPU virtualization in high performance cloud computing. Concurr. Comput. Pract. Exp. **30**(24), e4895 (2018)
17. Montella, R., Ruggieri, M., Kosta, S.: A fast, secure, reliable, and resilient data transfer framework for pervasive IoT applications. In: IEEE INFOCOM 2018-IEEE Conference on Computer Communications Workshops (INFOCOM WKSHPS). IEEE (2018)
18. Salimans, T., Goodfellow, I., Zaremba, W., Cheung, V., Radford, A., Chen, X.: Improved techniques for training GANs. In: Advances in Neural Information Processing Systems, pp. 2234–2242 (2016)
19. Tamilselvan, P., Wang, P.: Failure diagnosis using deep belief learning based health state classification. Reliab. Eng. Syst. Saf. **115**, 124–135 (2013)

20. Thirukovalluru, R., Dixit, S., Sevakula, R.K., Verma, N.K., Salour, A.: Generating feature sets for fault diagnosis using denoising stacked auto-encoder. In: 2016 IEEE International Conference on Prognostics and Health Management (ICPHM), pp. 1–7. IEEE (2016)

21. Verma, N.K., Sevakula, R.K., Dixit, S., Salour, A.: Intelligent condition based monitoring using acoustic signals for air compressors. IEEE Trans. Reliab. **65**(1), 291–309 (2016)

Binary Code for the Compact Palmprint Representation Using Texture Features

Agata Giełczyk[1]([✉])[iD], Gian Luca Marcialis[2][iD], and Michał Choraś[1]

[1] UTP University of Science and Technology Bydgoszcz, Bydgoszcz, Poland
agata.gielczyk@utp.edu.pl
[2] University of Cagliari, Cagliari, Italy

Abstract. In this paper, we present an effective approach to the biometric user verification using palmprints. The main idea and key innovation of the method is a compact 32-bit length vector to summarize the palmprint texture. This method provides the user verification with the accuracy reaching 92% in the experiments performed on the benchmark PolyU palmprint database. Moreover, the reported results show that the obtained accuracy appears to be hardly dependent on the number of enrolled samples. The proposed representation may be extremely useful in real life applications because of its compactness and effectiveness.

Keywords: Palmprint · Image processing · Biometrics ·
User verification · Texture features

1 Introduction

Identity verification has become an emerging and important challenge for the digital market and overall society recently. Establishing identity in an efficient manner is necessary in numerous applications including, but not limited to, access control (soft and hard targets, applications), aviation transport, e-banking and mobile devices. Thanks to the raising computing power of electronic devices, the traditional methods of identity verification (cards, passwords and PIN numbers) can be replaced by or coupled with biometrics. Several examples of successful, large scale implementations of biometric systems can be listed in sectors such as, among others: biometric passports (including fingerprints and face images), electronic and mobile banking for authentication and confirmation of transactions, criminal investigation (e.g. AFIS and police fingerprints databases in many countries) and in systems such as EURODAC.

Biometrics refers to the measurement and statistical analysis of people's biological (e.g., fingerprint) and behavioral (e.g., gait) characteristics, which can be used to recognize the identity of individuals [2].

Despite of the fact that fingerprint, face and iris recognition are now widespread [17], many other biometric features exist and can provide promising results: hand geometry, ear or palmprint, for example. The part of body or

M. Vento and G. Percannella (Eds.): CAIP 2019, LNCS 11679, pp. 132–142, 2019.
https://doi.org/10.1007/978-3-030-29891-3_12

the behaviour of a person has to meet some requirements in order to become a biometric trait: universality, distinctiveness, permanence, collectability, performance, acceptability and circumvention.

The palmprint can be recognized as one of the most promising biometric modalities. In a few words, it is the inner surface of the hand. The palmprint provides advantages such as: easy capturing process, relatively big surface, cost effectiveness, non-intrusive nature and rich texture [26]. Moreover, it is similar to the fingerprint, because it is made up of ridge and valleys of the skin. Since the palm's surface is larger than that of a finger, it is arguable that it contains more individual information.

Therefore, we present a texture-based image processing technique for efficient palmprint verification. The novelty of the paper is the very compact and effective palmprint representation, consisting in a feature vector of 32 bits, which is, to the best of our knowledge, the smallest representation of a palmprint (and maybe, of any other biometrics). Experiments on a well-known benchmark data set show the potentials of our representation in terms of achieved verification accuracy.

The paper is structured as follows: Sect. 2 overviews the related work and state of the art in palmprint recognition. In Sect. 3 the proposed method is presented in details. In Sects. 4 and 5 the experiments, results and conclusions are described.

2 Related Work

Even though the popularity of palmprint as a biometric modality is not comparable to that of the fingerprint or the iris, there are plenty of papers available. The state-of-the-art differs in each step of the pipeline: pre-processing, features extraction and classification. When it comes to the features extraction domain, the first approaches were based on the Gabor filter as it was presented for example in [19]. Such an approach was moved directly from the fingerprint recognition and was pretty successful, even without any machine learning methods was used in the matching step. For the Gabor filter, the Hamming distance or City Block distance has shown to be useful.

The other basic approach to the palmprint representation is the enhancement and description of the three palmprint's main lines: the heart line, the life line and the head line (Principal Line Analysis). Those lines are presented in Fig. 1. The advantages of such an approach have been reported in [16]: less sensibility to illumination conditions, being significantly more stable than wrinkles, a higher visibility even when the quality of the image is low.

Another possible approach is through the us of the hand geometry and palm texture simultaneously, as in [13,28]. In this case, apart from the texture of the inner part of the hand, the hand shape is analyzed - the length and width of fingers and the whole hand, the hand's area and perimeter, the shape of the convex hull built around the hand and others. This can be classified as a multimodal approach, which is considered to be more reliable to the following limitations: noisy data, intra-class variations, restricted degrees of freedom, non-universality, spoof attacks, and unacceptable error rates [27]. The palmprint can

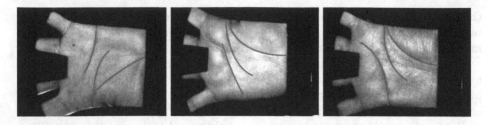

Fig. 1. Examples of principal lines presented on PolyU samples

be also coupled with the palm vein pattern [20]. A special device for palm vein image acquisition must be adopted in this case, which makes this system hardly movable to a mobile or even a widely implemented scenario.

The most challenging approaches are the ones trying to model a compact representation of the palmprint. Among other, the fractal theory-based approach [23], by Discrete Fourier Transform [12], Local Binary Patterns [21], SIFT descriptors [3,18].

Beside the above works, representing the palmprint as a binary string affects is even more challenging. In these approaches, the ROI is divided into non overlapping blocks and some operations are performed only over the limited element of the image, e.g. the Gabor filter. Using blocks allows to analyze local texture features (in palmprint e.g. wrinkles). Numerous approaches have been presented so far, also in the fingerprint domain [5,30] but it can be successfully moved to the palmprint recognition as presented in [11]. It is also possible to analyze the 3D image of the palmprint in order to identify the user. In [6] the authors proposed a system using the blocked surface type feature and Principal Component Analysis. It is also possible to analyse the multispectral palmprint images like in [4] or in [7], where the Gabor filter bank was used again.

Recently, several machine learning methods were implemented, due to the wide success of the Convolutional Neural Networs: the authors of [10] proposed running autoencoders; Dian and Dongmei [9] implemented another CNN-based architecture; Ref. [8] adopted a standard SVM. Finally, the authors of [32] proposed their own machine learning classifier called MPELM.

3   The Proposed Method

Among the approaches presented in the previous Section, ours falls on the kind of bit-code-based ones. As we pointed out, this is a very challenging problem, because it requires the ability of model a representative feature-based approach with the main constraints of compactness and effectiveness of a bit-code.

To this aim, we were inspired by the statistical method of texture analysis introduced by Haralick *et al.* in [14]. In order to extract features, the gray tone spatial dependence co-occurrence statistics are involved. Haralick defined the gray level co-occurrence matrix (GLCM) as descriptor of the relative frequencies with which two pixels separated by the certain distance under a specified

angle occur on the image. This approach was widely implemented in the past
[15]: objects identification on aerial, satellite and microscopic images, medical
applications and X-ray automatic analysis. All these studies achieved reasonable
results on different textures using gray tone co-occurrence. It was also successfully moved into the biometrics as presented in [24].

Therefore, we adapted the Haralick's method to the palmprint representation.
The overview of the proposed system is presented in Fig. 2.

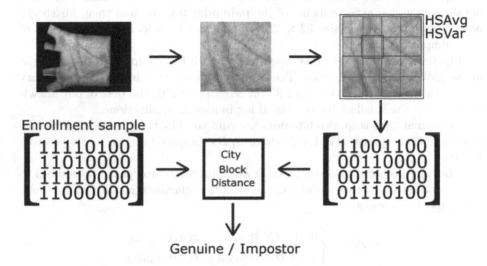

Fig. 2. The processing pipeline of the algorithm: ROI extraction, HSAvg and HSVar
calculation for the whole ROI and blocks, 32-bit length code generation, comparison
the generated code with the code obtained from the enrollment sample using City
Block Distance

Given a palmprint image, in the pre-processing step we use the ROI extraction algorithm reported in in [31]. The obtained ROI is a 128 × 128 px image.

For the feature extraction we used two measurements: the Haralick Sum
Average (HSAvg) and Haralick Sum Variance. They are calculated using the
Eqs. 1 and 2 respectively, where: N_g - number of gray levels (here: $N_g = 255$),
$p(i,j)$ - entry in GLCM spatial-dependency matrix, $HSEnt$ - Haralick Sun
Entropy expressed with the Eq. 4, $p_{x+y}(i)$ - entry in the marginal-probability
matrix obtained by summing the rows of $p(i,j)$ and expressed using Eq. 3

$$HSAvg = \sum_{i=2}^{2N_g} i \cdot p_{x+y}(i) \tag{1}$$

$$HSVar = \sum_{i=2}^{2N_g} (i - HSEnt)^2 \cdot p_{x+y}(i) \tag{2}$$

$$p_{x+y}(i) = \sum_{i=1}^{N_g} \sum_{j=1}^{N_g} p(i,j) \tag{3}$$

$$HSEnt = \sum_{i=2}^{2N_g} p_{x+y}(i) \cdot \log\{p_{x+y}(i)\} \tag{4}$$

The above-mentioned metrics are calculated first for the whole ROI, thus obtaining a global measurements of the palmprint texture, and then, for the 16 non-overlapping blocks (size 32×32), thus obtaining a local measurements of the palmprint texture.

Equations 5 and 6 were then used to compute the comparison between the above global and local metrics. The obtained bit value is included in a binary vector. In such a way, we obtain a 32 bit-length code. To the best of our knowledge, this is the smallest bit-code used for biometric applications.

In the matching step, two bit-codes are compared by the City Block Distance (CBD) which is expressed as Eq. 7, where A, B - compared vectors and n - vectors length.

The final decision is done by setting an appropriate acceptance threshold to the computed CBD, thus obtaining the standard classification in Genuine user and Impostors classes.

$$vec[a] = \begin{cases} 0 & \text{if } HSAvg_{local} \leq HSAvg_{global} \\ 1 & \text{if } HSAvg_{local} > HSAvg_{global} \end{cases} \tag{5}$$

$$vec[a] = \begin{cases} 0 & \text{if } HSVar_{local} \leq HSVar_{global} \\ 1 & \text{if } HSVar_{local} > HSVar_{global} \end{cases} \tag{6}$$

$$CBD = \sum_{k=1}^{n} |A_k - B_k| \tag{7}$$

4   Experiments and Results

Experiments were performed on the PolyU database - a benchmark palmprint database available online [1]. The PolyU contains images of palmprint captured by a contact-based capture device using various illumination conditions. In the research we there were 12 samples for each of 50 users involved. All samples were taken with normal lighting.

The evaluation parameter was the verification accuracy, which can be expressed with the Eq. 8, where TP - true positives, TN - true negatives, P - total number of genuine samples, N - total number of impostor samples.

$$Acc = \frac{TP + TN}{P + N} \cdot 100\% \tag{8}$$

The following experimental results are subdivided in three groups: the first one is aimed to show that using the *Haralick Sum Average* and *Haralick Sum Variance* together is more efficient than using one of them. This show that the bit-lenght is someway constrained to be not less than 32 bits, due to the fact that HSA and HSV encodes probably low correlated characteristics of the palmprint.

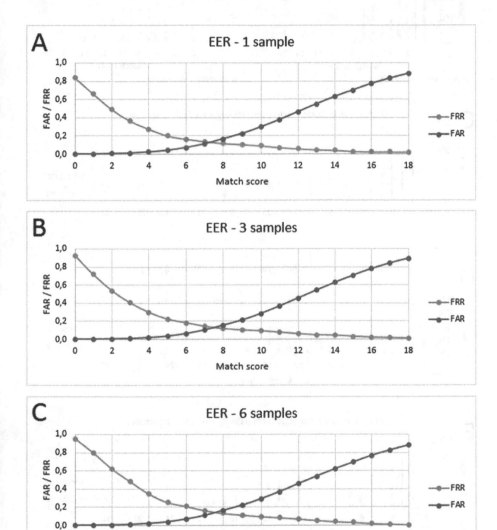

Fig. 3. Equal Error Rate for (A) 32-bit length code using HSAvg and HSVar - 1 enrollment sample, (B) 32-bit length code using HSAvg and HSVar - 3 enrollment samples, (C) 32-bit length code both HSAvg and HSVar - 6 enrollment samples

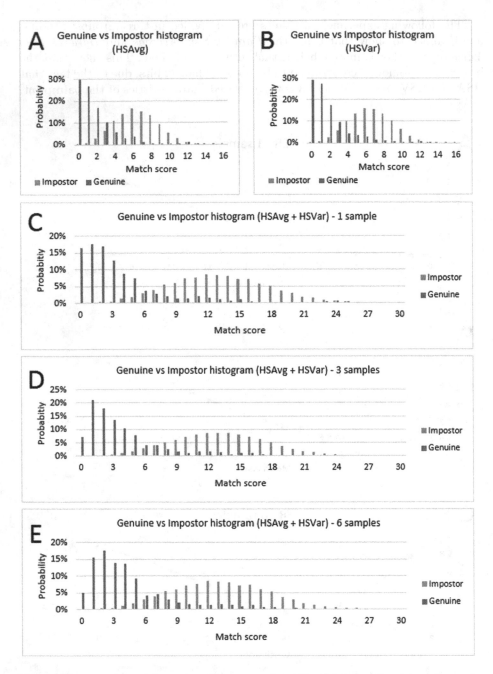

Fig. 4. The genuine vs impostor histograms for (A) 16-bit length code using only Haralick Sum Average, (B) 16-bit length code using only Haralick Sum Variance, (C) 32-bit length code using both HSAvg and HSVar - 1 enrollment sample, (D) 32-bit length code using both HSAvg and HSVar - 3 enrollment samples, (E) 32-bit length code using both HSAvg and HSVar - 6 enrollment samples

That is why, we perform our algorithm for each two possible sample pair three times: (1) using only *HSAvg* and 16-bits length vector (2) using only *HSVar* and 16-bits length vector (3) using both *HSAvg* and *HSVar* and the whole 32-bits length vector. The obtained results are presented in Fig. 4 A, B and C. Even though the probability of a proper verification for the positive sample is stable $(1 - FRR = 83\%)$, by means of two measures we were able to reduce the FAR error from 0.10 and 0.09 to 0.07. In Fig. 3 A there is presented the False Acceptance Rate (*FAR*) and the False Rejection Rate (*FRR*) for the 32-bits length vector. In this step we compared each possible pair of samples.

The second group of experiments was aimed to investigate the dependence on the number of templates. As a matter of fact, it is quite acknowledged that the accuracy may be increased by storing more templates into the system. Therefore, we used 3 and 6 templates per user. During testing the vector of features is compared to each enrollment sample and the average value is calculated. This average value is compared to an experimentally fixed threshold. Comparing the testing sample to the set of enrollment samples is essential also in the real live applications. The results of all experiments are provided in Table 1, while the Impostor/Genuine histograms are presented in Fig. 4D and E. The enlargement of the enrollment set size causes a slight increase of the accuracy (from 89.15% to 92.16%), however it may also due to some statistical fluctuation because of the random selection of the templates. In Fig. 3B and C there are presented the False Acceptance Rate (*FAR*) and the False Rejection Rate (*FRR*) for experiment using 3 and 6 enrollment samples. The obtained results demonstrate that the high accuracy of verification is weakly dependent on the number of templates.

Finally, in the third group of experiments, we compared our approach with other ones at the state-of-the-art on the PolyU data set. Results are reported in Table 2. It is easy to see that the obtained accuracy is comparable to the reported methods. What is remarkable, the proposed method uses only 32 bits (1 floating point number) in order to represent the palmprint, while other methods use longer or even far longer vector of features, as it can be noticed in the second column of Table 2.

Table 1. Obtained results: accuracy for each fold, standard deviation of the accuracy, average of the accuracy for each experiment - with 1, 3 and 6 enrollment samples

Experiment	Fold 01	Fold 02	Fold 03	Standard deviation	Accuracy
1 sample	–	–	–	–	91.96%
3 samples	87.50%	92.51%	87.45%	2.91%	89.15%
6 samples	90.95%	94.56%	90.97%	2.08%	92.16%

Table 2. Comparison with some state-of-the-art methods. The length of the features vectors and the accuracy obtained are reported.

Publication	Vector length	Accuracy
Younesi and Amirani [33]	6 floating point numbers	99.81%
Verma and Chandran [29]	117 points	99.81%
Mokni et al. [22]	47.104 floating point numbers	98.25%
Ray and Misra [25]	3 points	96.60%
Giełczyk et al.	32 bits	92.16%

5   Conclusions and Future Work

In this paper we presented an efficient approach to palmprint-based user verification. It uses a binary code in order to represent the image of a palmprint. As the key advantages of the proposed method we consider the compactness and the representativeness. Most importantly, it ensures a high accuracy reaching 92%. The obtained accuracy is also comparable to the state-of-the-art methods. What is remarkable, the proposed method uses only 32 bits (namely, 1 floating point number or 1 integer between 0 and $2^{32} - 1$) in order to represent the whole palmprint.

We believe that this representation is very promising. Thus, we are going to extend this approach in our future work. First of all, we will investigate the possibility of increasing the verification accuracy to extend the possible applications of the method.

As it is, we are thinking to a mobile scenario. The mobile biometrics has become increasingly popular recently due to the fact that the popularity of mobile devices is constantly raising, as well as the amount of private and sensitive messages and files processed using them. In these cases, the ratio between True Positive and True Negative rates may be less stringent with respect to high-security applications, thus the reported accuracy could be considered sufficient and easibly achievable in these contexts.

Beside this application, saving the proposed code on an RFID card is quite feasible. This may lead to the creation a multi-factor authentication system, that is considered to be the most robust way to secure sensitive data.

Last but not least, the proposed code can be used as a way of user authentication to service provided by cloud-based services. The popularity of could computing is increasing, thus the security level of such services has to be increased as well. This may be reached by the use of an improved version of our bit-code.

Acknowledgements. The research was conducted using the BSM 81/2017 project's wherewithal, which is founded by the Polish Ministry of Science and High Education.

References

1. Polyu database. http://www4.comp.polyu.edu.hk/~biometrics/. Accessed 03 Feb 2019
2. Akhtar, Z., Hadid, A., Nixon, M., Tistarelli, M., Dugelay, J.L., Marcel, S.: Biometrics: In: Search of Identity and Security (Q & A). IEEE MultiMedia (2017)
3. Almaghtuf, J., Khelifi, F.: Self-geometric relationship filter for efficient sift keypoints matching in full and partial palmprint recognition. IET Biom. **7**(4), 296–304 (2018)
4. Amraoui, A., Fakhri, Y., Kerroum, M.A.: Multispectral palmprint recognition based on fusion of local features. In: 2018 6th International Conference on Multimedia Computing and Systems (ICMCS), pp. 1–6. IEEE (2018)
5. Bai, C.c., Wang, W.q., Zhao, T., Wang, R.x., Li, M.q.: Deep learning compact binary codes for fingerprint indexing. Front. Inf. Technol. Electron. Eng. **19**(9), 1112–1123 (2018)
6. Bai, X., Gao, N., Zhang, Z., Zhang, D.: 3D palmprint identification combining blocked ST and PCA. Pattern Recognit. Lett. **100**, 89–95 (2017)
7. Bounneche, M.D., Boubchir, L., Bouridane, A., Nekhoul, B., Ali-Chérif, A.: Multispectral palmprint recognition based on oriented multiscale log-gabor filters. Neurocomputing **205**, 274–286 (2016)
8. Charfi, N., Trichili, H., Alimi, A.M., Solaiman, B.: Bimodal biometric system for hand shape and palmprint recognition based on sift sparse representation. Multimed. Tools Appl. **76**(20), 20457–20482 (2017)
9. Dian, L., Dongmei, S.: Contactless palmprint recognition based on convolutional neural network. In: 2016 IEEE 13th International Conference on Signal Processing (ICSP), pp. 1363–1367. IEEE (2016)
10. Elgallad, E.A., Charfi, N., Alimi, A.M., Ouarda, W.: Human identity recognition using sparse auto encoder for texture information representation in palmprint images based on voting technique. In: 2017 Sudan Conference on Computer Science and Information Technology (SCCSIT), pp. 1–8. IEEE (2017)
11. Franzgrote, M., et al.: Palmprint verification on mobile phones using accelerated competitive code. In: 2011 International Conference on Hand-Based Biometrics, pp. 1–6. IEEE (2011)
12. Giełczyk, A., Choraś, M., Kozik, R.: Hybrid feature extraction for palmprint-based user authentication. In: 2018 International Conference on High Performance Computing & Simulation (HPCS), pp. 629–633. IEEE (2018)
13. Giełczyk, A., Choraś, M., Kozik, R.: Lightweight verification schema for image-based palmprint biometric systems. Mob. Inf. Syst. **2019**, 9 pages (2019). https://doi.org/10.1155/2019/2325891
14. Haralick, R.M., Shanmugam, K., et al.: Textural features for image classification. IEEE Trans. Syst. Man Cybern. **6**, 610–621 (1973)
15. Haralick, R.M., et al.: Statistical and structural approaches to texture. Proc. IEEE **67**(5), 786–804 (1979)
16. Huang, D.S., Jia, W., Zhang, D.: Palmprint verification based on principal lines. Pattern Recognit. **41**(4), 1316–1328 (2008)
17. Jain, A.K., Nandakumar, K., Ross, A.: 50 years of biometric research: accomplishments, challenges, and opportunities. Pattern Recognit. Lett. **79**, 80–105 (2016)
18. Jaswal, G., Kaul, A., Nath, R.: Multiple feature fusion for unconstrained palm print authentication. Comput. Electr. Eng. **72**, 53–78 (2018)

19. Kong, W.K., Zhang, D.: Palmprint texture analysis based on low-resolution images for personal authentication. In: Object Recognition Supported by User Interaction for Service Robots, vol. 3, pp. 807–810. IEEE (2002)
20. Li, W., Yuan, W.q.: Multiple palm features extraction method based on vein and palmprint. J. Ambient. Intell. Hum. Comput., 1–15 (2018)
21. Luo, Y.T., et al.: Local line directional pattern for palmprint recognition. Pattern Recognit. **50**, 26–44 (2016)
22. Mokni, R., Elleuch, M., Kherallah, M.: Biometric palmprint identification via efficient texture features fusion. In: 2016 International Joint Conference on Neural Networks (IJCNN), pp. 4857–4864. IEEE (2016)
23. Mokni, R., Kherallah, M.: Novel palmprint biometric system combining several fractal methods for texture information extraction. In: 2016 IEEE International Conference on Systems, Man, and Cybernetics (SMC), pp. 002267–002272. IEEE (2016)
24. Mokni, R., Mezghani, A., Drira, H., Kherallah, M.: Multiset canonical correlation analysis: texture feature level fusion of multiple descriptors for intra-modal palmprint biometric recognition. In: Paul, M., Hitoshi, C., Huang, Q. (eds.) PSIVT 2017. LNCS, vol. 10749, pp. 3–16. Springer, Cham (2018). https://doi.org/10.1007/978-3-319-75786-5_1
25. Ray, K.B., Misra, R.: Palm print recognition using hough transforms. In: 2015 International Conference on Computational Intelligence and Communication Networks (CICN), pp. 422–425. IEEE (2015)
26. Tabejamaat, M., Mousavi, A.: Generalized gabor filters for palmprint recognition. Pattern Anal. Appl. **21**(1), 261–275 (2018)
27. Taouche, C., Batouche, M.C., Berkane, M., Taleb-Ahmed, A.: Multimodal biometric systems. In: 2014 International Conference on Multimedia Computing and Systems (ICMCS), pp. 301–308. IEEE (2014)
28. Travieso, C.M., Ticay-Rivas, J.R., Briceno, J.C., del Pozo-Baños, M., Alonso, J.B.: Hand shape identification on multirange images. Inf. Sci. **275**, 45–56 (2014)
29. Verma, S.B., Chandran, S.: Analysis of sift and surf feature extraction in palmprint verification system. In: International Conference on Computing, Communication and Control Technology (IC4T), pp. 27–30 (2016)
30. Wang, Y., Wang, L., Cheung, Y.M., Yuen, P.C.: Learning compact binary codes for hash-based fingerprint indexing. IEEE Trans. Inf. Forensics Secur. **10**(8), 1603–1616 (2015)
31. Wojciechowska, A., Choraś, M., Kozik, R.: Evaluation of the pre-processing methods in image-based palmprint biometrics. In: Choraś, M., Choraś, R. (eds.) IP&C 2017. AISC, vol. 681, pp. 43–48. Springer, Cham (2018). https://doi.org/10.1007/978-3-319-68720-9_6
32. Xu, X., Lu, L., Zhang, X., Lu, H., Deng, W.: Multispectral palmprint recognition using multiclass projection extreme learning machine and digital shearlet transform. Neural Comput. Appl. **27**(1), 143–153 (2016)
33. Younesi, A., Amirani, M.C.: Gabor filter and texture based features for palmprint recognition. Procedia Comput. Sci. **108**, 2488–2495 (2017)

Handwriting Analysis to Support Alzheimer's Disease Diagnosis: A Preliminary Study

Nicole Dalia Cilia[✉], Claudio De Stefano, Francesco Fontanella,
Mario Molinara, and Alessandra Scotto Di Freca

Department of Electrical and Information Engineering (DIEI), University of Cassino
and Southern Lazio, Via G. Di Biasio, 43, 03043 Cassino, FR, Italy
{nicoledalia.cilia,destefano,fontanella,m.molinara,a.scotto}@unicas.it

Abstract. Alzheimer's disease (AD) is the most common neurodegenerative dementia of old age and the leading chronic disease contributor
to disability and dependence among older people worldwide. Handwriting is among the motor activities compromised by AD, which is the
result of a complex network of cognitive, kinaesthetic and perceptive-
motor skills. Indeed, researchers have shown that the patients affected
by these diseases exhibit alterations in the spatial organization and poor
control of movement. In this paper, we present the preliminary results of
a study in which an experimental protocol (including the copy of words,
letters and sentence task) has been used to assess the kinematic properties of the movements involved in the handwriting. The obtained results
are very encouraging and seem to confirm the hypothesis that machine
learning-based analysis of handwriting can be profitably used to support
AD diagnosis.

Keywords: Handwriting · Classification algorithm ·
Alzheimer's disease

1 Introduction

Alzheimer's disease (AD) is the most prevalent brain neurodegenerative disorder
progressing to severe cognitive impairment and loss of autonomy (i.e., dementia)
in older people [9,10,15]. Criteria for clinical diagnosis of AD were proposed in
1984 [12] by the National Institute of Neurological and Communicative Disorders
and Stroke (NINCDS) and by the Alzheimer's Disease and Related Disorders
Association (ADRDA). According to these criteria, the diagnosis of AD needs
histopathologic confirmation (i.e., microscopic examination of brain tissue) in
autopsy or biopsy [1,2,17]. Nonetheless, an early diagnosis would greatly improve
the effectiveness of available treatments, but it is still a challenging task.

This work is supported by the Italian Ministry of Education, University and Research
(MIUR) within the PRIN2015-HAND project.

M. Vento and G. Percannella (Eds.): CAIP 2019, LNCS 11679, pp. 143–151, 2019.
https://doi.org/10.1007/978-3-030-29891-3_13

To date, clinical diagnosis of such diseases are performed by physicians and may be supported by tools such as imaging (e.g. magnetic resonance imaging), blood tests and lumbar puncture (spinal tap). Recently, researchers have shown that the patients affected by these diseases exhibit alterations in the spatial organization and poor control of movements. It follows that, in principle, some diagnostic signs of AD should be detectable by motor tasks. Among them, Handwriting (HW), which is the result of a complex network of cognitive, kinaesthetic and perceptive-motor skills [18] may be significantly compromised. For example, in the clinical course of AD, dysgraphia occurs both during the initial phase, and in the progression of the disorder [20]. However, in this field, many published studies have been conducted in the areas of medicine and psychology, where typically standard statistical tools (with ANOVA and MANOVA analysis) are used to investigate the relationship between the disease and the variables taken into account to describe a patient's handwriting. Conversely, as we have shown in [6], very few studies have been published, which use classification algorithms to detect people affected by AD from their handwriting.

From the literature reviewed, we found several open issues that need to be addressed: (i) the definition of an experimental protocol, composed of an ensemble of handwriting and drawing tasks the subjects should perform, to investigate whether there are specific features allowing us to detect the early signs of AD; (ii) a well-designed data set, large enough to allow an effective training of classification algorithms; (iii) the tools to be used for the automatic analysis of the handwriting tasks. To solve the first issue we proposed [3] a protocol consisting in 25 tasks (copy, reverse copy, free writing, drawing etc.) to analyse the impact of different tasks and different motor skills on AD patient performance.

In this paper, we present the results of a preliminary study in which we have considered only a subset of the tasks included in the above protocol, in order to assess the kinematic properties of the movements involved in the handwriting. We collected the data produced by 130 subjects using a graphic tablet. From these data, we have extracted the most common features in literature [6]. Finally, for the classification phase, we considered two effective and widely used classification methods, namely Random Forest and Decision Trees. The obtained results are very encouraging and seem to confirm the hypothesis that machine learning-based analysis of handwriting can be profitably used to support the diagnosis of AD.

2   Materials and Methods

In the following subsections, the dataset collection procedure and the protocol designed for collecting handwriting samples, are detailed.

2.1   Dataset Collection

The 130 subjects who participated to the experiments, namely 66 AD patients and 64 healthy controls, were recruited with the support of the geriatric ward,

Alzheimer unit, of the "Federico II" hospital in Naples. As concerns the recruiting criteria, we took into account clinical tests (such as PET, TAC and enzymatic analyses) and standard cognitive tests (such as MMSE). In these tests, the cognitive abilities of the examined subject were assessed by using questionnaires including questions and problems in many areas, which range from orientation to time and place, to registration recall. As for the healthy controls, in order to have a fair comparison, demographic as well as educational characteristics were considered and matched with the patient group. Finally, for both patients and controls, it was necessary to check whether they were on therapy or not, excluding those who used psychotropic drugs or any other drug that could influence their cognitive abilities.

The data were collected by using a graphic tablet, which allows the recording of pen movements during the handwriting process. During the trial, images and sound stimuli are also provided to the subject to guide the execution of the tasks. Finally, the subjects were also asked to follow the indications provided by the experimenter.

2.2   Protocol

The aim of the protocol is to record the dynamics of the handwriting, in order to investigate whether there are specific features that allow us to distinguish subjects affected by the above-mentioned diseases from healthy ones. The nine tasks considered for this study are selected from a larger experimental protocol presented in [3], and they are arranged in increasing order of difficulty, in terms of the cognitive functions required. The goal of these tasks is to test the patients' abilities in repeating complex graphic gestures, which have a semantic meaning, such as letters and words of different lengths and with different spatial organizations. The tasks have been selected according to the literature, which suggests that:

(i)   graphical tasks and free spaces allow the assessment of the spatial organization skills of the patient;
(ii) the copy and dictation tasks allow to compare the variations of the writing respect to different stimuli (visual or sound);
(iii) tasks involving different pen-ups allow the analysis of air movements, which it is known to be altered in the AD patients;
(iv) tasks involving different graphic arrangements, e.g. words with ascenders and/or descendants, or complex graphic shapes, allow testing fine motor control capabilities.

Furthermore, in order to evaluate patient responses under different fatigue conditions, these tasks should be provided by varying their intensity and duration.

(1) As in [19] or in [11], in the first task the subjects must copy three letters that have different graphic composition.

(2) The second task consists in copying four letters on adjacent rows. The aim of the cues is to test the spatial organization abilities of the subject [14].

(3–4) The task 3 and 4 require participants to write continuously for four times, in cursive, a single letter and a bigram, respectively [8,16]. These tasks allow the testing of the motion control alternation.

(5–8) The tasks 5, 6, 7 and 8 implies word copying, which is the most explored activity in the analysis of handwriting for individuals with cognitive impairment [8,13,19]. Moreover, to observe the variation of the spatial organization, we have introduced the copy of the same word without or with a cue.

(9) In the ninth task, subjects are asked to write, above a line (the cue), a simple phrase, dictated them by the experimenter. As in [7], the hypothesis is that the movements can be modified because of the lack of visualization of the stimulus.

2.3   Segmentation and Feature Extraction

The features extracted during the handwriting process have been exploited to investigate the presence of neurodegenerative diseases in the examined subjects. We used the MovAlyzer tool to process the handwritten trace, considering both on-paper and on-air traits. Their segmentation in elementary strokes was obtained by assuming as segmentation points both pen up and pen down, as well as the zero crossings of the vertical velocity profile. The feature values were computed for each stroke and averaged over all the strokes relative to a single task: we considered for each feature both the mean value and the maximum value for that task. Note that, as suggested in [19], we have separately computed the features over on-paper and on-air traits, because the literature shows significant differences in motor performance in these two conditions.

3   Experiments and Results

The software used for the classification was Weka. We decided to use three data groups: the data related to the on-air features; the data concerning the on paper features; and the overall data (on paper and on air). Each feature is present in the data set for the 9 tasks performed by the 130 subjects. For the experiments, we used two different classifiers: The Random Forest and the Decision Tree, namely J48. For both of them, 500 iterations were performed and a 5 fold validation strategy was considered. It is noteworthy that we have chosen the Random Forest classifier because it is widely recognized as a top of performing classifier. However, being an ensemble of classifiers, it does not provide easily interpretable models. We also have chosen Decision Tree because through the generated tree it is possible to identify the specific features used during the classification process.

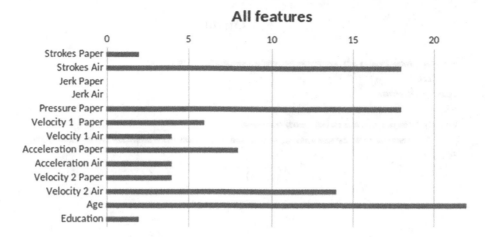

Fig. 1. Occurrences of all features.

The tables below summarize the values of Accuracy and False Negative Rate (FNR) for each task. The first column provides the number of tasks, the second the features used, the third the classifier employed, while in the fourth we report the value of accuracy and in the final column, we show the value of False Negative Rate. The False Negative Rate is very relevant in medical diagnosis applications since it indicates the ability of correctly identifying the patients, thus allowing their inclusion in the appropriate therapeutic pathway.

The preliminary results seem to encourage the use of classification algorithms as tools to support the diagnose of AD. From the tables shown below (Tables 1, 2, 3 and 4) we can point out that: firstly, for each task the max value (in bold) of accuracy is over 70%, reaching peak in some tasks, such as the fifth task with value of 76%. Secondly we can claim that, on average, emerges a better classification using the Random Forest classifier compared to J48. This is easily justifiable considering that Random Forest, unlike J48, is an ensemble of classifiers. However, as reported in the last column, FNR is lower using J48 classifier. In particular, the lower value of FNR occurs in the on-paper traits of the second task, with a value of 8.82%. Moreover, as shown in the histograms (Figs. 1 and 2), from a decision tree it is possible to identify the occurrences of the features for the classification. It is noteworthy that, using all features, the system mainly uses the strokes, the pressure and the subject age that is the most used one. Moreover, jerk, both on air and on paper, is never used. Instead, if we consider the two groups of features separately, subject age still remains the most used one for both groups, followed by the velocity (on air) and pressure (on paper).

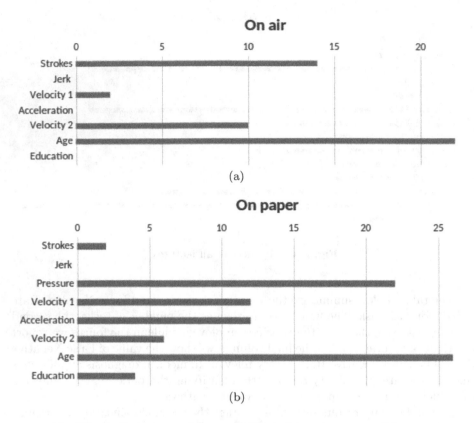

Fig. 2. Occurrence of features. On air (a) and on paper (b).

Table 1. Classification results of task 1 and 2.

Task	Features	Classifier	Accuracy	FNR
1	All	RF	71.96	28.79
	All	J48	66.66	19.70
	On paper	RF	**72.72**	28.79
	On paper	J48	65.90	27.27
	On air	RF	71.21	22.73
	On air	J48	68.18	18.18
2	All	RF	66.41	33.82
	All	J48	66.41	36.76
	On paper	RF	**72.38**	23.53
	On paper	J48	67.16	36.76
	On air	RF	60.44	33.82
	On air	J48	70.89	**8.82**

Table 2. Classification results of task 3 and 4.

Task	Features	Classifier	Accuracy	FNR
3	All	RF	**69.09**	44.90
	All	J48	61.81	40.82
	On paper	RF	68.18	44.90
	On paper	J48	63.63	30.61
	On air	RF	67.27	44.90
	On air	J48	66.36	22.45
4	All	RF	**71.42**	36.00
	All	J48	63.81	30.00
	On paper	RF	66.66	38.00
	On paper	J48	67.62	34.00
	On air	RF	61.90	42.00
	On air	J48	63.80	18.00

Table 3. Classification results of task 5, 6, 7, 8.

Task	Features	Classifier	Accuracy	FNR
5	All	RF	75.67	25.45
	All	J48	66.66	38.18
	On paper	RF	**76.57**	23.64
	On paper	J48	67.56	41.82
	On air	RF	64.68	34.55
	On air	J48	61.26	38.18
6	All	RF	69.29	39.22
	All	J48	64.91	41.18
	On paper	RF	68.41	43.14
	On paper	J48	**71.93**	21.57
	On air	RF	64.03	45.10
	On air	J48	63.15	39.22
7	All	RF	63.63	38.46
	All	J48	53.63	59.62
	On paper	RF	**64.54**	38.46
	On paper	J48	62.72	40.38
	On air	RF	63.63	38.46
	On air	J48	62.72	21.15
8	All	RF	70.43	36.54
	All	J48	69.56	38.46
	On paper	RF	68.69	38.46
	On paper	J48	66.95	38.46
	On air	RF	**72.17**	30.77
	On air	J48	67.82	34.62

Table 4. Classification results of task 9.

Task	Features	Classifier	Accuracy	FNR
9	All	RF	**72.30**	34.85
	All	J48	66.92	31.75
	On paper	RF	70.00	26.98
	On paper	J48	67.69	12.70
	On air	RF	70.00	34.92
	On air	J48	69.23	33.33

4   Conclusion and Open Issues

In this paper, we presented a novel solution for the early diagnosis of Alzheimer's disease by analyzing features extracted from handwriting. The preliminary results obtained are encouraging and the work is in progress to increase general performance. In particular, from the results obtained we can claim to have identified some simple tasks, features and classifiers, which support the diagnosis of Alzheimer's. In other words, this system could represent a low cost and non-invasive tool to support the diagnosis of Alzheimer's disease, in juxtaposition with actual diagnosis systems.

Starting from these results, the next steps to be taken could include the combination of all tasks taken into account in a suitable way (the task itself can be used as a new feature) [4,5]; introduction of a reject option in order to reduce false negative rate; introduction of new features evaluated on slant, loop surface, horizontal size and vertical size, etc; reduction of the unbalancing dataset caused by difficulties in recruiting young patients and old people without any cognitive disease.

References

1. Babiloni, C., et al.: Classification of single normal and Alzheimer's disease individuals from cortical sources of resting state EEG rhythms. Front. Neurosci. **10**, 47 (2016)
2. Bevilacqua, V., D'Ambruoso, D., Mandolino, G., Suma, M.: A new tool to support diagnosis of neurological disorders by means of facial expressions. In: Proceedings of the 2011 IEEE International Symposium on Medical Measurements and Applications, MeMeA 2011 (2011)
3. Cilia, N., De Stefano, C., Fontanella, F., Scotto di Freca, A.: An experimental protocol to support cognitive impairment diagnosis by using handwriting analysis. Procedia Comput. Sci. **141**, 466–471 (2018)
4. Cordella, L.P., De Stefano, C., Fontanella, F., Scotto di Freca, A.: A weighted majority vote strategy using Bayesian networks. In: Petrosino, A. (ed.) ICIAP 2013. LNCS, vol. 8157, pp. 219–228. Springer, Heidelberg (2013). https://doi.org/10.1007/978-3-642-41184-7_23

5. De Stefano, C., Fontanella, F., Folino, G., di Freca, A.S.: A Bayesian approach for combining ensembles of GP classifiers. In: Sansone, C., Kittler, J., Roli, F. (eds.) MCS 2011. LNCS, vol. 6713, pp. 26–35. Springer, Heidelberg (2011). https://doi.org/10.1007/978-3-642-21557-5_5
6. De Stefano, C., Fontanella, F., Impedovo, D., Pirlo, G., Scotto di Freca, A.: Handwriting analysis to support neurodegenerative diseases diagnosis: a review. Pattern Recognit. Lett. **121**, 37–45 (2018)
7. Hayashi, A., et al.: Neural substrates for writing impairments in japanese patients with mild Alzheimer's disease: a spect study. Neuropsychologia **49**(7), 1962–1968 (2011)
8. Impedovo, D., Pirlo, G.: Dynamic handwriting analysis for the assessment of neurodegenerative diseases: a pattern recognition perspective. IEEE Rev. Biomed. Eng. **12**, 209–220 (2019). https://doi.org/10.1109/RBME.2018.2840679
9. Jelic, V., Dierks, T., Amberla, K., Almkvist, O., Winblad, B., Nordberg, A., Tsukahara, N.: Longitudinal changes in quantitative EEG during long-term tacrine treatment of patients with Alzheimer's disease. Neurosci. Lett. **254**(4), 85–88 (1988)
10. Kang, J., Lemaire, H.G., Unterbeck, A., Salbaum, J.M., Masters, C.L., Grzeschik, K.H., et al.: The precursor of Alzheimer's disease amyloid A4 protein resembles a cell-surface receptor. Nature **325**, 733–736 (2015)
11. Lambert, J., Giffard, B., Nore, F., de la Sayette, V., Pasquier, F., Eustache, F.: Central and peripheral agraphia in Alzheimer's disease: From the case of auguste D. to a cognitive neuropsychology approach. Cortex **43**(7), 935–951 (2007)
12. McKhann, G., Drachman, D., Folstein, M., Katzman, R., Price, D., Stadlan, E.: Clinical diagnosis of Alzheimer's disease: report of the NINCDS-ADRDA work group under the auspices of department of health and human services task force on Alzheimer's disease. Neurology **34**, 939–944 (1984)
13. Onofri, E., Mercuri, M., Archer, T., Ricciardi, M.R., Massoni, F., Ricci, S.: Effect of cognitive fluctuation on handwriting in Alzheimer's patient: a case study. Acta Medica Mediterranea **3**, 751 (2015)
14. Onofri, E., Mercuri, M., Salesi, M., Ricciardi, M., Archer, T.: Dysgraphia in relation to cognitive performance in patients with Alzheimer's disease. J. Intellect. Disabil. Diagn. Treat. **1**, 113–124 (2013)
15. Price, D.L.: Aging of the brain and dementia of the Alzheimer type. Princ. Neural Sci., 1149–1168 (2000)
16. Slavin, M.J., Phillips, J.G., Bradshaw, J.L., Hall, K.A., Presnell, I.: Consistency of handwriting movements in dementia of the Alzheimer's type: a comparison with Huntington's and Parkinson's diseases. J. Int. Neuropsychol. Soc. **5**(1), 20–25 (1999)
17. Triggiani, A., et al.: Classification of healthy subjects and Alzheimer's disease patients with dementia from cortical sources of resting state EEG rhythms: a study using artificial neural networks. Front. Neurosci. **10**, 604 (2017)
18. Tseng, M.H., Cermak, S.A.: The influence of ergonomic factors and perceptual-motor abilities on handwriting performance. Am. J. Occup. Ther. **47**(10), 919–926 (1993)
19. Werner, P., Rosenblum, S., Bar-On, G., Heinik, J., Korczyn, A.: Handwriting process variables discriminating mild Alzheimer's disease and mild cognitive impairment. J. Gerontol. Psychol. Sci. **61**(4), 228–236 (2006)
20. Yan, J.H., Rountree, S., Massman, P., Doody, R.S., Li, H.: Alzheimer's disease and mild cognitive impairment deteriorate fine movement control. J. Psychiatr. Res. **42**(14), 1203–1212 (2008)

Geometrical and Statistical Properties of the Rational Order Pyramid Transform and Dilation Filtering

Kento Hosoya[1], Kouki Nozawa[1], and Atsushi Imiya[2](✉)

[1] School of Science and Engineering, Chiba University,
Yayoi-cho 1-33, Inage-ku, Chiba 263-8522, Japan
[2] Institute of Management and Information Technologies, Chiba University,
Yayoi-cho 1-33, Inage-ku, Chiba 263-8522, Japan
imiya@faculty.chiba-u.jp

Abstract. The pyramid transform of rational orders is described using matrix transform. This matrix expression of the rational order pyramid transform clarifies the eigenspace properties of the transform. The matrix-based expression, however, derives orthogonal base in each resolution. This orthogonal property of base of signals derive a unified computation of linear transformation to images any rational resolutions. Furthermore, the eigenspace property allows us to define the rational pyramid transform families using the discrete cosine transform. Numerical evaluation of the transform clarifies that rational order pyramid transform preserves the normalised distribution of grey-scale in images.

1 Introduction

In this paper, the pyramid transform [2–4] of rational orders [1] is reformulated from the viewpoints of discrete functional analysis. The rational order pyramid transform is introduced from the viewpoint of linear filtering of signals and images. This transform is a shift invariant linear transform, which is mathematically described using convolution by defining kernel function of the transform.

We reformulate the transform using the matrix expression of the convolution operation. This matrix expression of the rational order pyramid transform clarifies the eigenspace properties of the transform. In ref. [1] the rational order pyramid transform is designed form the viewpoint of synthesis of IIR filter banks by assuming biorthogonal relation for the kernels of pyramid transform and its dual transform. The matrix-based expression, however, derives orthogonal bases in each resolution. This eigenspace property allows us to define the rational pyramid transform families using the discrete cosine transform for any resolution. Since these orthogonal bases are related by scaling, the bases allow us to deal with the pyramid transform as scaling of arguments of bases and affine transform in vector space defined by dimension of images. Furthermore, We also clarify that rational order pyramid transform preserves the normalised distribution of grey-scale in images.

© Springer Nature Switzerland AG 2019
M. Vento and G. Percannella (Eds.): CAIP 2019, LNCS 11679, pp. 152–163, 2019.
https://doi.org/10.1007/978-3-030-29891-3_14

Resolutions of medical images depend on the modalities for data observation. These multiresolution images with different resolutions are essential nature on data in image-based retrievals, classification and diagnosis, for longitudinal medical image-analysis. For registration of a temporal sequence of images observed by different modalities with various resolutions, the normalisation and harmonisation of resolutions of images observed by the various modalities in different time are demanded. The rational order pyramid transform and dilation filtering achieve the normalisation and harmonisation of resolutions of images preserving statistical properties of the grey-value distribution of images. Therefore, the rational order pyramid transform is used as a resolution-conversion method.

2   Pyramid Transform

We assume that images are elements of the Sobolev space $H^2(\mathbf{R}^2)$. The downsampling and upsampling operation S_σ and U_σ, respectively, with factor σ are defined as

$$g(x,y) = S_\sigma f(x,y) = f(\sigma x, \sigma y), \quad f(x,y) = U_\sigma g(x,y) = \frac{1}{\sigma^2} g\left(\frac{x}{\sigma}, \frac{y}{\sigma}\right). \quad (1)$$

Since these operations satisfy the relations

$$\int_{-\infty}^{\infty} \int_{-\infty}^{\infty} U_\sigma g(x,y) f(x,y) dx dy = \int_{-\infty}^{\infty} \int_{-\infty}^{\infty} g(x,y) S_\sigma f(x,y) dx dy, \quad (2)$$

$$\int_{-\infty}^{\infty} \int_{-\infty}^{\infty} |g(x,y)|^2 dx dy = \int_{-\infty}^{\infty} \int_{-\infty}^{\infty} |U_\sigma g(x,y)|^2 dx dy \quad (3)$$

and $S_\sigma U_\sigma g(x,y) = g(x,y)$, $U_\sigma = S_\sigma^*$ and U_σ is a partial isometric operator.
    We deal with the linear transforms

$$g(x,y) = Rf(x,y) = \int_{-\infty}^{\infty} \int_{-\infty}^{\infty} w_\sigma(u) w_\sigma(v) f(\sigma x - u, \sigma y - v) du dv, \quad (4)$$

$$f(x,y) = Eg(x,y) = \frac{1}{\sigma^2} \int_{-\infty}^{\infty} \int_{-\infty}^{\infty} w_\sigma(u) w_\sigma(v) g\left(\frac{x-u}{\sigma}, \frac{y-v}{\sigma}\right) du dv, \quad (5)$$

where

$$w_\sigma(x) = \begin{cases} \frac{1}{\sigma}\left(1 - \frac{1}{\sigma}|x|\right), & \text{if } |x| \le \sigma, \\ 0, & \text{otherwise} \end{cases} \quad (6)$$

for $\sigma > 0$. These transforms perform downsampling with factor σ after shift-invariant smoothing and shift-invariant smoothing (interpolation) after upsampling with factor σ, respectively.
    We define metrics in two functional spaces.

Definition 1. *In both the defined domain and the range space of the transform R, the inner products of functions are defined as*

$$(f,g)_D = \int_{-\infty}^{\infty} \int_{-\infty}^{\infty} f(x,y) g(x,y) dx dy, \quad (7)$$

$$(Rf, Rg)_R = \int_{-\infty}^{\infty} \int_{-\infty}^{\infty} Rf(x,y) Rg(x,y) dx dy. \quad (8)$$

Since the transforms R and E satisfy the relation

$$\int_{-\infty}^{\infty}\int_{-\infty}^{\infty} Rf(x,y)g(x,y)dxdy = \int_{-\infty}^{\infty}\int_{-\infty}^{\infty} f(x,y)Eg(x,y)dxdy, \qquad (9)$$

that is, $(f, Rg)_R = (R^*f, g)_D$, these pair of transforms are mutually dual transforms.

The discrete version of Eq. (4) for $p \in \mathbf{Z}_+$ is

$$g_{mn} = h_{pm\,pn}, \quad h_{mn} = \sum_{\alpha,\beta=-(p-1)}^{(p-1)} \frac{p-|\alpha|}{p^2} \cdot \frac{p-|\beta|}{p^2} f_{m+\alpha\,n+\beta}. \qquad (10)$$

Equation (10) is the pyramid transform of order p. The dual transform of Eq. (10) is

$$f_{pm+\alpha\,pn+\beta} = \frac{1}{p^2}\left(\frac{p-\alpha}{p}\cdot\frac{p-\beta}{p}g_{pm\,pn} + \frac{\alpha}{p}\cdot\frac{\beta}{p}g_{p(m+1)\,p(n+1)}\right), \qquad (11)$$

for $\alpha, \beta = 0, 1, \cdots, (p-1)$. Equation (11) is the linear interpolation of $g_{pm\,pn}$ to generate f_{mn} for $m, n = 0, \pm 1, \cdots \pm \infty$ and $p, q \in \mathbf{Z}_+$.

Using the relation between Eqs. (10) and (11), we construct the pyramid transform of the rational order q/p for $p, q \in \mathbf{Z}_+$.

Definition 2. *The q/p-pyramid transform first achieves upsampling of order p by using linear interpolation. For the upsampled data, the pyramid transform of order q is applied.*

Definition 3. *The dual transform is achieved by downsampling to the result of the dual transform of the pyramid transform.*

For $\mu > 0$, the dilation filtering [5] is

$$h(x,y) = g(x,y) *_\mu f(x,y) = \int_{-\infty}^{\infty}\int_{-\infty}^{\infty} g(x-\mu u, y-\mu v)f(u,v)dudv$$

$$= \frac{1}{\mu^2}\int_{-\infty}^{\infty}\int_{-\infty}^{\infty} g(u,v)f\left(\frac{x-u}{\mu}, \frac{y-v}{\mu}\right)dudv. \qquad (12)$$

This formula coincides with Eq. (5) if we set $w_\mu(x) := g(x)$. Therefore, dilation filtering with the filter $w_\mu(x)$ is the dual transform of the pyramid transform.

For an absolute integrable function w and $f \in H^2(\mathbf{R}^2)$, the convolution $g = w * f$ of f and w satisfies the inequality

$$|g|_2^2 = |w * f|_2^2 \le |w|_1^2|f|_2^2, \quad g(x,y) = \int_{-\infty}^{\infty}\int_{-\infty}^{\infty} w(u,v)f(u-x,v-y)dudv, \qquad (13)$$

where

$$|f|_2^2 = \int_{-\infty}^{\infty}\int_{-\infty}^{\infty} |f(x,y)|^2 dxdy, \quad |f|_1 = \int_{-\infty}^{\infty}\int_{-\infty}^{\infty} |f(x,y)|dxdy. \qquad (14)$$

Equation (13) implies that the pyramid transform is a linear compact operation.

3   Eigenspace Analysis of Transforms

By using the q/p-pyramid transform for vectors, we derive matrix expressions for the q/p-pyramid transform for image arrays. The pyramid transform

$$g_n = \frac{1}{4}f_{2n-1} + \frac{1}{2}f_{2n} + \frac{1}{4}f_{2n+1} = \frac{1}{4}(f_{2n-1} + 2f_{2n} + f_{2n+1}) \qquad (15)$$

for the sequence $\{f_n\}_{n=-\infty}^{\infty}$ is redescribed as

$$g_n = h_{2n}, \quad h_n = \frac{1}{4}(f_{n-1} + 2f_n + f_{n+1}). \qquad (16)$$

These relations imply that the pyramid transform is achieved by downsampling after computing moving average.

Using the matrix D, which is the one-dimensional discrete Laplacian with the Neumann boundary condition, we define

$$W = \frac{1}{4}(D + 4I), \qquad D = \begin{pmatrix} -1 & 1 & 0 & 0 & \cdots & 0 & 0 \\ 1 & -2 & 1 & 0 & \cdots & 0 & 0 \\ 0 & 1 & -2 & 1 & \cdots & 0 & 0 \\ \vdots & \vdots & \vdots & \vdots & \ddots & \vdots & \vdots \\ 0 & 0 & 0 & \cdots & 0 & 1 & -1 \end{pmatrix}. \qquad (17)$$

Setting $S = I \otimes e_2$ for $e_2 = (1,0)^\top$ the matrix expression of the pyramid transform with the Neumann boundary condition is

$$R = SW. \qquad (18)$$

We extend Eq. (18) to the q/p-transform.

Let

$$D\Phi = \Phi\Lambda, \qquad \Phi^\top\Phi = I, \qquad \Lambda = ((\lambda_k \delta_{kl})) \qquad \lambda_k^{(n)} = 4\sin^2\frac{\pi k}{2n} \qquad (19)$$

be the eigendecomposition of D. The matrix

$$\Phi = \left(\left(\frac{1}{\sqrt{n}}s_j \cos\frac{(2j+1)i}{2n}\pi\right)\right) = (\varphi_0, \varphi_1, \cdots, \varphi_{n-1}), \qquad s_j = \begin{cases} 1, & \text{if } j = 0, \\ \frac{1}{\sqrt{2}}, & \text{otherwise} \end{cases} \qquad (20)$$

is the discrete cosine transform matrix of the type II for vectors in $\mathbf{R}^n$.

The matrix of downsampling operation for vectors is

$$S_q = I \otimes e_1^q, \qquad e_1^q = (1,0,\cdots,0)^\top \in \mathbf{R}^q. \qquad (21)$$

Furthermore, the $2p + 1$-dimensional diagonal matrix

$$N_p = ((n_{|i-j|})), \qquad n_k = \frac{p-k}{p}, \qquad 0 \le p \le k \qquad (22)$$

is expressed as

$$N_p = \sum_{k=0}^{p} a_k D^k, \qquad\qquad D^0 = I, \qquad (23)$$

for an appropriate collection of coefficients $\{a_k\}_{k=1}^{p}$. Using matrices N_p and S_p, the linear interpolation for order p is expressed

$$L_p = N_p S_p. \qquad (24)$$

as the matrix. Equation (24) implies the following property.

Property 1. Assuming that the domain of signals is $\mathcal{L}\{\varphi_i\}_{i=0}^{n-1}$, the range of signals upsampled using linear interpolation of order p is $\mathcal{L}\{\varphi_i\}_{i=0}^{pn-1}$.

The pyramid transform of order q is expressed as

$$R_q = \frac{1}{q} S_q N_q, \qquad (25)$$

since the pyramid transform is achieved by downsampling after shift-invariant smoothing, for which the matrix expression is N_q. Equation (25) implies the following theorem.

Theorem 1. *With the Neumann boundary condition, the pyramid transform of order q is a linear transform from $\mathcal{L}\{\varphi_i\}_{i=0}^{n-1}$ to $\mathcal{L}\{\varphi_i\}_{i=0}^{\frac{1}{q}n-1}$, assuming that $n = kq$.*

Equations (24) and (25) derive the following theorem.

Theorem 2. *The q/p-pyramid transform is expressed as*

$$R_{q/p} = \frac{1}{q} S_q N_q L_p = \frac{1}{q} S_q N_{q/p} S_p, \qquad\qquad N_{q/p} = N_q N_p. \qquad (26)$$

Theorem 2 implies the following theorem.

Theorem 3. *With the Neumann boundary condition, the q/p-pyramid transform is a linear transform from $\mathcal{L}\{\varphi_i\}_{i=0}^{n-1}$ to $\mathcal{L}\{\varphi_i\}_{i=0}^{\frac{p}{q}n-1}$.*

Since the matrix expressions of $R_{q/p}^{*}$ and $E_{q/p}$ are $R_{q/p}^{\top}$ and $E_{q/p}^{\top}$, respectively, we have the following theorem.

Theorem 4. *For a rational number q/p, the pyramid transform and its dual transform satisfy the relations,*

$$R_{q/p}^{*} = R_{q/p}^{\top} = E_{q/p} = R_{p/q}, \qquad\qquad E_{q/p}^{*} = E_{q/p}^{\top} = R_{q/p} = E_{p/q}, \qquad (27)$$

where A^* is the dual operation of the linear transform A.

Theorem 4 implies the following theorem.

Theorem 5. *If $R_{q/p}^\top = E_{s/r}$, the relation $q/p \times s/r = 1$ is satisfied for the rational-number pair q/p and s/r.*

For the pyramid transform, $R = R_{1/2} = S_2 N_1$ satisfies the relation $R^{k+1} = R^k(R)$. Furthermore, for the rational order pyramid transform $R_{q/p} = S_q N_{q/p} S_p$, we have the following relation

$$R_{r/q} R_{q/p} = \frac{1}{rq} S_r N_{r/q} S_q S_q N_{q/p} S_p = \frac{1}{rq} S_r N_{r/q} S_q N_{q/p} S_p \qquad (28)$$

since $S_q S_q = S_q^\top S_q = I_q$. Equation (28) derives the transform

$$R_{r/q/p} = \frac{1}{rq} S_r N_{r/q} S_q N_{q/p} S_p. \qquad (29)$$

The generalisation Eq. (28) is

$$R_{p_k/p_{k-1}\cdots/p_1} = \frac{1}{p_k p_{k-1} \cdots p_2} S_{p_k} N_{p_k/p_{k-1}} \cdots S_{p_2} N_{p_2/p_1} S_{p_1}. \qquad (30)$$

which is different from R^k. Furthermore, the dual transform of $R_{p_k/p_{k-1}\cdots/p_1}$ is

$$E_{p_k/p_{k-1}\cdots/p_1} = \frac{1}{p_k p_{k-1} \cdots p_2} S_{p_1} N_{p_1/p_2} \cdots S_{p_{k-1}} N_{p_{k-1}/p_k} S_{p_k}. \qquad (31)$$

The linear scale space transform is used for multiresolution image analysis. For a pair of positive number such that $p + q = 1$, the relation

$$\binom{n}{k} \sim \frac{1}{\sqrt{2\pi npq}} \exp\left(\frac{(k - np)^2}{2npq}\right) \qquad (32)$$

is called De Moivre-Laplace theorem. This theorem derives the discrete approximation of the linear scale space transform using the binomial distribution.

Table 1 summarises the relations between the p-pyramid transform for positive integers and the scaled linear scale-space transform for signals. This table clarifies the relation between the signals yielded by the p-pyramid transform and numerically approximated linear scale space transform.

The two-dimensional q/p-pyramid transform for the matrix F, which corresponds to two-dimensional array for image, is expressed as

$$G = R_{q/p} F R_{q/p}^\top. \qquad (33)$$

Equation (33) implies the following theorem.

Theorem 6. *With the Neumann boundary condition, the q/p-pyramid transform is a linear transform from $\mathcal{L}\{\varphi_i \varphi_j^\top\}_{i=0}^{n-1}$ to $\mathcal{L}\{\varphi_i \varphi_j^\top\}_{i,j=0}^{\frac{p}{q}n-1}$ assuming that $n = kq$.*

Since the vectors $\{\varphi_i\}_{i=0}^{n-1}$ satisfies the relation $\varphi_i^\top \varphi_j = \delta_{ij}$, the relation

$$(\varphi_i \varphi_j^\top)^\top \varphi_{i'} \varphi_{j'}^\top = \delta_{ii'} \delta_{jj'}. \qquad (34)$$

is satisfied. Therefore, the q/p-pyramid transform derives an orthogonal base system for q/p.

Table 1. Relations between the pyramid transform and linear scale-space transform

Pyramid Transform	Linear Scale Space Transform
$g_m = \sum_{k=-1}^{1} w_k f_{2m-k}$	$g_m = \sum_{k=-n}^{n} \frac{1}{(2n)!} \binom{2n}{n-k} f_{m-k}$
$g_m = h_{qm}$ $h_n = \sum_{\alpha=-(q-1)}^{(q-1)} \frac{p-\lvert\alpha\rvert}{q^2} k_{n+\alpha}$ $k_{m+\beta} = \frac{1}{p}\left(\frac{p-\beta}{p} f_m + \frac{\beta}{p} f_{m+1}\right)$	
$g(x) = \int_{-\infty}^{\infty} w_\sigma(y) f(\sigma y - x) dx$	$g(x) = \frac{1}{\sqrt{2\pi\tau}} \int_{-\infty}^{\infty} \exp\left(-\frac{y^2}{2\tau}\right) f(\sigma x - y) dy$

4 Statistical Properties of the q/p-Pyramid Transform

Figures 1, 2, and 3 show examples of the q/p-pyramid transform of a street view [6] and a natural scene [7]. In figures the first and third columns are images computed by the q/p-pyramid transform. The second and fourth columns are the grey-value histograms of the images in the first and third columns, respectively. In Fig. 1, from top to bottom, q/p is 2/1, 3/2 and 1/1. In Fig. 2, from top to bottom, q/p is 1/1, 3/4, 2/3 and 3/5. In Fig. 3, from top to bottom, 1/2, 2/5, 1/3 and 1/4. 1/1 and 1/2 indicate the original image and the image computed by the traditional pyramid transform, respectively.

For a positive function $f(x, y) \geq 0$ defined on the domain $\Omega = [0, a] \times [0, b]$, we define the function

$$f(x, y; u) = \begin{cases} f(x, y), & \text{if } f(x, y) < u, \\ u, & \text{otherwise.} \end{cases} \tag{35}$$

Since the total value of $f(x, y)$ which is smaller than $u \geq 0$ is

$$H(u; f(x, y)) = \int_0^a \int_0^b f(x, y; u) dx dy, \tag{36}$$

the total value for $f(x, y) = u$ is computed as

$$h(u; f(x, y)) = \frac{1}{\lvert a \times b \rvert} \lim_{\delta \to 0} \frac{H(u + \delta; f(x, y)) - H(u - \delta; f(x, y))}{2\delta}$$

$$= \frac{\partial}{\partial u} H(u; f(x, y)). \tag{37}$$

$h(u; f(x, y))$ is the normalised grey-value histogram of $f(x, y)$ on Ω.

The distance between a pair of normalised histograms $P(u) = h(u; f(x, y))$ and $Q(u) = h(u; g(x, y))$ is computed by the transportation

$$d_\alpha(P, Q) = \min_{c(x,y)} \sqrt[\alpha]{\int_0^{u_{\max}} \int_0^{u_{\max}} \lvert P(u) - Q(v) \rvert^\alpha c(u, v) du dv} \tag{38}$$

Table 2. Distance matrix of the normalised grey-value histograms for the images in the first column, where $\alpha = 2$.

	1/1	1/2	1/3	1/4	1/5	2/1	2/3	2/5	3/2	3/4	3/5	4/5
1/1	0	9.2874	10.031	10.139	9.6511	8.7058	9.4735	10.185	8.9554	9.7694	9.5414	9.2725
1/2	*	0	10.783	10.893	11.602	8.957	9.3465	11.228	9.1372	10.066	9.5539	10.325
1/3	*	*	0	11.362	12.508	10.048	10.268	10.856	10.797	10.065	9.5803	10.195
1/4	*	*	*	0	12.611	10.161	10.55	12.193	10.325	10.615	10.948	10.778
1/5	*	*	*	*	0	10.348	11.208	12.377	9.8662	10.706	10.639	10.747
2/1	*	*	*	*	*	0	8.9992	9.1722	8.281	8.6577	9.3642	8.8809
2/3	*	*	*	*	*	*	0	10.001	8.9412	9.9719	9.7911	10.017
2/5	*	*	*	*	*	*	*	0	10.06	10.813	10.415	10.411
3/2	*	*	*	*	*	*	*	*	0	9.7477	10.5	9.4746
3/4	*	*	*	*	*	*	*	*	*	0	9.8735	9.6991
3/5	*	*	*	*	*	*	*	*	*	*	0	9.9244
4/5	*	*	*	*	*	*	*	*	*	*	*	0

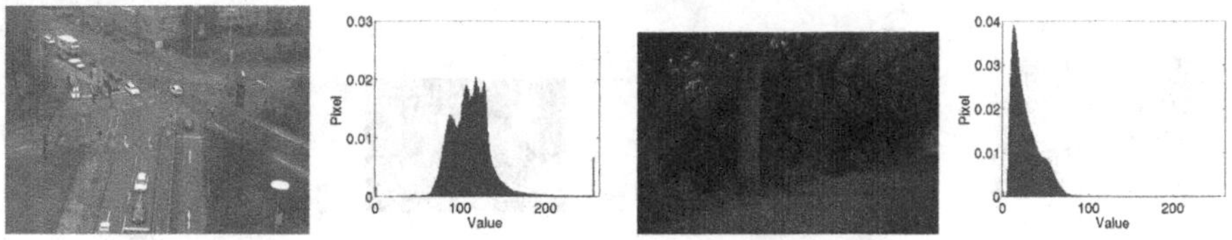

(a) 2/1	(b) 2/1	(c) 2/1	(d) 2/1
(e) 3/2	(f) 3/2	(g) 3/2	(h) 3/2
(i) 1/1	(j) 1/1	(k) 1/1	(l) 1/1

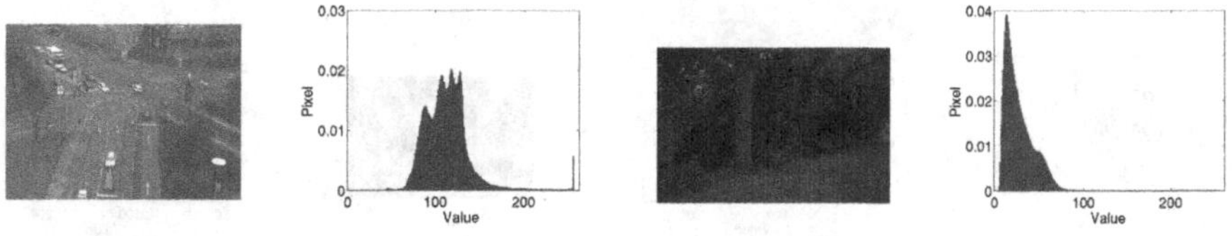

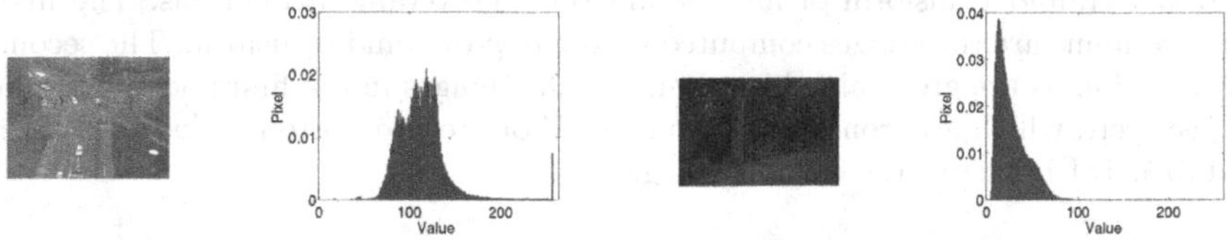

Fig. 1. Dilation filtering of images and their grey-value histograms. The first and third columns are the images computed by the q/p-pyramid transform. The second and fourth columns are grey-value histograms of the images in the first and third columns, respectively, which are from refs. [6] and [7]. From top to bottom, q/p is 2/1, 3/2 and 1/1. 1/1 indicates the original image.

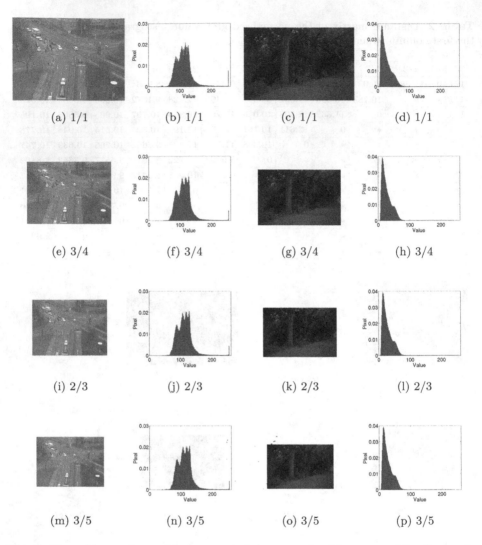

Fig. 2. Pyramid transform of images and their grey-value histograms. The first and third columns are the images computed by the q/p-pyramid transform. The second and fourth columns are grey-value histograms of the images in the first and third columns, respectively, which are from refs. [6] and [7]. From top to bottom, q/p is $1/1$, $3/4$, $2/3$ and $3/5$. $1/1$ indicates the original image.

for $\alpha > 0$ with the conditions

$$\int_0^{u_{\max}} c(u, v)du \leq Q(v), \qquad \int_0^{u_{\max}} c(u, v)dv \leq P(u).$$

Tables 2 and 3 show the distance matrices among the histograms in the second and fourth columns in Figs. 2 and 3, respectively, for $\alpha = 2$. In these tables, the elements in the upper triangles are computed, since the matrices are symmetric.

These numerical experiments imply that the grey-value distributions of the results of the q/p-pyramid transform possess the same distribution property as the original images, that is, the transform preserves the shapes of grey-value histograms of images for any rational numbers. Furthermore, the dilation convolution with the triangle kernel preserves the statistical properties of grey-values through the factors of dilation filtering, since the statistical properties of

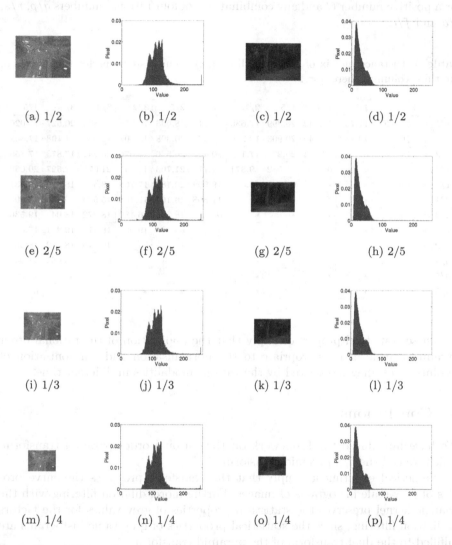

(a) 1/2   (b) 1/2   (c) 1/2   (d) 1/2

(e) 2/5   (f) 2/5   (g) 2/5   (h) 2/5

(i) 1/3   (j) 1/3   (k) 1/3   (l) 1/3

(m) 1/4   (n) 1/4   (o) 1/4   (p) 1/4

Fig. 3. Pyramid transform of images and their grey-value histograms. The first and third columns are the image computed by the q/p-pyramid transform. The second and fourth columns are grey-value histograms of the images in the first and third columns, respectively, which are from refs. [6] and [7]. From top to bottom, q/p is 1/2, 2/5, 1/3 and 1/4. 1/2 indicates the image computed by the traditional pyramid transform.

grey-value histograms are fulfilled to the dual transform of the pyramid transform. Moreover, setting $D(q/p, r/s)$ to be the transportation distance between a pair of the normalised grey-value histograms of images computed by the q/p- and r/s-pyramid transforms, Tables 2 and 3 show that

$$|D(q/p, r/s) - D(b/a, f/e)| \leq C \tag{39}$$

for a positive number C and any combinations of four rational numbers q/p, r/s, b/a and f/e.

Table 3. Distance matrix of the normalised grey-value histograms for the images in the third column, where $\alpha = 2$.

	1/1	1/2	1/3	1/4	1/5	2/1	2/3	2/5	3/2	3/4	3/5	4/5
1/1	0	18.961	17.769	19.042	20.399	17.636	18.311	18.098	16.558	18.833	20.527	15.026
1/2	*	0	19.112	18.745	20.903	18.229	17.47	20.398	19.001	18.535	17.108	17.852
1/3	*	*	0	22.494	20.237	17.146	20.432	20.526	17.076	20.241	17.873	17.858
1/4	*	*	*	0	21.582	19.871	17.775	21.703	19.445	21.073	21.527	20.063
1/5	*	*	*	*	0	18.555	19.909	20.188	17.708	18.453	18.629	18.337
2/1	*	*	*	*	*	0	17.808	18.107	15.763	15.974	16.523	16.606
2/3	*	*	*	*	*	*	0	18.206	16.189	18.972	18.04	19.536
2/5	*	*	*	*	*	*	*	0	19.291	18.474	19.421	17.662
3/2	*	*	*	*	*	*	*	*	0	16.216	18.172	18.399
3/4	*	*	*	*	*	*	*	*	*	0	16.685	17.546
3/5	*	*	*	*	*	*	*	*	*	*	0	18.29
4/5	*	*	*	*	*	*	*	*	*	*	*	0

These statistical properties imply that the application of the rational order pyramid transform is appropriate to the normalisation and harmonisation of resolutions of images observed by the various modalities in different time.

5   Conclusions

We have introduced the framework on the rational order pyramid transform, which we call the q/p-pyramid transform.

Numerical experiments imply that the transform preserves the curve profiles of grey-scale histograms of images. Furthermore, dilation filtering with the triangle kernel preserves the statistical properties of grey values for the factors of dilation filtering, since the statistical properties of grey-value histograms are fulfilled to the dual transform of the pyramid transform.

This research was supported by the Multidisciplinary Computational Anatomy and Its Application to Highly Intelligent Diagnosis and Therapy project funded by a Grant-in-Aid for Scientific Research on Innovative Areas from MEXT, Japan, and by Grants-in-Aid for Scientific Research funded by the Japan Society for the Promotion of Science.

References

1. Nguyen, H.T., Nguyen, L.-T.: The Laplacian pyramid with rational scaling factors and application on image denoising. In: 10th ISSPA, pp. 468–471 (2010)
2. Burt, P.J., Adelson, E.H.: The Laplacian pyramid as a compact image code. IEEE Trans. Commun. **31**, 532–540 (1983)
3. Thevenaz, P., Unser, M.: Optimization of mutual information for multiresolution image registration. IEEE Trans. Image Process. **9**, 2083–2099 (2000)
4. Kropatsch, W.G.: A pyramid that grows by powers of 2. Pattern Recognit. Lett. **3**, 315–322 (1985)
5. Yu, F., Koltun, V.: Multi-scale context aggregation by dilated convolutions. CoRR abs/1511.07122 (2015)
6. http://i21www.ira.uka.de/image_sequences/#dt
7. Geisler, W.S., Perry, J.S.: Statistics for optimal point prediction in natural images. J. Vis. **11**, 1–17 (2001)

Personal Identity Verification by EEG-Based Network Representation on a Portable Device

Giulia Orrú[1(✉)], Marco Garau[1], Matteo Fraschini[1], Javier Acedo[2],
Luca Didaci[1], David Ibáñez[2], Aureli Soria-Frish[2], and Gian Luca Marcialis[1]

[1] Department of Electrical and Electronic Engineering, University of Cagliari,
Cagliari, Italy
m.garau@gmail.com, fraschin@unica.it,
{giulia.orru,luca.didaci,marcialis}@diee.unica.it
[2] Starlab Barcelona S.L., Barcelona, Spain
{javier.acedo,david.ibanez,aureali.soria-frish}@starlab.es
https://www.starlab.es/

Abstract. EEG-based personal verification was investigated so far by using mainly standard non-portable device with a large number of electrodes (typically, 64) constrained to heavy headset configuration. Despite this equipment has been shown to be useful to investigate in depth EEG signal characteristics from a biomedical point of view, it may be considered less appropriate for designing real-life EEG-based biometric systems. In this work, EEG signals are collected by a portable and user-friendly device explicitly conceived for biometric applications, featured by a set of 16 channels. Investigated feature extraction algorithms are based on modelling the EEG channels as a network of mutually interacting units, which was shown to be effective for personal verification purposes when brain signals are acquired by standard EEG devices. This work shows that, even using a reduced set of channels, these approaches still remain effective. The aim of this paper is intended to stimulate research on the use of light and portable EEG headset configurations by adopting network-based representations of EEG brain signals, since a light headset represents a precondition in order to design real-life EEG-based personal verification systems.

Keywords: EEG · Person verification · Portable device

1 Introduction

The electroencephalogram (EEG) signal detected at scalp level has been proposed in the last decade as a biometric trait for personal recognition purposes [1–5], beside other well-known biometrics [7]. Despite its great potential, confirmed by the encouraging experimental results over different approaches [1–5], its main limitation relies on the large number of channels that strongly hinder the

M. Vento and G. Percannella (Eds.): CAIP 2019, LNCS 11679, pp. 164–171, 2019.
https://doi.org/10.1007/978-3-030-29891-3_15

use in practical applications. Furthermore, the standard EEG devices used so far are expensive, cumbersome and unfriendly. These devices require a heavy headset configuration of a large number of electrodes (64, in most cases) distributed over the scalp by means of which it is possible to acquire the time-variant EEG signals.

In this paper, we implemented a recently proposed feature extraction method for personal authentication [1], based on EEG network characteristics, by adopting a realistic, portable and low cost EEG device explicitly conceived for this application. In particular, the device is characterized by a small number of channels (only sixteen), considerably less than the number channels used for standard configuration (typically sixty-four) [1,2,5]. The feature extraction method allows to measure the importance of network nodes (EEG channels) estimating the network centrality (eigenvector centrality) from patterns of EEG phase synchronization between recordings sites. The network configuration is supposed to be unique from person to person and previous studies [1,4,5] have shown that a noticeable degree of individuality is embedded into the EEG signal and this can be exploited thanks to this representation.

We aim to show that a networks-based EEG representation is still able to convey individual and discriminant information, even when EEG signals are captured by a cheap and portable device, equipped with a limited set of channels. The relevance of the reported findings is in line with the requirement to develop EEG-based personal verification systems that can be used in real-life applications. In order to support our claim, the reported experimental results have been compared with those of previous works [1–5] which used a publicly available EEG dataset with a standard 64-channel configuration. In both cases, EEG signals were acquired during eyes-open resting-state condition.

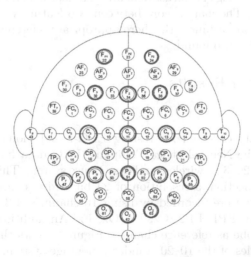

Fig. 1. Electrodes adopted for the 10–20 standard system montage on the subject's scalp. We pointed out the channels used by the portable device of this paper in red. (Color figure online)

2 The Method

We replicated the approach proposed in [1], based on the Eigenvector Centrality (EC) measurement. Given, per each person, a sample of n EEG signals, where n represents the number of channels, we performed the following:

- we filtered each signal by using a band-pass filter to obtain the correspondent band-limited signal in the range between 30 and 40 Hz, namely the gamma band [1–5];
- we computed the adjacency matrix that describes a graph of the functional brain network, where each node corresponds to a channel location and the weights are expressed by the Phase Lag Index (PLI). The PLI [2] allows to estimate the interdependence between channels pairs, as a sort of co-variance matrix. In particular, the PLI is defined as:

$$PLI = |<sign[sin(\Delta\phi(t_k))]>| \tag{1}$$

Where $\Delta\phi(t_k)$ represents the difference between instantaneous phases of two signals at the time t_k;

- from the adjacency matrix the importance of each node was computed by using the EC values as previously described in [1], which are, in summary, the eigenvalues of the diagonalized PLI matrix. According to [8], this approach is still highly competitive with respect to other feature extraction methods based for example on wavelet transform [9]. This is the first paper where it is shown its potentialities on a real, user-friendly device with a small number of channels.

In this way, starting from the raw EEG signals, we obtained, for each person, a feature vector consisting of n measurements, that is, the PLI matrix and the EC values of each node. The match score between two feature vectors is computed by using the Euclidean distance [1], where appropriate references to PLI and EC measurements can be also found.

3 Experimental Results

3.1 Data Set

A data set explicitly collected for testing EEG-based biometric systems has been provided by the Neuroelectrics Company. EEG data have been recorded by means of Enobio 20 [3], a wireless and easy to use system. This is characterized by a bluetooth connection, a resolution of 24 bit and a sampling frequency of 500 Hz. EEG signals were recorded by using 16 channels: P3, P4, P7, P8, O1, O2, C3, C4, F3, F4, FP1, FP2, Cz, Pz, Oz, Fz. An additional electrode was located on the earlobe as reference channel. Figure 1 shows the correspondence with the 64 electrodes of the 10–20 standard montage system.

The dataset consists of EEG recordings from 22 subjects. For each subject, two EEG signals were acquired. Each acquisition consists of one-minute eyes-open resting-state and a session of P300 Visual Event Related Potentials, made up of 10 trials, followed by 1 min of Spontaneous EEG. The trials were organized as follows:

- the subject relaxes for one minute;
- the subject identifies a target image showed asynchronously in 4 different orders (10 images selected from the 15 image set) and push a button. This task is repeated 10 times;
- after this step, randomized images (selected from the 15 image dataset) are shown, using 3 different inter-stimuli interval (ISI): 100 ms, 750 ms, 1100 ms, with a random variation of ±25 ms (uniform);
- the user is asked to count how many times he recognizes the target image.

In total, twenty one-minute trials for each person were captured.

We partitioned each one-minute long EEG sample in five non-overlapping epochs of 12 each. This allowed us to simulate five different traces of the EEG signal per subject as done in [1]. We refer to this dataset as Enobio, in the following.

For sake of comparison, the Physionet dataset was also used. This is a publicly available dataset that has been previously used for biometric applications [1–5]. The main difference with the Enobio is related with the acquisition protocol: the resting-state condition has been evaluated only after several kind of external stimuli[1], whilst in the Enobio dataset the resting state condition is evaluated before the external stimulus. In other words, subjects were free to concentrate themselves according to their own will. The Physionet dataset contains 109 subjects and the number of channels is 64.

Resting-state condition is considered as the ground-truth to evaluate the individuality of EEG signals of biometric applications, according to [4].

Table 1. The Equal Error Rate (where FAR = FRR) and the FRR at 1% FAR for the investigated algorithms on the "light" device adopted in this paper and a standard "heavy" device [1,4,5].

Experimental condition: resting state at open eyes						
Feat. vect.	EER			FRR at 1% FAR		
	Enobio	Phy64	Phy16	Enobio	Phy64	Phy16
EC	5.1%	4.5%	11.9%	16.0%	8.0%	45.8%
SC	22.9%	9.9%	-	65.5%	43.0%	-
PLI	5.0%	3.8%	7.8%	10.5%	99.6%	99.7%
PSD	28.6%	22.0%	26.8%	99.6%	99.9%	99.9%

---

[1] See in particular the website https://www.physionet.org/pn4/eegmmidb/.

3.2   Results

In order to have an appropriate "ground truth", we computed the so-called Power Spectral Density (PSD). This represents the basic measurement of the variations along the EEG signal [6]. We selected the γ band which was the most representative for the subject identification, according to [1].

Moreover, we implemented the method proposed in [5], based on another connectivity measurement called Spectral Coherence (SC). We performed experiments using the method based on the PLI and EC as described in the previous section, and adapting the one based on the SC.

The Likelihood Ratio hypothesis verification test was used for estimating the performance of all methods. Let X be the match scores from a certain method, and $f_{gen}(x)$ and $f_{imp}(x)$ be the conditional joint densities given the genuine users class and the impostors class, respectively. The optimal test for deciding whether a score vector X corresponds to a genuine user or an impostor is the likelihood ratio test (LLR) [1]. It is possible to define the binary hypothesis that a match score is sampled from the genuine users distribution if the related likelihood ratio is greater than a predefined threshold η, otherwise it is concluded that the match score is sampled from the impostors distribution. The likelihood ratio test is optimal only when the marginal densities are totally known. Since in practice these densities $f_{gen}(x)$ and $f_{imp}(x)$ are estimated from the training set of genuine and impostor match scores, the performance of likelihood ratio test depends on the accuracy of these estimations. Accordingly, as in [5], we used 70% of subjects (15 subjects) for computing the matching scores and estimating $f_{gen}(x)$ and $f_{imp}(x)$. For each subject, 10 genuine match scores and 350 impostor match scores were computed (14 impostors × 5 traces × 5 genuine traces). In the case of impostors, we excluded those match scores obtained by the same couple of samples, thus obtaining $14 \times 25 \times 13/2 = 2{,}275$ values. The total number of genuine scores were 150. On the basis of these, we estimated $f_{gen}(x)$ and $f_{imp}(x)$. Densities were estimated by a kernel density estimation methodWith regard to the Enobio dataset, a total number of 70 genuine match scores and $25 * 6 * 5/2 = 375$ impostor match scores were computed. This random partitioning was repeated 20 times and the mean performance is shown in Table 1.

Performance is given in terms of ROC curve (Fig. 2), which represent the percentage of wrongly accepted impostors (FAR) and the performance of wrongly rejected genuine users (FRR) in a unique plot, for each possible LLR threshold value. Two operational points in particular were pointed out: the Equal Error Rate point, where FAR = FRR, and the FRR correspondent to the threshold for which $FAR = 1\%$ (Table 1)[2].

As it can be seen from Table 1 and Fig. 2, the performance of the PLI and EC methods is very high even using the Enobio light headset configuration, and totally surpass the one obtained by the PSD and SC. Worth noting, the

---

[2] The authors of this paper are available for any clarification concerning the source code and the protocol adopted in order to assure the repeatability of experiments.

performance of PSD did not significantly change when passing from 16 to 64 channels, thus maintaining the meaning of "ground truth" as expected. The performance of PLI is even comparable with that of EC when 64 channels are used on the Physionet data set, when FAR values less than 4% are taken into account. This means that, although the FRR increases this is anyway less than that of the other investigated methods.

The same holds for EC and PLI for the EER values (Physionet columns). This means that, at the state of the art, with such a number of channels, the degree of individuality is good when it is expected that, over 100 recognition trials, 5 are taken into account to be false acceptances or false rejections. On the other hand, the performance drops roughly when more conservative operational points, namely, the FRR is calculated at FAR = 1%. It is worth noting that the performance of the EC -based method on the Enobio and Physionet datasets is still much higher than that obtained using the SC-based method, even when all 64 channels are adopted for this last method. The EER is more than two times the one obtained on Enobio when the number of channels and the channels are exactly the same on the Physionet dataset (Physionet column) for the EC-based method, whilst a slight decrease of the performance is observed when using the PLI-based method. This is probably due to the differences in the protocol for data acquisition, and suggests that the resting-state condition evaluated after the external stimuli appears to be more susceptible to cause intra-subjects and inter-subjects variations influencing the captured EEG signal. This effect is partially overcome by the PLI method (PLI row), where we obtained a FRR value close to that of EC using 64 channels. A possible explanation is that PLI encodes the possible lags of all channels in more measurements: each PLI feature vector is made up of 120 values, whilst the correspondent EC feature vector is made up of only 16 values. However, the very good performance of PLI at EER when using 64 channels is worth noting. This performance is still high even with the Enobio device, and maybe some modifications of the basic algorithms could also allow decreasing the error rate in other operational points as well.

According to the reported evidences, this biometric application appears to be still immature and unsuitable for large-scale applications, that means, when the number of possible users rapidly increases. On the other hand, it can be a good method to vehiculate the identity and the will of resources access for a small group of users when a high level of security is not necessary. For example, opening an internal house door or accessing to the own laptop when the subject is unable to do this because she/he is constrained at bed or cannot move. In other words, we are referring to the design of an appropriate BCI [3].

The significant decrease of the processing time and the reduced memory storage, especially by considering the PLI and EC methods, are noticeable. The low number of channels leads to feature vectors made up of 120 and 16 values, respectively. The amount of information to be processed was not only notably reduced, but the templates can be easily stored in mobile devices with limited storage memory.

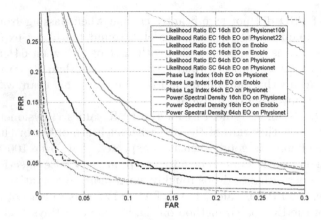

Fig. 2. ROC curves related to the Enobio data set for PSD, PLI, EC and SC methods. For sake of confirmation, we added the results obtained on the Physionet data set for the method at 16 and 64 channels. It is possible to see that Enobio and Physionet data sets led to similar results. However, the EER is more than two times the one obtained on Enobio when the number of channels and the channels are exactly the same (16) on the Physionet data set. This is probably due to some difference in the protocol for data acquisition.

4   Conclusions

On the basis of the performance comparison between the results obtained in this paper and the ones reported in previous works, we noted that whilst methods based on the EC and PLI are robust enough with respect to the decreased number of available channels, the one based on the SC has an important loss in performance. In other words, estimating the PLI or EC still maintains a sufficient representation of the brain network even in the case of the lightweight configuration of 16 channel of the Enobio device. In short, the classification rate is almost equivalent to that obtained on the 64-channel datasets, especially when considering low FAR values.

Another point of interest was the significant decrease of the processing time, due to the lower number of channels: the amount of information to be processed was notably reduced.

Although this first set of experiments was done on an apparently small data set, let us consider that achieved results are still close to that obtained on larger benchmarks. Therefore, we may expect that reported performance is a good starting point, especially by considering that it is unlikely that a recognition system or a BCI based on the EEG signal is designed to be large scaled, due to the difficulties related to the interactions among electrodes and the high cooperation level required to reduce any external noise during the signal acquisition.

On the other side, what reported strongly encourages a deeper analysis and development of network-based brain signals representations and their use for personal recognition as a part of future personal verification systems and Brain-Computer Interfaces.

References

1. Fraschini, M., et al.: An EEG-based biometric system using eigenvector centrality in resting state brain activity. IEEE Signal Process. Lett. **22**(6), 666–670 (2015)
2. Stam, C., et al.: Phase lag index: assessment of functional connectivity from multi channel EEG and MEG with diminished bias from common sources. Hum. Brain Mapp. **28**(11), 1178–1193 (2007)
3. Ramadan, R., Vasilakos, A.: Brain computer interface: control signals review. Neurocomputing **223**, 26–44 (2017)
4. Campisi, P., La Rocca, D.: Brain waves for automatic biometric-based user recognition. IEEE Trans. Inf. Forensics Secur. **9**(5), 782–800 (2014)
5. La Rocca, D., et al.: Human brain distinctiveness based on EEG spectral coherence connectivity. IEEE Trans. Biomed. Eng. **61**(9), 2406–2412 (2014)
6. Bascil, M.S., et al.: Spectral feature extraction of EEG signals and pattern recognition during mental tasks of 2-D cursor movements for BCI using SVM and ANN. Australas. Phys. Eng. Sci. Med. **39**(3), 665–676 (2016)
7. Sufyanu, Z., et al.: Enhanced face recognition using discrete cosine transform. Eng. Lett. **24**(1), 52–61 (2016)
8. Yang, S., et al.: Task sensitivity in EEG biometric recognition. Pattern Anal. Appl. **21**, 105 (2018). https://doi.org/10.1007/s10044-016-0569-4
9. Zheng, B., et al.: Recognition method based on Gabor wavelet transform and discrete cosine transform. Eng. Lett. **26**(2), 228–235 (2018)

A System for Controlling How Carefully Surgeons Are Cleaning Their Hands

Luca Greco, Gennaro Percannella$^{(\boxtimes)}$, Pierluigi Ritrovato, Alessia Saggese, and Mario Vento

Department of Computer and Electrical Engineering and Applied Mathematics, Via Giovanni Paolo II, 132, 84084 Fisciano, SA, Italy
{lgreco,pergen,pritrovato,asaggese,mvento}@unisa.it

Abstract. In this paper, we propose a method for the automatic compliance evaluation of the hand washing procedure performed by healthcare providers. The ideal cleaning procedure, as defined by the guidelines of the World Health Organization (WHO), is split into a sequence of ten distinct and specific hand gestures which have to be performed in the proper order. Thus, the conformance verification problem is formulated as the problem of recognizing that at a given time instant a specific gesture is carried out by the subject. The considered recognition problem is faced through a deep neural network inspired to AlexNet that classifies each image providing as output the guessed gesture class that the subject is performing. Images are captured by a depth camera mounted in a top-view position. The performance of the proposed approach has been assessed on a brand new dataset of about 131.765 frames obtained from 74 continuous recording from trained personnel. Preliminary evaluation confirms the feasibility of the approach with a recognition rate at the frame level that is about 77%, and is about 98% when using a mobile window of 1 s. The developed system will be deployed for training students of the medicine course on the surgical hand-washing procedure.

Keywords: Surgical hand washing · Gesture recognition · CNN · Public dataset

1 Introduction

Hospital infections are among the most frequent and severe complication of health care. According to a recent study conducted by the Center for Desease Control [2], each day about one in twenty-five hospital patients acquires a health care-associated infection, adding up to about 722,000 infections a year. Among such infected patients, 75,000 (about 10%) die of their infections.

It has been also shown that healthcare providers clean their hands less than half of the time they should; in [12] the authors report that this improper hand hygiene among healthcare workers is responsible for about 40% of healthcare-associated infections. It suggests that the hands of the operators are the most

© Springer Nature Switzerland AG 2019
M. Vento and G. Percannella (Eds.): CAIP 2019, LNCS 11679, pp. 172–181, 2019.
https://doi.org/10.1007/978-3-030-29891-3_16

common vehicle for the transmission of microorganisms from one patient to another, from one side to the other of the patient's body, as well as from operator to patient. The adoption of strategies to improve hand hygiene becomes thus mandatory for reducing the rates of infections related to health care, both in surgery and intensive care units, and in the hospital environment in general.

In the last years a particular interest of the scientific community has been devoted towards the surgical hand preparation, with the aim to reduce the risk of surgical site contamination with microorganisms originating from the surgeon's hands, although the presence of the gloves during the surgeries. Indeed, surgical hand preparation has a strategic importance in the reduction of infections. Nevertheless, as confirmed in [7], there is no standard procedure for evaluating the compliance with hand hygiene. The most common approaches for evaluating the compliance are the following: (1) direct observation of practice; (2) self-report of healthcare workers and (3) indirect calculation, based on the measurement of the products usage. According to the WHO [15], *direct observation* is the gold standard since it provides all information required for the analysis; however, it is only rarely used in practice since it is typically made by human observers, thus being time consuming and expensive. Haas and Larson [7] also notice that *self-report* is not really accurate, while *indirect calculation* based on the measurement of products does not provide information of non-compliance. In the last years some attempts have been made towards the monitoring of the hand preparation.

In [5] and [10] a method based on indirect calculation is proposed: the authors introduce a sensor able to automatically compute the level of alcohol, which is among the main compounds of the standard products to be used for hand washing. In case this level is not sufficient, then the access to the room is not guaranteed to that person. In [16] the authors analyse the effect of several data coming both from the hand washing system (i.e. the quantity of product used) and the washing operation (i.e. the time spent for washing the hands) in order to identify the probability of infection for a patient. In [13] a system for the automatic analysis of the hands after the washing has been proposed: the hands are washed with soap mixed with UV reflective powder; the operator has to insert his hands inside a case equipped with ultraviolet lighting and a digital camera. Although being among the most innovative solutions in this field, this system is not really usable in real environments for two main reasons: this is invasive and expensive, since it requires the adding of UV reflective powder in all the soap dispensers; furthermore, the introduction of the case in the equipment could be a further source of contamination.

The main problem of the above approaches is that a feedback is provided only at the end of the hand washing procedure. Therefore, there is a strong need of a solution able to (1) monitor the compliance with hand hygiene and also (2) to provide a real time feedback to the surgeon during the hand washing procedure, in order to allow him/her to improve the procedure and then to reduce the risk of infection for the patient.

Within this context, we propose a novel architecture for analysing in real time the sequence of gestures performed by the surgeon during the hand washing procedure. The latter can be considered as composed by a series of gestures that must be performed in a proper way, in a given order and for at least a minimum time period. It implies that the hand washing problem can be formulated in terms of a gesture recognition problem, in which a specific hand washing movement can be considered as a specific class of the procedure.

Hand gesture can be defined as the combination of those gestures and movements produced by hand or hand and arm [4]. It is considered as the best method for interacting with a computer or a robot without any peripheral devices [6,8,11]. In [3], the approaches for hand gesture recognition are partitioned in three main categories depending on the type of sensor used for analysing the movement: vision-based, glove-based and depth-based. The authors state that the first two approaches are not promising and natural enough, while the most promising methods available in the literature are based on depth cameras, which allows to exploit the third dimension related to the depth. Independently on the sensor adopted for acquiring the set of images, the best results are typically achieved by using deep learning methodologies, with particular reference to convolutional neural networks, which achieve outstanding results outperforming "non-deep" state-of-the-art methods [1].

Starting from the above considerations, in this paper we propose to solve the problem of the automatic compliance evaluation of the hand washing procedure by a method based on deep learning that automatically analyzes the sequence of images by recognizing the gestures performed by the subject and providing a score about its conformance to the guidelines; in case of a low score, the operator is alerted so as to immediately repeat only that gesture.

The main contributions of the paper can be summarized as follows:

- we propose a system to automatically evaluate the quality of the surgeon hand washing procedure; this has been achieved by formulating the problem as a gesture recognition problem; to the best of our knowledge this is the first attempt in the literature that address this problem in the literature;
- we also introduce a baseline approach for hand washing gesture recognition, where the gestures are analyzed and classified by means of a Convolutional Neural Network; furthermore, a sliding window based on a majority voting is introduced in order to provide a single information about the whole sequence;
- a new dataset composed by 74 different video sequences has been created and made publicly available for benchmarking purposes. There is no other dataset available in the literature for facing the same problem.

The paper is organized as follows: in Sect. 2 the procedure for surgeon hand washing is introduced and the method proposed for facing with this problem is detailed. Furthermore, we also describe the dataset used for assessing performance. In Sect. 3 we define the indices used for evaluating the performance of the proposed approach and comment on the results obtained by testing the approach on the adopted dataset.

2 Methods and Materials

2.1 Dataset

The medical community recognizes several hand hygiene washing procedures[1]. The procedures may vary with respect to the context (patient care, visit, surgical operation, etc.), but also with respect to the type of soap, the presence or absence of water, the use of specific tools like a nail cleaner or a sponge, etc. In this paper, we refer to surgical hand washing procedure as reported in [12] and [14] which comprises the ten gestures briefly described in Table 1. In the same table we attribute to each gesture an abbreviation that, for the sake of conciseness, will be used in the rest of the paper.

For the study proposed in this paper, we simulated in the laboratory an hospital environment by using a white plane that resembles a washbasin. The camera was mounted in a zenithal position in order to capture the movements of the hands of the person without occlusions. The camera is mounted at $D_{plane} = 0.9\,$m above the ground plane: this allows to capture entirely the area where the hand washing has place, and guarantees margin of maneuver for the medical doctor.

The dataset consists of 74 image sequences, where each sequence refers to the complete and continuous hand washing procedure performed by a person. The acquisitions were done using an Intel® RealSense™ Depth Camera D435 that is equipped with a depth sensor and an RGB sensor. Each registration comprises both the RGB stream (8 bits per each of the 3 channels) and depth stream (16 bits per channel, each sample representing the distance from the camera in millimeters) acquired with 640×480 pixels resolution and 15 frames per second.

For the experimental analysis reported in this paper, the dataset is divided into a training set of 50 sequences recorded among 41 different persons, and a test set which comprises the remaining 24 sequences recorded from 12 different subjects. We selected subjects with different heights and equally distributed between male and female in order to avoid introducing a bias in the learning phase with respect to the physical appearance of the subject. Before recording, each subject was instructed on the correct hand washing procedure; furthermore during the procedure he/she was guided gesture by gesture, through a video representing the procedure as performed by a medical doctor; finally, each sequence, both RGB and depth streams, has been validated by a medical doctor.

In Table 2, we report the composition of the dataset, and for each type of gesture we indicate the total number of frames and its average duration in seconds. We notice that the distribution of the classes is not balanced; in fact, referring to the train set, the duration of the sequences may range from a minimum of 4 s for the **W** and the **S** gestures, to a maximum of 23 s of the **N** gesture.

---

[1] See www.who.int/gpsc/5may/Hand_Hygiene_Why_How_and_When_Brochure.pdf.

Table 1. Description of the ordered sequence of gestures included in the hand washing procedure considered in this paper. For each gesture there are reported the rank of the gesture in the ordered sequence, the abbreviation and a short description.

Order	Abbreviation	Description	Figure
1	W	Wet the hands, the movement consists in getting wet from the hand up to the elbow.	
2	N	Clean the area under all nails through a nail cleaner.	
3	SN	Using a sponge, scrub the area under and over the nails.	
4	SH	Using a sponge, scrub the palms, the space between the finger and the back of both hands.	
5	S	Get soap from the dispenser using elbows.	
6	P	Rub the palms of the hands together.	
7	IF	With intertwined fingers, rub the interdigital space.	
8	BH	Rub the back of both hands with the palm of the other.	
9	F	Wrap each finger with the other hand and rub it in its entirety with circular movements. The gesture is repeated for both hands.	
10	FA	Wrap the wrist with the other hand, with slow circular movements rub the arm in its entirety rising towards the elbow. Repeat the gesture for both arms.	

Table 2. Consistence of the train and test datasets: in each cell they are reported both the number of frames and the average duration in seconds of the gesture indicated in the first column. The dataset comprises 50 and 24 sequences in the train and in the test sets, respectively.

Gesture	Train set	Test set
W	3'236/4 s	1'448/4 s
N	17'057/23 s	5'744/16 s
SN	10'850/14 s	3'906/11 s
SH	16'198/22 s	6'096/17 s
S	3'149/4 s	1'109/3 s
P	6'645/9 s	2'943/8 s
IF	6'424/9 s	2'856/8 s
BH	14'000/19 s	5'579/15 s
F	7'492/10 s	2'886/8 s
FA	1'0464/14 s	3'683/10 s
Total	95'515/127	36'250/101 s

2.2 Proposed Method

In this paper, the problem of assessing the conformance of the hand washing procedure carried out by a subject is cast to the problem of recognizing the performed gesture. To this aim we use a classifier that attributes each input frame to one of the ten classes reported in Table 1. The proposed classifier relies only on depth information, while discarding the RGB channel. The motivation behind this choice is that depth data guarantees higher immunity than data from the RGB channel with respect to problems given by variations of the background, lighting source, color of the human skin, soap and other objects used during the procedure as the sponge and the nail cleaner. The immunity assured by the selected information source is particularly important for the deployment of the system in real scenarios where large variations in the adopted washbasins, lighting sources, washing tools, are to be taken into account.

The classifiers adopted in this paper is based on AlexNet, the deep neural network proposed in [9]. The most prominent differences with respect to the original version of the network are related to size and type of the input, and the number of output neurons. In fact, AlexNet was designed to work with three channels (RGB) images with 1'000 classes while the network used for this work takes in input one channel images and has 10 output neurons (a neuron for each class). In order to reduce the dimension of data to provide in input to the network and speed-up computation at both training and inference time, the original images were proprocessed. In particular, the images were firstly cropped to 340×340 in order to consider only the central region of the image where the washing activity is carried out. Then, the image is rescaled to 170×170 by bicubic interpolation. Furthermore, we set to background all the pixels referring to points in the scene at a distance from the camera equal or greater than D_{th}, where the latter is fixed as $D_{th} = D_{plane} - \epsilon$, with D_{plane} as the distance of the bottom white plane from the camera. In this way, we remove from the scene elements which are not significant with respect to the classification problem. Finally, we halve the size of samples (from 16 bits to 8 bits) and rescale the values as follows:

$$s_r(i,j) = \begin{cases} M \cdot (1 - \frac{s_o(i,j)}{D_{th}}) & \text{if } 0 \leq s_o(i,j) \leq D_{th} \\ 0 & \text{otherwise} \end{cases} \tag{1}$$

where $s_o(i,j)$ and $s_r(i,j)$ are the values of the (i,j)-th pixel of the image before and after rescaling, respectively. For our tests, we set $\epsilon = 1$ cm (as anticipated, $D_{plane} = 90$ cm).

Data augmentation was also adopted for increasing the size of the train dataset with the aim of achieving a more robust classifier. In particular, we were interested to increase the robustness of the method with respect to the following two factors: (1) specularity of the hand movements performed by right-handed and left-handed subjects; (2) persons assuming an oblique position with respect to the washbasin. In order to account for these two sources of variability, all images of the train dataset were (1) flipped and (2) rotated by 10°, 20° and 30° in both directions. Larger rotations were considered unnecessary since they cannot physically take place. Finally, for the network training, we used softmax cross entropy loss function while the optimizer function is the gradient descent; a constant learning rate of 0.001 was set (Fig. 1).

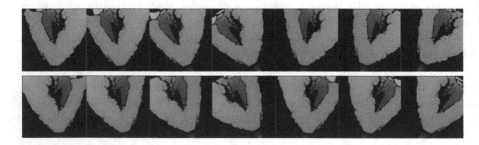

Fig. 1. Example of images generated after data augmentation. In the top-left corner there is the original image and in the bottom-left corner the flipped one, while proceeding from left to right in both rows there are reported the images rotated counterclockwise and then clockwise by 10°, 20° and 30°.

3   Experimental Results

3.1   Experimentation Protocol

As mentioned in the previous section, according to our knowledge it does not exist a dataset for automatically classify the movement for surgical handwashing. For this reason we limit the performance evaluation of the proposed approach to the measurement of accuracy using the confusion matrix on the test set data. It is worth to mention that the recording of the test set has been made over several days and under different conditions (illumination, part of the day) as per the training set. As detailed in Sect. 2 the test set is composed of 24 sequences recorded by 12 people.

Table 3. Test-set confusion matrix for single frame (values in %).

	W	N	SN	SH	S	P	IF	BH	F	FA
W	96,14	0,00	0,17	0,00	2,01	0,00	0,00	0,00	0,00	1,68
N	0,08	83,89	2,99	2,80	0,38	0,65	1,69	7,52	0,00	0,00
SN	1,09	12,14	67,29	7,91	0,26	2,02	0,57	8,73	0,00	0,00
SH	1,30	4,37	8,77	46,09	0,98	5,73	2,53	27,78	1,84	0,60
S	2,81	0,18	0,00	0,00	90,35	0,00	0,00	0,00	0,00	6,67
P	0,14	0,07	0,54	1,97	0,00	75,63	12,76	8,01	0,41	0,48
IF	0,26	0,65	0,13	1,87	0,00	6,13	82,89	7,10	0,90	0,06
BH	0,84	5,39	0,91	9,66	0,11	1,86	1,05	78,22	0,77	1,19
F	0,00	0,07	0,00	3,72	0,37	10,49	11,46	1,49	71,80	0,60
FA	7,01	0,49	0,00	0,16	1,58	0,43	0,00	3,10	0,00	87,23

3.2 Performance Analysis

The performance analysis of the proposed method has been twofold: we evaluated the performance on a single frame and on a sequence of frames. For the sequence of frames has been considered a mobile window of a length of 1 s (15 frames) with a step of 5 frames (2/3 overlap).

Table 3 presents the confusion matrix for single frame. Operating on single frame, the achieved overall accuracy of the system is equal to 73,82%. As evident from Table 3, the overall accuracy is highly influenced by the poor performance in SH (Sponge Hand) recognition where in almost 28% of the cases this action is confused with BH action. Errors ranging from 10% to 13% are also evident on the SN (Sponge Nail), P (Palms) and BH (Back of Hands) actions. Working on single frame the action that is more confused with the others is Fingers.

Performance improves substantially when we consider a mobile window. In Table 4 the confusion matrix for the sequence of frames is reported. In that case the overall accuracy increased to 81.93%, that is about 11% relative improvement with respect to the decision taken on single frames, although also with mobile windows the system confuses SH with BH action.

3.3 Robustness of the Proposed Approach

According to our experimentation, considering the mobile windows, the proposed method is quite robust with respect to changes in illumination, this is also due to use of the depth camera. On the contrary, the overall performance drop significantly (less than 50%), as soon as we change the height of the camera of

Table 4. Test-set confusion matrix for mobile windows (values in %).

	W	N	SN	SH	S	P	IF	BH	F	FA
W	92,95	0,00	0,00	0,00	0,00	0,00	0,00	0,00	0,00	7,05
N	1,76	89,34	1,92	1,92	0,38	0,00	0,38	3,91	0,00	0,38
SN	0,78	10,18	83,36	1,29	0,00	1,40	0,00	3,00	0,00	0,00
SH	0,63	2,19	4,75	62,15	0,00	2,79	0,00	27,49	0,00	0,00
S	0,00	0,00	0,35	3,86	88,42	0,00	0,00	1,23	0,00	6,14
P	0,00	0,00	0,00	0,41	4,14	86,08	3,39	5,63	0,00	0,34
IF	0,00	0,00	0,00	0,00	0,00	7,81	91,74	0,45	0,00	0,00
BH	0,00	2,94	0,00	13,80	0,00	2,49	2,07	78,61	0,11	0,00
F	0,00	0,07	0,00	0,45	0,00	6,85	6,18	2,98	83,48	0,00
FA	5,71	0,00	0,00	0,00	0,00	0,43	0,38	0,00	2,72	90,76

more than 10 cm. This is due to the fact the dataset augmentation process does not considered image re-sizing, but flip and rotations only.

4   Conclusions

In this paper we studied the a computer vision solution for facing the problem of automatic verification of the compliance with the WHO guidelines of the hand washing procedure performed by a medical doctor. The proposed approach is based on a deep neural network derived from the well known AlexNet and adapted to work on depth images.

The experimental analysis carried out on a dataset of more than 70 complete hand cleaning procedures demonstrated that the proposed approach is a viable solution for facing this problem, achieving an overall accuracy of $97,4\%$ in the recognition of the different hand gestures comprised by the hand washing protocol defined by the WHO. However, the analysis of the results shows that further research efforts should be directed to address the problem of the uneven accuracy distribution among the classes and in particular over the SH class that is often confused with F.

References

1. Asadi-Aghbolaghi, M., et al.: A survey on deep learning based approaches for action and gesture recognition in image sequences. In: IEEE International Conference on Automatic Face Gesture Recognition (FG 2017), pp. 476–483, May 2017. https://doi.org/10.1109/FG.2017.150
2. Centers for Disease Control and Prevention: Hand hygiene in healthcare settings (2018). https://www.cdc.gov/handhygiene/
3. Chen, L., Wang, F., Deng, H., Ji, K.: A survey on hand gesture recognition. In: International Conference on Computer Sciences and Applications, pp. 313–316, December 2013. https://doi.org/10.1109/CSA.2013.79

4. Cheng, H., Yang, L., Liu, Z.: Survey on 3D hand gesture recognition. IEEE Trans. Circuits Syst. Video Technol. **26**(9), 1659–1673 (2016). https://doi.org/10.1109/ TCSVT.2015.2469551
5. Edmond, M., Goodell, A., Zuelzer, W., Sanogo, K., Elam, K., Bearman, G.: Successful use of alcohol sensor technology to monitor and report hand hygiene compliance. J. Hosp. Infect. (2010). https://doi.org/10.1016/j.jhin.2010.07.006
6. Foggia, P., Percannella, G., Saggese, A., Vento, M.: Recognizing human actions by a bag of visual words. In: Proceedings of the 2013 IEEE International Conference on Systems, Man, and Cybernetics, SMC 2013, pp. 2910–2915 (2013). https://doi. org/10.1109/SMC.2013.496
7. Haas, J., Larson, E.: Measurement of compliance with hand hygiene. J. Hosp. Infect. (2007). https://doi.org/10.1016/j.jhin.2006.11.013
8. Kaur, H., Rani, J.: A review: Study of various techniques of hand gesture recognition. In: IEEE International Conference on Power Electronics, Intelligent Control and Energy Systems (ICPEICES), pp. 1–5, July 2016. https://doi.org/10.1109/ ICPEICES.2016.7853514
9. Krizhevsky, A., Sutskever, I., Hinton, G.E.: Imagenet classification with deep convolutional neural networks. In: Pereira, F., Burges, C.J.C., Bottou, L., Weinberger, K.Q. (eds.) Advances in Neural Information Processing Systems, vol. 25, pp. 1097–1105. Curran Associates, Inc. (2012)
10. Marra, A.R., et al.: The use of real-time feedback via wireless technology to improve hand hygiene compliance. Am. J. Infect. Control. **42**(6), 608–611 (2014). https:// doi.org/10.1016/j.ajic.2014.02.006
11. Sonkusare, J.S., Chopade, N.B., Sor, R., Tade, S.L.: A review on hand gesture recognition system. In: IEEE International Conference on Computing Communication Control and Automation, pp. 790–794, February 2015. https://doi.org/10. 1109/ICCUBEA.2015.158
12. Stilo, A., et al.: Hand washing in operating room: a procedural comparison. Epidemiol. Biostat. Public Health (2016)
13. Szilágyi, L., Lehotsky, A., Nagy, M., Haidegger, T., Benyó, B., Benyo, Z.: Steryhand: A new device to support hand disinfection. In: International Conference of the IEEE Engineering in Medicine and Biology, pp. 4756–4759, August 2010. https://doi.org/10.1109/IEMBS.2010.5626377
14. WHO: Surgical hand preparation: state-of-the-art. In: World Health Organization (ed.) WHO Guidelines on Hand Hygiene in Health Care: First Global Patient Safety Challenge Clean Care Is Safer Care, chap. 13, pp. 54–60. WHO, Genevra (2009), https://www.ncbi.nlm.nih.gov/books/NBK144036/
15. World Health Organization: WHO guidelines on hand hygiene in health care (2009)
16. Zhang, P., White, J., Schmidt, D., Dennis, T.: Applying machine learning methods to predict hand hygiene compliance characteristics. In: IEEE EMBS International Conference on Biomedical Health Informatics (BHI), pp. 353–356, February 2017. https://doi.org/10.1109/BHI.2017.7897278

Class-Conditional Data Augmentation Applied to Image Classification

Eduardo Aguilar[1,2(✉)] and Petia Radeva[2,3]

[1] Universidad Católica del Norte, Antofagasta, Chile
eaguilar02@ucn.cl
[2] Universitat de Barcelona, Barcelona, Spain
[3] Computer Vision Center, Bellaterra, Spain

Abstract. Image classification is widely researched in the literature, where models based on Convolutional Neural Networks (CNNs) have provided better results. When data is not enough, CNN models tend to be overfitted. To deal with this, often, traditional techniques of data augmentation are applied, such as: affine transformations, adjusting the color balance, among others. However, we argue that some techniques of data augmentation may be more appropriate for some of the classes. In order to select the techniques that work best for particular class, we propose to explore the epistemic uncertainty for the samples within each class. From our experiments, we can observe that when the data augmentation is applied class-conditionally, we improve the results in terms of accuracy and also reduce the overall epistemic uncertainty. To summarize, in this paper we propose a class-conditional data augmentation procedure that allows us to obtain better results and improve robustness of the classification in the face of model uncertainty.

Keywords: CNNs · Data augmentation · Deep learning ·
Epistemic uncertainty · Image classification · Food recognition

1 Introduction

Image classification has been an interesting topic for many years for the computer vision community. However, it was not until the arrival of Deep Convolutional Neural Networks (CNNs) that it was possible to tackle more difficult problems composed of images of a large number of different objects acquired in uncontrolled environments. Significant improvements in performance have been evidenced in the literature when we compare methods based on CNNs features with respect to using handcrafted image features. These improvements can be found in multiple contexts such as: object recognition [8], food image recognition [11], face recognition [15], among others. With the results achieved, CNNs seem to be a solution to solve most kinds of image analysis problems. However, CNN methods have an obstacle, they are prone to overfit when there is no enough data [5,10,14]. Instead of acquiring more data, that not always is possible, commonly

© Springer Nature Switzerland AG 2019
M. Vento and G. Percannella (Eds.): CAIP 2019, LNCS 11679, pp. 182–192, 2019.
https://doi.org/10.1007/978-3-030-29891-3_17

there are two types of regularization to avoid the overfitting: at the architecture level, for example through l_2 normalization [9], dropout [16], etc; and at data level, through data augmentation [8].

Data augmentation is called the process used during the training of the model that consists of applying image transformations to the original images with the aims to expanding data and its variability. The authors in [13], proposed that the techniques can be grouped as: traditional transformations [8], Generative Adversarial Networks [3,17] and texture transfer [4]. Specifically for the traditional transformations, as far as we know, they do not take into account that some techniques can be beneficial or detrimental to training, depending on the type of image that will be analyzed. For the latter, we propose to group these techniques in two groups: generic methods, those that apply geometric transformations to the images (eg. crops, reflection, zoom in, etc.), which are independent of the image class; and specific methods, those based on the pixel transforms of the images (eg. color, brightness, contrast, etc.), which are class-dependent. For example, in the context of food recognition adjusting the color balance could be counterproductive, when we have to learn the distinctive features of near classes as *white rice with brown rice* or *pumpkin soup with carrot or tomato soup*, among other.

Understanding the model uncertainty could be useful in determining which dependent methods of data augmentation are most appropriate to apply to the target image. There are two main types of uncertainty that can be modeled: Aleatoric Uncertainty, which captures noise inherent in the observation; and Epistemic Uncertainty, that captures the ignorance about which model generated the collected data [7]. Keep in mind that, in the case of Epistemic Uncertainty, we can reduce it given enough data. The fact of how this uncertainty is reduced, suggests that if we observe the variation of Epistemic Uncertainty for the samples of a particular class when we change data augmentation strategies, we could determine which method is likely to be beneficial for each class.

From the image classification side, in our work we validate our proposed method in two public datasets built to deal with the food recognition problem [2,6]. We focus on food recognition, since, to difference with other visual analysis problems, the high inter-class similarity and intra-class variability of the food classes [1,12], in addition of the small numbers of images available in the majority public datasets, makes this a challenging problem that could leverage by a correct data augmentation process.

Our main contributions in this paper are as follows:

1. We provide an epistemic uncertainty-based method, which allows incorporating additional image processing techniques, chosen according to the class in which the input images belong, to the traditional data augmentation process.
2. We demonstrate that it is possible to achieve better results when we add to the data augmentation process the chosen image enhancement strategies by the class which the image belongs to, instead of using the same process indistinctly for all images.
3. We present the Normalized Epistemic Uncertainty (NEU) metric that allows better analysis of the behavior of the model in terms of its stability.

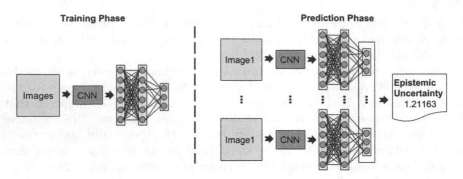

Fig. 1. The scheme of the proposed method: in both phases, the dropout must remain turned up. Note that, during the prediction phase, the same image is fed to the CNN several times to calculate the epistemic uncertainty given by the model for that image.

The remainder of this paper is organized as follows: first, in Sect. 2, we present the proposed method; second, in the Sect. 3, we present the datasets, the experimental setup and discuss the results; finally, in Sect. 4, we describe the conclusions.

2   Proposed Method

In this section, we explain each step involved in the proposed approach, which takes advantage of the epistemic uncertainty intrinsic in the data to determine the type of data augmentation process applying to the images during the training of the model.

2.1   Model Setup

The architecture used in our proposed approach is based on CNNs. At the top of the network, the output of the last convolution layer is flattened. Then, it is necessary to add a dropout layer after each hidden fully connected layer so that we are able to apply the Monte Carlo dropout (MC-dropout) sampling [7] to calculate the epistemic uncertainty. Finally, it is ended up with an output layer with softmax activation and neurons equal to the number of classes (see Fig. 1).

2.2   Class Epistemic Uncertainty

Once the model is trained, the next step is to determine the Epistemic uncertainty. This uncertainty can be obtained by applying MC-dropout sampling. In practical terms, it means to predict K times the same image using the model with the dropout layer turned on. Then, the Epistemic uncertainty will correspond to the predictive entropy calculated from the K predictions given.

Formally, the Epistemic Uncertainty (EU) can be expressed as follows:

Let $\overline{p(y_c = \hat{y}_c | x)}$ be the average probability that the prediction y_c is equal to ground-truth $\hat{y}_c$ given the image x, calculated from K MC-dropouts simulations. Then,

$$EU(x_t) = - \sum_{c=1}^{C} \overline{p(y_c = \hat{y}_c | x_t)} \ln(\overline{p(y_c = \hat{y}_c | x_t)}), \qquad (1)$$

where

$$\overline{p(y_c = \hat{y}_c | x)} = \frac{1}{K} \sum_{k=1}^{K} p(y_c^k = \hat{y}_c^k | x). \qquad (2)$$

As we discussed earlier, our intention is to determine, through the EU, which data augmentation technique is most appropriate for the images of a particular class. By definition, the EU tends to reduce when we increase the samples in the dataset. So, if we are able to reduce the EU for some classes, when we incorporate specific data augmentation techniques, it is likely that these techniques contribute to the learning of these classes. Therefore, in our case, it is interesting for us to know the average EU considering all the samples within each class, we will name it as Class Epistemic Uncertainty (CEU). In the proposed method, CEU is used to compare between a model trained with generic data augmentation techniques (eg. random crops and horizontal flips) with other models that incorporate the specific data augmentation techniques to the generic one. Then, we consider that the specific technique is appropriate for a class when the model trained with this technique incorporated in the data augmentation process obtains the lowest CEU value.

2.3   Class-Conditional Data Augmentation

The criterion contemplates in the proposed method how to determine the specific techniques of data augmentation for each class as following (see Fig. 2):

1. A model that considers generic data augmentation technique (GDA-model) is trained with the aim of being compared with the models that also incorporate a specific data augmentation technique.
2. A model is trained for each specific data augmentation technique (SDA-model) that we would like to incorporate into the process. Each model adds only a specific technique to the generic one, which will be used during the training.
3. The best model is chosen with respect to the accuracy obtained in the validation set for the models trained in steps 1 and 2.
4. CEU is computed for all models in step 3.
5. With the results in step 4, the GDA-model is compared with the SDA-model. To those classes in which the SDA-model obtains a lower CEU than the GDA-model, we assign them the respective specific technique used by that SDA-model.

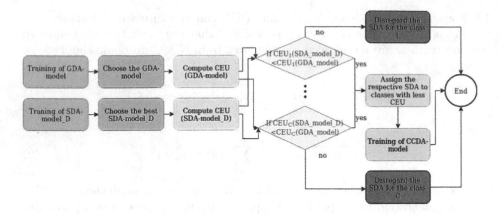

Fig. 2. Flowchart of the proposed class-conditional data augmentation (CCDA) procedure. SDA_model_D denotes the model which incorporate the Dth specific data augmentation technique (eg. color, contrast) into the generic data augmentation process.

6. Finally, considering the specific techniques selected for each class from step 5, we train a new model using data augmentation with generic techniques for all classes and also the selected one for each class.

3   Experiments

In this section, we first present the datasets used, second we describe the evaluation measures, third we present the experimental setup and last we describe the results obtained with our proposed approach.

3.1   Datasets

The two public datasets chosen to validate our hypothesis are described below.

Food-101. This is an international food dataset which contains the top 101 most popular food plates [2]. For each dish, the dataset provides of $1,000$ images collected from foodspotting.com. The distribution of the dataset given by the authors is of 75% for training and the remaining 25% for testing. In our case, we keep the same data for the test set, but we divide the train set leaving 90% for training and 10% for validation.

UECFOOD-256. This is a food image dataset, containing 256 dishes and $31,395$ images [6]. The dataset mainly includes Japanese dishes, but also consists of foods from several countries such as China, France, Indonesia, Italy, Thailand, United States and Vietnam. Each image has annotations for the type of dish and also the bounding box information where the dish is located. In addition, the authors provide a 5-fold cross validation annotations that include 28, 280 images, with a minimum, maximum and average of images per class of 87, 637 and 110.47. In our case, we used the first fold for the test and, from the remaining four folds, we randomly selected about 90% for training and 10% for validation. Note that, the object (food) bounding box information is not used in our experiments.

3.2   Metrics

In order to evaluate the performance of our approach, we used the overall Accuracy (Acc), which is a standard metric for object recognition, and additionally we check the Mean Epistemic Uncertainty. Note that, the maximum value of the latter depends on the numbers of classes, and for this reason we normalized it leaving the possible values between zero to one, which we call Normalized Epistemic Uncertainty (NEU). Both metrics are formally defined as follows:

$$Acc = \frac{1}{T} \sum_{c=1}^{C} TP_c, \tag{3}$$

where C is the number of classes, TP_c (True Positives) is the amount of images belonging to the class c classified correctly, and T is the total images evaluated.

$$NEU = \frac{1}{T} \sum_{t=1}^{T} \frac{EU(x_t)}{\ln(C) - \ln(1)}, \tag{4}$$

where $\ln(C) - \ln(1)$ corresponds to the normalization factor obtained when the average prediction for each class is equal to a random prediction.

3.3   Experimental Setup

We trained end-to-end a CNN architecture (see Fig. 1), based on ResNet-50 [5], using the categorical cross-entropy loss optimized with Adam. We modified this neural network by removing the output layer, and instead, we added one hidden fully connected layer of 2048 neurons, followed by a dropout layer with a probability of 0.5, and we ended up with an output layer with softmax activation and neurons equal to the number of classes of the respective dataset. In total, eight models were trained for each dataset based on the same architecture, but changing the data augmentation applied. The models are the following:

1. *ResNet50:* CNN Model trained without applying data augmentation.
2. *ResNet50+DA:* CNN model with the traditional randoms crops and horizontal flips strategies to data augmentation.
3. *ResNet50+DA+B:* The base is ResNet50+DA with the incorporation of a random adjustment of the image brightness in the data augmentation process.
4. *ResNet50+DA+CN:* The base is ResNet50+DA with the incorporation of a random adjustment of the image contrast in the data augmentation process.

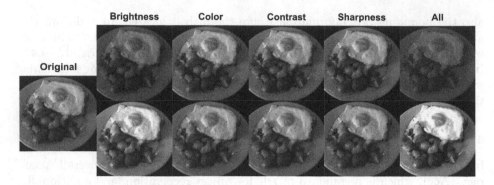

Fig. 3. An example of the resulting image when we apply the minimal (top) and maximal (bottom) values used in the experimentation for each strategy corresponding to the image enhancement methods.

5. *ResNet50+DA+CL:* The base is ResNet50+DA with the incorporation of a random adjustment of the image color in the data augmentation process.
6. *ResNet50+DA+S:* The base is ResNet50+DA with the incorporation of a random adjustment of the image sharpness in the data augmentation process.
7. *ResNet50+DA+A:* The base is ResNet50+DA with the incorporation of a random adjustment of the all image enhancement strategies (brightness, contrast, color, and sharpness) to the images in the data augmentation process.
8. *Proposed method:* The base is ResNet50+DA with the incorporation of a random adjustment of image enhancement strategies in the data augmentation process, which are selected according to the image class. Note that, in some cases, all or none of the strategies could be applied.

All models were re-trained, from a pre-trained model on ILSVRC dataset [8], during 50 epochs with a batch size of 16, and an initial learning rate of $2e-4$. In addition, we applied a decay of 0.2 every 8 epochs. The training was done using Keras with Tensorflow as backend.

Regarding the data augmentation process, for models 2 to 8, the original image is re-sized to (256,256) and then randoms crops with a size of (224,224) and horizontal flip with a 50% probability are applied. In the case of models 3 to 8, in addition, we apply image enhancement methods available from the image processing library PIL. With the aim that the application of specific techniques of data augmentation do not drastically affect the information contained in an image, we empirically select a range of values between 0.75 and 1.25 for all methods, where the value applied in the images will be obtained randomly in each iteration. Notice that a value equal to 1 means obtaining the same image. On the other hand, a value equal to 0 is obtained for the brightness, the color, the contrast or the sharpness, that is to obtain a black, black and white, solid gray or blurred image, respectively. Therefore, a factor less than 1 means, for example, less color and vice versa. Examples of the resulting images with the minimal and maximal value can be seen in the Fig. 3.

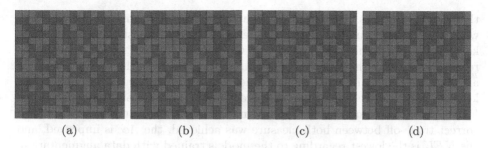

(a)   (b)   (c)   (d)

Fig. 4. From left to right: classes selected of UECFOOD-256 to apply adjustment of: (a) brightness, (b) color, (c) contrast and (d) sharpness. The class identifier (c_{id}) can be obtained for the formula: $c_{id} = 16 * col + row$, where the first position (upper-left corner) corresponds to $(row, col) = (0, 0)$. (Color figure online)

3.4   Results

In this section, we present the results obtained by the models in the datasets Food-101 and UECFOOD-256.

As we explained in Sect. 2, to train our proposed approach, we must first select the specific data augmentation (SDA) techniques that will be applied to each image taking into account the class to which the image belongs. For this purpose, we trained five models, one used as reference (ResNet50+DA) and other four models which incorporate one SDA technique each one (ResNet50+DA+B, ResNet50+DA+CN, ResNet50+CL and ResNet50+S). Once the models have been trained, we calculate the epistemic uncertainty of the samples contained in the validation sets. Then, we average the epistemic uncertainty of the samples within the same class (CEU). After that, we compared the CEU of the ResNet50+DA model with respect to the rest of the models for each class. If at least one of models have a CEU smaller than the reference model, we consider that the enhanced method incorporated in these models is likely to benefit the learning of this class. The results obtained by applying this procedure can be seen in Fig. 4. In this figure, we show in red color the SDA techniques selected for each class in the UECFOOD-256 datasets. For example: in case that images belong to the $c_{id} = 0$, we obtain that we must to adjust randomly the brightness, the color, the contrast and the sharpness; for the images belongs to $c_{id} = 15$, brightness and contrast; and so on.

Regarding the results during the test phase, these can be seen, in terms of *Acc* (with dropout turned down) and *NEU* (with dropout turned up), in Table 1 and Table 2 for the Food-101 and UECFOOD-256 datasets respectively. As one might expect, the lowest performance in terms of *Acc* was achieved in both datasets, when we trained the model without data augmentation (ResNet50). Despite this, it is interesting to highlight that this model has the best result in terms of *NEU*. Note that *NEU* is calculated from the predictive entropy, so, in essence, a high value also implies a high entropy and, consequently, the model is more prone to change the prediction when there are perturbations in the data that produces a loss of some discriminative feature. For this reason, a model with low NEU means that the model remains stable against the perturbation, keeping the good and bad predictions. On the other hand, when analyze the results obtained with ResNet50+DA+A, we can see that the incorporation of all SDA techniques into the data augmentation process negatively affects the learning of our model, reducing the correct prediction rate and model stability. Finally, when we compare our proposed method with the rest, we can see that a correct trade-off between both measure was achieved, the Acc is improved, and the NEU is the lowest regarding to the models trained with data augmentation.

Table 1. Results on Food-101 in terms of Acc and NEU for the models trained with different data augmentation techniques. For NEU, less is better.

Model	Acc	NEU
ResNet50	77.66%	19.85%
ResNet50+DA	82.65%	27.35%
ResNet50+DA+A	82.54%	29.45%
Proposed method	82.82%	26.25%

Table 2. Results on UECFOOD-256 in terms of Acc and NEU for the models trained with different data augmentation techniques. For NEU, less is better.

Model	Acc	NEU
ResNet50	61.00%	30.22%
ResNet50+DA	65.02%	33.55%
ResNet50+DA+A	64.65%	36.53%
Proposed method	65.54%	33,51%

4   Conclusions

In this paper, we proposed a method to perform class-conditional data augmentation based on epistemic uncertainty estimation. In our method, we differentiate the traditional data augmentation in two type, where one of them depends on the class of the image. For the latter, the techniques to be used are selected by the analysis of the epistemic uncertainty for each class of the same model trained with different data augmentation strategies. Note that the selection process can be considered computationally expensive. However, the cost involved in this process is only present in the training time. Therefore, it does not harm the model performance during the prediction regarding the use of resources computational or response time. From the results obtained, we observed that the proposed approach outperforms the results with respect to the rest of the model evaluated without affecting its stability. As a conclusion, we have shown that it is beneficial for model learning to incorporate specific data augmentation techniques taken into account the class to which the image belongs. As future work, we will explore the application of epistemic uncertainty to several problems such as, the outlier detection and the classifier selection.

Acknowledgement. This work was partially funded by TIN2015-66951-C2-1-R, 2017 SGR 1742, Nestore, Validithi, 20141510 (La MaratoTV3) and CERCA Programme/Generalitat de Catalunya. E. Aguilar acknowledges the support of CONICYT Becas Chile. P. Radeva is partially supported by ICREA Academia 2014. We acknowledge the support of NVIDIA Corporation with the donation of Titan Xp GPUs.

References

1. Aguilar, E., Bolaños, M., Radeva, P.: Regularized uncertainty-based multi-task learning model for food analysis. J. Vis. Commun. Image Represent. **60**, 360–370 (2019)
2. Bossard, L., Guillaumin, M., Van Gool, L.: Food-101 – mining discriminative components with random forests. In: Fleet, D., Pajdla, T., Schiele, B., Tuytelaars, T. (eds.) ECCV 2014. LNCS, vol. 8694, pp. 446–461. Springer, Cham (2014). https://doi.org/10.1007/978-3-319-10599-4_29
3. Frid-Adar, M., Klang, E., Amitai, M., Goldberger, J., Greenspan, H.: Synthetic data augmentation using GAN for improved liver lesion classification. In: 2018 IEEE 15th International Symposium on Biomedical Imaging, ISBI 2018, pp. 289–293. IEEE (2018)
4. Gatys, L.A., Ecker, A.S., Bethge, M.: Image style transfer using convolutional neural networks. In: Proceedings of the IEEE Conference on Computer Vision and Pattern Recognition, pp. 2414–2423 (2016)
5. He, K., Zhang, X., Ren, S., Sun, J.: Deep residual learning for image recognition. In: Proceedings of the IEEE Conference on Computer Vision and Pattern Recognition, pp. 770–778 (2016)
6. Kawano, Y., Yanai, K.: Automatic expansion of a food image dataset leveraging existing categories with domain adaptation. In: Agapito, L., Bronstein, M.M., Rother, C. (eds.) ECCV 2014. LNCS, vol. 8927, pp. 3–17. Springer, Cham (2015). https://doi.org/10.1007/978-3-319-16199-0_1
7. Kendall, A., Gal, Y.: What uncertainties do we need in Bayesian deep learning for computer vision? In: Advances in Neural Information Processing Systems, pp. 5574–5584 (2017)
8. Krizhevsky, A., Sutskever, I., Hinton, G.E.: ImageNet classification with deep convolutional neural networks. In: Advances in Neural Information Processing Systems, pp. 1097–1105 (2012)
9. Krogh, A., Hertz, J.A.: A simple weight decay can improve generalization. In: Advances in Neural Information Processing Systems, pp. 950–957 (1992)
10. Liu, S., Deng, W.: Very deep convolutional neural network based image classification using small training sample size. In: 2015 3rd IAPR Asian Conference on Pattern Recognition (ACPR), pp. 730–734. IEEE (2015)
11. Martinel, N., Foresti, G.L., Micheloni, C.: Wide-slice residual networks for food recognition. In: 2018 IEEE Winter Conference on Applications of Computer Vision (WACV), pp. 567–576. IEEE (2018)

12. Mezgec, S., Koroušić Seljak, B.: NutriNet: a deep learning food and drink image recognition system for dietary assessment. Nutrients **9**(7), 657 (2017)
13. Mikołajczyk, A., Grochowski, M.: Data augmentation for improving deep learning in image classification problem. In: 2018 International Interdisciplinary PhD Workshop (IIPhDW), pp. 117–122. IEEE (2018)
14. Ng, H.W., Nguyen, V.D., Vonikakis, V., Winkler, S.: Deep learning for emotion recognition on small datasets using transfer learning. In: Proceedings of the 2015 ACM on International Conference on Multimodal Interaction, pp. 443–449. ACM (2015)
15. Parkhi, O.M., Vedaldi, A., Zisserman, A., et al.: Deep face recognition. In: bmvc, vol. 1, p. 6 (2015)
16. Srivastava, N., Hinton, G., Krizhevsky, A., Sutskever, I., Salakhutdinov, R.: Dropout: a simple way to prevent neural networks from overfitting. J. Mach. Learn. Res. **15**(1), 1929–1958 (2014)
17. Zhang, H., et al.: Stackgan: text to photo-realistic image synthesis with stacked generative adversarial networks. In: Proceedings of the IEEE International Conference on Computer Vision, pp. 5907–5915 (2017)

Fabric Classification and Matching Using CNN and Siamese Network for E-commerce

Chandrakant Sonawane[✉], Dipendra Pratap Singh, Raghav Sharma,
Aditya Nigam, and Arnav Bhavsar

SCEE, Indian Institute of Technology Mandi, Mandi 175005, India
{t17140,t17132}@students.iitmandi.ac.in,
pratap_singh@projects.iitmandi.ac.in,
{aditya,arnav}@iitmandi.ac.in

Abstract. According to the Google-Kearney study (May 2016), the fashion industry in India has a tremendous scope and can easily surpass the electronic consumer product sector as early as 2020. However, the apparel sector faces a major limitation on the part of the subjectivity in judging the fabric quality. There is no doubt that the e-commerce industry can earn the highest rate of return from the apparel sector; still, its popularity often got limited. Any person purchasing apparel always first like to touch the fabric to get a 'feel' of the fabric and its texture to compare it with the mental/latent representation of other fabrics to assess the quality or equivalence. Though the 'feel' of any fabric texture cannot be physically quantified, the latent representation of fabric texture can be extracted and compared using Autoencoders and Siamese networks respectively. In this paper, we have utilized an inexpensive (less than 5% frugal cellular microscope for the data collection in contrast to any expensive fabric texture scanners. We have utilized Convolutional Neural Networks based Autoencoders and Siamese network for classification, clustering, and matching of similar fabric textures. We have shown that even with frugal data collection methods, the proposed CNN classifiers using the latent feature representation of fabric texture gives a higher accuracy of 98.40% for fabric texture classification.

Keywords: Fabric texture · Classification · Matching ·
Siamese network · CNN autoencoder · t-SNE · K-Means clustering

1 Introduction

In the textile industry, the classification of fabrics is usually manually done which requires a long time and considerable human efforts. With the rapid development of computer vision techniques, the automatic and efficient methods for fabric classification are highly desired. To predict the fabric class, the texture of that fabric is the best way for representation. In fabric texture classification, main challenges are varying lightening conditions, occlusion, rotation, etc.

© Springer Nature Switzerland AG 2019
M. Vento and G. Percannella (Eds.): CAIP 2019, LNCS 11679, pp. 193–205, 2019.
https://doi.org/10.1007/978-3-030-29891-3_18

which occur at the time of scanning the texture. Currently, texture identification is done using statistical and transform based methods. Examples are Gray-Level Co-occurrence Matrix (GLCM) [1] and Fast Fourier Transforms [2,3], Gabor filter and Wavelets transform methods respectively are used for texture identification with 90% identification accuracy. These methods perform well over simple and repetitive textures but give high classification errors over complex fabric textures. In general, at the time of fabric scanning, people use high-quality scanners whereas in this work we have replaced these costly scanners with a frugal cellular microscope and with the help of CNN feature representations we get comparable or better results. In this paper, we are utilizing a frugal cellular microscope for scanning of fabrics and applying the Convolutional Neural Networks (CNN) [4] for texture classification and matching to get better results which are based on more robust techniques of data collection.

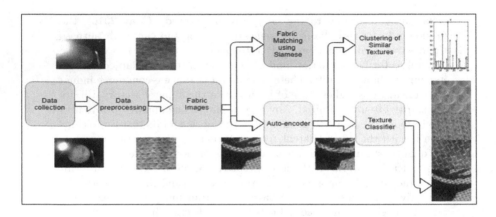

Fig. 1. Overall scope of this paper.

1.1 Motivation

In this online shopping era, E-commerce businesses' [5–7] growth is on it's peak. There are so many companies that are providing the facilities to choose the product based on the aspects of the specification, feature, brand, price, usage of items, etc. In particular, the consumer chooses garments by looking at its apparent/visual texture, color, brand, design, price, etc. but there is no way by which the consumer can predict the quality of the fabric by just looking at images. Also, the consumer cannot compare the similar type of textures of different brands for price evaluation. Dissatisfaction with the fabric quality is one of the major reasons for clothing returns that are around (40%) [8] for the e-commerce sector, others being fabric color and fitting issues. Thus, in this work, we address the problem of finding the solution to four basic user-generated queries. Queries are as follows:

– **Query 1:** Given a sample texture, a user wants similar textured fabrics.

- **Query 2:** A user wants to know the similarity between two fabric textures.
- **Query 3:** Given a fabric, a user wants to know the fabric of exactly the same texture.
- **Query 4:** A user wants to know all available fabric textures in the database.

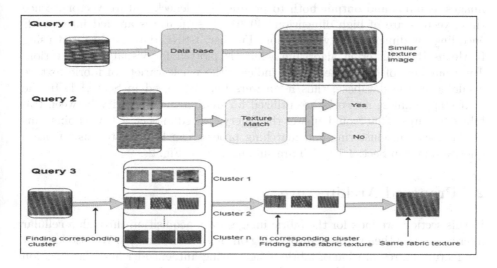

Fig. 2. Proposed solutions to user generated queries.

In addition to these addressed problems, we achieve the fast, automatic and reliable solution which can increase its utility for the E-commerce platform.

1.2   Related Work

In the field of texture identification, Ravandi *et al.* in [3] used Fourier transform method to identify the fabric structure with 90% accuracy, but it failed in identifying similar texture fabrics. In [1] and [9], authors have used gray-level co-occurrence matrix (GLCM) for identification of fabric texture with warp and weft floats. However poor identification of warp and weft floats especially in knitted fabric leads to a high classification error rate.

Recently, people have started deep learning techniques to study fabric textures. Since we could not find a good number of works based on deep learning we are mentioning a few works. In [10], Babar Khan *et al.* used deep Extreme Learning Model (ELM) with classification accuracy 97.5%. In all the works as mentioned above, people were using only classification techniques, but our work is different as we are applying to cluster for similar textures and finding the similarity between two textures along with classification.

1.3   Contribution

We have collected the data of one hundred twenty-three different fabric types using the cellphone-based microscope (Fig. 1). Classification of fabric textures is done using Convolutional Neural Networks (CNN) classifiers that have shown 98.40% of accuracy on our test dataset. An Autoencoder is trained using fabric images as input and output both to produce bottleneck feature vectors. Since these vectors are of high dimension (4096), these features are fed into t-SNE encoding for dimensionality reduction. Further, t-SNE data is clustered using K-Means [11] clustering algorithm which is plotted for visual interpretation. Total numbers of the cluster would indicate the whole variety of fabric texture available in the database; thus it answers Query4 raised in Sect. 1.1. In the next step, Siamese networks are utilized for finding the similarity between two fabric textures. That would answer the Query2 raised in Sect. 1.1. Combinations of classification, clustering and matching process can be used to answer other queries raised in Sect. 1.1 which are summarized in Fig. 2.

2   Proposed Architecture

In this section, we look for the fabric images data acquisition through a cellular microscope and then we do preprocessing on those fabric images. We also look for the feature representation of fabric images using autoencoder and classification of those images using a K-means clustering algorithm. Later in this section, we look for the similarity between fabric images through a siamese network.

2.1   Data Acquisition and Preprocessing

To train the CNN, we need a large amount of images data to estimate its huge number of parameters. To fulfill this need, we have collected the data using a cellular phone microscope (Fig. 3). This device is 30X Zoom LED Magnifier which is used to capture the microscopic view of fabric texture providing sufficiently fine details of any fabric. At the time of data collection, this device is mounted on Samsung Galaxy J7 (Fig. 4) prime mobile phone to collect the texture images of the variety of fabrics.

Fig. 3. Cellular microscope.   **Fig. 4.** Microscope mounted on mobile's camera.

Fig. 5. Images of fabric taken by a cellular phone microscope above and processed images data used to train CNN below.

These images can not be used directly to train the CNN as it contains fabric texture along with a cellular phone microscope boundary, lance light effect, and additional black background. To train the CNN, we need only fabric texture images and to obtain this we have applied the image processing techniques to extract the fabric texture from cellular microscope images. The process is explained in Algorithm 1.

Algorithm 1. Algorithm for Preprocessing

Require: Image I of size $m \times m$
Ensure: Cropped ROI image I_{ROI}, of size $n \times n$ where $n < m$
1: Convert I_{RGB} into I_{gray} using color channels merge
2: Detecting the edges in I_{gray}
3: Finding center(x, y) of isolated objects using Hough transform [12]
4: Finding radius r of circle region as isolated objects using Hough transform [12]
5: Extracting the squared region as I_{ROI} with center(x, y) and sides $n \times n$ where n is $r \times \sqrt{2}$

After applying Algorithm 1 on unprocessed images data, we get processed texture images data as shown in Fig. 5.

2.2 Feature Representation and Classification

Our first goal is to classify fabric images as well as clustering images with similar textures. The main challenges for this task are the unavailability of labeled training data and the high dimensionality of data. To overcome unavailability and to avoid handling of high dimensional training data we use unsupervised learning. To do this, an Autoencoder is trained to capture generative representative features. Autoencoder has two parts-Encoder and Decoder as shown in Table 1.

Encoder contains 24 layers convolution, batch normalization, and max-pooling layers. Encoder learns to extract the most informative features from the input image such that the decoder gets the original image back given the encoded feature. In this pair, the decoder part contains 22 layers involving convolution, batch normalization, and up-sampling layers.

Table 1. Autoencoder Architecture

Type of layer	Filter size	No. of filters	Output	Parameters
Encoder layers				
Conv2D	(7,7)	16	(128, 128, 16)	800
Max Pooling			(64, 64, 16)	0
Conv2D	(3,3)	32	(64, 64, 32)	4640
Conv2D	(3,3)	32	(64, 64, 32)	9248
MaxPooling			(32, 32, 32)	0
Conv2D	(3,3)	64	(32, 32, 64)	18496
Conv2D	(3,3)	64	(32, 32, 64)	36928
MaxPooling			(16, 16, 64)	0
Conv2D	(3,3)	128	(16, 16, 128)	73856
Conv2D	(3,3)	128	(16, 16, 128)	147584
MaxPooling			(8, 8, 128)	0
Conv2D	(3,3)	256	(8, 8, 256)	295168
Conv2D	(3,3)	256	(8, 8, 256)	590080
Conv2D	(3,3)	512	(8, 8, 512)	
Bottleneck feature vector				
Conv2D	(1,1)	64	(8, 8, 64)	32832
Decoder layers				
UpSampling			(16, 16, 64)	0
Conv2D	(3,3)	128	(16, 16, 128)	73856
Conv2D	(3,3)	128	(16, 16, 128)	147584
UpSampling			(32, 32, 128)	0
Conv2D	(3,3)	64	(32, 32, 64)	73792
Conv2D	(3,3)	64	(32, 32, 64)	36928
UpSampling			(64, 64, 64)	0
Conv2D	(3,3)	128	(64, 64, 32)	18464
Conv2D	(3,3)	128	(64, 64, 32)	9248
UpSampling			(128, 128, 32)	0
Conv2D	(3,3)	16	(128, 128, 16)	4624
Conv2D	(3,3)	16	(128, 128, 16)	2320
Conv2D	(7,7)	1	(128, 128, 1)	785

CNN Texture Classifier. With the help of this Autoencoder, the best possible generative feature representation is extracted which is used further in the classification procedure. It is observed here that instead of discriminative feature we have used the generative feature by which we have found a significant gain in the accuracy. While training in the Autoencoder pair both encoder and decoder were present. Whereas at the time of testing we have removed the decoder part, making the prediction with the encoder part only. To predict the class of a given test image, first, we obtain the encoded feature vector then fed into fully connected layers. In the last step, using a softmax layer, we give the class label. Classifier architecture is shown in Fig. 6.

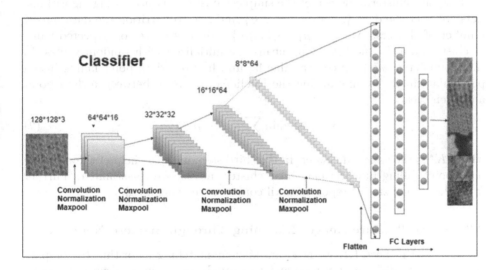

Fig. 6. Classifier architecture.

Clustering of Similar Textures. Apart from the classification of fabrics, the next goal of this work is to provide a range of similar textured fabrics when a customer is looking for fabrics of a particular texture. To perform this task, we must have some groups of fabrics based on their similar textures. To generate these types of groups, clustering of the similar fabric texture images is required which gives a limited set of clusters. At the time of clustering of high dimensional encoded feature vectors, we use t-SNE [13] and K-means clustering algorithm for dimensionality reduction and clustering, respectively.

t-distributed Stochastic Neighbor Embedding (t-SNE) algorithm [13] maps high dimensional data into its low dimensional representation while maintaining the distance proportion between any two points. In the first step, the algorithm converts euclidean distances between two points into the conditional probability of similarities between points in the high dimensional dimension. In the next step, the algorithm calculates pairwise affinities in the low dimension space. In the third step, the difference (Kullback–Leibler divergence) between conditional probabilities of high dimensional and low dimensional is minimized using a gradient descent method. The cost function (D) would be:

$$D = KL(P||Q) = \sum_i \sum_j p_{ij} log \frac{q_{ij}}{p_{ij}} \tag{1}$$

where $KL(P||Q)$ is Kullback–Leibler divergence between high dimensional space (P) and low dimensional space (Q). p_{ij} is the joint conditional probabilities of similarity between point i and point j in high dimensional space and q_{ij} is the joint conditional probabilities of similarities between point i and point j in low dimensional space.

K-Means clustering is one of the simplest unsupervised learning algorithms. Lets consider the data $\{x_1, x_2, x_3 \ldots \ldots x_N\}$ and aim to partition the data into K number of clusters. 'Means' $\{\mu_1, \mu_2, \ldots \ldots \mu_k\}$ indicates center or expected value of cluster data. In the first step, means are initialized with random values. In the second step, we keep center value fix and find out data point falling into a particular cluster by minimizing the Euclidean distance between a data point and their means.

$$K^* = \underset{k}{\operatorname{argmin}} \sum_{n=1}^{N} ||x_n - \mu_K||^2 \tag{2}$$

where K^* is the assigned cluster. In the third step, with the help of these cluster data point falling into the particular cluster, means are re-estimated. Further from the second step is repeated until convergence is achieved.

2.3   Fabric Texture Images Matching Through Siamese Network

As discussed in Sect. 1.1, we need an efficient matching algorithm to compare two fabrics of different textures and to provide fabric images with the same texture given a particular fabric texture. To accomplish this task, we use the siamese network as this network gives a similarity measure between two input images. To train the siamese network for a variety of image pairs, we provide two images coming from the same class *i.e.* the collection of images of the same fabric as a correct pair and two images from different classes as an incorrect pair. We have generated two different networks, first with contrastive loss and second with triplet loss, where the second network performs better than first.

Loss Function. Siamese network uses a shared CNN network to produce encodings $f(x_a)$, $f(x_p)$, $f(x_n)$ of Anchor Image (x_a), Positive Image (x_p) and Negative Image (x_n), respectively (Fig. 7). Encodings are merged such that the $L2$ Euclidean distance between Anchor encoding $(f(x_a))$ and Positive encoding $(f(x_p))$ is less than Anchor encoding $(f(x_a))$ and Negative encoding $(f(x_n))$.

$$||f(x_a) - f(x_p)||^2 - ||f(x_a) - f(x_n)||^2 \geq \alpha \tag{3}$$

where α as a regularizer is used so that distances between encodings should not become zero while training the network.

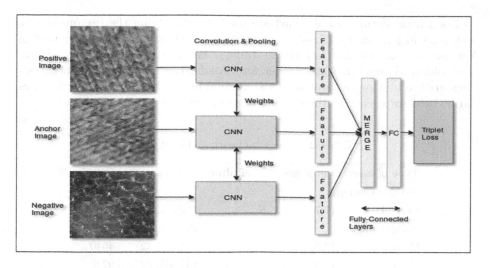

Fig. 7. Siamese network for image matching.

Triplet loss function can be defined as below:

$$L_{triplet}(x_a, x_p, x_n) = max(0, \alpha + ||f(x_a) - f(x_p)||^2 - ||f(x_a) - f(x_n)||^2) \quad (4)$$

If $\alpha + ||f(x_a) - f(x_p)||^2 - ||f(x_a) - f(x_n)||^2$ is less than zero, then $L_{triplet}(x_a, x_p, x_n)$ would be zero. However, if $\alpha + ||f(x_a) - f(x_p)||^2 - ||f(x_a) - f(x_n)||^2$ is greater than zero, then $L_{triplet}(x_a, x_p, x_n)$ would take that loss into consideration and try to reduce the overall loss.

3   Experimentation and Discussion

For experimental analysis, we have collected a dataset comprising of 123 types of fabrics having varied textures and colors. Images are resized to 128 pixels height and width after extracting images with Hough transformation. Images are subject to data augmentation techniques in which images were rotated with 10°. After doing the above mentioned pre-processing, images are fed into the CNN based Autoencoder whose architecture is given in Table 1. The aim of the Autoencoder, is to produce compact representative encoding but with the best generative features. Thus in the encoder part, we have allowed the model to expand till 512 layers of depth to increase the discrimination capacity of the network. We have reduced the dimension of feature vectors by applying a convolving filter of dimension $(1, 1)$ and applied 64 times to get the compact bottleneck encoding. We have built our models using Keras (1.0.0) and trained our model on Nvidia GeForce $GTX1080$ graphics card. We have used 'mean squared error' as our loss function and RMSprop as gradient descent with learning rate 0.001.

Bottleneck features so obtained are used for classifying the texture images with a 98.40% accuracy. Classifier network is based upon the Encoder part of Autoencoder Architecture is given in Table 1. We have selected bottleneck features obtained through Autoencoder for classification because bottleneck features are the best representative of the original image. Such bottleneck features can be used to regenerate the original image using the decoder (Table 2).

Table 2. Siamese network architecture

Type of layer	Filter size	No. of filters	Output	Details
Feature extraction				
Conv2D	(7,7)	16	(128, 128, 16)	800
Maxpooling2d			(64, 64, 16)	0
Conv2D	(3,3)	16	(64, 64, 32)	4640
Conv2D	(3,3)	16	(64, 64, 32)	9248
Maxpooling2d			(32, 32, 32)	0
Conv2D	(3,3)	64	(32, 32, 64)	18496
Conv2D	(3,3)	64	(32, 32, 64)	36928
Maxpooling2d			(16, 16, 64)	0
Conv2D	(3,3)	128	(16, 16, 128)	73856
Conv2D	(3,3)	128	(16, 16, 128)	147584
Maxpooling2d			(8, 8, 128)	0
Conv2D	(3,3)	256	(8, 8, 256)	295168
Conv2D	(3,3)	256	(8, 8, 256)	590080
Merging of features				
Flatten			16384	
Merge			16384	
Dropout				0.3
Dense			100	
Dropout				0.3
Dense			1	

Since the dimension of the bottleneck feature is quite high, thus we have used t-SNE encoding for dimension reduction from 4096 dimensional embedding to 2. After that, we have used K-means clustering on this to cluster similar texture fabrics together. Figure 8 shows the cluster signatures for each type of fabric texture. As shown in Fig. 8, fabric textures of Fig. 8(b_2) and (e_2) are similar, that is why they are converging into the same cluster no. 9 in our experiment which is shown in cluster graphs of Fig. 8(b_1) and (e_1) respectively. Similarly, textures of Fig. 8(c_2) and (d_2) also converged in the cluster no. 8.

Figure 9 shows the cluster composition of 10 clusters for 49 types of fabric textures. It shows the degree of similarity among fabric textures. Each cluster forms one true type of fabric texture. Thus the user can select the fabric from anyone cluster which would give fabrics of having similar textures. For fabric texture matching, we have implemented a Siamese network using both Contrastive and Triplet losses as shown in Eq. 4. During experimentation, We have observed Siamese network performed better with Triplet loss in comparison to Contrastive loss.

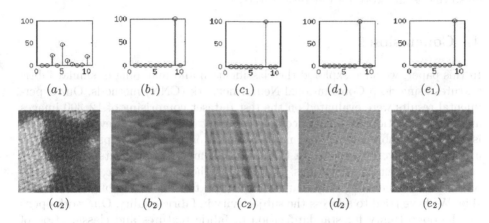

Fig. 8. Above is cluster signature of texture classes and below is sample image from that corresponding texture class.

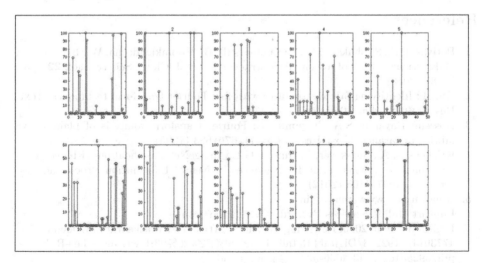

Fig. 9. Clustering of similar fabric texture images.

3.1   Failure Case Analysis

Our clustering experiment performs quite well in almost all the fabrics. However, our model shows its limitation over the fabrics in which color patterns of the fabric form the intrinsic feature of the fabric texture as shown in Fig. 8(a_2) and in case of fabric having the multiple textures. In such a case, clustered images do not converge into one type of fabric cluster but are diversified into many fabric clusters. Multiple texture fabric is expected to diversify into many texture clusters. However, the issue of the impact of color patterns on the fabric texture clustering is the work for our future study.

4   Conclusion

In this paper, we have explored the classification and matching of similar fabric textures using deep Convolutional Neural network (CNN) methods. Our experimental results were evaluated on the test dataset comprising of 12, 300 images and show exceptionally higher accuracy of about (98.40%). However, more work is needed for fabrics which are multi-textured or where color pattern itself is a part of the overall texture. In the era of e-commerce, products are classified according to their specifications. However, in the case of fabric, look and feel of texture is done using only manual inspection from both the buyer and seller side. We have tried to address the subjectivity in fabric quality. Our work opens up the opportunity for standardization of fabric textures and classification of fabric texture with minimum need for manual inspection.

References

1. Potiyaraj, P., Subhakalin, C., Sawangharsub, B., Udomkichdecha, W.: Recognition and re-visualization of woven fabric structures. Int. J. Cloth. Sci. Technol. **22**(2/3), 79–87 (2010)
2. Xu, B.: Identifying fabric structures with fast Fourier transform techniques. Text. Res. J. **66**(8), 496–506 (1996)
3. Hosseini Ravandi, S.A., Toriumi, K.: Fourier transform analysis of plain weave fabric appearance. Text. Res. J. **65**(11), 676–683 (1995)
4. Krizhevsky, A., Sutskever, I., Hinton, G.E.: ImageNet classification with deep convolutional neural networks. In: Advances in Neural Information Processing Systems, pp. 1097–1105 (2012)
5. Amazon inc. www.amazon.in
6. Flipkart Online Services Pvt. ltd. www.flipkart.com
7. Digital Retail in 2020: Rewriting the Rules. https://www.atkearney.in/documents/4773014/8192273/Digital+Retail+in+2020%E2%80%93Rewriting+the+Rules.pdf/392551c2-7b43-4666-938e-2168a6bd7f6d
8. Reagan, C.: A \$260 billion 'ticking time bomb': the costly business of retail returns (2016)
9. Guo, Z., Zhang, D., Zhang, L., Zuo, W.: Palmprint verification using binary orientation co-occurrence vector. Pattern Recognit. Lett. **30**(13), 1219–1227 (2009)

10. Khan, B., Wang, Z., Han, F., Iqbal, A., Masood, R.: Fabric weave pattern and yarn color recognition and classification using a deep ELM network. Algorithms **10**(4), 117 (2017)
11. Kanungo, T., Mount, D.M., Netanyahu, N.S., Piatko, C.D., Silverman, R., Wu, A.Y.: An efficient k-means clustering algorithm: analysis and implementation. IEEE Trans. Pattern Anal. Mach. Intell. **7**, 881–892 (2002)
12. Stanton, K.B., et al.: PSUBOT-a voice-controlled wheelchair for the handicapped. In: Proceedings of the 33rd Midwest Symposium on Circuits and Systems, pp. 669–672. IEEE (1990)
13. van der Maaten, L., Hinton, G.: Visualizing data using t-SNE. J. Mach. Learn. Res. **9**, 2579–2605 (2008)

Real-Time Style Transfer
with Strength Control

Victor Kitov[1,2]($\boxtimes$) (iD)

[1] Lomonosov Moscow State University, Moscow, Russia
[2] Plekhanov Russian University of Economics, Moscow, Russia
v.v.kitov@yandex.ru
https://victorkitov.github.io

Abstract. *Style transfer* is a problem of rendering a content image in the style of another style image. A natural and common practical task in applications of style transfer is to adjust the strength of stylization. Algorithm of Gatys et al. [4] provides this ability by changing the weighting factors of content and style losses but is computationally inefficient. *Real-time style transfer* introduced by Johnson et al. [9] enables fast stylization of any image by passing it through a pre-trained transformer network. Although fast, this architecture is not able to continuously adjust style strength. We propose an extension to real-time style transfer that allows direct control of style strength at inference, still requiring only a single transformer network. We conduct qualitative and quantitative experiments that demonstrate that the proposed method is capable of smooth stylization strength control and removes certain stylization artifacts appearing in the original real-time style transfer method. Comparisons with alternative real-time style transfer algorithms, capable of adjusting stylization strength, show that our method reproduces style with more details.

Keywords: Image processing · Image generation · Style transfer · Texture synthesis · Stylization strength · Residual network · Multi-task learning

1 Introduction

Gatys et al. [4] demonstrated that deep neural networks can represent not only the content but also the style of the image which can be described by the Gramm matrices, containing covariances between activations at different channels of the deep convolutional network. The disentanglement of content and style enabled neural style transfer - a technique to render any content image in the style taken from another style image using deep neural network. Since content image already possesses some inherent style, it becomes necessary to specify the amount of style that needs to be transferred from the style image. Original approach of Gatys et al. [4] allowed to do that by adjusting the weights besides content and

© Springer Nature Switzerland AG 2019
M. Vento and G. Percannella (Eds.): CAIP 2019, LNCS 11679, pp. 206–218, 2019.
https://doi.org/10.1007/978-3-030-29891-3_19

style components in the target loss function. However, this approach required computationally expensive optimization process in the space of pixel intensities of the stylized image.

Later works of Ulyanov et al. [16] and Johnson et al. [9] (which we refer to as *real-time style transfer* or *the baseline method* for short), proposed a fast framework for style transfer. In this approach an image transformer network was trained and then any image could be stylized in real-time by passing it through this network. Since transformer was trained using loss function of Gatys et al. consisting of a weighted sum of style and content loss components, a change in desired stylization strength implied a change in the optimization criteria and thus required training a separate transformer network. This incurred not only computational costs for training multiple models, but also storage costs for keeping them on disk. More importantly, this approach suffered from the limitation that stylization with only a discrete set of stylization strengths could be applied - one for each trained transformer network, whereas stylization strength is inherently a continuous feature.

We propose a modification for the style transfer approach of Johnson et al. [9], which we name *real-time style transfer with strength control*. Proposed algorithm retains the advantage of the original method - namely, it applies style to any image very fast by just passing it through a feed-forward transformer network. However, it additionally gives the possibility to continuously adjust stylization strength at inference time.

The proposed architecture yields comparable quantitative results to the baseline algorithm, measured by the total loss value that is minimized for both methods. Qualitatively, for higher stylization strength it gives stylization of comparable quality to the baseline. Interestingly, for smaller stylization strength proposed method gives results of higher quality by alleviating stylization artifacts consistently generated by the baseline method. This observation is illustrated on sample images and further supported by the results of the user evaluation study.

Qualitative comparison is provided with another modern stylization methods, capable to control stylization strength at inference time. Namely, we compare our method with AdaIn [8] and universal style transfer [11]. Results demonstrate that our method reproduces style with significantly more details, while AdaIn and universal style transfer drop much of the style information.

The paper is organized as follows. Section 2 gives an overview of related methods. Section 2 describes the proposed method in detail. Section 4 provides experimental results comparing proposed algorithm with existing real-time style transfer method qualitatively, quantitatively and by means of a user study. It also provides qualitative comparison of our method with two other methods capable of performing stylization with strength control. Finally, Sect. 5 concludes.

2 Related Work

The task of rendering image in given style, also known as style transfer and non-photorealistic rendering, is a long studied problem in computer vision. Earlier approaches [6,13,15] mainly targeted reproduction of specific styles (such as pencil drawings or oil paintings) and used hand-crafted features for that. Later work of Gatys et al. [4] proposed a style transfer algorithm based on deep convolutional neural network VGG [14]. This algorithm was not tied to specific style. Instead the style was specified by a separate style image. Key discovery of Gatys et al. was to find representation for content and style based on activations inside the convolutional neural network. Thus content image could produce target content representation and style image could produce target style representation and for any image we could measure its deviation in style and content, captured by content and style losses. Proposed approach was to find an image giving minimal weighted sum of the content and style loss. Stylization strength was possible by adjusting the weighting factor besides the style loss.

However, algorithm of Gatys et al. required computationally expensive optimization taking several minutes even on modern GPUs. To overcome this issue Ulyanov et al. [16] and Johnson et al. [9] proposed to train a transformer network for fast stylization. The content image there was simply passed through the transformer network for stylization. The network was trained using a weighted sum of content and style loss of Gatys et al. Thus it was tied to specific style and stylization strength, fixed in the loss function, so modification of stylization strength at inference time was not possible.

Further research targeted to propose a transformer network architecture capable of applying different styles simultaneously. Main idea was to hold most of architecture fixed and to vary only particular elements depending on the style. Chen et al. [2] used separate convolution filter for each style. Dumoulin et al. [3] used different parameters of instance normalization, but these coefficients still needed to be optimized. Ghiasi et al. [5] proposed to predict these parameters using a separate style prediction network, thus omitting expensive optimization. However, the problem of stylization strength control was not addressed in these works.

In alternative line of research stylization was performed by passing a content image through an autoencoder with linear scaling of intermediate image representation. Huang et al. [8] applied channel-wise scaling forcing channel-wise means and variances of the content image to match those of the style image. Li et al. [11] extended this approach by matching means and whole covariance matrix of activations at different channels instead. Moreover, in their approach a content image was passed through a sequence of deep and shallow autoencoders and content representation was adjusted in each of them. Stylization strength was possible in these methods by targeting a weighted combination of the content and style moments: higher coefficient besides the style moment imposed more style and vice versa.

Generative adversarial networks [7] (GANs) were also successfully applied to style transfer, for instance, in [1, 18]. The difference to the framework considered in this paper is that GANs retrieve style from multiple style images instead of just one.

3 Real-Time Style Transfer with Strength Control

3.1 Baseline Method

Our real-time style transfer with strength control architecture is built upon the baseline method – real-time style transfer of Johnson et al. [9] with minor improvements: batch-normalization layers are replaced with instance normalization layers, following [17], and transposed convolutions replaced by nearest neighbor upsampling and ordinary convolutions to omit checkerboard artifacts, following [12]. Other specifications of layers are not changed, training details are also fully reproduced except that it is empirically found that 80K images are sufficient for convergence of the transformer network. In this method a content image x_c is stylized by passing it through a transformer network $T_w(x_c)$ pretrained to reproduce given style with fixed stylization strength.

3.2 Proposed Extension

Proposed method is built upon the structure of the baseline method. Stylization is performed by passing a content image x_c through the transformer network: $x = T_w(x_c, \alpha)$, where parameter $\alpha \geq 0$ specifies stylization strength. During training transformer network is adapted to produce results for different α, so the user can adjust it at inference in real time. Building blocks of the proposed algorithm remain from the baseline, except residual blocks. In [9] traditional residual block $i = 1, 2, ...5$ for input u produces the output given by the sum of identity transformation and a non-linear transformation: $u + f_i(u)$. Our modified residual block i outputs $u + \gamma_i f_i(u)$, where

$$\gamma_i = 2\frac{|\alpha\beta_i|}{1 + |\alpha\beta_i|}, \tag{1}$$

and β_i is a block-specific trainable parameter, allowing the network to better distribute strength of stylization along blocks. Renormalization (1) is performed to ensure that for any α and β_i resulting factor $\gamma_i \in [0, 2)$ does not dominate the identity connection, allowing the network to propagate gradients well during training. Higher α increases the impact of the non-linear transformation $f_i(u)$ on the final result. Since $f_i(u)$ is responsible for applying style and identity skip-connection leaves input image as it is, γ_i and thus α, naturally control the amount of style added to the input.

The structure of the proposed method is shown on Fig. 1 with the new components, compared to the baseline method, highlighted in red.

3.3 Training

For given stylization strength α our method and the baseline method were trained using conventional style transfer loss from [9], consisting of content, style and total variation components:

$$\mathcal{L}(x, x_c, x_s, \alpha) = \mathcal{L}_c(x, x_c) + \alpha v_s \mathcal{L}_s(x, x_c) + v_{TV} \mathcal{L}_{TV}(x),$$

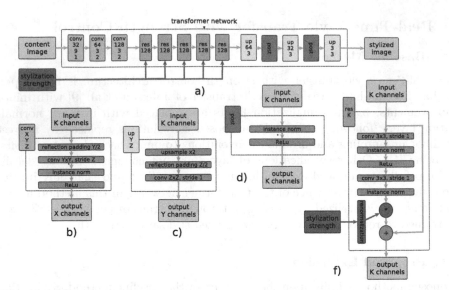

Fig. 1. Architecture of real-time style transfer with stylization strength control, differences from the structure of Johnson are highlighted in red. (a) transfer network (b)–(f) detailed schemes of convolutional, residual, upsampling and post-processing blocks respectively. (Color figure online)

applied to content image x_c, style image x_s and resulting image x with fixed predefined weights v_s and v_{TV}, controlling impact of the corresponding components. Separate baseline model was trained for each α from a grid, and our method used only a single model. To force adjustment of our method to different α, this parameter was sampled uniformly from the grid $[0, 0.1, \ldots 10.0]$ for each mini-batch. Sampling from exponential(1) distribution was also considered, but it didn't provide enough variance to yield sufficiently different results for different α.

Content images were taken from MS COCO 2014 training dataset [19], consisting of 80K images with a batch size 16. Each image was resized and cropped to 256×256. One epoch through the dataset was enough for convergence, and training one model took around 45 min on two NVIDIA GeForce GTX 1080 GPUs. We used Adam optimizer with learning rate 10^{-3}. Total variation strength is set to 10^{-5}.

4   Experiments

4.1   Qualitative Comparison with Real-Time Style Transfer

A complete implementation of our approach in pytorch with pretrained models is available for download[1]. By applying different styles to various content images in

---

[1] https://github.com/victorkitov/style-transfer-with-strength-control.

our experiments, it is observed that real-time style transfer of Johnson et al. [9], being a very powerful model, overfits to the target loss function. This results in sporadically appearing local artifacts when applying generator model trained with small stylization strength. Our model is based upon framework of Johnson et al. but is less flexible due to necessity to apply style with a whole range of different strengths. This additional constraint serves as regularization and reduces overfitting, alleviating observed artifacts during style transfer. It can be seen on Figs. 2 and 3 where our method gives visually more pleasing results without salient artifacts of the baseline model. These findings are consistent for different content and style images.

4.2   Quantitative Comparison with Real-Time Style Transfer

To compare the results quantitatively we consider 5K content images from MS COCO 2017 validation dataset resized and cropped to 256×256 and calculate average loss by the baseline method of Johnson et al. [9] and by our method for each style out of 8 styles from [10]. Average style loss is approximately 15 times bigger than average content loss and total variation loss is several orders of magnitude less and thus removed from consideration. Next we calculate average ratio between our method loss and baseline method loss as well as standard deviation of this ratio along different styles. Figure 4 shows ratios for total loss, content loss and style loss. It can be seen that our method closely reproduces total loss - it is close to the baseline total loss for style strength greater or equal to 1 and increases only 2 times for style strength dropping to 0.1. Style loss stays very close to the baseline in all cases, so change in the total loss occurs due to significant difference in the content loss. Baseline method indeed is able to achieve lower content loss by preserving content image in all pixels except local regions with strongly expressed style which appears as an artifact and is an undesirable property of the baseline stylizer.

4.3   User Evaluation Study

Proposed method and the baseline method of Johnson et al. [9] were compared on the representative set of 4 content images and 8 style images [10]. Each content was stylized using every style with stylization strength randomly chosen from $[0.1, 0.3, 0.6, 1, 3, 5, 10]$, giving a set of 32 stylizations. 9 respondents were sequentially shown pairs of stylizations in the same setup for our and the baseline method. For each pair they were asked to select stylization they like more. To omit position bias, stylizations of the two methods were placed in random order.

Table 1 gives a summary of the results. These results suggest that the proposed method gives visually more pleasing results than the baseline method of Johnson et al. in 2/3 of cases. This is an expected result since mentioned above artifacts of the baseline method appear consistently in cases of stylization with small strength.

Fig. 2. Johnson et al. [9] vs. our method. Proposed algorithm uses single generator network, while baseline needs separate network for each stylization strength. This single generator is enough to stylize with different strength. The method of Johnson et al. frequently generates local artifacts when performing stylization with small strength (second row). Proposed algorithm alleviates these artifacts and produces more pleasing results.

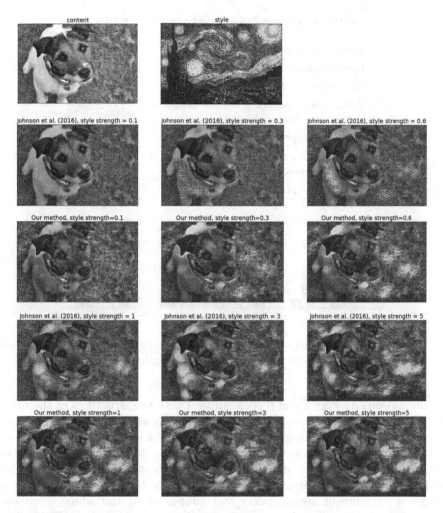

Fig. 3. Johnson et al. [9] vs. our method. Proposed algorithm uses single generator network, while baseline needs separate network for each stylization strength. This single generator is enough to stylize with different strength. The method of Johnson et al. frequently generates local artifacts when performing stylization with small strength (second row). Proposed algorithm alleviates these artifacts and produces more pleasing results.

4.4 Qualitative Comparison with Other Existing Methods

Since AdaIn [8] and universal style transfer [11] enable style strength control during inference, we present qualitative comparisons of our and their stylizations on Figs. 5 and 6. Style strength for these methods is controlled by special parameter which is limited to [0, 1] interval. So we adapt style strength levels of our method to qualitatively match parameter levels of the compared methods.

Table 1. Summary of the user evaluation study.

Total number of image pairs	32
Total number of respondents	9
Total number of responses	288
Number of responses when the proposed method was better than the baseline	192
The same as proportion	66.6%
Number of images that were better rendered by the proposed method	21
The same as proportion	65.6%

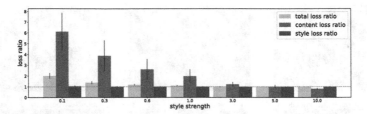

Fig. 4. Ratio of our loss function to the Johnson et al. 2016. Loss function for total, content and style loss evaluated for different style strengths.

Comparisons on Figs. 5 and 6 conform well with the structures of the methods. AdaIn applies style transfer by matching means and standard deviations of the intermediate content image representation to that of the style image. Representation is calculated on single layer of the autoencoder. This simple operation does not allow to reproduce style in detail and generates simplified cartoon-like result instead. Universal style transfer applies style by passing content image through a sequence of autoencoders and adapts mean and whole covariance matrix of the intermediate image representation on each of them. This allows to reproduce more characteristics of style but still without fine details due to limited capabilities of linear scaling. Also since universal style transfer applies style by passing content image through a sequence of deep autoencoders, the result becomes comparatively more blurry.

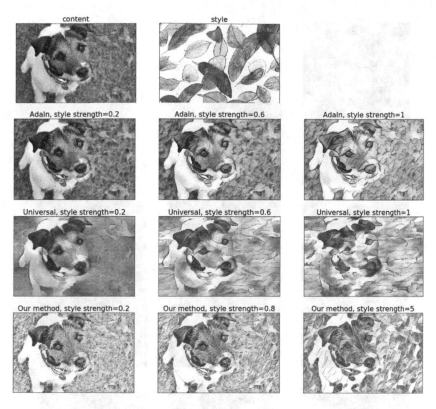

Fig. 5. Qualitative comparison of our method with AdaIn and universal style transfer. Our method better reproduces style details.

Instead of linear scaling our method applies stylization by multiple non-linear transformations which makes it more flexible and allows the method to reproduce style with fine details. Nevertheless, for some applications, such as cartoon-like poster creation, image simplifications obtained by AdaIn and universal style transfer are also desirable properties.

Fig. 6. Qualitative comparison of our method with AdaIn and universal style transfer. Our method better reproduces style details.

5 Conclusion

We have presented an extension to the real-time style transfer of Johnson et al. [9] which allows training a single image transformer network capable of stylization with adjustable stylization strength at inference time. Qualitative and quantitative comparisons show that the proposed architecture is good at applying stylization of different strength and produces results not worse than Johnson et al. Although average content loss obtained by their method is lower, it comes at a price of introducing distracting local artifacts to the stylized image. Proposed algorithm alleviates these artifacts, which may be attributed to the regularization effect of the training procedure forcing the model to solve not a particular task, but a range of tasks. Conducted user study supports our qualitative conclusions that the proposed method gives perceptually more appealing stylization results. Qualitative comparisons with other methods capable of real-time stylization strength control show that our algorithm better preserves details of the style. Thus the proposed algorithm is a viable style transfer solution when real-time control of stylization strength is important.

References

1. Cao, K., Liao, J., Yuan, L.: CariGANs: unpaired photo-to-caricature translation (2018)
2. Chen, D., Yuan, L., Liao, J., Yu, N., Hua, G.: StyleBank: an explicit representation for neural image style transfer. In: Proceedings of the IEEE Conference on Computer Vision and Pattern Recognition, pp. 1897–1906 (2017)
3. Dumoulin, V., Shlens, J., Kudlur, M.: A learned representation for artistic style. In: Proceedings of ICLR, vol. 2 (2017)
4. Gatys, L.A., Ecker, A.S., Bethge, M.: Image style transfer using convolutional neural networks. In: Proceedings of the IEEE Conference on Computer Vision and Pattern Recognition, pp. 2414–2423 (2016)
5. Ghiasi, G., Lee, H., Kudlur, M., Dumoulin, V., Shlens, J.: Exploring the structure of a real-time, arbitrary neural artistic stylization network. arXiv preprint arXiv:1705.06830 (2017)
6. Gooch, B., Gooch, A.: Non-photorealistic Rendering. AK Peters/CRC Press, New York (2001)
7. Goodfellow, I., et al.: Generative adversarial nets. In: Advances in Neural Information Processing Systems, pp. 2672–2680 (2014)
8. Huang, X., Belongie, S.: Arbitrary style transfer in real-time with adaptive instance normalization. In: Proceedings of the IEEE International Conference on Computer Vision, pp. 1501–1510 (2017)
9. Johnson, J., Alahi, A., Fei-Fei, L.: Perceptual losses for real-time style transfer and super-resolution. In: Leibe, B., Matas, J., Sebe, N., Welling, M. (eds.) ECCV 2016. LNCS, vol. 9906, pp. 694–711. Springer, Cham (2016). https://doi.org/10.1007/978-3-319-46475-6_43
10. Kitov, V.: Set of content and style images. https://github.com/victorkitov/style-transfer-with-strength-control. Accessed 1 Apr 2019
11. Li, Y., Fang, C., Yang, J., Wang, Z., Lu, X., Yang, M.H.: Universal style transfer via feature transforms. In: Advances in Neural Information Processing Systems, pp. 386–396 (2017)

12. Odena, A., Dumoulin, V., Olah, C.: Deconvolution and checkerboard artifacts. Distill (2016). https://doi.org/10.23915/distill.00003. http://distill.pub/2016/deconv-checkerboard

13. Rosin, P., Collomosse, J.: Image and Video-Based Artistic Stylisation, vol. 42. Springer, London (2012)

14. Simonyan, K., Zisserman, A.: Very deep convolutional networks for large-scale image recognition. arXiv preprint arXiv:1409.1556 (2014)

15. Strothotte, T., Schlechtweg, S.: Non-photorealistic Computer Graphics: Modeling, Rendering, and Animation. Morgan Kaufmann, San Francisco (2002)

16. Ulyanov, D., Lebedev, V., Vedaldi, A., Lempitsky, V.S.: Texture networks: feed-forward synthesis of textures and stylized images. In: ICML, vol. 1, p. 4 (2016)

17. Ulyanov, D., Vedaldi, A., Lempitsky, V.: Instance normalization: the missing ingredient for fast stylization. arXiv preprint arXiv:1607.08022 (2016)

18. Zhu, J.Y., Park, T., Isola, P., Efros, A.A.: Unpaired image-to-image translation using cycle-consistent adversarial networks. In: Proceedings of the IEEE International Conference on Computer Vision, pp. 2223–2232 (2017)

19. Lin, T.-Y., et al.: Microsoft COCO: common objects in context. In: Fleet, D., Pajdla, T., Schiele, B., Tuytelaars, T. (eds.) ECCV 2014. LNCS, vol. 8693, pp. 740–755. Springer, Cham (2014). https://doi.org/10.1007/978-3-319-10602-1_48

Faster Visual-Based Localization
with Mobile-PoseNet

Claudio Cimarelli, Dario Cazzato[⊠], Miguel A. Olivares-Mendez,
and Holger Voos

Interdisciplinary Center for Security, Reliability and Trust (SnT),
University of Luxembourg,
29, Avenue J. F. Kennedy, 1855 Luxembourg, Luxembourg
{claudio.cimarelli,dario.cazzato,miguel.olivaresmendez,
holger.voos}@uni.lu

Abstract. Precise and robust localization is of fundamental importance
for robots required to carry out autonomous tasks. Above all, in the case
of Unmanned Aerial Vehicles (UAVs), efficiency and reliability are critical aspects in developing solutions for localization due to the limited
computational capabilities, payload and power constraints. In this work,
we leverage novel research in efficient deep neural architectures for the
problem of 6 Degrees of Freedom (6-DoF) pose estimation from single
RGB camera images. In particular, we introduce an efficient neural network to jointly regress the position and orientation of the camera with
respect to the navigation environment. Experimental results show that
the proposed network is capable of retaining similar results with respect
to the most popular state of the art methods while being smaller and
with lower latency, which are fundamental aspects for real-time robotics
applications.

Keywords: Deep learning · Convolutional Neural Networks ·
6-DoF pose estimation · Visual-Based Localization · UAV

1 Introduction

At the present time, the popularity of Unmanned Aerial Vehicles (UAVs) is
rapidly increasing due to their peculiar characteristics. In fact, they are frequently adopted in a broad range of research projects and commercial applications, such as building inspections, rescue operations, and surveillance, which
require high mobility and flexible adaptation to complex situations [24]. The
ability of a drone to localize itself inside the surrounding environment is crucial
for enabling higher degrees of autonomy in the assigned tasks. Global Navigation
Satellite System (GNSS) is a common solution to the problem of retrieving a
global position, but it often fails due to signal loss in cluttered environments like
urban canyons or natural valleys. Moreover, its precision in the localization is

© Springer Nature Switzerland AG 2019
M. Vento and G. Percannella (Eds.): CAIP 2019, LNCS 11679, pp. 219–230, 2019.
https://doi.org/10.1007/978-3-030-29891-3_20

correlated with the number of satellites in direct line of sight [3], and the accuracy requirements are often not meet by GPS-like technology since the provided localization comes with an uncertainty up-to some meters.

As an alternative to GPS, Visual-Based Localization (VBL) [25] refers to the set of methods that estimate the 6-Degrees of Freedom (6-DoF) pose of a camera, that is, its translation and rotation with respect to the map of the navigation environment, solely relying on the information enclosed in the images. In robotics, VBL is commonly used to solve the kidnapped robot problem, whereas in a SLAM pipeline is part of a re-localization module which allows recovering the global position in the map after the tracking is lost or for loop-closing [37]. Visual localization methods can be categorized either as indirect methods, also called topological or appearance-based, or direct methods, sometimes referred to as metric [25]. On the one hand, indirect methods formulate localization as an image-retrieval problem, providing a coarse estimate of the position depending on the granularity of the locations with an image saved in the database [4,40]. On the other hand, direct methods cast localization as a pose regression problem and try to deliver an exact estimate of both position and orientation for each new view [18,31,34]. Thus, direct localization is more appropriate for robot navigation where the operating environment is confined to a well-defined area and we expect to obtain a pose as precise as possible when the tracking is lost.

In this paper, we address the problem of metric localization using as a feature extractor a neural network proposed by the recent research on efficient architectures. In particular, we adopt MobileNetV2 [29] previously trained for the image classification task, as a starting point to build a model for regressing the pose. This choice permits to achieve a trade-off between competitive performance and computation speed. As follows, our contribution is two-fold: from one side, as the best of our knowledge, this is the first attempt to use MobileNetV2 architecture for the localization problem. Moreover, the proposed approach is faster than main state-of-the-art works, while preserving the localization performance. The rest of the manuscript is organized as follows. In Sect. 2, a short review of methods proposed in the recent literature for visual localization is proposed. The methodology, the loss function and the overall structure of the deep learning model are described in Sect. 3. Subsequently, the experimental setup and the obtained results are shown in Sect. 4. Ultimately, Sect. 5 presents the conclusion and future research directions.

2 Related Work

In this section, we review the methods that have been proposed in the recent literature of visual localization techniques. Currently, the approaches to the direct localization problem go into three distinct directions: one is to rely on matching 2D image features with 3D points of a structured model of the environment; another is to use classic machine learning algorithms to learn the 3D coordinates of each the pixels in order to establish the matches; lastly, we can provide an end-to-end differentiable solution to regress the 6-DoF pose using Convolutional

Neural Networks (CNNs). Then, we briefly summarize the most efficient neural network architectures for image processing, and the main applications of CNNs to the field of UAVs navigation.

Local Feature-Based Localization is a family of methods usually supported by a 3D reconstruction of the environment created through a Structure-from-Motion (SfM) pipeline [33]. Hence, they establish correspondences between 2D features extracted from a query image, such as SIFT [23] or ORB [28], and those associated with the 3D points in the model. Finally, the pose of the camera is recovered providing the set of putative matches to a Perspective-n-Point (PnP) algorithm [14] inside a Random Sample Consensus (RANSAC) loop [27]. Irschara *et al.* [13] use methods of image retrieval in conjunction with a compressed scene representation composed of real and synthetic views. Li *et al.* [22] propose to invert the search direction using a prioritization scheme. Sattler *et al.* [30] enhance the 2D-3D matching with a Vocabulary-based Prioritized Search (VPS) that estimates the matching cost for each feature to improve the performances, and combine the two opposite search directions [31]. Despite being very precise when correct correspondences are found, the main drawbacks are the computational costs, which does not scale with the extent of the area to cover, and the need to store a 3D model [25].

Scene Coordinates Regression methods use machine learning to speed up the matching phase by directly regressing the scene coordinates of the image pixels. Shotton *et al.* [34] train a random forest on RGB-D images, and formulate the localization problem as an energy function minimization over the possible camera location hypothesis. Hence, they use the Kabsch algorithm [15] inside a RANSAC loop to iteratively refine the hypothesis selection. The downside of these methods is the need for depth maps and of high-resolution images to work well.

Deep Learning has been adopted only recently to solve the direct localization problem. Following the success of neural networks in many computer vision tasks ranging from image classification to object detection [21], PoseNet [18] is the first work in which CNNs are applied to the pose regression task. In particular, they reuse a pre-trained GoogLeNet [36] architecture on the ImageNet dataset [5], demonstrating the ability of the network to generalize to a completely different task thanks to transfer learning [6]. In later works, Walch *et al.* [39] extend PoseNet with LSTM [9] to encode contextual information, and Wu *et al.* [41] generates synthetic pose to augment the training dataset. Subsequently, Kendall *et al.* [16] introduce a novel formulation to remove any weighting hyperparameter from the loss function. Though these single CNN methods for pose regression were not able to surpass the average performance of classical approaches [32,34], they demonstrate themselves capable of handling the most visually difficult frames, being more robust to illumination variance, cluttered areas, and textureless surfaces [39].

Recently, Multi-Task networks [26,38] demonstrate that by leveraging auxiliary task learning, such as Visual Odometry or Semantic Segmentation, the neural network improves on the main task of global localization. As a result, they were able to outperform the state-of-the-art of feature-based and scene coordinate regression methods.

Since the current approaches rely on very deep network architectures, e.g. GoogLeNet, our proposal is to replace them with a more efficient architecture in order to produce a more appealing solution for the deployment on a UAV. Improving on the previous generation of "mobile" networks [10], MobileNeV2 [29] combine the *depthwise separable convolution* with a *linear bottleneck layer* drastically decreasing the number of operation and weights involved in the computation of the output. In this work, we show that this shallower network is able to run faster than other single CNN solutions without sacrificing the localization accuracy.

3   Methodology

Inspired by previous works on direct visual localization exploiting CNNs [16,41], our aim is to estimate the camera pose from a single RGB image by adding a regressor fed by the output of the network chosen as a base feature extractor. In the following subsections, we describe the representation of the pose vector, the loss function used to learn the task of pose estimation, and the architectural details of the deep learning model.

3.1   Pose Representation

The output for each input image consists of a 7-dimensional vector $\mathbf{p}$, representing both translation and rotation of the camera w.r.t. the navigation environment:

$$\mathbf{p} = [\mathbf{x}, \mathbf{q}] \tag{1}$$

where $\mathbf{x} \in \mathbb{R}^3$, represents the position in the 3D space, and the orientation $\mathbf{q} \in \mathbb{R}^4$ is expressed as a quaternion.

Our choice of using a quaternion over other representations for the orientation is motivated by the fact that any 4-dimensional vector can be mapped to a valid rotation by scaling its norm to unit length. Instead, opting for rotation matrices would require to enforce the orthonormality constraint, since the set of rotation matrices belongs to the special orthogonal Lie group, $SO(3)$ [16]. Other representations, such as Euler angles and axis-angle, suffer from the problem of periodic repetition of the angle values around 2π.

However, Wu *et al.* [41] proposed a variant of the Euler angles, named Euler6, to overcome the issue of periodicity in which they regress a 6-dimensional vector $e = [sin\phi, cos\phi, sin\theta, cos\theta, sin\psi, cos\psi]$. Notwithstanding in [41] the authors showed empirically an improvement over quaternions, we decided not to express the rotation as Euler6 for a closer comparison with the majority of the state-of-the-art approaches. Anyway, in Sect. 4 we also compare our solution with the aforementioned work.

3.2   Loss Function

In order to train the network for the task of pose estimation, we minimize the difference between the ground truth pose, $[\mathbf{x}, \mathbf{q}]$, associated with an image $\mathcal{I}$ in the training dataset, and the pose predicted by the deep learning model, $[\hat{\mathbf{x}}, \hat{\mathbf{q}}]$. Hence, the loss function aims to optimize the two components of the pose, translation and orientation, denoted by $\mathcal{L}_x$ and $\mathcal{L}_q$ respectively:

$$\mathcal{L}_x(\mathcal{I}) = \|\mathbf{x} - \hat{\mathbf{x}}\|_p \tag{2}$$

$$\mathcal{L}_q(\mathcal{I}) = \|\mathbf{q} - \frac{\hat{\mathbf{q}}}{\|\hat{\mathbf{q}}\|}\|_p \tag{3}$$

where with the notation $\|\cdot\|_p$ we refer to the p-norm. In our experiments, we apply $p = 2$, which corresponds to the Euclidean norm. Besides, the predicted quaternion is normalized to unit length to ensure a valid rotation representation.

Even though the Euclidean norm is a valid metric for 3D translation vectors, in the case of quaternions it does not take in consideration that the valid rotations lie on the unit 3-sphere, and that mapping from unit quaternion to the SO(3) group is 2-to-1 [11]. However, Kendall *et al.* [18] argue that, as the difference between the predicted and ground truth quaternions decreases, the Euclidean distance converges to the spherical distance.

Since the two components, $\mathcal{L}_x$ and $\mathcal{L}_q$ of the loss function that we want to minimize is on a different scale, a weight β is added to the quaternion error in order to balance the backpropagated gradient magnitude [18]. In light of this, the loss function is defined as:

$$\mathcal{L}(\mathcal{I}) = \mathcal{L}_x(\mathcal{I}) + \beta \cdot \mathcal{L}_q(\mathcal{I}) \tag{4}$$

In order to remove any hyperparameter from the loss function, [16] replaced β with two learnable variables, $\hat{s}_x$ and $\hat{s}_q$, in the formulation of the loss with *homoscedastic uncertainty*:

$$\mathcal{L}(\mathcal{I}) = \mathcal{L}_x(\mathcal{I}) \cdot exp(-\hat{s}_x) + \hat{s}_x + \mathcal{L}_q(\mathcal{I}) \cdot exp(-\hat{s}_q) + \hat{s}_q \tag{5}$$

Homoscedastic uncertainty captures the uncertainty of the model relative to a single task, for example, treating the regression of translation and rotation as two separated tasks, while learning multiple objectives at the same time. For this reason, is useful in multitask settings to weight the loss components based on the different measurement units relative to the particular task [17]. In our experiments, we initialized $\hat{s}_x$ and $\hat{s}_q$ to 0.5 and 0.1 respectively.

3.3   Deep Learning Model

In order to build a small network for localization, we decided to adapt the novel MobileNetV2 [29] by adding fulling connected layers to regress the pose; for this reason, we refer to our proposed network as *Mobile-PoseNet*. MobileNetV2 is an architectural design for neural networks that leverages efficient convolution

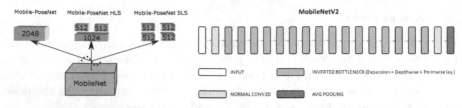

(a) Branching of the fully connected layers.   (b) Architecture of MobileNetV2. For more details on its structure refer to the original paper [29].

Fig. 1. MobilePoseNet's architecture.

operations, namely the *depthwise separable convolution*, and a novel layer, the *linear bottleneck* with *inverted residual* block, to produce a light weight network with optimized computation time.

The *depthwise separable convolution* reduces the number of parameters and of Multiply-Adds (MAdds) operations by decomposing the standard convolution operation with N filters of size $D_K \times D_K \times N$ into two steps: *depthwise convolution* and *pointwise convolution*. Having an input with M channels, the *depthwise convolution* is composed of M filters of size $D_K \times D_K \times 1$, operating on each m_{th} input channel separately. Then, the *pointwise convolution* applies N filters of size $1 \times 1 \times M$ to combine the channels into new features [10]. In addition, MobileNetV2's authors reformulate the original *residual block* [8], which is used to support the propagation of the gradient through deep stacked layer. On the one hand, they remove the non-linearity at the shortcut connected layers, where the *residual function* is computed, so that more information is preserved. On the other hand, they apply the shortcut connections directly at the bottleneck instead of the expansion layer; in this way, the authors assert, the memory footprint can be drastically reduced. Ultimately, MobileNetV2 allows tuning a *width multiplier* α in order to choose the preferred trade-off between accuracy and size of the network. We set $\alpha = 1$ to obtain a network with 3.4M parameters and 300M MAdds, resulting in a sensible shrinking compared to GoogLeNet with 6.8M parameters and 1500M MAdds.

Thus, we perform an average pooling on the output of MobileNetV2 last convolutional layer, deriving a vector of 1×1280 dimension that contains an high-dimensional feature representation of the input image. Therefore, we connect a fully connected layer of 2048 neurons followed by a *ReLu6* [20] non-linearity, which maps the features to the desired 7-dimensional pose vector. ReLu6, as stated by the authors, helps to learn a sparse feature representation earlier in the training. More importantly, it can be exploited to optimize fixed-point low-precision calculations [10].

Furthermore, to improve the generalization capability of the network, we add a *Batch Normalization* layer [12] before the non-linearity. Hence, this layer learns how to shift the mean and variance of the input batches after normalizing them. In addition, we adopt *Dropout* [35], which is an alternative form of activation regularization that reduces overfitting and indirectly induces sparsity by dropping random neurons at training time.

Ultimately, we test the branching technique proposed in [41] to regress the translation and rotation vectors separately (see Fig. 1a). Hence, we symmetrically split the neurons into two groups of 1024, so that we maintain the same total number intact. Additionally, we experiment with a third version of the network that keeps a common fully connected layer for translation and rotation of 1024 neurons and splits in half the rest forming two groups of 512. Our purpose is to compare the benefits of jointly learning position and orientation, that is, sharing the information enclosed in the common weights, against training two individual branches for each task. Therefore, we distinguish these design choices by referring to the first as *symmetric layer split (SLS)*, and to the latter as *half layer split (HLS)*.

4 Experiments and Results

In this section, we evaluate our proposed solutions on two datasets, *7-Scenes* [34] and *Cambridge Landmarks* [18]. The first includes indoor images, whereas the second one contains pictures captured in an outdoor urban environment. They have been chosen to demonstrate how the proposed method behaves in scenarios showing opposite characteristics.

4.1 Datasets

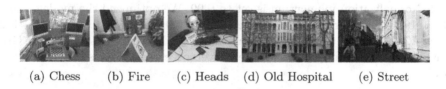

(a) Chess   (b) Fire   (c) Heads   (d) Old Hospital   (e) Street

Fig. 2. *7-Scenes* and *Cambridge Landmarks* sample images

7-Scenes [34] is a dataset for RGB-D designed to benchmark relocalization methods. Thus, it was collected through a Microsoft Kinect camera in seven indoor scenarios, which contains in total more than 40k frames with 640×480 resolution and an associated depth map. The challenging aspects of this dataset are its high variations in the camera pose in a small area generating motion blur, perceptual aliasing, and light reflections. These unique characteristics make the pose estimation particularly difficult for methods relying on handcrafted features, especially in views where textured areas are not clearly distinguishable [39].

Cambridge Landmarks was introduced in [18], and currently provides six outdoor scenarios. It contains more than 10k images, sampled from a high-resolution video captured by a smartphone. The ground truth labels were generated through an SfM reconstruction of the environment. Visual clutter caused by the presence of pedestrians and vehicle plus a substantial variance in the lighting conditions are the main challenges posed by this dataset (Fig. 2).

All the scenes in both datasets are subdivided in sequences, depending on the trajectories from which they were generated. In fact, each of the sequences shows a different perspective of the surrounding environment. Hence, for training and testing our model, we use the same partitioning of the datasets as provided by the respective authors. Thus, we create a separate "dev" set for evaluating the models during the training phase by taking a random sample of 10% of the frames from all the sequences in the training set. Anyway, we prefer to form the "dev" set from trajectories that are unseen in the training set in case we found a number of sequences high enough for a specific dataset scene; the purpose is to estimate more accurately the performance on the test set and choose wisely the parameters and stopping criteria for training.

4.2   Experimental Setup

The network is implemented using the TensorFlow-Slim open-source library [1, 2]. We initialized MobileNet with weights pre-trained on the ImageNet dataset, and the fully connected layers using the method proposed by He *et al.* [7]. Before training, we normalize the images by computing an RGB image that represents the standard deviation and the mean of a particular dataset scene. Then, for each image, we remove the mean and divide by the standard deviation in order to center the data and uniformly scale the pixel intensities. Dropout rate is set to 0.1, which means only 10% of the neurons are turned off during training, whereas Batch Normalization momentum is set to 0.99. We optimized the models using Adam [19] with a learning rate $\alpha = 1e^{-4}$, $\beta_1 = 0.9$, and $\beta_2 = 0.999$, on batches of size 128 shuffled at each new epoch, using an NVIDIA Tesla V100 16 GB. Thus, we let the training last until the convergence of the loss is reached on the "dev" set.

4.3   Discussion of the Results

In Table 1, we compare the results with three other CNN-based localization methods: PoseNet [18], PoseNet2 [16] with learned σ^2 weights in the loss, and BranchNet [41], which represents rotations with Euler6 and splits the network in two branches in order to regress the position and the orientation separately. Whereas we benchmark our result against PoseNet [18] because it pioneered the approach to the direct localization problem using CNNs, we share with the other methods some architectural choices. On the one hand, we adopt the *homoscedastic uncertainty* introduced by [16] to balance different loss components; on the other hand, we split the network layers following the work of [41], who showed significant improvements.

In general, it is evident that Mobile-PoseNet is able to outperform PoseNet and BranchNet in most of the scenarios. Interestingly, the more complex loss function is the main factor that gives us an advantage over these methods and is able to fill the initial gap between the two base networks. In fact, we noted poor

Table 1. Median localization error on the 7-Scenes and Cambridge Landmarks datasets. The large error reported in the Street dataset is possibly due to the repeated structure of the buildings and to the wide covered area.

	Area or Volume	BranchNet [41] Euler6	PoseNet [18] β weight	PoseNet2 [16] learn σ^2 weights	Mobile-PoseNet (proposed)	Mobile-PoseNet HLS (proposed)	Mobile-PoseNet SLS (proposed)
7-Scenes							
Chess	$6\,\text{m}^3$	0.20 m, 6.55°	0.32 m, 8.12°	0.14 m, 4.50°	0.17 m, 6.78°	0.18 m, 7.27°	0.19 m, 8.22°
Fire	$2.5\,\text{m}^3$	0.35 m, 11.7°	0.47 m, 14.4°	0.27 m, 11.8°	0.36 m, 13.0°	0.36 m, 13.6°	0.37 m, 13.2°
Heads	$1\,\text{m}^3$	0.21 m, 15.5°	0.29 m, 12.0°	0.18 m, 12.1°	0.19 m, 15.3°	0.18 m, 14.3°	0.18 m, 15.5°
Office	$7.5\,\text{m}^3$	0.31 m, 8.43°	0.48 m, 7.68°	0.20 m, 5.77°	0.26 m, 8.50°	0.28 m, 8.98°	0.27 m, 8.54°
Pumpkin	$5\,\text{m}^3$	0.24 m, 6.03°	0.47 m, 8.42°	0.25 m, 4.82°	0.31 m, 7.53°	0.38 m, 9.30°	0.34 m, 8.46°
Red Kitchen	$18\,\text{m}^3$	0.35 m, 9.50°	0.59 m, 8.64°	0.24 m, 5.52°	0.33 m, 7.72°	0.33 m, 9.19°	0.31 m, 8.05°
Stairs	$7.5\,\text{m}^3$	0.45 m, 10.9°	0.47 m, 13.8°	0.37 m, 10.6°	0.41 m, 13.6°	0.48 m, 14.4°	0.45 m, 13.6°
Cambridge Landmarks							
Great Court	$8000\,\text{m}^2$	—	—	7.00 m, 3.65°	8.68 m, 6.03°	8.12 m, 5.60°	8.60 m, 5.58°
King's College	$5600\,\text{m}^2$	—	1.92 m, 5.40°	0.99 m, 1.06°	1.13 m, 1.57°	1.20 m, 1.79°	1.14 m, 1.53°
Old Hospital	$2000\,\text{m}^2$	—	2.31 m, 5.38°	2.17 m, 2.94°	3.11 m, 4.11°	2.13 m, 3.73°	2.62 m, 4.21°
Shop Façade	$875\,\text{m}^2$	—	1.46 m, 8.08°	1.05 m, 3.97°	1.39 m, 6.37°	1.55 m, 5.64°	1.73 m, 6.19°
St. Mary's Church	$4800\,\text{m}^2$	—	2.65 m, 8.48°	1.49 m, 3.43°	2.34 m, 6.23°	2.16 m, 5.97°	2.18 m, 6.01°
Street	$50000\,\text{m}^2$	—	—	20.7 m, 25.7°	22.9 m, 36.3°	22.6 m, 32.6°	22.9 m, 36.2°

performances applying the β weighted loss to MobileNet during experiments. Instead, PoseNet2 obtains the best results in all the benchmark scenes apart from *Old Hospital* in which Mobile-PoseNet *HLS* is able to surpass the translation error by a small margin. However, we note that PoseNet2 uses frames with a resolution of 256 × 256, whereas our models require an input of 224 × 224 pixel images. Moreover, we do not augment the dataset trough random crops of the original images as in the competing approaches. Performing such operation would add an additional regularization effect, thus helping the generalization capabilities of the model and resulting in better performances overall. Besides, we observe that Mobile-PoseNet perform better on scenes spread on smaller areas overall. In contrast, Mobile-PoseNet *HLS* competitively gains higher scores in the scenarios of Cambridge Landmarks with an elevated spatial extent.

Finally, we run the network on a TegraTX2 to test the latency, that is, the time interleaving from the submission of one frame into the network to the moment of receiving the estimated pose. Hence, using the integrated TensorFlow tool for run-time statistics, we note that MobileNet-PoseNet takes on average 17.5 ms of run time, while the classic PoseNet 24 ms.

At last, we want to remark that the proposed solution employs a base feature extractor that carries half the number of parameters, in contrast to the aforementioned state-of-the-art methods with which we compare. This factor contributes to the lower accuracy of the output (Fig. 3).

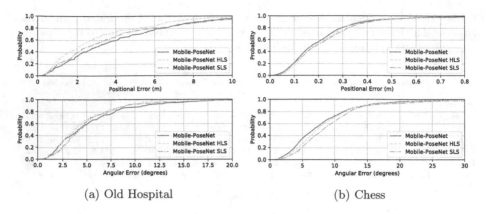

(a) Old Hospital   (b) Chess

Fig. 3. Cumulative probability distribution of the localization error.

5   Conclusion

In this paper, we introduce an efficient Convolutional Neural Network to solve the localization problem. In particular, we adapt MobileNetV2 with regressor layers to estimate the 6-DoF pose and propose a double modification of the architectural design by symmetrically splitting the neurons in the fully connected layer for learning independently the orientation and rotation. Comparison with state-of-the-art methods using a single CNN for direct pose regression shows that our method achieves competitive results, in spite of using a shallower network for feature extraction. In fact, contrary to the other approaches that make use of GoogLeNet, we employ MobileNetV2, which results in a faster and more suitable localization solution for being deployed on-board of a UAV.

Notwithstanding the empirical results in favor of using the Euclidean norm to compute the quaternion error, for future works, we will investigate the combination of quaternion with a different metric in the loss function or to adopt a totally different representation for the rotation.

References

1. MobileNetV2 source code. https://github.com/tensorflow/models/tree/master/research/slim/nets/mobilenet
2. Abadi, M., et al.: TensorFlow: large-scale machine learning on heterogeneous systems (2015). https://www.tensorflow.org/, software available from tensorflow.org
3. Araar, O., Aouf, N.: A new hybrid approach for the visual servoing of VTOL UAVs from unknown geometries. In: 22nd Mediterranean Conference on Control and Automation, pp. 1425–1432. IEEE (2014)
4. Cummins, M., Newman, P.: FAB-MAP: probabilistic localization and mapping in the space of appearance. Int. J. Robot. Res. **27**(6), 647–665 (2008)
5. Deng, J., Dong, W., Socher, R., Li, L.J., Li, K., Fei-Fei, L.: ImageNet: a large-scale hierarchical image database. In: IEEE Conference on Computer Vision and Pattern Recognition, pp. 248–255 (2009)

6. Donahue, J., et al.: DeCAF: a deep convolutional activation feature for generic visual recognition. In: International Conference on Machine Learning, pp. 647–655 (2014)
7. He, K., Zhang, X., Ren, S., Sun, J.: Delving deep into rectifiers: surpassing human-level performance on ImageNet classification. In: IEEE Conference on Computer Vision and Pattern Recognition, pp. 1026–1034 (2015)
8. He, K., Zhang, X., Ren, S., Sun, J.: Deep residual learning for image recognition. In: IEEE Conference on Computer Vision and Pattern Recognition, pp. 770–778 (2016)
9. Hochreiter, S., Schmidhuber, J.: Long short-term memory. Neural Comput. 9(8), 1735–1780 (1997)
10. Howard, A.G., et al.: MobileNets: efficient convolutional neural networks for mobile vision applications. arXiv preprint arXiv:1704.04861 (2017)
11. Huynh, D.Q.: Metrics for 3d rotations: comparison and analysis. J. Math. Imaging Vis. 35(2), 155–164 (2009)
12. Ioffe, S., Szegedy, C.: Batch normalization: accelerating deep network training by reducing internal covariate shift. arXiv preprint arXiv:1502.03167 (2015)
13. Irschara, A., Zach, C., Frahm, J.M., Bischof, H.: From structure-from-motion point clouds to fast location recognition. In: IEEE Conference on Computer Vision and Pattern Recognition, pp. 2599–2606. IEEE (2009)
14. Josephson, K., Byrod, M.: Pose estimation with radial distortion and unknown focal length. In: IEEE Conference on Computer Vision and Pattern Recognition, pp. 2419–2426. IEEE (2009)
15. Kabsch, W.: A solution for the best rotation to relate two sets of vectors. Acta Crystallogr. Sect. A Cryst. Phys. Diffr. Theor. Gen. Crystallogr. 32(5), 922–923 (1976)
16. Kendall, A., Cipolla, R.: Geometric loss functions for camera pose regression with deep learning. In: Camera Relocalization by Computing Pairwise Relative Poses Using Convolutional Neural Network, pp. 5974–5983 (2017)
17. Kendall, A., Gal, Y., Cipolla, R.: Multi-task learning using uncertainty to weigh losses for scene geometry and semantics. In: IEEE Conference on Computer Vision and Pattern Recognition, pp. 7482–7491 (2018)
18. Kendall, A., Grimes, M., Cipolla, R.: PoseNet: a convolutional network for real-time 6-DOF camera relocalization. In: IEEE International Conference on Computer Vision, December 2015
19. Kingma, D.P., Ba, J.: Adam: a method for stochastic optimization. arXiv preprint arXiv:1412.6980 (2014)
20. Krizhevsky, A., Hinton, G.: Convolutional deep belief networks on CIFAR-10. Unpublished manuscript 40(7) (2010)
21. LeCun, Y., Bengio, Y., Hinton, G.: Deep learning. Nature 521(7553), 436 (2015)
22. Li, Y., Snavely, N., Huttenlocher, D.P.: Location recognition using prioritized feature matching. In: Daniilidis, K., Maragos, P., Paragios, N. (eds.) ECCV 2010. LNCS, vol. 6312, pp. 791–804. Springer, Heidelberg (2010). https://doi.org/10.1007/978-3-642-15552-9_57
23. Lowe, D.G.: Distinctive image features from scale-invariant keypoints. Int. J. Comput. Vis. 60(2), 91–110 (2004)
24. Lu, Y., Xue, Z., Xia, G.S., Zhang, L.: A survey on vision-based UAV navigation. Geo Spat. Inf. Sci. 21(1), 21–32 (2018)
25. Piasco, N., Sidibé, D., Demonceaux, C., Gouet-Brunet, V.: A survey on visual-based localization: on the benefit of heterogeneous data. Pattern Recognit. 74, 90–109 (2018)

26. Radwan, N., Valada, A., Burgard, W.: VLocNet++: deep multitask learning for semantic visual localization and odometry. IEEE Robot. Autom. Lett. **3**(4), 4407–4414 (2018)
27. Raguram, R., Frahm, J.-M., Pollefeys, M.: A comparative analysis of RANSAC techniques leading to adaptive real-time random sample consensus. In: Forsyth, D., Torr, P., Zisserman, A. (eds.) ECCV 2008. LNCS, vol. 5303, pp. 500–513. Springer, Heidelberg (2008). https://doi.org/10.1007/978-3-540-88688-4_37
28. Rublee, E., Rabaud, V., Konolige, K., Bradski, G.: ORB: an efficient alternative to SIFT or SURF. In: IEEE Conference on Computer Vision and Pattern Recognition. IEEE (2011)
29. Sandler, M., Howard, A., Zhu, M., Zhmoginov, A., Chen, L.C.: MobileNetV 2: inverted residuals and linear bottlenecks. In: IEEE Conference on Computer Vision and Pattern Recognition, pp. 4510–4520 (2018)
30. Sattler, T., Leibe, B., Kobbelt, L.: Fast image-based localization using direct 2D-to-3D matching. In: International Conference on Computer Vision, pp. 667–674. IEEE (2011)
31. Sattler, T., Leibe, B., Kobbelt, L.: Improving image-based localization by active correspondence search. In: Fitzgibbon, A., Lazebnik, S., Perona, P., Sato, Y., Schmid, C. (eds.) ECCV 2012. LNCS, vol. 7572, pp. 752–765. Springer, Heidelberg (2012). https://doi.org/10.1007/978-3-642-33718-5_54
32. Sattler, T., Leibe, B., Kobbelt, L.: Efficient & effective prioritized matching for large-scale image-based localization. IEEE Trans. Pattern Anal. Mach. Intell. **39**(9), 1744–1756 (2017)
33. Schonberger, J.L., Frahm, J.M.: Structure-from-motion revisited. In: IEEE Conference on Computer Vision and Pattern Recognition, pp. 4104–4113 (2016)
34. Shotton, J., Glocker, B., Zach, C., Izadi, S., Criminisi, A., Fitzgibbon, A.: Scene coordinate regression forests for camera relocalization in RGB-D images. In: IEEE Conference on Computer Vision and Pattern Recognition, pp. 2930–2937 (2013)
35. Srivastava, N., Hinton, G., Krizhevsky, A., Sutskever, I., Salakhutdinov, R.: Dropout: a simple way to prevent neural networks from overfitting. J. Mach. Learn. Res. **15**(1), 1929–1958 (2014)
36. Szegedy, C., et al.: Going deeper with convolutions. In: IEEE Conference on Computer Vision and Pattern Recognition (2015)
37. Taketomi, T., Uchiyama, H., Ikeda, S.: Visual SLAM algorithms: a survey from 2010 to 2016. IPSJ Trans. Comput. Vis. Appl. **9**(1), 16 (2017)
38. Valada, A., Radwan, N., Burgard, W.: Deep auxiliary learning for visual localization and odometry. In: IEEE International Conference on Robotics and Automation, pp. 6939–6946. IEEE (2018)
39. Walch, F., Hazirbas, C., Leal-Taixe, L., Sattler, T., Hilsenbeck, S., Cremers, D.: Image-based localization using LSTMs for structured feature correlation. In: Camera Relocalization by Computing Pairwise Relative Poses Using Convolutional Neural Network, pp. 627–637 (2017)
40. Weyand, T., Kostrikov, I., Philbin, J.: PlaNet - photo geolocation with convolutional neural networks. In: Leibe, B., Matas, J., Sebe, N., Welling, M. (eds.) ECCV 2016. LNCS, vol. 9912, pp. 37–55. Springer, Cham (2016). https://doi.org/10.1007/978-3-319-46484-8_3
41. Wu, J., Ma, L., Hu, X.: Delving deeper into convolutional neural networks for camera relocalization. In: IEEE International Conference on Robotics and Automation, pp. 5644–5651. IEEE (2017)

Unsupervised Effectiveness Estimation Through Intersection of Ranking References

João Gabriel Camacho Presotto, Lucas Pascotti Valem,
and Daniel Carlos Guimarães Pedronette[✉]

Department of Statistics, Applied Mathematics and Computing,
State University of São Paulo (UNESP), Rio Claro, Brazil
daniel.pedronette@unesp.br

Abstract. Estimating the effectiveness of retrieval systems in unsupervised scenarios consists in a task of crucial relevance. By exploiting estimations which dot not require supervision, the retrieval results of many applications as rank aggregation and relevance feedback can be improved. In this paper, a novel approach for unsupervised effectiveness estimation is proposed based the intersection of ranking references at top-k positions of ranked lists. An experimental evaluation was conducted considering public datasets and different image features. The linear correlation between the proposed measure and the effectiveness evaluation measures was assessed, achieving high scores. In addition, the proposed measure was also evaluated jointly with rank aggregation methods, by assigning weights to ranked lists according to the effectiveness estimation of each feature.

Keywords: Effectiveness estimation · Image retrieval · Ranking

1 Introduction

The pervasive presence of mobile devices in the daily life, in conjunction with developments in image acquisition and sharing technologies have increased the growth of image collections. In this scenario, Content-Based Image Retrieval (CBIR) [11] systems have established as an indispensable tool, capable of indexing and searching the available data through its visual content. However, despite the successful use of CBIR approaches in many scenarios, some research challenges still remain as important obstacles.

A challenging limitation of supervised CBIR approaches relies on the need of obtaining labeled data in order to provide training sets for learning strategies. That is particularly relevant in scenarios with scarce labeled data and growing image collections. Therefore, unsupervised approaches capable of analyzing data without any training sets, have become of crucial importance.

Recently, various unsupervised approaches have been proposed for image and multimedia retrieval scenarios [2,21]. Unsupervised post-processing and metric

© Springer Nature Switzerland AG 2019
M. Vento and G. Percannella (Eds.): CAIP 2019, LNCS 11679, pp. 231–244, 2019.
https://doi.org/10.1007/978-3-030-29891-3_21

learning methods redefine a similarity/dissimilarity measure, based on the contextual information encoded in the datasets. Such methods capture the dataset manifold in order to compute a more global similarity measure. The global measures are expected to be more effective and, consequently produce more accurate retrieval results.

Several strategies have been exploited in order to compute such measures, including graph-based approaches [21] and diffusion processes [2]. One of the most promising approaches rely on the use of effectiveness estimation measures [16]. The key idea consists in estimating the quality of retrieval results through the analysis of consistence of the ranking references.

Actually, predicting the effectiveness of visual features is a very challenging task, specially in unsupervised scenarios, where no labeled data is available. In the late years, different approaches have been proposed aiming at estimating the effectiveness of image features [8, 16, 18, 29, 30]. The reciprocal neighborhood consists in a rich source information, which has been successfully exploited [16, 18] by effectiveness estimation measures. A more recent approach [30] consider the decay of similarity scores through ranked lists, where the effectiveness of a feature is estimated according to the area under a normalized score curve.

The effectiveness estimation measures are also fundamental in fusion tasks. Fusion approaches are generally divided into two categories [22]: early fusion and late fusion. Early fusion tasks are performed considering the raw features, while late fusion is performed generating representations from the features, like similarity matrices or ranked lists. Late fusion strategies have achieved promising results, but it is known that finding the optimal combination of ranked lists is an NP-hard problem [4]. Therefore, effectiveness estimation measures are fundamental to assign weights to each feature.

In this paper, we propose a novel unsupervised effectiveness estimation measure for image retrieval. The proposed Full-Intersection measure is based on the density of the ranking references at top-k positions of ranked lists. The intersection among ranked lists of different neighbors is computed in order to assign an effectiveness estimation score. The strategy is based on the premise that high-effective ranked lists tends to reference each other at top positions of ranked lists. Experimental results on public datasets assess the linear correlation between the proposed measure and ground-truth effectiveness measures. The proposed measure is also evaluated on fusion tasks, by deriving a rank aggregation method which estimates the weight of each feature.

This paper is organized as follows: Sect. 2 presents a formal definition of the ranking model used. Section 3 presents the proposed effectiveness estimation measure, while Sect. 4 discusses the rank aggregation method proposed. The experimental evaluation and obtained results are discussed in Sect. 5. Finally, Sect. 6 states our conclusions.

2 Retrieval and Rank Model

This section briefly defines the image retrieval model adopted along the paper. Let $C = \{img_1, img_2, \ldots, img_n\}$ be an image collection, where $n = |C|$ defines the size of the collection. Let D be an image descriptor. An image descriptor can be defined [23] as a tuple (ϵ, ρ):

- $\epsilon \colon \hat{I} \to \mathbb{R}^n$ is a function, which extracts a feature vector $v_{\hat{i}}$ from an image $\hat{I}$;
- $\rho \colon \mathbb{R}^n \times \mathbb{R}^n \to \mathbb{R}$ is a distance function that computes the distance between two images according to the distance between their corresponding feature vectors.

The distance between two images img_i and img_j is given by the value of $\rho(\epsilon(img_i), \epsilon(img_j))$. The notation $\rho(i, j)$ is used for readability purposes. A distance matrix A can be computed based on distance among all images, such that $A_{ij} = \rho(i, j)$.

The ranking model adopted is defined based on ranked lists [20]. A ranked list τ_q can be also computed for query image img_q, based on distance ρ. The ranked list $\tau_q = (img_1, img_2, \ldots, img_n)$ can be defined as a permutation of the collection $\mathcal{C}$. A permutation τ_q is a bijection from the set $\mathcal{C}$ onto the set $[N] = \{1, 2, \ldots, n\}$. The position (or rank) of image img_i in the ranked list τ_q, is denoted by $\tau_q(i)$. If img_i is ranked before img_j in the ranked list of img_q, that is, $\tau_q(i) < \tau_q(j)$, then $\rho(q, i) \leq \rho(q, j)$.

Taking every image $img_i \in \mathcal{C}$ as a query image img_q, a set of ranked lists $\mathcal{R}$ can be computed as follows:

$$\mathcal{R} = \{\tau_1, \tau_2, \ldots, \tau_n\}. \tag{1}$$

We can also define a neighborhood set that contains the most similar images to img_q as $\mathcal{N}(q, k)$. For the k-nearest neighbor query, we have $|\mathcal{N}(q, k)| = k$, which is formally defined as follows:

$$\mathcal{N}(q, k) = \{\mathcal{S} \subseteq \mathcal{C}, |\mathcal{S}| = k \wedge \forall img_i \in \mathcal{S}, img_j \in \mathcal{C} - \mathcal{S} : \\ \tau_q(i) < \tau_q(j)\}. \tag{2}$$

Based on the described retrieval model, next section presents the proposed unsupervised effectiveness measure.

3   Full-Intersection Measure

The size of intersection between top positions of ranked lists is of remarkable relevance in retrieval scenarios [5,20], broadly exploited as rank correlation measure. However, the intersection often consider pairs of ranked lists. In this paper, the proposed Full-Intersection measure computes the intersection among a set of ranked lists, defined by the k-neighborhood of a given query. The general objective is to analyze the density of ranking references among the ranked lists of k-neighbors, which is expected to be high.

In brief, the measure evaluates the number of co-occurrences of images in different ranked lists, defined by each k-neighbor. The analysis is performed by increasing the number of positions of the ranked lists being analyzed, from $d = 1$

until a predefined parameter k. In this way, the measure assigns higher weights to top positions of ranked lists. The higher the computed intersection between ranked lists (number of co-occurrences), the bigger is the effectiveness estimation of the ranked list.

The measure is formally defined as follows. Let $F_I(q)$ be the Full-Intersection score obtained to a query image $img_q \in \mathcal{C}$, it can be defined as:

$$F_I(q) = \sum_{d=1}^{k} \sum_{i \in \mathcal{N}(q,d)} \left(\sum_{j \in \mathcal{N}(q,d)} f(i,j) \right)^e , \qquad (3)$$

where $f(i,j) = |i \cap j|$ and e is a constant[1] which aims to underscore high intersections. The value of function is defined as $f(i,j) = 1$ when $i = j$, and 0 otherwise.

Algorithm 1 presents an algorithmic solution to compute the *Full-Intersection* measure.

Algorithm 1. Full Intersection

Require: Query image img_q; Ranked List τ_q; Parameter k; Constant e
Ensure: *Score $F_I(q)$*
   $F_I(q) \leftarrow 0$
   for all $img_i \in \tau_q \mid i \leq k$ **do**
      reset($currentList$)
      for all $img_j \in \tau_q \mid j \leq i$ **do**
         add img_j to $currentList$
      end for
      for all $img_j \in \tau_q \mid j \leq i$ **do**
         for all $img_l \in \tau_i \mid l \leq i$ **do**
            add img_j to $currentList$
         end for
      end for
      $sum \leftarrow 0$
      reset($processedSet$)
      for all $img_j \in currentList$ **do**
         if $img_j \notin processedSet$ **then**
            for all $img_l \in currentList \mid l > j$ **do**
               if $img_j = img_l$ **then**
                  $sum \leftarrow sum + 1$
               end if
            end for
         end if
         add img_j to $processedSet$
      end for
      $F_I(q) \leftarrow F_I(q) + sum^e$
   end for

---

[1] The constant e is set to 1.5 on the experimental evaluation.

Figure 1 illustrate Algorithm 1. The first iteration compare the image from the first image of the ranked lists τ_q and τ_i, which returns an empty intersection. The next iteration considers the top-2 positions of τ_q, τ_i, and τ_j, resulting in two co-occurrences of img_i. This procedure is repeated to the next images of τ_q, until a predefined k, obtaining in each iteration it's own score. The final result $F_I(q)$ of the method, is defined as the sum of the generated scores.

4   Rank Aggregation

This section discusses the use of the proposed method in rank aggregation tasks. The objective is to extend a traditional rank aggregation method in order to consider weights to each feature according to its effectiveness estimation.

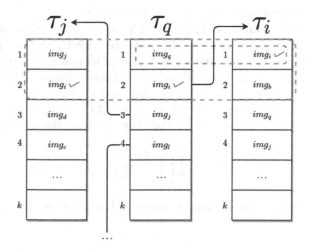

Fig. 1. Computation of *Full-Intersection* measure of the ranked list τ_q.

4.1   Borda Count

The traditional Borda Count method combines position information from different ranked lists, generated by different image features. The distance $F_B(q, i)$ between two images can be defined as follows:

$$F_B(q, i) = \sum_{j=0}^{m} \tau_{qD_j}(i) \qquad (4)$$

where $\tau_{qD_j}(i)$ denotes the position of image img_i in the ranked list τ_q according do the descriptor D_j.

The Borda Count method does not distinguish high-effective from low-effective ranked lists. With the objective of incorporating such information, we discuss a variation of proposed measure.

4.2 Intersection Rank Aggregation

The proposed Full-Intersection measure returns a score for each ranked lists. In rank aggregation tasks, we need to adapt $F_I(q)$ in order for assign a score for pairs of images. Thus, a Full Intersection Similarity $F_{SI}(q, i)$, can be defined as:

$$F_{SI}(q, i) = \sum_{d=1}^{k} \left(\sum_{j \in \mathcal{N}(q,d)} f(i,j) \right)^{e},$$

(5)

with $e = 1.5$, the same value used in *Full Intersection*.

In short, Intersection Rank Aggregation multiplies the value obtained from the Full-Intersection measure with the value obtained from the Borda Rank Aggregation Method. This is done for each pair of images (img_i, img_j) from the dataset. It is possible to use Intersection Rank Aggregation to combine m visual features (for the experimental evaluation, we used $m = 2$).

For the rank aggregation task, each (i, j) cell of the matrix constructed from the dataset will get the Intersection Rank Aggregation value $I(i, j)$, defined by:

$$I(i, j) = \prod_{l=1}^{m} \frac{F_B(i, j)}{1 + F_{SI}(i, j)},$$

(6)

where m is the number of descriptors combined, $D = d_1, d_2, ..., d_m$ and d_i is a descriptor.

5 Experimental Evaluation

In this section we present the experimental evaluation of the proposed Full-Intersection measure and the proposed rank aggregation method. Several experiments were conducted considering MPEG-7 [10], Soccer [28], and Brodatz [3] datasets. Considering the characteristic of the dataset, we selected different visual features, which takes in consideration features such as color, shape and texture, extracted from all images. Table 1 presents a overview of the datasets and visual features used in all experiments.

Table 1. Datasets and descriptors utilized in experiments.

Dataset	Size	Type	Overview	Descriptors
MPEG-7 [10]	1.400	Shape	A well known dataset composed of 1400 shape images divided in 70 classes. Usually used to evaluate unsupervised machine learning methods	Segment Saliences (SS) [24], Beam Angle Statistics (BAS) [1], Inner Distance Shape Context (IDSC) [12], Contour Features Descriptor (CFD) [19], Aspect Shape Context (ASC) [13] e Articulation-Invariant Representation (AIR) [6]
Soccer [28]	280	Color	Contains images from 7 soccer teams, containing 40 images per class.	Global Color Histogram (GCH) [26], Auto Color Correlograms (ACC) [7], Border/Interior Pixel Classification (BIC) [25] e Color Structure Descriptor [14]
Brodatz [3]	1.776	Texture	A popular dataset to evaluate texture descriptors which contains 111 different textures divided in 16 classes.	Local Binary Patterns (LBP) [15], Color Co-Occurrence Matrix (CCOM) [9] e Local Activity Spectrum (LAS) [27]

5.1   Effective Estimation Evaluation

The proposed measure was compared with two ground-truth measures, the Mean Average Precision (MAP) and P@X (Precision at x), the latter that computes the precision in the first x positions in a given ranked list. For the evaluation, the Pearson Correlation Coefficient between the measures was used, which is defined by the following equation:

$$r = \frac{\sum_{i=1}^{n}(X_i - \overline{X})(Y_i - \overline{Y})}{\sqrt{\sum_{i=1}^{n}(X_i - \overline{X})^2}\sqrt{\sum_{i=1}^{n}(Y_i - \overline{Y})^2}}, \tag{7}$$

where r returns values between 1 and -1. The value 1 indicates a perfect positive correlation between the measures and the latter a perfect negative correlation. In the experiments, we expect to obtain results close to 1, which indicates a strong correlation between the variables.

The obtained results of Full-Intersection measure were compared with two previously proposed measures: the Reciprocal Neighborhood Density [16,17] and the Authority Measure [16,18], using the same experimental protocol. The first is based on Reciprocal kNN Distance [17], which analyze the ranked lists of two images, counting the number of reciprocal neighbors between those ranked lists. Authority Measure [18] uses a graph-based approach to analyze the density of references among ranked lists of the top-k positions.

Experimental evaluation was conducted considering the top-k positions of the ranked lists, with k ranging from 10 to 20. Figures 2 and 3 show the correlation between the effective estimation methods previously described and the ground-truth measures MAP and $P@X$ with $k = 10$ using different image features. The last bar on chart is an average of all correlations previously obtained. Figures 4, 5, 6, 7 present the same analysis increasing the value of k in 5 for each test, finishing with $k = 20$. As we can observe, the highest average Pearson Correlation Coefficient is achieved by the Full-Intersection measure for $k = 15$. In addition, the propose measure is more robust to different values of k.

Next, we present a visual analysis between Full-Intersection and the ground-truth measures. Each value in x-axis represents the obtained score of a image in

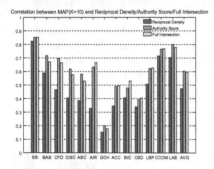

Fig. 2. Correlation between MAP and effective estimation measures ($k = 10$).

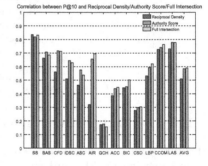

Fig. 3. Correlation between $P@10$ and effective estimation measures.

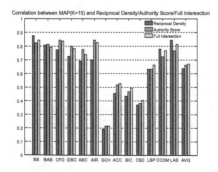

Fig. 4. Correlation between MAP and effective estimation measures ($k = 15$).

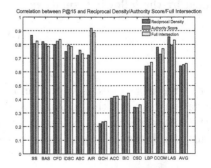

Fig. 5. Correlation between $P@15$ and effective estimation measures.

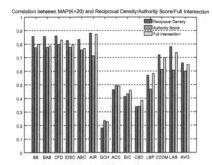

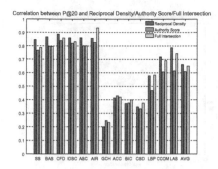

Fig. 6. Correlation between MAP and effective estimation measures $(k = 20)$.

Fig. 7. Correlation between $P@20$ and effective estimation measures.

Full Intersection and the values in y-axis represents the obtained score by the ground-truth measure. The score generated from Full-Intersection assumes high values, and in order to generate more readable x values, all the values obtained in the experiments were divided by the biggest one, so that we obtain a interval of $[0, 1]$ at the x-axis, as in the ground-truth measures.

The Figs. 8 and 9 illustrate this analysis for the texture and shape descriptors, LBP [15] and ACC [7], respectively, considering MAP as the ground-truth measure, with $k = 15$. Figures 10 and 11 presents the same analysis, now considering $P@15$ as the ground-truth measure and using shape and texture descriptors, CFD [19] and LBP [27].

It is worth mentioning that in the charts utilizing $P@15$, the obtained values in the y-axis presents a nearly fixed variation due to the definition of the measure, in which case, the percentage of images of the same category is based on the first 15 positions of the ranked list. This result in the spacing between y values in Figs. 10 and 11. It is possible to observe in all charts a approximately linear and positive behaviour, which can explain the high correlation values obtained.

Table 2 presents a analysis between the average correlation obtained in each experiment for each ground-truth effectiveness measure, as well as the average of those. We can observe good results in Full-Intersection.

Figures 12 and 13 presents some ranked lists analysed on the effective estimation experiments. Images different from the query (highlighted in green) are highlighted in red. In both images there is two ranked lists which obtained a high $F_I(q)$ and two ranked lists with a low $F_I(q)$. Figure 12 presents results obtained with the MPEG-7 [10] dataset and Fig. 13 with the Soccer [28] dataset. It is possible to see that the ranked lists with the highest $F_I(q)$ have less images with different classes than the query image. The opposite can be seen in the ranked lists with a low $F_I(q)$.

5.2   Rank Aggregation Evaluation

This section presents the effectiveness evaluation of the proposed Intersection Rank Aggregation compared with Borda Rank Aggregation Method and

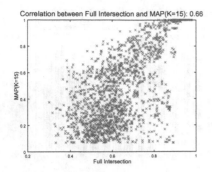

Fig. 8. Correlation between MAP and Full-Intersection: LBP [15] and $k = 15$.

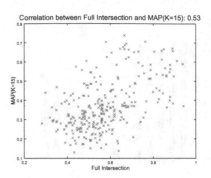

Fig. 9. Correlation between MAP and Full-Intersection - ACC [7] and $k = 15$.

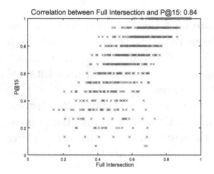

Fig. 10. Correlation between $P@15$ and Full-Intersection for the shape descriptor CFD [19].

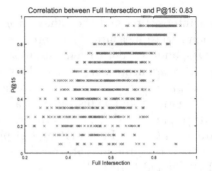

Fig. 11. Correlation between $P@15$ and Full-Intersection for the texture descriptor LAS [27].

Table 2. Comparison among unsupervised effectiveness estimation measures considering the Pearson correlation coefficient with ground-truth measures.

		Authority measure	Reciprocal neighborhood	Full intersection
K = 5	P@5	0.32	**0.40**	0.39
	MAP	0.20	**0.35**	0.31
K = 10	P@10	0.51	0.58	**0.59**
	MAP	0.47	**0.60**	**0.60**
K = 15	P@15	0.64	0.65	**0.66**
	MAP	0.64	0.66	**0.67**
K = 20	P@20	**0.66**	0.61	0.65
	MAP	**0.66**	0.60	0.65
K= 25	P@25	**0.62**	0.50	0.58
	MAP	**0.61**	0.48	0.57
Average		0.53	0.54	**0.57**

Fig. 12. Ranked lists of MPEG-7 [10] dataset and their Full-Intersection score. (Color figure online)

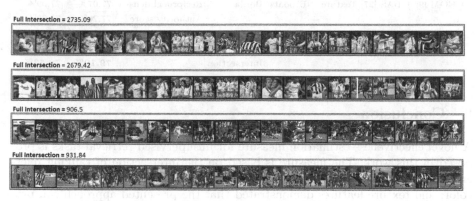

Fig. 13. Ranked lists of Soccer [28] dataset and their Full-Intersection score. (Color figure online)

Reciprocal Rank Fusion [16], both rank aggregation methods that use a effective estimation measure to assigns weights to each feature in order to improve the retrieval results.

Table 3 presents the effectiveness results of related methods and the proposed Intersection Rank Aggregation. The evaluation considers the MAP (Mean Average Precision), with $k = 15$ and $k = 20$.

Table 3. Comparison between different rank aggregation methods to several combination of visual descriptors.

Descriptor	Visual property	Dataset	Aggregation method	Effectiveness estimation	MAP ($k = 15$)	MAP ($k = 20$)
CFD [19] + ASC [13]	Shape	MPEG-7	Borda	Reciprocal density	93.63%	94.06%
				Authority score	93.93%	94.13%
			Reciprocal	Reciprocal density	95.36%	95.53%
				Authority score	**95.85%**	95.92%
			Intersection	-	95.70%	**96.06%**
BIC [25] + ACC [7]	Color	Soccer	Borda	Reciprocal density	42.06%	42.24%
				Authority score	42.24%	42.39%
			Reciprocal	Reciprocal density	42.06%	42.23%
				Authority score	**42.26%**	**42.42%**
			Intersection	-	40.97%	40.54%
CCOM [9] + LAS [27]	Texture	Brodatz	Borda	Reciprocal density	77.07%	77.09%
				Authority score	77.20%	76.92%
			Reciprocal	Reciprocal density	77.85%	77.84%
				Authority score	78.04%	77.98%
			Intersection	-	**79.10%**	**78.53%**

6   Conclusion

A novel effectiveness estimation measure for unsupervised retrieval tasks is proposed in this work. The measure is based on the intersection of ranking references among top retrieval results. An experimental evaluation involving shape, color, and texture features demonstrated that the presented approach can provide accurate prediction of the retrieval effectiveness performance. The measure was evaluated according to its linear correlation to effectiveness measures based on ground-truth labels, as precision and MAP. In addition, a novel rank aggregation method is derived based on the proposed measure. As future work, we intend to exploit the proposed measure in relevance feedback methods and in other multimedia retrieval tasks.

Acknowledgments. The authors are grateful to the São Paulo Research Foundation - FAPESP (grants #2017/02091-4,#2018/15597-6, #2017/25908-6, and #2019/04754-6), the Brazilian National Council for Scientific and Technological Development - CNPq (grant #308194/2017-9), and Petrobras (grant #2017/00285-6).

References

1. Arica, N., Vural, F.T.Y.: BAS: a perceptual shape descriptor based on the beam angle statistics. Pattern Recognit. Lett. **24**(9–10), 1627–1639 (2003)
2. Bai, S., Bai, X., Tian, Q., Latecki, L.J.: Regularized diffusion process on bidirectional context for object retrieval. IEEE Trans. Pattern Anal. Mach. Intell. **41**(5), 1213–1226 (2019)

3. Brodatz, P.: Textures: A Photographic Album for Artists and Designers. Dover, New York (1966)
4. Dwork, C., Kumar, R., Naor, M., Sivakumar, D.: Rank aggregation methods for the web. In: Proceedings of the 10th International Conference on World Wide Web, WWW 2001, pp. 613–622 (2001)
5. Fagin, R., Kumar, R., Sivakumar, D.: Comparing top k lists. In: ACM-SIAM Symposium on Discrete Algorithms, SODA 2003, pp. 28–36 (2003)
6. Gopalan, R., Turaga, P., Chellappa, R.: Articulation-invariant representation of non-planar shapes. In: Daniilidis, K., Maragos, P., Paragios, N. (eds.) ECCV 2010. LNCS, vol. 6313, pp. 286–299. Springer, Heidelberg (2010). https://doi.org/10.1007/978-3-642-15558-1_21
7. Huang, J., Kumar, S.R., Mitra, M., Zhu, W.J., Zabih, R.: Image indexing using color correlograms. In: IEEE Conference on Computer Vision and Pattern Recognition, CVPR 1997, pp. 762–768 (1997)
8. Jia, Q., Tian, X.: Query difficulty estimation via relevance prediction for image retrieval. Signal Process. 110(C), 232–243 (2015)
9. Kovalev, V., Volmer, S.: Color co-occurence descriptors for querying-by-example. In: International Conference on Multimedia Modeling, p. 32 (1998)
10. Latecki, L.J., Lakmper, R., Eckhardt, U.: Shape descriptors for non-rigid shapes with a single closed contour. In: IEEE Conference on Computer Vision and Pattern Recognition, CVPR 2000, pp. 424–429 (2000)
11. Lew, M.S., Sebe, N., Djeraba, C., Jain, R.: Content-based multimedia information retrieval: state of the art and challenges. ACM Trans. Multimed. Comput. Commun. Appl. (TOMM) 2(1), 1–19 (2006)
12. Ling, H., Jacobs, D.W.: Shape classification using the inner-distance. IEEE Trans. Pattern Anal. Mach. Intell. 29(2), 286–299 (2007)
13. Ling, H., Yang, X., Latecki, L.J.: Balancing deformability and discriminability for shape matching. In: Daniilidis, K., Maragos, P., Paragios, N. (eds.) ECCV 2010. LNCS, vol. 6313, pp. 411–424. Springer, Heidelberg (2010). https://doi.org/10.1007/978-3-642-15558-1_30
14. Manjunath, B., Ohm, J.R., Vasudevan, V., Yamada, A.: Color and texture descriptors. IEEE Trans. Circ. Syst. Video Technol. 11(6), 703–715 (2001)
15. Ojala, T., Pietikäinen, M., Mäenpää, T.: Multiresolution gray-scale and rotation invariant texture classification with local binary patterns. IEEE Trans. Pattern Anal. Mach. Intell. 24(7), 971–987 (2002)
16. Pedronette, D.C.G., da Silva Torres, R.: Unsupervised effectiveness estimation for image retrieval using reciprocal rank information. In: 2015 28th SIBGRAPI Conference on Graphics, Patterns and Images, pp. 321–328 (2015)
17. Pedronette, D.C.G., Penatti, O.A.B., Calumby, R.T., da Silva Torres, R.: Unsupervised distance learning by reciprocal kNN distance for image retrieval. In: International Conference on Multimedia Retrieval, ICMR 2014 (2014)
18. Pedronette, D.C.G., Penatti, O.A., da Silva Torres, R.: Unsupervised manifold learning using reciprocal kNN graphs in image re-ranking and rank aggregation tasks. Image Vis. Comput. 32(2), 120–130 (2014)
19. Pedronette, D.C.G., da Silva Torres, R.: Shape retrieval using contour features and distance optmization. In: International Joint Conference on Computer Vision, Imaging and Computer Graphics Theory and Applications, VISAPP 2010, vol. 1, pp. 197–202 (2010)
20. Pedronette, D.C.G., da Silva Torres, R.: Image re-ranking and rank aggregation based on similarity of ranked lists. Pattern Recognit. 46(8), 2350–2360 (2013)

21. Pedronette, D.C.G., Gonçalves, F.M.F., Guilherme, I.R.: Unsupervised manifold learning through reciprocal kNN graph and Connected Components for image retrieval tasks. Pattern Recognit. **75**, 161–174 (2018)
22. Piras, L., Giacinto, G.: Information fusion in content based image retrieval: a comprehensive overview. Inf. Fusion **37**(Supplement C), 50–60 (2017)
23. da Silva Torres, R., Falcão, A.X.: Content-based image retrieval: theory and applications. Revista de Informática Teórica e Aplicada **13**(2), 161–185 (2006)
24. da Silva Torres, R., Falcão, A.X.: Contour salience descriptors for effective image retrieval and analysis. Image Vis. Comput. **25**(1), 3–13 (2007)
25. Stehling, R.O., Nascimento, M.A., Falcão, A.X.: A compact and efficient image retrieval approach based on border/interior pixel classification. In: ACM Conference on Information and Knowledge Management, CIKM 2002, pp. 102–109 (2002)
26. Swain, M.J., Ballard, D.H.: Color indexing. Int. J. Comput. Vis. **7**(1), 11–32 (1991)
27. Tao, B., Dickinson, B.W.: Texture recognition and image retrieval using gradient indexing. J. Vis. Comun. Image Represent. **11**(3), 327–342 (2000)
28. van de Weijer, J., Schmid, C.: Coloring local feature extraction. In: Leonardis, A., Bischof, H., Pinz, A. (eds.) ECCV 2006, Part II. LNCS, vol. 3952, pp. 334–348. Springer, Heidelberg (2006). https://doi.org/10.1007/11744047_26
29. Xing, X., Zhang, Y., Han, M.: Query difficulty prediction for contextual image retrieval. In: Gurrin, C., et al. (eds.) ECIR 2010. LNCS, vol. 5993, pp. 581–585. Springer, Heidelberg (2010). https://doi.org/10.1007/978-3-642-12275-0_52
30. Zheng, L., Wang, S., Tian, L., He, F., Liu, Z., Tian, Q.: Query-adaptive late fusion for image search and person re-identification. In: 2015 IEEE Conference on Computer Vision and Pattern Recognition (CVPR), pp. 1741–1750, June 2015

Joint Correlation Measurements for PRNU-Based Source Identification

Vittoria Bruni[1,2](✉), Alessandra Salvi[2], and Domenico Vitulano[2]

[1] Department of Basic and Applied Sciences for Engineering,
Sapienza, Rome University, Via Antonio Scarpa 16, 00161 Rome, Italy
vittoria.bruni@uniroma1.it
[2] Institute for Calculus Applications M. Picone, National Research Council,
Via dei Taurini 19, 00185 Rome, Italy
d.vitulano@iac.cnr.it

Abstract. Camera fingerprint, namely PRNU, is a multiplicative noise source contained in each image captured by a given sensor. Source camera identification derives from similarity assessment between camera fingerprint and a candidate image; it requires the extraction of image PRNU and the estimation of camera fingerprint. To this aim, a denoising procedure is commonly applied in both cases and correlation is used for assessing similarity. However, correlation measure strongly depends on the accuracy of camera fingerprint estimation and PRNU image extraction. This paper presents a method for making more robust correlation-based source camera identification. It consists of more than one estimation of camera fingerprint; then, identification consists of the quantification of the amount of concurrence between correlation measures. It is expected higher correspondence between measures whenever the candidate image has been captured by a given device (match case); while lack of correspondence is expected whenever the image does not come from the considered device (no match case). Preliminary experimental results show that the proposed joint correlation measurements contribute to improve the precision of correlation-based source camera identification methods, especially in terms of a reduced number of false positives.

Keywords: Photo Response Non Uniformity pattern noise ·
Camera identification · Correlation

1 Introduction

Source camera identification is an important issue and a great challenge in digital forensics. It mainly consists of determining which specific device has captured a given image and, if possible, independently of eventual format changes, as for example the ones due to uploads and downloads from social networks or to storage in smarter formats as jpg.

One of the most common approaches to the problem is the extraction of the Photo Response Non Uniformity pattern noise (PRNU) which is a noise source

© Springer Nature Switzerland AG 2019
M. Vento and G. Percannella (Eds.): CAIP 2019, LNCS 11679, pp. 245–256, 2019.
https://doi.org/10.1007/978-3-030-29891-3_22

which characterizes each single device since caused by sensor imperfections. As a result, it represents a distinct fingerprint in the image without the need of additional information, as for example metadata. Although this nice property, the extraction of PRNU does not represent a trivial task since it is a multiplicative noise source hidden in the image.

Approaches to source camera identification are mainly feature based. The aim is to extract PRNU or some of its typical features and then compare them—for a complete review of camera identification approaches, please refer to, for example, [1,6,9,10]. In the first case, comparison is performed through the use of a proper metric directly to PRNU images extracted from the analysed image and the one of the device—the reference work for this kind of approach is the one proposed by Lukas et al. [7]; in the second case classification and/or clustering on features vector is applied depending on the scenario—some recent approaches are [1,8]. In the first case, natural images or flat field (FF) images captured by the device are necessary; in the second case a robust training process is needed. It is also worth observing that the best kind of approach to use depends on the working scenario [5]. For example, the comparison between PRNU images and camera fingerprint can be applied if PRNU of one or more devices can be estimated (natural images or FF are available). On the contrary, clustering methods are more suitable when any information concerning the device is available but we are interested in determining if two images have been captured by the same device. In both cases, the way the features are extracted plays a crucial role in the identification process. For example, most of approaches define device PRNU as the average of the residual images obtained by applying a denoising filter to a set of images captured by the same device; or as the average of flat field images (i.e. images without details—uniform illumination) related to the same device. However, the way denoising and averaging process are performed can affect the metric and then the final result. That is why, studies concerning the selection of the best denoiser and proper similarity metrics have been presented [3,8].

The aim of this paper is not to propose a novel method for PRNU extraction but to make more robust camera identification process. To this aim the pioneering method in [7] has been considered. The working scenario is the following: a dataset of images (natural or FF) are available for a set of devices, a set of candidate images is to be analysed and the task is to establish if candidate images have been captured by available devices. The main idea is to collect more than one correlation measure for each candidate image by considering three different image regions (the whole image), only homogeneous image regions (edges are excluded), only edge regions, and more than one estimation of camera fingerprint (for example coming from different averaging processes). Correlation values, separately evaluated for each image region, represent a feature vector and each camera fingerprint provides a different feature vector. If a candidate image has been captured by a given device, we expect higher correlation between the feature vector associated to camera fingerprint; in the opposite case, due to the random nature of noise, lack of correlation is expected.

Preliminary experimental results on Dresden database [4] show that the proposed approach is able to improve identification results of denoising-based approaches, as the one in [7], in terms of accuracy and precision. In addition, the proposed procedure is computationally efficient and does not require training procedures. The remainder of the paper is the following. Next section presents details concerning the proposed approach and the corresponding algorithm. The third section contains some experimental results and comparative studies, while the last section draws the conclusions.

2 The Proposed Method

The dominant part of noise pattern in images captured by a device is represented by the PRNU component. The latter is caused by pixels non-uniformity (PNU), or by the different sensitivity to light of sensor photosites, which originates during device manufacturing. This noise component is totally independent of factors related to surrounding environment or temperature, as it is caused by intrinsic structural properties of the individual sensor. Due to its strong relationship with the specific sensor, PRNU represents the most significant and distinctive fingerprint of a device and, therefore, represents a fundamental characteristic in source identification, image authentication and tampering detection processes. The mathematical model that is commonly adopted for the output of imaging sensor is the following [2]

$$I(i,j) = I_0(i,j) + I_0(i,j)K(i,j) + \Theta(i,j) \tag{1}$$

where I represents the acquired image, (i,j) are pixel row and column indices, I_0 is the noise-free image, K represents PRNU noise whose elements are typically close to zero, while Θ is a combination of random noises such as shot noise, read out noise and quantization noise—in the sequel pixel coordinates will be omitted for simplicity. PRNU is a multiplicative zero-mean noise component and represents sensor fingerprint. To extract the component of interest K from I, it is necessary to remove the contribution of I_0 which, however, is unknown. This is the reason why a regularization (denoising) filter is applied to I in order to get an estimate for I_0, i.e. $I_0 \approx J = D(I)$, where D represents the regularization operator. Hence, PRNU is estimated from the residual signal R which is defined as follows

$$R = I - J = IK + \Phi,$$

where Φ is a noise component and refers to the distortion introduced by the regularization operator.

Therefore, if $\Phi = 0$, PRNU matrix simply is $K = R/I$. Unfortunately, in real cases it is not so; hence, the residual image is extracted from different images $I_1, I_2, ..., I_N$ captured by the same sensor using maximum-likelihood estimate [2], i.e.

$$R_n = I_n K + \Phi_n, \qquad n = 1, ..., N$$

and then

$$K \approx \hat{K} = \frac{\sum_{n=1}^{N} R_n I_n}{\sum_{n=1}^{N} I_n^2}. \tag{2}$$

The use of a set of images maximizes the probability that the average error of denoising is zero, thus providing a more precise estimate for camera fingerprint, that will be denoted as reference pattern.

Hence, in order to assess if the image I comes from the camera whose PRNU is K, a similarity metric is necessary. The most common is Pearson correlation, defined as follows

$$\rho(A, B) = \frac{< (A - \bar{A}), (B - \bar{B}) >}{\|A - \bar{A}\|_2 \|B - \bar{B}\|_2} \tag{3}$$

where $< *, * >$ is the inner product operator, A and B are the matrices to be compared while $\bar{A}$ and $\bar{B}$ represent their sample mean. In the specific case $A = R$ and $B = IK$.

The estimation of the reference pattern (camera fingerprint) can be independent of the denoising procedure if flat field images are available for each device. Flat field images do not contain scene content and have an (approximate) uniform illumination. As a result, by denoting with $F_1, ..., F_N$, N flat field images related to a specific device, the model in Eq. (1) can be simplified as follows

$$F_n = c_n + c_n K + \Theta_n, \quad n = 1, ..., N \tag{4}$$

where c_n is the constant illumination value in F_n. It is straightforward that the pointwise average of N flat field images is a denoising procedure from which estimating K. By denoting with $\bar{c}$ the average of the constant values c_n, we have

$$\bar{F} = \frac{1}{N} \sum_n F_n = \bar{c} + \bar{c} K + \bar{\Theta}.$$

If N is sufficiently large, $\bar{\Theta} \approx 0$, and then $K = \frac{\bar{F} - \bar{c}}{\bar{c}}$. It is also worth observing that since K is zero-mean, $\bar{c}$ is the mean value of $\bar{F}$. On the basis of similar arguments, in the literature the maximum likelihood estimation of K, as in Eq. (2), is substituted for the sample mean of residuals and correlation directly is evaluated between image residual and residuals sample mean.

In practical cases, previous relations and assumptions are not exact; hence, different methods could be used for getting K estimation, as for example a different denoiser, a different way for getting image sample mean and so on. It is obvious that the closer to the ideal case we are, the more K estimations coincide.

The main idea in this paper is to exploit the fact that if an image matches with a given sensor, with high probability it matches with almost all estimations of the reference pattern; on the contrary, if the image does not match the sensor, then matching results with the different estimations of the reference pattern can be random—as shown in Fig. 1. In other words, we expect that the problem is well conditioned in the match case with respect to errors in camera fingerprint estimation, while it is not so for the no match case.

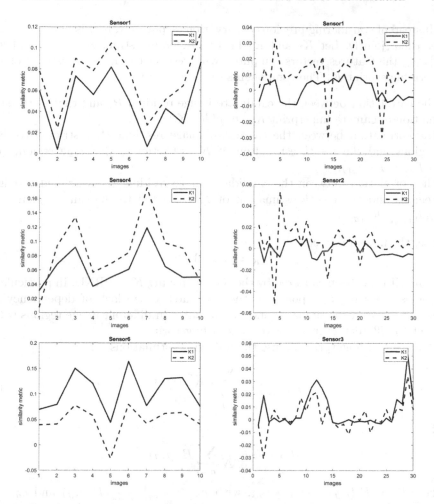

Fig. 1. Correlation measures estimated by comparing image PRNU with two different estimations of camera fingerprints (K_1 and K_2): match case (*left*); no match case (*right*). Plots refer to results related to 10 images in the match case and 30 images in the no match case.

In addition, for a fixed camera fingerprint estimation, if only flat regions or only edge regions are considered in the candidate image, higher correlation is expected in the match case in terms of relations between similarity metrics in the different regions, while non predictable behaviour is expected in the non match case—an example is shown in Fig. 2. In particular, in the match case it is reasonable to expect that the similarity metric measured in the non edge regions is comparable or greater than the one measured on the whole image and much more greater than the one measured on edge regions, where eventual denoising errors are more evident.

Instead of considering previous observations separately, in this paper we consider them jointly. Let K_1 and K_2 be two different estimations of K and let $\{V_i\}_{i=1,2}$ the features vectors computed with respect to the $i-th$ estimation of camera fingerprint K. The components of each V_i are

1. the correlation between the candidate image residual R_I and the $i-th$ estimation of camera fingerprint K, i.e. $\rho(R_I, K_i)$,
2. the correlation between the candidate image residual R_I restricted to flat regions and the $i-th$ estimation of K restricted to the same region, i.e. $\rho(R_{I_{flat}}, K_{i,flat})$,
3. the correlation between the candidate image residual R_I restricted to edge regions and the $i-th$ estimation of K restricted to the same region, i.e. $\rho(K_{I_{edge}}, K_{i,edge})$.

Hence, the inner product

$$\tau_{I.K} = <V_1, V_2> \tag{5}$$

indicates if I has been captured by the sensors having K as PRNU. In particular, $\tau_{I.K}$ close to zero corresponds to the no match case—lack of dependency is expected between the similarity metric evaluated in different image regions with respect to different estimations of camera fingerprint.

For camera fingerprint we use the following estimations

$$K_1(i,j) = \sum_{n=1}^{N} \frac{F_n(i,j) - c_n}{c_n} \tag{6}$$

and

$$K_2(i,j) = \frac{1}{N} \sum_{n=1}^{N} H_n(i,j) \tag{7}$$

where $H_n = F_n(i,j) - c_{n,j} - c_{n,i}$, with $c_{n,j} = \frac{1}{Nrows} \sum_i F_n(i,j)$ and $c_{n,i} = \frac{1}{Ncols} \sum_j (F_n(i,j) - c_{n,j})$.

Hence, the idea is to measure how is correlated the behaviour of some similarity measures with respect to different but close estimations of K; since in case of match we expect that both candidate image PRNU and K estimations have much in common with the actual K, it is reasonable to expect the same behaviour when they are estimated using a subset of image pixels; on the contrary, in the no match case, it is expected to observe different behaviour due to the fact that candidate image PRNU and K estimations do not have too much in common with the actual K. Independently of the inner dependency between the similarity metric evaluated in image subregions, we expect that these dependencies are preserved more in the match case whenever K estimation slightly changes.

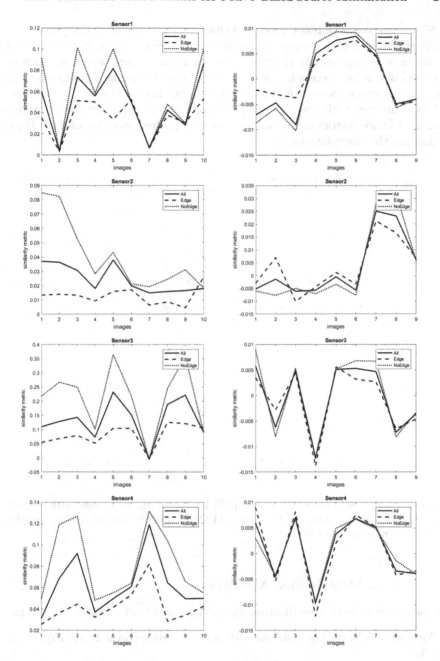

Fig. 2. Correlation measures estimated by comparing image PRNU in three different image regions: the whole image (*All*), smooth regions (*NoEdge*), edge regions (*Edge*). Match case (*left*); No match case (*right*). Plots refer to ten images (*x axis*).

Figure 3 shows the inner product values $(\tau(V_1, V_2))$, as in Eq. (5), for some candidate images with respect to seven sensors. For each plot, the first value corresponds to the matching device, the remaining ones represent no match cases. As it can be observed, $\tau(V_1, V_2)$ in the match case is significantly higher than the no match cases—i.e., for each candidate image, the feature vectors V_1 and V_2 computed with respect to the corresponding device are more correlated than the feature vectors computed with respect to devices different from the one originating the candidate image.

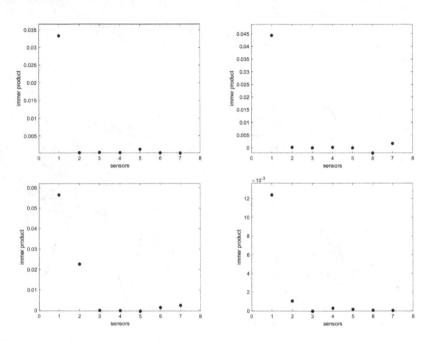

Fig. 3. Inner product computed as in Eq. (5) for four different images with respect to seven devices. Only one device has captured the candidate image: the one providing the highest inner product value.

2.1   Camera Identification Algorithm

The proposed camera identification algorithm consists of the following steps:

- For each device in the database estimate the fingerprint using Eqs. (6) and (7)
- For each candidate image I,
  - apply a denoising filter and extract the residual image
  - apply an edge detector, extract the edge map and apply a dilation to the map
  - compute the feature vectors V_1 and V_2 with respect to the s-th device, as described in the previous section, evaluate $\tau_s(V_1, V_2)$, as in Eq. (5).

- compute $\bar{s} = argmax_s(\tau_s(V_1, V_2))$. If $|\tau_{\bar{s}}| > T$, then I has been captured by the $\bar{s}$−th device with high probability, otherwise I does not derive from available devices.

3   Experimental Results

The proposed method has been tested on publicly available database in the forensics field, the Dresden Image Database [4]. It includes hundred images (natural and flat field) captured by several camera models and devices. A subset of uncompressed images and devices, listed in Table 1, have been used in our tests. We use the result in two different ways: *(i)* as in [7], a threshold for each device has been considered and then match and no match cases have been determined by comparing the adopted similarity metric with the threshold value; *(ii)* for each image, the device giving the highest value of the similarity metric has been selected as the original one. A wavelet based denoiser has been used for extracting residual images and Canny edge detector has been employed for extracting edge image regions—a dilation parameter equal to 5 has been used in all tests.

Table 1. Devices from Dresden database [4] used for tests.

Device	No. FF images	No. candidate images	Image size
Olympus 1050SW	50	25	3648 × 2736
Panasonic DMC-FZ50	25	25	3648 × 2736
Pentax Optio W60	50	25	3648 × 2736
Ricoh Capilo GX100	25	25	3648 × 2736
Samsung NV15	50	25	3648 × 2736
Sony DSC-T77 4	50	25	3648 × 2736
Sony DSC-W170	50	25	3648 × 2736

The basic method in [7] has been considered and the amount of improvement provided by the proposed method has been evaluated. Results have been measured in terms of F1 score, Specificity (True Negative Rate (TNR)), and Accuracy (A). F1 score is the harmonic mean between sensitivity (True Positive Rate (TPR) or recall) and Precision (Positive Predictive value, PPV), i.e. $F1 = 2\frac{TPR\,PPV}{TPR+PPV}$. TPR measures the percentage of success in assigning to each analysed image the corresponding original sensor and is defined as $TPR = \frac{TP}{TP+FN}$, where TP denotes the number of *true positive* (i.e. the number of images correctly classified) and FN denotes the *false negative*, i.e. the number of images that have not been correctly classified. PPV quantifies the amount of success in correctly identifying the sensor originating a given image with respect to the found associations and it is defined as $PPV = \frac{TP}{FP+TP}$, where FP denotes the *false positive*, i.e. the number of not correct match.

Table 2. Precision, Sensitivity, F1score, Specificity and Accuracy values obtained for the subset of sensors and images extracted from Dresden database, by using the source camera identification method in [7] and the proposed refinement.

Method	Precision	Sensitivity	F1 score	Specificity	Accuracy
Method in [7]	0.626	**0.957**	0.757	0.905	0.912
Proposed method	**0.730**	0.929	**0.818**	**0.943**	**0.941**

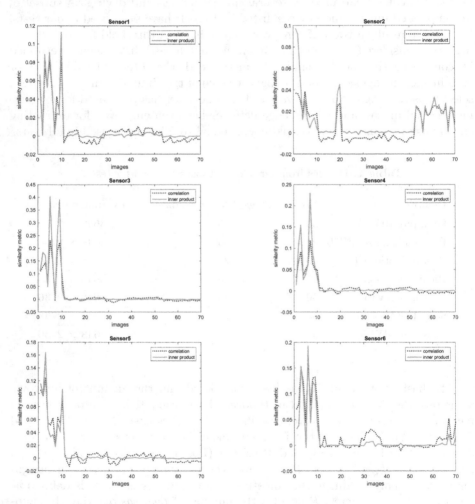

Fig. 4. Correlation values computed with respect to fingerprint estimation K_2 and inner products computed as in Eq. (5). Plots refer to six sensors: only 10 images over 70 have been captured by each sensor—they are the first 10 in the plot for each sensor (match case). In the no match case (last 60 images for each plot) the inner product is very close to zero, while it is higher, on average, in the match case.

Specificity (TNR) measures the percentage of success in assessing that a given image does not come from a given sensor and it is defined as $TNR = \frac{TN}{FP+TN}$, where TN denotes the *true negative*, i.e. the number of recognized no match.

Finally, accuracy quantifies the number of correct assessments with respect to the number of all assessments, i.e., $A = \frac{TP+TN}{TP+FP+TN+FN}$.

Results are in Table 2. As it can be observed the proposed method actually improves the basic source camera identification algorithm in [7]. In particular, F1 score, Specificity and Accuracy increase mainly due to the fact that the number of false positives significantly reduces (about 50%); as a result the proposed method increases precision in source identification process. This is motivated by the fact that in the no match case inner products assume values very close to zero, as Fig. 4 shows—the figures refers to seven sensors and 70 images: each sensor captured only ten images. It is evident that a simple threshold could be applied to the inner products signal in order to clearly assess correspondences between images and sensor. Results remain almost unchanged whenever natural images are used for fingerprint estimation instead of flat fields images—in this case K_1 is the maximum likelihood estimation in Eq. (2) since more robust. It is worth stressing that, even in this case, the proposed improvement method contributes to considerably reduce the number of false positives. The same advantage is provided whenever images subjected to a moderate resizing or images downloaded from a social network, like Facebook, are considered.

Finally, it is worth stressing that the additional computational effort required by the proposed method is very moderate—5% of additional computing time is required with respect to the basic algorithm in [7]—a Matlab (2018b) code has been run on a Intel(R) Core(TM) i5 having 1.70 GHz CPU and 12 GB RAM.

4   Conclusions

In this paper a method for making more robust source camera identification based on correlation as similarity metric has been proposed. The goal is reached on the basis of two main observations: if a camera has been captured by a given sensor, precise relationships between similarity metric evaluated in image subregions having specific characteristics (with or without edges) are expected, while it is not so for the no match case; in the match case the computation of correlation is numerically better conditioned with respect to the no match case. As a result the correlation between feature vectors derived from different estimations of camera fingerprint has been defined as new similarity metric to use in the final step of camera identification process. In order to quantify the actual advantage provided by the proposed approach, the pioneering method in [7] has been considered. Preliminary experimental results have shown that the proposed procedure is able to increase accuracy and precision of source camera identification methon in [7], thanks to the significant reduction of detected false positives. In addition, the proposed method is robust to the use of natural images in camera fingerprint estimation process instead of flat field as well as images downloaded from a social network. Future research will be devoted to refine the proposed method by extending it to different similarity metrics and by embedding it in more recent methods for source camera identification as well as to evaluate its robustness to image manipulation.

Acknowledgments. This research has been partially funded by Regione Lazio, POR FESR Aerospace and Security Programme, Project COURIER - COUntering RadIcalism InvEstigation platform - CUP F83G17000860007.

References

1. Akshatha, K.R., Karunakar, A.K., Anitha, H., Raghavendra, U., Shetty, D.: Digital camera identification using PRNU: a feature based approach. Digit. Investig. **19**, 69–77 (2016)
2. Chen, M., Fridrich, J., Goljan, M., Lukas, J.: Determining image origin and integrity using sensor noise. IEEE Trans. Inf. Forensics Secur. **3**(1), 74–90 (2008)
3. Chierchia, G., Parrilli, S., Poggi, G., Sansone, C., Verdoliva, L.: On the influence of denoising in PRNU based forgery detection. In: Proceedings of ACM Workshop on Multimedia in Forensics, Security and Intelligence, pp. 117–122. ACM, New York (2010)
4. Gloe, T., Bhme, R.: The Dresden image database for benchmarking digital image forensics. J. Digit. Forensic Pract. **3**(2–4), 150–159 (2010)
5. Farinella, G.M., Giuffrida, M.V., Digiacomo, V., Battiato, S.: On blind source camera identification. In: Battiato, S., Blanc-Talon, J., Gallo, G., Philips, W., Popescu, D., Scheunders, P. (eds.) ACIVS 2015. LNCS, vol. 9386, pp. 464–473. Springer, Cham (2015). https://doi.org/10.1007/978-3-319-25903-1_40
6. Li, R., Li, C.-T., Guan, Y.: Inference of a compact representation of sensor fingerprint for source camera identification. Pattern Recognit. **74**(74), 556–567 (2018)
7. Lukas, J., Fridrich, J.J., Goljan, M.: Digital camera identification from sensor pattern noise. IEEE Trans. Inf. Forensics Secur. **1**(2), 205–214 (2006)
8. Marra, F., Poggi, G., Sansone, C., Verdoliva, L.: Blind PRNU-based image clustering for source identification. IEEE Trans. Inf. Forensics Secur. **12**(9), 2197–2211 (2017)
9. Thaia, T.H., Retraintband, F., Cogranne, R.: Camera model identification based on the generalized noise model in natural images. Digit. Signal Process. **00**, 1–15 (2015)
10. Tuama, A., Comby, F., Chaumont, M.: Camera model identification with the use of deep convolutional neural networks. In: Proceedings of IEEE International Workshop on Information Forensics and Security (WIFS) (2016)

Detecting Sub-Image Replicas: Retrieval and Localization of Zoomed-In Images

Afraà Ahmad Alyosef$^{(\boxtimes)}$ (ID) and Andreas Nürnberger (ID)

Department of Technical and Business Information Systems,
Faculty of Computer Science, Otto von Geruicke University Magdeburgy,
Magdeburg, Germany
{afraa.ahmad-alyosef,andreas.nuernberger}@ovgu.de

Abstract. Zoomed-in image retrieval is a special field of near-duplicate image retrieval. It allows determining the sight, panorama or landscape image where a zoomed-in image belongs to. In addition, it can help to detect copyright violations of images that have been cropped and rescaled from panorama images. So far, only few research have been done on this problem using supervised learning techniques. We present a method to retrieve and localize zoomed-in images with respect to the whole scene based on correlating groups of features. Feature grouping is used to filter features that do not contribute to identifying relations between images. The remaining features are used to estimate the scale and location of the zoomed-in image with respect to the whole scene. We provide results of a benchmark data study using the proposed method to detect zoomed-in images and to localize them in the correlating whole scene images. We compare our method with the RANSAC model in case of zoomed-in retrieval and localization. The results indicate that our approach is more robust than the RANSAC model and can detect the relation and localize zoomed-in images even when most matched features are not correlated or only a few matches can be found.

Keywords: Zoomed-in retrieval · Triangles of features · Zoomed-in localization

1 Introduction

Near-duplicate (ND) image retrieval has been discussed in various studies, since it allows reducing the redundancy in image datasets, discovering copyright violation and classifying images that belong to the same scene. Zoomed-in images retrieval is a specific field of ND image retrieval where the zoomed-in image shows details of a part of a panorama, sight, satellite or landscape image. To improve the ND retrieval, various techniques have been introduced to refine feature extraction, progress feature structuring models or develop matching processes [2,6,10,19,35,37]. However, to the best of our knowledge, only a few research have been considered a particular case, when a ND image is a zoomed-in image of a whole scene. This field of research is important due to the strong

© Springer Nature Switzerland AG 2019
M. Vento and G. Percannella (Eds.): CAIP 2019, LNCS 11679, pp. 257–268, 2019.
https://doi.org/10.1007/978-3-030-29891-3_23

increase of captured images of the same sights in various resolutions or zooming levels, e.g. social media. Moreover, nowadays there are a lot of applications that can be applied to fake an image by altering its resolution, crop part of a high resolution or panorama image and increase or decrease its resolution or apply other effects on it. Such applications produce a large number of fake images that need a lot of processes to clarify scenes that such images belongs to. Therefore, the main goal of this work is to improve the retrieval of zoomed-in images. More especially, to predict the correlating group of matched features between the whole scene and zoomed in images and use this correlation to minimize the non-relevant but still retrieved images. The computation of the correlating set of matches provides us with valuable information about the scale difference and location of a zoomed-in image in the whole scene. The advantage of our proposed method is the capability to estimate the correlating group of matches regardless of the amount of false matched features (outliers) or even when only a few matches are detected.

The most similar research task to ours is discussed in [28], where a bag of feature model and an inverted index are applied to rank the retrieved images concerning a given query image. However, our work differs significantly in the following aspects. First, a query can be any part of the whole scene and it is not determined by users. Secondly, in our work, the resolution of a query could be higher or lower of the resolution of the whole scene. Third, the core idea of our study is to determine the correlating group of matched features between the zoomed-in and whole scenes and use this group of features to filter the retrieved set and estimate the location of a zoomed-in image in the whole scene. To achieve our goal, we utilize the SIFT algorithm to extract the features. We employ kd-trees and nearest neighbor search to structure and match the features. After that, we apply our method to determine the correlating group of matched features and reject the matches, that do not contribute to identify any relation between images. Finally, we filter the matched features to predict the scale and location of a zoomed-in image in the whole scene.

The remainder of this paper is structured as follows. Section 2 gives an overview of the prior works related to ND retrieval algorithms. Section 3 details the proposed method to improve the retrieval and localization of zoomed-in images. Section 4 describes the constructed dataset, evaluation measures, settings of our experiments and discusses the results. Finally, Sect. 5 presents the conclusion of this work and discusses possible future work.

2 Related Work

This section reviews the related approaches to near-duplicate image retrieval, specifically zoomed-in image retrieval. Convolution neural networks (CNN) have been involved in recent research of ND retrieval [16,31]. Such approaches require a huge amount of images and the known relation between them to complete the training process.

Almost all of the ND retrieval approaches require several processing steps that build up on each other. The first step is to extract features from images.

Keypoints features, more specifically, SIFT keypoints [26] are the most popular methods to extract features in the ND retrieval field. This is, due to its invariant properties to different kinds of image transformations and their robustness to viewpoint change, adding noise or blur to images. Therefore, various researches have presented improvements of the SIFT descriptor to reduce the time of matching and improve the performance of ND retrieval [2, 4, 18, 22]. In [18], the principle component analysis is applied to obtain the $64D$ SIFT descriptors. In [22] the dimensionality of the SIFT descriptor has been reduced by ignoring and averaging some component in the SIFT descriptor to get $96D$, $64D$ or $32D$ descriptors. In other research, the descriptor vectors of the SIFT features have been compressed to build compressed region SIFT$-64D$, $32D$ or $16D$ [2, 4]. The invariant and robust properties of the reduced SIFT descriptors have been verified in [2, 4] in the field of ND retrieval.

The next step is to structure the extracted features. For this, a lot of researches have used a bag of feature model representation of local features. The goal of using a bag of feature model is to accelerate the process of retrieval. This bag of feature model has been built using $k-$means clustering [14, 21, 25, 36] or a combination of hierarchical $k-$means clustering and inverted files [17, 29]. Hashing functions are other methods to structure the bag of feature model [6, 11]. Opposite to clustering methods, the application of hash functions requests no training stage. Therefore various kinds of hashing functions are combined with a bag of feature model to improve ND image retrieval. The $kd-$tree have been used to structure and identify the nearest neighbor features between two images [7]. It has been applied to obtain matched keypoints to solve tasks of finding the similarity and identifying duplicate regions in images [5, 15, 30]. The $kd-$tree is binary tree suitable to structure $k-$dimensional features. Therefore, it is appropriate to structure high dimensional descriptors such as the SIFT and the SURF descriptors.

After matching features of two images, the outliers should be filtered by thresholding the Euclidean distance among matched features [9, 15, 30]. A similarity measure based on the correlation coefficient between two features has been presented in [8]. Finally, to predict the relation or the transformation between two images a post-processing step is required. For this step, the Random Sample Consensus (RANSAC) method has been proposed as one of the most appropriate approaches to estimate the scale and rotation between images [13, 23]. The purpose of the RANSAC algorithm is to compute the homography matrix H concerning four matched features selected randomly. The matrix H is calculated iteratively for various samples. After that, the iteration with the highest number of inliers is selected to filter the remain matched features as inlier or outlier. Modifications of the RANSAC model have been discussed in [27, 32]. However, the focus of Self-Similarities approaches [34] and GOODSAC approach [27] is on tracing particular objects in images. Whereas we are looking for an object independent approach i.e., there is no previous knowledge about the content and size of processed images. The least median of squares (LMS) is a different approach to estimate the geometrical transformation between two matched images.

The main idea of this approach is to replace the sum with the median of the squared residuals [33]. However, the performance of both the RANSAC and the LMS decrease when the number of outlier increase [12].

In this work, we aim to improve the retrieval and localization of zoomed-in images even when a lot of matches are filtered as outliers or when only a few matches are detected. Therefore, we need to identify the correlating group of matched features and use this group to filter outliers and estimate the scale and location of the zoomed-in image in the whole scene. For this task, the computation costs of the RANSAC and the LMS are very expensive. Moreover, the RANSAC algorithm fails in estimating the correct relation or is not able to determine the relation at all when the matched features include a lot of outliers or when too few matches are detected. Therefore, in this work, we propose our novel method to predict outliers and specify the location of zoomed-in images in the corresponding whole scenes even if the matches include a lot of outliers or only few matched features are detected.

3 Proposed Approach

In this work, we aim to estimate the correlation between zoomed-in and whole scene images. To achieve this, we suggest to define the correlating group of matched features and uses them in further processing to filter the outliers, which do not indicate any meaningful information about the zoomed-in/whole scene relation. Based on the remaining set of matched features (correlating group), we estimate the scale and location of the zoomed-in image in the whole scene.

3.1   Correlation Estimation

In the optimal case, the matched features of the zoomed-in image form a dense region in the whole scene. However, in practice, sets of false matches may appear and also construct other dense regions in the whole scene (see Fig. 2(a)). Even when the matches form a dense region, they may contain a set of false matches. This is, because of the repeated pattern or similar texture in the whole scene or zoomed-in image. Therefore, in this work, we analyze the correlation between matched features using location information of features. Given a set M matches and their locations $L_z = \{l_{z1}, l_{z2}, ..., l_{zm}\}$, $L = \{l_1, l_2, ..., l_m\}$ in zoomed-in and whole scene images respectively. We pick three samples matches l_{zi}, l_{zj}, l_{zk} of L_z, that are non collinear, and their correspondence l_i, l_j, l_k of L. To consider them as a part of the correlating group, the edges joining these points should satisfy the following:

$$\left| \frac{e_{zi}}{max\{e_{zi}, e_{zj}, e_{zk}\}} - \frac{e_i}{max\{e_i, e_j, e_k\}} \right| < \epsilon \tag{1}$$

$$\left| \frac{e_{zj}}{max\{e_{zi}, e_{zj}, e_{zk}\}} - \frac{e_j}{max\{e_i, e_j, e_k\}} \right| < \epsilon \tag{2}$$

$$\left| \frac{e_{zk}}{max\left\{e_{zi}, e_{zj}, e_{zk}\right\}} - \frac{e_k}{max\left\{e_i, e_j, e_k\right\}} \right| < \epsilon \tag{3}$$

where e_{zi}, e_{zj}, e_{zk} and e_i, e_j, e_k are the edges of the constructed triangles in both of zoomed-in and whole scene images respectively. Theoretically, the differences in 1, 2 and 3 should be zeros. But because of the approximate localization of features, we allow a difference smaller than a predefined threshold ϵ. To avoid the effect of zooming-in and resolution change, for each selected set l_{zi}, l_{zj}, l_{zk} of L_z we justify that no identification case occur between l_i, l_j, l_k of L_z. So that, all matches are accepted, that their locations satisfy the following condition.

$$d\left(l_{zi}, l_{zj}\right) > dis\_thr * min\{h_z, w_z\} \wedge d\left(\{l_i, l_j\}\right) > dis\_thr * min\{h, w\} \tag{4}$$

where h_z, w_z and h, w are the height and width of the zoomed-in and whole scene images respectively. dis_thr is a selected threshold defined during our experiments. This process is repeated iteratively for all possible combinations of matches. If a specific amount of samples (greater than a predefined threshold $corr\_thr$) fulfills relations 1, 2, 3 and 4, then the correlation between matches is confirmed. Otherwise, no correlation can be defined furthermore the retrieved image is recommended to be non-relevant.

3.2 Scale and Location Estimation

After estimating the correlation among matches, we filter out the matches that, they do not indicate any information about the relation between images. For this step, based on the locations of matched features, we form all possible triangles in zoomed-in and whole scene images. After that, the average edge ratios are computed and stored as follow:

$$avg = \left(\frac{e_{zi}}{e_i} + \frac{e_{zj}}{e_j} + \frac{e_{zk}}{e_k} \right) / 3 \tag{5}$$

So that, for each matched feature, a vector, of edge ratios, is formed. To filter the outlier, the median and absolute deviation of all vectors around the median are calculated as described in [24]. All matches that their vectors contain many irrelevant edges greater than a specific threshold $reject\_thr$ are excluded. The remained matches form the correlating group. The relations between matches in the filtered group are analyzed again to determine the robust matches that will be the candidates to estimate the scale and location information of the zoomed-in image in the whole scene.

4   Evaluation

To evaluate the performance of our proposed method, we construct a suitable image dataset (see Subsect. 4.1). This dataset contains the zoomed-in images that, they cover patches of various sizes and various resolution of panorama images. Furthermore, we introduce the evaluation measures (see Subsect. 4.2) that we use to evaluate the performance. Afterward, we discuss the results of our experiment in the Subsect. 4.3.

4.1 Dataset

To verify the robustness of our method, we construct our image dataset using panorama images downloaded from [1]. Ten various percentages are used to determine the area of panorama images that are covered by the zoomed-in images. These percentages are: 56%, 40%, 35%, 30%, 25%, 20%, 15%, 10%, 5% and 2% of the size of original panorama images. For each percentage, two zoomed-in images of different locations are chosen randomly. After that, the cubic interpolation model [20] is employed to scale up (i.e. increase the resolution) the zoomed-in image. The scaled-up image has a 150% resolution of the original zoomed-in image. Using the same model, we create four scaled-down zoomed-in images. These scaled-down images have 70%, 50%, 30% or 15% of the resolution of original zoomed-in images. Based on these settings, 200 zoomed-in images are generated for each panorama image. Using 250 panoramas, a zoomed-in dataset of size 50,000 is constructed. We reduce the resolution of panorama images four times too to build four sets of query images, each contains 250 images. The built set of query images are Q_Scale1, Q_Scale2, Q_Scale3 and Q_Scale4 and they have 60%, 30% 15% and 5% of the resolution of the original panoramas respectively. Using these sets, we can analyze the effect of scale change on correlation detection and determine which scale is more appropriate to estimate the correlation and localize the zoomed-in images.

4.2 Evaluation Measures

To evaluate the retrieval performance of our proposed method, we compute the mean recall MR as follow [3]:

$$MR = \frac{1}{Q} \sum_{q=1}^{Q} Recall(q) \quad \text{where} \quad Recall(q) = \frac{N_{qr}}{N_q} \tag{6}$$

where Q, is the total number of query images and $Recall(q)$ is the recall of a query image q. N_q is the number of zoomed-in images, which are relevant to a specific query whole scene image. N_{qr} is the number of retrieved and relevant zoomed-in images. To present the distribution of recall values around the MR, we compute the variance of the recall VR as follow:

$$VR = \frac{1}{Q} \sum_{q=1}^{Q} (Recall(q) - MR)^2 \tag{7}$$

To evaluate the performance based on the ranking of the results, we compute the mean average precision MAP, which presents the distribution of the relevant zoomed-in images in the retrieved results and is defined as:

$$MAP = \sum_{q=1}^{Q} \frac{Ap(q)}{Q} \quad \text{where} \quad AP(q) = \frac{1}{n} \sum_{i=1}^{n} p(i) \times r(i) \tag{8}$$

where $Ap(q)$ is the average precision for q, $r(i) = 1$ if the ith retrieved image is relevant otherwise $r(i) = 0$. $p(i)$ is the precision at the ith position.

To compute the relative error of zoomed-in image localization, we divide the offset errors by length of width of query images depending on the direction in which the offset occurs. In this way, we avoid the bias of the computed error to the resolution of the query image. To present the error of localization in pixels, we compute the absolute error as the sum of offsets in horizontal and vertical directions. After that, we compute the mean and variance of the relative error to describe the scatter of the individual localization errors around the mean relative error.

4.3 Result

The features of both zoomed-in dataset and panorama (query) images are extracted utilizing the SIFT algorithm. Since the values of scale and contrast parameters of the SIFT algorithm affect the retrieval process [3], we suggest giving them fix values during all of our experiments. The features are structured by creating the $kd-$tree. The nearest neighbor and Euclidean distance are used to define the matched features. The resulted images are sorted based on their similarity to the query image. As each query image has 200 relevant images in the dataset, the top 200 ranked images are recommended to be the retrieved set. The Experiments discuss three scenarios: First, the effect of scale change of query images on the ranking of retrieved results. Second, estimate and exclude the non-relevant zoomed-in images of the retrieved results. Third and finally, determine the location of the zoomed-in image in the whole scene.

Down Scale Effect. To explain the effect of scale change on the retrieved results, we scale query images using various rates as explained in Sect. 4.1. Afterward, we evaluate the retrieved results as described in Sect. 4.2. Table 1 presents the results when query images are scaled using various percentages. The results show the best performance when query images are downscaled to 30% of the size of the original image. Both mean recall and average precision decrease when query images have the original size or downscaled to 60% of the original one. The reason is the high resolution, which causes producing more features and later increases the possibility of getting false matches. Moreover, Table 1 describes that the variance of mean recall increases when the scale decrease to cover only 15% or 5% of the resolution of original queries.

Exclude Non-relevant Results. To filter the results, we apply the relations 1, 2, 3 and 4 of Sect. 3.1 on the best 200 retrieved zoomed-in images. In the experiment, we find that a reasonable value of ϵ could be in a range $[0.02, 0.09]$. The dis_thr relies on the size and resolution of query images. For our experiment, we identify its value to be in the range $[0.008, 0.03]$. Table 2 presents the average of rejected non-relevant and retrieved zoomed-in images. It shows that the query with 30% of the resolution of original queries (i.e. Q_Scale2) retrieves the

Table 1. Comparison of retrieval performance when query images are scaled down using various scale levels. The average mean recall and the average variance of the recall are computed based on the top 200 retrieved images.

Scale down ratio	Mean recall %	Variance of recall %	Average precision %
Q_Scale1: 60%	67.77	1.88	53.36
Q_Scale2: 30%	**80.00**	**1.38**	**67.09**
Q_Scale3: 15%	73.70	2.03	61.86
Q_Scale4: 5%	70.94	2.17	60.43

best results. However, our method detects all non-relevant results even when the query downscaled to cover only 5% (i.e. Q_Scale4) of the resolution of the original queries. Furthermore, Table 2 clarifies that our suggested method detects a part of retrieved and relevant results as non-relevant. The least amount of rejected relevant results are found by query images of set Q_Scale2 and then by Q_Scale1.

Table 2. The performance of our suggested method to detect non-relevant retrieved images (first row). Through this process, some of the relevant and retrieved results are detected as non-relevant (second row). For this experiment, we set $\epsilon = 0.05$ and correlating threshold $corr\_thr = 30\%$ of the size of average edge vector (see Subsect. 3.2).

Scale down ratio	Q_Scale1	Q_Scale2	Q_Scale3	Q_Scale4
Rejected non-relevant & retrieved (%)	97.22	**99.96**	99.86	99.82
Rejected relevant & retrieved (%)	7.20	**4.02**	15.16	21.85

Fig. 1. An example where our proposed method estimates the correlation group of matches (green lines) and localize the zoomed-in image in the whole scene successfully. Whereas, the RANSAC model fails to predict the relation. In this example, the detected features are 530 and 35 in the whole scene and zoomed-in images respectively. The total number of matches is five and there are no detected outliers. (Color figure online)

Localize Zoomed-In Images. After estimating the correlating group of matches, the locations of zoomed-in images are identified as explained in Subsect. 3.2. For our experiment, we employ a threshold to reject the irrelevant edges. This threshold is $reject\_thr = 25\%$. We compare the performance of our method with the performance of the RANSAC model to estimate the correlation between images and localize the zoomed-in image in the whole scenes. The results describe that our method is further robust than the RANSAC model in estimating the correlation and location of zoomed-in images in whole scenes. Table 3 presents that the performance of the RANSAC model decreases faster than the performance of our approach when the resolution of query images decreases like in Q_Scale3 and Q_Scale4. This is, due to the instability of the RANSAC model when the number of outliers increases. Figure 1 shows an example where our proposed method assesses the correlation between the matches and predicts the location of the zoomed-in image successfully even when only five found matches. Whereas, these matches are not sufficient to estimate the correlation when the RANSAC model is applied. Figure 2(a) shows an instance of having a lot of outliers between matches. In this case, our method predicts the correlation and location of a zoomed-in image even when more than half of matches are marked being outliers. When the amount of known outliers is lesser than the half of matches, the RANSAC model, as well as our method, estimates the correlation among the correlating group as detailed in Fig. 2(b). The third row in Table 3 indicates the least relative localization error found by Q_Scale1 next by Q_Scale2. Whereas, the least absolute error of localization is found by Q_Scale4 and next by Q_Scale2. However, the localization shifting is trivial through all established scales. Consequently, the localization is performable even when the resolution decreases a lot. We do not calculate the localization errors detected by the RANSAC model because it estimates the homography change between two images based on the correlating group of matches. When the RANSAC model

Table 3. The performance of the RANSAC model versus our proposed method given below. The results present the rate of exact localized zoomed-in images applying our method and projected images using the RANSAC model. RANSAC model estimates the transformation matrix but does not return any information about locations. Therefore, we compute the localization errors only for our method.

Scale down ratio	Q_Scale1	Q_Scale2	Q_Scale3	Q_Scale4
RANSAC model (%)	83.92	79.33	60.32	42.76
Proposed method (%)	**95.00**	**94.68**	87.00	73.40
Relative error by proposed method (%)	$\mathbf{1.90 \cdot 10^{-3}}$	$3.09 \cdot 10^{-3}$	$1.05 \cdot 10^{-2}$	$7.15 \cdot 10^{-2}$
Absolute error by proposed method (pixel)	2.53	2.48	3.12	**1.11**

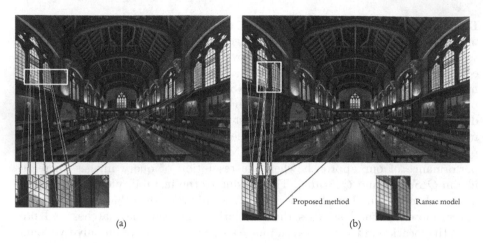

Fig. 2. (a) An example where our proposed method determines correctly the correlating group of matched features and localized the zoomed-in image in the whole scene whereas, the RANSAC model fails to predict the relation. In this example, the extracted features in the whole scene and zoomed-in images are 359 and 48 respectively. The total number of matches is 17. Additionally, more than half of matches are detected as outliers (i.e. ten outliers). (b) An example shows that our proposed method and the RANSAC model find successfully the zoomed-in image and predict its location in the whole scene. In this example, the detected features are 359 and 70 in the whole scene and zoomed-in images respectively. The total number of matches is 16. Only six matches are identified as outliers (pink). (Color figure online)

estimates the transformation correctly, we suggest that the retrieved image is localized unless the model predicts no correlation between images.

5   Conclusion

In this work, we proposed a method to improve zoomed-in image retrieval and localization. We achieved this by identifying the correlating group of features between zoomed-in and whole scene images. We computed the correlation by estimating the symmetry of all constructed triangles that are built based on the locations of matched features. Based on the correlating group, we decided whether a zoomed-in image is a part of a given whole scene. After that, we used the correlating group to determine the location of the zoomed-in image in the whole scene without any previous information about the relation between them. The results characterized that our proposed method is more robust than the RANSAC model to assess the correlation and localize zoomed-in images even when the matches contain many outliers or only a set of few matches are found.

In a future study, we intend to extend our approach to predict the intersection relation between two images. Furthermore, we aim to analyze the performance of our proposed approach when additional modifications are applied to the zoomed-in or whole scene images.

References

1. Source for panorama images. Last proceeding, August 2018. http://en.wikipedia. org/wiki/User:Diliff#/media
2. Alyosef, A.A., Nürnberger, A.: Adapted SIFT descriptor for improved near duplicate retrieval. In: Proceedings of the 5th ICPRAM, pp. 55–64 (2016)
3. Alyosef, A.A., Nürnberger, A.: The effect of SIFT features properties in descriptors matching for near-duplicate retrieval tasks. In: Proceedings of the 6th International Conference on Pattern Recognition Applications and Methods, pp. 703–710 (2017)
4. Ahmad Alyosef, A., Nürnberger, A.: Near-duplicate retrieval: a benchmark study of modified SIFT descriptors. In: Fred, A., De Marsico, M., Sanniti di Baja, G. (eds.) ICPRAM 2016. LNCS, vol. 10163, pp. 121–138. Springer, Cham (2017). https://doi.org/10.1007/978-3-319-53375-9_7
5. Amerini, I., Ballan, L., Caldelli, R., Bimbo, A.D., Serra, G.: A SIFT-based forensic method for copy-move attack detection and transformation recovery. IEEE Trans. Inf. Forensics Secur. **6**, 1099–1110 (2011)
6. Auclair, A., Vincent, N., Cohen, L.A.: Hash functions for near duplicate image retrieval. In: WACV (2009)
7. Beis, J.S., Lowe, D.G.: Shape indexing using approximate nearest neighbour search in high-dimensional spaces. In: IEEE Conference on Computer Vision and Pattern Recognition, pp. 1000–1006 (1997)
8. Bravo-Solorio, S., Nandi, A.K.: Exposing duplicated regions affected by reflection rotation and scaling. In: Proceedings of International Conference on Acoustics Speech and Signal Processing, pp. 1880–1883 (2011)
9. Christlein, V., Riess, C., Angelopoulou, E.: On rotation invariance in copy-move forgery detection. In: Proceedings of IEEE Workshop on Information Forensics and Security, pp. 129–134 (2010)
10. Chum, O., Philbin, J., Isard, M., Zisserman, A.: Scalable near identical image and shot detection. In: Proceedings of CIVR (2007)
11. Chum, O., Philbin, J., Zisserman, A.: Near duplicate image detection: min-Hash and tf-idf weighting. In: British Machine Vision Conference (2008)
12. Dubrofsky, E.: Homography estimation: Masters essay carleton university. The University of British Columbia, pp. 1–32 (2009)
13. Fishler, M., Bolles, R.: Random sample consensus: a paradigm for model fitting with applications to image analysis and automated cartography. Commun. ACM **6**, 381–395 (1981)
14. Grauman, K., Darrell, T.: The pyramid match kernel: efficient learning with sets of features. J. Mach. Learn. Res. **8**, 725–760 (2007)
15. Huang, H., Guo, W., Zhang, Y.: Detection of copy-move forgery in digital images using SIFT algorithm. In: Proceedings of Pacific-Asia Workshop on Computational Intelligence and Industrial Application (2008)
16. Huang, S., Hang, H.M.: Multi-query image retrieval using CNN and SIFT features. In: Asia-Pacific Signal and Information Processing Association Annual Summit and Conference (2017)
17. Jiang, M., Zhang, S., Li, H., Metaxas, D.N.: Computer-aided diagnosis of mammographic masses using scalable image retrieval. IEEE Trans. Biomed. Eng. **62**, 783–792 (2015)
18. Ke, Y., Sukthankar, R.: PCA-SIFT: a more distinctive representation for local image descriptors. In: CVPR, pp. 506–513 (2004)

19. Ke, Y., Sukthankar, R., Huston, L., Chang, S.: Efficient near-duplicate detection and sub image retrieval. In: IEEE Trans. Proceedings of ACM International Conference on Multimedia, pp. 869–876 (2004)
20. Keys, R.: Cubic convolution interpolation for digital image processing. IEEE Trans. Acoust. Speech Signal Process. **29**, 1153–1160 (1981)
21. Grauman, K., Darrell, T.: Pyramid match kernels: Discriminative classification with sets of image features. In: Proceedings of ICCV (2005)
22. Khan, N., McCane, B., Wyvill, G.: SIFT and SURF performance evaluation against various image deformations on benchmark dataset. In: DICTA (2011)
23. Lee, J.J., Kim., G.Y.: Robust estimation of camera homography using fuzzy RANSAC. In: ICCSA 07: International Conference on Computational Science and Its Applications (2007)
24. Leys, C., Ley, C., Klein, O., Bernard, P., Licata, L.: Detecting outliers: do not use standard deviation around the mean use absolute deviation around the median. J. Exp. Soc. Psychol. **49**, 764–766 (2013)
25. Li, J., Qian, X., Li, Q., Zhao, Y., Wang, L., Tang, Y.Y.: Mining near duplicate image groups. Multimedia Tools Appl. **74**, 655–669 (2014)
26. Lowe, D.: Distinctive image features from scale-invariant keypoints. J. Comput. Vis. **60**, 91–110 (2004)
27. Michaelsen, E., von Hansen, W., Kirchhof, M., Meidow, J., Stilla, U.: Estimating the essential matrix: GOODSAC versus RANSAC. In: Proceedings of the Photogrammetric Computer Vision, pp. 1–6 (2006)
28. Mikulik, A., Chum, O., Matas, J.: Image retrieval for online browsing in large image collections. In: Brisaboa, N., Pedreira, O., Zezula, P. (eds.) SISAP 2013. LNCS, vol. 8199, pp. 3–15. Springer, Heidelberg (2013). https://doi.org/10.1007/978-3-642-41062-8_2
29. Nistèr, D., Stewènius, H.: Scalable recognition with a vocabulary tree. In: CVPR, pp. 2161–2168 (2006)
30. Pan, X., Lyu, S.: Region duplication detection using image feature matching. IEEE Trans. Inf. Forensics Secur. **5**, 857–867 (2010)
31. Radenovic, F., Tolias, G., Chum, O.: Fine-tuning CNN image retrieval with no human annotation. In arXiv (2017)
32. Raguram, R., Frahm, J.-M., Pollefeys, M.: A comparative analysis of RANSAC techniques leading to adaptive real-time random sample consensus. In: Forsyth, D., Torr, P., Zisserman, A. (eds.) ECCV 2008. LNCS, vol. 5303, pp. 500–513. Springer, Heidelberg (2008). https://doi.org/10.1007/978-3-540-88688-4_37
33. Rousseeuw, P.: Least median of squares regression. J. Am. Stat. Assoc. **79**, 871–880 (1984)
34. Shechtman, E., Irani, M.: Matching local self-similarities across images and videos. In: Proceedings IEEE Conference on Computer Vision and Pattern Recognition, pp. 1–8 (2007)
35. Xu, D., Cham, T., Yan, S., Duan, L., Chang, S.: Near duplicate identification with spatially aligned pyramid matching. IEEE Trans. Circ. Syst. Video Technol. **20**, 1068–1079 (2010)
36. Yang, Y., Newsam, S.: Comparing SIFT descriptors and Gabor texture features for classification of remote sensed imagery. In: Proceedings of the 15th IEEE on Image Processing, pp. 1852–1855 (2008)
37. Zhang, D.Q., et al.: Detecting image near-duplicate by stochastic attribute relational graph matching with learning. In: Proceedings of the 12th Annual ACM International Conference on Multimedia (2004)

Homogeneity Index as Stopping Criterion for Anisotropic Diffusion Filter

Fernando Pereira dos Santos(✉) and Moacir Antonelli Ponti

Institute of Mathematical and Computer Sciences (ICMC),
University of São Paulo (USP), São Carlos, SP, Brazil
{fernando_persan,ponti}@usp.br
http://www.icmc.usp.br/~moacir

Abstract. The Anisotropic Diffusion Filter is an image smoothing method often applied to improve segmentation and classification tasks. Because it is an adaptive and iterative method, one should define some stopping criterion in order to avoid unnecessary computational cost while producing the desired output. However, state-of-the-art methods in this regard consider costly comparative functions computed at each iteration or allowing extra iterations before actually stopping. Therefore, in this paper we propose a new stopping criterion to overcome this difficulty that defines the number of iterations without additional comparisons during the image processing. Our stopping criterion is based on the image homogeneity index and the constants included in the filter definition, which can be calculated before the first iteration. Using three different measures of similarity in grayscale and colorful images from different domains with variation of tonality, our results indicate that the proposed stopping criterion reduces the number of iterations and, simultaneously, maintains the quality of the diffused images. Consequently, our method can be applied to images from different sources, color composition, and levels of noise.

Keywords: Anisotropic Diffusion Filter · Stopping criterion · Smoothing

1 Introduction

A diffusion filter $I(x, y; t) = I_0(x, y) * G(x, y; t)$ consists of applying convolutions of a noisy image I_0 with a Gaussian filter G to obtain derived images I_t during successive iterations t [16]. The filters based on the diffusion equation aim to achieve smoothing and, simultaneously, maintain the boundaries of the objects contained in the image. However, in regions where the process of diffusion is very intense, the original boundaries of the image are lost. To solve this issue, the Anisotropic Diffusion Filter was developed to smooth the internal regions while maintaining border regions [3]. The number of iterations of this method is usually defined according to the amount of noise present in the image, applying

M. Vento and G. Percannella (Eds.): CAIP 2019, LNCS 11679, pp. 269–280, 2019.
https://doi.org/10.1007/978-3-030-29891-3_24

an adaptive mask that changes according to the properties defined in the current iteration [15]. Despite its applicability and good results in practice, the computational cost of this filter is high mainly because it is an iterative method. For each iteration of the process, the diffusion coefficient must be calculated on each pixel based on its neighborhood [6]. In addition, in order to avoid loss of relevant information, it is necessary to control the number of iterations by stipulating a stopping criterion [1].

In the literature, the stopping criterion vary in its conception, from fixed values determined by the level of Gaussian noise present [3] to the adaptive methods which apply some function to determine if the diffused image is the most adequate. The adaptive methods apply validations to each iteration, such as local gradient between flat regions and borders [22] or entropy to maximize the correlation between the diffused and original image [7]. Another possibility is to apply similarity metrics as an attempt to minimize the distance between the images, in which a previously defined threshold is required [23]. While fixed methods may cause oversmoothing, the adaptive ones carry higher processing cost due to constant validations in the diffused image. Hence, a method that offers a good compromise in terms of image quality and computational cost is still to be investigated.

When the application involves medical diagnosis, such as skin lesions [15], 3D computational microscopy [17], magnetic resonance imaging [18], or X-radiography [10], the images may have very high resolution, increasing the computational cost of each iteration. Contrarily, in applications that demand immediate responses, such as fingerprint [8], unnecessary iterations may delay the image validation. Due to these requirements, the stopping criterion must be generalizable to different resolutions, in both grayscale and colorful images without increasing processing. With this objective, we propose a new stopping criterion for the Anisotropic Diffusion Filter, which consists of properties from the noisy image and parameters from the filter definition. In our method, the number of iterations is stipulated only once considering the Homogeneity Index, aiming at reducing the computational cost and guaranteeing the diffused image quality.

2   Anisotropic Diffusion Filter

The original equation of the Anisotropic Diffusion Filter $u_t = g \cdot | \bigtriangledown u|$ [16] was improved by the addition of terms, such as mean curvature flow $div(\bigtriangledown u/| \bigtriangledown u|)$ [2], forcing term $(u - I)$ [14], and moderated selector $(1 - g)$ [3], as in Eq. 1. In this equation, u is the diffused image at iteration t of an original image I. Additionally, the equation has a diffusion speed λ, a divergence operator div, and the gradient of u, $\bigtriangledown u$.

$$u_t = g \cdot | \bigtriangledown u| \cdot \text{div} \left(\frac{\bigtriangledown u}{| \bigtriangledown u|} \right) - \lambda \cdot (1 - g) \cdot (u - I), \tag{1}$$

where g is a nonincreasing smooth function, in which $g(0) = 1$, $g(s) \geq 0$, and $g(s) \to 0$ when $s \to \infty$. Consequently, when g (see Eq. 2, where K is a parameter to be manually defined) is equivalent to 1, the region is heavily smoothed and when it approaches 0, the smoothing effect is negligible [3].

$$g_{i,j} = \frac{1}{1 + K \cdot (|\nabla (G_\sigma * u_{i,j})|)^2} \tag{2}$$

The convolution $G_\sigma * u_{i,j}$ (defined in Eq. 3) is a Gaussian scale space of g. Hence, the Gaussian kernel G_σ of a coordinate (i,j), described in Eq. 4, considers the standard deviation of the noise σ and a positive constant A.

$$G_\sigma * u_{i,j} = \frac{1}{36} \cdot \Big[G_\sigma(1,1) \cdot u_{(i-1,j-1)} + G_\sigma(-1,1) \cdot u_{(i+1,j-1)}$$

$$+ G_\sigma(1,-1) \cdot u_{(i-1,j+1)} + G_\sigma(-1,-1) \cdot u_{(i+1,j+1)} + 16 \cdot G_\sigma(0,0) \cdot u_{(i,j)}$$

$$+ 4 \cdot G_\sigma(0,1) \cdot u_{(i,j-1)} + 4 \cdot G_\sigma(1,0) \cdot u_{(i-1,j)} + 4 \cdot G_\sigma(-1,0) \cdot u_{(i+1,j)} \tag{3}$$

$$+ 4 \cdot G_\sigma(0,-1) \cdot u_{(i,j+1)} \Big]$$

$$G_\sigma(i,j) = \frac{1}{A \cdot \pi \cdot \sigma^2} \cdot e^{\frac{-|i^2+j^2|}{A \cdot \sigma^2}} \tag{4}$$

Based on the equations that define the Anisotropic Diffusion Filter, one should evaluate Eq. 5 at each pixel of the image to be smoothed. The discrete approximation of this filter is given below, in which parameter Δt defines the temporal evolution between iterations. For brevity of description, we refer to [3] and [4] for details of all steps to obtain the discrete equation.

$$u_{i,j}^{t+1} = u_{i,j}^t + \Delta t \cdot g_{i,j}^t \cdot \Bigg[\frac{\left(\frac{u_{i+1,j}^t - u_{i-1,j}^t}{2}\right)^2 \cdot (u_{i,j+1}^t - 2 \cdot u_{i,j}^t + u_{i,j-1}^t)}{\left(\frac{u_{i+1,j}^t - u_{i-1,j}^t}{2}\right)^2 + \left(\frac{u_{i,j+1}^t - u_{i,j-1}^t}{2}\right)^2}$$

$$- \frac{((u_{i+1,j}^t - u_{i-1,j}^t) \cdot (u_{i,j+1}^t - u_{i,j-1}^t)) \cdot \left(\frac{u_{i+1,j+1}^t - u_{i+1,j-1}^t - u_{i-1,j+1}^t + u_{i-1,j-1}^t}{2}\right)}{\left(\frac{u_{i+1,j}^t - u_{i-1,j}^t}{2}\right)^2 + \left(\frac{u_{i,j+1}^t - u_{i,j-1}^t}{2}\right)^2}$$

$$+ \frac{\left(\frac{u_{i,j+1}^t - u_{i,j-1}^t}{2}\right)^2 \cdot (u_{i+1,j}^t - 2 \cdot u_{i,j}^t + u_{i-1,j}^t)}{\left(\frac{u_{i+1,j}^t - u_{i-1,j}^t}{2}\right)^2 + \left(\frac{u_{i,j+1}^t - u_{i,j-1}^t}{2}\right)^2} \Bigg] - \lambda \cdot (1 - g_{i,j}^t) \cdot (u_{i,j}^t - u_{i,j}^0)$$

$$\tag{5}$$

2.1   Homogeneity Index as Stopping Criterion

The Anisotropic Diffusion Filter requires a stopping criterion to interrupt the smoothing process. Many of the stopping criterion in the literature do not consider the properties of the image, being dependent only on the parameters that define the filter equations. A widely used stopping criterion is the Optimal

Smoothing Time (OST) [3] that relates the standard deviation of Gaussian noise σ to the value of the constant A contained in the Gaussian function: $T = \frac{\sigma^2}{A}$. Although widely used in many applications, this method does not consider the properties from each image, considering a fixed value of iterations for the same scenario. By ignoring the image content, unnecessary iterations increase computational cost. Due to this fact, in this paper we propose a new stopping criterion which is based on an image homogeneity measure that allows to define the number of iterations that is appropriate to some image homogeneity characteristics. In Eq. 6 is defined the Homogeneity Index which considers the value of the pixel p in each coordinate (i, j) of an $N \times M$ image.

$$Homogeneity = \sum_{i=0}^{N-1} \sum_{j=0}^{M-1} \frac{p(i,j)}{1 + |i - j|} \tag{6}$$

Based on the Homogeneity Index, we propose and analyze two novel stopping criterion for the Anisotropic Diffusion Filter: Basic Homogeneity Index Stopping Criterion (BHISC); and Complete Homogeneity Index Stopping Criterion (CHISC). BHISP (defined in Eq. 7) considers, besides the terms A and σ from the OST Equation, the maximum Homogeneity Index ($maxHomo$) among all channels that compose the image. Therefore, this criterion can be applied in both color and gray levels images. In the latter is not necessary to verify the maximum index because it has only one to be considered.

$$BHISC = \frac{maxHomo \cdot A}{\sigma^2} \tag{7}$$

Depending on the image resolution to be smoothed, each iteration can be very computationally costly. For this reason, BHISC is a good approximation of our most accurate method: CHISC (see Eq. 8). CHISC is also based on the Homogeneity Index, however it allows extra iterations by adding a proportion between the temporal evolution Δt and noise σ by the smoothing constant K.

$$CHISC = BHISC + \frac{\Delta t \cdot \sigma}{K} \tag{8}$$

BHISC and CHISC are computed only once, before the first iteration of the filter, not requiring comparisons along the iterations [7], neither performing other complex analysis during filtering [11]. The rationale behind our approach is that homogeneous images require fewer iterations, whereas heterogeneous images need more smoothing. With this new approach, the stopping criterion is defined according to both the image properties (homogeneity) and the parameters that compose the filter implementation.

3   Experimental Setup

Six images were studied in our experiments, two in grayscale and four in RGB, with the purpose of analyzing a different homogeneity in tonality. With this variation, we aim to generalize our stopping criterion for both gray and colorful representations and, simultaneously, in homogeneous and heterogeneous images. To this context, we adopted three classic images (Cameraman, Lena, and Mandrill) and three others from datasets of different domains, often used for recognition tasks: Kangaroo [24] (kangaroo 10041); 102 Flower [13] (flower 00254); and HAM10000 [19] (skin lesion 25234), as presented in Fig. 1.

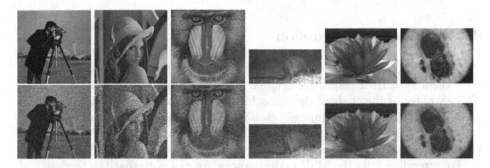

Fig. 1. Images applied into the experiments: Cameraman (436 × 436); Lena (220 × 220); Mandrill (450 × 449); Kangaroo (200 × 430); Flower (500 × 667); and Skin lesion (450 × 600). The images on top are the original ones and the images on bottom are the respective noisy images (applying $\sigma = 0.1$).

The maximum homogeneity (among the three channels) from the original images are, approximately: 1913 (Cameraman); 988 (Lena); 2539 (Mandrill); 845 (Kangaroo); 2456 (Flower); and 2616 (Skin lesion). This fluctuation implies a wide range of contrasts, indicating our experiment is appropriate for our method validation. For each image, Gaussian noise was applied varying $\sigma = 0.025, 0.05, 0.1$. This is important to evaluate the behavior of the stopping criterion in different levels of noise. For color images, we perform noise addition and filtering on the three channels separately.

3.1 Parameters Definition

The Anisotropic Diffusion Filter has as parameters the standard deviation of the noise σ, the diffusion speed λ, the temporal evolution Δt, the positive constant from Gaussian function A, and the smoothing constant K. In all experiments, we adopted $\Delta t = 0.1$, $K = 0.0008$, and $\lambda = \sigma$ as suggested in [4,15]. We defined a maximum number of iterations as $T = 100$, and to guarantee this we need to ensure $T = \sigma^2/A = 100$. Therefore, A must be computed according to the level of Gaussian noise. Consequently, for $\sigma = 0.025, 0.05$, and 0.1, A corresponded respectively to $625 \cdot 10^{-5}, 25 \cdot 10^{-4}$, and $1 \cdot 10^{-3}$.

3.2 Evaluation

To evaluate the improvement in those noisy images, three measures were adopted: Mean Square Error (MSE) [20]; Peak Signal-to-Noise Ratio (PSNR) [5];

and Structural Similarity (SSIM) [21]. MSE is a measure intensely applied for similarity comparison between images, in which the difference between all matching pixels is calculated, in which low values represent better results. PSNR is a logarithmic measure that considers MSE in the equation and its main application is for image reconstruction. SSIM is a more complex measure in relation to MSE and PSNR, determining the similarity in a range of $[0, 1]$. For PSNR and SSIM higher values are better [9,12].

4   Results and Discussion

We applied the Anisotropic Diffusion Filter (Eq. 5) to the noisy images and compare them with their respective original representation (before noise addition). The graphics in Fig. 2 show the smoothing performances of the filter along all iterations (0 to 100) for all images (each row is a different image) and in relation to each measure: in the first column MSE; in the central column PSRN; and in the latter one SSIM.

By attending only the MSE performances, we can note that the tendency of successive iterations is to reduce the initial dissimilarity until some optimal number of iterations (in which we observe the highest similarity with original image), representing an equilibrium of smoothing and detail maintenance. In contrast, PSRN and SSIM aim to find their ideal performance with more iterations. In this scenario, the "Cameraman", "Mandrill", "Flower", and "Skin lesion" images have progressive performance curves that tend to establish the optimal stopping point with few iterations and remain practically stable. However, the "Kangaroo" image presents highest irregularity, since it is a homogeneous image and the smoothing found the ideal point more quickly. After that, it begins a progressive degradation until regains its equilibrium.

An important detail in all measures is the curvature of convergence to the ideal value. With few iterations, the variation is more intense, indicating noise still contaminates the image. However, after all noise the filter was designed to reduce was removed, the results show little variation between iterations. Due to the lack of improvement after the break-even point, more iterations are unnecessary, implying only computational cost. Additionally, as we can observe by the behavior of the curves that express the measurements, this ideal point is located somewhere between the first and half the number of maximum iterations. Note also that, as expected, noisier images have greater dissimilarity with their respective original representation, even with the application of the filter.

Based on the metrics at each iteration, we highlight the better results and the respective iteration for each noisy image. Table 1 shows the performance with MSE, in which we compared the result of the calculated iteration designated (Eqs. 7 and 8 for BHISC and CHISC) with OST [3] by 100 iterations.

By inspecting the better results, we observed that there is a large variation of the ideal iteration number ("Kangaroo" with 0.025 of Gaussian noise requires only 3 iterations while "Skin lesion" with 0.05 of Gaussian noise requires 70 iterations). Therefore, applying the same filter with 100 iterations causes wastage

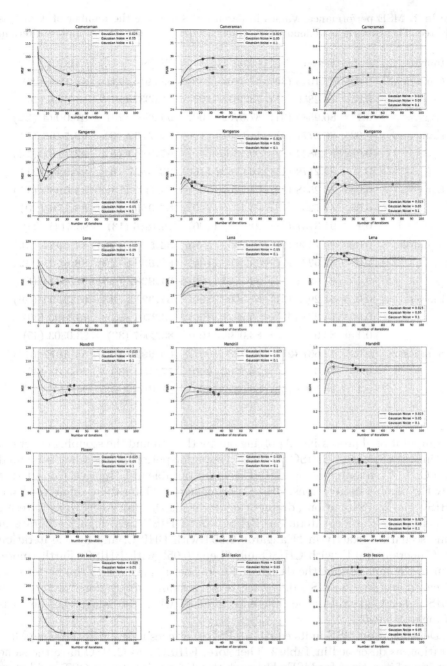

Fig. 2. Performance graphics of the Anisotropic Diffusion Filter during consecutive iterations. The zero iteration represents the original noisy image, i.e. without smoothing. The red dots represent the best result; the black ones represent CHISC. Each row represents an image and each column a different evaluation measure (from left to right: MSE, PSNR, and SSIM). (Color figure online)

Table 1. MSE performance. Values in parentheses indicate the number of iterations selected. The values in bold denote performance superior to the OST stopping criterion.

Image	σ	Better	OST [3]	BHISC	CHISC
Cameraman	0.025	67.1045 (32)	67.7167 (100)	69.4914 (19)	68.2729 (22)
	0.05	78.2859 (41)	78.5017 (100)	81.0337 (19)	79.1346 (26)
	0.1	86.9587 (31)	87.5759 (100)	90.2608 (20)	**87.0044 (32)**
Kangaroo	0.025	86.2771 (3)	110.3914 (100)	**92.7162 (8)**	**98.5406 (11)**
	0.05	87.9844 (8)	99.13 (100)	**87.9844 (8)**	**92.1161 (14)**
	0.1	93.2179 (11)	103.7822 (100)	**93.5827 (8)**	**97.945 (21)**
Lena	0.025	83.2548 (22)	84.2207 (100)	85.2445 (13)	**84.0989 (17)**
	0.05	87.7298 (14)	93.1926 (100)	**87.9854 (13)**	**89.176 (20)**
	0.1	91.3737 (47)	91.7285 (100)	95.1886 (13)	93.4141 (25)
Mandrill	0.025	80.7409 (9)	85.2392 (100)	**84.5601 (26)**	**84.5984 (29)**
	0.05	87.628 (17)	89.3796 (100)	**88.6364 (25)**	**88.6501 (32)**
	0.1	91.6814 (33)	92.1624 (100)	**91.9282 (25)**	**91.8344 (37)**
Flower	0.025	61.2926 (31)	61.4067 (100)	**61.3213 (33)**	**61.3504 (36)**
	0.05	73.273 (49)	73.2971 (100)	73.3701 (33)	73.3196 (39)
	0.1	83.0363 (63)	83.0506 (100)	83.2067 (32)	83.0803 (45)
Skin lesion	0.025	64.667 (27)	64.728 (100)	**64.6929 (30)**	**64.6877 (34)**
	0.05	76.9182 (70)	76.9285 (100)	77.0341 (30)	76.9548 (36)
	0.1	86.5808 (52)	86.6272 (100)	87.1024 (30)	86.7338 (42)

of computational processing. Applying our method to find the stopping criterion, for this set of images, BHISC provides 9 superior performances when compared with OST. Even more precise, CHISC is more suitable in 11 images. Considering only the number of iterations, BHISC performed 21.39 iterations on average and CHISC had 28.78 iterations, dramatically reducing the processing time. In terms of identifying the ideal iteration, BHISC and CHISC were highly accurate in some scenarios: exactly in "Kangaroo 0.05" with BHISC; and by one iteration in "Cameraman 0.1" with CHISC and "Lena 0.05" with BHISC. Furthermore, even in the images that the designated iteration is not close to the better one, we can note that the MSE difference is a maximum of 3.81 for "Lena 0.1" in BHISC. For OST, this same difference is 24.11 when the image considered is "Kangaroo 0.025".

Dependent on MSE in its equation, PSNR reaches its apex in the same MSE iteration, as described in Table 2. Therefore, BHISC and CHISC have the same averages of iterations for MSE. Although the difference between OST and better performance is always smaller or closer than 1.0, BHISC and CHISC stand out: BHISC has 8 higher performances and 2 equivalents (when the difference is less than 0.005) while CHISC has 9 superior performances and 5 equivalents.

Table 2. PSNR performance. Values in parentheses indicate the number of iterations selected. The values in bold denote performance superior to the OST stopping criterion. The * indicates performance equivalent to OST.

Image	σ	Better	OST [3]	BHISC	CHISCB
Cameraman	0.025	29.8632 (32)	29.8238 (100)	29.7114 (19)	29.7883 (22)
	0.05	29.1939 (41)	29.182 (100)	29.0441 (19)	29.1471 (26)
	0.1	28.7376 (31)	28.7069 (100)	28.5758 (20)	**28.7353 (32)**
Kangaroo	0.025	28.7718 (3)	27.7014 (100)	**28.4592 (8)**	**28.1946 (11)**
	0.05	28.6867 (8)	28.1687 (100)	**28.6867 (8)**	**28.4874 (14)**
	0.1	28.4358 (11)	27.9695 (100)	**28.4188 (8)**	**28.2209 (21)**
Lena	0.025	28.9267 (22)	28.8766 (100)	28.8241 (13)	**28.8828 (17)**
	0.05	28.6993 (14)	28.4369 (100)	**28.6866 (13)**	**28.6283 (20)**
	0.1	28.5225 (47)	28.5057 (100)	28.3449 (13)	28.4266 (25)
Mandrill	0.025	29.0598 (9)	28.8244 (100)	**28.8591 (26)**	**28.8571 (29)**
	0.05	28.7043 (17)	28.6184 (100)	**28.6546 (25)**	**28.654 (32)**
	0.1	28.5079 (33)	28.4851 (100)	**28.4963 (25)**	**28.5007 (37)**
Flower	0.025	30.2567 (31)	30.2486 (100)	**30.2546 (33)**	30.2526 (36)*
	0.05	29.4813 (49)	29.4799 (100)	29.4756 (33)*	29.4785 (39)*
	0.1	28.9381 (63)	28.9373 (100)	28.9287 (32)	28.9358 (45)*
Skin lesion	0.025	30.0239 (27)	30.0198 (100)	30.0222 (30)*	30.0225 (34)*
	0.05	29.2705 (70)	29.2699 (100)	29.2639 (30)	29.2684 (36)*
	0.1	28.7565 (52)	28.7542 (100)	28.7304 (30)	28.7489 (42)

Considering the SSIM measure, the best performances (column named "Better") occur with variation from 7 ("Mandrill 0.025") to 70 iterations ("Kangaroo 0.1"). In this measure, BHISC and CHISC also stand out the OST for ensuring values closer to the ideal result with fewer iterations: BHISC is only surpassed in 3 images (18 of total) and CHISC in 4 images. In addition, BHISC has equivalent performance (difference of less than 0.005) to the better performance in 8 images and CHISC in 7 images. Due to the variety of homogeneity among the selected images and the results obtained, BHISC and CHISC are efficient approaches to determine the amount of iterations necessary to smooth images for the Anisotropic Diffusion Filter in both gray and colorful levels.

In Fig. 3, we presented the resulting images after Anisotropic Diffusion Filter for $\sigma = 0.1$. In this view, we can compare the differences among the Better Image with OST, BHISC, and CHISC. Simply by visual comparison it is difficult to assess which sample is more similar to the original. Therefore, the measure analysis is important in this scenario to confirm the quality of the proposed method.

Table 3. SSIM performance. Values in parentheses indicate the number of iterations selected. The values in bold denote performance superior to the OST stopping criterion. The * indicates performance equivalent to OST.

Image	σ	Better	OST [3]	BHISC	CHISC
Cameraman	0.025	0.5401 (33)	0.5359 (100)	0.5064 (19)	0.5226 (22)
	0.05	0.4334 (45)	0.4319 (100)	0.3871 (19)	0.4177 (26)
	0.1	0.3485 (59)	0.3483 (100)	0.2928 (20)	0.3424 (32)
Kangaroo	0.025	0.5434 (20)	0.4079 (100)	**0.4395 (8)**	**0.4681 (11)**
	0.05	0.3892 (12)	0.351 (100)	0.3546 (8)*	**0.3838 (14)**
	0.1	0.3849 (70)	0.067 (100)	**0.2681 (8)**	**0.3689 (21)**
Lena	0.025	0.8503 (23)	0.7751 (100)	**0.8408 (13)**	**0.8433 (17)**
	0.05	0.8447 (13)	0.686 (100)	**0.8447 (13)**	**0.8183 (20)**
	0.1	0.7872 (42)	0.7773 (100)	0.7766 (13)*	0.7692 (25)
Mandrill	0.025	0.8197 (7)	0.7666 (100)	**0.7805 (26)**	**0.7776 (29)**
	0.05	0.7587 (9)	0.7283 (100)	**0.7348 (25)**	**0.7345 (32)**
	0.1	0.7141 (41)	0.7118 (100)	0.7121 (25)*	0.7135 (37)*
Flower	0.025	0.9143 (28)	0.9134 (100)	0.9142 (33)*	0.9141 (36)*
	0.05	0.8817 (36)	0.8812 (100)	0.8817 (33)*	0.8817 (39)*
	0.1	0.8333 (55)	0.8331 (100)	0.8313 (32)*	0.8332 (45)*
Skin lesion	0.025	0.8933 (28)	0.893 (100)	0.8933 (30)*	0.8932 (34)*
	0.05	0.8366 (38)	0.8365 (100)	0.8363 (30)*	0.8366 (36)*
	0.1	0.7577 (54)	0.7579 (100)	0.7542 (30)*	0.7578 (42)*

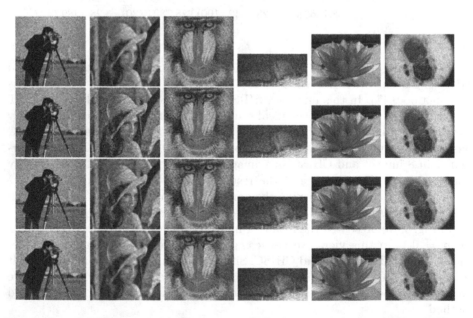

Fig. 3. Smoothed images: in the first row with the better results considering MSE; in the second row with OST (100 iterations); in the third row with BHISC; and in the last row with CHISC.

5   Conclusion

In this paper we presented a new stopping criterion for the Anisotropic Diffusion Filter. Our method considers both the parameters in the filter design and the Homogeneity Index computed directly on the image. Our stopping criterion computes the number of necessary iterations, which is obtained before the first iteration, without including extra computational costs between iterations to stop filtering. Our method was evaluated with three important similarity metrics between representations in different image domains and noise levels. Also, our method guarantees reduction in the number of iterations, without impacting the final image quality. Due to the great applicability of this filter, we believe that our stopping criterion should be applied and evaluated in other scenarios in which early stop is required for computational performance. Future work may include the use of other appearance features that complement the homogeneity index proposed in this paper.

Acknowledgment. The authors would like to thank CNPq (grant 307973/2017-4). This study was financed in part by the Coordenação de Aperfeiçoamento de Pessoal de Nível Superior - Brasil (CAPES) - Finance Code 001 and by the CEPID-CeMEAI (FAPESP grant #2013/07375-0).

References

1. Albarqouni, S., Baust, M., Conjeti, S., Al-Amoudi, A., Navab, N.: Multi-scale graph-based guided filter for de-noising cryo-electron tomographic data. In: BMVC, p. 17-1. Citeseer (2015)
2. Alvarez, L., Lions, P.L., Morel, J.M.: Image selective smoothing and edge detection by nonlinear diffusion. SIAM J. Numer. Anal. **29**(3), 845–866 (1992)
3. Barcelos, C.A.Z., Boaventura, M., Silva, E.: A well-balanced flow equation for noise removal and edge detection. IEEE Trans. Image Process. **12**(7), 751–763 (2003)
4. Barcelos, C.A.Z., Pires, V.: An automatic based nonlinear diffusion equations scheme for skin lesion segmentation. Appl. Math. Comput. **215**(1), 251–261 (2009)
5. Cappabianco, F.A., da Silva, P.P.: Non-local operational anisotropic diffusion filter. arXiv preprint arXiv:1812.04708 (2018)
6. Frommer, Y., Ben-Ari, R., Kiryati, N.: Shape from focus with adaptive focus measure and high order derivatives. In: BMVC, p. 134-1 (2015)
7. Khan, M.A., Khan, T.M., Kittaneh, O., Kong, Y.: Stopping criterion for anisotropic image diffusion. Optik **127**(1), 156–160 (2016)
8. Khan, T.M., Khan, M.A., Kong, Y., Kittaneh, O.: Stopping criterion for linear anisotropic image diffusion: a fingerprint image enhancement case. EURASIP J. Image Video Process. **2016**(1), 6 (2016)
9. Kowalik-Urbaniak, I.A., et al.: Modelling of subjective radiological assessments with objective image quality measures of brain and body CT images. In: Kamel, M., Campilho, A. (eds.) ICIAR 2015. LNCS, vol. 9164, pp. 3–13. Springer, Cham (2015). https://doi.org/10.1007/978-3-319-20801-5_1
10. Malarvel, M., Sethumadhavan, G., Bhagi, P.C.R., Kar, S., Saravanan, T., Krishnan, A.: Anisotropic diffusion based denoising on x-radiography images to detect weld defects. Digit. Signal Process. **68**, 112–126 (2017)

11. Manzinali, G., Hachem, E., Mesri, Y.: Adaptive stopping criterion for iterative linear solvers combined with anisotropic mesh adaptation, application to convection-dominated problems. Comput. Methods Appl. Mech. Eng. **340**, 864–880 (2018)
12. Mustaniemi, J., Kannala, J., Heikkilä, J.: Disparity estimation for image fusion in a multi-aperture camera. In: Azzopardi, G., Petkov, N. (eds.) CAIP 2015. LNCS, vol. 9257, pp. 158–170. Springer, Cham (2015). https://doi.org/10.1007/978-3-319-23117-4_14
13. Nilsback, M.E., Zisserman, A.: Automated flower classification over a large number of classes. In: 2008 Sixth Indian Conference on Computer Vision, Graphics & Image Processing, pp. 722–729. IEEE (2008)
14. Nordström, K.N.: Biased anisotropic diffusion: a unified regularization and diffusion approach to edge detection. Image Vis. Comput. **8**(4), 318–327 (1990)
15. Oliveira, R.B., Marranghello, N., Pereira, A.S., Tavares, J.M.R.: A computational approach for detecting pigmented skin lesions in macroscopic images. Expert Syst. Appl. **61**, 53–63 (2016)
16. Perona, P., Malik, J.: Scale-space and edge detection using anisotropic diffusion. IEEE Trans. Pattern Anal. Mach. Intell. **12**(7), 629–639 (1990)
17. Ponti, M., Helou, E.S., Ferreira, P.J.S., Mascarenhas, N.D.: Image restoration using gradient iteration and constraints for band extrapolation. IEEE J. Sel. Top. Signal Process. **10**(1), 71–80 (2015)
18. Srivastava, A., Bhateja, V., Tiwari, H.: Modified anisotropic diffusion filtering algorithm for MRI. In: 2015 2nd International Conference on Computing for Sustainable Global Development (INDIACom), pp. 1885–1890. IEEE (2015)
19. Tschandl, P., Rosendahl, C., Kittler, H.: The HAM10000 dataset, a large collection of multi-source dermatoscopic images of common pigmented skin lesions. Sci. Data **5**, 180161 (2018)
20. Wang, Z., Bovik, A.C.: Mean squared error: love it or leave it? A new look at signal fidelity measures. IEEE Signal Process. Mag. **26**(1), 98–117 (2009)
21. Wang, Z., Bovik, A.C., Sheikh, H.R., Simoncelli, E.P., et al.: Image quality assessment: from error visibility to structural similarity. IEEE Trans. Image Process. **13**(4), 600–612 (2004)
22. Xu, J., Jia, Y., Shi, Z., Pang, K.: An improved anisotropic diffusion filter with semi-adaptive threshold for edge preservation. Signal Process. **119**, 80–91 (2016)
23. Yilmaz, E., Kayikcioglu, T., Kayipmaz, S.: Noise removal of CBCT images using an adaptive anisotropic diffusion filter. In: 2017 40th International Conference on Telecommunications and Signal Processing (TSP), pp. 650–653. IEEE (2017)
24. Zhang, T., Wiliem, A., Hemsony, G., Lovell, B.C.: Detecting kangaroos in the wild: the first step towards automated animal surveillance. In: 2015 IEEE International Conference on Acoustics, Speech and Signal Processing (ICASSP), pp. 1961–1965. IEEE (2015)

Adaptive Image Binarization Based on Multi-layered Stack of Regions

Hubert Michalak[ID] and Krzysztof Okarma[(✉)][ID]

Department of Signal Processing and Multimedia Engineering,
Faculty of Electrical Engineering,
West Pomeranian University of Technology, Szczecin,
26 Kwietnia 10, 71-126 Szczecin, Poland
{michalak.hubert,okarma}@zut.edu.pl

Abstract. The main purpose of conducted research is the development of a new image thresholding method, which is faster than typical adaptive methods and more accurate than global binarization. Since natural images captured by cameras are usually unevenly illuminated, due to unknown and various lighting conditions, an appropriate binarization influences the results of further image analysis significantly.

In this paper, the analysis of multi-layered stack of regions, being the enhancement of the single-layer version, is proposed to calculate the local image properties. Since the balance between the global and local adaptive thresholding requires the choice of an appropriate number of shifted layers and block size, its verification has been made using a database of test images. The proposed local threshold value is chosen as the mean local intensity corrected using two additional parameters subjected to optimization.

The developed procedure allows for more accurate and faster binarization, which can be applied in many technical systems. It has been verified by the example of text recognition accuracy for the non-uniformly illuminated document images in comparison to alternative global and local methods of similar of lower computational complexity.

Keywords: Document images · Adaptive thresholding · Image binarization

1 Introduction

Dynamic progress in many industrial systems and technologies, which can be observed in recent years, is closely related to the development of interdisciplinary solutions integrating knowledge derived from various scientific disciplines, creating the foundations of "Industry 4.0". Good examples of such interdisciplinary areas might be the applications of pattern recognition and machine vision in mechatronics and robotics, even more commonly used not only for localization, path following and autonomous navigation, but also in automatic map construction, monitoring and inspection or detection of risky situations. However, in

© Springer Nature Switzerland AG 2019
M. Vento and G. Percannella (Eds.): CAIP 2019, LNCS 11679, pp. 281–293, 2019.
https://doi.org/10.1007/978-3-030-29891-3_25

many solutions utilizing cameras and video analysis, particularly applied in outdoor scenarios, there is a necessity of analysis of natural images captured in unknown or varying lighting conditions, which may be troublesome in practical implementation, especially for low computational power systems.

Since one of the key steps in most of image analysis algorithms applied in industrial machine vision applications is image binarization, due to its significant influence on the results of further analysis, the use of classical global methods such as well-known Otsu thresholding [13] is often insufficient. Therefore, some new computational approaches were proposed, including adaptive algorithms [17,18], although usually much more computationally demanding. As the hardware implementation of simpler methods in electronic devices, e.g. FPGA modules, can be efficiently made, the computational effort of more sophisticated algorithms, which require the analysis of the neighbourhood of each pixel, may be too high for some applications. Therefore a solution filling the gap between the global and adaptive local image thresholding would be needed, which can utilize the region based approach.

The most typical approach for the verification of newly developed image binarization methods is the use of degraded document images, e.g. during yearly DIBCO events using some typical metrics applied for comparisons of each pixel of the resulting image with provide "ground truth" binary images [12]. On the other hand, such developed general purpose image binarization metrics can also be verified in a more general way as some small imperfections may not necessarily influence further stages of image analysis, especially in applications related to Optical Character Recognition (OCR), Optical Mark Recognition (OMR), QR codes or register plates. For this reason, in this paper, the intentionally prepared database of unevenly illuminated document images has been used, subjected to text recognition using the commonly applied Tesseract OCR engine developed by Google, and the calculated metrics are based on the comparison of recognized characters instead of individual pixels.

2   Brief Overview of Image Binarization Methods

The most popular image thresholding methods are based on the assumption of bimodal histogram of the image brightness allowing for a reasonable choice of the threshold in the histogram's valley. Such an approach should lead to an efficient separation of bright objects from dark background, or reversely, for well illuminated images. Since the use of fixed threshold is usually insufficient and may lead to classification of some of the pixels representing the same object into two opposite classes, the classic solution of this problem is the application of Otsu thresholding [13], where the threshold is determined to maximize the inter-class variance, or minimize the sum of intra-class variances for the pixels classified as zeros and ones (finally representing black and white colours). A similar global thresholding method was also proposed later [4] with the use of entropy instead of variance. A solution for unimodal histograms was published by Rosin [14], who proposed to compute the global threshold searching for a histogram's corner.

Since many natural images may be non-uniformly illuminated, a single global threshold may be hard or even impossible to determine due to the presence of darker and brighter background areas. Therefore, some adaptive methods were proposed which require the analysis of the local neighbourhood of each pixel. One of the most popular, proposed by Niblack [11], is based on the choice of threshold as the sum of the local average and standard deviation multiplied by a constant coefficient which may be tuned depending on the chosen window size. Some of the modifications of this algorithm can be found in the survey papers [5,17] as well as its faster implementation proposed by Samorodova [15]. One of the most widely known adaptations [16] is referred as Sauvola method additionally using the dynamic range of the standard deviation and the multiplication of the local mean value by the term containing the normalized standard deviation.

Some other popular adaptive methods are: Bradley [2], based on the assumption that pixels darker more than T percent from the local average should be set as black (implemented in MATLAB as *adaptthresh* function), and Wolf [20] being the modification of Sauvola algorithm, as well as the simple use of the local average referred as *meanthresh* method. The use of the local contrast was proposed in Bernsen method [1], where the local threshold is set as the average of the local minimum and maximum intensity but all low contrast areas are classified as background.

Feng [3] proposed the criterion of maximization of the local contrast utilizing the local mean, minimum and standard deviation. Nevertheless, due to the use of median filter and additional bilinear interpolation, this method is quite slow, as shown in further experiments.

Some more sophisticated methods were also introduced by various researchers and their comparative analysis can be found in survey papers [8,17,18].

3   Region Based Image Binarization

Finding a reasonable balance between the fast global image thresholding methods, which are not accurate for unevenly illuminated images, and much slower adaptive binarization, is possible using the region based approach. Such idea was initially applied for the combination of local and global Otsu and Kapur methods [7], as well as the utilization of Niblack's approach for image regions applied for barcode detection in images captured by smartphones [6]. Although this method utilizes simple Niblack's formula based on the mean value and standard deviation of the image region (block), the additional application of the Support Vector Machine (SVM) classification increases the computational efforts. Nevertheless, the application of Kulyukin's method for general purpose image binarization not always leads to satisfactory results, especially for unevenly illuminated images. An extension of this approach with additional lowering coefficient (b) applied for the Niblack's formula and optimization of the block size [10] was verified for the modified DIBCO datasets using the pixel-level comparisons, leading to even better results than obtained for popular adaptive methods.

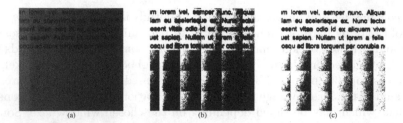

Fig. 1. Illustration of exemplary highly non-uniformly illuminated document image (a) and blocking artifacts obtained using the method proposed in the paper [9] with different parameters (b, c).

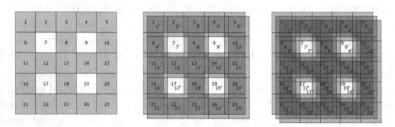

Fig. 2. Illustration of overlapping of stacks for exemplary 25 regions (layers marked with apostrophes and quotation marks are applied with offset – in this example less than 50% for better visibility).

The initial idea of the application of the region based binarization for text recognition was presented assuming the application of document images containing predefined text [9]. The proposed improved method assumes the division of the image into regions of $N \times N$ pixels. For each of the regions the local threshold can be determined as:

$$T = a \cdot mean(X) - b \,, \tag{1}$$

where $mean(X)$ is the average brightness of the image region and the parameters a and b are subjected to optimization.

4   Proposed Method

The application of region based image binarization method may cause the presence of blocking artifacts, particularly for unevenly illuminated natural images, as shown in Fig. 1. One of the possible solutions of this issue might be the decrease of the block size, allowing for less rapid changes of local threshold values calculated for smaller regions. However, such approach increases the computational effort and may lead to loss of details for some images.

The proposed improved algorithm is based on the same idea of calculation of the local thresholds as the average brightness corrected by two parameters, however the number of regions is higher than would result from the resolution of the image and therefore they partially overlap each other. In this case for each sub-region more threshold values are calculated depending on the number of overlapping blocks covering the sub-region. The resulting local threshold is determined as the average of the threshold values calculated for the number of regions dependent on the assumed number of layers and overlapping factor. A general idea of the proposed improved method utilizing a multi-layered stack of regions is illustrated in Fig. 2. The rationale for such an approach is a better tolerance of rapid illumination changes with the ability of a correct image binarization.

The first experiments were made assuming the simplest case of 50% overlapping factor and two layers. Therefore the corners of all blocks at the second layer were located in the centres of the blocks at the first layer (and reversely). In such case the calculation of average values should be made for smaller regions containing $\frac{N}{2} \times \frac{N}{2}$ pixels. Nevertheless, due to such approach it is possible to obtain significantly better results than for the simple respective increase of the number of blocks. A similar approach can be applied for more layers, although increase of their number by more than 8 layers does not lead to further substantial improvements increasing the computational complexity, as verified experimentally. The additional limitation of the conducted experiments is the assumed "original" size of the block which should be the multiple of the smallest block size in the considered stack of regions. Since some of the shifted blocks may be expanded outside the original image plane, the additional preprocessing should be made to expand the image before the computations and final trimming to the original resolution.

5   Experimental Verification

Assuming the binarization of non-uniformly illuminated document images captured by a camera, followed by text recognition using the OCR engine, recognition accuracy, as well as F-Measure, can be easily determined counting the number of properly recognized characters [19]. Additionally, as a metric typical for comparison of the strings of text, Levenshtein distance may be applied, which is defined as the minimum number of edits (insertions, deletions or substitutions) of single characters required to change the compared text string into the original one. A similar approach is also used in this paper, calculating the F-Measure values for the characters instead of its typical use for pixels, therefore defined as:

$$FM = 2 \cdot \frac{PR \cdot RC}{PR + RC}, \tag{2}$$

where PR and RC denote the precision (ratio of true positives to the sum of all positives) and recall (true positives to the sum of true positives and false negatives), respectively. In this case, positives and negatives are considered as properly and improperly recognized characters.

The experimental verification of the proposed method was made using an intentionally developed test database containing non-uniformly illuminated document image captured by a midrange Digital Single Lens Reflex Camera (DSLR).

All the images contain the same generated text (well known "Lorem ipsum"), consisting of 3782 characters (with spaces), 563 words and 6 paragraphs. This text was printed 20 times using the combination of five different font shapes (Arial, Times New Roman, Calibri, Courier and Verdana) and four styles (normal, bold, italics and bold+italics). Such set of 20 sheets of printed documents was photographed 7 times in different lighting conditions. The first "easy" scenario (a) – used mainly for comparisons with fast global methods – was the uniform illumination, and the six others contained: side shading (b), shading from the bottom (c), 45° angle shading (d), irregular shadows with sharp edges (e), arc type shadows (f) as well as the overexposure in the central part of the page with underexposed boundaries (g). Each of these types of illumination was analysed independently to verify if the proposed algorithm, and the others used for comparisons, would allow for an appropriate binarization, being good enough for the proper text recognition using the OCR engine. An illustration of the described types of illuminations is shown in Fig. 3.

All experiments, presented in this paper, were conducted using MATLAB environment and integrated Tesseract OCR engine, developed by Google. The algorithm was implemented as the M-file avoiding the use of slower solutions such as *for* loops in favour of matrix processing allowing for minimization of the computation time. For comparison purposes, some codes developed by the Authors of respective algorithms as well as publicly available open source implementations were used. Some methods, available in MATLAB toolboxes, were used in the heavily optimized form of built-in functions (e.g. Otsu or adaptive Bradley methods) and for this reason their computation time may be shorter.

6   Discussion of Results

The first part of the conducted experiments was intended to preliminary checking if the algorithm works properly as well as to determination of the optimal parameters, such as the number of layers, size of blocks and additional coefficients a and b for the prepared database. The optimal values for all mentioned parameters were calculated using this database of images allowing for the maximization of the OCR accuracy. For this purpose a series of tests and computations was performed aimed to finding the optimal size of blocks assuming their squared shape to make the implementation easier. Additionally, their size was assumed as the power of two to simplify the application of the multi-layered modifications. Therefore the size of the block was chosen as 8, 16, 32, 48, 64, 96, 128, 192, 256, 384, 512, 786 and 1024 pixels, both for horizontal and vertical dimensions, and the number of layers was set to 1, 2, 4, 8 and 16. For the verification of the final character recognition accuracy, F-Measure and Levenshtein distance were used and the obtained results are presented in Fig. 4.

As can be observed, the optimal size of the block for the analysed database, independently on number of layers, is 32×32 pixels. It can also be noted that the increase of the number of layers lead to better recognition accuracy, although the use of more than 8 layers does not cause significant increase of the performance.

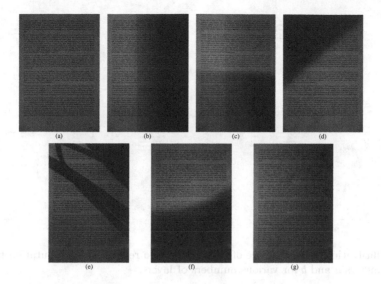

Fig. 3. Exemplary uniformly illuminated image (a) and various types of unevenly illumination considered in experiments (b–g).

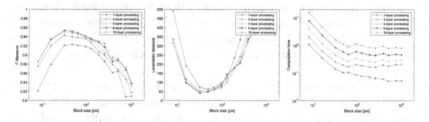

Fig. 4. Illustration of dependence of text recognition results and computation time on the block size and the number of layers.

To verify additionally the influence of the chosen size of block and number of layers on the processing time, some additional measurements were conducted. Their results are illustrated in Fig. 4 as well.

An interesting, although easily predictable, observation is the increase of the computation time caused by higher number of layers. However, the dependence on the block size is not always monotonic, although in general the choice of more smaller blocks requires more operations related to switching between blocks, additions, etc. causing the increase of the overall processing time. Knowing the relationship between the number of layers and the computation time it is possible to balance dynamically the required quality and the time needed for binarization.

The next stage of experiments was the optimization of the additional coefficients a and b. Obtained results, presented in Fig. 5, show also the relation between the recognition accuracy and the number of layers, similarly as for the number of blocks. The optimal choice of parameters, used in further calculations

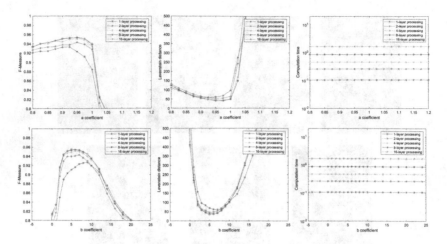

Fig. 5. Illustration of dependence of text recognition results and computation time on the parameters a and b for various numbers of layers.

was the combination of $a = 0.95$ and $b = 7$. Additionally, the influence of the choice of both parameters on the processing time was examined. According to expectations, obtained processing speed was constant, so the impact of both parameters is negligible. Therefore, an appropriate choice of both considered parameters may influence the binarization results without additional computational cost.

Finally, the above values of both parameters were selected for the 32×32 pixels blocks. Since the single layer method was analysed in the paper [9], the main contribution of this research is its extension into multi-layered stack of regions. Due to its application, a significant improvement of F-Measure and Levenshtein distance parameters can be achieved, competitive also in comparison to some other popular global and local thresholding algorithms. The results of such comparisons for the whole prepared database, containing 5 font shapes, 7 shadow types and 4 font styles, are presented in Table 1.

Omitting the binarization algorithm forces the Tesseract OCR engine to apply its own default binarization method, according to its documentation Otsu thresholding is applies, although some slight differences in obtained results can be noticed in comparison to those achieved for the binary input images subjected to prior global Otsu thresholding. Both approaches, although being very fast, lead to poor recognition results.

The remaining methods used in comparisons are the most popular adaptive thresholding algorithms leading to much better binarization results, also in terms of further text recognition accuracy. Nevertheless, the computational complexity of each of those algorithms is much higher due to the necessity of the analysis of the local neighbourhood of each pixel using the sliding window approach, similarly as in popular convolutional filters applied in image processing. It is also worth to note that during the experiments the optimized implementation

Table 1. Comparison of experimental results obtained for the whole database using various binarization methods (results for uniform illumination shown in parentheses)

Binarization algorithm	F-Measure	Levenshtein distance	Computation time [ms]
None	0.7290 (0.9638)	1299.88 (56.35)	0.15 (0.15)
Otsu [13]	0.7356 (0.9614)	1280.41 (62.70)	2.78 (3.89)
Feng [3]	0.7283 (0.9109)	1057.71 (66.35)	316.24 (309.90)
Bernsen [1]	0.7646 (0.8473)	773.49 (191.80)	298.90 (297.49)
Meanthresh	0.8091 (0.9595)	510.98 (24.90)	59.51 (59.37)
Bradley [2] (Gaussian)	0.8384 (0.9663)	644.37 (27.25)	324.03 (318.94)
Niblack [11]	0.8760 (0.9614)	284.49 (30.45)	110.92 (109.81)
Bradley [2] (mean)	0.8925 (0.9665)	296.20 (26.55)	32.85 (54.02)
Sauvola [16]	0.9387 (0.9709)	108.98 (20.65)	109.30 (106.84)
Wolf [20]	0.9298 (0.9661)	174.29 (21.45)	112.16 (110.15)
Single layer [9]	0.9230 (_0.9704_)	60.93 (20.05)	53.97 (38.35)
Proposed – 2 layers	0.9429 (0.9664)	53.73 (20.60)	93.44 (91.76)
Proposed – 4 layers	0.9500 (0.9669)	47.14 (18.75)	167.62 (161.17)
Proposed – 6 layers	0.9526 (0.9674)	44.19 (_17.15_)	248.82 (240.15)
Proposed – 8 layers	_0.9536_ (0.9640)	41.57 (17.45)	318.40 (311.22)
Proposed – 12 layers	0.9527 (0.9701)	_41.06_ (17.55)	467.19 (464.12)
Proposed – 16 layers	0.9525 (0.9663)	43.10 (17.55)	621.37 (612.14)

Table 2. Comparison of experimental results obtained using the proposed method for various font shapes and styles

Font shape/style	Average (all adaptive methods)		Average (all proposed methods)	
	F-Measure	Levenshtein distance	F-Measure	Levenshtein distance
Arial	0.9051	223.06	0.9541	27.07
Times New Roman	0.9116	242.05	0.9597	25.11
Calibri	0.8994	250.26	0.9519	26.01
Courier	0.8695	367.56	0.9171	131.43
Verdana	0.9046	229.98	0.9510	27.33
Normal	0.8928	296.75	0.9439	67.11
Bold	0.9071	220.59	0.9542	30.43
Italic	0.8939	293.02	0.9443	59.29
Bold+italic	0.8985	239.98	0.9447	32.72

of both Bradley methods was used, which is available in MATLAB environment as the *adaptthresh* function. The rest of the codes, except Otsu (implemented in MATLAB *graythresh* function) were used in the forms proposed by their authors and other researchers, being comparable with our implementations.

Table 3. Comparison of experimental results obtained using the proposed method for various shading types

Type of shading	Average (all adaptive methods)		Average (all proposed methods)	
	F-Measure	Levenshtein distance	F-Measure	Levenshtein distance
Shown in Fig. 3a	0.9555	34.69	0.9674	18.44
Shown in Fig. 3b	0.8679	356.22	0.9440	63.34
Shown in Fig. 3c	0.9090	260.67	0.9486	56.36
Shown in Fig. 3d	0.8841	330.33	0.9642	18.15
Shown in Fig. 3e	0.8143	504.46	0.8810	100.72
Shown in Fig. 3f	0.9041	302.48	0.9497	62.51
Shown in Fig. 3g	0.9504	49.22	0.9726	12.20

The use of additional layers in the proposed algorithm decreases the Levenshtein distance, increasing the F-Measure values, for the price of longer computations. Nevertheless, the obtained results, even for two layers, are better than those achieved applying Sauvola method both in terms of F-Measure and Levenshtein distance. Using only two layers, they can be achieved during a comparable, even slightly shorter, time. Further increase of the number of layers (up to 8 layers) allows for even more enhancements of text recognition results, although the computational effort increases noticeably and therefore the application of such versions of the proposed approach should be dependent on hardware resources and time constraints.

Analysing the results shown in Table 1, obtained for uniformly illuminated document images (the values in parentheses), the differences are not as remarkable, although the use of at least 4 layers in the proposed method allows for the best results in terms of Levenshtein distance. The differences in computational efforts can also be noticed easily. Tables 2 and 3 illustrate the results obtained for various subsets of the database, averaged for all adaptive methods (only without Otsu and including also the proposed approaches), as well as the proposed method (as the average values achieved for the single layer and all considered multi-layered versions), divided according to font shapes and styles as well as the type of shading. Poor results obtained for Courier font are caused by its thinness whereas the thickness of bold fonts makes the text recognition easier.

Considering the type of shading, according to expectations, the best results were obtained for uniformly illuminated documents, whereas the worst for the irregular shadows with sharp edges. Hence, the advantages of the proposed method can be observed mostly for the natural lighting with visible smooth gradients.

7   Concluding Remarks

The proposed approach to computation of thresholds for image binarization purposes based on multi-layered stack of regions may be a useful solution in many industrial applications as it combines good image preprocessing properties for further text recognition with reasonably low computational effort. The verification of its usefulness for the challenging unevenly illuminated document images proves its potential applicability for the analysis of natural images, particularly captured in outdoor scenarios where the lighting conditions may be hard to predict. Some exemplary areas of applicability may include electronic devices with integrated cameras used for automatic video surveillance purposes, traffic monitoring and vehicle tracking in Intelligent Transportation Systems, as well as video support systems for navigation of mobile robots, Unmanned Aerial Vehicles and modern autonomous vehicles, especially in low computational power systems where the application of deep learning methods is not possible.

Promising results of the verification of the proposed method for the demanding problem of text recognition in non-uniformly illuminated document images do not mean that it is specific only for this purpose, as the main reason for the preparation of the image database is the lack of ground truth images, which might be compared with the binarization results using the pixel level computations. It would require a precise calibration of the external (e.g. location, zoom) and internal parameters of cameras or the use of synthetic images instead of natural photos. Nevertheless, the applicability of the proposed method is not limited and it may be utilized in all machine vision systems where a reliable image binarization is necessary, not only for OCR purposes but also for the recognition of QR codes, shape recognition and classification, non-destructive testing, automated warehouses, etc.

Since the proposed method is flexible and may be further extended towards even better overall results with only slight potential increase of the computational complexity, our future experiments may be concentrated on the development of the reasonably fast automatic detection of the text height and its relation to the appropriate block size. Another direction of research will be the optimization of the method for the recognition of QR codes and line detection based on Hough transform for the navigation of autonomous mobile robots. Another direction of our further experiments may be the application of the Monte Carlo method to minimize the computation time due to the reduction of the number of the analysed pixels in each block and finding the optimal balance between the computation time and the obtained OCR accuracy.

References

1. Bernsen, J.: Dynamic thresholding of grey-level images. In: Proceedings of International Conference on Pattern Recognition (ICPR), pp. 1251–1255 (1986)
2. Bradley, D., Roth, G.: Adaptive thresholding using the integral image. J. Graph. Tools **12**(2), 13–21 (2007). https://doi.org/10.1080/2151237X.2007.10129236

3. Feng, M.L., Tan, Y.P.: Adaptive binarization method for document image analysis. In: 2004 IEEE International Conference on Multimedia and Expo (ICME), vol. 1, pp. 339–342 (2004). https://doi.org/10.1109/ICME.2004.1394198

4. Kapur, J., Sahoo, P., Wong, A.: A new method for gray-level picture thresholding using the entropy of the histogram. Comput. Vis. Graph. Image Process. **29**(3), 273–285 (1985). https://doi.org/10.1016/0734-189X(85)90125-2

5. Khurshid, K., Siddiqi, I., Faure, C., Vincent, N.: Comparison of Niblack inspired binarization methods for ancient documents. In: Document Recognition and Retrieval XVI, vol. 7247, pp. 7247–7247-9 (2009). https://doi.org/10.1117/12.805827

6. Kulyukin, V., Kutiyanawala, A., Zaman, T.: Eyes-free barcode detection on smartphones with Niblack's binarization and Support Vector Machines. In: Proceedings of the 16th International Conference on Image Processing, Computer Vision, and Pattern Recognition, IPCV 2012, vol. 1, pp. 284–290. CSREA Press (2012)

7. Lech, P., Okarma, K., Wojnar, D.: Binarization of document images using the modified local-global Otsu and Kapur algorithms. Przegląd Elektrotechniczny **91**(1), 71–74 (2015). https://doi.org/10.15199/48.2015.02.1

8. Leedham, G., Yan, C., Takru, K., Tan, J.H.N., Mian, L.: Comparison of some thresholding algorithms for text/background segmentation in difficult document images. In: Proceedings of 7th International Conference on Document Analysis and Recognition, ICDAR 2003, pp. 859–864 (2003). https://doi.org/10.1109/ICDAR.2003.1227784

9. Michalak, H., Okarma, K.: Region based adaptive binarization for optical character recognition purposes. In: Proceedings of International Interdisciplinary PhD Workshop (IIPhDW), pp. 361–366, Świnoujście, Poland (2018). https://doi.org/10.1109/IIPHDW.2018.8388391

10. Michalak, H., Okarma, K.: Fast adaptive image binarization using the region based approach. In: Silhavy, R. (ed.) CSOC2018 2018. AISC, vol. 764, pp. 79–90. Springer, Cham (2019). https://doi.org/10.1007/978-3-319-91189-2_9

11. Niblack, W.: An Introduction to Digital Image Processing. Prentice Hall, Englewood Cliffs (1986)

12. Ntirogiannis, K., Gatos, B., Pratikakis, I.: Performance evaluation methodology for historical document image binarization. IEEE Trans. Image Process. **22**(2), 595–609 (2013). https://doi.org/10.1109/TIP.2012.2219550

13. Otsu, N.: A threshold selection method from gray-level histograms. IEEE Trans. Syst. Man Cybern. **9**(1), 62–66 (1979). https://doi.org/10.1109/TSMC.1979.4310076

14. Rosin, P.L.: Unimodal thresholding. Pattern Recognit. **34**(11), 2083–2096 (2001). https://doi.org/10.1016/S0031-3203(00)00136-9

15. Samorodova, O.A., Samorodov, A.V.: Fast implementation of the Niblack binarization algorithm for microscope image segmentation. Pattern Recognit. Image Anal. **26**(3), 548–551 (2016). https://doi.org/10.1134/S1054661816030020

16. Sauvola, J., Pietikäinen, M.: Adaptive document image binarization. Pattern Recognit. **33**(2), 225–236 (2000). https://doi.org/10.1016/S0031-3203(99)00055-2

17. Saxena, L.P.: Niblack's binarization method and its modifications to realtime applications: a review. Artif. Intell. Rev. 1–33 (2017). https://doi.org/10.1007/s10462-017-9574-2

18. Shrivastava, A., Srivastava, D.K.: A review on pixel-based binarization of gray images. In: Satapathy, S.C., Bhatt, Y.C., Joshi, A., Mishra, D.K. (eds.) Proceedings of the International Congress on Information and Communication Technology. AISC, vol. 439, pp. 357–364. Springer, Singapore (2016). https://doi.org/10.1007/978-981-10-0755-2_38

19. Sokolova, M., Lapalme, G.: A systematic analysis of performance measures for classification tasks. Inf. Process. Manag. **45**(4), 427–437 (2009). https://doi.org/10.1016/j.ipm.2009.03.002

20. Wolf, C., Jolion, J.M.: Extraction and recognition of artificial text in multimedia documents. Form. Pattern Anal. Appl. **6**(4), 309–326 (2004). https://doi.org/10.1007/s10044-003-0197-7

Evaluating Impacts of Motion Correction on Deep Learning Approaches for Breast DCE-MRI Segmentation and Classification

Antonio Galli, Michela Gravina, Stefano Marrone[(✉)], Gabriele Piantadosi,
Mario Sansone, and Carlo Sansone

DIETI, University of Naples Federico II, Naples, Italy
{anto.galli,mi.gravina}@studenti.unina.it,
{stefano.marrone,gabriele.piantadosi,mario.sansone,
carlo.sansone}@unina.it

Abstract. Dynamic Contrast Enhanced-Magnetic Resonance Imaging
(DCE-MRI) is a diagnostic method suited for the early detection and
diagnosis of cancer, involving the serial acquisition of images before
and after the injection of a paramagnetic contrast agent. Dealing with
long acquisition times, DCE-MRI inevitably shows noise (artefacts) in
acquired images due to the patient (often involuntary) movements. As
a consequence, over the years, machine learning approaches showed that
some sort of motion correction technique (MCT) have to be applied in
order to improve performance in tumours segmentation and classification. However, in recent times classic machine learning approaches have
been outperformed by deep learning based ones, thanks to their ability to
autonomously learn the best set of features for the task under analysis.
This paper proposes a first investigation to understand if deep learning
based approaches are more robust to the misalignment of images over
time, making the registration no longer needed in this context. To this
aim, we evaluated the effectiveness of a MCT both for the classification
and for the segmentation of breast lesions in DCE-MRI by means of some
literature proposal. Our results show that while MCTs seems to be still
quite useful for the lesion segmentation task, they seem to be no longer
strictly required for lesion classification one.

Keywords: Deep convolutional neural network · DCE-MRI · Breast ·
Cancer · Motion correction

1 Introduction

Breast cancer is one of the most common causes of death and a major public
health problem worldwide. After skin cancers, it is the most diagnosed cancer
among women, accounting for nearly one out of three. Researchers have identified hormonal, lifestyle and environmental factors that may increase the risk

© Springer Nature Switzerland AG 2019
M. Vento and G. Percannella (Eds.): CAIP 2019, LNCS 11679, pp. 294–304, 2019.
https://doi.org/10.1007/978-3-030-29891-3_26

of breast cancer, but it's not clear why some people who have no risk factors develop it while other people with high-risk factors never do. Breast cancer is one of the most common cancers among women and still nowadays the key for reducing its death rate is early diagnosis: the later a tumour is diagnosed the more difficult and uncertain the treatment will be. To this aim, the World Health Organization (WHO) suggests mammography as the main breast cancer screening methodology for its fast processing and high diagnostic value [21] but, unfortunately, this methodology is not suitable for under-forty women (showing hyperdense glandular tissues).

In the last few years, researchers have been focusing on Dynamic Contrast Enhanced-Magnetic Resonance Imaging (DCE-MRI) as a complementary tool for early detection of breast cancer, demonstrating its potential both for staging newly diagnosed patients and in assessing therapy effects [6]. DCE-MRI advantages include its ability to acquire 3D dynamic (functional) information, not available with conventional RX imaging [24], its limited invasiveness, since it does not make use of any ionising radiations or radioactive contrast agent, and its suitability for under-forty women and for high-risk patients [1].

Consisting in the acquisition of multiple 3D volumes over time, DCE-MRI can be considered as 4-dimensional data (Fig. 1a), obtained by combining different images acquired before (pre) and after (post) the intravenous injection of a paramagnetic contrast agent (usually Gadolinium-based). As a consequence, each voxel (a three-dimensional pixel over time) is associated with a Time Intensity Curve (TIC) representative of the temporal dynamics of the acquired signal (Fig. 1b) that reflects the absorption and the release of the contrast agent, following the vascularisation characteristics of the tissue under analysis [23].

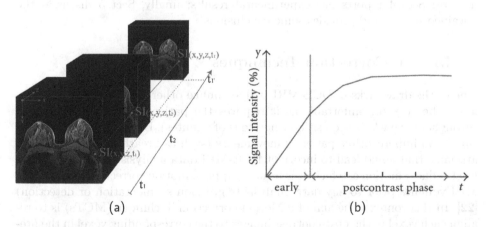

(a)   (b)

Fig. 1. DCE-MRI and Time Intensity Curves. (a) A representation of the four dimensions (3 spatial + 1 temporal) of a typical breast DCE-MRI. In red, an exemplification showing a voxel (of coordinates x, y, z) acquisitions over different time intervals (t_1 to t_T); (b) Illustration of a Time Intensity Curve for a voxel: the t axes represents the different acquisitions along time, highlighting the pre-contrast (early) and postcontrast injection phases; the y axes reports the acquired signal (and thus the voxel luminance) variation. (Color figure online)

While the use of DCE-MRI has proved to improve breast cancer diagnosis [8], it is a very time-consuming and error-prone task that involves analysis of a huge amount of data [11]. It follows that radiologist can hardly inspect DCE-MRI data without the use of a Computer Aided Detection/Diagnosis (CAD) system designed to reduce such amount of data, allowing them to focus attention only on regions of interest. Typical CAD system consists of different modules, each intended to address a given task, including lesion detection, segmentation and diagnosis. Although several papers propose the use of machine learning, still today it is not easy to identify the definitive set of features for an accurate lesion diagnosis and segmentation.

For this reason, several works explored the applicability of Deep Learning (DL) approaches in CAD system, in order to exploit their ability to learn compact hierarchical features that well fit the specific task to solve. CAD systems usually include some pre-processing stages intended to prepare data before the execution of the main phases, mainly in order to optimize image quality. Among them, Motion Correction Techniques (MCT) are used to face problems related to patient involuntary movements, such as breathing, that could introduce noise into the acquired images.

The aim of this paper is to analyze if deep learning based approaches are more robust to these small misalignments of images over time, reducing the need for MCTs. In particular, we evaluated the effectiveness of a MCT both for the classification and for the segmentation of breast lesions in DCE-MRI by means of some literature proposal.

The rest of the paper is organized as follows: Sect. 2 introduces MCTs; Sect. 3 describes the analyzed deep learning approaches, also introducing the considered dataset; Sect. 4 reports our experimental results; finally, Sect. 5 discusses the obtained results and provides some conclusions.

2   Motion Correction Techniques

One of the drawbacks of DCE-MRI is that, unlike other acquisition techniques, it can be very uncomfortable as it requires the patient to remain motionless throughout the whole acquisition time (tens of minutes). During this period, even small and imperceptible patient's movements (such as breathing) can introduce artefacts that could lead to incorrect DCE-MRI data analysis. To remove (or at least reduce) motion artefacts it is usual to apply a motion correction of the DCE-MRI volumes prior to any data analysis (e.g. lesion segmentation or detection) [22]. In this context, the aim of a Motion correction Technique (MCTs) is to re-align each voxel in the post-contrast images to the corresponding voxel in the pre-contrast (reference) image (Fig. 2), trying to maximize an objective function that is assumed to be maximal when the images are correctly aligned. In literature, several MCTs have been proposed [22,25], some of which have been adapted to be used in diagnostic medical imaging. Many surveys on motion correction agree in categorizing the techniques on the basis of the type of transformation used to realign two images:

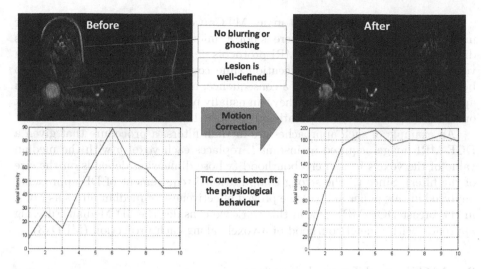

Fig. 2. Example of motion artefacts in a DCE-MRI Breast slice (upper images) and the TIC associated to the marked region (down images), before (left column) and after (right column) the application of a MCT.

- **Rigid/Non Rigid:** a rigid transformation (or affine) provides a set of transformations that include translations, scaling, homothety, similarity transformations, reflections, rotations, shear mapping, and compositions of them in any combination and sequence. Affine transformations are not able to model all possible anatomic deformations, especially those resulting in artefacts of soft tissues (i.e. breast), making elastic (non-rigid) transformations more suited in this cases [19]. Both rigid and elastic transformations can be applied on two-dimensional surfaces or on three-dimensional volumes [12].
- **Mono-modal/Multi-modal:** the term "modal" refers to the kind of scanner/sensor used to acquire the images. For multi-modal images, the correction technique aligns (register) images obtained from different scanners. The multi-modal registration is widely used in the medical field of complementary surveys such as CT/MRI brain and PET/CT total body [7].
- **Spatial or frequency domain:** The spatial methods operate in the domain of the image, by comparing the characteristics and/or the intensity pattern. On the other hand, in the frequency domain, it is possible to apply "phase correlation" methods which consist in rephrasing an image in relation to another. This phase-shift in the field of frequencies corresponds to an alignment that, unlike many algorithms in the spatial domain, is able to reduce the noise, the occlusion, and other defects typical of medical images.
- **Intensity or features based:** methods based on intensity rely on similarity measures that take into account the brightness values of each pixel/voxel. Feature-based techniques require targets images that, using some fixed points manually set or automatically determined, are used as the reference in the optimization process of minimizing the Euclidean distance between the image under correction and the target.

It is worth noticing that (i) many MTCs were not originally designed for medical imaging and (ii) that there is not a unique MCT that works best across different patients and different MRI protocols [9,14]. Moreover, MCTs are often very complex and their long execution time could make them not suitable to be used in a clinical context. As a consequence, many times simpler registration approaches are preferred, since they can usually perform as well as more complex ones, but requiring less computational effort [8,13].

An example of such approaches are median filters, a procedure that given a DCE-MRI image acquired at instant t, replaces each voxel v with the median value of the voxels in its neighbourhood (whose dimension depends on the size of the filter). Since (i) the strong computational requirement of DL approaches analyzed in this paper and (ii) the proved effectiveness of median filters as MCT in the breast DCE-MRI [15], in this work we consider the 3D Median Filtering approach, with a neighbourhood of 3 voxels along each projection (MEDx3).

3   MCTs and Deep Learning

In recent years, Deep learning (DL) approaches have gained popularity in many pattern recognition tasks thanks to their ability to learn compact hierarchical features that well fit the specific task to solve. Among these approaches, we can cite Convolutional Neural Networks (CNN) that are composed of different convolutional layers stacked in a deep architecture meant to automatically learn the best data representation. Their main characteristic consists in the fact that filters used for convolution operations are not known *a priori*, but are learned during the training stage. In other words, the network learns the best filters in order to create the best mapping between the set of inputs and the set of outputs. As a consequence, this characteristic results in no need for the feature extraction and selection phase. However, misalignment of images due to patient movement may still represent an open issue and, therefore, **the aim of this work is to be a first investigation on whether deep learning approaches are able to learn a set of features able to automatically mitigate the effects of motion correction artefacts**. To this aim, we evaluate the real effectiveness of MCTs for two deep models proposed in the literature, implemented respectively for lesion classification (diagnosis) and segmentation (detection). Both models have been re-implemented according to our best interpretation of the authors' papers and suitably evaluated to be fairly compared.

3.1   Lesion Segmentation

For the lesion segmentation task, we considered the use of a U-Shaped CNN, as proposed in [16] for the breast segmentation task. The approach consists of three main steps:

- Removing all the foreign tissues (bones, muscles, etc) and air background, by using an automatically segmented breastmask

- Extraction of *slices* by cutting the DCE-MRI 4D data along the axis with the highest resolution
- Slice-by-slice segmentation with a U-Net CNN.

The core of the approach is a U-Shaped CNN, an encoder-decoder architecture originally designed for biomedical electron microscopy (EM) images multiclass pixel-wise semantic segmentation [17]. Some modifications have been introduced in the original U-Net proposal: (a) the output feature-map of the network has been set to one channel to speed up the convergence during the training; (b) zero-padding with a size-preserving strategy has been applied for preserving the output shapes; (c) batch normalization (BN) layers after each convolution has been applied to improve the training stability.

3.2   Lesion Diagnosis

For the lesion classification task we considered the work proposed by Haarburger et al. [3] consisting in the use of a ResNet34 [4] CNN architecture pre-trained on the ImageNet dataset. The network is fine-tuned to work with breast DCE-MRI images and to face a binary classification problem (malignant vs benign lesions).

During fine-tuning on the DCE-MRI data, all layers are trained simultaneously using cross entropy loss (therefore no layers weights have been frozen). Moreover, since the network expects three input channels, a subset of the acquired images (T, see Fig. 1a) is needed. To this aim, authors provide an experimental comparison of all possible subset of images provided by the acquisition protocol and determine the best combination for malignancy classification.

3.3   Experimental Setup

Both CNNs have been implemented with the Keras high-level neural networks API in Python 3.6, by using TensorFlow (v1.6) as back-end for the U-Net CNN and Pytorch for the Haarburger et al. [3] work. The Python scripts have been evaluated on a physical server hosted in our university HPC centre equipped with 2 x Intel(R) Xeon(R) Intel(R) 2.13 GHz CPUs (4 cores), 32 GB RAM and an Nvidia Titan Xp GPU (Pascal family) with 12 GB GRAM.

The U-Net model for Lesion segmentation has been trained by minimizing a task-specific loss defined as follows:

$$\text{loss} = 1 - \text{DSC}(y_{\text{network}}, y_{\text{gold-standard}}) \tag{1}$$

$$\text{DSC} = (2 \cdot n(GS \cap SEG))/(n(GS) + n(SEG)) \tag{2}$$

where DSC represents the Dice Similarity Coefficient and $n(\cdot)$ represents the number of voxels in the enclosed volume. The network kernel weights have been initialized to random numbers from a standard distribution $\mathcal{N}(0, \sqrt{2/(\text{fan}_i + \text{fan}_o)})$ [2] where fan_i and fan_o are respectively the input and output size of the convolution layer, while the bias weights have been initialized to a constant value of 0.1. ADAM optimizer [5] was used, with $\beta_1 = 0.9$, $\beta_2 = 0.999$ and lr $= 0.001$ using an inverse time decay strategy.

Haarburger et al. [3] network has been pre-trained on ImageNet dataset. Authors employed stochastic gradient descent using a momentum of 0.9, with a decaying learning rate starting at 0.001 and decreasing with a factor of 0.05 every 7 epochs.

3.4   Dataset

The dataset consists of 42 women breast DCE-MRI 4D data (average age 40 years, in range 16–69) with benign or malignant lesions histopathologically proven: 42 regions of interest (ROIs) were malignant and 25 were benign, for a total of 67 ROIs.

All patients underwent imaging with a 1.5 T scanner (Magnetom Symphony, Siemens Medical System, Erlangen, Germany) equipped with breast coil. DCE T1-weighted FLASH 3D coronal images were acquired (TR/TE: 9.8/4.76 ms; flip angle: 25°; field of view 370 × 185 mm × mm; matrix: 256 × 128; thickness: 2 mm; gap: 0; acquisition time: 56 s; 80 slices spanning entire breast volume). One series (t_0) was acquired before and 9 series (t_1–t_9) after intravenous injection of 0.1 mmol/kg of a positive paramagnetic contrast agent (gadolinium-diethylene-triamine penta-acetic acid, Gd-DOTA, Dotarem, Guerbet, Roissy CdG Cedex, France). An automatic injection system was used (Spectris Solaris EP MR, MEDRAD, Inc., Indianola, PA) and the injection flow rate was set to 2 ml/s followed by a flush of 10 ml saline solution at the same rate.

As **gold-standard** for the segmentation stage, an experienced radiologist delineated suspect ROIs using T1-weighted and *subtractive* image series. Starting from DCE-MRI acquired data, the subtractive image series is defined by subtracting t_0 series from t_4 series. In subtractive images, any tissue that does not absorb the contrast agent is suppressed. Manual segmentation stage was performed in Osirix [18], that allows the user to define ROIs at a sub-pixel level. All the lesion was histopathologically proven. The evidence of malignity was used as **gold-standard** for the lesion classification task.

4   Results

This section reports the results of the approaches described in Sect. 3 with and without applying the MEDx3 Motion Correction Technique. Performance is evaluated using a 10-fold cross validation, in turn using each fold for testing and the reaming ones for training and validation. In our case, if the fold i is used for testing, the previous one is then used for validation and all the other ones for training. It is worth noticing that, although each lesion is composed of different slices, the lesion diagnosis task has to predict a single class for the whole lesion. For this reason, **it is very important to perform a patient-based instead of a slice-based cross validation**, in order to reliably compare different models by avoiding mixing intra-patient slices in the evaluation phase.

Considering as the positive class the malignant one, segmentation performance are evaluated in terms of dice (DSC), Specificity (SPE) and Sensitivity (SEN), while classification performance are assessed in terms of Sensitivity (SEN), Specificity (SPE), F1-Score (F1) and Area under ROC curve (AUC).

Table 1 shows the results obtained by implementing U-Net for lesion segmentation with and without the use of the MEDx3 MCT.

Table 1. Results obtained by implementing the U-Net for lesion segmentation with and without the MEDx3 MCT.

	SPE	SEN	DSC
Piantadosi et al. [16]	100%	53.93%	**57.69%**
Piantadosi et al. [16] with MEDx3	100%	66.23%	**66.01%**

Similarly, Table 2 reports the results obtained by implementing Haarburger et al. [3] method without applying any MCTs and by applying the MEDx3 MCT. Since the network performs a slice-by-slice classification, a combining strategy is required in order to classify each lesion. As proposed in the original work [3], we aggregated all the lesion's slices predictions by taking the class of the slice with the maximum probability as the overall malignancy class for the lesion.

Table 2. Results obtained by implementing Haarburger et al. [3] model with and without the MEDx3 MCT.

	SPE	SEN	F1	AUC
Haarburger et al. [3]	42.86%	76.19%	71.11%	**70.75%**
Haarburger et al. [3] with MEDx3	50.00%	76.19%	72.73%	**69.73%**

Finally, since results with and without MC seems to suggest that lesions classification with DL approaches no longer needs a MC stage, for the sake of completeness, in Table 3 we compare the CNN performance with those obtained on the same task by using a non-deep approaches previously proposed in the literature [20], evaluating the performance in terms of AUC.

Table 3. Comparison in terms of AUC of CNN results with those obtained by using a non-deep approach.

	No Reg	MEDx3
Haarburger et al. [3]	70.75%	69.73%
Lavasani et al. [20]	65.31%	72.11%

5 Discussion and Conclusions

The aim of this paper was to carry a preliminary study in order to investigate if deep learning approaches are able to automatically mitigate the motion artefacts effects to the extent of making motion correction techniques no longer needed. We consider our previous work [8,13] where MEDx3, a simple MCT, was demonstrated to overcome the most advanced MCTs in the task of mitigating the artefacts in DCE-MRI breast images. All the evaluations are conducted with respect to the result in the tasks of segmentation and/or classification. Table 1 shows how MEDx3 can still effectively improve the performance of the lesion segmentation task that, therefore, still seems to be affected by the noise due to the patient's movements. On the other hand, Table 2 shows that the performance of Deep Learning based approaches for the lesion classification are not very impacted by the execution of a MEDx3 Motion Correction Technique. Therefore, in order to determine if this property is related on the task and not to the used MC approach, in Table 3 we compared the performance of the deep and of a non-deep approach, showing that in the latter case the use of MEDx3 can improve results up to 7%. These preliminary results seem to suggest that the lesion segmentation task can still be positively affected by the use of a simple MCT, that is MEDx3, while the lesion classification task is more robust to motion artefacts. A possible interpretation could be that while CNNs could learn motion invariant features for the diagnosis task, the need for a precise voxel-based segmentation can be strongly affected by the voxel misalignment over time. However, on the other ends, as already stated in [10], performance of current CNN for the lesion classification task are still no outstanding enough to sustain such a claim and, therefore, it is very important to push research in that direction.

As a final remark, we would like to highlight that a limitation of this study is the population size: our finding should be confirmed on a larger dataset. Moreover, in order to produce more general and robust claims, the effect of different MCTs should be analyzed. With this aim, future work will focus on exploring the effect of different MCTs on other deep approaches.

Acknowledgments. The authors gratefully acknowledge the support of NVIDIA Corporation with the donation of the Titan Xp GPU used for this research, the availability of the Calculation Centre SCoPE of the University of Naples Federico II and thank the SCoPE academic staff for the given support. The authors are also grateful to Dr. Antonella Petrillo, Head of Division of Radiology and PhD Roberta Fusco, Department of Diagnostic Imaging, Radiant and Metabolic Therapy, "Istituto Nazionale dei Tumori Fondazione G. Pascale" - IRCCS, Naples, Italy, for providing data. This work is part of the "Synergy-net: Research and Digital Solutions against Cancer" project (funded in the framework of the POR Campania FESR 2014–2020 - CUP B61C17000090007).

References

1. El-Kwae, E.A., Fishman, J.E., Bianchi, M.J., Pattany, P.M., Kabuka, M.R.: Detection of suspected malignant patterns in three-dimensional magnetic resonance breast images. J. Digit. Imaging Off J. Soc. Comput. Appl. Radiol. **11**, 83–93 (1998)
2. Glorot, X., Bengio, Y.: Understanding the difficulty of training deep feedforward neural networks. In: Proceedings of the Thirteenth International Conference on Artificial Intelligence and Statistics, pp. 249–256 (2010)
3. Haarburger, C., et al.: Transfer learning for breast cancer malignancy classification based on dynamic contrast-enhanced MR images. Bildverarbeitung für die Medizin 2018. I, pp. 216–221. Springer, Heidelberg (2018). https://doi.org/10.1007/978-3-662-56537-7_61
4. He, K., Zhang, X., Ren, S., Sun, J.: Deep residual learning for image recognition
5. Kingma, D.P., Ba, J.: Adam: a method for stochastic optimization. arXiv preprint arXiv:1412.6980 (2014)
6. Levman, J., Leung, T., Causer, P., Plewes, D., Martel, A.L.: Classification of dynamic contrast-enhanced magnetic resonance breast lesions by support vector machines. IEEE Trans. Med. Imaging **27**, 688–696 (2008)
7. Maintz, J., Viergever, M.A.: A survey of medical image registration. Med. Image Anal. **2**(1), 1–36 (1998). http://www.sciencedirect.com/science/article/pii/S1361841501800268
8. Marrone, S., Piantadosi, G., Fusco, R., Petrillo, A., Sansone, M., Sansone, C.: Automatic lesion detection in breast DCE-MRI. In: Petrosino, A. (ed.) ICIAP 2013. LNCS, vol. 8157, pp. 359–368. Springer, Heidelberg (2013). https://doi.org/10.1007/978-3-642-41184-7_37
9. Marrone, S., Piantadosi, G., Fusco, R., Petrillo, A., Sansone, M., Sansone, C.: A novel model-based measure for quality evaluation of image registration techniques in DCE-MRI. In: 2014 IEEE 27th International Symposium on Computer-Based Medical Systems (CBMS), pp. 209–214. IEEE (2014)
10. Marrone, S., Piantadosi, G., Fusco, R., Petrillo, A., Sansone, M., Sansone, C.: An investigation of deep learning for lesions malignancy classification in breast DCE-MRI. In: Battiato, S., Gallo, G., Schettini, R., Stanco, F. (eds.) ICIAP 2017. LNCS, vol. 10485, pp. 479–489. Springer, Cham (2017). https://doi.org/10.1007/978-3-319-68548-9_44
11. Nodine, C.F., Kundel, H.L., et al.: Using eye movements to study visual search and to improve tumor detection. Radiographics **7**(6), 1241–1250 (1987)
12. Penney, G.P., Weese, J., Little, J.A., Desmedt, P., Hill, D.L.G., Hawkes, D.J.: A comparison of similarity measures for use in 2-d-3-d medical image registration. IEEE Trans. Med. Imaging **17**(4), 586–595 (1998)
13. Piantadosi, G., Fusco, R., Petrillo, A., Sansone, M., Sansone, C.: LBP-TOP for volume lesion classification in breast DCE-MRI. In: Murino, V., Puppo, E. (eds.) ICIAP 2015. LNCS, vol. 9279, pp. 647–657. Springer, Cham (2015). https://doi.org/10.1007/978-3-319-23231-7_58
14. Piantadosi, G., Marrone, S., Fusco, R., Petrillo, A., Sansone, M., Sansone, C.: Data-driven selection of motion correction techniques in breast DCE-MRI. In: 2015 IEEE International Symposium on Medical Measurements and Applications (MeMeA), pp. 273–278. IEEE (2015)

15. Piantadosi, G., Marrone, S., Fusco, R., Sansone, M., Sansone, C.: Comprehensive computer-aided diagnosis for breast T1-weighted DCE-MRI through quantitative dynamical features and spatio-temporal local binary patterns. IET Comput. Vis. **12**(7), 1007–1017 (2018)

16. Piantadosi, G., Sansone, M., Sansone, C.: Breast segmentation in MRI via U-Net deep convolutional neural networks. In: 2018 24th International Conference on Pattern Recognition (ICPR), pp. 3917–3922. IEEE (2018)

17. Ronneberger, O., Fischer, P., Brox, T.: U-Net: convolutional networks for biomedical image segmentation. In: Navab, N., Hornegger, J., Wells, W.M., Frangi, A.F. (eds.) MICCAI 2015. LNCS, vol. 9351, pp. 234–241. Springer, Cham (2015). https://doi.org/10.1007/978-3-319-24574-4_28

18. Rosset, A., Spadola, L., Ratib, O.: OsiriX: an open-source software for navigating in multidimensional DICOM images. J. Digit. Imaging **17**, 205–216 (2004)

19. Rueckert, D., Sonoda, L.I., Hayes, C., Hill, D.L., Leach, M.O., Hawkes, D.J.: Nonrigid registration using free-form deformations: application to breast MR images. IEEE Trans. Med. Imaging **18**(8), 712–721 (1999)

20. Navaei Lavasani, S., Fathi Kazerooni, A., Saligheh-Rad, H., Gity, M.: Discrimination of benign and malignant suspicious breast tumors based on semi-quantitative DCE-MRI parameters employing support vector machine. Front. Biomed. Technol. **2**(2), 87–92 (2015)

21. Smith, R.A., et al.: American cancer society guidelines for breast cancer screening: update 2003. CA Cancer J. Clin. **53**(3), 141–169 (2003)

22. Tanner, C., Hawkes, D.J., Khazen, M., Kessar, P., Leach, M.O.: Does registration improve the performance of a computer aided diagnosis system for dynamic contrast-enhanced MR mammography? In: 3rd IEEE International Symposium on Biomedical Imaging: Nano to Macro, pp. 466–469. IEEE (2006)

23. Tofts, P.S.: T1-weighted DCE imaging concepts: modelling, acquisition and analysis. Magneton Flash Siemens **3**, 30–39 (2010)

24. Twellmann, T., Saalbach, A., Müller, C., Nattkemper, T.W., Wismüller, A.: Detection of suspicious lesions in dynamic contrast enhanced MRI data. In: Annual International Conference of the IEEE Engineering in Medicine and Biology Society, vol. 1, pp. 454–457 (2004)

25. Zitová, B., Flusser, J.: Image registration methods: a survey. Image Vis. Comput. **21**(11), 977–1000 (2003). http://www.sciencedirect.com/science/article/pii/S0262885603001379

A Two-Step System Based on Deep Transfer Learning for Writer Identification in Medieval Books

Nicole Dalia Cilia, Claudio De Stefano, Francesco Fontanella,
Claudio Marrocco, Mario Molinara$^{(\boxtimes)}$, and Alessandra Scotto Di Freca

Department of Electrical and Information Engineering (DIEI), University of Cassino
and Southern Lazio, Via G. Di Biasio, 43, Cassino, FR, Italy
{nicoledalia.cilia,destefano,fontanella,c.marrocco,m.molinara,
a.scotto}@unicas.it

Abstract. In digital paleography, recent technology advancements are used to support paleographers in the study and analysis of ancient documents. One main goal of paleographers is to identify the different *scribes* (writers) who wrote a given manuscript. Deep learning has recently been applied to many domains. However, in order to overcome its requirement of large amount of labeled data, transfer learning have been used. This approach typically uses previously trained large deep networks as starting points to solve specific classification problems. In this paper, we present a two step deep transfer learning based tool to help paleographers identify the parts of a manuscript that were written by the same writer. The suggested approach has been tested on a set of digital images from a Bible of the XII century. The achieved results confirmed the effectiveness of the proposed approach.

Keywords: Deep transfer learning · Object detection ·
Writer identification · Digital paleography

1 Introduction

Digital paleography uses computer-based approaches to analyze and represent ancient and medieval documents and its main purpose is to support the paleographical analysis of these documents by the paleographers [2]. These approaches can be used either to replace traditional qualitative measurements with modern computer-vision tools, or by using the recently emerged AI and pattern recognition based approaches which have been proven to be effective in processing the many currently available high-quality digital images of ancient and medieval manuscripts [7–9]. These approaches can be categorized according to the two types of features taken into account: global or local. The former are focused on measures from the whole page, whereas the latter are based on the analysis of the single words, letters and signs of the written trace. In this framework, one

M. Vento and G. Percannella (Eds.): CAIP 2019, LNCS 11679, pp. 305–316, 2019.
https://doi.org/10.1007/978-3-030-29891-3_27

of the most important problems faced by paleographers is to identify the writers who participated to the handwriting process of a given manuscript.

In the last few years, due to their ability to deal with complex and hard image classification tasks, deep learning (DL) based approaches have been receiving increasing attention from researchers and have been successfully applied to numerous real-world applications [4,24], and they have shown to be able to learn high-level features from mass data. These features are typically extracted from the available data by using unsupervised or semi-supervised feature learning algorithms and hierarchical feature extraction. On the contrary, traditional machine learning methods [3,5] need a preliminary feature engineering step involving the expert of the application field, increasing the application development cost. Although DL-based approaches have proven to be effective in many computer vision problems, their performance strongly depends on the availability of massive training data. Unfortunately, the insufficient training data problem cannot be easily solved in many application domains. This is because the collection of labeled data may require a long and expensive process.

In order to overcome the problem of insufficient data, the transfer learning approach can be used. According to this approach, pre-trained networks, typically trained on huge datasets containing millions of images and thousands of classes, are used as starting points for the learning process of new networks. To date, the transfer learning paradigm is widely applied to computer vision and natural language processing tasks.

Previous DL approaches for ancient document analysis have been mainly used for identifying elements of interest inside document pages. In [14], for example, the authors use a Fully Convolutional Neural Network (FCNN) to locate handwritten annotations in historic German documents. In [20], instead, the authors introduced a database containing annotated pages of medieval manuscripts. They also tested the performance of a Convolutional Auto Encoder in the layout analysis of the database pages. In [17], Oliveira et al. addressed the problem of performing multiple tasks simultaneously; they considered tasks such as page extraction, baseline extraction and layout analysis.

Also transfer learning based approaches have been used for document analysis. In [1], for example, the authors used a deep Convolutional Neural Network (CNN) based approach using ImageNet to recognize ads, forms and scientific writings. As concerns historical documents, in [12] the authors used a FCNN for word spotting. The works presented in [25] and [6], instead, were devoted to Optical Character Recognition (OCR). In particular, in [25] the authors used a transfer learning based approach to recognize Hindi, Arabic, and Bangla handwritten numerals in ancient documents. As for the work presented in [6], it aimed at recognizing Chinese characters by using a deep neural network pretrained on Latin characters. Finally, at the best of our knowledge, there are no DL-based works for writer identification in ancient documents. However, in [16], the authors identify writers in ancient handwritten documents by using a DL-based technique for denoising and hand-crafted descriptor features for the writer identification task.

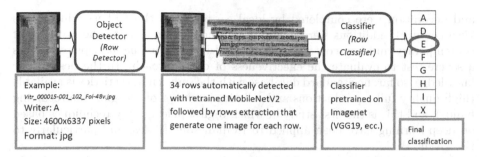

Fig. 1. The general structure of the computational chain

In this paper, we present a novel approach based on deep transfer learning for the recognition of the writers in ancient documents. We propose a two step solution: in the first step we are able to detect rows in the pages and in the second step we classify these rows producing the classification of the entire page. As concerns the first phase, we used an object detection system pretrained on MS-COCO dataset [15] and based on MobileNet V2 [19]. As concerns the second phase, we used five different networks, all pretrained on the ImageNet database [18] and suitable to solve a multiclass problem.

A representation of the entire system is depicted in Fig. 1 where the row detector and the row classifier are showed.

The overall system has been tested on the "Avila Bible". The manuscript was written in Italy by, at least, eight scribes within the third decade of the 12th century. Then it was sent to Spain, where its text and decoration were completed by local scribes. Because of the presence of writers from different ages, this manuscript represents a challenge for evaluating the effectiveness of our approach.

The remainder of the paper is organized as follows: in Sect. 2, we will detail the materials and methods used to develop the proposed system, while, in Sect. 3, we will illustrate the experimental results. Finally, in Sect. 4 some conclusions are drawn.

2   Materials and Methods

In the following subsections, the dataset used to test the proposed approach, the models adopted as starting points of the learning process, the architecture of the new classifier, as well as the preprocessing and the training procedure are detailed.

2.1   Dataset Construction

The "Avila Bible" was written in Italy by, at least, twelve scribes within the third decade of the 12th century and then it was sent to Spain, where its text and decoration were completed by local scribes; in a third phase (during the 15th century), additions were made by another writer. Due to the presence of contemporary and non-contemporary scribal hands, this manuscript represents a severe test to evaluate the effectiveness of our approach. To the best of our knowledge, so far, no standard database with the same characteristics is available (high quality full reproductions and a limited number of recognizable recurring hands), and this is the first study in which digital paleography techniques based on deep learning have been applied to Romanesque Bibles, and particularly to the "Avila Bible".

The Avila Bible consists of 870 two-column pages, but we considered only 749 pages where the paleographic analysis has individuated the presence of at least eight scribal hands. Two examples of pages from the Avila Bible, with a resolution of about 6000 × 4000 pixels, are shown in Fig. 2. All 749 pages are labeled with a letters that identify each scriba (A, D, E, F, G, H, I, X).

Experimental phase has been conducted in three steps: (i) training and testing of row detector, (ii) training and testing of row classifier, (iii) a final test with the complete chain (row detector + row classifier) aimed to assign to each page a single scriba (see Fig. 1). The first two steps have been conducted on a subset of 96 (12 for each scriba) images randomly selected. In the following sections some details are given. The third step has been conducted on the remain 653 images, never seen by the system. On these 96 annotated pages divided in 56 images for training, 16 for validation and 24 for testing, the row detector and the row classifier have been fine tuned.

Fig. 2. (a) An example of manually annotated page. (b) An example of page with automatically detected rows

Fig. 3. How from pages have been obtained two dataset: xml+png for row detection, single rows for row classifier

Dataset for Row Detection: as showed in Fig. 2(a), in each page all rows have been annotated with a tool named "LabelImg"; annotation has been saved in a XML file (one for each page) by using the PASCAL VOC format (see Fig. 3). These 96 images with related XML files have been used for re-train the object detector (row detector).

Dataset for Row Classification: the same 96 pages have been used for row classifier training. Starting from the bounding boxes contained into the XML files, a set of subimages containing only a single row has been extracted from pages (see Fig. 3). As reported in Table 1, from each class has been selected 7, 3 and 2 pages for extracting rows for training, testing and validation respectively.

Table 1. From images to rows. The number of images for each class adopted for the rows dataset creation in training, testing and validation sets.

Classes	Train	Test	Val
A	7	3	2
D	7	3	2
E	7	3	2
F	7	3	2
G	7	3	2
H	7	3	2
I	7	3	2
X	7	3	2
TOT	56	24	16
Extracted Rows	7197	3031	1871
TOT rows		12099	

2.2   The Adopted Models for Row Detection

During the last years different models of Deep Neural Networks (DNNs) for object detection have been trained on public datasets like MS-COCO [15], obtaining, year by year, the highest performance in this kind of challenge. One of the most promising and versatile model is the MobileNetV2 [19], a Single Shot Detector fully scalable network ready to run on different target, from workstation to mobile device.

With MobileNetV1 a depthwise separable convolution has been introduced with the idea to reduce the model size and complexity. Moreover width multiplier and resolution multiplier parameters has been introduced by which has been possible to modify drastically the number of Multiplications and Additions involved in the inference process.

In MobileNetV2, a better module is introduced with inverted residual structure so when adopted for feature extraction, the state-of-the-art performances are also achieved for object detection and semantic segmentation.

For MobileNetV2 we selected in a preliminary experimental phase the following hyperparameters:

– Root mean square with learning rate = 0.004, momentum = 0.9
– max epochs equal to 200000
– patience (a limits for epochs if validation loss does not improve for a while) equal to 200
– batch size 24
– accuracy as a measure of performance
– images resized as 1200×800 (the original pages are around 6000×4000 pixels).

2.3   The Adopted Models for Row Classification

As regards row classification, the so called transfer learning is becoming very popular and different CNN have been trained on ImageNet [11], obtaining, year by year, the highest performance in this kind of challenge.

In this paper five models spanning between 2015 and 2017 have been adopted: VGG19 [21], ResNet50 [13], InceptionV3 [23], InceptionResNetV2 [22], NASNet-Large [26].

These models evolved in two main directions: first, by introducing new structural elements (inception, residual, dropout, etc); second, by increasing the number of layers. As a consequence the number of parameters has increased from 25 millions in VGG19 to 97 millions in NASNetLarge and the number of layers (convolutional, dropout, inception, etc.) has grown from the nineteen of VGG to some hundred of NASNetLarge.

The five DNNs adopted are characterized by two main sections: a section for Feature Extraction (FE) that receives the images as input and produces features as output in correspondence of the (so called) bottleneck; and a section for classification (C) realized with some kind of fully connected network. This two-steps architecture has been modified by replacing the original classifier (C) with a unique classifier as described below.

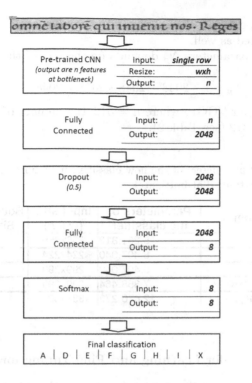

Fig. 4. The adopted classifier

2.4   Data Augmentation and Preprocessing for Row Classifier

Images have been normalized from the original size to the maximum input size $w \times h$ of the network as reported in Table 2; after that, a simple rescaling has been adopted, automatically adjusted by the employed network. The chosen parameters turned out to be the best ones in accordance to previous tests and have been augmented by:

- rotation with angle selected in $[0, 30°]$
- zoom with ratio selected in $[0, 30\%]$
- width and height shift with values selected in $[0, 30\%]$.

2.5   The Architecture of the New Row Classifier

As mentioned above, for each network adopted, the original classifier has been substituted with a new classifier (see Fig. 4) based on two fully connected layers with 2048 nodes, an intermediate dropout was introduced to improve the generalization capability of the network alongside with a softmax layer that generates the confidence degrees of the output class in the range $[0, 1]$.

The size of the input image $(w \times h)$, automatically rescaled by the employed network, and the size n at bottleneck (number of features extracted) for each of the models is reported in Table 2 where the number of the parameters of the classifier are reported as well.

The number of parameters N_p depends on the size of the bottleneck n and in general is:

$$N_p = n * 2048 + 2048 * 2048 + 2048 * 8 \tag{1}$$

As an example, for VGG19 where $n = 512$, the number of classifier parameters become $5, 261, 312$ (see Table 2).

Table 2. Number of parameters of the new classifier, maximum image input size and number of features extracted at bottleneck.

Model	Parameters of the classifier	Input size (w x h)	Bottleneck Size (n)
VGG19	5.261.312	256x256	512
ResNet50	8.407.040	224x224	2.048
InceptionV3	8.407.040	299x299	2.048
InceptionResNetV2	7.358.464	299x299	1.536
NASNetLarge	12.470.272	331x331	4.032

2.6   Training: Transfer Learning and Fine Tuning for Row Classifier

The training of the row classifier models has been realized in two steps: Transfer Learning (TL) and Fine Tuning (FT). During the TL step, all the parameters of the module FE are frozen whereas the parameters of the classifier C are randomly initialized and trained. During the FT step, both modules (FE and C) are involved in the training process and all the parameters are unfrozen. The FT assumes that the parameters are initialized with the ImageNet training for FE and the final values of TL for C.

For the TL and FT steps, the following hyper parameters and settings have been used:

- Stochastic Gradient Descent (SGD) with learning rate = 0.0001, momentum = 0.9
- max epochs equal to 2, 000
- patience (a limits for epochs if validation loss does not improve for a while) equal to 200
- batch size 16
- accuracy as a measure of performance

where one epoch means one pass of the full training set and it contains a number of iterations equal to *epochs/batch*. The training phase was conducted by using a validation set in order to reduce or avoid overfitting of the network on training set.

3   Experiments and Results

The experiments were performed by using an Intel Core i7-7700 CPU @ 3.60 GHz 256 GB of RAM with a GPU Titan Xp. As framework, we used Keras 2.2.2 with TensorFlow 1.10.0 as backend. A time ranging from 2 h to 24 h was involved in TL and FT phases with the maximum of 24 h on NASNetLarge during the FT where there were 97 millions of parameters to learn. The final test have been made on 653 Avila pages. By applying the object detector a mean of about 40% of the total rows are correctly identified page by page. These rows are submitted to the row classifier (one of the five selected in turns). A page is assigned to the majority class or, in other words, to the class to which the largest number of rows has been assigned.

Applying the overall system to these 653 images it is possible to evaluate the Accuracy and the $F1 - score$ as reported in Table 3. The accuracy Acc_i for class i is evaluated as:

$$Acc_i = \frac{\text{pages correctly classified as class } i}{(\text{number of pages in class } i)} \qquad (2)$$

The F1 score can be interpreted as a weighted average of the precision and recall, where an F1 score reaches its best value at 1 and worst score at 0. The relative contribution of precision and recall to the F1 score is equal. F1 is evaluated by using the $precision_i$ and $recall_i$. For multiclass problems $precision_i$ is equal to Acc_i while $recall_i$ is:

$$recall_i = \frac{\text{pages correctly classified as class } i}{(\text{number of pages classified as } i)} \qquad (3)$$

$$F1_i = 2 * \frac{precision_i * recall_i}{precision_i + recall_i} \qquad (4)$$

Global Acc and $F1$ are evaluated as mean of the values associated with each class.

In Table 3 the obtained performances are organized as follows:

- columns are related to each class
- rows are related to the different models
- each model row is divided in two subrows: one for TL and one for FT,
- each TL/FT row is divided in other two subrows: one for Acc and one for $F1$
- the last column contains the mean values of the performance index on the entire test set
- last row contains the number of rows available in each class.

From the table it can be observed that: (i) there is generally an important improvement by passing from TL to FT; (ii) the best results have been produced with InceptionV3 after FT where Acc and $F1$ reach 88% and 83%, respectively; (iii) the best results with only TL, have been produced with ResNet50 where Acc and $F1$ reach 73% and 72%, respectively.

Table 3. Performance of the complete chain with the retrained MobileNetV2 row detector and with five different classifier for row classification applied on the entire test set.

			A	D	E	F	G	H	I	X	Average
VGG19	TL	Acc	0.28	0.37	0.03	0.62	0.00	0.38	0.88	0.13	0.33
		F1	0.39	0.27	0.05	0.39	0.00	0.43	0.47	0.22	0.28
	FT	Acc	0.93	0.95	0.59	0.89	0.75	0.97	0.69	0.31	0.76
		F1	0.93	0.67	0.64	0.86	0.63	0.97	0.77	0.42	0.74
ResNet50	TL	Acc	0.82	0.89	0.58	0.82	0.58	0.90	0.58	0.69	**0.73**
		F1	0.84	0.68	0.71	0.73	0.50	0.93	0.72	0.61	**0.72**
	FT	Acc	0.87	0.84	0.65	0.84	0.67	0.97	0.60	0.81	0.78
		F1	0.88	0.68	0.77	0.80	0.59	0.97	0.72	0.68	0.76
InceptionV3	TL	Acc	0.71	1.00	0.20	0.23	0.00	0.97	0.71	0.09	0.49
		F1	0.65	0.27	0.30	0.35	0.00	0.93	0.47	0.17	0.39
	FT	Acc	0.89	1.00	0.85	0.82	0.83	0.97	0.77	0.91	0.88
		F1	0.92	0.79	0.90	0.84	0.69	0.86	0.82	0.81	0.83
Inception ResNetV2	TL	Acc	0.50	1.00	0.17	0.08	0.33	0.79	0.73	0.13	0.47
		F1	0.36	0.11	0.34	0.23	0.00	0.65	0.36	0.06	0.26
	FT	Acc	0.90	1.00	0.86	0.82	0.88	0.97	0.67	0.63	**0.84**
		F1	0.92	0.81	0.93	0.81	0.52	0.88	0.82	0.68	**0.80**
NASNet	TL	Acc	0.23	1.00	0.32	0.13	0.00	0.97	0.56	0.03	0.41
		F1	0.36	0.11	0.34	0.23	0.00	0.65	0.36	0.06	0.26
	FT	Acc	0.90	1.00	0.89	0.72	0.92	0.97	0.75	0.75	0.86
		F1	0.92	0.81	0.93	0.81	0.52	0.88	0.82	0.68	0.80
Num of pages by class			93	77	82	80	88	77	81	75	Tot 653

4   Conclusions

In this paper, we presented a deep transfer learning based approach to solve one of the most important problems faced by paleographers, i.e. the identification of the writers who participated to the handwriting process of ancient manuscripts. The proposed approach consists of two modules. The first uses an object detection system based on the MobileNet V2 network to automatically detect end extract the rows in the page images. The second one, instead, classifies the extracted rows. In both cases a deep transfer learning approach has been used and in particular object detection module has been pretrained on MS-COCO while the classifier module has been pretrained by ImageNet.

The proposed approach has been tested on the "Avila Bible", a XII century manuscript. Because of the presence of writers from different ages, this manuscript represented a challenging task to evaluate the effectiveness of the proposed approach.

From the experimental results, the following conclusions can be drawn: (i) *TL* without *FT* generally produces a weak classifier; (ii) models trained on a completely different dataset, after a refinement in the training phase, can be used effectively on datasets like Avila; (iii) more parameters do not imply better performance; in fact, the best results have been obtained with InceptionV3, characterized by 30 million parameters, and not NASNetLarge, characterized by 97 million parameters. In [10] and [7] the authors, using Machine Learning techniques, have achieved excellent performances in the recognition of writers in this same type of documents. However, while in this study the annotated images are only 96, in that study the annotated images were about the 50% of 749, with features extracted ad hoc for Avila. The main novelty of the present study was to apply transfern learning techniques, not previously used in literature, without the definition of features specifically designed to recognize writers in ancient manuscripts. The performances were promising and the future work will include the extensions of test experiments on other datasets and with other intra and inter database training/testing.

Acknowledgment. The authors gratefully acknowledge the support of NVIDIA Corporation for the donation of the Titan Xp GPUs.

References

1. Afzal, M.Z., et al.: Deepdocclassifier: document classification with deep convolutional neural network. In: 2015 13th International Conference on Document Analysis and Recognition (ICDAR), pp. 1111–1115, August 2015
2. Antonacopoulos, A., Downton, A.C.: Special issue on the analysis of historical documents. IJDAR **9**(2–4), 75–77 (2007)
3. Bria, A., Marrocco, C., Karssemeijer, N., Molinara, M., Tortorella, F.: Deep cascade classifiers to detect clusters of microcalcifications. In: Tingberg, A., Lång, K., Timberg, P. (eds.) IWDM 2016. LNCS, vol. 9699, pp. 415–422. Springer, Cham (2016). https://doi.org/10.1007/978-3-319-41546-8_52
4. Bria, A., et al.: Improving the automated detection of calcifications by combining deep cascades and deep convolutional nets. In: Progress in Biomedical Optics and Imaging - Proceedings of SPIE, vol. 10718 (2018)
5. Bria, A., Marrocco, C., Molinara, M., Tortorella, F.: A ranking-based cascade approach for unbalanced data. In: 2012 21st International Conference on Pattern Recognition (ICPR), pp. 3439–3442. IEEE (2012)
6. Ciresan, D.C., Meier, U., Schmidhuber, J.: Transfer learning for Latin and Chinese characters with deep neural networks. In: The 2012 International Joint Conference on Neural Networks (IJCNN), pp. 1–6 (2012)
7. De-Stefano, C., Maniaci, M., Fontanella, F., Scotto di Freca, A.: Reliable writer identification in medieval manuscripts through page layout features: the "avila" bible case. Eng. Appl. Artif. Intell. **72**, 99–110 (2018)
8. De Stefano, C., Maniaci, M., Fontanella, F., Scotto di Freca, A.: Layout measures for writer identification in mediaeval documents. Measurement **127**, 443–452 (2018)
9. De Stefano, C., Fontanella, F., Maniaci, M., Scotto di Freca, A.: A method for scribe distinction in medieval manuscripts using page layout features. In: Maino, G., Foresti, G.L. (eds.) ICIAP 2011. LNCS, vol. 6978, pp. 393–402. Springer, Heidelberg (2011). https://doi.org/10.1007/978-3-642-24085-0_41
10. De Stefano, C., Fontanella, F., Maniaci, M., Scotto di Freca, A.: Exploiting page layout features for scribe distinction in medieval manuscripts. In: Proceedings of the 15th International Graphonomics Society Conference (IGS 2011). pp. 106–109 (2011)
11. Deng, J., Dong, W., Socher, R., Li, L.J., Li, K., Li, F.F.: Imagenet: a large-scale hierarchical image database. In: CVPR, pp. 248–255. IEEE Computer Society (2009). http://dblp.uni-trier.de/db/conf/cvpr/cvpr2009.html#DengDSLL009
12. Granet, A., Morin, E., Mouchère, H., Quiniou, S., Viard-Gaudin, C.: Transfer learning for handwriting recognition on historical documents. In: International Conference on Pattern Recognition Applications and Methods. Madeira, Portugal, January 2018. https://hal.archives-ouvertes.fr/hal-01681126

13. He, K., Zhang, X., Ren, S., Sun, J.: Deep residual learning for image recognition. CoRR abs/1512.03385 (2015). http://dblp.uni-trier.de/db/journals/corr/corr1512.html#HeZRS15
14. Kölsch, A., Mishra, A., Varshneya, S., Liwicki, M.: Recognizing challenging handwritten annotations with fully convolutional networks. CoRR abs/1804.00236 (2018). http://arxiv.org/abs/1804.00236
15. Lin, T.-Y., et al.: Microsoft COCO: common objects in context. In: Fleet, D., Pajdla, T., Schiele, B., Tuytelaars, T. (eds.) ECCV 2014. LNCS, vol. 8693, pp. 740–755. Springer, Cham (2014). https://doi.org/10.1007/978-3-319-10602-1_48
16. Ni, K., Callier, P., Hatch, B.: Writer identification in noisy handwritten documents. In: 2017 IEEE Winter Conference on Applications of Computer Vision (WACV). vol. 00, pp. 1177–1186, March 2017. http://doi.ieeecomputersociety.org/10.1109/WACV.2017.136
17. Oliveira, S.A., Seguin, B., Kaplan, F.: dhsegment: a generic deep-learning approach for document segmentation. CoRR abs/1804.10371 (2018). http://arxiv.org/abs/1804.10371
18. Russakovsky, O., et al.: Imagenet large scale visual recognition challenge. Int. J. Comput. Vision **115**(3), 211–252 (2015)
19. Sandler, M., Howard, A., Zhu, M., Zhmoginov, A., Chen, L.C.: Mobilenetv 2: inverted residuals and linear bottlenecks. In: The IEEE Conference on Computer Vision and Pattern Recognition (CVPR), June 2018
20. Simistira, F., Seuret, M., Eichenberger, N., Garz, A., Liwicki, M., Ingold, R.: Divahisdb: a precisely annotated large dataset of challenging medieval manuscripts. In: 2016 15th International Conference on Frontiers in Handwriting Recognition(ICFHR), vol. 00, pp. 471–476, October 2016
21. Simonyan, K., Zisserman, A.: Very deep convolutional networks for large-scale image recognition. CoRR abs/1409.1556 (2014). http://dblp.uni-trier.de/db/journals/corr/corr1409.html#SimonyanZ14a
22. Szegedy, C., Ioffe, S., Vanhoucke, V.: Inception-v4, inception-resnet and the impact of residual connections on learning. CoRR abs/1602.07261 (2016). http://dblp.uni-trier.de/db/journals/corr/corr1602.html#SzegedyIV16
23. Szegedy, C., Vanhoucke, V., Ioffe, S., Shlens, J., Wojna, Z.: Rethinking the inception architecture for computer vision. CoRR abs/1512.00567 (2015). http://dblp.uni-trier.de/db/journals/corr/corr1512.html#SzegedyVISW15
24. Trovini, G., et al.: A deep learning framework for micro-calcification detection in 2D mammography and c-view. In: Progress in Biomedical Optics and Imaging - Proceedings of SPIE, vol. 10718 (2018)
25. Tushar, A.K., Ashiquzzaman, A., Afrin, A., Islam, M.R.: A novel transfer learning approach upon Hindi, Arabic, and Bangla numerals using convolutional neural networks. CoRR abs/1707.08385 (2017). http://arxiv.org/abs/1707.08385
26. Zoph, B., Vasudevan, V., Shlens, J., Le, Q.V.: Learning transferable architectures for scalable image recognition. CoRR abs/1707.07012 (2017). http://dblp.uni-trier.de/db/journals/corr/corr1707.html#ZophVSL17

Restoration of Colour Images Using Backward Stochastic Differential Equations with Reflection

Dariusz Borkowski[✉][iD]

Faculty of Mathematics and Computer Science, Nicolaus Copernicus University, Chopina 12/18, 87-100 Toruń, Poland
dbor@mat.umk.pl
http://www.mat.umk.pl/~dbor

Abstract. Colour image denoising methods based on the chromaticity-brightness decomposition are well-known for their excellent results. We propose a novel approach for chromaticity denoising using advanced techniques of stochastic calculus. In order to solve this problem we use backward stochastic differential equations with reflection. Our experiments show that the new approach gives very good results and compares favourably with deterministic differential equation methods.

Keywords: Inverse problem ·
Backward stochastic differential equations with reflection ·
Stochastic processes · Chromaticity denoising · Image reconstruction

1 Introduction

One of the most important issues of digital image processing and computer vision is a problem of image denoising. A key element in most image processing algorithms is efficient and effective reconstruction of images. Reconstruction algorithms allow us to pre-process the data for further analysis, which is very important in many disciplines, especially in astronomy, biology and medicine.

Let D be a bounded, convex domain in $\mathbf{R}^2$, $u : \overline{D} \to \mathbf{R}^3$ be an original RGB image and $u_0 : \overline{D} \to \mathbf{R}^3$ be the observed image of the form $u_0 = u + \eta$, where η stands for a white Gaussian noise (independently added to all coordinates). We are given u_0, the problem is to reconstruct u.

There are many different techniques to solve the above inverse problem. We can mention here linear filtering, DCT [28], wavelets theory [12], variational modelling [24], methods driven by nonlinear diffusion equation [18,23,26] and the stochastic approach, which typically relies on the theory of Markov fields and Bayesian theory [16]. Moreover, there is another class of methods that uses the non local similarity of patches in the image. We can list non local means [5], BM3D [20], NL-Bayes [4] and K-SVD [1].

© Springer Nature Switzerland AG 2019
M. Vento and G. Percannella (Eds.): CAIP 2019, LNCS 11679, pp. 317–329, 2019.
https://doi.org/10.1007/978-3-030-29891-3_28

Most methods for the colour images have been formulated on channel-by-channel and vectorial models [3,18,23]. In this paper we study the restoration based on the chromaticity-brightness decomposition [6–8]. This model is known to be close to human perception of colours and gives good results [9]. The general idea of the chromaticity-brightness approach is as follows. The brightness component is defined by the Euclidean norm $|u_0|$. The chromaticity component is given by $u_0/|u_0|$ and takes values in S^2, the unit sphere in $\mathbf{R}^3$. The core of this method is to restore these two components independently. In the case of restoring the brightness we apply the backward stochastic differential equations (in short BSDEs) and we need model from [2]. In order to reconstruct the chromaticity component we propose a novel method driven by backward stochastic differential equations with reflection (in short RBSDEs). Unfortunately, in the case of RBSDEs we can not apply the above reasoning directly. The problem of the existence and uniqueness of RBSDEs for non-convex domains is presently still open [22]. Here we consider a model of the chromaticity given by a convex triangle T^2 in $\mathbf{R}^3$ and the brightness as a mean of red, green and blue component [19,27]. Next, as before, we restore these components independently.

The paper is constructed as follows. In Sect. 2 we recall model of filtering in terms of BSDEs taken from [2]. Section 3 provides new results of RBSDE restoration of noisy chromaticity. We give here the algorithm of chromaticity denoising. Finally, in Sect. 4 experimental results and comparison to other methods are presented.

2   Restoration of the Brightness

Let

$$u_0^b(x) = \frac{u_0^R(x) + u_0^G(x) + u_0^B(x)}{3}. \tag{1}$$

be the brightness of the noisy image, where

$$u_0(x) = \left(u_0^R(x), u_0^G(x), u_0^B(x)\right) \tag{2}$$

is given RGB noisy image.

To restore the brightness u^b of the original image u we apply method from [2]. The reconstructed grayscale pixel $u^b(x)$ is defined as Y_0 satisfying the following BSDE equation:

$$\begin{cases} X_t = x + \displaystyle\int_0^t \sigma(s, X_s)\, dW_s + K_t^{\overline{D}}, & t \in [0, T], \\ Y_t = u_0^b(X_S) + \displaystyle\int_t^T c(s)(Y_s - u_0^b(X_s))ds - \int_t^T Z_s\, dW_s, & t \in [0, T], \end{cases} \tag{3}$$

where

$$\sigma(s, X_s) = \begin{bmatrix} -\left(1 - \dfrac{c(s)}{c}\right) \dfrac{(G_\gamma * u_0^b)_{x_2}(X_s)}{|\nabla(G_\gamma * u_0^b)(X_s)|}, & \dfrac{c(s)}{c} \dfrac{(G_\gamma * u_0^b)_{x_1}(X_s)}{|\nabla(G_\gamma * u_0^b)(X_s)|} \\ \left(1 - \dfrac{c(s)}{c}\right) \dfrac{(G_\gamma * u_0^b)_{x_1}(X_s)}{|\nabla(G_\gamma * u_0^b)(X_s)|}, & \dfrac{c(s)}{c} \dfrac{(G_\gamma * u_0^b)_{x_2}(X_s)}{|\nabla(G_\gamma * u_0^b)(X_s)|} \end{bmatrix} \tag{4}$$

$$c(t) = \begin{cases} 0 & \text{if } t < S \text{ or } |\nabla(G_\gamma * u_0^b)(x)| < d, \\ c & \text{if } t \geq S \text{ and } |\nabla(G_\gamma * u_0^b)(x)| \geq d. \end{cases} \tag{5}$$

$S \in \mathbf{R}_+ < T \in \mathbf{R}_+$, $d \in \mathbf{R}_+$, $c \in \mathbf{R}_+$, $\gamma \in \mathbf{R}_+$ – parameters,

$\{X_t \in \overline{D}\}_{t \in [0,T]}$, $\{Y_t \in \mathbf{R}\}_{t \in [0,T]}$, $\{K_t^{\overline{D}} \in \mathbf{R}^2\}_{t \in [0,T]}$, $\{Z_t \in \mathbf{R}\}_{t \in [0,T]}$ – stochastic processes,

$$u_{x_i}(y) = \frac{\partial u}{\partial x_i}(y), \nabla(u(y)) = \begin{bmatrix} \frac{\partial u}{\partial x_1}(y) \\ \frac{\partial u}{\partial x_2}(y), \end{bmatrix}, (G_\gamma * u)(x) = \int_{\mathbf{R}^2} \frac{1}{2\pi\gamma} e^{-\frac{|x-y|}{\gamma}} u(y) dy.$$

For a fixed pixel x we consider a certain equation of (3) type. The values of the process X determines pixels from domain of the image $\overline{D}$ which we will use in process reconstruction. We can say that this process determines neighbourhood of the pixel x (with irregular shape). The reconstructed value $u(x)$ is the sum of pixels from its neighbourhood multiplied by some weights. The weight values are determined by the process Y. Appropriate definition of Y allows as to give weight values (also negative) which depend on direction and distance from reconstructed pixel. In this model we deblur in gradient direction from time T to S and smooth out in perpendicular to gradient direction from S to 0. To avoid false detections due to noise, u_0^b is convolved with a Gaussian kernel G_γ (in practice 3×3 Gaussian mask). Parameter T defines the size of the neighbourhood used in the reconstruction procedure. The parameter d determines which pixels will be reconstructed with using smoothing model (only in gradient direction) and which with using enhancing model (in gradient and in perpendicular to gradient direction). The parameter c is responsible for effect of edge sharpening. If reconstructed pixel x belongs to the edge (the condition $|\nabla(G_\gamma * u_0^b)(x)| \geq d$ is true) the process X has values along edges (from time 0 to S) and pixels in gradient direction (from time S to T). If the condition $|\nabla(G_\gamma * u_0^b)(x)| \geq d$ is false then we explore only pixels along edges with positive weights and resign from sharpening effect.

2.1   Algorithm

Consider a time discretization

$$0 < t_0 < t_1 < \cdots < t_j \leq S < t_{j+1} < \cdots < t_m = T, t_i - t_{i-1} = \frac{T}{m}.$$

In the first step we generate trajectory of the process X for $t_0, t_1, \ldots, t_{m-1}$ using the Euler formula [25]

$$X_0 = x, X_{t_k} = \Pi_{\overline{D}}[X_{t_{k-1}} + \sigma(t_{k-1}, X_{t_{k-1}})(W_{t_k} - W_{t_{k-1}})], \tag{6}$$

where $\Pi_{\overline{D}}(x)$ denotes a projection of x on the set $\overline{D}$. The difference $W_{t_k} - W_{t_{k-1}}$ is approximated using random number generator and is equal to two independent values (vector) obtained using generator of the normal distribution with parameters $\mathcal{N}(0, t_k - t_{k-1})$. Example of this sequence is shown on Fig. 1(a). The image has two areas: gray and white. Process X starts from the reconstructed pixel x located on the edge. Next, the process X has values along the edge until time S, then after time S moves towards the gradient. From a definition of BSDE

$$Y_{t_m} := u_0^b(X_{t_j}).$$

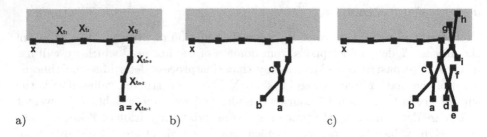

Fig. 1. Illustration of the algorithm.

Now, we backwardly count values $Y_{t_{m-1}}, Y_{t_{m-2}}, \ldots, Y_0$ [21].

$$Y_{t_{m-1}} := \mathbf{E}\left[Y_{t_m}|\mathcal{F}_{t_{m-1}}\right] + \frac{T}{m}c(t_{m-1})\left(\mathbf{E}\left[Y_{t_m}|\mathcal{F}_{t_{m-1}}\right] - u_0^b(X_{t_{m-1}})\right)$$

Since Y_{t_m} is $\mathcal{F}_{t_{m-1}}$ measurable we have

$$Y_{t_{m-1}} = Y_{t_{m-1}}^a = u_0^b(X_{t_j}) + \frac{T}{m}c(t_{m-1})\left(u_0^b(X_{t_j}) - u_0^b(a)\right).$$

Next, for t_{m-2} we define

$$Y_{t_{m-2}} := \mathbf{E}\left[Y_{t_{m-1}}|\mathcal{F}_{t_{m-2}}\right] + \frac{T}{m}c(t_{m-2})\left(\mathbf{E}\left[Y_{t_{m-1}}|\mathcal{F}_{t_{m-2}}\right] - u_0^b(X_{t_{m-2}})\right).$$

Since $Y_{t_{m-1}}$ is not $\mathcal{F}_{t_{m-2}}$ measurable, we need to count $\mathbf{E}\left[Y_{t_{m-1}}|\mathcal{F}_{t_{m-2}}\right]$ by using Monte Carlo method with M iterations. We start M-times from point $X_{t_{m-2}}$. Example for $M = 3$ is shown on Fig. 1(b) (in practise we need to use about 10 iterations). As before we count $Y_{t_{m-1}}^b$ and $Y_{t_{m-1}}^c$ and then

$$\mathbf{E}\left[Y_{t_{m-1}}|\mathcal{F}_{t_{m-2}}\right] \approx \frac{Y_{t_{m-1}}^a + Y_{t_{m-1}}^b + Y_{t_{m-1}}^c}{3},$$

$$Y_{t_{m-2}} \approx Y_{t_{m-2}}^{a,b,c} = \frac{Y_{t_{m-1}}^a + Y_{t_{m-1}}^b + Y_{t_{m-1}}^c}{3}$$

$$+ \frac{T}{m}c(t_{m-2})\left(\frac{Y_{t_{m-1}}^a + Y_{t_{m-1}}^b + Y_{t_{m-1}}^c}{3} - u_0^b(X_{t_{m-2}})\right).$$

Next, value for t_{m-3} is equal to

$$Y_{t_{m-3}} := \mathbf{E}\left[Y_{t_{m-2}}|\mathcal{F}_{t_{m-3}}\right] + \frac{T}{m}c(t_{m-3})\left(\mathbf{E}\left[Y_{t_{m-2}}|\mathcal{F}_{t_{m-3}}\right] - u_0^b(X_{t_{m-3}})\right)$$

and again, similarly to $Y_{t_{m-2}}$ we need to count it by using Monte Carlo method. For $M = 3$ (see Fig. 1(c)) we have formula

$$Y_{t_{m-3}} \approx Y_{t_{m-3}}^{a,b,c,d,e,f,g,h,i} = \frac{Y_{t_{m-2}}^{a,b,c} + Y_{t_{m-2}}^{d,e,f} + Y_{t_{m-2}}^{g,h,i}}{3}$$
$$+ \frac{T}{m} c(t_{m-3}) \left(\frac{Y_{t_{m-2}}^{a,b,c} + Y_{t_{m-2}}^{d,e,f} + Y_{t_{m-2}}^{g,h,i}}{3} - u_0^b(X_{t_{m-3}}) \right).$$

The above reasoning should be repeated until we determine Y_0 which is a reconstructed value i.e. $u^b(x)$.

More details about numerical implementation, especially how to speed up calculations, are presented in the paper [2].

3   Restoration of the Chromaticity

The RGB space can be used to define *rg chromaticity* [27] in the usual way

$$u_0^c(x) = \left(u_0^r(x), u_0^g(x), u_0^b(x) \right) \in T^2 \tag{7}$$

where

$$u_0^r(x) = \frac{u_0^R(x)}{u_0^R(x) + u_0^G(x) + u_0^B(x)},$$

$$u_0^g(x) = \frac{u_0^G(x)}{u_0^R(x) + u_0^G(x) + u_0^B(x)},$$

$$u_0^b(x) = \frac{u_0^B(x)}{u_0^R(x) + u_0^G(x) + u_0^B(x)},$$

$$T^2 = \left\{ ((x_1, x_2, x_3) \in \mathbf{R}^3; x_1 + x_2 + x_3 = 1 \right\}.$$

If $u_0(x) = (0, 0, 0)$ then we assume that $u_0^c(x) = (1/3, 1/3, 1/3)$. Note that, we consider this model in $\mathbf{R}^3$ space (not triangle in $\mathbf{R}^2$) because this will allow us to adopt the DiZenzo geometry used for RGB images [10, 11].

3.1   DiZenzo Geometry

Let $u : D \to \mathbf{R}^n$ be a vector valued image and fix $x \in D$. Consider the function $F_x : V \to \mathbf{R}$, $F_x(v) = \left| \frac{\partial u}{\partial v}(x) \right|^2$, where $V = \{ v \in \mathbf{R}^2; |v| = 1 \}$. We are interested in finding the arguments $\theta_+(u, x), \theta_-(u, x)$ and corresponding values $\lambda_+(u, x) = F_x(\theta_+(u, x))$, $\lambda_-(u, x) = F_x(\theta_-(u, x))$ which maximize and minimize the function F_x, respectively. Note that F_x can be rewritten as $F_x(v) = F_x([v_1, v_2]^T) = v^T \mathbf{G}(x) v$. In the useful case of colour RGB images $\mathbf{G}$ is defined by the following

$$\mathbf{G}(x) = \begin{bmatrix} \sum_{i=1}^{3} \left(\frac{\partial u_i}{\partial x_1}(x) \right)^2, & \sum_{i=1}^{3} \frac{\partial u_i}{\partial x_1}(x) \frac{\partial u_i}{\partial x_2}(x) \\ \\ \sum_{i=1}^{3} \frac{\partial u_i}{\partial x_1}(x) \frac{\partial u_i}{\partial x_2}(x), & \sum_{i=1}^{3} \left(\frac{\partial u_i}{\partial x_2}(x) \right)^2 \end{bmatrix} \tag{8}$$

The interesting point about $\mathbf{G}(x)$ is that its positive eigenvalues $\lambda_+(u, x)$, $\lambda_-(u, x)$ are the maximum and the minimum of F_x while the orthogonal eigenvectors $\theta_+(u, x)$ and $\theta_-(u, x)$ are the corresponding variation orientations. Three different choices of vector gradient norms $N(u, x)$ have been proposed in the literature:

$$\sqrt{\lambda_+(u, x)}, \sqrt{\lambda_+(u, x) - \lambda_-(u, x)}, \sqrt{\lambda(u, x) + \lambda_-(u, x)}.$$

In this paper we use $N(u, x) = \sqrt{\lambda_+(u, x)}$ as a natural extension of the scalar gradient norm viewed as the value of maximum variations.

3.2   RBSDE Model for Chromaticity

We propose the following RBSDE model to restoration of the chromaticity $u^c(x)$.

$$\begin{cases} X_t = x + \displaystyle\int_0^t \sigma(s, X_s)\, dW_s + K_t^{\overline{D}}, & t \in [0, T], \\ Y_t = u_0^c(X_S) + \displaystyle\int_t^T c(s)(Y_s - u_0^c(X_s))ds - \int_t^T Z_s\, dW_s + K_T^{T_\epsilon^2} - K_t^{T_\epsilon^2}, & t \in [0, T], \end{cases} \tag{9}$$

where

$$\sigma(s, X_s) = \left[\left(1 - \frac{c(s)}{c}\right) \theta_-(G_\gamma * u_0^c, X_s), \frac{c(s)}{c}\theta_+(G_\gamma * u_0^c, X_s) \right] \tag{10}$$

$$c(t) = \begin{cases} 0 & \text{if } t < S \text{ or } N(G_\gamma * u_0^c, x) < d, \\ c & \text{if } t \geq S \text{ and } N(G_\gamma * u_0^c, x) \geq d \end{cases} \tag{11}$$

$\{Z_t \in \mathbf{R}^3\}_{t \in [0,T]}$ and $\{K^{T_\epsilon^2} \in \mathbf{R}^3\}$ is a correction process for values of chromaticity i.e. $\{Y_t \in T_\epsilon^2\}_{t \in [0,T]}$. We keep these values in the set

$$T_\epsilon^2 = \{(x_1, x_2, x_3), 1 - \epsilon \leq x_1 + x_2 + x_3 \leq 1 + \epsilon\},$$

where ϵ is very small number needed to obtain domain with non empty interior. This assumption is required for theoretical results for RBSDEs [15].

3.3   Algorithm

Consider a time discretization

$$0 < t_0 < t_1 < \cdots < t_j \leq S < t_{j+1} < \cdots < t_m = T, t_i - t_{i-1} = \frac{T}{m}.$$

and trajectory of the process X for $t_0, t_1, \ldots, t_{m-1}$

$$X_0 = x, \ X_{t_k} = \Pi_{\overline{D}}[X_{t_{k-1}} + \sigma(t_{k-1}, X_{t_{k-1}})(W_{t_k} - W_{t_{k-1}})], \tag{12}$$

From definition of RBSDE it is known that $Y_{t_m} := u_0^c(X_{t_j}) \in T^2$. The steps of the algorithm are similar to the gray level case but here we need to additionally define Y as projection Π_{T^2} on the chromaticity space.

$$Y_{t_{m-1}} := \Pi_{T^2} \left[u_0^c(X_{t_j}) + \frac{T}{m} c(t_{m-1}) \left(u_0^c(X_{t_j}) - u_0^c(a) \right) \right],$$

$$Y_{t_{m-2}} := \Pi_{T^2} \left[\mathbf{E} \left[Y_{t_{m-1}} | \mathcal{F}_{t_{m-2}} \right] + \frac{T}{m} c(t_{m-2}) \left(\mathbf{E} \left[Y_{t_{m-1}} | \mathcal{F}_{t_{m-2}} \right] - u_0^c(X_{t_{m-2}}) \right) \right],$$

$$\vdots$$

$$Y_{t_0} := \Pi_{T^2} \left[\mathbf{E} \left[Y_{t_1} | \mathcal{F}_{t_0} \right] + \frac{T}{m} c(t_1) \left(\mathbf{E} \left[Y_{t_1} | \mathcal{F}_{t_0} \right] - u_0^c(X_{t_0}) \right) \right],$$

where the restored pixel is $u^c(x) = Y_{t_0} \in T^2$.

4   Experimental Results

Fig. 2. (a) Original image 256×256 pixels (b) Noisy image $\rho = 10$ (c) CTV (S^1, l^1) ($PSNR = 28.90$) (d) TV ($PSNR = 30.12$) (e) PTV ($PSNR = 30.54$) (f) RBSDE ($PSNR = 29.28$).

In this section we present experimental results illustrating the difference of our algorithm (in short RBSDE) and other method based on differential equations. We use the implementation of compared methods from Image Processing On Line: Total Variation Denoising using Split Bregman [17] (in short TV), Chambolle's Projection Algorithm [13] (in short PTV) and Collaborative TV Regularization [14] (in short CTV). Parameters of these approaches were set to the default values as recommended by the authors. Our algorithm has only one

Table 1. PSNR for food.png 256×256

	$\rho = 10$	$\rho = 20$	$\rho = 30$	$\rho = 40$	$\rho = 50$
TV	30.12	25.85	23.20	21.15	19.45
PTV	**30.54**	27.04	25.28	**24.10**	**23.14**
CTV ($l^{1,1,1}$)	26.46	25.71	24.07	23.36	21.80
CTV ($l^{2,1,1}$)	28.20	27.11	25.46	23.24	20.98
CTV ($l^{2,2,1}$)	29.20	27.51	24.89	22.12	19.73
CTV ($l^{\infty,1,1}$)	29.08	27.48	25.06	22.30	19.97
CTV ($l^{\infty,\infty,1}$)	30.06	26.08	23.26	20.39	18.23
CTV ($l^{\infty,2,1}$)	30.17	27.48	24.07	20.99	18.58
CTV ($l^{2,\infty,1}$)	29.81	27.19	23.75	20.85	18.65
CTV (S^{1},l^{1})	28.90	**27.59**	**25.48**	22.92	20.53
CTV (S^{∞},l^{1})	29.09	27.15	24.38	21.60	19.32
RBSDE	29.28	27.00	25.21	23.44	22.32

parameter i.e. a standard noise deviation ρ. Others parameters depend only on the value of ρ. Choosing their values, we followed the principle of maximizing the Peak Signal to Noise Ratio (in short PSNR). We can also release parameter c, which is responsible for sharpening the image. However, too high value of this parameter has a negative impact on the value of PSNR (although the picture is more readable for our eyes).

In Table 1 and Fig. 2 we can see results of the reconstruction of the *food.png* image 256×256 pixels. We obtained a very good result by the PTV method. Our algorithm has obtained a decent result regardless of the noise value. The analysis of the image shows that our method keeps details in the image.

The RBSDE algorithm gives much better results for higher resolution images: *kodim14.png* (from KODAK database) and *traffic.png* (from IPOL database). In this test, we omit the CTV because online IPOL implementation of this method does not allow for processing of higher resolution images. The analysis of the measures of image quality from Tables 2 and 3 shows that the new method performs better. In the picture Fig. 3 we have confirmation of earlier observation that RSBDE retains more details, in particular the edges are sharper. An interesting example is Fig. 4 in which you should look at the black slat on the car door. Our method very well removed the noise from the edges compared to PTV and TV.

Table 2. PSNR for kodim14.png 768 × 512

	$\rho = 10$	$\rho = 20$	$\rho = 30$	$\rho = 40$	$\rho = 50$
TV	31.39	27.99	25.99	24.39	22.98
PTV	31.50	28.21	26.56	25.52	24.75
RBSDE	**32.03**	**29.06**	**27.57**	**26.32**	**25.16**

Table 3. PSNR for traffic.png 704 × 469

	$\rho = 10$	$\rho = 20$	$\rho = 30$	$\rho = 40$	$\rho = 50$
TV	31.31	27.40	25.01	23.29	21.84
PTV	**31.74**	28.26	26.51	25.39	**24.63**
RBSDE	31.32	**28.48**	**26.87**	**25.50**	24.26

Table 4. Time for food.png 512 × 512

	$\rho = 10$	$\rho = 20$	$\rho = 30$	$\rho = 40$	$\rho = 50$
CPU time	21 s	22 s	21 s	22 s	20 s

The reconstruction time of our method on 1 × CPU: 1.7 GHz Intel Core i7 2 × core, is shown in the table Table 4. The number of iterations of the Monte Carlo method was selected in such a way that this time would be the same for the whole range of noise.

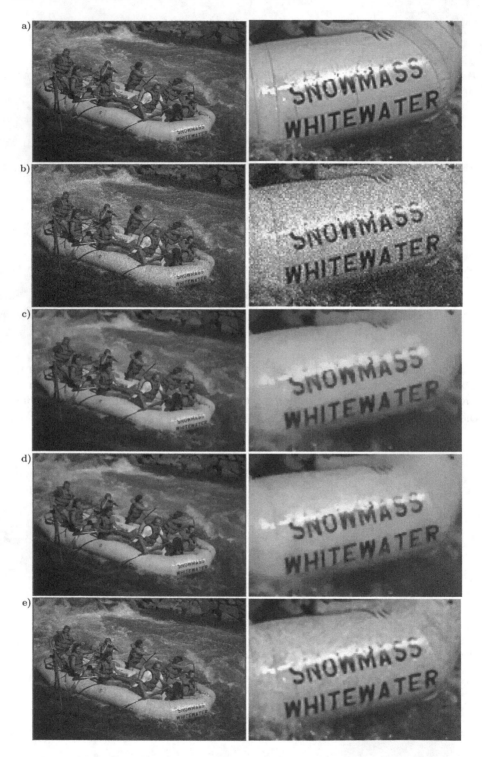

Fig. 3. (a) Original image 768×512 pixels (b) Noisy image $\rho = 30$ (c) TV ($PSNR =$ 25.99) (d) PTV ($PSNR = 26.56$) (e) RBSDE ($PSNR = 27.57$).

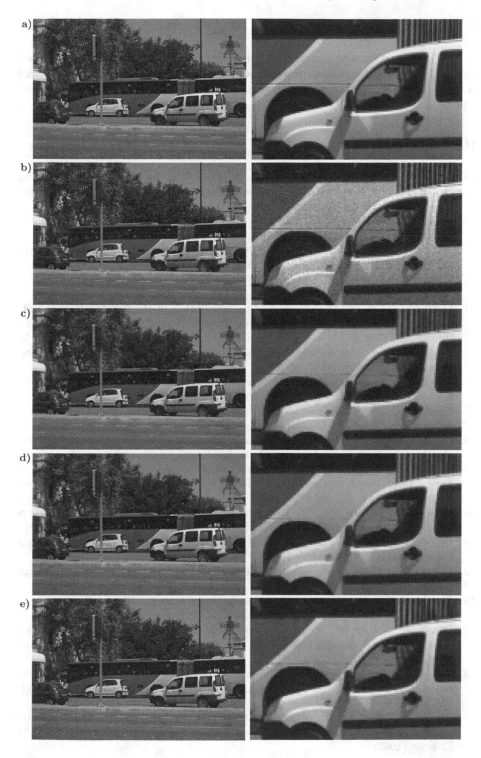

Fig. 4. (a) Original image 704×469 pixels (b) Noisy image $\rho = 10$ (c) TV ($PSNR = 31.31$) (d) PTV ($PSNR = 31.74$) (e) RBSDE ($PSNR = 31.32$).

5 Conclusions

In this paper we present a new method of image denoising based on backward stochastic differential equations with reflection. The main purpose of this work is to present a new tool for reconstructing of digital images, and the work itself will become the starting point for further exploration of RBSDEs methods.

References

1. Aharon, M., Elad, M., Bruckstein, A., et al.: K-SVD: an algorithm for designing overcomplete dictionaries for sparse representation. IEEE Trans. Signal Process. **54**(11), 4311 (2006)
2. Borkowski, D.: Forward and backward filtering based on backward stochastic differential equations. Inverse Prob. Imaging **10**(2), 305–325 (2016)
3. Borkowski, D., Jańczak-Borkowska, K.: Image denoising using backward stochastic differential equations. In: Gruca, A., Czachórski, T., Harezlak, K., Kozielski, S., Piotrowska, A. (eds.) ICMMI 2017. AISC, vol. 659, pp. 185–194. Springer, Cham (2018). https://doi.org/10.1007/978-3-319-67792-7_19
4. Buades, A., Lebrun, M., Morel, J.: Implementation of the non-local bayes (NL-Bayes) image denoising algorithm. Image Process. Line **3**, 1–44 (2013)
5. Buades, A., Coll, B., Morel, J.M.: A non-local algorithm for image denoising. In: 2005 IEEE Computer Society Conference on Computer Vision and Pattern Recognition (CVPR 2005), vol. 2, pp. 60–65. IEEE (2005)
6. Caselles, V., Sapiro, G., Tang, B.: Color image enhancement via chromaticity diffusion. IEEE Trans. Image Process. **10**(5), 701–707 (2001)
7. Cecil, T., Osher, S., Vese, L.: Numerical methods for minimization problems constrained to S^1 and S^2. J. Comput. Phys. **198**(2), 567–579 (2004)
8. Chan, T., Shen, J.: Variational restoration of nonflat image features: models and algorithms. SIAM J. Appl. Math. **61**(4), 1338–1361 (2000). (electronic)
9. Chan, T.F., Kang, S.H., Shen, J.: Total variation denoising and enhancement of color images based on the CB and HSV color models. J. Vis. Commun. Image Represent. **12**(4), 422–435 (2001)
10. Deriche, R., Tschumperlé, D.: Diffusion pde's on vector-valued images: local approach and geometric viewpoint. IEEE Signal Process. Mag. **19**(5), 16–25 (2002)
11. Di Zenzo, S.: A note on the gradient of a multi-image. Comput. Vis. Graph. Image Process. **33**(1), 116–125 (1986)
12. Donoho, D.L., Johnstone, J.M.: Ideal spatial adaptation by wavelet shrinkage. Biometrika **81**(3), 425–455 (1994)
13. Duran, J., Coll, B., Sbert, C.: Chambolle's projection algorithm for total variation denoising. Image Process. Line **3**, 311–331 (2013)
14. Duran, J., Moeller, M., Sbert, C., Cremers, D.: On the implementation of collaborative TV regularization; application to cartoon+ texture decomposition. Image Process. Line **6**, 27–74 (2016)
15. Gegout Petit, A., Pardoux, E.: Equations différentielles stochastiques rétrogrades réfléchies dans un convexe. Stochast. Int. J. Probab. Stoch. Process. **57**(1–2), 111–128 (1996)
16. Geman, S., Geman, D.: Stochastic relaxation, GIBBS distributions, and the bayesian restoration of images. In: Readings in Computer Vision, pp. 564–584. Elsevier (1987)

17. Getreuer, P.: Rudin-osher-fatemi total variation denoising using split bregman. Image Process. Line **2**, 74–95 (2012)
18. Gilboa, G., Sochen, N., Zeevi, Y.Y.: Forward-and-backward diffusion processes for adaptive image enhancement and denoising. IEEE Trans. Image Process. **11**(7), 689–703 (2002)
19. Groot, W., Kruithof, A.A.: The colour triangle. Philips Techn. Rev. **12**(5), 137–144 (1950)
20. Katkovnik, V., Danielyan, A., Egiazarian, K.: Decoupled inverse and denoising for image deblurring: variational BM3D-frame technique. In: 2011 18th IEEE International Conference on Image Processing, pp. 3453–3456. IEEE (2011)
21. Ma, J., Protter, P., San Martin, J., Torres, S., et al.: Numerical method for backward stochastic differential equations. Ann. Appl. Probab. **12**(1), 302–316 (2002)
22. Pardoux, E., Răşcanu, A.: Stochastic Differential Equations, Backward SDEs, Partial Differential Equations. SMAP, vol. 69. Springer, Cham (2014). https://doi.org/10.1007/978-3-319-05714-9
23. Perona, P., Malik, J.: Scale-space and edge detection using anisotropic diffusion. IEEE Trans. Pattern Anal. Mach. Intell. **12**(7), 629–639 (1990)
24. Rudin, L.I., Osher, S., Fatemi, E.: Nonlinear total variation based noise removal algorithms. Physica D **60**(1–4), 259–268 (1992)
25. Słomiński, L.: Euler's approximations of solutions of sdes with reflecting boundary. Stochast. Proces. Appl. **94**(2), 317–337 (2001)
26. Weickert, J.: Theoretical foundations of anisotropic diffusion in image processing. In: Kropatsch, W., Klette, R., Solina, F., Albrecht, R. (eds.) Theoretical Foundations of Computer Vision, vol. 11, pp. 221–236. Springer, Vienna (1996). https://doi.org/10.1007/978-3-7091-6586-7_13
27. Wikipedia contributors: RG chromaticity from Wikipedia, the free encyclopedia (2019). Accessed 01 Feb 2019
28. Yaroslavsky, L.P., Egiazarian, K.O., Astola, J.T.: Transform domain image restoration methods: review, comparison, and interpretation. In: Nonlinear Image Processing and Pattern Analysis XII, vol. 4304, pp. 155–170. International Society for Optics and Photonics (2001)

Sound Transformation: Applying Image Neural Style Transfer Networks to Audio Spectograms

Xuehao Liu[✉], Sarah Jane Delany, and Susan McKeever

Technological University Dublin, Dublin, Ireland
xuehao.liu@mydit.ie, {sarahjane.delany,susan.mckeever}@dit.ie

Abstract. Image style transfer networks are used to blend images, producing images that are a mix of source images. The process is based on controlled extraction of style and content aspects of images, using pre-trained Convolutional Neural Networks (CNNs). Our interest lies in adopting these image style transfer networks for the purpose of transforming sounds. Audio signals can be presented as grey-scale images of audio spectrograms. The purpose of our work is to investigate whether audio spectrogram inputs can be used with image neural transfer networks to produce new sounds. Using musical instrument sounds as source sounds, we apply and compare three existing image neural style transfer networks for the task of sound mixing. Our evaluation shows that all three networks are successful in producing consistent, new sounds based on the two source sounds. We use classification models to demonstrate that the new audio signals are consistent and distinguishable from the source instrument sounds. We further apply t-SNE cluster visualisation to visualise the feature maps of the new sounds and original source sounds, confirming that they form different sound groups from the source sounds. Our work paves the way to using CNNs for creative and targeted production of new sounds from source sounds, with specified source qualities, including pitch and timbre.

Keywords: Audio morphing · Neural network · Image style transfer · Generative adversarial network

1 Introduction

With the success of deep learning techniques for image classification [15], researchers have continued to achieve improved classification rates, with image classifiers now outperforming the ability of humans to recognise images. For example, the combination of Res-Net and an Inception V3 Convolutional Neural Network (CNN) can classify images with a 96.91% success rate [22]. Until recently, CNNs have been treated as a black box, with a limited understanding of how images are represented at each layer of the CNN. Gatys et al. [6] addressed this by examining how specific images features are captured at particular layers

© Springer Nature Switzerland AG 2019
M. Vento and G. Percannella (Eds.): CAIP 2019, LNCS 11679, pp. 330–341, 2019.
https://doi.org/10.1007/978-3-030-29891-3_29

of the CNN. They used this knowledge to generate images that mix the content and style of two source images. This image generation process, adopting the style or texture of one image and the content or contour of another image is termed *image style transfer*. Gatys et al. noted that higher layers of the CNN preserve the spatial structure or content in comparison to the capture at lower layers of image textures or style qualities in the image [13].

The purpose of this paper is to investigate image style transfer using neural networks for blending of sounds. An audio signal can be represented as a spectrogram, preserving audio frequency and amplitude. Instead of visual image inputs, audio spectrograms are fed into the image transfer process, producing a blended spectogram output. An early investigation of style transfer using spectrograms has been done by [23]. This work used AlexNet [15], a relatively shallow CNN, to extract feature maps and generate two illustrative audio spectrograms using the style transfer method. In addition to the limited number of outputs, there is no evaluation of the resultant spectrograms and thus limited insight into the nature of the generated sounds. In our work, we extend the work of [23], investigating the application of three image neural style transfer techniques [6,13,24] to the task of blending audio spectrogram inputs. We use classification models to demonstrate that the generated mixed sounds are new sounds distinguishable from the source sounds.

Audio morphing is a closely related field to our work as it focuses on the synthesis of audio signals. Audio morphing aims to find a middle ground between two audio signals, which share the properties from both sides [21]. Image neural style transform, when applied to audio, enables transformation of audio source sounds to produce a new sound, akin to audio morphing.

2   Related Work

The traditional approach to audio morphing [21] is to match pitch and temporal components between two audio signals. Another approach is to deduce the sinusoids of one audio signals and fill them with magnitude from another sound's sinusoids [19]. More recently, the methods for determining a mix of two sounds have become more complex. Different kinds of spectral envelopes can be applied on the morphing process [1]. A common factor of these methods is that, unlike neural network style transfer, they require manual feature extraction from the audio signals.

Recent research works have applied CNNs to audio processing tasks. For example, Dieleman [2] tested audio classification models, using CNNS trained on raw audio file input and the corresponding audio spectrogram input. Spectrograms were found to have a slightly higher prediction accuracy than the raw audio, suggesting that spectrograms are a richer information source. Han et al. [8] used a CNN (termed ConvNet) to classify musical instrument sounds. Hersehey et al. [11] used GoogleNet and Res-Net to do a similar classification task, but using a much larger video dataset, YouTube-100M. Their results with a 0.930 AUC demonstrated that good classification accuracies can be achieved using spectogram representation of audio signals. These works indicate that audio spectograms are a useful and valid representation of audio inputs with neural networks. In neural style transfer of audio, feature extraction will be done automatically by the network. Our neural style transfer work in this paper is inspired by image style transfer networks. In such networks, specific layers from the CNN are associated with *content* (objects) versus *style* (texture). Gatys et al. [6] demonstrated this by reconstructing an image, preserving its content, but changing the texture of the image to the style of Van Gogh's Starry Night. Johnson et al. [13] produced a faster version of Gatys et al.'s network, reducing time for one image blend from hundreds of seconds to less than one second. Frigo et al. [5] proposed a new style transfer method basing on Johnson et al.'s work, splitting the content and style images into small grids (adaptive quadtrees) and doing the style transfer operations on those similar small parts from the content and style images. Our work is also inspired by *image translation networks* which focus on translating just a specific portion of the image. For example, Isola et al. used conditional GANs to translate street maps to satellite maps [12]. In the work of Zhu et al. [24], they transform style on a portion of the image content using a cyclical generative adversarial network termed cycleGAN. An example of their work is the transformation of a horse in the image to a zebra, without changing the background of the content image, as shown in Fig. 1(d). Next, we provide a more detailed explanation of three image style transfer networks that represent a good coverage of the range of networks available and which will feature in our approach:

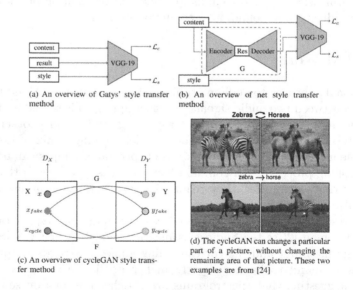

(a) An overview of Gatys' style transfer method

(b) An overview of net style transfer method

(c) An overview of cycleGAN style transfer method

(d) The cycleGAN can change a particular part of a picture, without changing the remaining area of that picture. These two examples are from [24]

Fig. 1. An overview of three kinds of structures used in this paper, and a GAN example.

Gatys et al. [6] image neural style transfer results are used as the baseline by other image style transfer methods [5,13]. The purpose of their network, as shown in Fig. 1(a), is to produce a blended image which consists of the content of one image and the style of another image. Looking at their configuration, the two sources images (one for content, one for style) are fed into the VGG-19 CNN [20]. The CNN extracts the content and style features, generating a blended result image. The result image is initialised as random noise, and on each training iteration the result image is adjusted to minimise the sum of content and style loss comparing to the result image.

Johnson et al. [13] proposed a method of image neural style transfer that performs significantly faster than that of Gatys et al. Their method shown in Fig. 1(b) produces a blended result image produced from a sample image that will provide the content, but the style is pre-defined. The underlying concept is that style can be pre-captured, whereas content from image to image will vary. Instead of initialising the input as random noise they pass the output of a generative network G, into the pre-trained VGG-19. The input to the generative network G is the content image. After each result iteration, the loss in respect to both the fixed style image and the content image is compared and gradient descent is performed on the generative network G. The advantage of their method is that style transfer can be applied at close to real-time processing speed.

Zhu et al. [24] created a cyclical generative adversarial network, termed *cycle-GAN*, for style transfer. The target task in their work is to translate a specific portion of the image, rather than transforming the style of the full image. In Fig. 1(d), a sample from their network demonstrates how a horse in an image is transferred to a zebra. The structure of cycleGAN is shown in Fig. 1(c). There are two classes X and Y in the dataset where the style of X can be transformed to Y. A generative network G generates a candidate y_{fake} from each x image and a discriminate network D_Y will evaluate whether it is a real Y image. A generative network F then generates x_{cycle} from y_{fake} and uses the discriminate network D_X to evaluate whether it is a real X image.

Applying this to Zhu et al.'s [24] example in Fig. 1(d), classes X and Y are zebra and horse respectively. The output in the figure are x_{fake} and y_{fake}. The training process of G and F is to build the mapping between X (zebra) and Y (horse). x_{fake} (fake zebra) may not exist, but we can minimize the distance between x_{cycle} and x to make a more realistic y_{fake} (fake horse). With a perfect G and a perfect F, x_{cycle} should equal to x, and y_{cycle} should equal to y. The horse should be the exact same one after changing it to a zebra and changing it back to horse. x_{fake} (fake zebra) and y_{fake} (fake horse) will be the transfer of X and Y we want.

To evaluate our results, we will need to determine whether coherent consistent sounds are being produced. According to [9], if we describe multiple audio signals as being the same kind of sound, their spectrograms are identical from the point view of timbre. As previously explained, CNNs can be used to successfully classify instruments basing on their timbre [8,11]. Classification has also been used in the image generation domain as an approach to verifying results of image generation [12]. Given these approaches, we will use classification methods (using CNNs) to test whether our generated sounds can be distinguished from the source sounds, and to test the timbre consistency of generated sounds.

3 Approach

Our approach used for audio style transfer follows the approaches used for image style transfer in other works [11,13,23,24]. The first step in image style transfer involves training a CNN on labelled images - producing a network with embedded content and style feature maps at known layers in the CNN. Applying this approach to audio, we train a CNN classification network with labelled audio spectogram inputs of the types of source sounds we will later aim to blend. The second step in image style transfer is the blending process itself - using the trained CNN and the relevant image style transfer technique with source inputs to produce a blended result output. For audio neural style transfer, the input to the trained network will be the spectogram representation of the two audio signals to be mixed. Figure 2(a) and (b) are two spectrogram examples of input to the CNN. Using the layers of this CNN, we will use three methods of image style transfer to the audio following the baseline transfer method of Gatys et al., the faster transfer method of Johnson et al. and Zhu et al.'s cycleGAN transfer method, as described in the Related Work section.

3.1 Datasets

We use the Nsynth corpus [4] which is a high-quality, large-scale musical instrument audio corpus. Every instance in the corpus is a 4 s long, 16 kHz audio snippet that covers the whole sound envelope. For our work, we will mix two different musical instrument sounds. We extract a subset dataset from the Nsynth corpus consisting of the flute and keyboard classes: 8000 clips randomly selected from acoustic keyboard sounds and 8000 flute clips. The flute clips include all the acoustic flute and a small amount of synthetic flute.

3.2 Training the Classification Network

We train the classification network to distinguish between the keyboard and flute sounds. Our CNN follows the structure of VGG-19 [20]. VGG-19 does not have any shortcuts or concatenation of feature maps and it has many layers at different feature levels. Thus it provides a rich source of image feature knowledge and is used in a variety of image style transfer networks [6,7,13]. We call our classification network audio-VGG. The only difference between our audio classification network and the original VGG-19 is the first layer. Since we use spectrograms as input, and there is only one channel in the spectrogram (the absolute value of the Short Time Fourier Transfer) the spectrogram will be represented as a grey-scale image. For the training process, 1000 clips from each class were used as the holdout set. The remaining 14000 clips (7000 for each class) were used for a 7-fold cross-validation. The accuracy achieved on the test set was 99.99% with a five epoch training process and a 0.0001 learning rate. This shows that the network can fully distinguish the two instrument sound types, with the internal layers capturing the features of flute and keyboard. Next, we apply three separate transfer networks to blend keyboard and flute sounds.

3.3   Using the Neural Style Transfer Networks for Sound Mixing

Baseline Slow Transfer: Our first transfer process uses Gatys et al.'s [6] network. The aim is to mix two source sounds, treating the flute spectrogram as the content image and the keyboard spectrogram as the style image. The audio spectrograms of the flute and keyboard sounds are passed as input into our pretrained audio-VGG network. The target blended sound spectrogram is initialised as random Gaussian noise. The training process uses gradient descent on the Gaussian noise based on total loss$\mathcal{L}$, where total loss$\mathcal{L}$ is calculated by comparing the outputs from different layers of audio-VGG network. On completion of the gradient descent, the Gaussian noise input spectrogram has been transformed to a mix of the visual content and style of our source sound and keyboard spectograms. The transfer process is slow, taking several hours to generate a single mixed sound even using the modern GPUs (GTX 1080). The content loss is between two outputs of layers `relu3_3` in that audio-VGG. In the style loss $\mathcal{L}_s$, the Gram matrix loss $\mathcal{L}_g$, energy loss $\mathcal{L}_e$, and frequency loss $\mathcal{L}_f$ are balanced [23]. The style loss is computed on layer `relu1_2`, `relu2_2`, `relu3_3` and `relu4_3`. The interpolation factor λ is equal to 1e-2.

Faster Fixed Style Transfer: The second method of style transfer used is Johnson et al.'s [13] faster fixed-style and generative network approach to speed up the transfer process. With this transfer process, we are generating multiple flute snippets which have the visual spectrogram style feature of a single keyboard snippet. The structure of the network [13] starts with a three-layer encoder and ends with another three-layer decoder, connected by residual blocks. We trained the generative net G using a learning rate of 0.0002 for 10 epochs. The input of the generative network is the content spectrogram (a spectrogram of a flute snippet) and the output is the spectrogram of the mixed or blended sound. The mixed spectrogram, the content spectrogram (flute), and the style spectrogram (keyboard) will be passed into audio-VGG in the same way of the baseline slow transfer process. The difference is that the gradient descent will be done on the generative network. The style spectrogram is a keyboard clip. The content spectrograms are the same 8000 flute clips in the training VGG-19 process.

CycleGAN Transfer: Our third style transfer approach uses the structure and parameters of Zhu et al's discriminate and generative networks, more fully described in [24]. X is flute. Two new sounds are generated: The x_{fake} result is the flute with a keyboard content; y_{fake} is the keyboard with a flute content. The generative networks G and F have a similar structure to that used in Faster Fixed Style transfer. Instead of padding before the residual blocks in Johnson et al's work [13], we followed the structure in [24], which does the padding between every layer in the residual blocks. The discriminators D_X and D_Y are two Markovian discriminators (PatchGAN), which is also used in [12]. This Markovian discriminator randomly chops the input image into a smaller 70×70 patch. According to [12], this smaller patch of input will be sufficient for the network to discriminate fake images from real ones. Also it is faster and has a smaller number of parameters. We trained the networks for 10 epochs with a 0.0001 learning rate using the same audio clips above (flute(X) and keyboard(Y)).

4   Results

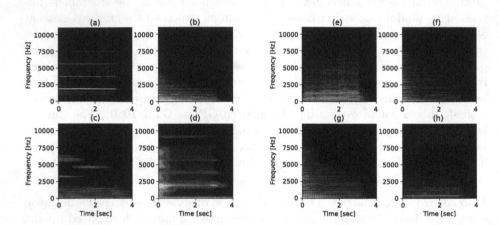

Fig. 2. (a)–(d): The spectrogram examples of slow transfer and faster fixed style transfer from the same source flute and keyboard. (a) the source flute, (b) the source keyboard, (c) the output spectrogram of slow transfer, (d) The output spectrogram of Faster Fixed Style transfer. (e)–(h): Spectrogram examples of the cycleGAN transfer. (e) the original flute x, (f) the original keyboard y, (g) the x_{fake} output, (h): the y_{fake} output.

The resulting audio clips are published online[1]. Listening to the resulting sounds, we can hear that they are different to our source sounds. However, we need objective mechanisms to determine whether the resulting sounds are consistent with each other, and distinctly separate from the source sounds. Following previous work on processing and evaluation of audio signals [8,14,17,18], we interpret our generated sound results using three methods: (1) Visual assessment of the generated audio spectrograms (2) Consistency tests on the generated sounds, using classification models and (3) Examination of the audio signal clusters.

4.1   Visual Assessment of Generated Spectrograms

Figure 2(a)–(d) shows two sample spectrograms of slow transfer and faster fixed style transfer. We observe that they both have the contour of the flute sound. With the baseline slow transfer, the harmonic is not clear, and the part higher than 6000 Hz is discarded. In the faster transfer, the lower frequency is emphasized, and there is an onset (beginning) of the note, which is missing in the

---

[1] https://www.xuehaoliu.com/audio-show.

slow transfer. Although the loss functions are the same, how these two methods learned from the keyboard are entirely different. With the slow transfer method, the generation of mixed spectrograms is initialised from Gaussian noise, whereas in faster fixed style transfer, the transfer has to follow the shape of content.

Figure 2(e)–(h) shows a mixed spectrograms resulting from the cycleGAN transfer. After the transfer, from flute to keyboard, the lower frequencies of the flute are emphasised, and the higher frequencies disappear. From keyboard to flute, the frequencies are denser. These two sample spectrograms show that this transfer will not change the harmonic, but the magnitude of each frequency is changed. This is similar to the model proposed by Serra et al. [19]. It is interesting to see that is how the model interprets the flute to/from keyboard transfers. With image transfer [24], the model should change the horse into zebra with the background intact. In this transfer process, what has been changed is the part that cycleGAN interpret as the key difference between flute and keyboard.

4.2 Sound Consistency Testing Using Classification

Classification is a common way to evaluate the output from style transfer network [3,12,24]. This is a quantitative way to examine the consistency of the outputs of the network. We tested whether our generated sounds are consistent on timbre via classification.

As a first simple test of consistency, we test whether the generated sounds are considered consistently closer to flute or keyboard by our audio-VGG, *which has had no exposure to the new sounds*. We took 1000 random selected clips of each of the three kinds of new generated mix sounds into the audio-VGG classification CNN. The classification returned for these test clips will show whether the audio-VGG defines the mixed sounds as closer to a flute or a keyboard.

Table 1 how of the mixed sounds are classified by the audio-VGG. Almost all of the mixed sounds are classified as a flute. We surmise that the generated mixed sounds therefore have common features that cause the audio-VGG classify them as the same sound.

Table 1. Number of instances per class when testing generated sounds using original audio-VGG

	Flute	Keyboard
Faster fixed style transfer	1000	0
cycleGAN keyboard to flute	998	2
cycleGAN flute to keyboard	992	8

The next step was to verify whether the generated sounds are consistent with each other, and distinguishable and consistent from the source sounds, when classified by a model that has been exposed to the new generated sounds. For each style transfer method, we trained a classifier to distinguish between the source keyboard sounds, source flute sounds and the generated mixed sound. We are dealing with four types of mixed sounds, from: the baseline slow transfer, the faster fixed style transfer, the two results of cycleGAN: the x_{fake} from G and the y_{fake} from F. For the baseline slow transfer, it is impractical to generate a large number of mixed spectrogram results needed for training, due to long processing time. We exclude this transfer process from our classification task. That leaves us with the three remaining generated sound types. For each of these three, we generated 8000 clips, and do the same train-test split as done in the previous training section (6000-1000-1000).

For each of our three generate sound types, we train a four-class classification network. The four classes consist of the original flute sounds, original keyboard sounds, the generated sounds from the relevant style transfer network and a fourth class - guitar sounds from the Nysnth dataset. The guitar class is a dummy class to introduce a class which is neither from the source sounds nor the generated mixed sounds. The structure of the network used was the VGG-19 network structure. The network was trained over 5 epochs, with a 0.0002 learning rate.

Table 2 shows the classification results across for four classes, for each of the faster fixed style transfer, cycleGAN form flute to keyboard and cycleGAN from keyboard to flute approaches.

Table 2. Class accuracy for 4 class VGG-19 for three generated sound types: Faster fixed style transfer and cycleGANs

	Overall accuracy	Recall			
		Flute	Keyboard	Guitar	Mixture
Faster fixed style transfer	0.9947	0.995	0.996	0.988	1.000
cycleGAN flute to keyboard	0.9872	0.986	0.985	0.978	1.000
cycleGAN keyboard to flute	0.9735	0.993	0.933	0.969	1.000

The table gives the overall accuracy and the class accuracy for each class for each network. The overall performance of each network is high, indicating that the generated sounds are consistent and distinguishable from the natural sounds. The class accuracy for the generated sounds for all style transfer approaches is perfect. The small number of errors made are between the natural sounds with the keyboard class accuracy the lowest.

We then need to determine whether the generated sounds from the different style transfer approaches are different from each other. To check this, we trained a six-class classifier: the three different natural sounds, keyboard, flute and guitar and the three different generated sounds from the different style transfer methods, faster fixed style transfer, cycleGAN from flute to keyboard and from keyboard to flute. The structure of this network is also VGG-19 It is trained under the same train-test strategy and the same 5 epoch.

Table 3. Class accuracy for the 6 Classification network of source and generated sounds in a single model

	Recall
Flute	0.914
Keyboard	0.944
Guitar	0.981
Faster fixed style transfer	0.999
cycleGAN from flute to keyboard	0.996
cycleGAN from keyboard to flute	1.000

Table 3 shows the classification result from the network trained on six classes. The high recall score of three mixed sounds classes shows that the network can distinguish the new generated audio signals from both natural sounds and from each other. We note that there is also some error in distinguishing the natural sounds. This may be because there are overlapping frequencies in the harmonics between those natural sounds [14].

4.3   Visualisation of Clusters

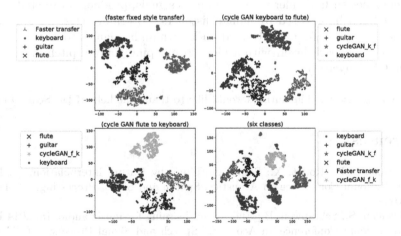

Fig. 3. t-SNE mapping of pool5

T-SNE [3,16] is a clustering method used in visualization tasks of classification networks [7,10], which we use to examine whether our new style transfer classes appear as clear clusters - and as separate clusters from the other classes. It is using a student-t distribution on the Stochastic Neighbor Embedding (SNE). SNE calculates the similarity by computing the conditional probability using

Euclidean distances between instances. We apply t-SNE on the Pooling Layer 5 [10] of every classification network.

Figure 3 shows the t-SNE mapping of layer pooling 5 for each classification network. Each dot represents a sound clip. Each kind of sound has its own color and shape. The "cycleGAN_f_k" denotes "cycleGAN from flute to keyboard" and vice versa. The generated mixed audio signals appear as clearly separated clusters from the original natural sounds clusters. It is interesting to see that for a classification network, it is easier to tell the difference between new generated mixed sounds and natural sounds, but it may get a little confused when classifying the classes which are all natural sounds.

5 Conclusions

Inspired by image neural style transfer, we applied three neural style transfer methods to audio mixing. All three methods can mix audio signals by mixing the visual style and content of audio spectrograms. The new generated audio signals are recognised by CNNs as individual classes. The t-SNE mapping shows that the new sounds are separate groups from the original sounds and from each other.

These new generated audio clips can be seen as a kind of morphing of two different kinds of audio signals, using visual concepts of style and content as our basis for mixing audio spectrograms. The next phase of work is to expand our techniques with a wider variety of audio signals, producing targeted sounds mixes that can be assessed by human listeners. To achieve this, we propose to examine the layers of a CNN trained on known audio signals to distinguish the feature maps at each layer, with a view to mapping timbre, pitch and tone to specific CNN layers.

Acknowledgement. The authors would like to thank the help of Dr. Sean O'Leary.

References

1. Caetano, M.F., Rodet, X.: Sound morphing by feature interpolation. In: IEEE International Conference on Acoustics, Speech and Signal Processing, pp. 11–231 (2011)
2. Dieleman, S., Schrauwen, B.: End-to-end learning for music audio. In: 2014 IEEE International Conference on Acoustics, Speech and Signal Processing (ICASSP), pp. 6964–6968. IEEE (2014)
3. Donahue, J., Krähenbühl, P., Darrell, T.: Adversarial feature learning. arXiv preprint arXiv:1605.09782 (2016)
4. Engel, J., et al.: Neural audio synthesis of musical notes with wavenet autoencoders. In: Proceedings of the 34th International Conference on Machine Learning, vol. 70, pp. 1068–1077 (2017). JMLR.org
5. Frigo, O., Sabater, N., Delon, J., Hellier, P.: Split and match: Example-based adaptive patch sampling for unsupervised style transfer. In: Proceedings of the IEEE Conference on Computer Vision and Pattern Recognition, pp. 553–561 (2016)

6. Gatys, L.A., Ecker, A.S., Bethge, M.: Image style transfer using convolutional neural networks. In: Proceedings of the IEEE Conference on Computer Vision and Pattern Recognition, pp. 2414–2423 (2016)
7. Ghiasi, G., Lee, H., Kudlur, M., Dumoulin, V., Shlens, J.: Exploring the structure of a real-time, arbitrary neural artistic stylization network. arXiv preprint arXiv:1705.06830 (2017)
8. Han, Y., Kim, J., Lee, K., Han, Y., Kim, J., Lee, K.: Deep convolutional neural networks for predominant instrument recognition in polyphonic music. IEEE/ACM Trans. Audio Speech Lang. Process. (TASLP) 25(1), 208–221 (2017)
9. Handel, S.: Timbre perception and auditory object identification. Hearing 2, 425–461 (1995)
10. Haque, A., Guo, M., Verma, P.: Conditional end-to-end audio transforms. arXiv preprint arXiv:1804.00047 (2018)
11. Hershey, S., et al.: Cnn architectures for large-scale audio classification. In: 2017 IEEE International Conference on Acoustics, Speech and Signal Processing (ICASSP), pp. 131–135. IEEE (2017)
12. Isola, P., Zhu, J.Y., Zhou, T., Efros, A.A.: Image-to-image translation with conditional adversarial networks. arXiv preprint (2017)
13. Johnson, J., Alahi, A., Fei-Fei, L.: Perceptual losses for real-time style transfer and super-resolution. In: Leibe, B., Matas, J., Sebe, N., Welling, M. (eds.) ECCV 2016. LNCS, vol. 9906, pp. 694–711. Springer, Cham (2016). https://doi.org/10.1007/978-3-319-46475-6_43
14. Kaneko, T., Kameoka, H., Hiramatsu, K., Kashino, K.: Sequence-to-sequence voice conversion with similarity metric learned using generative adversarial networks. In: Proceedings Interspeech, pp. 1283–1287 (2017)
15. Krizhevsky, A., Sutskever, I., Hinton, G.E.: Imagenet classification with deep convolutional neural networks. In: Advances in Neural Information Processing Systems, pp. 1097–1105 (2012)
16. Maaten, L.V.D., Hinton, G.: Visualizing data using t-sne. J. Mach. Learn. Res. 9(Nov), 2579–2605 (2008)
17. Marchi, E., Vesperini, F., Eyben, F., Squartini, S., Schuller, B.: A novel approach for automatic acoustic novelty detection using a denoising autoencoder with bidirectional LSTM neural networks. In: 2015 IEEE International Conference on Acoustics, Speech and Signal Processing (ICASSP), pp. 1996–2000. IEEE (2015)
18. Schlüter, J., Grill, T.: Exploring data augmentation for improved singing voice detection with neural networks. In: ISMIR, pp. 121–126 (2015)
19. Serra, X., et al.: Musical sound modeling with sinusoids plus noise. Musical Signal Processing, pp. 91–122 (1997)
20. Simonyan, K., Zisserman, A.: Very deep convolutional networks for large-scale image recognition. arXiv preprint arXiv:1409.1556 (2014)
21. Slaney, M., Covell, M., Lassiter, B.: Automatic audio morphing. In: 1996 IEEE Inter Conference on Acoustics, Speech, and Signal Processing. ICASSP-96. Conference, Proceedings. vol. 2, pp. 1001–1004. IEEE (1996)
22. Szegedy, C., Ioffe, S., Vanhoucke, V., Alemi, A.A.: Inception-v4, inception-resnet and the impact of residual connections on learning. In: AAAI, vol. 4, p. 12 (2017)
23. Verma, P., Smith, J.O.: Neural style transfer for audio spectograms. arXiv preprint arXiv:1801.01589 (2018)
24. Zhu, J.Y., Park, T., Isola, P., Efros, A.A.: Unpaired image-to-image translation using cycle-consistent adversarial networks. arXiv preprint (2017)

Timber Tracing with Multimodal Encoder-Decoder Networks

Fedor Zolotarev[1]([⊠]), Tuomas Eerola[1], Lasse Lensu[1], Heikki Kälviäinen[1],
Heikki Haario[1], Jere Heikkinen[2], and Tomi Kauppi[2]

[1] Lappeenranta-Lahti University of Technology LUT, School of Engineering Science,
Department of Computational and Process Engineering, Machine Vision and Pattern
Recognition Laboratory, P.O. Box 20, 53851 Lappeenranta, Finland
{fedor.zolotarev,tuomas.eerola,lasse.lensu,heikki.kalviainen,
heikki.haario}@lut.fi
[2] Finnos Oy, Tukkikatu 5, 53900 Lappeenranta, Finland
{jere.heikkinen,tomi.kauppi}@finnos.fi

Abstract. Tracking timber in the sawmill environment from the raw
material (logs) to the end product (boards) provides various benefits
including efficient process control, the optimization of sawing, and the
prediction of end-product quality. In practice, the tracking of timber
through the sawmilling process requires a methodology for tracing the
source of materials after each production step. The tracing is especially difficult through the actual sawing step where a method is needed
for identifying from which log each board comes from. In this paper,
we propose an automatic method for board identification (board-to-log
matching) using the existing sensors in sawmills and multimodal encoder-
decoder networks. The method utilizes point clouds from laser scans of
log surfaces and grayscale images of boards. First, log surface heightmaps
are generated from the point clouds. Then both the heightmaps and
board images are converted into "barcode" images using convolutional
encoder-decoder networks. Finally, the "barcode" images are utilized to
find matching logs for the boards. In the experimental part of the work,
different encoder-decoder architectures were evaluated and the effectiveness of the proposed method was demonstrated using challenging data
collected from a real sawmill.

Keywords: Convolutional neural networks ·
Encoder-decoder networks · Multimodal translation · Machine vision ·
Sawmilling

1 Introduction

Sawmilling is a complex process with a large number of different stages and
variables. A typical sawmill contains various measuring devices, such as laser
scanners and RGB cameras. These devices measure both the raw material and
end products during the different process stages. These measurements are not

© Springer Nature Switzerland AG 2019
M. Vento and G. Percannella (Eds.): CAIP 2019, LNCS 11679, pp. 342–353, 2019.
https://doi.org/10.1007/978-3-030-29891-3_30

connected with each other which prevents the full utilization of the measured information. The measurements are typically used to sort the logs or the boards to various categories, but the information about an individual log or board is lost while the material moves to the next process stage. However, tracing the material through the whole process is of great interest as it would allow various improvements for the sawmill process, such as better process control, the optimization of sawing, the prediction of the end-product quality in early stages of the process, and more accurate grading of the final product using sensor fusion. Other benefits include ensuring the legality and sustainability of the product origin [3] and avoiding faulty products at an earlier production step [5].

Tracking material is challenging in a typical sawmill environment where the raw material does not go through a straightforward process pipeline. In the multiple process stages, the material is stored in warehouses or storage areas without record keeping of individual items. This happens, for example, after the log measurements and during drying. Tracking of the material becomes even more difficult due to the various transformations the raw material goes through during debarking of the logs and sawing. Invasive tracking techniques such as labels or tags have been proposed [3]. However, they are too expensive to be used in the large scale, are easily damaged or corrupted during processing, and do not typically provide the means to track every board obtained from a single labeled log. This calls for non-invasive tracking techniques that utilize the measurable properties of the material itself to implement the matching.

In this paper, we propose a method to match grayscale images of boards to the laser scans of the surfaces (point clouds) of the corresponding logs. The method starts with the construction of heightmaps from the point clouds and utilizes a multimodal encoder-decoder network to translate the images and the heightmaps into matchable representations. The encoder-decoder network is trained using "barcode" images representing the starting and end points of knot clusters obtained from discrete X-ray tomography. The resulting network is able to generate similar "barcodes" from both the board images and the log surface heightmaps. Using these "barcodes", simple cross-correlation can be applied to find the best match for each board, i.e., the log where the board was sawn from. The proposed approach is visualized in Fig. 1.

It should be noted that the discrete X-ray tomography data is required only for the training phase. Once the networks have been trained, only the laser scanners and the cameras are required for the production deployment. We demonstrate the effectiveness of the proposed method with a challenging data set collected from a real sawmill.

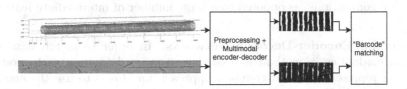

Fig. 1. Board-to-log matching. Given the point clouds of log surfaces and an image of a board, the task is to find the matching log for the board.

2   Related Work

2.1   Timber Tracing

Various solutions for tracing timber in sawmills have been proposed. Most of the solutions focus either on the re-identification of logs before sawing (log-to-log matching) or on matching boards before and after drying (board-to-board matching). The methods include cross-section images of the log ends [11], laser scans and RFID-tags for logs [2], and image-based matching for boards [8,9]. While the existing solutions provide a high tracing accuracy for the beginning and the end of the sawmill process, extending the tracing to cover the actual sawing (board-to-log matching) remains a challenge due to the following obvious reasons: (1) the material goes through a remarkable transformation and (2) the imaging modalities are different.

In [4], a method was proposed where knot clusters visible in X-ray scans of logs were matched with knots detected from boards. The presented preliminary results were promising. This approach, however, relies heavily on the performance of the knot detectors. Moreover, it requires an expensive X-ray scanner in front of the saw. To find a remedy for these restrictions, we utilize an end-to-end multimodal translation approach to translate the log measurements and board images into similar representations that can be matched to each other.

2.2   Multimodal Translation

Fully Convolutional Networks. The concept of fully convolutional networks was introduced in [7]. Its core idea is to remove the fully connected layers at the end of the network and instead make the input and output of the network to be of the same size. The fully convolutional networks are widely used for a variety of tasks, including multimodal translation, although a large proportion of them were initially created for the purpose of semantic segmentation. U-Net [10] is an example of such a network. It consists of the sequentially connected contracting and expansive paths, meaning that an image is first downsampled, and then upsampled back to the original size. The first part can be considered as an encoder and the second part as a decoder. It also utilizes skip connections that transfer features directly from the first half of the network to the second. This approach allows to capture smaller details and avoids the loss of resolution in the resulting image. The somewhat similar approach is used in SegNet [1] where the idea is to perform upsampling according to the indices that were selected during the max pooling operations. Compared to U-Net, only the indices are transferred using skip connections, as opposed to a large number of intermediate features.

Multimodal Encoder-Decoder Networks. In order to match data with different modalities, a method is needed to convert data from each modality to similar representations. A common approach for this is to use the encoder-decoder network. For example, in [6], U-Net is used as the encoder-decoder to translate data to different modalities. The latent representations, i.e., the outputs of the encoders, are concatenated for all the modalities and then decoded. Instead of concatenating different latent representations, the authors of [13] enforce the alignment of the latent space, meaning that any object should have one latent representation, independent of the modality. This common latent representation is used to align the encoder-decoder pairs, allowing for the direct translation between the modalities that do not have explicit pairs of examples.

3 Proposed Method

The proposed method to determine the corresponding log for each board consists of the following three steps:

1. Generate a heightmap from the laser point cloud.
2. Use encoders and decoders to transform the heightmap and the board image into the knot "barcodes".
3. Transform the "barcodes" into one-dimensional signals and perform cross-correlation to find the matching log for the board.

3.1 Generating Heightmaps

Information about the log surface is obtained in the form of the 3D point clouds. In the beginning it is necessary to remove data outliers generated due to the noise and obstructions during the data retrieval process. The point cloud is processed in layers that correspond to the circular cross sections of the log. First, the log center is calculated for the layer by using the median of all points. The points further than $2.5 \cdot \text{MAD}$ are removed, where MAD is the median absolute deviation of distances from the center. After that, the circle is fitted to the points using the least squares method. If the residual error of the fit is larger than a given threshold t ($t = 200$ has been used in this work), the layer is considered too noisy and removed. For the fitted circle with radius r, points with distance greater than $1.1r$ or less than $0.9r$ from the center are removed next. An example of the resulting point cloud can be seen in Fig. 2.

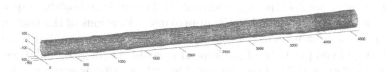

Fig. 2. Log point cloud after the removal of outliers.

A straightforward way to generate the heightmap is to fit a circle to each layer and to map the distance between each point and the circle. However, it was noticed that the resulting heightmaps contained large elevated areas making this approach unsuitable for our task. Those elevations appeared as a result of the log shape not being perfectly round but instead being the shape of a deformed circle that smoothly changes along the length of the trunk. The solution was to average each layer to generate the approximate smooth surface of the log. This was done by using moving average on the distances to the center of the fitted circle. First, averaging with a window of size 15 is done on each layer, and then averaging is performed along the length of the log with a window of size 35. The final heightmap is calculated by using the distance from the measured point to the smoothed surface. This way the large elevations are eliminated and only small bumps that correspond to the locations of branches remain. Horizontal dimension corresponds to the length of a log, vertical corresponds to an angle to the log center. A visual comparison of the two approaches can be seen in Fig. 3.

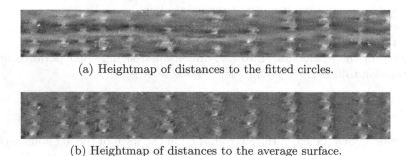

(a) Heightmap of distances to the fitted circles.

(b) Heightmap of distances to the average surface.

Fig. 3. Different approaches for generating a heightmap. (a) uses distances to the fitted circles, while (b) uses distance to the averaged surface. Large areas of elevation in (a) arise from the variance of the general shape of the log. (b) highlights only small bumps that roughly correspond to the locations of branches.

3.2   Multimodal Encoder-Decoder Networks

Multimodal encoder-decoder networks provide a tool to translate from one image modality to another. The following three modalities are considered in this work: log heightmaps, board images, and "barcode" images. The log heightmaps and the board images are 2D representations of the logs and the boards, respectively, and the "barcodes" correspond to the approximate locations of the knot clusters in the log. The information in the "barcodes" is essentially a one-dimensional list of the start and end positions of the knot clusters in the longitudinal direction of the log presented as a 2D binary image. This information is extracted from the logs using an X-ray scanner before they are sawn. The log heightmap and the board image are the source modalities (input) and the "barcode" image is the target modality (output of the translation process). Therefore, the X-ray generated "barcodes" form the ground truth to train the encoder-decoder networks. However, it should be noted that the "barcodes", generated from discrete X-ray tomography, are only used during the training phase and, therefore, an X-ray scanner is not required in order to deploy this method into production.

The schematic of the translation process of heightmaps and images to barcodes is presented in Fig. 4. By using only a single decoder on the latent representations of any other modality, we aim to align them. Skip connections from the encoders are also used along with the latent representation. The following three architectures were chosen for the encoder-decoder networks: U-Net [10], Segnet [1], and All Convolutional U-Net. The main difference between U-net and Segnet is the use of the skip connections. Before any downsampling operations, U-net transfers all features directly to the decoder, allowing for the preservation of the small details. Segnet, on the other hand, transfers only max pooling indices that are used to upsample the image. The advantage of this approach is the invariance to the modality-specific features. All Convolutional U-Net is a modification of the classic U-Net that was inspired by [12]. Instead of using the pooling and upsampling operations, the network learns the down- and upsampling operations by utilizing strided convolutions and strided transposed convolutions, respectively. It is done by completely removing max pooling and adding strides to the preceding convolution layers. The same operation is performed for the upsampling layers, except that the convolution layers are changed to transposed convolutions in order to perform the upsampling. Horizontal alignment of knots along the length of the log is used as a ground truth, which is essentially one-dimensional. Vertical locations of individual knots can differ even for matching logs and boards, owing to the fact that they depend on the measuring angle (in case of a heightmap) and the sawing angle (in case of a board image). Consequently, the loss function has been constructed to specifically optimize the horizontal intensity distribution in the resulting images. The loss function has the following form

$$\bar{p} = \sum_{y=0}^{h-1} P[y, x], \qquad \bar{t} = \sum_{y=0}^{h-1} T[y, x], \qquad loss(P, T) = \frac{\bar{p} \cdot \bar{t}}{||\bar{p}|| \, ||\bar{t}||}, \qquad (1)$$

where P, T are predicted and true images respectively, h is the height of an image. It is essentially a cosine of an angle between vectors representing horizontal alignment of knots. The value range is $[0, 1]$ due to the fact that each vector element is nonnegative (vector elements are sums of pixel values, which are normalized to $[0, 1]$ range). The training is performed on pairs of matching log and board: loss from Eq. 1 is calculated using the log and board "barcodes" as predicted images and x-ray cluster locations as true images. Both losses are then summed up to get the final loss for the iteration. This is done in order to train decoder on both modalities simultaneously.

3.3 "Barcodes" Cross-Correlation

After the heightmap and the board image are translated into the "barcode" images it is possible to measure their similarity. This is done by summing up barcodes along their height dimension which results in 1D signals representing the locations of knots along the length of logs or boards. Before the matching, the signals are normalized to be unit vectors. The similarity of the normalized

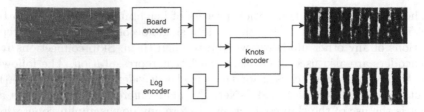

Fig. 4. Schematic of the multimodal translation process. It should be noted that there is only a single decoder.

signals is computed by using cross-correlation. The log that contains the highest similarity with the given board is selected as a match.

The conversion to 1D signals, instead of using the "barcodes" directly, is done in order to emphasize the similar properties of logs and boards. As was previously mentioned, vertical locations of knots differ even in the matching pairs of logs and boards. The proposed approach is invariant to the vertical locations of knots as it does the matching based on the horizontal knot distribution.

4   Experiments and Results

4.1   Data

The data for the experiments consisted of 50 logs and 274 boards sawn from them. The logs were selected from 5 different categories with varying diameters and quality, 10 logs from each category. The logs in Category 1 were numbered from 1 to 10, the logs in Category 2 from 11 to 20 and so on. The logs in Categories 1 to 3 (log numbers 1–30) were low quality logs with a larger amount of knots enabling easier matching while the logs in Categories 4 to 5 (log numbers 41–50) were high quality logs with a small amount of knots. A laser scanner was used to generate point clouds of the log surfaces, and an X-ray scanner to extract the locations of the knot clusters. Each log was color coded manually so that it was possible to track them through the sawing process providing the ground truth for the board-to-log matching.

After the logs were sawn, the resulting boards were imaged with an RGB camera system. The boards representing the main yield were imaged from both upper and lower sides while the side boards were imaged only from one side resulting in 393 board images in total. The different sides of the same board were treated as separate samples in the experiments. The images were converted to grayscale, rescaled to 448×160, and the colors were inverted. Inverting the colors was done to make the knots appear as white instead of black. Examples of the data used for training are presented in Fig. 5.

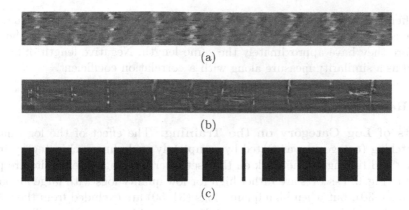

Fig. 5. Examples of preprocessed data: (a) A log heightmap; (b) A board image; (c) A "barcode" image of the knot clusters.

4.2   Experimental Arrangements

The encoders and the decoders were trained simultaneously on pairs of log heightmaps and board images from the same log as shown in Fig. 4. After the conversion of the heightmap and the board image the loss function was computed as described in Sect. 3.2 using the ground truth "barcode" images, generated using discrete X-ray tomography. During the training, data was augmented by random flips, small gaussian noise and vertical cyclical shift of the heightmaps. The vertical shift emulates different log rotations during laser measurements. Networks were trained by using Adam optimizer with the default parameters and learning rate of 0.001 and batches of size 7. Precision, recall and F-score for each log were calculated by treating the logs as classes for the board identification. The quality of the board-to-log matching was assessed using the weighted average F-score for all the logs. First, F-score is calculated for each class, then average is calculated by weighting each class score according to the support size of that class.

Due to the heterogeneous nature of the available data (5 different log categories), it is necessary to evaluate the effects of different categories on the training. In order to do that, one log category was completely excluded from the training and used as a test set. After that, 10 randomly selected logs from the rest were used for validation, and remaining logs were used to train the network, repeating this procedure 10 times for each test category. In order to compare the selected architectures of encoder-decoder networks, each network was trained 20 times, and results on the whole dataset and validation subsets was compared. Out of the 50 logs, 15 were used for validation and were excluded from the training set. Boards sawn from those logs were also excluded, meaning that approximately 30% of data was used for the validation. Finally, usage of additional information was studied. Similarly to [4], the lengths of the logs and the boards were used in the matching process. The results with and without the augmentation were compared. The augmentation was done simply by subtracting the difference of lengths from the cross-correlation value. Before subtracting, the difference was multiplied by 0.001. Boards are sawn along the length of the log, therefore they have approximately the same length. Negative length difference is used as a similarity measure along with a correlation coefficient.

4.3 Results

Effects of Log Category on the Training. The effect of the log quality on matching (category) was tested by completely excluding each category from training and testing the network on that set after training. The results are presented in Fig. 6. F-scores are rather high for low quality logs with large amounts of knots (1–30), but when high quality logs (31–50) are excluded from the training, the network is unable to generalize the learned features to them. This could mean that the higher the quality of the log, the more representative it is and possesses more subtle features. Whereas on the low quality logs the network quickly overfits on the few more prominent features that are inherent for the low quality wood. Therefore, it might be a good rule of thumb to include more high quality logs into the training procedure.

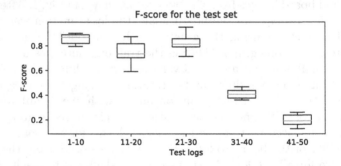

Fig. 6. The distribution of average F-scores on the test dataset. The box spans from lower to higher quartiles with a line at the median value. Lines extended from the box show the range of data with outliers depicted as white circles.

Architecture Comparison. The results of training 20 models of each encoder-decoder architecture are presented in Fig. 7. Validation set used comprised of 15 logs in total, 3 logs were taken from each category of quality. This was done in order to make the training set more representative. U-net and Convolutional U-net have similar scores on the validation set, both outperforming Segnet. All Convolutional U-net also has the highest score ceiling. When tested on the whole dataset, Convolutional U-net has the highest median score. Thus, All Convolutional U-net can be considered as the best architecture overall. The large spread of the scores can be explained by the nature of this particular translation task. In contrast to an ordinary classification task, there is an additional step of computing 1D signals and matching them together. This makes the result dependent not only on the sample itself, but on a large number of other samples that are used in the cross-correlation. Moreover, the sample size is rather small, and deep neural networks are notoriously dependent on the amount of the available training data. Keeping in mind results of the experiment from Sect. 4.3, the training could be made more robust by including more high quality logs into the training set.

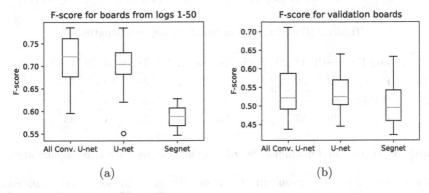

Fig. 7. The distribution of average F-scores for the selected architectures of the encoder-decoder networks: (a) All logs and boards used as input; (b) Only boards in the validation set used as input and matched to all logs.

Utilizing Log and Board Lengths. Table 1 shows results of matching for the All Convolutional U-Net network. The results presented are mean values of scores calculated with each of 20 networks trained in Sect. 4.3. Each 10 logs represent a category of increasing quality. It can be seen that as the quality increases the matching accuracy drops. This is expected as the main features that are used during the matching, i.e., knots, are less prevalent or completely absent in the high quality wood. The overall quality of matching is still reasonably high, reaching almost perfect scores for the logs of lower quality. The overall F-score of 0.72 is already reasonably high, but it can be improved even further by utilizing the lengths of boards and logs. It is evident from Table 2 that the size information itself is not enough to perform precise matching. However, as it can be seen from Table 3, augmenting the "barcode" matching with the size information shows a significant improvement in the matching accuracy, especially for the high quality logs. This demonstrates the flexibility of the approach, allowing for the utilization of the additional information that is available in a sawmill.

Table 1. Average board matching scores over all runs without size augmentation. Maximum scores over all runs are presented in parentheses. P is precision, R is recall and F is F-score.

Log IDs	1–10	11–20	21–30	31–40	41–50	1–30	31–50	1–50	Validation
P (%)	99 (100)	98 (100)	96 (98)	82 (96)	74 (87)	95 (97)	74 (84)	77 (83)	65 (80)
R (%)	95 (98)	92 (99)	85 (93)	61 (75)	56 (70)	91 (96)	58 (73)	74 (81)	52 (66)
F (%)	97 (99)	93 (99)	87 (95)	67 (79)	60 (73)	91 (96)	62 (75)	72 (79)	54 (71)

Table 2. Board matching results using only lengths.

Log IDs	1–10	11–20	21–30	31–40	41–50	1–30	31–50	1–50
P (%)	68	50	41	51	82	38	54	34
R (%)	42	34	26	25	52	34	38	36
F (%)	49	37	31	33	60	35	41	33

Table 3. Average and maximum board matching scores with size augmentation.

Log IDs	1–10	11–20	21–30	31–40	41–50	1–30	31–50	1–50	Validation
P (%)	99 (100)	99 (100)	97 (98)	93 (99)	91 (100)	98 (100)	89 (96)	87 (92)	87 (94)
R (%)	98 (100)	96 (100)	93 (98)	72 (80)	72 (83)	96 (99)	72 (81)	83 (88)	68 (78)
F (%)	98 (100)	97 (100)	94 (98)	78 (87)	77 (88)	96 (99)	76 (85)	81 (87)	73 (81)

5   Conclusion

A multimodal translation-based method for matching sawn timber to the logs from which they were sawn was proposed. The method uses the board images and the laser scanner data of the log surfaces as the input and utilizes the discrete X-ray tomography data to train a multimodal encoder-detector network translating the board and log data to a matchable representations. It should be noted that the X-ray data about the knot clusters is required only in the training phase. Once the network has been trained only the laser scanner and camera systems are needed providing a cost-effective method for timber tracing. The effects of different log categories on the training were studied and it can be concluded that the proposed method generalizes best when trained on higher quality logs. Three different architectures of the encoder-decoder networks were evaluated and a modified version of U-Net was chosen based on the evaluation. Furthermore, it was shown that the method performance can be improved by using additional information, such as lengths of boards and logs. The future work includes the evaluation of the method with larger datasets. In addition, modifying this method to utilize features not limited to the knots could greatly improve its effectiveness when working with high quality wood.

Acknowledgements. The research was carried out in the DigiSaw project (No. 2894/31/2017) funded by Business Finland and the participating companies. The authors would like to thank Finnos Oy, FinScan Oy, and Stora Enso Wood Products Oy Ltd for providing the data for the experiments.

References

1. Badrinarayanan, V., Kendall, A., Cipolla, R.: Segnet: a deep convolutional encoder-decoder architecture for image segmentation. IEEE Trans. Pattern Anal. Mach. Intell. **39**, 2481–2495 (2017)
2. Chiorescu, S., Grönlund, A.: The fingerprint method: Using over-bark and under-bark log measurement data generated by three-dimensional log scanners in combination with radiofrequency identification tags to achieve traceability in the log yard at the sawmill. Scand. J. For. Res. **19**(4), 374–383 (2004)
3. Dykstra, D.P., et al.: Technologies for wood tracking: verifying and monitoring the chain of custody and legal compliance in the timber industry. World Bank, Washington, DC (2002)
4. Flodin, J., Oja, J., Grönlund, A.: Fingerprint traceability of sawn products using industrial measurement systems for x-ray log scanning and sawn timber surface scanning. Forest Prod. J. **58**(11), 100–105 (2008)
5. Kozak, R.A., Maness, T.C.: A system for continuous process improvement in wood products manufacturing. Holz als Roh- und Werkstoff **61**(2), 95–102 (2003)
6. Kuga, R., Kanezaki, A., Samejima, M., Sugano, Y., Matsushita, Y.: Multi-task learning using multi-modal encoder-decoder networks with shared skip connections. In: ICCV Workshops (2017)
7. Long, J., Shelhamer, E., Darrell, T.: Fully convolutional networks for semantic segmentation. In: CVPR (2015)
8. Pahlberg, T., Hagman, O., Thurley, M.: Recognition of boards using wood fingerprints based on a fusion of feature detection methods. Comput. Electron. Agric. **111**, 164–173 (2015). Please supply the page range for Ref. [9].
9. Põlder, A., Juurma, M., Tamre, M.: Wood products automatic identification based on fingerprint method. Journal of Vibroengineering **14**(2), (2012)
10. Ronneberger, O., Fischer, P., Brox, T.: U-net: convolutional networks for biomedical image segmentation. In: MICCAI (2015)
11. Schraml, R., Hofbauer, H., Petutschnigg, A., Uhl, A.: Tree log identification based on digital cross-section images of log ends using fingerprint and iris recognition methods. In: Azzopardi, G., Petkov, N. (eds.) CAIP 2015. LNCS, vol. 9256, pp. 752–765. Springer, Cham (2015). https://doi.org/10.1007/978-3-319-23192-1_63
12. Springenberg, J., Dosovitskiy, A., Brox, T., Riedmiller, M.: Striving for simplicity: the all convolutional net. In: ICLR (workshop track) (2015)
13. Wang, Y., van de Weijer, J., Herranz, L.: Mix and match networks: encoder-decoder alignment for zero-pair image translation. In: CVPR (2018)

A Challenging Voice Dataset for Robotic Applications in Noisy Environments

Antonio Roberto$^{(\boxtimes)}$, Alessia Saggese, and Mario Vento

Department of Information Engineering, Electrical Engineering
and Applied Mathematics (DIEM), University of Salerno,
Via Giovanni Paolo II, 132, 84084 Fisciano, SA, Italy
{aroberto,asaggese,mvento}@unisa.it

Abstract. Artificial Intelligence plays a fundamental role in the speech-based interaction between humans and machines in cognitive robotic systems. This is particularly true when dealing with very crowded environments, such as museums or fairs, where cognitive systems could be profitably used. The existing datasets *"in the wild"* are not sufficiently representative for this purposes, thus there is a growing need to make publicly available a more complex dataset for speaker recognition in extremely noisy conditions. In this paper, we propose the Speaker Recognition dataset in the Wild (SpReW), a novel and more challenging Italian audio database for speaker recognition tasks. Moreover, we report a quantitative evaluation of a novel CNN architecture for Speaker Identification tasks called SincNet, on the proposed dataset. SincNet has been chosen as a baseline architecture since it has obtained impressive results on widely used controlled datasets. Experimental results demonstrate the difficulties when dealing with very noisy test sets and few clearly acquired samples for training.

Keywords: Cognitive robotics · Speaker Identification ·
Deep Learning

1 Introduction

One of the most promising weddings of the last decades is surely between artificial intelligence and robotics; the result of this wedding is the so called *cognitive robot* namely a robot able (1) to perceive the information about the environment, (2) to reason about the acquired information and finally, based on the current status, (3) to interact, through verbal and not communication, with the surroundings in a proper way. Within this context, speech-based interaction plays a crucial role due to the fact that it is potentially a much more natural and powerful method for communicating with machines with respect to traditionally used graphics-based interfaces. In particular, when the robot has to interact with different people it is not only important to recognize what they have said (speech to text) but also to identify the person who is currently speaking; this task is termed Speaker Identification [3] and it is the main topic of this paper.

© Springer Nature Switzerland AG 2019
M. Vento and G. Percannella (Eds.): CAIP 2019, LNCS 11679, pp. 354–364, 2019.
https://doi.org/10.1007/978-3-030-29891-3_31

Currently, the main focus of the research community is about obtaining good performance with a lot of people in the database, usually in controlled conditions; of course, when the surrounding environment is very noisy (*"in the wild"*) the performance drastically decreases. For instance, a robot for assisting medical staff in a hospital sector where the background noise variability is characterized by a high frequency (based on robot position in the hospital sector, the number of visitors, and the time of the day) and a non-repetitive behaviour. In this kind of applications, the number of people to identify is extremely smaller, the environment is extremely noisy but the application needs high robustness.

Hence the need to make a good estimation of the performance in real applications in order to design a robust speaker identification system even in completely noise conditions. At the best of our knowledge, there are two widely used datasets for speaker recognition tasks in the wild: VoxCeleb [2,12] and the Speakers In The Wild (SITW) Speaker Recognition Database [10]. The first one is a large-scale database designed for Deep Learning Architecture training and acquired automatically from YouTube videos; Despite SITW is a smaller dataset, it contains hand-annotated speech samples also acquired from open-source media channels. Both of them are designed to train a system robust to audio setup, in fact, audios are acquired in different situations with several microphones, etc., nevertheless, they are not suitable to test the performance in crowded environments with highly variable background noise.

Within this context, the main contribution in this paper is a novel challenging dataset for cognitive robotics applications with few people and very noisy and real environments, called SpReW, which has been made publicly available. Furthermore, as a baseline, we report an experimental evaluation of a recently proposed CNN architecture, namely SincNet [14], has been performed for the first time in non-controlled conditions, with the aim to understand the impact on the performance of the wild scenarios. The proposed dataset allows estimating the performance of systems applied in very noisy environments when trained with few clearly acquired audio samples of the speakers to identify; this is a very common situation when dealing with real identification systems.

The paper is organized as follows. Section 2 provides an overview of the state-of-the-art methods for speaker identification. The baseline architecture is presented in Sect. 3. The SpReW data set is described in Sect. 4, while the experimental results are presented in Sect. 5. Finally, conclusions are drawn in Sect. 6.

2   Related Works

There are mainly three macro-groups of methods which are used when dealing with speaker recognition and other audio classification tasks: (1) traditional methods, (2) Deep Neural Network (DNN) or more specifically Convolutional Neural Network (CNN) applied to an image-based representation of the audio, and (3) deep-architecture trained over raw audio data.

Traditional methods usually take as input hand-crafted features, e.g. Mel-Frequency Cepstral Coefficients and Wavelet-based coefficients and combine them with classifiers such as NN, LVQ or SVM. For instance, the GMM-UBM framework [15] classifier has been largely employed over literature for several audio recognition tasks. It has been used mainly for Speaker Verification tasks by using the Gaussian Mixture Model (GMM) to represent the target speaker features and the Universal Background Model (UBM) for all other people and then, compare them with the test data. Nevertheless, the GMM-UBM model has been employed also in Speaker Identification task by using the MAP adaptation procedure [1] to extract feature vectors termed *"GMM Mean Supervector"*. Moreover, other traditional proposed methods were based on the use of Support Vector Machine and the *bag of words* [8] approach.

The state-of-the-art in the field of speaker recognition was longly defined by i-vectors [5], a feature extraction method which allows reducing supervector dimension, given in input to several classifiers (e.g. heavy-tailed PLDA and GaussPLDA [4]). Furthermore, i-vectors have been also computed by replacing the UBM stage with a DNN one to compute the frame posterior probabilities [19].

Guided by the success achieved in computer vision, CNN has been largely used to classify audio represented through images. The input was usually time-frequency representation like spectrograms [18]. Several image-based features have been proposed, for instance, the gammatonegram [7] which is a representation inspired by the human auditory system.

Recently, opposed to standard spectral features several neural networks have been proposed to create a high level representation directly from raw data. Raw waveform neural network models have been successfully applied in the field of automatic speech recognition (ASR) [9,17] and Spoofing Detection [6].

3   The Baseline Architecture

In this paper, we propose SincNet [14] as baseline architecture. The network has been chosen since it has proved to be very performing on Speaker Identification tasks by obtaining an impressive Classification Error Rate of 0.85% on the TIMIT dataset [16] and 0.96% on the Librispeech database [13]; both of the datasets are acquired in controlled conditions and are very widely used for speaker recognition.

Before presenting the classifier architecture, we are going to provide an overall description of the baseline architecture. According to the authors, the main advantage of SincNet is that it is able to perform well even if in presence of dataset composed by few data. Unlike common convolutional architectures which learn all the elements of each filter, it replaces the first layer filters with parametric ones (Fig. 1).

More formally, the first convolutional layer is defined as follows:

$$y[n] = x[n] * g[n, f_1, f_2] \tag{1}$$

$$g[n, f_1, f_2] = 2f_2 sinc(2\pi f_2 n) - 2f_1 sinc(2\pi f_1 n) \tag{2}$$

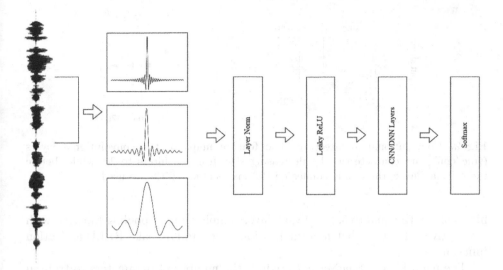

Fig. 1. SincNet architecture. The first layer takes in input the raw waveform and is based on a sinc filter bank which acts as multiband-pass filter able to learn the frequencies of interest. The remaining levels can be arbitrarily designed (Normalization Layer, Activation Functions, Convolutional/Fully-Connected Layer, etc.).

where $x[n]$ is the sampled input signal, $y[n]$ is the filtered output, and g is a pass-band function that depends just on two parameters which are the cut-off frequencies f_1 and f_2.

As for the computer vision, where has been experimentally proved that making a fine-tuning on a pre-trained network in a similar problem allows to achieve better performance, SincNet initializes the first layer using frequencies in according with the Mel-scale filter-bank [11], which has the advantage of directly allocating more filters in the lower part of the spectrum, where more crucial clues about the speaker identity are located. To assure that f_1 and the bandwidth $(f_2 - f_1)$ are positive, the parameters are re-defined as follows:

$$f_1' = |f_1| \tag{3}$$

$$f_2' = f_1' + |f_2 - f_1| \tag{4}$$

The FIR filters are designed by windowing the original IIR (Infinite Impulse Response) filter adopting the Hamming window, defined as follows:

$$w[n] = 0.54 - 0.46 * cos(\frac{2\pi n}{L}) \tag{5}$$

where L is the length of the window.

The network architecture (shown in Fig. 2) is composed of three convolutional layer, comprehensive of the Sinc layer, and three Fully-Connected layers. The feature maps and filter kernels size decrease along the network layers, in particular, the sinc-layer implements filters of length L equal to 251, while others use

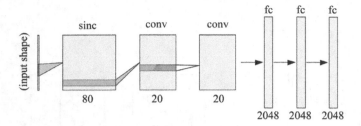

Fig. 2. Convolutional architecture. The feature maps of the convolutional layers (sinc/conv) are characterized by decreasing size, from 80 filters to 20, while, before the softmax layer, three fully-connected (fc) layers of size 2048 are used.

filters of length equal to 5. Finally, all layers employ a max-pooling function with a receptive field of 3, a batch normalization stage, and a Leaky-RELU activation function.

The main idea of SincNet is to reduce the number of parameters to train in the first convolutional layer by adding a constraint on the shape of the first layer and, therefore, to achieve a better generalization even when dealing with small datasets (e.g. in Speaker Identification *real applications* the amount of data is a crucial point). Furthermore, the use of band-pass filters allows to learn low and high cutoff frequencies of interest directly from data; this representation is extremely simple to interpret with respect to other approaches, allowing several *a posteriori* considerations.

3.1   Classifier Architecture

The system architecture, shown in Fig. 3, takes in input raw sampled waveform of duration T_w. The audio input has then split in chunks by using a sliding window of size 200 ms and overlap T_{ov}. The posterior probabilities over the targeted speakers for each obtained chunk are retrieved by using SincNet and then, the final decision is derived by averaging the chunk probabilities for each speaker and choosing the one with the higher score.

4   The Dataset

The task of identifying a speaker in very noisy conditions is the main problem of real applications, especially in a robotic system. Existing datasets are more focused on the generalization of the background and the acquisition system and are not representative of this kind of applications. Indeed, they are composed of audio samples acquired on open sources and, therefore, recorded with different audio setup and background noise without any filtering based on the application.

SpReW is an Italian audio dataset acquired in both controlled and very crowded environments. The audio samples have been recorded using the Samson UB1 omnidirectional microphone with a sampling rate of 16 KHz in four different sites. The details of the dataset composition are reported in Table 1.

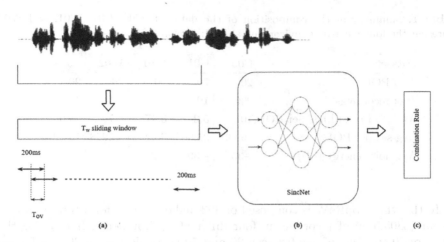

Fig. 3. System architecture. The test samples are obtained by splitting the input audio signal using an overlapped outer sliding window of size T_w and shift equal to 200 ms. After that, adopting an inner overlapped sliding window, the audio sample to classify is in turn split in chunks of size 200 ms, which is the SincNet input size *(a)*. The posterior probabilities of each chunk are estimated by the network *(b)* and then, the decision is derived by averaging them over targeted speakers and choosing the one with higher score *(c)*.

The dataset is composed of four recording environment: two of them are silent sites while the other two are in the wild. In particular, C00 is a fully controlled environment with a background characterized by very low energy (-35 dB); C01 is also a controlled environment near to a very transited pedestrian area (-30 dB); finally, W01 and W02 are two extremely crowded sites with loud background voices (-20 dB and -17 dB).

In order to be as similar as possible to the real conditions, only the samples of the environment C00 have to be used for training; indeed, usually, just a few clear recordings of the speaker to identify, acquired during the startup configuration of the system, are provided to the system. Furthermore, the use of an omnidirectional microphone jointly with different recording distances introduces another source of complexity by simulating a non-direct communication (e.g. a directive given to the robot while it is doing another task and, therefore, it is not directed towards the operator).

Currently, VoxCeleb [2,12] and the Speakers In The Wild (SITW) Speaker Recognition Database [10] are the mainly used datasets for Speaker Recognition tasks in the wild. Differently from them, SpReW has been acquired with a specific goal, i.e. with the aim to create a benchmarking database in crowded environments with highly variable background noise, where cognitive systems could be profitably used. On the contrary, VoxCeleb and SITW are focused on system robustness in its most general sense, e.g. with respect to the audio setup and the acquisition scene.

Table 1. Summary of the composition of the data set. C00, C01, W01, and W02 represent the four recording environments. POI: Person Of Interest.

Dataset	C00	C01	W01	W02	Total
# of POI	20	20	20	20	20
# of recordings	200	104	104	85	493
Avg # of recordings per POI	10	5.2	5.47	4.72	24.65
Avg sec per POI	66.995	33.968	36.218	33.228	165.276
Avg noise energy (dB)	−35	−30	−20	−17	-

In the whole, SpReW is composed of 493 audio samples for a total of about 1 hour (3305.52 s) of recording in four different environments. It contains the voices of 20 speakers of age between 20 and 50 years old with a 30% of female people. Furthermore, SpReW contains audio samples of each speaker recorded in all the proposed environments.

The SpReW dataset can be downloaded at the MIVIA Public Datasets Download page[1]. The dataset files are structured in a multi-folder organization, in particular, the first level divides the audio samples by the environment while the second level divides them by speaker. Finally, in order to easily get the ground truth from each file, their names are defined as follows: $G\_C\_ENV\_REC.wav$; where G represents the gender of the speaker (M/F), C is the class identifier, ENV represents the environment code, and REC is the record id (e.g. $F\_9\_W02\_0005.wav$).

5 Experiments

The SincNet architecture hyper-parameters has been tuned over the C00 audio samples; as suggested in [14], the network has been trained with a minibatch of size 128 composed by random chunks from all the available, with a duration of 200 ms. The weights have been optimized using the RMSprop optimizer with a learning rate $lr = 0.001, \alpha = 0.95, \epsilon = 10^{-7}$.

The evaluation over the test set has been conducted by varying the duration T_w of the recording provided to the system for the classification and the overlap T_{ov} between two consecutive inner sliding windows. In order to obtain a more reliable estimation of the future performance all the possible recordings windows from the original audio sample have been considered by using an outer sliding window of duration T_w and shift equal to 200 ms. In particular, the parameters used for the evaluation are:

- $T_w \in \{200\,\text{ms}, 500\,\text{ms}, 1\,\text{s}, all\_the\_sentence\}$
- $T_{ov} \in \{0\,\text{ms}, 50\,\text{ms}, 100\,\text{ms}, 150\,\text{ms}\}$

---

[1] https://mivia.unisa.it/datasets-request/.

Table 2. Summary of results, in terms of accuracy (%), as a function of the input duration T_w (s) and the overlap T_{ov} (ms) between two consecutive sliding windows computed over all the environments.

T_w/T_{ov}	0	50	100	150
0.2	21,28	21,28	21,28	21,28
0.5	**26,72**	25,85	25,63	25,43
1	30,81	**31,91**	31,41	31,41
Sentence	40,95	40,61	**43**	42,66

where $T_w = all\_the\_sentence$ represents the use of all obtainable chunks for the classification; this setting simulates a system composed by an *ideal* speech-recognition technique followed by the reference architecture. On the other hand, the use of $T_w = 200$ ms results in the chunk-based evaluation.

We evaluate the performance of the reference architecture in terms of Accuracy.

5.1 Results

In Table 2 we report the summary of the results, in terms of accuracy, achieved by the reference architecture over the SpReW test set. The table does not show high performance, in fact, the SincNet does not exceed 50% even in the case of the *sentence* classification. These results prove how difficult it is for speaker identification systems to deal with real applications, i.e. where few target recordings acquired in a single silent environment are available.

Note that the performance increases with increment in size of the outer sliding window; this result is, in fact, this environment is the one with the higher background noise energyèxtita posteriori due to the fact that a bigger window allows more classifications and, therefore, to reduce the probability of errors.

For more accurate analysis, we report in Table 3 the performance achieved by SincNet grouped by the environment. The main result shown by the table is

Table 3. Summary of results, in terms of accuracy (%), as a function of the input duration T_w (s) and the overlap T_{ov} (ms) between two consecutive sliding windows computed for each environment.

T_w/T_{ov}	C01				W01				W02			
	0	50	100	150	0	50	100	150	0	50	100	150
0.2	24,08	24,08	24,08	24,08	23,05	23,05	23,05	23,05	16,7	16,7	16,7	16,7
0.5	**30,59**	29,93	29,24	28,77	**29,3**	27,67	27,8	27,57	**20,3**	19,92	19,82	19,95
1	36,38	**37,31**	36,31	36,92	33,32	34,05	**34,38**	33,65	22,73	**24,35**	23,57	23,64
Sentence	48,07	47,11	**49,03**	**49,03**	44,68	44,68	**47,87**	44,68	29,47	29,47	31,57	**33,68**

the accuracy achieved by the reference network in C01: even if the samples are acquired in a controlled condition the results are around 50%. As expected, the accuracies decrease when the system is applied in the wild up to a gap of about 20%. It is well-known that models provide competitive performance when more training audio samples are provided in different environments and surroundings but they expensive to obtain. Under the challenging conditions proposed in this work with SpReW, the results point out the need for more reliable training techniques.

Finally, we report in Fig. 4 the accuracy trend as a function of the number of speakers taken into consideration. The plots show a high decrease in performance

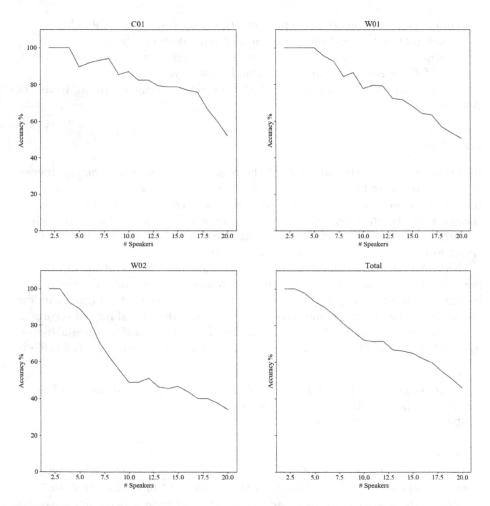

Fig. 4. Accuracy trend as a function of the number of speakers taken into consideration, calculated for the entire test set (Total) and for each individual environment.

in W02; this result is reasonable, in fact, this environment is the one with the higher background noise energy.

6   Conclusions

In this paper, we have presented a new dataset, called the Speaker Recognition dataset in the Wild (SpReW), which is the most representative of real application conditions in the wild available in the literature; i.e. the training set is composed by few audio samples acquired in controlled conditions while the test set contains recordings obtained in very crowded sites.

Furthermore, we have reported an experimental evaluation of the performance of SincNet, a recently proposed CNN architecture, on the proposed dataset. The results have shown the difficulties when dealing with very noisy environment and when the training is composed of few target recordings acquired in a single silent environment.

References

1. Campbell, W.M., Sturim, D.E., Reynolds, D.A.: Support vector machines using GMM supervectors for speaker verification. IEEE Signal Process. Lett. **13**(5), 308–311 (2006). https://doi.org/10.1109/LSP.2006.870086
2. Chung, J.S., Nagrani, A., Zisserman, A.: VoxCeleb2: deep speaker recognition. In: Proceedings of Interspeech 2018, pp. 1086–1090 (2018). https://doi.org/10.21437/Interspeech.2018-1929
3. Cordella, L.P., Foggia, P., Sansone, C., Vento, M.: A real-time text-independent speaker identification system. In: ICIAP (2003)
4. Cumani, S., Plchot, O., Laface, P.: Probabilistic linear discriminant analysis of i-vector posterior distributions. In: 2013 IEEE International Conference on Acoustics, Speech and Signal Processing, pp. 7644–7648, May 2013. https://doi.org/10.1109/ICASSP.2013.6639150
5. Dehak, N., Kenny, P.J., Dehak, R., Dumouchel, P., Ouellet, P.: Front-end factor analysis for speaker verification. Trans. Audio Speech Lang. Proc. **19**(4), 788–798 (2011). https://doi.org/10.1109/TASL.2010.2064307
6. Dinkel, H., Qian, Y., Yu, K.: Investigating raw wave deep neural networks for end-to-end speaker spoofing detection. IEEE/ACM Trans. Audio Speech Lang. Process. **26**(11), 2002–2014 (2018). https://doi.org/10.1109/TASLP.2018.2851155
7. Foggia, P., Saggese, A., Strisciuglio, N., Vento, M.: Cascade classifiers trained on gammatonegrams for reliably detecting audio events. In: 2014 11th IEEE International Conference on Advanced Video and Signal Based Surveillance (AVSS), pp. 50–55, August 2014. https://doi.org/10.1109/AVSS.2014.6918643
8. Foggia, P., Petkov, N., Saggese, A., Strisciuglio, N., Vento, M.: Reliable detection of audio events in highly noisy environments. Pattern Recognit. Lett. **65**, 22–28 (2015). https://doi.org/10.1016/j.patrec.2015.06.026. http://www.sciencedirect.com/science/article/pii/S0167865515001981
9. Hoshen, Y., Weiss, R.J., Wilson, K.W.: Speech acoustic modeling from raw multi-channel waveforms. In: 2015 IEEE International Conference on Acoustics, Speech and Signal Processing (ICASSP), pp. 4624–4628, April 2015. https://doi.org/10.1109/ICASSP.2015.7178847

10. McLaren, M., Ferrer, L., Castán Lavilla, D., Lawson, A.: The speakers in the wild (SITW) speaker recognition database, pp. 818–822, September 2016. https://doi.org/10.21437/Interspeech.2016-1129

11. Moore, B.: Hearing. Handbook of Perception and Cognition, 2nd edn. Elsevier Science (1995). https://books.google.it/books?id=OywDx9pxCMYC

12. Nagrani, A., Chung, J.S., Zisserman, A.: VoxCeleb: a large-scale speaker identification dataset. In: INTERSPEECH (2017)

13. Panayotov, V., Chen, G., Povey, D., Khudanpur, S.: LibriSpeech: an ASR corpus based on public domain audio books. In: 2015 IEEE International Conference on Acoustics, Speech and Signal Processing (ICASSP), pp. 5206–5210, April 2015. https://doi.org/10.1109/ICASSP.2015.7178964

14. Ravanelli, M., Bengio, Y.: Speaker recognition from raw waveform with SincNet, August 2018

15. Reynolds, D.A., Quatieri, T.F., Dunn, R.B.: Speaker verification using adapted Gaussian mixture models. Digit. Signal Process. **10**(1), 19–41 (2000). https://doi.org/10.1006/dspr.1999.0361. http://www.sciencedirect.com/science/article/pii/S1051200499903615

16. Garofolo, J.S., Lamel, L., Fisher, W.M., Fiscus, J., Pallett, S.D., Dahlgren, L.N., Zue, V.: TIMIT acoustic-phonetic continuous speech corpus. Linguistic Data Consortium, November 1992

17. Sainath, T., Weiss, R.J., Wilson, K., Senior, A.W., Vinyals, O.: Learning the speech front-end with raw waveform CLDNNs. In: Interspeech (2015)

18. Salamon, J., Bello, J.P.: Deep convolutional neural networks and data augmentation for environmental sound classification. CoRR abs/1608.04363 (2016). http://arxiv.org/abs/1608.04363

19. Zhong, J., Hu, W., Soong, F., Meng, H.: DNN i-vector speaker verification with short, text-constrained test utterances, pp. 1507–1511, August 2017. https://doi.org/10.21437/Interspeech.2017-1036

Binary Classification Using Pairs of Minimum Spanning Trees or N-Ary Trees

Riccardo La Grassa[1] , Ignazio Gallo[1(✉)] , Alessandro Calefati[1] ,
and Dimitri Ognibene[2]

[1] University of Insubria, Varese, Italy
ignazio.gallo@uninsubria.it
[2] University of Essex, Colchester, Essex, UK

Abstract. One-class classifiers are trained only with target class samples. Intuitively, their conservative modeling of the class description may benefit classical classification tasks where classes are difficult to separate due to overlapping and data imbalance. In this work, three methods leveraging on the combination of one-class classifiers based on non-parametric models, Trees and Minimum Spanning Trees class descriptors (MST_CD) are proposed.

These methods deal with inconsistencies arising from combining multiple classifiers and with spurious connections that MST-CD creates in multi-modal class distributions. Experiments on several datasets show that the proposed approach obtains comparable and, in some cases, state-of-the-art results.

Keywords: One-class classifiers · Minimum spanning tree ·
Instance-based approaches · Non-parametric models

1 Introduction

With the rise of social platforms and internet, data produced by users has grown exponentially enabling the use of data greedy machine learning algorithms in several applications, still in many domains of practical interests, data are still scarce and require more data efficient methods especially for non-trivial classification tasks where classes are difficult to separate due to overlapping and data imbalance. One-class classifiers are trained with target class only samples under the strong assumption that data from the other classes are not available or have low quality. Intuitively, their conservative modeling of the data distribution may benefit classical classification tasks if they were combined in a effective manner.

In this work, three methods are proposed which leverage on the combination of one-class classifiers based on non-parametric models, K-Nearest Neighbour, Trees and Minimum Spanning Trees class descriptors (MST-CD), to tackle binary classification problems.

In the first model, we train classifiers using Minimum Spanning Tree Class Descriptor (MST_CD) in the training step and then apply a new technique to

© Springer Nature Switzerland AG 2019
M. Vento and G. Percannella (Eds.): CAIP 2019, LNCS 11679, pp. 365–376, 2019.
https://doi.org/10.1007/978-3-030-29891-3_32

provide a more reliable prediction. The second model creates a more powerful classifier based on MST_CD combining results according to an ensemble method. The third model is very similar to the previous one but uses a tree starting to the closest neighbour to the target pattern for each classifier and finally it leverages on the ensemble technique.

In the next Section related works are shown, the proposed approach is described in Sect. 4, Experiments are in Sect. 6 and Conclusions in Sect. 7.

2   Related Work

In the feature selection field, many approaches have been proposed and used with classifiers to obtain better accuracy [1,2,7,12]. Krawczyk *et al.* [8] proposes a generic model that improves the performance of many common classifiers showing des standard and des-threshold methodologies. They are based on a k-Nearest Neighbour (k-NN) technique that assigns a pattern to a class on the basis of the class of its nearest k neighbours. The approach shows good results and authors compare it with classical models. However, they do not consider the case in which no classifier is "activated" and, thus, when it is not possible to obtain a prediction for a new instance x. Duin *et al.* [14] proposes a simple approach to assign these refused objects to the class with largest prior probability, but they do not describe a method in the scenario where the two decision boundaries overlap. Our approach combines part of the approach described in [8,14] using MSTs with other methodologies to improve the accuracy and considering also the overlapping. Abpeykar *et al.* [1] proposes a survey that sums up the performance of many classifiers on well-known datasets from UCI repository. A milestone on one-class classifier comes from Pekalska *et al.* [6] with their MST descriptor. The original idea was to try to search a pattern from all training sets in order to create a MST that represents the model on which will be done some geometrical operations with the goal to generate a border for a specific class. Segui *et al.* [11] focuses on the research of noise within a target class and removes it in order to have better accuracy at testing time. They confirm that a graph-based one-class classifier, like MST_CD obtains good results than other approaches, especially dealing with small samples cardinalities and high data dimensionalities. Quinlan [9] proposes a general method that allows predictions using both mixed approach of instance-based and model-based learning. He proves that these composite methods often produce better results in term of predictions than using only a single methodology.

3   Minimum Spanning Tree Class Descriptor

As widely described in [6] a MST_CD is a non-parametric classifier able to create a structure, seeing only data of the single class of interest. This structure is based on Minimum Spanning Tree, basic elements of this classifier are not only vertices but also edges of the graph, giving a richer representation of the data. Considering edges of the graph as target class objects, additional virtual target objects are generated. The classification of a new object x is based on the distance to the nearest vertex or edge. The key of this classifier is to track a shape around the training set not considering only all instances of the training but also edges of the graph, in order to have more structured information. Therefore, in prediction phase, the classifier considers two important elements:

- Projection of point x on a line defined by vertices x_i, x_j
- Minimum Euclidean distance between (x, x_i) and (x, x_j)

The Projection of x is defined as follow:

$$p_{e_{i,j}}(x) = x_i + \frac{(x_j - x_i)^T (x_j - x_i)}{||x_j - x_i||^2}(x_j - x_i)$$

if $p_{e_{i,j}}(x)$ lies on the edge $e_{i,j} = (x_i, x_j)$, we compute $p_{e_{i,j}}(x)$ and the Euclidean distance between x and $p_{e_{i,j}}(x)$, more formally:

$$0 <= \frac{(x_j - x_i)^T (x_j - x_i)}{||x_j - x_i||^2} <= 1$$

then

$$d(x|e_{i,j}) = ||x - p_{e_{i,j}}(x)||$$

Otherwise we compute the Euclidean distance of x and pairs (x_i, x_j), precisely:

$$d(x|e_{i,j}) = min(||x - x_j||, ||x - x_i||)$$

Therefore, a new object x is recognized by MST_CD if it lies in proximity of the shape built in training phase, otherwise the object is considered as outlier. The decision whether an object is recognized by classifier or not is based on threshold of the shape created during the training phase, more formally:

$$d_{MST\_CD}(x|X) <= \theta$$

Authors set the threshold θ as the median of the distribution of the edge weights $w_{ij} = ||e_{ij}||$ in the given MST. Given $\hat{e} = (||e_1||, ||e_2||, ..., ||e_n||)$ as an ordered edge weights values, they define θ as $\theta = ||e_{[\alpha n]}||$, where $\alpha \in [0, 1]$. For instance, with $\alpha = 0.5$, we assign the median value of all edge weights into the MST.

4   Proposed Approach

The main objective of a one-class classifier is to recognize instances of a selected class from a set of samples. All instances that are not classified by this model will be considered as outliers (or alien class), while others will be recognized as belonging to the same class of the training set. In this context, we cannot say anything about the refused objects (outlier), but if we have a one-class classifier for each label of the dataset we can not have outliers because if a classifier refuses an object, it should be accepted by the others classifiers. In this work, we use two one-class classifiers trained on two different classes. We assume a discriminant function f_{ab} on a binary classification problem to classify a new object considering acceptation and rejection from both our classifiers. Given X a MST and x a new object, we define a function that assigns a label such that:

$$f_{ab}(x, X) = \begin{cases} 1 & \text{if } d_{MST\_CD_0}(x|X) <= \theta \text{ and } d_{MST\_CD_1}(x|X) > \theta_1 \\ 0 & \text{if } d_{MST\_CD_0}(x|X) > \theta \text{ and } d_{MST\_CD_1}(x|X) <= \theta_1 \end{cases} \tag{1}$$

However, we may have two anomaly cases:

1. both classifiers refuse the pattern to be predicted
2. both classifiers accept the pattern to be predicted

In this specific case we can apply a simple technique to assign a pattern to two possible classes depending on its distance to clusters. More formally, given x a target vector, i and j are all elements of the dataset belonging to both classes, we define:

$$d(x|i) = (|x - i_0|, |x - i_1|, ..., |x - i_{n_0}|)$$
$$d'(x|j) = (|x - j_0|, |x - j_1|, ..., |x - j_{n_1}|)$$

where n_0 and n_1 are cardinalities of first and second class respectively.

Then we take the k nearest elements for each class, such that:

$$k <= min(n_0, n_1)$$

We compute the vector difference as:

$$Vector_{diff} = [(d_1 - d'_1), (d_2 - d'_2), ..., (d_k - d'_k)]$$

Finally, We assume a new function f'_{ab} to classify the object as:

$$f'_{ab}(x, Vector_{diff}) = \begin{cases} 1 & \text{if } |Vector_{diff}(k <= 0)| > |Vector_{diff}(k > 0)| \\ 0 & \text{otherwise} \end{cases} \tag{2}$$

4.1   First Approach

Our first approach combines two one-class classifiers based on Minimum Spanning Tree class descriptor and solve both above mentioned issues. When one of the two issues appear, e.g. both classifiers accept (classifiers overlap) or reject (uncovered) the input sample, an approach similar to K-NN majority vote is applied. Using the already computed euclidean distances between the sample and the elements of the two MSTs, the K elements of each MST (MST_1, MST_2) nearer to the sample are selected to check which of the two MSTs is consistently closer to the sample. This is done by internally sorting the two sets of K elements in increasing distance order from the sample then subtracting the 2 corresponding K-ary vectors (D_1, D_2) of distances and finally counting how many positive elements are in the resulting vector $R = D_1 - D_2$. If R contains more positive than negative elements the sample is associated to MST_2 as its elements are closer to the sample. This method allows to integrate the generalization capabilities of the MST with the robustness offered by the K-NN vote strategy to deal with binary classification strategies. See the pseudo-code in Algorithm 1.

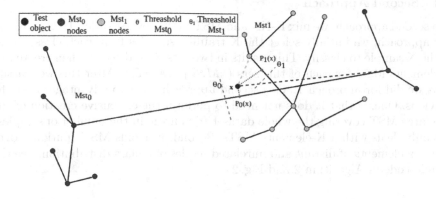

Fig. 1. MST_CD model: In this figure, we show the problem about the competence area into two different classifiers in a toy scenario. In this case the object x will be predicted as blue class instead of green class. This happens because the orthogonal projection of x is nearer to an edge that contains an outlier and the object is located into a non-competence area of the blue-classifier making a wrong prediction.

Algorithm 1. MST CD OVA

1: **for** $v \in \mathcal{G}_0$ **do**
2:     all euclidean distances $\leftarrow ||x - v||$
3: **end for**
4: NodeX = Take min(all euclidean distances)
5: EdgeNodeX $\leftarrow$ Search inc/out edge nodeX and return (u, v)
6: **for** $u, v \in \mathcal{E}(NodeX)$ **do**
7:     **if** $0 <= \dfrac{(x_j - x_i)^T * (x - x_i)}{||x_j - x_i||^2} <= 1$ **then**
8:       $P_{e_{ij}}(x) = x_i + \dfrac{(x_j - x_i)^T * (x - x_i)}{||x_j - x_i||^2} * (x_j - x_i)$
9:       $d(x|e_{ij}) \leftarrow ||x - P_{e_{ij}}(x)||$
10:     **else**
11:       $d(x|e_{ij}) \leftarrow min\{||x - x_i||, ||x - x_j||\}$
12:     **end if**
13: **end for**
14: **Repeat line 1-13 for graph** G_1
15: min dist0 = $min(d(x|e_{ij}))$
16: min dist1 = $min(d1(x|e_{ij}))$
17: $1 \leftarrow$ if $d_{MST\_CD_0}(x|X) <= \theta$ and $d_{MST\_CD_1}(x|X) > \theta_1$
18: $0 \leftarrow$ if $d_{MST\_CD_0}(x|X) > \theta$ and $d_{MST\_CD_1}(x|X) <= \theta_1$
19: **if** min dist0 $<= \theta$ and min dist1 $<= \theta_1$ **then**
20:     knn weight1=order($d_1(x|u)$) and take k_1-elements
21:     knn weight0=order($d_0(x|v)$) and take k_1-elements
22:     euclidean distance vectors = (knn weight1 - knn weight0)
23:     positive = Count $n_i > 0$ in euclidean distance vectors
24:     negative = Count $n_i < 0$ in euclidean distance vectors
25:     **if** negative >= positive **then**
26:       prediction $\leftarrow 1$
27:     **else**
28:       prediction $\leftarrow 0$
29:     **end if**
30: **end if**
31: **if** min dist0 $> \theta$ and min dist1 $> \theta_1$ **then**
32:     The approach is equal to lines [20-29]
33: **end if**

4.2   Second Approach

In a second approach, we mix K-NN and MST in the reverse order. Using a K-NN like approach, we initially select the K training samples from each class closest to the X sample to classify. This results in two sets S_1 and S_2, we then create two K-elements MST for each of this sets ($kMST_1$, $kMST_1$). After this we classify X as we did for approach 1. This second approach has two advantages over the previous. One, is that it does not need to perform the expensive creation of the two large MST covering the whole dataset (quadratic in the number of samples) but only deals with a K-elements MSTs. Second, it avoids MST spurious edges between elements of distant and unrelated modes of a class distribution. See the pseudo-code in Algorithm 2 and Fig. 2.

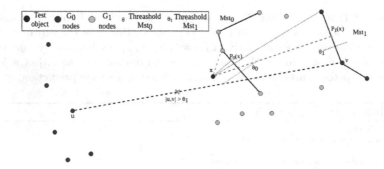

Fig. 2. MST_CD_GP model: A different approach on the same toy example considering a combination built on two small MST starting from nodes with a minimum distance from target pattern.

Algorithm 2. MST CD with Gamma parameters

```
1: function CREATE SMALL MST(g0 weight sorted, g1 weight sorted)
2:     smallG_0 = first gamma index sorted values in g0 weight sorted
3:     edges couple ← all combinations nodes small g0
4:     for u, v ∈ ]dgescouple do
5:         small G_0 ← (node u, node v, weight = (u, v))
6:     end for
7:     small MST_0 = ComputeMST(small G_0)
8:     Same approach for MST_1
9:     e(small MST0) = (||e_0||, ||e_1||, ..||e_n||)
10:     e(small MST1) = (||e_0||, ||e_1||, ..||e_n||)
11:     θ_0 = ||e_(αn)||
12:     θ_1 = ||e_(αn)||
13: return small MST_0, smallMST_1
14: end function
```

4.3   Third Approach

The third is similar to the second one but instead of selecting the K nearest elements to the sample X to classify, it selects only the nearest element E to the sample and then selects the K-1 elements of the training set nearest to E. It then creates a tree having E as root and it uses it as a classifier like in previous cases. This further extends the robustness to outliers and spurious connections between far nodes. See the pseudo-code in Algorithm 3 and Fig. 3.

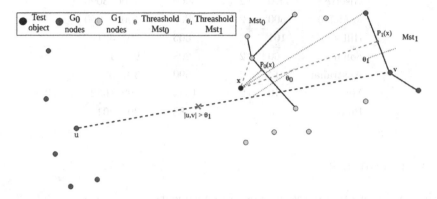

Fig. 3. N-ary model: A different approach on the same toy example. Using a N-ary model makes less complex the prediction phase ignoring outliers from the structure.

Algorithm 3. N-ary model

```
 1: function CREATE_N_ARY(subG₀ weight sorted, subG₁ weight sorted, gamma index)
 2:     n_ary₀ = first gamma index sorted values in g0 weight sorted
 3:     n_ary₁ = first gamma index sorted values in g1 weight sorted
 4:     for u, v ∈ ∫ubG_0weightedsorted do
 5:         n_ary₀ ← (nodeu, nodev, weight = (u, v))
 6:     end for
 7:     for u, v ∈ ∫ubG_1weightedsorted do
 8:         n_ary₁ ← (nodeu, nodev, weight = (u, v))
 9:     end for
10:     return n_ary₀, n_ary₁
11: end function
```

---

5 Datasets

We use five low-dimensional datasets (*Hill, Sonar, Australian, Mofn, Pima*) and three high-dimensional datasets (*Arcene, Gisette, Madelon*), all taken from the UCI repository [3]. All of them have two classes. Table 1 shows the details of all datasets. To evaluate our approach in a more robust way, we selected datasets with a huge variability in term of number of features and number of instances. For all the datasets we use 5-fold Cross Validation. We replace the missing values in the datasets with the average value for the missing features.

Table 1. Number of features, classes, instances and positive-negative samples for all the datasets used in our experiment.

Datasets	Features	Classes	Instances	pos-neg
Arcene	10000	2	100	44–56
Gisette	5000	2	6000	3000–3000
Madelon	500	2	2000	1000–1000
Hill	101	2	606	305–301
Sonar	60	2	208	97–111
Australian	14	2	690	307–383
Mofn	10	2	1324	292–1032
Pima	8	2	688	305–301

6   Experiments

In this section we report two groups of experiments,

- to study the effect on the parameters in our models,
- to compare the proposed models with the results available in the literature on some well known benchmarks.

6.1   Parameters Evaluation

For each classifier, we extract some common metrics to evaluate the performance, such as Sensitivity, Precision and F1 Score. Starting from these values we create confusion matrix and obtain the final accuracy considering True/False positive and True/False negative samples.

Table 2. These are the results of both classifiers using our MST_CD model about Sensitivity, Precision, F1 Score and Total accuracy on Sonar dataset. Last line contains the average for each column.

MST_CD

Fold	$Sensitivity^0$	$Sensitivity^1$	$Precision^0$	$Precision^1$	$F1^0$	$F1^1$	Accuracy
1	0,867	0,900	0,867	0,900	0,867	0,900	0,886
2	0,833	0,944	0,938	0,850	0,882	0,895	0,889
3	0,800	1,000	1,000	0,833	0,889	0,909	0,900
4	0,688	0,880	0,786	0,815	0,733	0,846	0,805
5	0,714	0,850	0,769	0,810	0,741	0,829	0,794
Average	0,780	0,915	0,872	0,842	0,822	0,876	**0,855**

Table 3. Details of our third model N-ary considering the same measures than above table. We show an accuracy of 87.3% with gamma=20 and gamma=10 in N-ary model against 85.5% in our first model. Results of each lines are extracted using an average on k=5 fold-validation.

N-ary							
Gamma	$Sensitivity^0$	$Sensitivity^1$	$Precision^0$	$Precision^1$	$F1^0$	$F1^1$	Accuracy
30	0,791	0,915	0,873	0,850	0,829	0,881	0,860
20	0,793	0,915	0,873	0,850	0,830	0,881	0,861
10	0,820	0,915	0,879	0,869	0,847	0,890	**0,873**
8	0,830	0,906	0,869	0,876	0,847	0,890	**0,873**
6	0,816	0,880	0,849	0,854	0,830	0,865	0,851
4	0,808	0,882	0,852	0,848	0,826	0,863	0,848
3	0,787	0,861	0,830	0,832	0,804	0,844	0,829

Table 4. Parameters set

Parameters	Arcene	Madelon	Gisette	Mofn	Australian	Pima	Sonar	Hills
Threshold	0.25	0.25	0.2	0.05	0.05	0.05	0.1	0.9
Neighbours	4	12	4	2	6	6	2	2

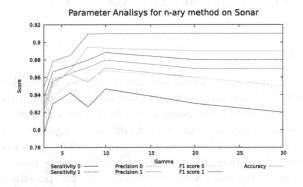

Fig. 4. Best Gamma parameter search for method using the Sonar dataset. We use the average accuracy to select the best parameter.

Table 5. 5-fold Cross-Validation accuracy results on 6 datasets. Results obtained with our three models (MST_CD, MST_CD_GP, N-ary) are compared with results published in [7] on same datasets.

Dataset	Krakovna et al. [7]										Our models		
	Bart	c5.0	Cart	Lasso	LR	NB	RF	SBFC	SVM	TAN	CD	CD_GP	N-ary
Arcene	71.6	66	63	65.6	52	69	71.8	72.2	72	-	79.6	77.7	**80.3**
Madelon	76	75.8	**78.2**	60.7	60	59.8	67.1	63.4	62	54.2	75	75.2	75.3
Gisette	**97.7**	94.8	90.8	97.2	88.1	90.3	97	95.2	96.9	-	96.8	-	-
Mofn	100	84.8	83.9	100	100	86.4	92.4	86.2	94.6	92.1	100	100	100
Australian	86.9	86.7	84.2	85.6	86.8	85.7	**87.8**	86.9	86	86.8	69.0	70.6	70.3
Pima	78.2	76.8	75.7	78	78.3	78	77.8	**78.9**	78.1	**78.9**	70.1	71.7	74.1

Table 6. 5-fold Cross-Validation accuracy results on five different datasets. Results obtained with our three models (MST_CD, MST_CD_GP, N-ary) are compared with the results of different ensemble methods published in [1].

Dataset	Abpeykar et al. [1]									Our models		
	AdaB	Bagg	Dagg	LogitB	Mod	Decor	Grad	Mt.B	Stack.C	CD	CD_GP	N-ary
Arcene	79.5	82.5	74.5	85.5	**86.0**	-	56.0	80.0	56.0	79.6	77.7	80.3
Madelon	63.4	75.0	57.2	63.0	52.5	73.3	50.1	61.7	50.1	75	75.2	**75.3**
Sonar	71.6	76.9	69.7	79.3	70.6	84.1	53.3	74.5	53.3	85.4	85.2	**88**
Hills	50.4	50.2	50.4	50.4	-	-	50.4	50.4	50.4	58.1	57.9	**61.1**
Gisette	88.9	75.0	82.2	89.4	-	82.2	48.1	82.7	48.1	**96.8**	-	-

Table 7. 5-fold Cross-Validation accuracy results on five datasets. The results obtained with our three models are compared with the results of different machine learning methods published in [1].

Datasets	Abpeykar et al. [1]					Our models		
	Dt	k-NN	NB	RF	SVM	MST_CD	MST_CD_GP	N-ary
Arcene	67.2	66.7	69.7	71.4	71.4	79.6	77.7	**80.3**
Madelon	**82.7**	74.8	79.3	77.9	78.4	75	75.2	75.3
Sonar	79.5	80.4	77.6	81.4	82.3	85.4	85.2	**88.0**

6.2   Comparison

We evaluated the proposed models on the well known benchmark datasets described in Sect. 5. In particular, we compared our methods using the results published in [1,7] and shown the comparison in Tables 5, 6 and 7. In our work, we have two one-class classifiers and the rate of True/Negative samples has been computed considering two different models. For instance if an object has been predicted correctly True positive by a classifier the others must be refuse and label it as True negative, otherwise, we consider all the possible combinations (2^2) in our case (two classifiers). The final accuracy is obtained from average of Cross-Validation. In our experiments, we set γ parameter into the second and third model within the range [2, 30] nodes and take the maximum accuracy obtained from Cross-Validation methods considering always the same dimension training/test (80%–20%) see Table 3. Threshold measures and k-neighbours are set as we show into Table 4 on each specific dataset. In Table 5 we compare results of our models with many references used to examine the performance of classifiers (Moradi and Rostami 2015). Our models do not use feature selection techniques, therefore for each instance we exploit all available features. Comparing our models with the ensemble methods known as AdaboostM1 [4], Bagging [15], Dagging [15], LogitBoost [5], MODLEM [13], Decorate (Melville and Mooney 2003), Grading [10], MultiBoostAB [16] and StackingC (Seewald 2002), our models overcome the accuracy of other ensembles classifier (except for Arcene dataset where Bagging, LogitBoost and Modlem have higher accuracy than our models).

7   Conclusion

The presented results show that the solutions proposed are competitive both with ensemble and classical classifiers. The second and third method that aimed at increasing the robustness to outliers and spurious MST connections were proved to consistently ameliorate accuracy. Also the latter methods avoid the initial computation of expensive large MST while requiring the computation of small MST at runtime and provide higher accuracy. This makes the latter methods more convenient with large datasets for which the complete MST computation may be too expensive. We are also confident that these methods can be highly optimized using caching methods to further improve online computation performance. Future work will tackle the issue of feature scaling and selection as well as the possibility to combine the approach with ensemble methods.

References

1. Abpeykar, S., Ghatee, M., Zare, H.: Ensemble decision forest of RBF networks via hybrid feature clustering approach for high-dimensional data classification. Comput. Stat. Data Anal. **131**, 12–36 (2019)
2. Budak, H., Taşabat, S.: A modified t-score for feature selection. Anadolu Üniversitesi Bilim Ve Teknoloji Dergisi A-Uygulamalı Bilimler ve Mühendislik (2016)
3. Dua, D., Graff, C.: UCI machine learning repository (2019), http://archive.ics.uci.edu/ml
4. Eibl, G., Pfeiffer, K.P.: How to make AdaBoost.M1 work for weak base classifiers by changing only one line of the code. In: Elomaa, T., Mannila, H., Toivonen, H. (eds.) ECML 2002. LNCS (LNAI), vol. 2430, pp. 72–83. Springer, Heidelberg (2002). https://doi.org/10.1007/3-540-36755-1_7
5. Frank, E., Holmes, G., Kirkby, R., Hall, M.: Racing committees for large datasets. In: Lange, S., Satoh, K., Smith, C.H. (eds.) DS 2002. LNCS, vol. 2534, pp. 153–164. Springer, Heidelberg (2002). https://doi.org/10.1007/3-540-36182-0_15
6. Juszczak, P., Tax, D.M., Pe, E., Duin, R.P., et al.: Minimum spanning tree based one-class classifier. Neurocomputing **72**(7–9), 1859–1869 (2009)
7. Krakovna, V., Du, J., Liu, J.S.: Interpretable selection and visualization of features and interactions using bayesian forests. Stat. Interface **11**, 503–513 (2018)
8. Krawczyk, B., Galar, M., Woźniak, M., Bustince, H., Herrera, F.: Dynamic ensemble selection for multi-class classification with one-class classifiers. Pattern Recogn. **83**, 34–51 (2018)
9. Quinlan, J.R.: Combining instance-based and model-based learning. In: Proceedings of the Tenth International Conference on Machine Learning, pp. 236–243 (1993)
10. Seewald, A.K., Fürnkranz, J.: An evaluation of grading classifiers. In: Hoffmann, F., Hand, D.J., Adams, N., Fisher, D., Guimaraes, G. (eds.) IDA 2001. LNCS, vol. 2189, pp. 115–124. Springer, Heidelberg (2001). https://doi.org/10.1007/3-540-44816-0_12
11. Seguí, S., Igual, L., Vitrià, J.: Weighted bagging for graph based one-class classifiers. In: El Gayar, N., Kittler, J., Roli, F. (eds.) MCS 2010. LNCS, vol. 5997, pp. 1–10. Springer, Heidelberg (2010). https://doi.org/10.1007/978-3-642-12127-2_1

12. Singh, B., Vyas, O.: Maximum spanning tree based redundancy elimination for feature selection of high dimensional data. Int. Arab J. Inf. Technol. **15**, 831–841 (2018)
13. Stefanowski, J.: The rough set based rule induction technique for classification problems. In: Proceedings of 6th European Conference on Intelligent Techniques and Soft Computing EUFIT, vol. 98 (1998)
14. Tax, D.M., Duin, R.P.: Using two-class classifiers for multiclass classification. In: Object recognition supported by User Interaction for Service Robots, vol. 2, pp. 124–127. IEEE (2002)
15. Ting, K.M., Witten, I.H.: Stacking bagged and dagged models (1997)
16. Webb, G.I.: Multiboosting: a technique for combining boosting and wagging. Mach. Learn. **40**(2), 159–196 (2000)

Estimating the Noise Level Function
with the Tree of Shapes and
Non-parametric Statistics

Baptiste Esteban, Guillaume Tochon[✉], and Thierry Géraud

EPITA Research and Development Laboratory (LRDE), Le Kremlin-Bicêtre, France
{baptiste.esteban,guillaume.tochon,thierry.geraud}@lrde.epita.fr

Abstract. The knowledge of the noise level within an image is a valuable information for many image processing applications. Estimating the noise level function (NLF) requires the identification of homogeneous regions, upon which the noise parameters are computed. Sutour *et al.* have proposed a method to estimate this NLF based on the search for homogeneous regions of square shape. We generalize this method to the search for homogeneous regions with arbitrary shape thanks to the tree of shapes representation of the image under study, thus allowing a more robust and precise estimation of the noise level function.

Keywords: Noise level function · Tree of shapes · Non-parametric rank correlation

1 Introduction

Natural images are inherently corrupted by digital noise resulting from the various imperfections occuring during the acquisition chain (such as sensor noise, quantization noise, and so on). Efficiently handling or removing the noise is a fundamental task in image processing, but it requires a precise knowledge of the noise attributes. By providing the relationship between the intensity of the image pixels and the noise variance, the noise level function [16] (NLF) is a valuable information to estimate, not only for image denoising purposes [3], but also for image segmentation [11], image compression [23] or super-resolution [12]. When the noise is signal-independent, classical separation approaches can be applied to estimate its properties [10,17]. For signal-dependent noise (such as Poisson and Poisson-Gaussian), variance stabilization techniques have first to be applied [18,21], but their optimal use requires a certain knowledge of the noise, leading to a chicken-and-egg situation. As an alternative to separation techniques, Beaurepaire *et al.* [2] proposed to first identify some homogeneous regions in the image, on which the noise parameters can be further evaluated. In order to be independent of the noise statistical distribution, Sutour *et al.* [22] proposed a non-parametric method to detect these homogeneous areas. However, their definition as square blocks does not facilitate their detection, as their shape

M. Vento and G. Percannella (Eds.): CAIP 2019, LNCS 11679, pp. 377–388, 2019.
https://doi.org/10.1007/978-3-030-29891-3_33

makes them unsuited to the image content. The use of patches adapting locally to the image morphological content would allow a better identification of these homogeneous regions, and therefore yield a more robust estimation of the NLF. This idea of adaptive patches has already been investigated in the literature for image denoising purposes [8,9], but to the best of our knowledge, it has never been implemented to estimate the NLF.

In this article, we extend the NLF estimation method developed by Sutour *et al.* [22]. More specifically, we no longer seek for square homogeneous blocks, but we rather search for arbitrarily shaped homogeneous regions based on the tree of shapes (ToS) [1,19] representation of the considered image. This hierarchical representation naturally provides areas whose contours follow the level lines of the image (seen as a topographic map), thus adapted to its morphological content. We show that the extraction of the most relevant shapes from the ToS allows to obtain a more robust NLF estimation than in the case of square blocks.

The present article is organized as follows: Sect. 2 summarizes the method proposed by Sutour *et al.* [22]. In Sect. 3, we introduce our generalized search for homogeneous regions of arbitrary shapes, based on a Mumford-Shah simplification of the ToS representation. Qualitative and quantitative comparisons between the method proposed by Sutour *et al.* [22] and ours are presented in Sect. 4, while Sect. 5 concludes and draws some perspectives of our work.

2   NLF Estimation with Square Blocks

The NLF estimation proposed by Sutour *et al.* [22] is decomposed in two steps:

1. the detection of homogeneous square blocks through a non-parametric statistical test based on Kendall τ rank correlation coefficient,
2. the identification of the NLF, *i.e.* the relation linking the intensity of the image pixels to the noise variance.

In the following, $f : \Omega \subset \mathbb{Z}^2 \to \mathbb{R}$ will denote an image that associates a numeric value $x_i = f(i)$ to any pixel $i \in \Omega$.

2.1   The Kendall τ Coefficient

The ith block of pixels $b_i \subset \Omega$ is said to be homogeneous if its pixel values fluctuate only because of the noise, and not because of the image content. In order not to depend on any assumption on the nature of the noise, the homogeneous block detection step is formulated as a non-parametric hypothesis test using the Kendall τ rank correlation coefficient [15]. Let $x \in \mathbb{R}^n$ and $y \in \mathbb{R}^n$ be two sequences of n observations of two random variables X and Y. The Kendall τ coefficient $\tau(x, y)$ is defined on the interval $[-1, 1]$ by:

$$\tau(x, y) = \frac{1}{n(n-1)} \sum_{1 \leq i,j \leq n} \text{sign}(x_i - x_j)\, \text{sign}(y_i - y_j), \tag{1}$$

with $x_i \neq x_j$ and $y_i \neq y_j$, $\forall i \neq j$.

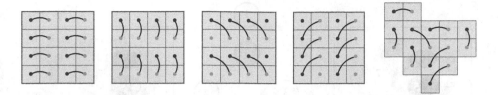

Fig. 1. First four cases: the tested region has a square shape, its pixel values are divided in sequences x and y following the horizontal, vertical, diagonal, and anti-diagonal relationships. When the tested region is extracted from the ToS and has an arbitrary shape (rightmost case), the splitting in sequences x and y is performed randomly.

In the associated statistical test, $\tau(x, y) = 0$ constitutes the null hypothesis H_0 and indicates an absence of correlation between the values of x and y. Equation (1) can be reformulated to take into account any tied pairs (if $x_i = x_j$ or $y_i = y_j$) [14]. Under H_0 (absence of correlation between X and Y), the z-score associated with $\tau(x, y)$ follows a standard normal distribution $\mathcal{N}(0, 1)$ [22, Proposition 3.6]. Conversely, the alternative hypothesis H_1 is declared when $\tau(x, y) \neq 0$, that is, when the fluctuation of the pixel values in b_i cannot be explained by the noise only (because of the presence of an edge within the block for instance).

2.2   Detection of Homogeneous Blocks

In Sutour *et al.* [22], the studied image is divided in blocks b_i of size 16×16 pixels. The pixel values of each block b_i are split in two sequences x and y for which the Kendall τ coefficient $\tau(x, y)$ is computed. If the p-value $p = \mathbb{P}(\tau(X, Y) > \tau(x, y) | H_0)$ is greater than a predefined detection threshold α, the null hypothesis H_0 is accepted, meaning that the values of the two sequences x and y are uncorrelated. The block b_i is thus declared homogeneous.

In practice, b_i is split in $K = 4$ sequences $x^{(k)}$ and $y^{(k)}$ following the horizontal, vertical, diagonal and anti-diagonal neighborhood relationships, as displayed by Fig. 1. b_i is then declared homogeneous if all K p-values p_k exceed the detection threshold:

$$\min_k \left\{ p_k = \mathbb{P}\left(\tau(X, Y) > \tau(x^{(k)}, y^{(k)}) \, | \, H_0 \right) \right\} > \alpha. \tag{2}$$

2.3   NLF Estimation

The NLF defines the relation between the intensity of the image pixels and the variance of the noise corrupting them. Sutour *et al.* [22] proposed a positively increasing second degree polynomial relation for the NLF: $\sigma_i^2 = \text{NLF}_{(a,b,c)}(x_i) = ax_i^2 + bx_i + c$, with $(a, b, c) \in (\mathbb{R}^+)^3$. This notably allows to model the additive Gaussian noise (whose NLF $\sigma_i^2 = c$ is constant, hence $(a, b) = (0, 0)$), the Poisson noise (with linear NLF $\sigma_i^2 = bx_i$, thus $(a, c) = (0, 0)$), the multiplicative/Gamma

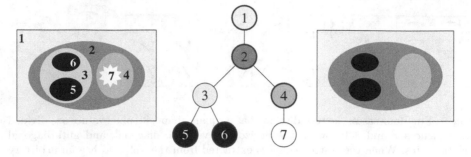

Fig. 2. Left: input image; Middle: corresponding tree of shapes; Right: Mumford-Shah simplification where the optimal partition is composed of the level lines of the nodes circled in blue. (Color figure online)

noise (whose NLF $\sigma_i^2 = ax_i^2$ is parabolic, hence $(b, c) = (0, 0)$), and their different mixtures (such as the Poisson-Gaussian noise for instance).

First, the empirical mean $\hat{\mu}_i = \mathbb{E}[b_i]$ and empirical variance $\hat{\sigma}_i^2 = \mathrm{Var}[b_i]$ of each homogeneous block b_i are calculated. Following, the NLF coefficients are estimated as those minimizing the residual error between the empirical variance $\hat{\sigma}_i^2$ and the variance predicted by the NLF relation $\mathrm{NLF}_{(a,b,c)}(\hat{\mu}_i)$ for all homogeneous block b_i:

$$(\widehat{a, b, c}) = \underset{(a,b,c)\in(\mathbb{R}^+)^3}{\mathrm{argmin}} \sum_i \|\mathrm{NLF}_{(a,b,c)}(\hat{\mu}_i) - \hat{\sigma}_i^2\|_1. \tag{3}$$

Despite being more complex to solve than a L^2 minimization (which could be solved by classical least-square estimation), the L^1 minimization used in Eq. (3) is more robust to outliers and is solved in practice thanks to the preconditioned primal-dual Chambolle-Pock algorithm [6].

3   NLF Estimation with the Tree of Shapes

The drawback of searching for homogeneous square blocks is that their shape is not adaped to the morphological content of the image. Thus, depending on the input image, it might be complicated to detect sufficiently enough of these blocks in order to get a robust and precise estimation of the NLF. Here, we relax the constraint on the shape of the sought homogeneous regions. For that purpose, we propose to use regions adapted to the image content, extracted from the ToS representation of the considered image.

3.1   The Tree of Shapes

The tree of shape (ToS) is a hierarchical structure belonging to the field of mathematical morphology [19]. For $\lambda \in \mathbb{R}$, we define the lower level set of f (of level λ) as $[f < \lambda] = \{i \in \Omega \mid f(i) < \lambda\}$ and the upper level set as $[f \geq \lambda] = \{i \in \Omega \mid f(i) \geq \lambda\}$. A *shape* $\mathcal{C} \subset \Omega$ is a connected component belonging to one

Fig. 3. Input noisy image (left) and examples of Mumford-Shah simplifications applied to its ToS with regularization parameter $\nu = 500$ (center) and $\nu = 2000$ (right).

of these two sets, with its holes filled [13]. The ToS $\mathcal{T}$ of an image encodes the inclusion relationship between the different shapes of the image in a hierarchical manner. The border $\partial \mathcal{C}_i$ of each shape $\mathcal{C}_i$ corresponds to a level line of the image (when seen as a topographic relief). The ToS therefore represents the inclusion of all level lines of the image, as displayed in Fig. 2.

Note that the ToS can be computed very efficiently: an algorithm with a linear complexity with respect to the number of pixels exists [5], and it can be parallelized [7].

3.2 Mumford-Shah Simplification of the Tree of Shape

After its construction, the ToS representation is composed of meaningful shapes (in terms of image content description), but it also contains small and/or meaningless shapes (notably the leaves and regions close to the root of the tree). Thus, prior to conducting the homogeneity test, a simplification of the ToS according to the Mumford-Shah functional is performed in order to filter out those meaningless shapes. This ToS simplification procedure is based on the Mumford-Shah image segmentation principle [20]. If $\pi = \bigsqcup_i R_i$ is a partition of Ω, and if $\bar{f}_i$ is the mean value of f on region $R_i \subset \Omega$, the (piecewise constant) Mumford-Shah functional of f on π is defined as

$$E_\nu(f, \pi) = \sum_{R_i \in \pi} \left(\iint_{R_i} (\bar{f}_i - f)^2 dx dy + \frac{\nu}{2} |\partial R_i| \right), \qquad (4)$$

where $|\partial R_i|$ is the length of the border of R_i and ν is a regularization parameter of the functional. Finding the partition π that minimizes Eq. (4) without any further constraint on π remains an arduous and non-convex optimization task.

When this energy minimization procedure is subordinated to the ToS structure however, the region borders ∂R_i are fixed since they are defined as the contours $\partial \mathcal{C}_i$ of the shapes $\mathcal{C}_i \in \mathcal{T}$. It thus becomes possible to find the optimal segmentation with a greedy algorithm that iteratively removes shapes to decrease the energy functional (see [24] for more details). In practice, the Mumford-Shah

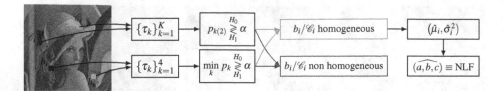

Fig. 4. Illustration of the stages for the NLF estimation from blocks b_i and from shapes $\mathcal{C}_i$.

simplification of $\mathcal{T}$ yields a simplified ToS $\mathcal{T}_\nu^\star$ where some initial shapes have been filtered out, such that the segmentation $\partial\mathcal{T}_\nu^\star$ formed by the union of the level lines of the remaining shapes in $\mathcal{T}^\star$ minimizes the Mumford-Shah functional (4) for a given value of the regularization parameter:

$$\mathcal{T}_\nu^\star = \underset{\mathcal{T}_\nu'}{\operatorname{argmin}} \, E_\nu\left(f, \partial\mathcal{T}_\nu'\right), \tag{5}$$

where $\mathcal{T}_\nu'$ is a simplified ToS with some shapes of $\mathcal{T}$ have been removed, and $\partial\mathcal{T}_\nu'$ is the partition of Ω that is obtained by taking the union of the level lines of all shapes in $\mathcal{T}_\nu'$. An example of Mumford-Shah simplification is presented in Fig. 2, where the shapes $\mathcal{C}_3$ and $\mathcal{C}_7$ have been filtered out from the original ToS, leading to the rightmost partition obtained as the union of the level lines of the remaining shapes (circled in blue).

3.3 Detection of Homogeneous Shapes

The ToS representation of the noisy input image f is composed of shapes with very irregular contours, and with a limited depth of inclusion. Thus, we first smooth f with a Gaussian filter prior to the construction of its ToS. This yields an increased number of shapes with regularized contours, and a greater depth of inclusion in the ToS.

The obtained ToS is simplified according to the Mumford-Shah functional for several values of the regularization parameter ν, yielding several simplified ToS $\mathcal{T}_\nu^\star$ whose shapes are pooled together in a set of candidate shapes $\mathcal{C}^\cup = \bigcup_\nu \{\mathcal{C} \in \mathcal{T}_\nu^\star\}$ of various sizes and complexities, as illustrated in Fig. 3.

The homogeneity test is then conducted on all candidate shapes $\mathcal{C}_i \in \mathcal{C}^\cup$ with the pixel values of the noisy image $f(\mathcal{C}_i)$ and not those of the filtered image. In order to compute the Kendall $\tau(x, y)$ coefficient, it is necessary to divide the values of the pixels in $\mathcal{C}_i$ in two sequences x and y. However, the shape of $\mathcal{C}_i$ being arbitrary (as opposed to a square block of 16×16 pixels), it does not guarantee the validity of the neighborhood relationships used by Sutour *et al.* [22]. The division into two sequences x and y is therefore done randomly (by imposing that the two sequences are of the same length, potentially dropping one pixel if the total number of pixel values to be split is odd). This random splitting strategy, as opposed to the horizontal, vertical, diagonal, and anti-diagonal splitting applied to square blocks, is illustrated in Fig. 1. In practice,

Fig. 5. Images *building, city, cobble, monument, shell* and *wall.*

the random division in sequences $x^{(k)}$ and $y^{(k)}$ is repeated K times in order to mitigate stochastic effects, and K p-values p_k of coefficients $\tau(x^{(k)}, y^{(k)})$ are calculated. The shape $\mathcal{C}_i$ is stated to be homogeneous if the 2nd order statistic (the second smallest p-value) $p_{k(2)}$ exceeds the detection threshold α (in order to prevent the case where a test would be rejected only because of a particular arrangement of the division and not due to the inhomogeneity of the considered shape). The empirical mean $\hat{\mu}_i$ and variance $\hat{\sigma}_i^2$ of all homogeneous shapes further lead to the estimation of the NLF coefficients $\widehat{(a, b, c)}$ according to Eq. (3). These different steps are illustrated in Fig. 4.

4   Results

4.1   Experimental Set-Up

We evaluate our method on 6 images of dimensions 720×540 pixels shown in Fig. 5. These are extracted from a high definition image database[1], for which the acquisition noise can be neglected. They were chosen to be as representative as possible in terms of morphological content, *i.e.*, to feature large homogeneous areas as well as small details and some textured regions. More precisely, we evaluate the robustness and the accuracy of the NLF estimated by our approach and by the method of Sutour *et al.* [22]. In a first step, we assess the robustness of the estimated NLF to the nature of the added noise. For that purpose, we add a non-mixed noise of varying intensity (setting to 0 the other two coefficients of the NLF), and we evaluate the ability of the NLF estimation method to practically estimate the right coefficient to be nonzero. If a Gaussian noise was added for instance, $(a, b) = (0, 0)$ in the corresponding NLF, and we thus check that it is also the case in the estimated NLF.

---

[1] http://www.gipsa-lab.grenoble-inp.fr/~laurent.condat/imagebase.html

Table 1. Number of times (among the 6 trials) each NLF estimation method correctly retrieves the nature of the noise.

	building	city	cobble	monument	shell	wall
With blocks [22]	1/0/1	0/1/3	0/0/0	6/0/0	0/1/0	0/0/1
With shapes	6/4/4	4/3/5	4/2/6	0/5/4	2/3/6	0/0/6

In a second step, we evaluate the estimation accuracy by artificially adding a mixed noise whose coefficients a, b and c (controling the NLF) are derived from a normal law $\mathcal{N}(0.01, 0.003)$ with mean 0.01 and standard deviation 0.003 (rounding to 0 negative coefficient). Note that the pixel values have been rescaled in the $[0:1]$ interval beforehand. In order to measure the estimation quality of NLF parameters, we calculate the mean relative error (MRE) between the reference $\text{NLF}_{(a,b,c)}$ and the estimated $\text{NLF}_{\widehat{(a,b,c)}}$ by

$$\text{MRE}(\widehat{a, b, c}) = \frac{1}{|I|} \sum_{x_i \in I} \frac{|\text{NLF}_{(a,b,c)}(x_i) - \text{NLF}_{\widehat{(a,b,c)}}(x_i)|}{\text{NLF}_{(a,b,c)}(x_i)}, \qquad (6)$$

where I is a discretization of the pixel intensities interval $[0:1]$ in the image.

In any case, each noisy image is pre-filtered by a Gaussian filter with variance $\sigma = 1$ on which is built the ToS. The latter is simplified according to the Mumford-Shah functional, and we set the regularization parameter ν to be $200, 500, 1000, 2000$ and 5000. In the resulting simplified images, we consider only the shapes $\mathcal{C}_i$ whose size is greater than 250 pixels, on which the homogeneity test is conducted. This minimum size guarantees a reliable estimate of the Kendall coefficient of $\mathcal{C}_i$, as well as its empirical mean $\hat{\mu}_i$ and variance $\hat{\sigma}_i^2$ (note that in [22], the minimum size for a block b_i is $16 \times 16 = 256$ pixels). For each shape, the pixel values are randomly split $K = 10$ times in sequences $x^{(k)}$ and $y^{(k)}$, therefore leading to $K = 10$ Kendall tests. The second smallest p-value $p_{k(2)}$ is used to validate the homogeneity of the shape, namely whether it exceeds or not the detection threshold α fixed at $\alpha = 0.4$. This very restrictive detection threshold allows to really guarantee the homogeneity of all shapes detected as such.

4.2   Robustness of the Estimated NLF

To evaluate the capacity of the NLF estimation method to retrieve the correct nature of the noise polluting the input image, we add a non-mixed noise of varying intensity, setting the other two parameters at 0 in the NLF. For each type of noise (multiplicative, Poisson, Gaussian), its associated parameter in the NLF (a, b and c, respectively) is set successively to 0.01, 0.015, 0.02, 0.025, 0.03 and 0.5 and we count how many times (among those 6 settings) the two NLF estimation methods practically estimate only the correct coefficient to be nonzero (note that we do not focus here on the accuracy of this estimated nonzero coefficient).

Table 2. Mean and standard deviation (in parenthesis) of the MRE between the reference NLF and the estimated NLF using square blocks and using shapes from the ToS. The given percentage corresponds to the number of times (with respect to the 20 draws) the use of shapes yields a NLF estimation with lower MRE than the use of square blocks.

	building	*city*	*cobble*	*monument*	*shell*	*wall*
With blocks [22]	0.0481	0.0926	0.8701	0.2235	0.1212	0.1075
	(0.0234)	(0.1007)	(0.7031)	(0.0966)	(0.0743)	(0.1064)
With shapes	**0.0349**	**0.0462**	**0.0346**	**0.0552**	**0.0385**	**0.0513**
	(0.0134)	(0.0116)	(0.0121)	(0.0201)	(0.0124)	(0.0102)
	65%	85%	100 %	95%	100%	75%

Table 1 presents the obtained results, where a $x/y/z$ entry means that the multiplicative noise $((b, c) = (0, 0))$ has been correctly identified x out of 6 times, the Poisson noise $((a, c) = (0, 0))$ has been correctly identified y out of 6 times, and the Gaussian noise $((a, b) = (0, 0))$ has been correctly identified z out of 6 times. Except for the multiplicative noise a on the image *monument*, our proposed NLF estimation method consistently obtains better results than the NLF estimated by square blocks. Note also that, in general, the estimation of a Gaussian noise seems much easier than for a multiplicative noise or Poisson noise, for which the L^1 minimization seems in general not to succeed nulling the c coefficient (corresponding to the offset).

4.3   Accuracy of the Estimated NLF

To assess the accuracy of the estimated NLF coefficients, we add a mixed noise whose parameters a, b and c are drawn from a normal law $\mathcal{N}(0.01, 0.003)$ with mean 0.01 and standard deviation 0.003. We then compute the MRE between the true parameters (a, b, c) and the ones $(\widehat{a, b, c})$ that have been estimated using square blocks and shapes extracted from the ToS. We repeat this experiment 20 times for each image, and report in Table 2 the overall mean and standard deviation of the obtained MRE for both methods, as well as the percentage of times (with respect to the 20 draws) the NLF estimation based on shapes yields a lower (hence, better) MRE than its square blocks counterpart.

For the six studied images, the estimated NLF using shapes from the ToS consistently outperforms the NLF estimated with square blocks in terms of mean MRE, and with lower standard deviation. In the tighter case (being the *building* image), the proposed method still provides better results than the one of Sutour *et al.* [22] 13 times out of the 20 different draw (65%). This confirms sfrom a quantitative standpoint that the use of shapes adapted to the image content yields a more reliable and more robust estimation of the NLF.

To get a qualitative insight of this conclusion, Fig. 6 presents the square blocks and shapes detected as homogeneous for the *building* image polluted with a mixed noise of coefficients $(a, b, c) = (1.22.10^{-2}, 0.82.10^{-2}, 0.82.10^{-2})$, as well as the estimated NLF coefficients in each case. In the first case, 104

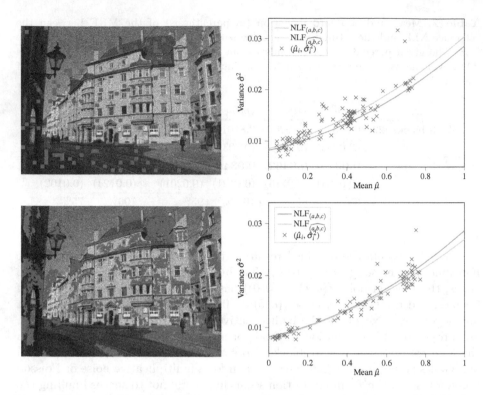

Fig. 6. First row: *blocks* detected as homogeneous for a mixed noise added to the *building* image (left) and estimated NLF compared to the reference NLF (right). Second row: *shapes* detected as homogeneous for the same noise (left), and corresponding estimated NLF compared to the reference NLF (right).

square blocks were detected as homogeneous, leading to the coefficient estimates $(\widehat{a, b, c}) = (1.12.10^{-2}, 1.07.10^{-2}, 0.85.10^{-2})$ and a MRE of $7.56.10^{-2}$. In the second case, 81 homogeneous shapes were detected from the various Mumford-Shah simplifications of the ToS constructed on the *building* image, leading to $(\widehat{a, b, c}) = (0.93.10^{-2}, 0.98.10^{-2}, 0.78.10^{-2})$ for the NLF coefficient estimation and a MRE of $2.96.10^{-2}$. While the number of homogeneous regions used to estimate the NLF coefficients is of the same order of magnitude for both competing methods (although being smaller when using the ToS), the size of the detected homogeneous regions drastically differs. In [22], square blocks are limited to $16 \times 16 = 256$ pixels since the image content is unknown *a priori* and cannot be assumed to comprise large homogeneous areas. Since this limitation vanishes with the use of regions adapting to the image content, shapes of significantly larger sizes are detected as homogeneous. This lead to a more precise evaluation of their empirical mean $\hat{\mu}_i$ and variance $\hat{\sigma}_i^2$ since more samples are used, hence a less vertically dispersed scatterplot $\{(\hat{\mu}_i, \hat{\sigma}_i^2)\}$, as it can be seen on Fig. 6, resulting in a more accurate and more robust estimation of the NLF coefficients with fewer regions.

5   Conclusion

In this article, we have presented an extension of the method of Sutour *et al.* [22] to estimate the NLF of some noisy images. The key idea is to replace the search for homogeneous square blocks by that of homogeneous shapes, extracted from a tree of shapes simplified using the Mumford-Shah functional. As a consequence, the computation of the noise statistics is performed on regions adapted to the morphological content of the image, making the NLF estimation more robust and more accurate. Eventually, we are able to better identify the nature and characteristics of the noise polluting the image. A major perspective of our work is to adapt the NLF estimation to color images, since a definition of the tree of shapes already exists for multivariate images [4].

References

1. Ballester, C., Caselles, V., Monasse, P.: The tree of shapes of an image. ESAIM Control. Optim. Calc. Var. **9**, 1–18 (2003)
2. Beaurepaire, L., Chehdi, K., Vozel, B.: Identification of the nature of noise and estimation of its statistical parameters by analysis of local histograms. In: 1997 IEEE International Conference on Acoustics, Speech, and Signal Processing, vol. 4, pp. 2805–2808. IEEE (1997)
3. Buades, A., Coll, B., Morel, J.M.: A review of image denoising algorithms, with a new one. Multiscale Model. Simul. **4**(2), 490–530 (2005)
4. Carlinet, E., Géraud, T.: MToS: a tree of shapes for multivariate images. IEEE Trans. Image Process. **24**(12), 5330–5342 (2015)
5. Carlinet, E., Géraud, T., Crozet, S.: The tree of shapes turned into a max-tree: a simple and efficient linear algorithm. In: Proceedings of the 24th IEEE International Conference on Image Processing (ICIP), Athens, Greece, pp. 1488–1492 (2018)
6. Chambolle, A., Pock, T.: A first-order primal-dual algorithm for convex problems with applications to imaging. J. Math. Imaging Vis. **40**(1), 120–145 (2011)
7. Crozet, S., Géraud, T.: A first parallel algorithm to compute the morphological tree of shapes of nD images. In: Proceedings of the 21st IEEE International Conference on Image Processing (ICIP), Paris, France, pp. 2933–2937 (2014)
8. Dabov, K., Foi, A., Katkovnik, V., Egiazarian, K.: BM3D image denoising with shape-adaptive principal component analysis. In: SPARS 2009-Signal Processing with Adaptive Sparse Structured Representations (2009)
9. Deledalle, C.A., Duval, V., Salmon, J.: Non-local methods with shape-adaptive patches (NLM-SAP). J. Math. Imaging Vis. **43**(2), 103–120 (2012)
10. Donoho, D.L.: De-noising by soft-thresholding. IEEE Trans. Inf. Theory **41**(3), 613–627 (1995)
11. Droske, M., Rumpf, M.: Multiscale joint segmentation and registration of image morphology. IEEE Trans. Pattern Anal. Mach. Intell. **29**(12), 2181–2194 (2007)
12. Freeman, W.T., Jones, T.R., Pasztor, E.C.: Example-based super-resolution. IEEE Comput. Graph. Appl. **2**, 56–65 (2002)

13. Géraud, T., Carlinet, E., Crozet, S., Najman, L.: A quasi-linear algorithm to compute the tree of shapes of nD images. In: Hendriks, C.L.L., Borgefors, G., Strand, R. (eds.) ISMM 2013. LNCS, vol. 7883, pp. 98–110. Springer, Heidelberg (2013). https://doi.org/10.1007/978-3-642-38294-9_9

14. Kendall, M.G.: The treatment of ties in ranking problems. Biometrika **33**(3), 239–251 (1945). http://www.jstor.org/stable/2332303

15. Kendall, M.G.: A new measure of rank correlation. Biometrika **30**(1/2), 81–93 (1938)

16. Liu, C., Freeman, W.T., Szeliski, R., Kang, S.B.: Noise estimation from a single image. In: 2006 IEEE Computer Society Conference on Computer Vision and Pattern Recognition, vol. 1, pp. 901–908. IEEE (2006)

17. Liu, X., Tanaka, M., Okutomi, M.: Single-image noise level estimation for blind denoising. IEEE Trans. Image Process. **22**(12), 5226–5237 (2013)

18. Mäkitalo, M., Foi, A.: Noise parameter mismatch in variance stabilization, with an application to poisson-Gaussian noise estimation. IEEE Trans. Image Process. **23**(12), 5348–5359 (2014)

19. Monasse, P., Guichard, F.: Fast computation of a contrast-invariant image representation. IEEE Trans. Image Process. **9**(5), 860–872 (2000)

20. Mumford, D., Shah, J.: Optimal approximations by piecewise smooth functions and associated variational problems. Commun. Pure Appl. Math. **42**(5), 577–685 (1989)

21. Pyatykh, S., Hesser, J.: Image sensor noise parameter estimation by variance stabilization and normality assessment. IEEE Trans. Image Process. **23**(9), 3990–3998 (2014)

22. Sutour, C., Deledalle, C.A., Aujol, J.F.: Estimation of the noise level function based on a nonparametric detection of homogeneous image regions. SIAM J. Imaging Sci. **8**(4), 2622–2661 (2015)

23. Walker, J.S.: Combined image compressor and denoiser based on tree-adapted wavelet shrinkage. Opt. Eng. **41**(7), 1520–1528 (2002)

24. Xu, Y., Géraud, T., Najman, L.: Hierarchical image simplification and segmentation based on Mumford-Shah-salient level line selection. Pattern Recognit. Lett. **83**, 278–286 (2016)

Deep Convolutional Neural Networks for Plant Species Characterization Based on Leaf Midrib

Leonardo F. S. Scabini[1(✉)], Rayner M. Condori[2], Isabella C. L. Munhoz[1], and Odemir M. Bruno[1]

[1] São Carlos Institute of Physics, University of São Paulo, São Carlos, SP, Brazil
scabini@ifsc.usp.br
[2] Institute of Mathematics and Computer Science, University of São Paulo, São Carlos, SP, Brazil

Abstract. The automatic characterization and classification of plant species is an important task for plant taxonomists. On this work, we propose the use of well-known pre-trained Deep Convolutional Neural Networks (DCNN) for the characterization of plants based on their leaf midrib. The samples studied are microscope images of leaf midrib cross-sections taken from different specimens under varying conditions. Results with traditional handcrafted image descriptors demonstrate the difficulty to effectively characterize these samples. Our proposal is to use DCNN as a feature extractor through Global Average Pooling (GAP) over the raw output of its last convolutional layers without the application of summarizing functions such as ReLU and local poolings. Results indicate considerably performance improvements over previous approaches under different scenarios, varying the image color-space (gray-level or RGB) and the classifier (KNN or LDA). The highest result is achieved by the deeper network analyzed, ResNet (101 layers deep), using the LDA classifier, with 99.20% of accuracy rate. However, shallower networks such as AlexNet also provide good classification results (97.36%), which is still a significant improvement over the best previous result (83.67% of combined fractal descriptors).

Keywords: Deep Convolutional Neural Networks ·
Global average pooling · Plant classification · Leaf midrib

1 Introduction

In the whole world, several plant species play a critical role in the ecosystem functioning since they supply food to nearly all terrestrial organisms, maintain the atmosphere due to photosynthesis and recycle matter. In order to understand these plants better, it is indispensable the classification of plant species properly, which can be, even for specialists, a hard task [29]. Traditionally, taxonomists use identification keys to discover the unknown species that is being analyzed; this

© Springer Nature Switzerland AG 2019
M. Vento and G. Percannella (Eds.): CAIP 2019, LNCS 11679, pp. 389–401, 2019.
https://doi.org/10.1007/978-3-030-29891-3_34

approach is time-consuming and can lead to problems (especially with species that are similar). To surpass problems brought via manual identification processes, studies using machine learning techniques have been conducted, many of them using Deep Learning frameworks [38].

Applications of Deep Convolutional Neural Networks (DCNN) in plant science have emerged in the last years since the boom caused by the first models such as AlexNet [16]. The first works [4,34] describing the use of deeper convolutional architectures for plant classification were proposed for the 2014 Image-CLEF/LifeCLEF challenge[1], which consists in the identification of about 500 plant species. The winner of the competition [4] proposed the training of the AlexNet network [16] from scratch (random initial weights). In [34] the authors propose the use of a pre-trained DCNN as a generic leaf feature extractor, using the output of intermediate convolutional layers to feed an ensemble of extremely randomized trees to perform the classification. This process is known as transfer learning [2] and can also be employed through the reuse of trained weights by replacing the network's last fully-connected layer (classification layer) and training the architecture again in the target application, with the proper number of output neurons. The outstanding results achieved by DCNN in the 2014 challenge led the 2015 edition to be dominated by this kind of approach. For instance, in [27] the authors propose the use of the fine-tuning technique, in which a pre-trained architecture is used transferring its learning capability for plant identification. Still, in 2015, DCNN were employed to learn unsupervised feature representations for 44 different plant species [18] in a similar fashion. Interestingly, the authors have shown through a visualization technique (deconvolutional networks) that leaf venations of different order have been chosen to uniquely represent each of the plant species. These works use DCNN pre-trained on the well-known ImageNet dataset [6], which consists of millions of images for a general object classification problem with 1000 classes. The knowledge the convolutional networks obtain from this large variety of images allows the achievement of impressive results in various scenarios, thus popularizing the portability of pre-trained models. This technique and also the proposal of new network models are found in further works about plant species classification [8,32], plant disease detection [12,33], and other plant science areas [23,37].

Most works employing DCNN in plant science focus on leaf images in the macroscopic scale, that is the most common and broader available data. However, in the context of plant taxonomy environmental conditions can affect the leaf structure, reflecting on its visual properties. Moreover, many scientists work with microscopic images, analyzing molecular and cellular plant structures. In this context, this work focuses on microscopic leaf midrib cross-sections, which are more robust to environmental effects. The dataset comprises 50 Brazilian plant species [30] with samples collected from different individuals, in a total of 606 high-quality RGB images. These images have expressive texture patterns that vary between species, which suggests that texture descriptors could be useful for identification. However, results with handcrafted gray-level descriptors [30]

---

[1] www.imageclef.org.

show the difficulty to effectively distinguish between all the considered species. This happens due to several image variations such as rotation, scale and also morphological and structural differences between specimens of the same species. We then employ the use of pre-trained DCNN as a feature extractor through global average pooling (GAP) over its last convolutional layer, which has shown significant performance improvements compared to previous results with hand-crafted descriptors.

2 Theoretical Background

2.1 Plant Taxonomy

Taxonomy is the science of describing, classifying and ordering organisms, based on their similarity [29]. The process of plant identification can be done in two different manners: through a manual approach or an automated one. The manual process consists in the use of an identification key, in which taxonomists answer a series of questions about the unknown plant, and, based on relevant characteristics, the amount of candidates is narrowed down [38]. Even though it is a common way to identify plant species, this traditional process is time-consuming and low-efficient [22]. Both specialists and non-specialists can have a hard time when identifying plants manually, firstly due to difficulties with species that are morphologically similar [7] and secondly when the analysis depends on plant structures that appear only in specific times of the year, such as flowers [30].

The automated process to identify plants, on the other hand, can be an alternative to overcome the limitations of the traditional approach. Using automated methodologies, the process of identification can be more accurate, less time-consuming and more replicable [7]. Nowadays, the automated identification field may lie on molecular methods, such as DNA sequencing, or can make use of machine learning techniques to classify images from different plant structures [7].

Different studies have been conducted to develop better strategies in automated plant classification when using computer vision, and, a majority of them utilizes leaves for plant discrimination [38]. It is possible to find studies using images of whole leaves [39] and others using some external parts of leaves, such as veins [10]. Although the use of these structures may be an interesting option since leaves are available for sampling throughout the year, environmental conditions can cause these structures to vary drastically [14]. In order to avoid this environmental effect, some internal structures that potentially store information as discrimination patterns can be used in plant identification [30]. One of them, called leaf midrib, is composed of sets of specialized tissues, phloem and xylem, and other cells [15]. As shown in previous studies, these structures may become potential plant identifiers, because they are less plastic than other regions of the leaf, they are stable when submitted to the image acquisition process and their characteristics vary among different species [30]. Our work uses images from leaf midribs to evaluate if they are indeed possible structures to discriminate between different plant species.

2.2   Deep Learning and Convolutional Neural Networks

A convolutional neural network is a type of neural network that is mainly used for analyzing images or videos in a supervised setting. There are two well-defined components in a convolutional neural network: (i) the feature extraction part and (ii) the classification part. In this regard, the latter component is usually organized into one or more *fully-connected layers*. On the other hand, the feature extraction part has evolved throughout the years. Initially, it comprised a few convolutional and pooling layers [17]. Then, since the introduction of the *deep learning* concept, a growing number of publications have been proposing convolutional neural networks with innovative architectural properties, deeper filter banks, and many other new techniques. Therefore, DCNN models have rapidly become the state-of-art in several computer vision tasks [5,9,20].

The input of any layer in the feature extraction part of a DCNN consists of a set of $n_{\mathbf{A}^{(l)}}$ 2-D feature maps of equal size, where l indicates the layer's depth and $\mathbf{A}_j^{(l)}$ represents the j-th input feature map ($1 \leq j \leq n_{\mathbf{A}^{(l)}}$). In this paper, every time the term "feature map" appears, it refers to this 2-D representation. In the case of *convolutional layers*, the trainable weights are organized into a set of $n_{\mathbf{F}^{(l)}}$ filters of fixed size. This set, also known as the *filter bank* ($\mathbf{F}^{(l)}$), is in charge of computing a new set of feature maps $\mathbf{A}^{(l+1)}$ by convolving $\mathbf{A}^{(l)}$ with every filter in $\mathbf{F}^{(l)}$. In the case of *pooling layers*, they do not have any trainable variables because they apply a fixed mathematical operation, typically the maximum or average value, over the set of regions in a given feature map $\mathbf{A_j}^{(l)}$ obtained by a sliding window approach. In addition, there are vastly more types of layers in a DCNN that also yield a feature map, for example, the Dropout layer, the concatenation layer, and batch normalization. In this paper, we use the Global Average Pooling (GAP) layer to transform a given set of feature maps $\mathbf{A}^{(l)}$ into a feature vector. More information about the GAP is in the following section.

3   Proposed Methodology

In the following sections, we give detailed information regarding the proposal of this work and the plant species dataset.

3.1   Dataset

The dataset used in this study is introduced by [30] and consists of leaf images from 50 different plant species found in the Cerrado biome in central Brazil, at IBGE Ecological Reserve. The leaves (at least four for each species) were obtained from the third and fourth nodes from the branch tip and the images of midribs were captured in a 10x objective, using a trinocular microscope Axio Lab A1 coupled to a digital camera Axiocam ICc 1. Details about the specific plant species and the number of samples per class can be consulted in [30], and the dataset is available on the Scientific Computing Group website[2].

---

[2] www.scg.ifsc.usp.br/dataset/Midrib.php.

Figure 1 shows some samples of the dataset for 4 classes, where it is possible to notice different image variations within/between classes.

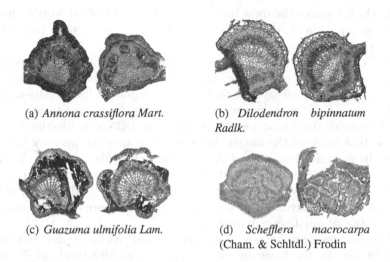

(a) *Annona crassiflora Mart.*

(b) *Dilodendron   bipinnatum Radlk.*

(c) *Guazuma ulmifolia Lam.*

(d) *Schefflera   macrocarpa* (Cham. & Schltdl.) Frodin

Fig. 1. Two samples for each of some classes of the dataset, representing the midrib cross-section microscopy image of the corresponding plant species. Images present several geometrical variations in size, rotation and also morphological variations between individuals.

3.2   Pre-trained DCNN for the Characterization of Leaf Midrib

The dataset available is composed of 606 images, which is an insufficient amount to train DCNN from scratch considering that these models are usually trained with millions of images. Therefore, we take advantage of well-known pre-trained architectures. This practice is common when the number of samples of the application domain is restricted or when it is not possible to train DCNN from scratch due to lack of time and hardware. Using available pre-trained models is a more practical way to benefit from well-validated DCNN, which are already trained with millions of images. Moreover, the computational cost to apply these networks to only extract descriptors for single images is much smaller than the cost to train them. The training process usually consists of thousands of iterations over millions of images, being hugely dependent on graphics processing unit (GPU) cards, and can take over many days.

A given DCNN is employed by removing its classification part, thus we focus on the output information of its convolutional layers only (the feature extraction part). The last convolutional layer outputs a set of $n_{\mathbf{A}^{(l)}}$ feature maps. Every feature map $\mathbf{A}_j^{(l)}$, $(1 \leq j \leq n_{\mathbf{A}^{(l)}})$ contains rich information about the processed image. It comprises the processing of all the previous layers and its neuron activation, resulting in a descriptive data structure related to the image patterns.

As the combination of feature maps from the last convolutional layer is a three-dimensional structure, we apply another technique in order to obtain a single image descriptor. As proposed by [19], a Global Average Pooling (GAP) is performed, which reduces the data into a single vector. In other words, this layer takes the mean value of every feature map $\mathbf{A}_j^{(l)}$, concatenating it into a feature vector of size $n_{\mathbf{A}^{(l)}}$.

The GAP technique is broadly used in convolutional networks to summarize the information output of some layer, and it is usually employed to flatten the output of a convolutional layer so that it can be inputted into a fully-connected layer. The use of GAP as the output of pre-trained networks is a transfer learning approach in which there is no necessity to train the DCNN, unlike the fine-tuning technique that replaces the output layer and readapts the network weights to perform the classification in the target application, which is costly. Therefore, there is no special need for powerful computers or GPU cards when using GAP as the DCNN is only used as a feature extractor. The image descriptor obtained can then be fed into any machine learning technique, where the user can explore different artificial intelligence paradigms.

The techniques described so far are generic and can be applied to most pre-trained DCNN. In the following, we explain the architectural details of each analyzed network model and how we obtain image descriptors from them.

AlexNet: This network [16] (2012) was the first DCNN to achieve high visibility due to the impressive results obtained in the 2012 ImageNet challenge [6]. It is 8 layers deep, of which 5 are convolutional and 3 are fully-connected layers and has an input layer of size $227 \times 227 \times 3$. The raw output of the fifth convolutional layer, before the activation and its max pooling, is used to compose the feature maps, which are then reduced to a single vector through GAP.

VGG: Proposed by the Visual Geometry Group (VGG) [31] (2014), this model has a deeper architecture in comparison to AlexNet, performing among the top participants of the ImageNet 2014 challenge. We analyzed two variations of this model, the VGG16 (13 convolutional and 3 fully-connected) and VGG19 (16 convolutional and 3 fully-connected). These networks have an input size of $224 \times 224 \times 3$, and we take the output of its last convolutional layer (without applying ReLU and max-pooling).

GoogLeNet (InceptionV3): This network [36] (2016) is an improved version of the GoogLeNet architecture [35]. In comparison to traditional networks that are mostly feed-forward, the InceptionV3 is known for having inception modules paralleling local convolutions, forming different pathways along with the network layers. In certain parts, the parallel path outputs are combined and fed to the following layer. The whole network is composed of 42 layers, where the input layer has sizes $299 \times 299 \times 3$. An image descriptor is obtained by applying GAP over the feature maps produced by the last concatenation performed over the last inception module of the network (without the subsequent local average pooling).

ResNet: Deep Residual Networks [13] (2016) have shortcut connections that skip one or more convolutional layers, easing the training of substantially deeper architectures. We analyze the use of two versions of ResNet: ResNet50 (50 layers deep) and ResNet101 (101 layers deep). This model has input sizes of 224 × 224 × 3 and an image descriptor is obtained with GAP over the output of the last addition, which is the output of the last convolutional layer combined with a residual connection (without ReLU and local average pooling).

Considering that these models have a defined architecture, all images of the Midrib dataset are resized to fit the network according to its respective input size. As a matter of demonstration, we analyzed the possibility to process the entire images by modifying the network architecture, however, there are images up to 9551 × 9935 × 3 that have caused a GPU Nvidia Titan X of 12 GB to run out of memory. Moreover, the performance achieved with the resized images is highly satisfactory, eliminating the need to analyze the samples in its original sizes. It is also important to notice that we have adopted the raw values from the output of the last convolutional layers before the use of common summarizing techniques such as ReLU and local average/max pooling to avoid the loss of information. For instance, the application of the ReLU function can generate sparse feature maps, and the local average/max pooling reduces the information of the layer output.

Following the steps previously described it is possible to use each of the DCNN to obtain image descriptors. This information can then be fed into a machine learning method to build a model for the problem at hand. In our case, it consists of a supervised classification procedure for the characterization of plant species based on its leaf midrib. In the next section, we explain the following steps of the classification and the experimental protocol adopted.

4   Results and Discussion

In this section, we present the classification results obtained with DCNN descriptors and compare them with other literature methods. We employ the same experimental protocol as in [30], that we describe in the following. To validate the results, the dataset is split into a 10-fold cross-validation scheme. In this scenario, all samples are randomly divided into 10 groups, and the validation consists in an iterative process where 1 group is used for the test at each step, while the remaining is used to train the model. The supervised classifier Linear discriminant analysis (LDA) [28] is used considering its good performance and to make possible a direct comparison with the results presented in [30]. We also included results using the supervised k-nearest neighbors (KNN) classifier with $k = 1$, one of the simplest classification methods based on the nearest training sample. We considered this alternative because the use of a simpler classifier highlights the quality of the computed features, besides reducing the computational cost of the classification procedure. In this context, it remains as an alternative for the user who can ponder between efficiency and performance.

We compare results between the DCNN techniques and other handcrafted texture descriptors using either the image gray-levels or its color information from the RGB space. For DCNN, in the gray-level scenario, we replicate the information for all the three image color-channels as the network inputs demand a 3-channel image. As a baseline, we considered an intensity histogram descriptor, which is a non-spatial approach (first-order statistic) that computes the occurrence of pixel values. An image descriptor is obtained by first discretizing pixel values into 32 bins, computing the pixel occurrence (histogram) and then calculating a probability density function from it. This method is applied in two ways: using the histogram from the image gray-levels (luminance) or concatenating histograms from each color-channel of the RGB space. The following traditional descriptors from the literature are also considered in the comparisons: Gabor filters [21] (1994), Binary Gabor Patterns (BGP) [40] (2012), Local Binary Patterns (LBP) [24] (2002), Local Phase Quantization (LPQ) [25] (2008) and Complete Local Binary Patterns (CLBP) [11] (2010). We analyzed these techniques in their original fashion, i.e. computing descriptors from the image gray-levels, or in an integrative approach, by concatenating descriptors from each color-channel of the RGB space. Another interesting type of handcrafted texture descriptors are based on fractal geometry, technique that have demonstrated notable results on plant analysis [1,3,26,30]. This is a consequence of the complex nature intrinsic to fractals, which makes them quite similar to many structures found in nature and, particularly, in plant leaves [30]. Therefore, we considered the results obtained through the Midrib dataset with a technique based on the combination of Boulingand-Minkowski and Fourier fractal descriptors [30] (2015) for gray-level image characterization. All the classification results are presented in Table 1, measured by the mean accuracy of 10-fold cross-validation and the corresponding error/standard deviation.

According to the obtained classification results, it is notable that DCNN performs significantly better than handcrafted descriptors. Traditional texture descriptors have a similar behavior under different scenarios, where most perform around (or below) 50%, with exception of some cases of Gabor, CLBP, and BGP that perform above 70%. It is also possible to notice that color play an important role in the plant midrib characterization, where practically all results were improved in relation to the gray-level approach. The results obtained by Intensity histograms show that the pixel distribution alone has better discrimination than spatial methods in almost all cases; for instance, it has the best performance using KNN in the RGB space (78%). This calls the applicability of traditional handcrafted descriptors and their variations for the plant midrib characterization into question. On the other hand, the results of fractal descriptors obtained in [30] reflect its superiority above the traditional methods for plant characterization. It achieves 83.67% using the image gray-levels and the LDA classifier, overcoming all the previous methods. However, significantly superior results can be achieved through DCNN descriptors using both the KNN and the LDA classifier. Although the deeper network ResNet achieved the highest accuracy rates (using LDA with 99.02% for gray-level and 99.20% for RGB), the difference between the other networks is small. For instance, the VGG16 network achieves a better performance together with the KNN classifier under

Table 1. Classification results of the 50 analyzed plant species with traditional and DCNN-based descriptors using a 10-fold cross-validation scheme in different scenarios: varying the image color-space (gray-level or RGB) and the classifier (KNN or LDA). The error (standard deviation) is shown in brackets, and the best results are highlighted in bold type.

Method		KNN		LDA	
		Gray-level	RGB	Gray-level	RGB
Handcrafted	Intensity histograms	70.75 (±4.0)	78.14 (±5.9)	51.19 (±4.8)	68.18 (±8.4)
	Gabor	72.21 (±6.9)	76.02 (±5.6)	42.04 (±0.7)	40.70 (±9.8)
	BGP	35.95 (±7.3)	41.59 (±5.8)	55.75 (±5.9)	74.13 (±4.9)
	LBP	46.20 (±5.4)	50.63 (±5.0)	49.12 (±0.6)	64.35 (±6.8)
	LPQ	45.67 (±6.6)	44.76 (±4.1)	49.75 (±8.4)	61.52 (±4.5)
	CLBP	66.60 (±5.5)	70.00 (±5.7)	43.10 (±6.2)	58.24 (±11.9)
	Combined fractal [30]			83.67 (±0.7)	
DCNN	AlexNet	91.93 (±2.8)	95.53 (±2.2)	96.64 (±1.4)	97.36 (±1.7)
	VGG16	**96.84** (±1.5)	96.00 (±2.4)	98.21 (±2.1)	98.62 (±1.5)
	VGG19	95.24 (±2.1)	93.86 (±3.3)	97.80 (±2.3)	98.57 (±1.4)
	InceptionV3	96.37 (±2.0)	94.59 (±3.3)	98.45 (±1.4)	97.45 (±1.5)
	ResNet50	96.57 (±2.8)	**97.06 (± 1.2)**	98.48 (±1.0)	98.90 (±1.0)
	ResNet101	96.58 (±2.3)	96.92 (±1.2)	**99.02** (±1.2)	**99.20 (± 0.8)**

gray-level images, 96.84% against 96.58% of ResNet101. The lower DCNN result is obtained by AlexNet with the KNN classifier under gray-level images, with 91.93% of accuracy rate. However, it is still considerably superior to the highest result of handcrafted methods obtained by the combined fractal technique.

Interestingly, the results of DCNN between gray-level or RGB images vary very little despite the highest ones been achieved using the colored information. On the other hand, the results of most traditional descriptors are significantly improved when using color. This happens due to the increase in its number of descriptors, as they are applied in an integrative way (combining descriptors from each channel). However, even with this increase, these methods perform below the Combined fractal technique, which uses only the image gray-levels. It shows that beyond the importance of color on the characterization there are complex patterns on the leaf midrib that could be related to shape and structural composition. Moreover, the DCNN superior performance can be explained by their ability to automatically identify regions of interest on the image. Therefore, they have more flexibility to deal with the different image variations present on the midrib samples.

We analyze in depth the result obtained using ResNet101 with the LDA classifier and RGB images (the confusion matrix for this experiment is shown in Fig. 2(a)). It is possible to notice that only 5 errors occur, where (b) shows one of the incorrectly classified images. This is a sample from the *Byrsonima subterranea* species, which was considered as *Byrsonima verbascifolia*. However, there is a high visual similarity between these both species, as (c) shows. Moreover, they belong to the same family (*Malpighiaceae*), corroborating to its structural similarity.

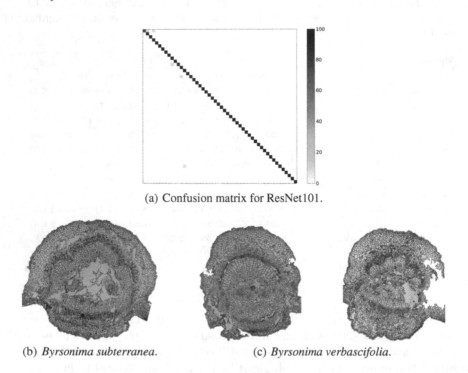

(a) Confusion matrix for ResNet101.

(b) *Byrsonima subterranea.*   (c) *Byrsonima verbascifolia.*

Fig. 2. Confusion matrix for the result of ResNet101 using LDA and RGB images (a). Sample of *Byrsonima subterranea* missclassified as *Byrsonima verbascifolia* by the method (b) and its corresponding true class (c).

5   Conclusion

This work explores the applicability of pre-trained DCNN for the characterization of 50 plant species based on microscope images of leaf midrib cross-sections. This is done through transfer learning using the output of the last convolutional layers of these networks, and image descriptors are obtained with GAP. We considered four well-known network architectures: AlexNet, VGG (16 and 19 layers), GogLeNet/InceptionV3 and ResNet (50 and 101 layers). We compare results with traditional handcrafted descriptors and a combination of fractal techniques proposed in [30], and a significant improvement is achieved over the previously available results on the literature. Most of the grey-level handcrafted descriptors perform poorly on this task and when color is included, the majority of the results are increased (using both KNN and LDA classifiers). On the other hand, DCNN features achieve a higher performance in all scenarios, corroborating to the robustness of DCNN models, considering that the studied dataset presents different image variations such as rotation, scale, sample position and also complex structural variations within specimens of the same species. This evidences the ability of these models to tackle intrinsic morphological patterns presented in the 50 plant species analyzed. Therefore, our results indicate that pre-trained DCNN can be used to obtain high-quality image features to distinguish plant species based on their leaf midribs.

Acknowledgements. Leonardo F. S. Scabini acknowledges support from CNPq (Grant number #142438/2018-9). Rayner M. Condori acknowledges support from FONDECYT, an initiative of the National Council of Science, Technology and Technological Innovation-CONCYTEC (Peru). Odemir M. Bruno acknowledges support from CNPq (Grant #307797/2014-7 and Grant #484312/2013-8) and FAPESP (grant #14/08026-1 and #16/18809-9).

References

1. Backes, A.R., Casanova, D., Bruno, O.M.: Plant leaf identification based on volumetric fractal dimension. Int. J. Pattern Recognit. Artif. Intell. **23**(06), 1145–1160 (2009)
2. Bengio, Y.: Deep learning of representations for unsupervised and transfer learning. In: Proceedings of ICML Workshop on Unsupervised and Transfer Learning, pp. 17–36 (2012)
3. Bruno, O.M., de Oliveira Plotze, R., Falvo, M., de Castro, M.: Fractal dimension applied to plant identification. Inf. Sci. **178**(12), 2722–2733 (2008)
4. Chen, Q., Abedini, M., Garnavi, R., Liang, X.: IBM research Australia at Life-CLEF2014: plant identification task. In: CLEF (Working Notes), pp. 693–704 (2014)
5. Cimpoi, M., Maji, S., Kokkinos, I., Vedaldi, A.: Deep filter banks for texturerecognition, description, and segmentation. Int. J. Comput. Vis. **118**(1), 65–94 (2016). https://doi.org/10.1007/s11263-015-0872-3
6. Deng, J., Dong, W., Socher, R., Li, L.J., Li, K., Fei-Fei, L.: ImageNet: a large-scale hierarchical image database. In: IEEE Conference on Computer Vision and Pattern Recognition, CVPR 2009, pp. 248–255. IEEE (2009)
7. Gaston, K.J., O'Neill, M.A.: Automated species identification: why not? Philos. Trans. R. Soc. Lond. B Biol. Sci. **359**(1444), 655–667 (2004)
8. Ghazi, M.M., Yanikoglu, B., Aptoula, E.: Plant identification using deep neural networks via optimization of transfer learning parameters. Neurocomputing **235**, 228–235 (2017)
9. Girshick, R., Donahue, J., Darrell, T., Malik, J.: Region-based convolutional networks for accurate object detection and segmentation. IEEE Trans. Pattern Anal. Mach. Intell. **38**(1), 142–158 (2016). https://doi.org/10.1109/TPAMI.2015.2437384
10. Grinblat, G.L., Uzal, L.C., Larese, M.G., Granitto, P.M.: Deep learning for plant identification using vein morphological patterns. Comput. Electron. Agric. **127**, 418–424 (2016)
11. Guo, Z., Zhang, L., Zhang, D.: A completed modeling of local binary pattern operator for texture classification. IEEE Trans. Image Process. **19**(6), 1657–1663 (2010)

12. Hanson, A., Joel, M., Joy, A., Francis, J.: Plant leaf disease detection using deep learning and convolutional neural network. Int. J. Eng. Sci. **5324** (2017)
13. He, K., Zhang, X., Ren, S., Sun, J.: Deep residual learning for image recognition. In: Proceedings of the IEEE Conference on Computer Vision and Pattern Recognition, pp. 770–778 (2016)
14. Junior, J.J.d.M.S., Rossatto, D.R., Kolb, R.M., Bruno, O.M.: A computer vision approach to quantify leaf anatomical plasticity: a case study on Gochnatia polymorpha (Less.) Cabrera. Ecol. Inform. **15**, 34–43 (2013)
15. Keating, R.C.: Leaf histology and its contribution to relationships in the Myrtales. Ann. Mo. Bot. Gard., 801–823 (1984)
16. Krizhevsky, A., Sutskever, I., Hinton, G.E.: ImageNet classification with deep convolutional neural networks. In: Advances in Neural Information Processing Systems, pp. 1097–1105 (2012)
17. LeCun, Y., Bengio, Y., Hinton, G.: Deep learning. Nature **521**, 436–444 (2015). https://doi.org/10.1038/nature14539
18. Lee, S.H., Chan, C.S., Wilkin, P., Remagnino, P.: Deep-plant: plant identification with convolutional neural networks. In: 2015 IEEE International Conference on Image Processing (ICIP), pp. 452–456. IEEE (2015)
19. Lin, M., Chen, Q., Yan, S.: Network in network. CoRR abs/1312.4400 (2013). http://arxiv.org/abs/1312.4400
20. Lu, H., Cao, Z., Xiao, Y., Fang, Z., Zhu, Y.: Toward good practices for fine-grained maize cultivar identification with filter-specific convolutional activations. IEEE Trans. Autom. Sci. Eng. **15**(2), 430–442 (2018). https://doi.org/10.1109/TASE.2016.2616485
21. Manjunath, B.S., Ma, W.Y.: Texture features for browsing and retrieval of image data. IEEE Trans. Pattern Anal. Mach. Intell. **18**(8), 837–842 (1996)
22. Mokeev, V.V.: On application of convolutional neural network for classification of plant images. In: 2018 Global Smart Industry Conference (GloSIC), pp. 1–6. IEEE (2018)
23. Mortensen, A.K., Dyrmann, M., Karstoft, H., Jørgensen, R.N., Gislum, R., et al.: Semantic segmentation of mixed crops using deep convolutional neural network. In: CIGR-AgEng Conference, 26–29 June 2016, Aarhus, Denmark. Abstracts and Full papers, pp. 1–6. Organising Committee, CIGR 2016 (2016)
24. Ojala, T., Pietikainen, M., Maenpaa, T.: Multiresolution gray-scale and rotation invariant texture classification with local binary patterns. IEEE Trans. Pattern Anal. Mach. Intell. **24**(7), 971–987 (2002)
25. Ojansivu, Ville, Heikkilä, Janne: Blur insensitive texture classification using local phase quantization. In: Elmoataz, Abderrahim, Lezoray, Olivier, Nouboud, Fathallah, Mammass, Driss (eds.) ICISP 2008. LNCS, vol. 5099, pp. 236–243. Springer, Heidelberg (2008). https://doi.org/10.1007/978-3-540-69905-7_27
26. Plotze, R.d.O., et al.: Leaf shape analysis using the multiscale Minkowski fractal dimension, a new morphometric method: a study with Passiflora (Passifloraceae). Can. J. Bot. **83**(3), 287–301 (2005)
27. Reyes, A.K., Caicedo, J.C., Camargo, J.E.: Fine-tuning deep convolutional networks for plant recognition. In: CLEF (Working Notes) (2015)
28. Ripley, B.D.: Pattern Recognition and Neural Networks. Cambridge University Press, Cambridge (1996)
29. Seeland, M., Rzanny, M., Boho, D., Wäldchen, J., Mäder, P.: Image-based classification of plant genus and family for trained and untrained plant species. BMC Bioinform. **20**(1), 4 (2019)

30. da Silva, N.R., Florindo, J.B., Gómez, M.C., Rossatto, D.R., Kolb, R.M., Bruno, O.M.: Plant identification based on leaf midrib cross-section images using fractal descriptors. PLoS ONE **10**(6), e0130014 (2015)

31. Simonyan, K., Zisserman, A.: Very deep convolutional networks for large-scale image recognition. arXiv preprint arXiv:1409.1556 (2014)

32. Singh, A.K., Ganapathysubramanian, B., Sarkar, S., Singh, A.: Deep learning for plant stress phenotyping: trends and future perspectives. Trends Plant Sci. (2018)

33. Sladojevic, S., Arsenovic, M., Anderla, A., Culibrk, D., Stefanovic, D.: Deepneural networks based recognition of plant diseases by leaf image classification. Comput. Intell. Neurosci. **2016** (2016)

34. Sünderhauf, N., McCool, C., Upcroft, B., Perez, T.: Fine-grained plant classification using convolutional neural networks for feature extraction. In: CLEF (Working Notes), pp. 756–762 (2014)

35. Szegedy, C., et al.: Going deeper with convolutions. In: The IEEE Conference on Computer Vision and Pattern Recognition (CVPR), June 2015

36. Szegedy, C., Vanhoucke, V., Ioffe, S., Shlens, J., Wojna, Z.: Rethinking the inception architecture for computer vision. In: The IEEE Conference on Computer Vision and Pattern Recognition (CVPR), June 2016

37. Ubbens, J., Cieslak, M., Prusinkiewicz, P., Stavness, I.: The use of plant models in deep learning: an application to leaf counting in rosette plants. Plant Methods **14**(1), 6 (2018)

38. Wäldchen, J., Mäder, P.: Plant species identification using computer vision techniques: a systematic literature review. Arch. Comput. Methods Eng. **25**(2), 507–543 (2018)

39. Yigit, E., Sabanci, K., Toktas, A., Kayabasi, A.: A study on visual features of leaves in plant identification using artificial intelligence techniques. Comput. Electron. Agric. **156**, 369–377 (2019)

40. Zhang, L., Zhou, Z., Li, H.: Binary Gabor pattern: an efficient and robust descriptor for texture classification. In: 2012 19th IEEE International Conference on Image Processing (ICIP), pp. 81–84. IEEE (2012)

Towards an Automatic Annotation of French Sign Language Videos: Detection of Lexical Signs

Hussein Chaaban[1,2,3,4](✉), Michèle Gouiffès[1,2,3,4], and Annelies Braffort[2,3,4]

[1] Paris Sud University, Orsay, France
hussein.chaaban@u-psud.fr
[2] Paris-Saclay University, Saint-Aubin, France
[3] Laboratoire d'Informatique pour la Mécanique et les Sciences de l'Ingénieur LIMSI, Orsay, France
[4] Centre national de la recherche scientifique CNRS, Paris, France

Abstract. This paper presents an approach towards an automatic annotation system for French Sign Language (LSF). Such automation aims to reduce the processing time and the subjectivity of manual annotations done by linguists in order to study the sign language and simplify indexing for automatic signs recognition. The described system uses face and body keypoints collected from 2D RGB standard LSF videos. A naive Bayesian model was built to classify gestural units using the collected keypoints as features. We started from the observation that, for many signers, the production of lexical signs is very often accompanied by mouthing. Effectively, the results showed that the system is capable of detecting lexical signs, with highest success rate, using only information about mouthing and head direction.

Keywords: LSF videos · Annotations · Lexical signs · Mouthing

1 Introduction

Sign Languages (SL) are visuo-gestural languages used mainly by the deaf community. Very few linguist studies have been produced to explain and formalize their rules and grammar. The first contemporary linguist to study SL was Stokoe [17] who described the language in terms of phonemes (or cheremes) and built a written transcription of it. This work has laid the groundwork and paved the way for deeper research on SL. Today, linguists collect and annotate videos of signers in natural contexts in order to extract knowledge from them. Currently, most of the SL videos are manually annotated using a software like ELAN [21] or ANVIL [10]. Though this process consumes a lot of time and the produced annotations are usually non-reproducible since they depend on the subjectivity and the experience of the annotator. An automatic annotation system could certainly accelerate the work and enhance the reproducibility of the results.

© Springer Nature Switzerland AG 2019
M. Vento and G. Percannella (Eds.): CAIP 2019, LNCS 11679, pp. 402–412, 2019.
https://doi.org/10.1007/978-3-030-29891-3_35

Cues about the hands (shape and motion), face expressions, gaze orientation, mouthing are useful to be annotated. When talking about SL, most of the non SL signers tend to think directly of the hands. In fact, two communication channels exist: Manual Components (MC) consisting of the hand shapes, orientations and motions and, Non-Manual Components (NMC) consisting of face features and body pose. Cuxac's model [5] presents two ways of signifying using a combination of 4 different MC and 4 NMC:

(1) "saying and showing" with an illustrative intent which consists of **Highly Iconic Structures (HIS)** that include Transfers in Sizes and Shapes (TSS) of objects, in Situations (ST) and in Persons (PT);
(2) "without showing" which consists of **Lexical Signs (LS)**, *i.e.* predefined signs in a dictionary, and pointing. More than 65% of the signs are lexical [8].

Thus, distinguishing these two classes, LS and HIS, would be a first step before applying a dedicated processing for each of them. To do so, this paper proposes to determine the more relevant body and face features to detect LS in a SL discourse. Then, it illustrates this result by testing a classification method. The experiments are made on a French Sign Language (LSF) video dataset consisting of standard RGB videos. Thus, it is not required to use any specific sensor or wearable device, which enlarges its possible use-cases. This pre-annotation intends to facilitate the work of the linguists and can be useful to constitute annotated data for further deep learning strategies.

The remainder of the paper is structured as follows. The next section discusses the previous work conducted on annotation of SL videos. Section 3 describes the datasets that are studied in this paper. Then, Sects. 4 and 5 describe respectively the features and classification methods. To finish, Sect. 6.3 discusses the results.

2 Related Work

In the literature, few papers explored the automatic annotation of SL. The majority of these works on SL annotation study the American Sign Language (ASL) as it is the richest one in terms of databases. The conducted studies on ASL may not be necessarily suitable nor applicable to LSF since SL are not universal languages: each country has its own SL and grammar.

The first attempts of SL recognition were conducted on isolated signs. The general idea was to extract some features from images in order to identify signs using a classifier such as SVM [7,16], neural networks [9], HMM [1], KNN [15]. These works were mainly focusing on the MC as features as it was believed that hands had the main information in an SL speech. Nowadays, many image processing and object segmentation techniques were developed [20] and with the revolution in machine learning, the systems are capable of estimating and tracking face [18] and body [19] in real time with high success rate using only 2D image features. Most works on SL recognition focus on specific datasets, made in controlled environments (uniform background, signer with dark clothes) and dealing with a specific topic, such as weather [11]. But the real challenge in SL recognition remains in identifying dynamic signs, *i.e.* signs in real SL speech, and most importantly independently of the signer [12]. Such work requires a huge annotated dataset, which is not available for LSF.

Concerning automatic annotation, most of the proposals try to annotate the segments by describing facial and body events as mouthing, gaze, occlusion, hands placements, handshapes, and movements [14]. Few of them go further and exploit these events by combining MC and NMC to add a second level annotation such as LS and HIS. In fact, [6] succeeded to annotate pointing in LSF videos by combining MC and NMC. In [13], the MC and NMC are tracked in order to categorize LS. However, an actual annotation of LS was lacking, and the tracking of NMC was done on controlled videos of the head. In our work, we tested some combinations of MC and NMC to figure out which components are the most effective to classify LS.

3   Data

The dataset is a portion of MOCAP dataset, which collects RGB videos in LSF produced in our lab for other purposes[1]. The videos show the signer from hip up face view. These videos are standard (2D, 720×540 pixels, 25 FPS). We used 49 videos with 4 different signers with randomly picked combinations for learning and test sets. The length of videos varies between 15 to 34 s (average of 24 s, 19.63 min in total). In the videos the signers were asked to describe what they see in an image (Fig. 1). The given images represented 25 different scenes (Fig. 2) such as a living room, a forest, a wine store, a library, a city, a monument, a construction site... The images were chosen to have a variety of LS and HIS. All the videos were annotated manually by one expert. The annotations include gaze, LS and HIS. 1011 signs were annotated, 709 were LS and 304 were HIS.

Fig. 1. Sequence of lexical sign "Salon"

---

[1] Because of privacy policies, these videos are not available online https://www.ortolang.fr/market/corpora/mocap1.

Fig. 2. Examples of scenes to be described by the signers

4   Features Extraction

As far now, linguists did not establish a unified way for annotation nor a pre-defined list of MC and NMC to track. Checking the literature, most papers were interested in studying the handshapes, their placements, motion, direction and symmetry between them as MC and mouthing, mouth gestures, gaze and eyebrows as NMC.

To extract the features, we use OpenPose [4], a recent real time pose estimation library for face and body, which provides the coordinates of keypoints (body articulators and face elements). We have processed these coordinates to provide more evolved features described hereafter.

Mouthing. Based on the work of [3] which proves that mouth features are important indicators of LS, our first work has consisted in tracking the mouthing. Then other MC and NMC features were successively added to see how the classification improves. OpenPose provides the coordinates of 20 points that define the outer-line of the lips (Fig. 3(a)).

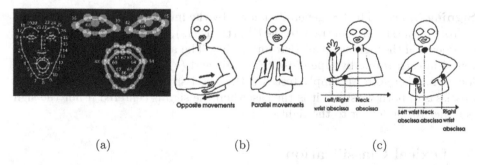

(a)   (b)   (c)

Fig. 3. (a) Facial Keypoints of OpenPose. (b) Relative movements of hands. (c) Placement of signs.

We assume that a mouthing is detected whenever the signer opens his mouth due to the pronunciation of a vowel, which is not the case for mouth gesture.

To detect the opening of the mouth, we calculated the isoperimetric ratio (or circularity) of the interior of the lips using the formula: $IR = \frac{4\pi a}{p^2}$ where a is the area and p is the perimeter. The higher the ratio is, the more the mouth is open, which is the sign of a mouthing.

However, mouth is often occluded when the signs are formed in front of the head. To handle the problem, a temporal analyzing window of 5 frames is used in which the last relevant IR value is kept, $i.e.$ $IR \leq 1$. The occlusion is detected when the distance between hands and mouth falls under a threshold (80 pixels in our dataset) and when lips coordinates are null.

Gaze/Head Direction. Gaze plays an important role in HIS, when the signer places objects in the signing space in front of him, and wants to draw the attention of the partner on something in the signing space.

Our facial features are detected using OpenFace [2]. Theoretically, the gaze could be tracked from this model. However, because of the low resolution of the images under consideration, we had to use only the head direction (which is generally close). We define the head direction as a ratio, where 0 refers to the signer head in center position, and negative/positive values stands for left and right respectively.

Bi-manual Motion. During HIS, the signer can draw objects in the signing space, generally with both hands moving in a symmetrical or opposite way. With OpenPose, we can get with high precision the coordinates of both wrists and elbows. Using these coordinates we deduce the velocity and direction of the hands movements to create a motion characteristic vector for each arm. The correlation of the two vectors of the two arms can give us an information about the relative movements of arms: symmetrical (both velocity and direction are similar), opposite (similar velocity and opposite directions).

Signing Space. The LS, generally known by the interlocutor, are mostly made in front of the signer. Contrary to the HIS (transfers), they require less placement of objects in the signing space (left and right). The abscissas of neck and wrists, found in each frame by OpenPose (Fig. 3(b) and (c)) are used to evaluate this location. Therefore we simply tested if the abscissa of the neck is between the abscissas of both wrists. If it is the case then the sign is centered if not the sign is either to the left or to the right.

5   Lexical Classification

Since we do not have a huge dataset for learning, a simple classifier has been chosen, instead of convolutional neural networks. The first step in building our classifier was finding the decision rule. Using the extracted features from the learning data and combining them with the annotations of LS and HIS, we drew the distribution of each parameter between the two types of signs along the frames of the videos. Since the values of our features are continuous, we took the assumption that their distributions are normal with mean μ_k and variance σ_k^2. In Fig. 4, it can be seen how the features values (for instance IR) distributed between LS and HIS for a specific learning set. These functions represent the probability distribution of each feature (x) given a sign type (C). $P(x_i \mid C)$ can be computed by plugging x_i into the equation for a Normal distribution parameterized by μ_k and σ_k^2

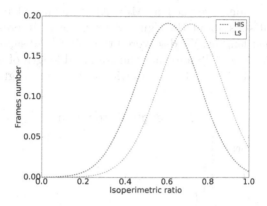

Fig. 4. Distribution of isoperimetric ratio IR between the two types of signs (LS and HIS.

$$P(x = x_i \mid C) = \frac{1}{\sqrt{2\pi\sigma_k^2}} e^{-\frac{(x_i - \mu_k)^2}{2\sigma_k^2}} \tag{1}$$

The discussion so far has derived the independent feature model, that is, the naive Bayes probability model. The naive Bayes classifier combines this model with a decision rule. One common rule is to pick the hypothesis that is the most probable; this is known as the maximum *a posteriori* or MAP decision rule. The corresponding Bayes classifier assigns a class label $\hat{y} = C_k$ for some k as follows:

$$\hat{y} = \text{argmax}_{k \in \{1,\dots,K\}} \; P(C_k) \prod_{i=1}^{n} p(x_i \mid C_k). \tag{2}$$

with the believe that all the features are independents.

After creating our model using the learning dataset, for each new frame in the testing dataset we calculate:

$$P(Lexical \mid F1, F2, F3, F4) = P(Lexical) \prod_{i=1}^{4} P(x_i \mid Lexical). \tag{3}$$

$$P(HIS \mid F1, F2, F3, F4) = P(HIS) \prod_{i=1}^{4} P(x_i \mid HIS). \tag{4}$$

where $F1$ is Mouthing, $F2$ is head pose, $F3$ is hands symmetry and $F4$ is sign placement. Then we compare (3) and (4), if the result of (3) is bigger then the result of (4) the new frame is part of LS if not then it is part of HIS sign.

6   Experiments and Results

6.1   Preliminary Analysis

The manual annotations provided in MOCAP were useful in a first time to establish some statistics about the signs. We were most interested in the signs frequencies and their lengths. We discovered that 69.99% of signs in the database are lexical where 30% are HIS and that the standard length of a sign is between 3 and 10 frames, as shown by the distribution of the sign lengths on Fig. 5.

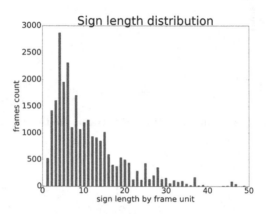

Fig. 5. The distribution of sign lengths in the dataset MOCAP.

6.2   Evaluation

The proposed method is applied to the dataset detailed in Sect. 3.

The classification results of LS are compared to the manual annotations. Fig. 6 shows, for one of the videos, and for each frame, an example of classification result (in red) compared to the annotation (in blue). Because of the subjectivity of the annotations, an annotated LS is considered as correctly detected when 3 consecutive frames (smallest sign length of a LS) classified as lexical fall in the range of the annotated sign.

For the evaluation metrics, we counted the true positives (TP) among detected lexical signs, false positives (FP), true negatives (TN) and false negatives (FN) in each video in the test dataset. Then we compute the TP and TN rates (TPR and TNR), the positive prediction value (PPV) and F1-score:

$$TPR = \frac{TP}{TP+FN} \quad TNR = \frac{TN}{TN+FP} \quad PPV = \frac{TP}{TP+FP} \quad F_1 = 2\frac{PPV.TPR}{PPV+TPR}$$

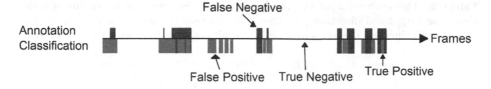

Fig. 6. Counting of false/true positives and false/true negatives (Color figure online)

6.3   Classification Results

First, the results of our method are evaluated for each signer individually and then combined to check if the classification is independent of the signer. For each experiment, the Mouthing (M) is tested alone, and the other ones are successively added: Head direction (H), Bi-manual motion (B) and Sign placement (S).

Intra-signer Study. For each signer, the videos are divided into 3 subsets L_1, L_2, and L_3. Two of them $(L_i, L_j) = (L_1, L_2), (L_1, L3), (L_2, L_3)$ are used for learning and the last one for testing. A cross-validation is performed, by collecting the results of each experiment. The averages and standard deviations of the results are shown in Table 1.

Table 1. The evaluation of the results for intra-signer classification using the features Mouthing (M), Head direction (H), Bi-manual motion (B) and Sign placement (S)). The shown values are the average of all the results coming from each signer separately

Features	TPR		TNR		PPV		F1 score	
	μ	σ	μ	σ	μ	σ	μ	σ
M	0.24	0.09	0.80	0.15	0.55	0.24	0.32	0.10
M + H	0.57	0.11	0.56	0.19	0.48	0.17	0.50	0.13
M + H + B	0.57	0.13	0.56,	0.18	0.46	0.17	0.48	0.14
M + H + B + S	0.57	0.10	0.55	0.18	0.46	0.16	0.48	0.12

Inter-signer Study. Here, the videos are divided into 4 subsets L_1, L_2, L_3 and L_4, each subset includes all the videos from the same signer. Again we tried all the different combinations of subsets for learning and testing with three subsets for learning and one subset for testing and the results are shown in Table 2.

By analysing the Tables 1 and 2, mouthing and head orientation appear to be the most relevant features for distinguishing LS from HIS. While, the bimanual signing and the placement of signs seem not adding any relevant information for this task. The similarity between the results obtained for intra-signer and for inter-signer experiments confirms the generality of our approach. The performance of the results seems to be low compared to more standard gesture recognition applications. This is explained by the huge variety of the motion

Table 2. The evaluation of the results for inter classification using the features Mouthing (M), Head direction (H), Bi-manual motion (B) and Sign placement (S)). The shown values are the average of all the results coming from all signers combined

Features	TPR		TNR		PPV		F1 score	
	μ	σ	μ	σ	μ	σ	μ	σ
M	0.25	0.09	0.80	0.08	0.52	0.15	0.33	0.10
M + H	0.61	0.11	0.57	0.19	0.50	0.16	0.53	0.09
M + H + B	0.62	0.12	0.57	0.17	0.51	0.15	0.53	0.09
M + H + B + S	0.58	0.12	0.57	0.17	0.49	0.14	0.50	0.09

made for signs, the imperfection and subjectivity of the annotations and the error margin of OpenPose and OpenFace during the features extraction since we are working on low resolution videos. However, our application consists of a semi automatic annotation of SL. It will be of great help for linguists, who will just have to confirm or not the correctness of the classification.

6.4   Impact of the Segmentation

As mentioned previously, the manual annotations of the videos are both subjective and imprecise. Each annotator has his own rules to define the beginning and the end of each sign. We wanted to find how many of the False Positive classified LS actually refer to a neighbour existing sign in the annotation to test the hypothesis that this classified sign was considered as False detection due to the subjectivity of the annotation and a delay of between the annotation and the detection (Fig. 7).   Thus we enlarged each detected sign by 3 frames (smallest length of a LS) at the beginning and the end of the sign and recalculated the evaluation results. The new values in Table 3 show an improvement of the classification rate. Even if the improvement is not that high it definitely makes us more curious about the importance of the segmentation of detected signs.

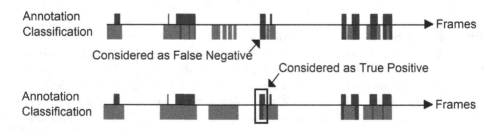

Fig. 7. Before enlarging detected signs (upper image) and after (lower image)

Table 3. The evaluation of the results for inter and intra classification after enlarging the detected signs

Intra-signer								
Features	TPR		TNR		PPV		F1 score	
	μ	σ	μ	σ	μ	σ	μ	σ
M + H	0.54	0.15	0.74	0.14	0.64	0.16	0.57	0.12
M + H + B + S	0.54	0.16	0.73	0.13	0.63	0.14	0.56	0.12
Inter-signer								
Features	TPR		TNR		PPV		F1 score	
	μ	σ	μ	σ	μ	σ	μ	σ
M + H	0.57	0.15	0.73	0.14	0.63	0.12	0.57	0.08
M + H + B + S	0.52	0.16	0.73	0.13	0.63	0.13	0.54	0.11

7 Conclusion

This paper has proposed a tool that will be useful for linguists to pre-annotate Sign Language (SL) videos, in order to alleviate the annotation burden. This first step distinguishes temporal segments that correspond to lexical signs from other segments, such as the highly iconic ones. According to the study made on the features, it has been shown that mouthing and head orientation are the most discriminant features for this task. This work has several perspectives. First, the impact of other features will be tested and other classifiers such as SVM will be used just to compare the results and observe the impact of the classification system on the results. Then, once a lexical sign is detected in the video, we will have to refine the temporal segmentation around this detection. After segmentation, it will be possible to launch a sign recognition algorithm on the resulting LS segments. It will be interesting also to test our approach on other SL, in order to test its universality.

References

1. Assaleh, K., Shanableh, T., Fanaswala, M.: Persian sign language (PSL) recognition using wavelet transform and neural networks. J. Intell. Learn. Syst. Appl. **2**, 19–27 (2010). https://doi.org/10.4236/jilsa.2010.21003
2. Baltrušaitis, T., Zadeh, A., Chong Lim, Y., Morency, L.P.: OpenFace 2.0: facial behavior analysis toolkit. In: IEEE International Conference on Automatic Face and Gesture Recognition (2018)
3. Balvet, A., Sallandre, M.A.: Mouth features as non-manual cues for the categorization of lexical and productive signs in French sign language (LSF). In: 6th Workshop on the Representation and Processing of Sign Languages: Beyond the Manual Channel, halshs-01079270, Reykjavik, France, May 2014
4. Cao, Z., Hidalgo, G., Simon, T., Wei, S.E., Sheikh, Y.: OpenPose: realtime multi-person 2D pose estimation using Part Affinity Fields. arXiv preprint arXiv:1812.08008 (2018)

5. Cuxac, C.: La langue des signes française (lsf). les voies de l'iconicité. Bibliothèque de Faits de Langues (15–16). Ophrys, Paris (2000)
6. Garcia, B., Sallandre, M.A., Schoder, C., L'Huillier, M.T.: Typologie des pointages en langue des signes française (lsf) et problématiques de leur annotation (2011)
7. Huang, C.L., Tsai, B.L.: A vision-based Taiwanese Sign Language Recognition. 20th International Conference on Pattern Recognition, ICPR, Istanbul, Turkey, pp. 3683–3686, August 2010. https://doi.org/10.1109/ICPR.2010.1110
8. Johnston, T.: Lexical frequency in sign languages. J. Deaf. Stud. Deaf. Educ. **17**(2), 163–193 (2012). https://doi.org/10.1093/deafed/enr036
9. Karami, A., Zanj, B., KianiSarkaleh, A.: Persain sign language (PSL) recognition using wavelet transform and neural networks. Expert. Syst. Appl. **38**(3), 2661–2667 (2011). https://doi.org/10.1016/j.eswa.2010.08.056
10. Kipp, M.: Anvil - a generic annotation tool for multimodal dialogue. INTER-SPEECH (2001)
11. Koller, O., Forster, J., Ney, H.: Continuous sign language recognition: towards large vocabulary statistical recognition systems handling multiple signers. Comput. Vis. Image Underst. **141**, 108–125 (2015)
12. Liang, Z.j., Liao, S.b., Hu, B.z.: 3D convolutional neural networks for dynamic sign language recognition. Comput. J. **61**(11), 1724–1736 (2018). https://doi.org/10.1093/comjnl/bxy049
13. Hrúz, M., Krňoul, Z., Campr, P., Müller, L.: Towards automatic annotation of sign language dictionary corpora. In: Habernal, I., Matoušek, V. (eds.) TSD 2011. LNCS (LNAI), vol. 6836, pp. 331–339. Springer, Heidelberg (2011). https://doi.org/10.1007/978-3-642-23538-2_42
14. Naert, L., Reverdy, C., Caroline, L., Gibet, S.: Per channel automatic annotation of sign language motion capture data. In: Workshop on the Representation and Processing of Sign Languages: Involving the Language Community, LREC, Miyazaki Japan, May 2018. https://hal.archives-ouvertes.fr/hal-01851404
15. Nandy, A., Prasad, J.S., Mondal, S., Chakraborty, P., Nandi, G.C.: Recognition isolated indian sign language gesture in real time. Inf. Process. Manag. Commun. Comput. Inf. Sci. **70**, 102–107 (2010)
16. Rashid, O., Al-Hamadi, A., Michaelis, B.: Utilizing invariant descriptors for finger spelling american sign language using SVM. In: Bebis, G., et al. (eds.) ISVC 2010. LNCS, vol. 6453, pp. 253–263. Springer, Heidelberg (2010). https://doi.org/10.1007/978-3-642-17289-2_25
17. Stokoe, W., Casterline, D., Croneberg, C.: A Dictionary of American Sign Language on Linguistic Principles, revised edn. Linstok Press, Silver Spring (1976)
18. Viola, P.A., Jones, M.J.: Robust real-time face detection. Int. J. Comput. Vis. **57**, 137–154 (2004). https://doi.org/10.1023/B:VISI.0000013087.49260.fb
19. Wei, S., Ramakrishna, V., Kanade, T., Sheikh, Y.: Convolutional pose machines. CoRR abs/1602.00134, August 2016. http://arxiv.org/abs/1602.00134. dblp computer science bibliography. https://dblp.org
20. Wiley, V., Lucas, T.: Computer vision and image processing: a paper review. Int. J. Artif. Intell. Res. **2**(1), 28–36 (2018). https://doi.org/10.29099/ijair.v2i1.42
21. Wittenburg, P., Levinson, S., Kita, S., Brugman, H.: Multimodal annotations in gesture and sign language studies. LREC (2002)

Orthogonal Affine Invariants
from Gaussian-Hermite Moments

Jan Flusser[1], Tomáš Suk[1(✉)], and Bo Yang[2]

[1] The Czech Academy of Sciences, Institute of Information Theory and Automation,
Pod vodárenskou věží 4, 182 08 Praha 8, Czech Republic
{flusser,suk}@utia.cas.cz
[2] School of Automation, Northwestern Polytechnical University,
127 West Youyi Road, Xi'an 710 072, Shaanxi, People's Republic of China
bo.yang@hotmail.fr
https://www.utia.cas.cz

Abstract. We propose a new kind of moment invariants with respect to
an affine transformation. The new invariants are constructed in two steps.
First, the affine transformation is decomposed into scaling, stretching and
two rotations. The image is partially normalized up to the second rotation, and then rotation invariants from Gaussian-Hermite moments are
applied. Comparing to the existing approaches – traditional direct affine
invariants and complete image normalization – the proposed method is
more numerically stable. The stability is achieved thanks to the use of
orthogonal Gaussian-Hermite moments and also due to the partial normalization, which is more robust to small changes of the object than the
complete normalization. Both effects are documented in the paper by
experiments. Better stability opens the possibility of calculating affine
invariants of higher orders with better discrimination power. This might
be useful namely when different classes contain similar objects and cannot be separated by low-order invariants.

Keywords: Affine transformation · Invariants · Image normalization ·
Gaussian-Hermite moments

1 Introduction

Recognition of objects that have undergone an unknown affine transformation
has been the aim of extensive research work. The importance of affinely-invariant
recognition techniques is mainly due to the fact, that 2D images are often projections of 3D world. As such, 2D images of 3D objects are perspective projections

This work has been supported by the Czech Science Foundation (Grant No. GA18-
07247S) and by the Praemium Academiae, awarded by the Czech Academy of Sciences.
Bo Yang has been supported by the Fundamental Research Funds for the Central
Universities (No. 3102018ZY025) and the Fund Program for the Scientific Activities of
the Selected Returned Overseas Professionals in Shaanxi Province (No. 2018024).

© Springer Nature Switzerland AG 2019
M. Vento and G. Percannella (Eds.): CAIP 2019, LNCS 11679, pp. 413–424, 2019.
https://doi.org/10.1007/978-3-030-29891-3_36

of their "ideal" views. Since perspective transformation is non-linear and difficult to cope with, in simplified imaging models it is often modelled by *affine transformation*. Such an approximation is justified if the object size is small comparing to the distance from the camera, because the perspective effect becomes negligible. For this reason, *affine invariants* play an important role in the view-independent object recognition and have been widely used not only in tasks where image deformation is intrinsically affine but also commonly substitute projective invariants.

Among the existing affine invariants, *moment invariants* are the most frequently studied, cited in the literature and used in applications (see [9] for an exhaustive survey). Their history can be traced back to Hilbert and other famous mathematicians of the last century [10, 11, 14, 21, 28, 29], who elaborated the traditional theory of algebraic invariants. Currently, we may recognize two major approaches to the design of affine moment invariants (AMIs). In direct derivation, explicit formulas for the invariants are found by various techniques. Reiss [19] and Flusser and Suk [8] adopted the algebraic theory, Suk and Flusser applied graph theory [25, 27] and Hickman proposed the method of transvectants [13]. All reported AMIs are composed of *geometric moments*, which are simple to work with theoretically but they are unstable in numerical implementation. When calculating them, we face the problem of precision loss due to the floating-point underflow and/or overflow. In theory of moments, a popular way of overcoming numerical problems is the use of orthogonal (OG) moments (i.e. moments defined as projections on an orthogonal polynomial basis) instead of the geometric ones. Since OG polynomials have a bounded range of values and can be calculated in a stable way by recurrent relations [4], the precision loss is by several orders less than that of geometric moments. Unfortunately, all known sets of OG polynomials are transformed under an affine transformation in so complicated manner, that a direct derivation of OG AMIs has not been reported yet.

Image normalization is an alternative way of obtaining invariants. The object is brought into certain canonical (also called normalized) position, which is independent of the actual position, rotation, scale, and skewing. The canonical position is usually defined by constraining the values of some moments, the number of which is the same as the number of free parameters of the transformation. Plain moments, calculated from the normalized object, are affine invariants of the original object. Affine image normalization was first proposed by Rothe et al. [20] and followed by numerous researchers [18, 22, 26, 39].

Normalization approach seems to be attractive because of its simplicity. We can override the numerical problems by taking OG moments of the normalized image. Lin [16] used Chebyshev moments, Zhang [38] used Legendre moments, and Canterakis [3], Mei [17] and Amayeh [1] adopted Zernike moments for this purpose. Another advantage is that no actual spatial transformation of the original object is necessary. Such a transformation would slow down the process and would introduce resampling errors. Instead, the moments of the normalized object can be calculated directly from the original object using the normalization constraints. However, a major drawback of image normalization lies in the instability of the canonical position. Two visually very similar shapes may be brought, under the same normalization constraints, to distinct canonical positions. The difference in canonical positions propagates into all normalized moments and these shapes are no longer recognized as similar. This used to be the main argument against the normalization method.

In this paper, we propose an original "hybrid" approach, which should suppress the instability while keeping all the positive aspects of normalization, namely the possibility of working with OG moments. The main idea is to decompose affine transformation into anisotropic scaling and two rotations, normalize w.r.t. the first rotation and anisotropic scaling only, and then use moment invariants from OG moments w.r.t. the second rotation. Thanks to using OG moments, this method is numerically more stable than direct AMIs. At the same time, skipping the normalization w.r.t. the second rotation makes the canonical position robust to small changes of the object. Figure 1 shows the differences between these three approaches graphically.

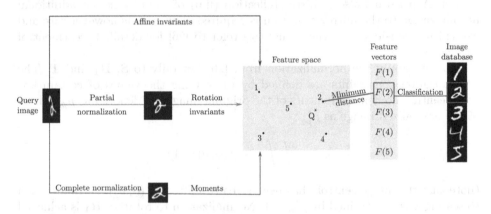

Fig. 1. Three approaches to reaching affine invariance. Direct affine invariants (top), partial normalization (middle), and complete normalization (bottom). We propose to use partial normalization followed by applying Gaussian-Hermite rotation invariants.

2 Affine Transformation and Its Decomposition

Affine transformation in 2D is defined as

$$\mathbf{x}' = \mathbf{A}\mathbf{x} + \mathbf{b} \tag{1}$$

where $\mathbf{A}$ is a regular 2×2 matrix with constant coefficients and $\mathbf{b}$ is a vector of translation. Normalization w.r.t. translation is achieved easily by shifting the coordinate origin into the object centroid. Thus, $\mathbf{b}$ vanishes and we will not consider it in the sequel.

Normalization w.r.t. $\mathbf{A}$ is based on a decomposition of $\mathbf{A}$ into a product of single-parameter matrices and subsequent normalizations w.r.t. each matrix.

Several decompositions can be used for this purpose. Rothe et al. [20] proposed two different decompositions – XSR decomposition into skewing, nonuniform scaling and rotation, and XYS decomposition into two skews and nonuniform scaling. Their method was later improved by Zhang [39], who studied possible ambiguities of the canonical position. Pei and Lin [18] tried to avoid the skewing matrix and proposed a decomposition into two rotations and a nonuniform scaling between them. A generalized and improved version of this decomposition was later published by Suk and Flusser [26]. We apply the decomposition scheme from [26] in this paper. We recall its basics below.

Affine matrix $\mathbf{A}$ is decomposed as

$$\mathbf{A} = \mathbf{R}_2 \mathbf{T} \mathbf{R}_1 \mathbf{S} \tag{2}$$

where $\mathbf{S}$ is a uniform scaling, $\mathbf{R}_1$ is the first rotation, $\mathbf{T}$ is so-called *stretching* which means $\mathbf{T}$ is diagonal and $T_{11} = 1/T_{22}$, and $\mathbf{R}_2$ is the second rotation. If $\mathbf{A}$ is regular, then such a decomposition always exists and is unique. If $\det(\mathbf{A}) < 0$, then $\mathbf{A}$ performs also a mirror reflection (flip) of the object and additional normalization to the mirror reflection is required. This case is however rare and we will not consider it in the sequel (we refer to [26] for detailed treatment of this case).

Now we apply the normalization from [26] but only to $\mathbf{S}$, $\mathbf{R}_1$ and $\mathbf{T}$. The normalization constraints are defined by prescribing the values of certain low order central moments. Moments of the original image are denoted as μ_{pq}, those of the normalized image as μ'_{pq}

$$\mu_{pq} = \int \int x^p y^q f(x, y) \mathrm{d}x \mathrm{d}y \tag{3}$$

(note that the image centroid has been already shifted to $(0, 0)$). Normalization to scaling $\mathbf{S}$ is constrained by $\mu'_{00} = 1$. Normalization to rotation $\mathbf{R}_1$ is achieved by the principal axis method (see [9], Chap. 3), when we diagonalize the second-order moment matrix and align the principal eigenvector with the x-axis. This is equivalent to constraints $\mu'_{11} = 0$ and $\mu'_{20} > \mu'_{02}$ and leads to the normalizing angle

$$\alpha = \frac{1}{2} \arctan\left(\frac{2\mu_{11}}{\mu_{20} - \mu_{02}}\right). \tag{4}$$

(If $\mu_{11} = 0$ and $\mu_{20} = \mu_{02}$, then we consider the image is already normalized to rotation and set $\alpha = 0$; if $\mu_{11} \neq 0$ and $\mu_{20} = \mu_{02}$, we set $\alpha = \pi/4$.) Normalization to stretching is done by imposing the constraint $\mu''_{20} = \mu''_{02}$.

In traditional "complete" normalization, the last normalization step – normalization w.r.t. $\mathbf{R}_2$ – is done by means of higher-order moments, which may lead to an unstable canonical position. An example of such instability is shown in Fig. 2. We used a T-like shape (we assumed it had already passed the normalization w.r.t. $\mathbf{S}$, $\mathbf{R}_1$ and $\mathbf{T}$) and varied its width t from 68 to 78 pixels. We normalized it w.r.t. rotation $\mathbf{R}_2$ by means of third-order moments as proposed in [26]. The canonical positions for $t = 68, 73$ and 78 pixels, respectively, are shown in Fig. 2 (b)–(d). We can see they differ from one another significantly, which leads to a strong discontinuity of any features calculated from the canonical form. In this paper, we propose to skip the last normalization and calculate rotation invariants from the canonical position achieved by normalization w.r.t. $\mathbf{S}$, $\mathbf{R}_1$ and $\mathbf{T}$. A similar idea was proposed by Heikkilä [12], who used Cholesky factorization of the second-order moment matrix for derivation of partial normalization constraints and then continued with geometric rotation moment invariants from [7].

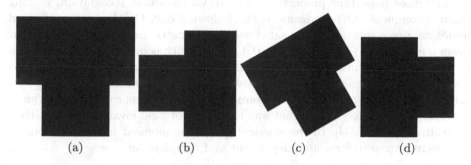

(a)   (b)   (c)   (d)

Fig. 2. The test shape of the thickness $t = 73$ before the normalization to $\mathbf{R}_2$ (a). The canonical positions after the $\mathbf{R}_2$-normalization has been applied for $t = 68$ (b), $t = 73$ (c), and $t = 78$ (d).

The rotation invariants we recommend to use are composed of Gaussian–Hermite (GH) moments. A brief introduction to GH moments along with an explanation why we chose GH moments for this purpose is given in the next section.

3 Gaussian–Hermite Moments and Invariants

Gaussian–Hermite moments and their use in image processing were exhaustively studied in [2, 6, 23, 24, 30, 32–34, 36]. Hermite polynomials are defined as

$$H_p(x) = (-1)^p \exp\left(x^2\right) \frac{d^p}{dx^p} \exp\left(-x^2\right). \tag{5}$$

They are orthogonal on $(-\infty, \infty)$ with a Gaussian weight function

$$\int_{-\infty}^{\infty} H_p(x)H_q(x) \exp\left(-x^2\right)dx = 2^p p! \sqrt{\pi}\delta_{pq} \tag{6}$$

and they can be efficiently computed by the following three-term recurrence relation

$$H_{p+1}(x) = 2xH_p(x) - 2pH_{p-1}(x) \quad \text{for } p \geq 1, \tag{7}$$

with the initial conditions $H_0(x) = 1$ and $H_1(x) = 2x$. For the definition of Gaussian–Hermite moments, we scale Hermite polynomials by a parameter σ and modulate them by a Gaussian function with the same parameter. Hence, the Gaussian–Hermite moment (GHM) $\overline{\eta}_{pq}$ of image $f(x, y)$ is defined as

$$\overline{\eta}_{pq} = \int\limits_{-\infty}^{\infty} \int\limits_{-\infty}^{\infty} H_p\left(\frac{x}{\sigma}\right) H_q\left(\frac{y}{\sigma}\right) \exp\left(-\frac{x^2 + y^2}{2\sigma^2}\right) f(x, y) \mathrm{d}x \mathrm{d}y. \tag{8}$$

The most important property of the GHMs for object recognition, making them "prominent" OG moments, is the following one. GHMs are transformed under an image rotation in the same way as geometric moments. In particular, given a functional $I(f, \mu_{pq})$, $p, q = 0, 1, \cdots, r$ which is invariant under rotation of image f, then functional $I(f, \overline{\eta}_{pq})$ is also an invariant. This theorem was discovered by Yang et al. [36]. Recently, the proof has been given in [31] that GHMs are the only orthogonal polynomials possessing this property. The Yang's theorem offers an easy and elegant way to design rotation invariants from GHMs of arbitrary orders [34]. In the classical geometric moment invariants from [7] that were proven to form an independent and complete set

$$\Phi_{pq} = \left(\sum_{k=0}^{q_0} \sum_{j=0}^{p_0} \binom{q_0}{k}\binom{p_0}{j}(-1)^{p_0-j} i^{p_0+q_0-k-j} \mu_{k+j, p_0+q_0-k-j}\right)^{p-q} \tag{9}$$
$$\cdot \sum_{k=0}^{p} \sum_{j=0}^{q} \binom{p}{k}\binom{q}{j}(-1)^{q-j} i^{p+q-k-j} \mu_{k+j, p+q-k-j}$$

where $p \geq q$ and p_0, q_0 are fixed user-defined indices such that $p_0 - q_0 = 1$, we only replace all μ_{pq}'s with corresponding $\overline{\eta}_{pq}$'s. These invariants are finally applied to the partially normalized image.

The idea of partial normalization is not fixed to any particular type of moments. In principle, any moments generating rotation invariants could be employed here. However, our experiments show that the GHMs perform better than all tested alternatives. We could use, similarly to [12], directly geometric moment invariants (9) but OG moments in general ensure better numerical stability and hence offer the possibility of using higher-order invariants [9]. Among OG moments, the moments orthogonal on a unit circle such as Zernike and Fourier-Mellin moments, provide an immediate rotation invariance and could be used here as well. Their application, however, requires mapping the image inside the unit circle, which introduces additional errors due to resampling and requires an extra time. So, moments orthogonal on a square appear to be an optimal choice because they are inherently suitable to work on a pixel grid directly. Finally, as proved in [31], GHMs are the only moments orthogonal on a square and yielding rotation invariants in the explicit form[1]. In this sense, GHMs provide an optimal solution.

4   Partial Normalization Method

In this section, we present the entire method step by step.

1. Let $f(x, y)$ be an input image, possibly deformed by unknown affine transformation $\mathbf{A}$. Compute the normalization parameters w.r.t. partial matrices $\mathbf{S}$, $\mathbf{R}_1$ and $\mathbf{T}$ as described in Sect. 2. Do not transform/resample the image $f(x, y)$, do not generate the normalized image $f'(x, y)$.
2. Calculate the transformed coordinates

$$\begin{pmatrix} x' \\ y' \end{pmatrix} = \mathbf{T}\mathbf{R}_1\mathbf{S} \begin{pmatrix} x \\ y \end{pmatrix}. \tag{10}$$

3. Calculate the GHMs (8) of the original image $f(x, y)$ with the Gaussian-Hermite polynomials computed on the normalized coordinates from the previous step. To do so, we have to know how GH polynomials are transformed under rotation and scaling. Fortunately, both relations are well known: GHMs are under rotation transformed as geometric moments [36]

$$\overline{\eta}'_{pq} = \sum_{k=0}^{p} \sum_{j=0}^{q} \binom{p}{k} \binom{q}{j} (-1)^j \, \sin^{p-k+j} \alpha \, \cos^{q+k-j} \alpha \, \overline{\eta}_{k+j,p+q-k-j}. \tag{11}$$

The behavior of GHMs under scaling was analyzed in [35]. Scaling affects not only the coordinates of Hermite polynomials but also the variance of the Gaussian modulation, which must be compensated by dividing the coordinates by $\sqrt{\mu_{00}}$. Since scaling is separable, we need just a 1D transformation for both 2D scaling and stretching. Thanks to this, we obtain the GHMs of $f'(x, y)$ without actually creating the normalized image.
4. Substitute the GHMs into (9) and calculate Gaussian-Hermite affine moment invariants (GHAMIs) of $f(x, y)$. They constitute the feature vector for invariant image description and classification.

5   Numerical Experiment

In this section, we test how the GHAMIs perform numerically and compare them to their two closest competitors, which are direct AMIs from geometric moments

---

[1] The reader may recall the so-called "indirect approach" to constructing rotation invariants from Legendre [5,15] and Krawtchouk [37] moments. The authors basically expressed geometric moments in terms of the respective OG moments and substituted into (9). They ended up with clumsy formulas of questionable numerical properties.

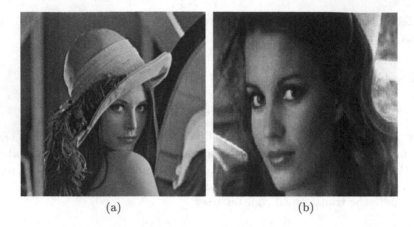

(a)   (b)

Fig. 3. Original test images: (a) Lena, (b) Lisa.

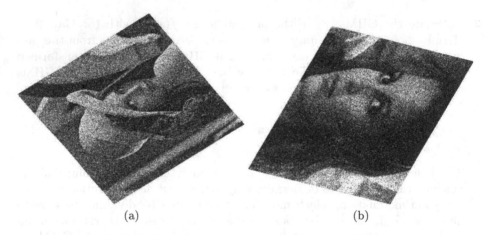

(a)   (b)

Fig. 4. Examples of the transformed and noisy test images: (a) Lena, (b) Lisa.

by Reiss and Suk [19,27] and partial normalization along with rotation invariants by Heikkila [12]. We choose direct AMIs for comparison since they are well-established and most cited affine invariants based on moments. Heikkila's method was chosen because it uses a similar idea of a partial normalization as we do. Comparison to other affine invariant methods is mostly irrelevant or unfair. For instance, the instability of complete normalization methods illustrated in Fig. 2 so much degrades their invariants, that these methods are seriously handicapped, even if the instability occurs on certain objects only. That is why we did not include any complete normalization method in this experimental study. We took two commonly used test images (see Fig. 3), generated 200 random affine transformations of both and added heavy Gaussian white noise of SNR = 0 dB to every image (see Fig. 4 for an example). For each image, we calculated a complete set of invariants up to the 12th moment order by three methods mentioned

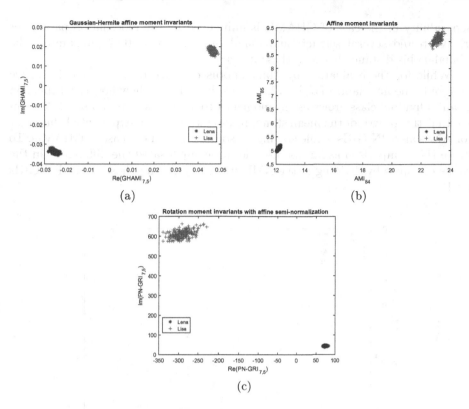

Fig. 5. The subspaces of two invariants of order 12 out of 85 invariants calculated: (a) GHAMIs, (b) AMIs, (c) PN-GRIs.

above. We choose the order 12 as a compromise – it allows to demonstrate the higher-order properties while still being numerically tractable. The complete set up to the 12th order consists of 85 independent invariants.

As a quality criterion, we chose the between-class separability measured by Mahalanobis distance

$$M = \sqrt{(\mathbf{m}_1 - \mathbf{m}_2)^T (\mathbf{S}_1 + \mathbf{S}_2)^{-1} (\mathbf{m}_1 - \mathbf{m}_2)}, \tag{12}$$

where $\mathbf{m}_i$ is the class mean and $\mathbf{S}_i$ is the covariance matrix. To demonstrate the higher-order effects, we used only the invariants of the highest (i.e. the 12th in this case) order. There are 13 invariants of the 12th order in each method.

The best separability was achieved by the proposed method using GHAMIs ($M = 173$), the worst one was provided by partial normalization and geometric rotation invariants (PN-GRIs, $M = 103$), and the AMIs performed somewhere in between yielding $M = 131$. The best performance of the GHAMIs is because the geometric moments, employed in the other two reference methods, suffer from the precision loss when calculating higher-order moments. The subspaces of two invariants are shown in Fig. 5 for illustration. It should be noted, that the separability in the case of GHAMIs is influenced by the modulation parameter σ. We tested several settings and found out that $\sigma = 0.525$ maximizes the Mahalanobis distance between these images.

While for the evaluation by Mahalanobis distance between two classes we used only the invariants of order 12, the graphs in Fig. 6 show how the dispersion of an individual class grows as the moment order increases from 3 to 12. We can see that the growth of the mean standard deviation has an exponential character for AMIs and PN-GRIs, while staying reasonably low in the case of GHAMIs. To make this comparison as fair as possible, we compensated the differences in the range of values by dividing of the AMIs values by 10 and those of the PN-GRIs by 100.

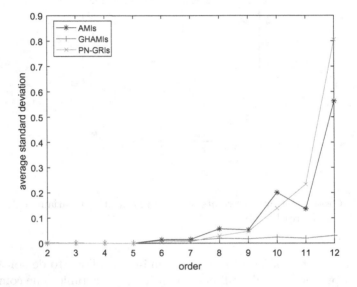

Fig. 6. Mean standard deviations of the GHAMIs, AMIs, and geometric rotation moment invariants for the Lena cluster. The average was calculated over all invariants of each order. Note the rapid growth of AMIs and PN-GRIs caused by the precision loss.

6   Conclusion

We proposed a new kind of moment invariants w.r.t. affine transformation. The new invariants are constructed in two steps. First, the image is partially normalized up to a rotation, and then recently proposed rotation invariants from Gaussian-Hermite moments are applied. Comparing to the existing approaches – direct affine invariants and complete normalization - the proposed method is more numerically stable and opens the possibility of using affine invariants of higher orders than before. This might be useful namely when different classes contain similar objects and cannot be separated by low-order invariants.

References

1. Amayeh, G., Kasaei, S., Bebis, G., Tavakkoli, A., Veropoulos, K.: Improvement of Zernike moment descriptors on affine transformed shapes. In: 9th International Symposium on Signal Processing and Its Applications ISSPA 2007, pp. 1–4. IEEE (2007)
2. Belghini, N., Zarghili, A., Kharroubi, J.: 3D face recognition using Gaussian Hermite moments. Int. J. Comput. Appl. Spec. Issue Softw. Eng., Databases Expert. Syst. **SEDEX**(1), 1–4 (2012)
3. Canterakis, N.: 3D Zernike moments and Zernike affine invariants for 3D image analysis and recognition. In: Ersbøll, B.K., Johansen, P. (eds.) Proceedings of the 11th Scandinavian Conference on Image Analysis SCIA 1999. DSAGM (1999)
4. Chihara, T.S.: An Introduction to Orthogonal Polynomials. Gordon and Breach, New York (1978)
5. Deepika, C.L., Kandaswamy, A., Vimal, C., Satish, B.: Palmprint authentication using modified Legendre moments. Procedia Comput. Sci. **2**, 164–172 (2010). Proceedings of the International Conference and Exhibition on Biometrics Technology ICEBT'10
6. Farokhi, S., Sheikh, U.U., Flusser, J., Yang, B.: Near infrared face recognition using Zernike moments and Hermite kernels. Inf. Sci. **316**, 234–245 (2015)
7. Flusser, J.: On the independence of rotation moment invariants. Pattern Recognit. **33**(9), 1405–1410 (2000)
8. Flusser, J., Suk, T.: Pattern recognition by affine moment invariants. Pattern Recognit. **26**(1), 167–174 (1993)
9. Flusser, J., Suk, T., Zitová, B.: 2D and 3D Image Analysis by Moments. Wiley, Chichester (2016)
10. Grace, J.H., Young, A.: The Algebra of Invariants. Cambridge University Press, Cambridge (1903)
11. Gurevich, G.B.: Foundations of the Theory of Algebraic Invariants. Nordhoff, Groningen (1964)
12. Heikkilä, J.: Pattern matching with affine moment descriptors. Pattern Recognit. **37**, 1825–1834 (2004)
13. Hickman, M.S.: Geometric moments and their invariants. J. Math. Imaging Vis. **44**(3), 223–235 (2012)
14. Hilbert, D.: Theory of Algebraic Invariants. Cambridge University Press, Cambridge (1993)
15. Hosny, K.M.: New set of rotationally Legendre moment invariants. Int. J. Electr. Comput. Syst. Eng. **4**(3), 176–180 (2010)
16. Liu, Q., Zhu, H., Li, Q.: Image recognition by affine Tchebichef moment invariants. In: Deng, H., Miao, D., Lei, J., Wang, F.L. (eds.) AICI 2011, Part III. LNCS (LNAI), vol. 7004, pp. 472–480. Springer, Heidelberg (2011). https://doi.org/10.1007/978-3-642-23896-3_58
17. Mei, Y., Androutsos, D.: Robust affine invariant shape image retrieval using the ICA Zernike moment shape descriptor. In: 16th IEEE International Conference on Image Processing (ICIP), pp. 1065–1068, November 2009
18. Pei, S.C., Lin, C.N.: Image normalization for pattern recognition. Image Vis. Comput. **13**(10), 711–723 (1995)
19. Reiss, T.H.: The revised fundamental theorem of moment invariants. IEEE Trans. Pattern Anal. Mach. Intell. **13**(8), 830–834 (1991)

20. Rothe, I., Süsse, H., Voss, K.: The method of normalization to determine invariants. IEEE Trans. Pattern Anal. Mach. Intell. **18**(4), 366–376 (1996)
21. Schur, I.: Vorlesungen über Invariantentheorie. Springer, Berlin (1968). https:// doi.org/10.1007/978-3-642-95032-2. in German
22. Shen, D., Ip, H.H.S.: Generalized affine invariant image normalization. IEEE Trans. Pattern Anal. Mach. Intell. **19**(5), 431–440 (1997)
23. Shen, J.: Orthogonal Gaussian-Hermite moments for image characterization. In: Casasent, D.P. (ed.) Intelligent Robots and Computer Vision XVI: Algorithms, Techniques, Active Vision, and Materials Handling, vol. 3208, pp. 224–233. SPIE (1997)
24. Shen, J., Shen, W., Shen, D.: On geometric and orthogonal moments. Int. J. Pattern Recognit. Artif. Intell. **14**(7), 875–894 (2000)
25. Suk, T., Flusser, J.: Graph method for generating affine moment invariants. In: Proceedings of the 17th International Conference on Pattern Recognition ICPR 2004, pp. 192–195. IEEE Computer Society (2004)
26. Suk, T., Flusser, J.: Affine normalization of symmetric objects. In: Blanc-Talon, J., Philips, W., Popescu, D., Scheunders, P. (eds.) ACIVS 2005. LNCS, vol. 3708, pp. 100–107. Springer, Heidelberg (2005). https://doi.org/10.1007/11558484_13
27. Suk, T., Flusser, J.: Affine moment invariants generated by graph method. Pattern Recognit. **44**(9), 2047–2056 (2011)
28. Sylvester assisted by F. Franklin, J.J.: Tables of the generating functions and groundforms for simultaneous binary quantics of the first four orders taken two and two together. Am. J. Math. **2**, 293–306, 324–329 (1879)
29. Sylvester assisted by F. Franklin, J.J.: Tables of the generating functions and groundforms for the binary quantics of the first ten orders. Am. J. Math. **2**, 223–251 (1879)
30. Yang, B., Dai, M.: Image analysis by Gaussian-Hermite moments. Signal Process. **91**(10), 2290–2303 (2011)
31. Yang, B., Flusser, J., Kautsky, J.: Rotation of 2D orthogonal polynomials. Pattern Recognit. Lett. **102**(1), 44–49 (2018)
32. Yang, B., Flusser, J., Suk, T.: Steerability of Hermite kernel. Int. J. Pattern Recognit. Artif. Intell. **27**(4), 1–25 (2013)
33. Yang, B., Flusser, J., Suk, T.: 3D rotation invariants of Gaussian-Hermite moments. Pattern Recognit. Lett. **54**(1), 18–26 (2015)
34. Yang, B., Flusser, J., Suk, T.: Design of high-order rotation invariants from Gaussian-Hermite moments. Signal Process. **113**(1), 61–67 (2015)
35. Yang, B., Kostková, J., Flusser, J., Suk, T.: Scale invariants from Gaussian-Hermite moments. Signal Process. **132**, 77–84 (2017)
36. Yang, B., Li, G., Zhang, H., Dai, M.: Rotation and translation invariants of Gaussian-Hermite moments. Pattern Recognit. Lett. **32**(2), 1283–1298 (2011)
37. Yap, P.T., Paramesran, R., Ong, S.H.: Image analysis by Krawtchouk moments. IEEE Trans. Image Process. **12**(11), 1367–1377 (2003)
38. Zhang, H., Shu, H., Coatrieux, G., Zhu, J., Wu, J., Zhang, Y., Zhu, H., Luo, L.: Affine Legendre moment invariants for image watermarking robust to geometric distortions. IEEE Trans. Image Process. **20**(8), 2189–2199 (2011)
39. Zhang, Y., Wen, C., Zhang, Y., Soh, Y.C.: On the choice of consistent canonical form during moment normalization. Pattern Recognit. Lett. **24**(16), 3205–3215 (2003)

A Web-Based System to Assess Texture Analysis Methods and Datasets

Alex J. F. Farfán[1], Leonardo F. S. Scabini[2(✉)], and Odemir M. Bruno[2]

[1] Institute of Mathematics and Computer Science, University of São Paulo,
São Carlos, SP, Brazil
[2] São Carlos Institute of Physics, University of São Paulo, São Carlos, SP, Brazil
`scabini@ifsc.usp.br`

Abstract. Texture analysis is an active area of research in computer vision and image processing, being one of the most studied topics for image characterization. When facing with texture analysis in a novel application a researcher needs to evaluate different texture methods and classifiers to verify which are the most suitable for each type of image. This usually leads the researcher to spend time setting code to make comparisons and tests. In this context, we propose a research and collaboration platform for the study, analysis, and comparison of texture descriptors and image datasets. This web-based application eases the creation of experiments in texture analysis that consists of extracting texture features and performing a classification over these features. It has a collection of methods, datasets, and classification algorithms while also allows the user to upload the code of new descriptors, the files of new texture datasets and to perform various tasks over them. Another interesting feature of this application is its interactive confusion matrix in which the researcher can identify correctly and incorrectly classified images.

Keywords: Texture classification · Feature extraction ·
Web-based application

1 Introduction

The scientific community benefits from using web-based tools to study, analyze, and share data coming from texture analysis. A web-based system promotes the research and collaboration among scientists, providing facilities to experiment with new texture descriptors over traditional or new image datasets. Thus, a researcher can modify with ease the settings of an experiment of texture classification, that is, the texture descriptors and its parameters, the image datasets, and the classifiers.

There are examples of web-based systems seeking to help in the analysis of images in fields such as biological, medical, and educational. [4] describes a web application to analyze photomicrographs of protozoan parasites using

© Springer Nature Switzerland AG 2019
M. Vento and G. Percannella (Eds.): CAIP 2019, LNCS 11679, pp. 425–437, 2019.
https://doi.org/10.1007/978-3-030-29891-3_37

morphologic characteristics of shape and texture. [3] presents a web application for image analysis to assist researchers in the analysis of medical image data. [18] proposes a web-based system to analyze images of the vascular structure of the eye fundus because it provides vital information to diagnose retinopathy. [6] presents a tool that helps in the teaching of the undergraduate course of electronics and image processing.

This paper is organized in six sections. Section 2 presents important concepts to understand this paper. Section 3 details the proposal of this paper. Section 4 presents the interfaces of the system. Section 5 presents some experiments made. Section 6 presents the conclusions.

2   Background

Human beings use vision to receive most part of the surrounding information, even 50% of the brain is intended to vision [15]. Almost every daily task we perform relies on our ability to see. Computer vision systems have been focusing on identification tasks in order to reduce or remove the human interference on simple vision tasks. In some cases, an automated system performs much faster than us, for instance when measuring geometric properties of objects such as area, volume, etc.

Among the computer vision research, texture analysis is one of the mostly studied topics for image characterization. Texture is a characteristic present in many images that allows understanding its content. Consequently, texture plays an important role in computer vision and image processing applications. Because of the important role of texture analysis, researchers are continually devising and developing texture descriptors, aiming to improve the modeling of the features of an image. It is important to note that a texture descriptor can perform differently in many image dataset.

The success of a texture descriptor strongly depends on a performance analysis, which also implies making a comparison among techniques. Whenever a researcher devises a texture descriptor or makes an improvement to an existing technique, he or she needs to spend time in literature code to make comparisons and tests, apart from focusing on his own algorithms. Thus, when employing texture analysis to a specific new application, a researcher needs to evaluate different methods for a consistent choice of the best approach.

2.1   Texture Descriptors

Several texture descriptors have been proposed over the years. We considered a initial set of descriptors:

– **DTCWT:** Dual Tree Complex Wavelet Transform [8] consists on finding the directional and spatial/frequency characteristics of the texture patterns. The method works applying a 2D-CWT to decompose an image into 8 subimages. The feature vector is composed of the mean and standard deviations of the L subimages with the largest averaged energies.

- **riu2LBP:** The Local Binary Pattern operator captures local spatial patterns of intensity changes in a neighborhood around a central pixel. A binary value 1 is obtained when a pixel has intensity greater or equal to the central pixel, and 0 otherwise. These values describe the local binary pattern of each pixel, and characterization can be done by computing its histogram [13].
- **LPQ:** This method is robust to image blurring and uses the local phase information extracted using the 2D Fourier transform computed over a rectangular neighborhood around each pixel position [14]. The feature vector is a 256-dimensional histogram of the quantized values that occur along the image.
- **MFS:** Multi Fractal Spectrum [19] is based on the Fractal dimension of the texture. The method computes the fractal dimensions of some categorization of the image, which is the local density function. Then a discretized histogram of densities is computed as the feature vector. This approach is invariant under view-point changes, non-rigid deformations, and local affine illumination.
- **CLBP:** The method is similar to the original LBP, however the local region is represented by its center pixel and a local difference sign-magnitude transform. This transform decomposes the image local structure into two complementary components, the different signs, and magnitudes. Similarly to LBP, this information is coded into binary and its histogram can be computed as feature vector [7].
- **LTP:** Local Ternary Pattern [17] is a generalization of LBP that considers uncontrolled lighting conditions. The LTP descriptors works with 3-valued codes, ternary codes $[-1, 0, 1]$. It uses a threshold t, which is both added and subtracted from the central pixel c, then the ternary code consists on zeros where the neighbor intensity is around $c \pm t$, 1 if it is greater and -1 if it is smaller. For characterization it split the binary codes into positive and negative parts, composing two histograms.
- **LCP:** The Linear Configuration Model [20] works encoding linear relationships among neighboring pixels, exploring local structural information and microscopic configuration information that involves image configuration and pixel-wise interaction relationships.
- **RLBP:** Rotated LBP [12] is a rotation invariant version of LBP. This is achieved by circularly shifting the weights according to the dominant direction in the pixel neighborhood, which is the index of the neighbor whose difference to the central pixel is a maximum.

2.2 Texture Datasets

It is important to evaluate texture descriptors with datasets that include realistic image transformations such as rotation, view-point, scale and illumination changes.

Outex: A framework for texture analysis, designed to test texture classification and segmentation algorithms. It has natural scenes and surface textures captured under variations in terms of illumination direction, surface rotation, and spatial resolution [10]. There are 16 tests suites used for classification. The suite Outex-10 dataset is frequently used to test texture descriptor because contains images rotated at nine angles (0, 5, 10, 15, 30, 45, 60, 75, 90 degrees). Outex-10 is divided in 24 texture classes, with 180 samples per class, making a total of 4320 images.

UIUC: Contains texture surfaces coming from albedo variations, 3D shapes, and a combination of both, captured with uncontrolled lighting conditions. The textures appear with changes in rotation, scale and viewpoint, also present a high intra-class variation [11]. UIUC dataset is divided into 25 classes, with 40 samples per class, making a total of 1000 gray-scale images.

USPTex: Contains a variety of color images of textures found on a daily basis, such as rice, vegetation, clouds, etc. They were captured with a digital camera and divided in non overlapping windows [2]. USPTex dataset is divided into 191 classes, with 12 samples per class, making a total of 2292 texture color images.

Midrib: It was created at the University of São Paulo with the purpose to identify plant species using microscopic images of the cross-sections of leaf midrib. The images were collected at the Cerrado biome in central Brazil [16]. The Midrib is divided into 50 classes (plant species), with a variable number of samples per class, ranging from 10 to 20, in total there are 606 images.

2.3   Classifiers

The choice of classifiers can impact on the final results, as different classification paradigms fit better on specific data. The following classifiers were used due to their performance, computational cost and ease of use.

KNN: The k-nearest neighbors [1] classifier is a supervised method that considers the Euclidean distance between the training and test samples. Given a labeled training set, a new sample with feature vector x is labeled with the predominant label of the k nearest neighbors of x. Most works use KNN with $1 \leq k \leq 3$.

Random Forest: A decision tree is a tree-like structure in which each internal node represents a test on a feature, each branch represents the outcome of the test, and each leaf node represents a class label. A Random Forest classifier is a combination of several tree predictions such that each tree depends on the values of a random vector, sampled independently and with the same distribution for all trees in the forest. Random forests correct the problem of single trees which tends to overfit the training set [9].

Logistic Regression: This is a statistical learning method for classification (not regression!) which relies on the logistic function. The idea consists on fitting a linear model to the feature space. The proposed web system consider a Logistic Regression classifier that builds a multinomial logistic regression model with a ridge estimator [5].

3 Proposed System

3.1 Overview

The application is a research and collaboration tool with the purpose of ease the task of texture classification. The application consists of two main components: the first dedicated to extract texture features from an image dataset, and the second deals with the classification of these features, see Fig. 1. The Feature Extraction component receives as input a texture dataset, a set of images identified with its corresponding classes (or labels), and returns as output a feature file, a set of feature vectors with the labels of the images. The Classification component classifies the data contained in the feature file and returns the classification results. This initial design constitute the basis for the design of the architecture and database of the system.

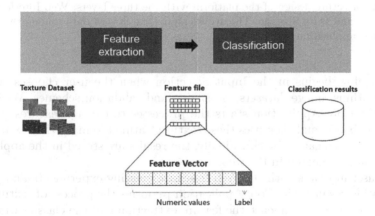

Fig. 1. An overview of the application highlighting the two main components of the platform: Feature extraction and Classification.

3.2 Architecture

The application is based on a three-layer architecture, appropriate for a web application. The layers are the Web Interface, the Core Application, and the Data Storage. Figure 2 depicts the architecture design of the system, it shows the relationships among the components and the flow of data between them.

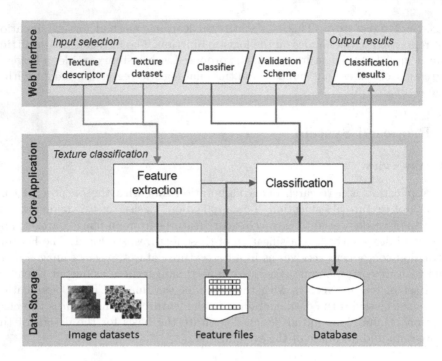

Fig. 2. Architecture design of the platform with the three layers: Web Interface, Core Application, and Data Storage. The arrows signal the flow of data among the components of the application.

The data flow begins in the Input Selection when the user chooses the texture algorithms, image datasets, classifiers, and validation schemes. With these inputs, the Core Application starts the processes to extract features (Feature Extraction block) and then uses these texture features to make the texture classification (Classification block). Finally, the results are stored in the application database and presented in the web.

The user interacts with the Web Interface creating experiments and getting classification results. The Core Application performs the process of texture classification, running in sequence the feature extraction and the classification. The Data Storage stores the data generated by the application, this includes the image datasets, the data of the experiments, the feature files, and the results of the classification.

4   Interfaces

As a web-based application, the application provides a familiar environment to use and share information using a standard browser. The application can be accessed at http://scgcluster.ifsc.usp.br:7000.

The user interacts with the application to make experiments of texture classification, to test new texture descriptors, to classify new texture image datasets, to review classification results, and to interact with the confusion matrix.

4.1   Make Experiments of Texture Classification

To setup an experiment for texture classification the user chooses texture descriptors, image datasets, classifiers, and validation schemes. When choosing texture descriptors the user can enter ranges of values (start, step and stop values) for its parameters.

Figure 3 shows the interface to make an experiment. The interface presents input boxes to select multiples values. In this case, for the feature extraction process, the user selected 1 image dataset (Outex-10), and 1 texture algorithm (CLBP.m) and customized its parameters, the parameter **radius** is set to 2, the parameter **points** has $start = 8$, $step = 4$, and $stop = 17$, so the parameter **points** has three values $\{8, 12, 16\}$. With this setting the user has at once 3 different values for CLBP, that is, $(2, 8)$, $(2, 12)$, and $(2, 16)$. For the classification process, the user selected 3 classifiers (kNN, RandomForest, and Logistic Regression), and 1 validation scheme (10-fold). Thus, at the end of the experiments the user will get 9 classification results, which comes from 3 texture descriptors, 1 dataset, 3 classifiers and 1 validation scheme, that is $3 \times 1 \times 3 \times 1 = 9$.

4.2   Test New Texture Descriptors

The platform allows the uploading of source code to test new texture descriptors. The source code can be in the following programming languages: Matlab, Python

Fig. 3. The interface to make experiments of texture classification. In this case the user has chosen 1 texture descriptor, 1 texture dataset, 3 classifiers and one validation scheme. The user customized the range of values for the parameters of the descriptors.

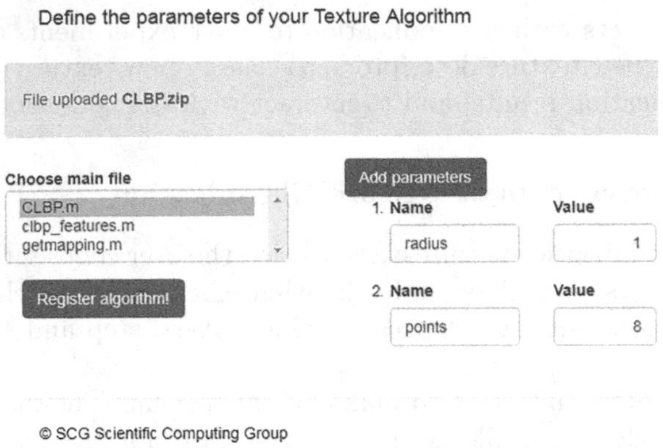

Define the parameters of your Texture Algorithm

File uploaded **CLBP.zip**

Choose main file

CLBP.m
clbp_features.m
getmapping.m

Register algorithm!

Add parameters

1. **Name**   Value

radius   1

2. **Name**   Value

points   8

© SCG Scientific Computing Group

Fig. 4. Interface to define the parameters of a texture descriptor. The user chooses the main file, and specify the name and values of the parameters.

or Java. The descriptors need to meet the following requirements to be used in the platform:

1. **Number and type of parameters.** The algorithm has at least two parameters. The first corresponds to an input image, the second and subsequent are specific to the algorithm.
2. **Type and size of images.** The texture descriptor works with gray scale and color images, when necessary the input image is converted to gray scale. Ideally, there is no restriction in the size of the input images. The algorithm handles the formats *jpg, png, bmp, ras, pnm, and tiff.*
3. **Output of the algorithms.** The output is a set of numbers representing the feature vector of the input image. This feature vector is used to build the feature file that will be used in the step of classification.
4. **Post processing steps.** There are no steps of post-processing, like those aiming to reduce the number of features over the whole set of features.

To upload an algorithm in the platform, the user chooses a file, in this case, a compressed file *CLBP.zip*. After the uploading, the application presents the interface shown in Fig. 4 to define the main file, that is, the entry point for the texture algorithm, and each time the user clicks the button *Add parameters* the interface presents two input boxes to enter the name and the value of a parameter. To register the algorithm in the platform the user clicks in *Register algorithm!*

4.3   Classify New Texture Datasets

Many researchers working in a specific field have their own texture image datasets. The platform provides the option to upload new image datasets. This allows the researcher to classify their image datasets with ready to use texture descriptor.

To be used in the platform, the name of the dataset need to be unique, the allowed file type is a compressed **zip** file, and the texture dataset can be organized in two ways: as a single directory or a root directory with subdirectories. As a single directory, the images have the format *class_sample.extension* to identify the classes and the samples of each class, for example, the filename *D31_08.bmp* represents the class *D*31, and sample 08, with extension *bmp*. As a root directory with subdirectories, the root directory identifies the dataset, the name of each subdirectory identify the classes, and the images inside a subdirectory are the corresponding samples.

4.4 Review Classification Results

To review and examine the classification results, the user enters to the Search interface. The interface is similar to the interface to make an experiment. There are four select boxes to choose among the texture descriptors, texture datasets, classifier, and the value of validation. The classification results are presented as a table, each row contains the following values: Descriptor, Dataset, Classifier, Validation, Accuracy and a link for detailed metrics. The results are presented in descending order according to their accuracy.

4.5 Interact with the Confusion Matrix

A confusion matrix is a tool that helps to visualize the results of a classifier. The application presents an interactive confusion matrix to identify the images correctly classified and those misclassified. It is of size $n \times n$ where n is the number of classes. The rows correspond to the true classes and the columns to the predicted classes. The Fig. 5 corresponds to the confusion matrix for the UIUC dataset using the LPQ descriptor (*LPQdesc.m* in the image) applying the Random Forest classifier. At the top of the image appears a summary of the result of classification. The cells of the diagonal are more bluish indicating a greater number of successes of classification. To interact with the confusion matrix the user can move the mouse over the cells of the matrix, it will appear a description corresponding to the actual class, the predicted class, and the number of instances classifieds. Making a click at a cell in the confusion matrix at the right will appear the correspondent images.

5 Experiments

In order to test the capacities of the application, we made experiments using the texture descriptors, the datasets and the classifiers described in Sect. 2. The following graphics were generated using the application. Figure 6 shows the classification results for the LCP descriptor applied over the UIUC dataset. The *radius* varies from 1 to 5, while the number of *points* stay constant. The Logistic Regression classifier has the best performance when $radius = 3$, and $points = 8$.

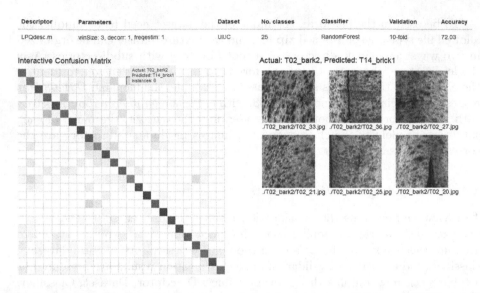

Descriptor	Parameters	Dataset	No. classes	Classifier	Validation	Accuracy
LPQdesc.m	winSize: 3, decorr: 1, freqestim: 1	UIUC	25	RandomForest	10-fold	72.03

Fig. 5. Confusion matrix showing the results of classification of LPQ over UIUC, using RandomForest with 10-fold cross validation. The cell clicked with red border indicates that 6 images were misclassified as *T14_brick1* instead of the actual class *T02_bark2*. The correspondent images appear at the right of the confusion matrix.

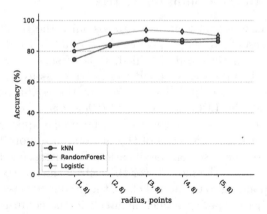

Fig. 6. Classification results for the LCP descriptor in the UIUC dataset, varying the radius and keeping the points constant. The Logistic Regression classifier performs the best when $radius = 3$, and $points = 8$.

It is interesting to note the improvement of the performance of the kNN and RandomForest classifiers when the parameter *radius* increases.

Figure 7 shows the accuracy of the texture descriptors studied applied over the UIUC dataset. In this case the best performance corresponds to the features extracted by CLBP, LCP and Rotated_LBP in order. The classifiers are not shown.

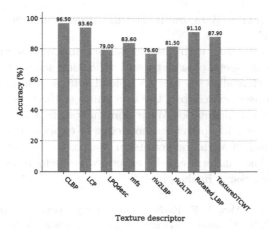

Fig. 7. Best result of classification in the UIUC dataset using the texture methods studied. The features extracted by the CLBP algorithm describes better this dataset.

Figure 8 shows the accuracy in the dataset studied using the texture features obtained by the CLBP descriptor. The accuracy is over 90% in benchmark datasets Outex-10, UIUC and USPTex, and over 89% in the more challenging dataset Midrib.

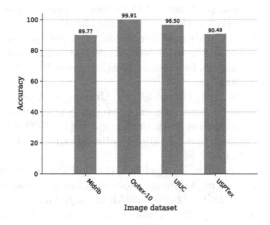

Fig. 8. Best result of classification of the CLB descriptor in the four datasets studied.

6   Conclusions

In this paper we propose a web-based system that provides a friendly environment to perform texture analysis experiments. The proposed platform is a collaboration and research tool for texture analysis. It also has the intent to promote access to texture data, methods and datasets and encourage collaboration among researchers.

The researcher can assess with ease the performance of different texture methods using different datasets, classifiers, and validation schemes. This is the first web-based system that allows a user to upload source code of new descriptors and new image datasets. Therefore, the user can test their own new descriptors with existing texture benchmarks. With domain-specific datasets, the platform can give insights that add up to the knowledge of experts in a field. Moreover, it is possible to interact with the confusion matrix to effectively discover misclassified images. The platform can be extended to include steps of image and classification preprocessing in the pipeline.

Acknowledgements. Alex J. F. Farfán acknowledges support from CNPq (Grant number #160871/2015-8) and CAPES (Grant number #PROEX-9527567/D). Leonardo F. S. Scabini acknowledges support from CNPq (Grant number #142438/2018-9). Odemir M. Bruno acknowledges support from CNPq (Grant #307797/2014-7 and Grant #484312/2013-8) and FAPESP (grant #14/08026-1 and #16/18809-9).

References

1. Aha, D., Kibler, D.: Instance-based learning algorithms. Mach. Learn. **6**, 37–66 (1991)
2. Backes, A.R., Casanova, D., Bruno, O.M.: Color texture analysis based on fractal descriptors. Pattern Recogn. **45**(5), 1984–1992 (2012)
3. Barnathan, M., Zhang, J., Megalooikonomou, V.: A web-accessible framework for the automated storage and texture analysis of biomedical images. In: 5th IEEE International Symposium on Biomedical Imaging: From Nano to Macro, ISBI 2008, pp. 257–259. IEEE (2008)
4. Castañón, C.A., Fraga, J.S., Fernandez, S., Gruber, A., Costa, L.d.F.: Biological shape characterization for automatic image recognition and diagnosis of protozoan parasites of the genus Eimeria. Pattern Recogn. **40**(7), 1899–1910 (2007)
5. le Cessie, S., van Houwelingen, J.: Ridge estimators in logistic regression. Appl. Stat. **41**(1), 191–201 (1992)
6. Garcia, I., Guzmán-Ramírez, E., Pacheco, C.: ColFDImap: a web-based tool for teaching of FPGA-based digital image processing in undergraduate courses. Comput. Appl. Eng. Educ. **23**(1), 92–108 (2015). https://doi.org/10.1002/cae.21581
7. Guo, Z., Zhang, L., Zhang, D.: A completed modeling of local binary pattern operator for texture classification. IEEE Trans. Image Process. **19**(6), 1657–1663 (2010)
8. Hatipoglu, S., Mitra, S.K., Kingsbury, N.: Texture classification using dual-tree complex wavelet transform (1999)
9. Ho, T.K.: Random decision forests. In: Proceedings of the Third International Conference on Document Analysis and Recognition, vol. 1, pp. 278–282. IEEE (1995)
10. Hossain, S., Serikawa, S.: Texture databases - a comprehensive survey. Pattern Recogn. Lett. **34**(15), 2007–2022 (2013). Smart Approaches for Human Action Recognition

11. Lazebnik, S., Schmid, C., Ponce, J.: A sparse texture representation using local affine regions. IEEE Trans. Pattern Anal. Mach. Intell. **27**(8), 1265–1278 (2005). https://doi.org/10.1109/TPAMI.2005.151

12. Mehta, R., Egiazarian, K.O.: Rotated local binary pattern (RLBP)-rotation invariant texture descriptor. In: ICPRAM, pp. 497–502 (2013)

13. Ojala, T., Pietikäinen, M., Mäenpää, T.: Multiresolution gray-scale and rotation invariant texture classification with local binary patterns. IEEE Trans. Pattern Anal. Mach. Intell. **24**(7), 971–987 (2002)

14. Ojansivu, V., Heikkilä, J.: Blur insensitive texture classification using local phase quantization. In: Elmoataz, A., Lezoray, O., Nouboud, F., Mammass, D. (eds.) ICISP 2008. LNCS, vol. 5099, pp. 236–243. Springer, Heidelberg (2008). https://doi.org/10.1007/978-3-540-69905-7_27

15. Pietikäinen, M., Hadid, A., Zhao, G., Ahonen, T.: Computer Vision Using Local Binary Patterns, vol. 40. Springer, London (2011). https://doi.org/10.1007/978-0-85729-748-8

16. da Silva, N.R., Batista Florindo, J., Gómez, M.C., Rossatto, D.R., Kolb, R.M., Bruno, O.M.: Plant identification based on leaf midrib cross-section images using fractal descriptors. Plos One **10**, e0130014 (2015)

17. Tan, X., Triggs, B.: Enhanced local texture feature sets for face recognition under difficult lighting conditions. IEEE Trans. Image Process. **19**(6), 1635–1650 (2010)

18. Tramontan, L., Poletti, E., Fiorin, D., Ruggeri, A.: A web-based system for the quantitative and reproducible assessment of clinical indexes from the retinal vasculature. IEEE Trans. Biomed. Eng. **58**(3), 818–821 (2011). https://doi.org/10.1109/TBME.2010.2085001

19. Xu, Y., Ji, H., Fermüller, C.: Viewpoint invariant texture description using fractal analysis. Int. J. Comput. Vis. **83**(1), 85–100 (2009)

20. Yimo Guo, G.Z., Pietikäinen, M.: Texture classification using a linear configuration model based descriptor. In: Proceedings of the British Machine Vision Conference, pp. 119.1–119.10. BMVA Press (2011). https://doi.org/10.5244/C.25.119

TRINet: Tracking and Re-identification Network for Multiple Targets in Egocentric Videos Using LSTMs

Jyoti Nigam[✉] and Renu M. Rameshan

Indian Institute of Technology, Mandi, H.P., India
jyoti_nigam@students.iitmandi.ac.in, renumr@iitmandi.ac.in

Abstract. We present a recurrent network based novel framework for tracking and re-identifying multiple targets in first-person perspective. Even though LSTMs can act as a sequence classifier, most of the previous works in multi target tracking use their output with some distance metric for data association. In this work, we employ an LSTM as a classifier and train it over the memory cells output vectors corresponding to different targets obtained from another LSTM. This classifier, based on appearance and motion features, discriminates the targets in two consecutive frames as well as re-identify them in a time interval. We integrate this classifier as an additional block in a detection free tracking architecture which enhances the performance in terms of re-identification of targets and also indicates the absence of targets. We propose a dataset of *twenty* egocentric videos containing multiple targets to validate our approach.

Keywords: Re-identification · LSTM · Sequence classification · Cells output vector

1 Introduction

Multiple target tracking is a key element for many computer vision tasks, such as group activity recognition, surveillance, and social gathering analysis. In this task a tracker locates all targets of interest in a video and maintains their identities over time. There are two broad categories of multi-target tracking, (i) detection based and (ii) detection free tracking. In the latter, the tracker starts with a certain number of targets and tracks them in subsequent frames. In general these trackers keep predicting the location of bounding boxes even when the target leaves the frame (it may be noted that this behavior can be controlled by considering the score values or an equivalent metric). However in detection based tracking the number of targets can vary between frames, thus requiring

This publication is an outcome of the R & D work undertaken project under the Visvesvaraya PhD Scheme of Ministry of Electronics and Information Technology, Government of India, being implemented by Digital India Corporation.

M. Vento and G. Percannella (Eds.): CAIP 2019, LNCS 11679, pp. 438–448, 2019.
https://doi.org/10.1007/978-3-030-29891-3_38

detections at each frame. In this paper we propose a tracking strategy which includes the advantages from both the mentioned strategies.

Use of deep learning techniques has advanced research in computer vision tremendously in recent years. In-spite of this we found only limited work related to multi-target tracking. The main difficulty is due to the lack of annotated data for training as deep neural networks require massive amount of data for training. In this direction there are two works which exploit ImageNet [4] annotated dataset as well as synthetic data for tracking. The first work by Anton et al. [3] addresses the problem of data association and trajectory estimation by a deep neural network. For pedestrian tracking only limited annotated data is available hence the authors opted for a synthetic generation model learned from real data. They employ recurrent neural networks (RNNs) for predicting target locations and long short term memory (LSTM) for data association. This work shows only satisfactory result on MOT Challenge dataset [14], and it also depends on the available detections at each frame.

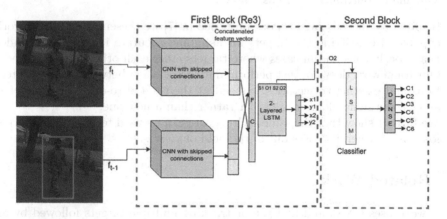

Fig. 1. Overview: consecutive cropped images are fed to the first block of the network architecture. The output of convolutional layers is propagated to LSTM to predict the location of target in the current frame. Input for LSTM in second block is the cells output vector $O_2 \in \mathcal{R}^{1024}$ of LSTM in the first block. The last layer of the network classifies the input sequence to assign identity to the target along with the prediction of presence/absence.

The algorithm proposed in [7] does not depend on detections at each frame but tracks a given number of targets throughout the video. It uses a recurrent neural network to track different objects in various natural situations and scenes. The authors propose a training methodology for a recurrent tracking network which translates the image embedding into the location coordinates while at the same time updates the internal appearance and motion model. Due to detection free approach the tracker keeps predicting the target location in its absence also. Our proposed method addresses this problem and predicts the loss of target without utilizing the detections.

Although there have been substantial advances in recent years, tracking with re-identification is still a challenging task. The term re-identification often comes in multi-target multi-camera scenario, where a particular target is being tracked in different video streams captured from a camera network. As a target may be captured from different cameras at different time stamps, each camera should depict that target as same person. We consider the problem of tracking a given number of targets in an egocentric video of social interaction which can be compared to multi camera case due to the following: the natural head motion of wearer and closeness of targets leads to the targets leaving the field of view of camera and re-entering at a later time. When a target re-enters the field of view it is not known whether it is a new target or one which was already seen. This demands re-identification of the target. In [15], the authors address similar problem but for a single target. Our proposed architecture addresses this issue along with the tracking of multiple targets. The overview of this architecture is shown in Fig. 1.

Our main contributions are as follows:

- Inspired by the existing network proposed in [7] we present a LSTM network capable of classifying the targets for assigning accurate identity even under heavy occlusions and in cases where targets cross each other.
- Our framework does not just perform data association between current detections and existing trajectories. Instead at the time of re-entry of a target it assigns the same identity as earlier rather than a new one.
- We further show that the same architecture can be used to predict the target loss event (when it moves out of the field of view).

2   Related Work

This work uses CNNs and LSTMs for tracking multiple targets followed by an additional LSTMs as classifier to re-identify the targets. We review the related work in two aspects: deep learning based multi-target tracking and person re-identification.

2.1   Deep Learning Based Multi-target Tracking

Multi-target tracking has been explored in great depth by computer vision community. Kitti [1], a benchmark suite for vision and robotics, performs on cars and people tracking. Earlier tracking approaches were based on CNNs and due to offline training they can handle only predefined object classes, *e.g.*, pedestrian, [2,9]. The method proposed in algorithm [7] exploit huge amount of visual tracking data to pre-train a CNN and acquire effective representations.

Though CNNs provide state-of-the-art results in tracking they are restrictive in their output pattern. As opposed to this, recurrent neural networks (RNNs) [6] offer a recursive relation between its input and output. This not only enables simulating a memory effect, but also allows for mapping input sequences to arbitrary output sequences, as long as the sequence alignment and the input and output dimensions are known in advance. In [3], the authors use RNN-based approach to learn trajectory predictions and an LSTM network to learn data association. The one-to-one assignment is done by computing Euclidean distance between LSTM state vectors whereas in the proposed method the LSTM cells output vectors are being classified to predict the target identity. Furthermore, in the proposed method in the absence of any target the trajectory is paused instead of being terminated as there is a scope of re-entry of any target. To the best of our knowledge, the output vectors of LSTM cells are used for the first time to classify targets in real-world videos.

2.2 Person Re-identification

In person re-identification, one can focus on two key-points: feature extraction and metric learning. In [18], methods like Boosting [8], Rank SVM [16], PLS [16] and metric learning [12,19] were used on the extracted features and they were found to be more discriminative compared with standard distance measures i.e. ℓ_1, ℓ_2 norm. In [18], a siamese neural network is proposed which differs from conventional neural networks, as this architecture consists two subnetworks sharing the same parameters. In general a siamese network is used to evaluate the similarity of two signature samples and in [17], it is used for verifying faces. The objective function used in siamese guides the end-to-end neural network to learn an optimal metric towards discriminating targets automatically. Note that this network uses only static features extracted from a CNN. We propose to use dynamic features in addition to the static ones, which helps in re-identification.

Our work is motivated by the recent success of RNNs and their application to language modeling [13]. Although we use LSTMs for location predictions, our method is substantially different from existing tracker [7] because we use the LSTM cells output values as a sequence to predict the target loss along with re-identifying these targets.

3   Proposed Method

The proposed tracking architecture, shown in Fig. 1, contains two blocks where the first block, taken from Re3 network [7], predicts the location of targets in upcoming frame and second block classifies the targets as well as predict the target absence. Although we follow the detection free tracking method, a detector [10] is used at every *tenth* frame to check for the target re-entry. In our experiments the videos are captured at 30 FPS with the image size of 720×1280 (height × width). We observe that the width of the bounding box of pedestrians ranges between 100 to 300 pixels and the events of leaving and re-entering the field of view are not single frame events, it takes $5-15$ number of frames. In a social gathering video the individual velocities are quite less. In the recording set up the distance between camera wearer and targets varied in the range of 1 to 10 m. A rough calculation shows that choosing to run a detector after every *ten* frames more or less captures target re-entry (this is only a rough calculation, and can lead to target not being tracked in certain cases).

The first block consists of convolutional layers to represent the target appearance, recurrent layers to memorize motion and appearance information, followed by a regression layer to generate the target location. The second block accepts the output vectors from the memory cells of LSTM of first block and trains a recurrent layer over them to abstract the target identity by exploring the ordered patterns of memory cells vectors corresponding to different targets. This is the dynamic feature as the LSTM cells values change at each time stamps according to the varying targets. The last layer is the classification layer which assigns identities to targets. We train the recurrent network of second block on real first-person videos of group formation. At test time, unlike Re3 [7], we do not rely on the predictions of first block; instead we check the output vector of first LSTM to predict the target identity or absence.

Network Input: At every frame, similar to [7], we feed the first block of network a pair of cropped image sequence. The first crop is centered at x_i^{t-1}, y_i^{t-1} (i^{th} target location) in the previous image f_{t-1}, whereas the second crop is in the same location, but in the current image f_t. Each cropped image is padded to be twice the size of the target's bounding box to provide context to the network. These crops are warped to be 227×227 pixels prior to be fed into the network. The second block connects with the first one at the recurrent layer cells output. At this position we obtain four memory cells vectors $s_1, o_1, s_2, o_2 \in \mathcal{R}^{1024}$ from 2–layered LSTM (s_1, o_1 from first layer and s_2, o_2 from second layer). We consider the final output vector o_2 as the sequential pattern representing one target (Fig. 2).

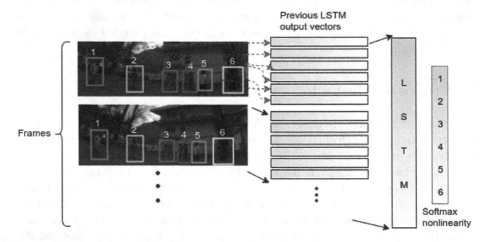

Fig. 2. Training procedure of LSTM classifier (second block). The ground truth is sequence obtained from cell gate values while tracking the targets along with their identities.

3.1   LSTMs as Sequence Classifier

Sequence classification involves predicting a class label for a given input sequence. In this section, we describe an LSTM-based network that learns the classification of targets from training data. An LSTM uses its memory cells to memorize long-range information and in tracking procedure it keeps track of moving pattern and varying features of a target. The activations of these cells are stored in the recurrent parameters of the network which can hold long-range temporal information.

Cell Output as Target Specific Sequence: In [11], it is proposed that in LSTMs different cells turn on to remember different types of information. Since in [7], a single LSTM is used for tracking multiple targets, in this experiment we exploit the values of multiple cells as a sequence to denote a specific target. Though, a sequence is being generated at a single time stamp we observe the on/off pattern of the cells across sequences to identify a target (different cells act as indicators for different targets).

Unrolling During Training: We consider a 1024–dimensional sequence (o_2) of LSTM output values from the first block of the proposed architecture corresponding to each target. This sequence is fed as input to the LSTM of the next block with the ground truth of class label. To learn the specific acting pattern of memory cells, the classifier LSTM look back through entire sequence of 1024 size.

3.2   Training Methodology

We use LSTM cells output vectors generated by Re^3 [7] (first block) over first-person videos to train our LSTM classifier (second block). The initial 200 frames from all *twenty* videos are considered where all the *six* targets are present throughout. Altogether we train our network on 24,000 number of different samples. Since in training we involve the initial frames which are captured during initial stage of group formation, the targets are at sufficient distance and do not occlude each other. This results in proper training data *i.e.* sequences with correct class labels. Once we initiate the tracker, we give the initial bounding boxes for each target with an identity and the tracker keeps following them further. These identities are being concatenated with the LSTM cells output sequences as class labels. These concatenated sequences are shown to LSTM for training and enable it to discriminate these sequences. The 25% of training data is split as validation set. The categorical cross entropy loss is used with softmax nonlinearity at the final layer. The number of neurons at the last layer are decided by considering the number of different targets throughout the videos. We label a target across different videos with the same identity while initializing the tracking procedure.

Network Output: The output of first block is, x_1, y_1, x_2, and y_2, the predicted coordinates of the target. The same LSTM predicts the locations for all input targets sequentially. The next block receives a 1024–dimensional LSTM cells

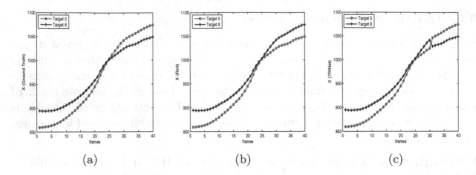

(a)   (b)   (c)

Fig. 3. The plots are showing robustness to identity switching between target 5 and 6, (a) ground truth, (b) Re3 results, and (c) TRINet results. The x coordinates are shown for *forty* frames of video-8. Near the 25th frame the targets cross each other and their identities are swapped by Re3 tracker whereas TRINet corrects the switch in 5 frames.

output vector as a sequence and predicts the class *i.e.* identity of the target. In the case, target leaves the field of view, the input sequence does not belong to any class and the prediction probability remains low for each class and we infer the absence of the target.

Tracking at Test Time: The remaining frames from each video are used for testing. In first frame of testing data we provide the locations of bounding boxes with the same identities of targets as defined in training procedure. As soon as the first block predicts the location of these targets the LSTM classifier of second block looks at the LSTM cells output sequences and predicts the classes or absence of targets.

(a)   (b)   (c)   (d)

Fig. 4. The images show the need of re-identification of a target within a video.

4   Experiments and Results

The proposed method, TRINet, is compared with Re3 [7] tracking method on the proposed dataset in aspects of overall performance, robustness to occlusion, and in the case of target loss and re-entry.

Implementation Details: We employ Keras and Tensorflow [5] (at back end) for training our LSTM classifier of second block. The LSTM model constitutes of a single layer with 256 cell units with 0.2 dropout. The ADAM gradient optimizer is used with the default momentum and learning rate of 10^{-5}. We set the batch size to 32 as in Re3, at the time of testing they update the LSTM states at every 32 number of time stamps. Hence, this setting allow us to capture a continuous flow of LSTM cells output vectors. We use categorical cross entropy loss for training which goes down till 0.0002 value in 500 number of epochs. All training and testing were carried out using a Nvidia 1080 Txi GPU @ 2.20 GHz.

Proposed Dataset: To validate our proposed approach we generate *twenty* egocentric videos where the first-person is surrounded by some targets (called agents as they perform an action of group formation). Initially they all were scattered randomly and then they start moving to form a group. Apart from first-person there are six different agents. The number of frames varies from 600 to 1000 in these videos, which results in a significant training as well as testing data for each class. In our choreographed videos, towards the ending frames eventually the targets form the groups and due to proximity they start merge and split (one target occluding another completely for few frames and then moving apart). In addition to this, due to head motion of first-person few targets start leaving the field of view and re-entering in subsequent frames. The merge and split and re-entry of targets make these videos more challenging in the aspect of preserving the same identity.

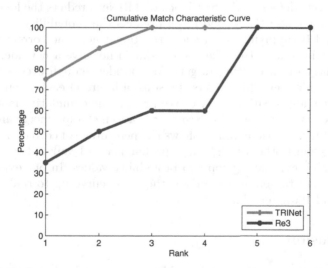

Fig. 5. Cumulative match characteristic (CMC) curve up to rank 6 to compare TRINet and Re3.

Robustness to Identity Switching: We present results to show that the TRINet performs significantly better during merge and split of targets. In the case when a target crosses another target their bounding boxes get same features and when they move apart the existing trackers get confused and their identities get swapped. However, TRINet looks at the recurrent features coming from the bounding boxes and classifies them accordingly. Note that without demanding the detections at every frame TRINet predicts the correct class of target and prevent the tracker from incorrect identity assignments while tracking. For instance, in video number 8 from frame number 260 to 300, two targets with identities *five* and *six* cross each other. Fig. 3 shows the tracking results for these *two* targets where the values of x-coordinates (reflect the merge and split process) at each frame are plotted. Here, the identities of targets are represented by different colors and patterns. It is evident from these plots the TRINet predicts the identities close to ground truth.

Re-identification of Targets: Generally, a person re-identification system maintains a gallery of subject/target images for matching with probe/query image. Whereas in our proposed method different cells of a single LSTM encapsulate the appearance and motion information of different targets which is useful for re-identifying a target. The importance of re-identification of a target in first-person videos can be seen through the sub figures of Fig. 4. Here, the sample images at different time stamps for target 6 from video 3 are shown. We first describe our re-identification method: we apply the face detector at every *tenth* frame for including the lost targets and resume their tracking. As soon as a new target gets detected, the first block of TRINet predicts the location in the consecutive frame and the second block predicts the probability values against each class and by applying the *argmax* the target gets the correct class label. In this way it is assured that the tracker should not give a new identity at the time of re-entry of an existing target. We consider enough events to evaluate situations in which multiple targets (persons of interest) each re-enters once or multiple time stamps within a video. We present the cumulative match characteristic (CMC) curve in Fig. 5 for *twenty six* cases including merge and split and re-entering of targets. Here, rank 1 shows the percentage of correct match for the given target against others with highest probability and rank 2 shows percentage of correct match considering top two probability values. In our experiment we have *six* different targets so we present the CMC curve up to rank 6 and after rank 2 we find 100% matching.

5   Conclusion

In this work, we focus on the use of LSTMs as sequence classifier to re-identify the targets in multi-target tracking. We conclude that the appearance and motion features extracted by one LSTM internal states can be used effectively to train another LSTM to discriminate the targets. In general re-identification methods maintain a gallery set for matching but this type of learning offers a gallery free re-identification as a single LSTM keeps information about all the targets.

We observe significant gain in tracking performance of a detection free tracker by adding an extra classifier which guides it in re-identifying the lost targets and in pausing the location predictions in the absence of targets.

References

1. Bernardin, K., Stiefelhagen, R.: Evaluating multiple object tracking performance: the clear mot metrics. J. Image Video Process. **2008**, 1 (2008)
2. Bertinetto, L., Valmadre, J., Henriques, J.F., Vedaldi, A., Torr, P.H.S.: Fully-convolutional Siamese networks for object tracking. In: Hua, G., Jégou, H. (eds.) ECCV 2016. LNCS, vol. 9914, pp. 850–865. Springer, Cham (2016). https://doi.org/10.1007/978-3-319-48881-3_56
3. Chen, L., Ai, H., Shang, C., Zhuang, Z., Bai, B..: Online multi-object tracking with convolutional neural networks. In: ICIP (2017)
4. Deng, J., Dong, W., Socher, R., Li, L.J., Li, K., Fei-Fei, L.: ImageNet: a large-scale hierarchical image database. In: CVPR (2009)
5. Girija, S.S.: TensorFlow: large-scale machine learning on heterogeneous distributed systems (2016). Software tensorflow.org
6. Goller, C., Kuchler, A.: Learning task-dependent distributed representations by backpropagation through structure. In: Proceedings of International Conference on Neural Networks (ICNN 1996), vol. 1, pp. 347–352. IEEE (1996)
7. Gordon, D., Farhadi, A., Fox, D.: Re3: real-time recurrent regression networks for object tracking. arXiv preprint arXiv:1705.06368, 3 (2017)
8. Gray, D., Tao, H.: Viewpoint invariant pedestrian recognition with an ensemble of localized features. In: Forsyth, D., Torr, P., Zisserman, A. (eds.) ECCV 2008. LNCS, vol. 5302, pp. 262–275. Springer, Heidelberg (2008). https://doi.org/10.1007/978-3-540-88682-2_21
9. Held, D., Thrun, S., Savarese, S.: Learning to track at 100 fps with deep regression networks. In: Leibe, B., Matas, J., Sebe, N., Welling, M. (eds.) ECCV 2016. LNCS, vol. 9905, pp. 749–765. Springer, Cham (2016). https://doi.org/10.1007/978-3-319-46448-0_45
10. Hu, P., Ramanan, D.: Finding tiny faces. In: Proceedings of the IEEE Conference on Computer Vision and Pattern Recognition, pp. 951–959 (2017)
11. Karpathy, A., Johnson, J., Fei-Fei, L.: Visualizing and understanding recurrent networks. arXiv preprint arXiv:1506.02078 (2015)
12. Koestinger, M., Hirzer, M., Wohlhart, P., Roth, P.M., Bischof, H.: Large scale metric learning from equivalence constraints. In: 2012 IEEE Conference on Computer Vision and Pattern Recognition, pp. 2288–2295. IEEE (2012)
13. Mikolov, T., Karafiát, M., Burget, L., Černockỳ, J., Khudanpur, S.: Recurrent neural network based language model. In: Eleventh Annual Conference of the International Speech Communication Association (2010)
14. Milan, A., Leal-Taixé, L., Reid, I.D., Roth, S., Schindler, K.: MOT16: a benchmark for multi-object tracking. CoRR abs/1603.00831 (2016). http://arxiv.org/abs/1603.00831
15. Nigam, J., Rameshan, R.M.: EgoTracker: pedestrian tracking with re-identification in egocentric videos. In: Proceedings of the IEEE Conference on Computer Vision and Pattern Recognition Workshops, pp. 40–47 (2017)
16. Prosser, B.J., Zheng, W.S., Gong, S., Xiang, T., Mary, Q.: Person re-identification by support vector ranking. In: BMVC, vol. 2, p. 6 (2010)

17. Schroff, F., Kalenichenko, D., Philbin, J.: FaceNet: a unified embedding for face recognition and clustering. In: Proceedings of the IEEE Conference on Computer Vision and Pattern Recognition, pp. 815–823 (2015)
18. Yi, D., Lei, Z., Liao, S., Li, S.Z.: Deep metric learning for person re-identification. In: 2014 22nd International Conference on Pattern Recognition, pp. 34–39, August 2014. https://doi.org/10.1109/ICPR.2014.16
19. Zheng, W.S., Gong, S., Xiang, T.: Reidentification by relative distance comparison. IEEE Trans. Pattern Anal. Mach. Intell. **35**(3), 653–668 (2013)

Digital Signature Based Control Integrity for JPEG HDR Images

Meha Hachani[✉] and Azza Ouled Zaid[✉]

SysCom Laboratory, National Engineering School of Tunis, University of Tunis el Manar, B.P.37, le Belvedere, 1002 Tunis, Tunisia
meha.hachani@isi.utm.tn, azza.ouledzaid@isi.rnu.tn

Abstract. *"A ship is always safe at the shore, but that is not what it is built for."*-Albert Einstein. The same philosophy is applied to picture files saved safety on storage devices. This is, however, not always the case. Sharing and exchanging image data through computer networks affect their security. The issue that arises is how to protect these visual contents from malicious attacks. To alleviate this problem, an image verification feature can be exploited to automatically verify the integrity of these contents. In this way, users can detect any intentional corruptions, which can occur at any time during transmission.

In the present work, we propose a selective authentication system adapted to HDR images. The main contribution consists in verifying the integrity of several parts from JPEG-HDR files by using a content-based watermarking method. Specifically, a couple of local digital thumbprint and digital signature is calculated based on the *SHA-2(256 bits)* secure hash algorithm. Then, a verification process is performed by using two different secret keys (private and public *RSA* keys). Our HDR image verification scheme is applied in the DCT transform domain and maintains backwards compatibility with the legacy JPEG standard. A performance analysis and comparison with related work demonstrate the effectiveness of the proposed approach.

Keywords: Integrity verification · JPEG-HDR images ·
SHA-256-bits hash algorithm · Secret keys

1 Introduction

In the field of computer networks, cryptography and cryptanalysis are two inter-related issues that provide means of ensuring authentication, confidentiality and integrity of data shared between actors. Security of data transmissions aims to prevent a third party from exploiting confidential data. This is by enabling a variety of security services such as confidentiality, integrity verification, source authentication or conditional access.

Today, High Dynamic Range (HDR) [6] imaging is an increasingly approved issue and has been the main focus in serval research areas. In fact, the wide

M. Vento and G. Percannella (Eds.): CAIP 2019, LNCS 11679, pp. 449–458, 2019.
https://doi.org/10.1007/978-3-030-29891-3_39

spread use of HDR content in multimedia applications, makes the exchange of HDR images a common practice. However, the global information sharing offered by omnipresent computer networks has caused a multitude of security threats that may affect the privacy protection. Consequently, the development of security services, for protecting HDR image access and distribution is becoming a matter of necessity. On the other hand, JPEG [5] is recognized to be the most popular image format which has been retained for image storage an displaying via smart phones, digital cameras, and computers. For these reasons, JPEG encoder has been extended to JPEG-HDR in order to compress HDR images.

Among the security tools, ones stand out the integrity verification in the image content. Some research studied were focused on watermarking based integrity control systems to protect JPEG-HDR images. Among these, the method presented in [4] propose to apply a tone mapping operator (TMO) on the HDR image. Then, perform the cryptographic hash to check the integrity of the obtained LDR image, in the discrete cosine transform (DCT) domain.

The main objective of this work is to verify if the JPEG-HDR content has not been modified in an unauthorized manner. To this end, we proposed to incorporate an integrity verification scheme into JPEG-HDR coding scheme. The proposed verification method performs in the frequency domain by using an hash algorithm. The key feature of the proposed solution is to check the integrity of several selected parts from JPEG-HDR image, while maintaining backwards and forward compatibility with JPEG coding technologies.

The rest of this paper is organized as follows. In Sect. 2, we present same existing studies conducted on the discussed field. In Sect. 3, we describe in detail the various blocks constituting our watermarking based integrity control scheme. In Sect. 4, we investigate the performance of the proposed system. Finally, in Sect. 5, we conclude with our final remarks.

2   Related Work

A variety of research studies have been carried out in literature to address the high demand on privacy [13,14,17,18] and security services [15,16] for image data sharing. Most solutions, involve standard digital signatures such as signed cryptographic hashes of the image content. Upon verification, these solutions yield a binary decision regarding image authenticity. On the other hand, several popular algorithms are based on simple statistical features such as histogram and moments, statistics of low-level quantization or random projection and quantization. In this context, Lin and Chang [2] proposed to adapt an old and popular robust authentication approach to JPEG images. Their method explores invariance of inter-block relations between pairs of DCT coefficients. A sequence of hash values are calculated for randomly choose block pairs. This sequence of features is encrypted using an asymmetric cipher. Recently, an image authentication scheme has been developed by Yan and Pan [1]. It consists in generating a couple of global and local hashes. This method is based on binary ranking signatures and performs multi-scale analysis of hash difference maps. In order to improve localization performance, the authors proposed to combine local and global signatures. Authors in [4] developed an integrity verification scheme, based on secret key image watermarking, to detect any change in JPEG-HDR files. Their method is based on A cryptographic hash algorithm that extracts a secure signature from pixel blocks. The verification procedure consists in comparing signatures. More recently, authors in [3] designed a new watermarking-based integrity control system for authenticating JPEG images. The proposed method is performed on the quantized DCT coefficients while determining the locations of the embedded watermark bits. Authors [3] proposed to extend the LSB plane to the higher bit planes according to the magnitudes of the DCT coefficients in order to find more flexible places to embed the watermark.

3   Proposed Method

JPEG-HDR is a lossy HDR compression scheme and is the pioneer backwards-compatible extension to the standard JPEG. After a tone mapping process, a color transformation is applied on the obtained LDR image followed by a DCT transformation. A residual data stored as an additional information into JPEG bitstream. This allows to render a tone-mapped version using any conventional JPEG decoder. For more detail about JPEG-HDR coding mechanism the reader can refer to [6]. The main contribution of our work is to propose an integrity verification system in conjunction with JPEG-HDR engine. The integrity control process is based on the secure hash algorithm SHA-2 [7] described subsequently in the next subsections. Mainly, the proposed system is parsed into three steps; First a RSA-key and a thumbprint (hash values) of the whole image are calculated. After that, the input HDR image is split into 32×32 blocks. For each block, a signature is computed according to the SHA-2 [7] thumbprint. Finally a signature verification step is performed by comparing the original thumbprint and the extracted one for each block of the image.

3.1   Thumbprint and Signature Calculation

An $n - bit$ hash is a shift from message of arbitrary length to $n - bit$ hash values. Particularly, hash functions are effective cryptographic primitives used for digital signatures and password protection. The secure hash algorithm SHA-2 [7] is a $256 - bit$ cryptographic hash function. It consists in providing 128 $bits$ for security against collision attacks. An arbitrary length message can be hashed using SHA-2 [7] algorithm by padding with its length so that the outcome corresponds to a multiple of 256 $bits$. long. Then the latter, will be splitted into a set of 256 bit word blocks $M^{(1)}, M^{(2)}, ..., M^{(N)}$. These word blocks are processed one at a time: Starting with a defined initial hash value $H(0)$, sequentially compute (Fig. 1):

$$H^i = H^{i-1} + C_{M(i)}(H^{i-1}); \tag{1}$$

with C is the SHA-256 [7] compression function and $+$ means word-wise mod 2^{32} addition. $H^{(N)}$ is the hash of M. The SHA-256 [7] compression function

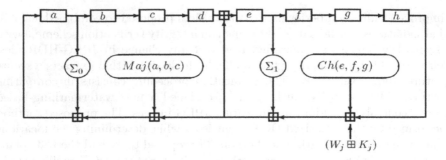

Fig. 1. j^{th} inner stage of the SHA-256 compression function C.

is represented as follows: The watermark based verification procedure is performed in the DCT domain. Specifically, after performing the tone mapping step on the HDR image, the obtained color LDR image (which represented in the RGB format) is converted into the equivalent luminance and chrominance images (Y, U, and V). The watermark is then inserted in the luminance Y image. Its is worth noting that the watermark based verification mechanism is essentially based on SHA-2 hash and RSA [8] asymmetric encryption algorithms. Therefore, we are required to determine a couple of secret key (public and private key) generated by RSA algorithm. According to SHA principal, each image data has its own unique identifier called *thumbprint*, which will be used in order to sign high data volume. Consequently, a secure hash function is applied to the whole image data. The obtained hash values or *thumbprint* are used in conjunction with the private key to compute a digital signature for each block of 32×32 samples. This step is considered as an encryption process and consists in hiding the calculated signatures into each block of the tone-mapped HDR image. To verify the signature, a decryption process is performed using the public key and the original thumbprint. The block diagram of the proposed control integrity scheme is depicted in Fig. 2. Our HDR image verification scheme is applied in the DCT transform domain and maintains backwards compatibility with the legacy JPEG standard. Figure 3, shows the legacy JPEG HDR compression scheme including our watermarking process.

3.2   Signature Verification

The verification procedure is performed at the receiver side. To successfully extract the signature from each block, a decryption step is applied to the encoded signed HDR image using the public key. In order to verify the authenticity in each block, new hash values are computed and compared with the original thumbprint. The encrypted public key and the original thumbprint are transmitted by the sender side in a specific APP marker of JPEG-HDR bitstream header as illustrated in Fig. 4. It is worth noting that an APP marker is a generic concept that is commonly used by JPEG baseline compression for inserting and extracting additional information to and from JPEG image.

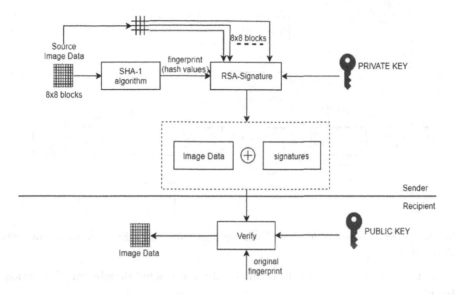

Fig. 2. Block diagram of the proposed image integrity verification framework.

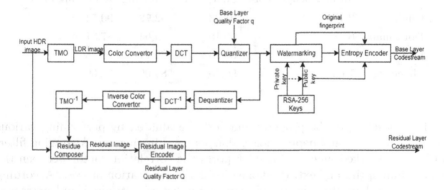

Fig. 3. Main building blocks of integrity process/JPED HDR compression system.

4   Experimental Results

Simulations where performed using four HDR images named: Chairs of size 343×231, Doll small of size 462×450, Memorial of size 512×768 and Room of size 1840×1224. These images are in pfm format and coded with 96 bits/pixel.

In Fig. 5, the LDR versions of the tested HDR images with and without watermarking are shown. From this figure, we can clearly notice that for each test image, the visual qualities of the watermarked images are undistinguishable from those of the original ones. In other words, the signed LDR images look visually identical to the originals. This demonstrates that the proposed method has no visual impact on the processed image.

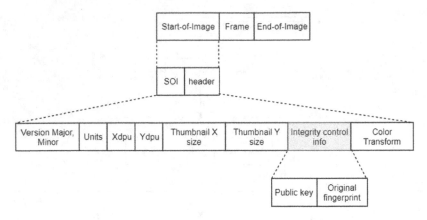

Fig. 4. JPEG compatible base-layer codestream including control integrity information.

Table 1. Correlation between the original and the extracted thumbprint after various attacks.

	Salt and pepper noise	Sharpening	Blurring	Averaging filter
Chairs	92.17	91.38	92.72	90.54
Doll_small	88.23	90.16	89,64	87.31
Room	90.33	88.15	89.11	90.18
Memorial	87.62	90.75	89.09	91.66

The robustness of the proposed method is evaluated by performing various attacks such as salt and pepper noise, sharpening, blurring and Averaging filter, on the watermarked images. Table 1 reports the correlation factor between the original thumbprint and extracted one during the verification process. According to the reported results, the correlation factor between original and extracted thumbprint attains an average of $89,94\%$ ($\simeq 0,9$), for the four test images, which is relatively high. This proves that our verification watermarking approach has strong robustness to common attack scenarios. It is worth outlining that the conducted experiments are quite preliminary. Particularly, it is interesting to examine the robustness against other attacks like volumetric scaling and low (or high) pass filtering.

4.1   Performance Evaluation

In this section we evaluate the performance of the proposed integrity verification scheme with respect to the quality of the marked image and the localization capability. To evaluate the impact of the integrity process on the HDR image quality, we proposed to use use two different metrics. The first one is an objective measure called the Multi-Exposure Peak Signal Noise Ratio (mPSNR) [9] and

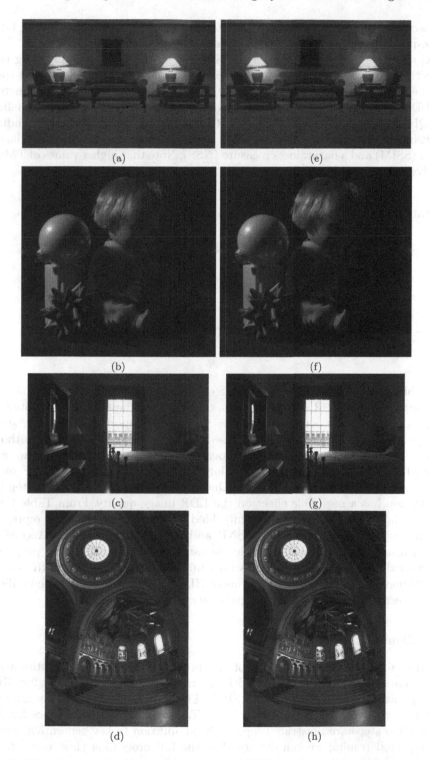

Fig. 5. Visual comparison between the original LDR versions of the test images ((a) Chairs, (b) Doll small, (c) Room, (d) Memorial) and the corresponding watermarked images ((e) Chairs, (f) Doll small, (g) Room, (h) Memorial).

the second one is a perceptually-based metric named HDR-VDP2 [12]. The later corresponds to the subjective mean opinion score QMOS.

Qualitative assessment was also carried out, in the LDR domain, using two objective metrics, Naturalness Image Quality Evaluator (NIQE) [11] and tone mapped image quality index (TMQI) [10] metrics. NIQE is a no-reference metric for LDR image evaluation. Low NIQE values entail better LDR image quality. TMQI was defined to evaluate the LDR image quality using its corresponding HDR image as a reference. It is based on a combination of a structural similarity index (SSIM) and a naturalness measure (NSS). Note that higher values of TMQI involve better visual quality.

Table 2. TMQI [10] and NIQE [11] measures with and without watermarking.

	Without watermarking		With watermarking	
	TMQI	NIQE	TMQI	NIQE
Chairs	0,873	5,77	0,861	5,52
Doll_small	0,675	4,60	0,646	4,57
Room	0,534	2,57	0,537	2.43
Memorial	0,554	2,50	0,559	2,41

Tables 2 and 3 illustrate the baseline evaluations of the proposed framework by using LDR and HDR representations, respectively. These results are obtained using a fixed quality compression ($q = 9$). Results reported in Table 2, show the quality evaluation of the compressed LDR test images with and without embedding the integrity verification process. From the reported results, we can notice that TMQI values are very similar. The results, in terms of NIQE measure, confirm the same interpretation. One may thus conclude that the integrity verification has a negligible effect on the LDR image quality. From Table 3, we analyze the imperceptibility of the embedded signature using the HDR representation, respectively in terms of mPSNR and HDR-VDP2 measures. According to the results reported in this Table we can clearly notice that our proposed scheme exhibits high HDR-VDP2 scores upper than 84. The mPSNR results also demonstrate that the lost in terms of HDR quality, induced by the verification watermarking is relatively insignificant.

4.2 Complexity Calculation

In order to assess the complexity of the proposed framework, execution-time tests were conducted on a laptop with an Intel Core 5 CPU M350 at 2.5 GHz, and operating system Windows 10 SP 1. The control integrity procedure was combined to JPEG HDR coding chain. In Table 4, the processing times for the verification steps are illustrated separately in addition to key generation. From the reported results, we can deduce that the full processing time varies from

Table 3. mPSNR [9] and HDR-VDP [12] evaluations with and without watermarking.

	Without watermarking		With watermarking	
	mPSNR	HDR-VDP	mPSNR	HDR-VDP
Chairs	21,229	82,864	20,213	83,136
Doll_small	30,572	83,025	29,413	84,807
Room	25,548	70,971	24,511	71,918
Memorial	21,796	74,935	20,758	75,540

0.047 to 0.146 ms depending on the image size. One may also notice that the execution time, for the watermark insertion, is higher than that needed for the integrity check. Obviously, this is due to the time required for the key generation and the thumbprint computation during the first stage.

Table 4. Average execution time of the integrity verification process

	Chairs	Doll_small	Memorial	Room
Watermarking (ms)	0,039	0,073	0,092	0,047
Verification (ms)	0,008	0,041	0,054	0,033

5 Conclusion

In this paper, we have described an integrity verification method to address the issue of secure HDR images. Preliminary experimental results have demonstrated the effectiveness of the proposed scheme in terms of qualitative and objective assessment, with respect to the quality of the marked HDR image and the localization capabilities.

In our future work, we plan to perform the integration-verification procedure on multiple selected regions. This in turn requires different secret keys and a single digital signature.

References

1. Yan, C.P., Pun, C.M.: Multi-scale difference map fusion for tamper localization using binary ranking hashing. IEEE Trans. Inf. Forensics Secur. **12**(9), 2144–2158 (2017)
2. Lin, C., Chang, S.: A robust image authentication method distinguishing JPEG compression from malicious manipulation. IEEE Trans. Circ. Syst. Video Technol. **11**(2), 153–168 (2001)
3. Kwon, O.J., Choi, S., Lee, B.: A watermark-based scheme for authenticating JPEG image integrity. IEEE Access **6**, 46194–46205 (2018)

4. Mzougi, S., Ouled Zaid, A.: Privacy protection and integrity verification of HDR images. In: International Conference on Computer Graphics and Digital Image Processing (2017)
5. Wallace, G.K.: The JPEG still picture compression standard. Multimedia engineering digital equipment corporation Maynard, Massachusetts. IEEE Trans. Consum. Electron. **38**, 1022–2027 (1992)
6. Ward, G., Simmons, M.: JPEG-HDR: A backwards-compatible, high dynamic range extension to JPEG. ACM SIGGRAPH Courses (2006)
7. FIPS PUB 180–1, NIST: Secure Hash Standard (SHS), April 1995
8. Rivest, R.L, Shamir, A., Adleman, L.M.: A method for obtaining digital signatures and public-key cryptosystems. In: ACM Proceedings of Communications, pp. 120–126 (1978)
9. Clarberg, P., Hasselgren, J., Akenine-Möller, T.: High dynamic range texture compression for graphics hardware. ACM Trans. Graph. **25**(3), 698–706 (2006)
10. Yeganeh, H., Wang, Z.: Objective quality assessment of tone-mapped images. IEEE Trans. Image Process. **22**(2), 657–667 (2013)
11. Mittal, A., Soundararajan, R., Bovik, A.C.: Making a completely blind image quality analyzer. IEEE Signal Process. Lett. **20**(3), 209–212 (2013)
12. Mantiuk, R., Kim, K., Rempel, A., Heidrich, W.: HDR-VDP-2: a calibrated visual metric for visibility and quality predictions in all luminance conditions. ACM Trans. Graph. **30**(4) (2001)
13. Yuan, L., Korshunov, P., Ebrahimi, T.: Privacy-preserving photo sharing based on a secure JPEG. In: IEEE Conference on Computer Communications (2015)
14. Yuan, L., David McNally, D., Küpçü, A., Ebrahimi, T.: Privacy-preserving photo sharing based on a public key infrastructure. In: SPIE (2015)
15. Ebrahimi, T., Grosbois, R.: SSecure JPEG 2000 - JPSEC. In: ICASSP Conference Proceedings 2003, pp. 716–719 (2000)
16. Wonga, P.W., Memon, N.: Secret and public key authentication watermarking schemes that resist vector quantization attack. In: SPIE (2000)
17. Niimi, M., Masutani, F., Noda, H.: Protection of privacy in JPEG files using reversible information hiding. In: International Symposium on Intelligent Signal Processing and Communications Systems, pp. 441–446, November 2012
18. Dufaux, F., Ebrahimi, T.: Toward a secure JPEG. In: Proceedings of SPIE (2006)

FS2Net: Fiber Structural Similarity Network (FS2Net) for Rotation Invariant Brain Tractography Segmentation Using Stacked LSTM Based Siamese Network

Ranjeet Ranjan Jha[1]([⊠]), Shreyas Patil[2], Aditya Nigam[1], and Arnav Bhavsar[1]

[1] School of Computing and Electrical Engineering,
Indian Institute of Technology, Mandi, Mandi 175005, India
ranjanjharanjeet@gmail.com, {aditya,arnav}@iitmandi.ac.in
[2] Department of Electrical Engineering, Indian Institute of Technology, Jodhpur,
Jodhpur, Rajasthan, India
patil.3@iitj.ac.in

Abstract. In this paper, we propose a novel deep learning architecture combining stacked Bi-directional LSTM and LSTMs with the Siamese network architecture for segmentation of brain fibers, obtained from tractography data, into anatomically meaningful clusters. The proposed network learns the structural difference between fibers of different classes, which enables it to classify fibers with high accuracy. Importantly, capturing such deep inter and intra class structural relationship also ensures that the segmentation is robust to relative rotation among test and training data, hence can be used with unregistered data. Our extensive experimentation over order of hundred-thousands of fibers shows that the proposed model achieves state-of-the-art results, even in cases of large relative rotations between test and training data.

Keywords: Brain tractography · Siamese · Deep learning · LSTM

1 Introduction

Inferences about brain structure is crucial in the diagnosis of numerous disorders and for surgical preparations. A very large number of neuronal connections exists in the human brain that connect various subdivisions, which help in communicating between several parts of brain. The resulting sequences (or pathways) form what we know as fiber tracts. Tractography on diffusion tensor imaging (DTI) data helps in extracting such fiber tracts of the human brain.

The left portion of Fig. 1 shows one such visualization of brain fiber tracts. Estimating clusters of fibers with similar property and follow similar paths (right parts of Fig. 1), can provide very useful information for high-level inference. The human brain consist of millions of such fibers and are hierarchically classified. Broadly, there are two kinds of fibers, namely gray matter and white matter

© Springer Nature Switzerland AG 2019
M. Vento and G. Percannella (Eds.): CAIP 2019, LNCS 11679, pp. 459–469, 2019.
https://doi.org/10.1007/978-3-030-29891-3_40

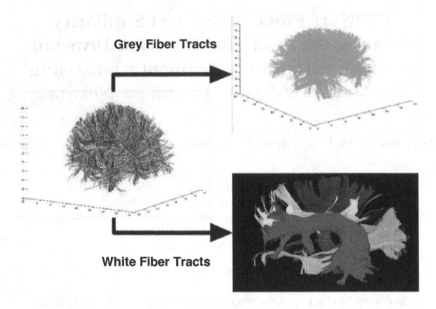

Fig. 1. Brain fiber tracts

fibers. The white fibers can be further divided into 8 important subdivisions: Arcute, Cingulum, Corticospinal, Forceps Major, Fornix, Inferior Occipitofrontal Fasciculus, Superior Longitudinal Fasciculus and Uncinate. As shown in Fig. 1 right, the grey fibers are spread in the periphery of the brain, and the eight classes of white matter fibers follow distinctive but highly non-linear paths each linking two different brain regions.

Classification of brain fibers has important applications in the field of surgical planning involving clipping of brain tissues, and for analysis and treatment of degenerative disorders. However, manual classification of brain fiber tracts can be tedious as there exist millions of such neuronal connections in any given human brain and requires very high level of proficiency. Hence, the need for an automated brain fiber segmentation techniques is vital. Moreover, as in practice it is common to encounter deformations due to patient motion, or while considering data across different patients, hence an automated approach should also consider the issue of non-registered training and testing brain data.

1.1 Related Work

Brain fiber classification has been considered in some contemporary works with both unsupervised and supervised techniques. In [1,5] unsupervised approaches have been reported. Such unsupervised clustering methods involve manual extraction of region of interests. The authors in [7] have employed Hausdorff distance as a similarity measure, and generate a white matter atlas with spectral clustering. The authors in [6] have considered a key set containing only important fiber points of each class and depending upon the proximity of a fiber with a particular set, the fiber is classified either belonging to same class or not. In [11], a hierarchical Dirichlet process is used to determine the number of clusters. Another supervised approach presented in [8], selects few major points of the fiber having maximum curvature and uses these in a clustering algorithm. The training cluster centers are then used to classify test fibers. Few approaches based on deep learning employ recurrent neural networks (RNN) [9], and long-short term memory (LSTM) [2]. The approach in [2] which uses curvature based pruning and bi-directional LSTMs achieves state-of-the-art performance. However, an important concern not addressed in recent works has been robustness against handling unregistered training and test data, commonly consisting of a relative rotation. In contrast to [2], the Siamese network architecture in the proposed approach is an important aspect, as the learning in [2] is of the particular path pattern. However, in the proposed approach the learning is of the difference in the path patterns of various classes of fibers. Another major difference between the approach in [2] and our proposed approach is the architecture of the network formed using various LSTM nodes. In [2] the number of nodes in the network remains constant whereas in the proposed approach the number of nodes are gradually decreased so as to provide condensed feature vectors for the comparison using the Siamese network architecture.

1.2   Contributions

(1) A new fiber structural similarity network (FS2Net) has been proposed using a moderately deep network built with LSTMs and bi-directional LSTM, in a Siamese architecture, for classification of DTI fiber tracts. (2) The classification is carried out at coarser level (*Grey*, *White* matter), as well as on a finer level of white fibers (into 8 classes). (3) In addition to registered brain data, we also discuss and demonstrate the effectiveness of the proposed approach even in cases of relative rotation between training and test data. (4) The proposed architecture and training strategy is computationally efficient; we demonstrate state-of-the-art results with only 11,000 brain fiber pairs used for training.

2   Proposed Model

2.1   Tractography Data

The tractography data used in this work is acquired from University of Pittsburg, and was used in the Pittsburg Brain Competition on Brain Connectivity conducted with the IEEE Int. Conf. on Data Mining, 2009. The data consists of brain fiber tracts for three subjects and their respective labels. The ground-truth labels are assigned manually by clinical neurology experts. Overall, the data consists of 250,000 fibers per subject. Each data point of a fiber is denoted by a 3-dimensional vector. The fibers are varying length containing 36 to 120 3D vectors each. The data is highly skewed in nature, so that almost 90% of

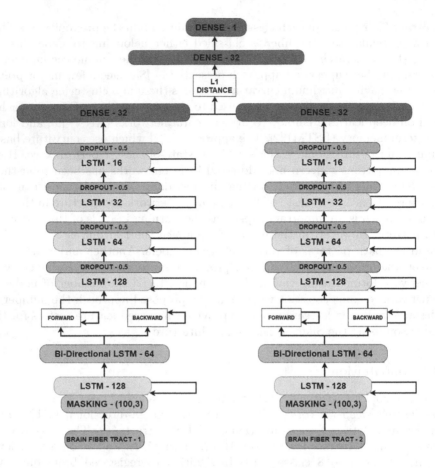

Fig. 2. Proposed FS2Net architecture

fibers belongs to Grey matter class and the rest belongs to finer fiber classes of White matter. Note that while the data belongs to only 3 subjects, the number of fiber samples to be classified is very large (order of hundred thousands). Also, as discussed later, the proposed network processes pairs of fibers to learn their similarity. Thus, the total number of pairs involved are $3 \times 250{,}000 \times 249{,}999/2$, which, from a pattern classification perspective, is a significantly large data. Interestingly, we obtain state-of-the-art results using only 11,000 pairs for training.

2.2   Curvature Based Data Pre-processing

Considering the fiber data is of varying length, data pruning has been performed at the beginning to make all inputs of the same size. The pre-processing step considers the important curvature points on the fiber. From the fiber projection on three planes, the sum of gradients have been computed at the points high

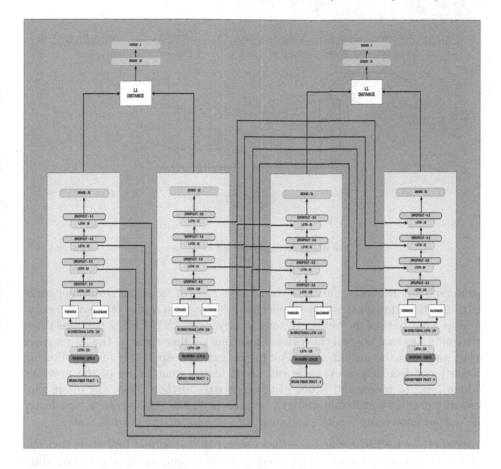

Fig. 3. Proposed FS2Net architecture with detailed use of LSTMs

curvature. The gradients are computed using one preceding point and one succeeding point, as well as with respect to point four preceding and succeeding points to attain scale invariance. Finally, 25% of the 3D vectors with smaller gradients are pruned, and the remaining 75% are padded with zeros, if required, to construct features of length 100 × 3.

2.3 Model Architecture

Below, we briefly discuss the components used in the proposed method viz. stacked LSTM, Bi-directional LSTMs (BLSTM), and Siamese network, followed by description of our model, and its training and testing.

Long Short Term Memory (LSTM) Elements: RNNs [10] are a class of neural networks that contain a loop so as to cater for the input from previous hidden layers. This loop acts as memory element, which allows it to exhibit

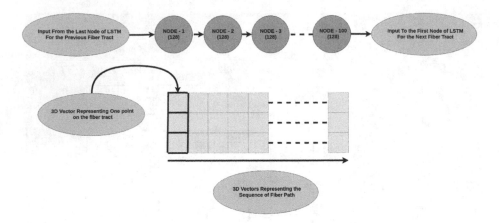

Fig. 4. Detailed use of LSTMs

dynamic temporal behaviour. LSTMs [3] are a class of recurrent neural networks that have the additional ability to selectively learn from nodes of previous iterations or what part of the history to retain. Any given LSTM block contains three different gates that control the forward information flow namely: the forget gate, input gate and the output gate. The forget gate is responsible for the filtering of the input from the previous state, i.e. it learns what nodes of the previous hidden layer to forget and which of these to pass further. Next, the input gate basically decides which values are to be present in the current state, and lastly the output gate computes the output of the present or the current state.

Bi-direction LSTMs: The basic idea behind Bi-directional LSTMs is that the output is connected both to the preceding state as well as the succeeding state wherein it is possible to predict based on the information from the past as well as from the future. The neuron of a regular LSTM layer is split into two directional neurons, one for positive time direction (forward states), and another for negative time direction (backward states). By using two time directions, input information from the past and future of the current time frame can be used unlike that in standard LSTM.

Siamese Network Based Fiber Comparator: In Siamese structure [4], two identical networks work in parallel with two different data point inputs, and the dissimilarity is learned between two classes by computing the L1 distance between the corresponding output feature vectors. The network yields a single binary output which specifies whether the two data points belong to the same class (True) or not (False). Hence, the network learns the difference between data points from two dissimilar classes or similarities between those from the same class. We have devised a Siamese LSTM based fiber comparator that can capture the deep inter-class differences and intra-class structural similarity of fibers.

Model Justification: The motivation for selecting LSTMs as the basic nodes for building the proposed network model is due to the reasoning that segmentation involves learning the sequencing of the 3D vectors (fiber representations). The BLSTMs cater to the consideration that curvature points of a fiber sequence are crucial in identifying its class label, and the curvature is defined by derivatives in both the directions. The Siamese network architecture has been used to learn the similarities or dissimilarities between paths of fiber tracts for different classes. Importantly, in effect, the network is not just learning the overall fiber trajectory but also the similarities (or differences) between fibers. This aspect allows the model to classify (rotationally) unregistered test fibers relative to the training data, as elaborated in Sect. 2.5.

The use of LSTMs as memory units so as to learn the specific path patterns has been depicted in Figs. 3 and 4, we can see here that the input masking of the 3 dimensional vectors is done so as to provide the input as a time sequence. Figure 4 shows the unwrapped structure of the first LSTM layer where the input dimension of $(100, 3)$ representing 100 vectors of $(1, 3)$ dimension spreading out into 128 nodes of the consequent layer of the neural network and the outputs of these being passed into the next time sequence input. As a result of such architecture the proposed network learns the specific path pattern related to each of the brain fiber class.

The bi-directional LSTMs are mainly used for the purpose of understanding the curvature of the given path pattern, as the inputs to the bi-directional LSTM nodes are the current 3 dimensional vector and also the output of the previous as well as the next state.

In Fig. 3 we can see that the first block is connected to the third and so on forming one part of the Siamese and the second is connected to fourth and so on forming the second part of the Siamese, hence effectively learning from the differences not only in the given path sequence as well as the consequent path sequences.

2.4 Training

We now discuss the training process for the proposed $FS2Net$. Here, 4 models are trained on the tractography data from three subjects: Three separate models from data of each of the three subjects, and a fourth model using the combined dataset. The models are trained both for coarse and fine levels.

Fiber Pairing: The first step of the training process is the pairing of fibers so as to pass them through the network and consequently learn similarities or dissimilarities. The ratio of number of similar pairs to the number of dissimilar pairs used was 4 : 7 for fine level classification and 5 : 6 for coarse level classification. The batch size of 11 pairs has been used in our approach, where, in a batch, all the similar pairs belonged to one class, and the dissimilar pair were made corresponding to the same class with equal number of pairs to each of the other classes. The labels for the pairs of same class is given as 1 (True) and different class as 0 (False). One of the advantages of pairing and measuring the similarity

Table 1. Performance analysis of the proposed *FS2Net* for registered data.

Patient	Accuracy (%)						Recall (%)		
	Macro			Micro			Macro		
	ANN	BrainSegNet	FS2Net	ANN	BrainSegNet	FS2Net	ANN	BrainSegNet	FS2Net
Intra: Trained and tested over same brain									
B1	98.02	98.88	99.23	97.34	98.12	99.01	82.1	94.98	96.14
B2	96.14	97.84	98.87	93.49	99.96	99.92	65.2	80.68	90.34
B3	96.69	96.42	98.68	95.96	97.45	98.97	57.6	73.45	81.49
Inter: Trained on B1 and tested on B2 and B3									
B2	91.32	—	97.45	88.05	—	94.58	30.9	—	58.55
B2	94.03	—	98.98	93.66	—	95.76	34.4	—	60.56
Inter: Trained on B2 and tested on B1 and B3									
B1	—	93.30	95.51	—	99.55	99.67	—	49.00	62.54
B3	—	94.47	96.11	—	96.18	97.89	—	49.60	59.09
Merged: Trained and tested over merged brain data									
	94.87	96.65	98.12	93.95	95.51	97.76	80.6	83.46	90.55

is that the skewed nature of the dataset is eliminated, as for pairs there must be equal number of all classes of fibers.

Training Process: After obtaining the pairs from the above mentioned process each fiber pair is passed through the network to obtain a output feature vector of size 32 after the dense layer as shown in Fig. 2. The L1 distance is then computed between two feature vectors and finally a single node at the end represents the similarity between the input fibers as 1 if they belong to the same class and 0 otherwise. The *ReLu* activation function is used for all the dense layers except for the last were *sigmoid* activation is used.

Network Hyper-parameters: Number of Iteration - 1000 (In one iteration only a single batch is passed), Batch Size - 11, Activation Functions - *ReLu* and *Sigmoid*, Optimizer - *Adam*, Loss Function - *Mean Squared Error*.

2.5   Testing Strategy

The above discussion indicates that the network essentially decides whether the two input fiber data belong to the same class or not. This, by itself, is not enough to perform an overall labeling. Thus, a default set of labeled brain fiber data is constructed for the purpose of comparison of the test fiber. The test fiber is paired with each one of the default set fibers and passed through the network and then the labeled brain fiber for which this pass obtains the maximum score in a scale from 0 to 1 is assigned that class or label.

In the default set of fibers the rotated fibers of all the classes also have been included so as to give rotation invariance during testing to cater for the unregistered data. Note that rotated brain data is not necessarily required for training the network. As the network is learning only similarity between fibers, it is enough to include the labeled rotated data only in this default set.

3   Experimental Analysis

For each subject, the brain data contains 250,000 fibers. As mentioned earlier, we perform a two level hierarchical classification: (a) Coarse (Macro) Level - involving binary fiber classification with respect to two classes viz. Grey and the white matter (where data imbalance is a major challenge), (b) Finer (Micro) Level - where fibers are classified into one of the 8 sub-classes of white fibers.

The training and testing of our proposed network *FS2Net* has been performed under the following protocols:

(a) **Intra Brain Testing:** Partitioning the data from the same patient into training and testing. We have reported results for data from one of the three patients. Note that such a strategy can be useful considering a practical case, where manual labeling is required only for a part of the data.

(b) **Inter Brain Testing:** Training over one of the three patient's data, and testing on a fraction of the data from other two patients. We have reported our results only when trained over patient 2 (i.e. Brain 2) data and tested over remaining Brain 1 and Brain 3 data.

(c) **Merged Brain Testing:** Training over merged data of all the three patients, such that (randomly chosen) 4000 of the data points from each brain has been considered for training, while remaining data is used for testing.

All the above mentioned training protocols have been performed for both macro and micro level testing and also for various degrees of rotations. *Accuracy* and *Recall*, defined below, have been used to quantify the performance.

$$Accuracy = \frac{\#correctly\ classified\ fibers}{Total fibers}$$

$$Recall = \frac{\#\ white\ fibers\ predicted}{Total\ white\ fibers}$$

We have defined *Recall* as above, so as to quantify the ability of our model to handle skewed data, considering the large difference in white and grey matter fibers numbers.

Comparative Analysis: The results of the proposed approach, in accordance with the testing strategy used in [8] and BrainSegNet [2] for fair comparisons, are depicted in Table 1. One can observe that we achieve state-of-the-art results in almost all the test cases. The accuracy in the inter-brain case falls compared to that of the intra-brain, due to possible variations between the structure of two brains in terms of size and fiber shape/path. However, the drop in accuracy is much lower that in the other approaches. The recall values in Table 1, signify the superiority of the proposed *FS2Net* in classifying white fibers (fewer in number), suggesting that the proposed model handles data imbalance better. The computational efficiency of the proposed network also surpasses that of the previous state-of-the-art. In [2], 80,000 fibers and 25 epochs have been used

Table 2. Performance with rotated unregistered test data.

Patient	Accuracy (%) - Micro			
Method	BrainSegNet	FS2Net		
Rotation angle	30	10	20	30
Intra: Trained over same brain				
Brain 1	56.68	90.21	87.74	85.56
Brain 2	49.51	91.12	88.67	86.23
Brain 3	51.32	88.96	86.78	83.12
Merged: Trained over merged brain data				
	43.56	87.91	86.01	82.87
	Accuracy (%) - Macro			
Intra: Trained over same brain				
Brain 1	58.98	91.73	88.44	84.19
Brain 2	52.01	92.91	89.99	88.03
Brain 3	53.69	90.12	89.11	85.09
Merged: Trained over merged brain data				
	46.11	88.36	85.91	83.38

whereas, here we have only used a total of 11,000 pairs in a batch size of 11 with 1000 iterations.

Rotational Invariance: The results corresponding to the rotation of test cases relative to the training set is shown in Table 2. Even here, the proposed approach achieves high classification accuracy. Note that as the rotation increases, the accuracy drops slightly, but this may also depend on the labeled samples that are included in the default fiber set used during testing. One can observe that the BrainSegNet method [2] performs poorly in case of rotations. This is because, it learns the absolute fiber structure/path, which can change significantly under rotation. However, the proposed network achieves rotation invariance via learning similarities rather than absolute structure. When a rotated test fiber is paired with a rotated default set fiber of the same class, the network provides a feature vector based on the similarity between these fibers. Thus, providing a wide range of fiber rotations in the default set enables rotational invariance. Considering a large and diverse dataset with small training samples, we believe that the achieved results are very encouraging. The while the similarity estimation between pairs is carried out during training, the testing strategy (as elaborated in Sect. 2.5) addresses the complete fiber classification task, via such a similarity computation.

4   Conclusion

We propose a novel Siamese LSTM-BLSTM architecture for classifying brain fiber tracts, which also caters for unregistered brain data involving rotations. We suggest a two-level hierarchical classification (a) White vs Grey matter and (b) White matter clusters. Our experimental evaluation shows that the proposed network achieves state-of-the-art classification accuracies, for registered as well as unregistered cases, with significant improvements in some evaluation scenarios.

References

1. Catani, M., Howard, R.J., Pajevic, S., Jones, D.K.: Virtual in vivo interactive dissection of white matter fasciculi in the human brain. Neuroimage **17**(1), 77–94 (2002)
2. Gupta, T., Patil, S.M., Tailor, M., Thapar, D., Nigam, A.: BrainSegNet: a segmentation network for human brain fiber tractography data into anatomically meaningful clusters. arXiv:1710.05158 (2017)
3. Hochreiter, S., Schmidhuber, J.: Long short-term memory. Neural Comput. **9**(8), 1735–1780 (1997)
4. Koch, G., Zemel, R., Salakhutdinov, R.: Siamese neural networks for one-shot image recognition. In: ICML Deep Learning Workshop, vol. 2 (2015)
5. Maddah, M., Mewes, A., Haker, S., Grimson, W., Warfield, S.: Automated atlas-based clustering of white matter fiber tracts from DTMRI. In: Medical Image Computing And Computer-Assisted Intervention–MICCAI 2005, pp. 188–195 (2005)
6. Nikulin, V., McLachlan, G.J.: Identifying fiber bundles with regularised κ-means clustering applied to the grid-based data. In: The 2010 International Joint Conference on Neural Networks (IJCNN), pp. 1–8, July 2010
7. O'Donnell, L.J., Westin, C.-F.: Automatic tractography segmentation using a high-dimensional white matter atlas. IEEE Trans. Med. Imaging **26**(11), 1562–1575 (2007)
8. Patel, V., Parmar, A., Bhavsar, A., Nigam, A.: Automated brain tractography segmentation using curvature points. In: Proceedings of the Tenth Indian Conference on Computer Vision, Graphics and Image Processing, p. 18. ACM (2016)
9. Poulin, P., et al.: Learn to track: deep learning for tractography. bioRxiv, p. 146688 (2017)
10. Sutskever, I.: Training recurrent neural networks. Ph.D. thesis, University of Toronto (2013)
11. Wang, X., Grimson, W.E.L., Westin, C.-F.: Tractography segmentation using a hierarchical dirichlet processes mixture model. NeuroImage **54**(1), 290–302 (2011)

Master and Rookie Networks for Person Re-identification

Danilo Avola[1], Marco Cascio[1], Luigi Cinque[1], Alessio Fagioli[1],
Gian Luca Foresti[2], and Cristiano Massaroni[1(✉)]

[1] Department of Computer Science, Sapienza University,
Via Salaria 113, 00198 Rome, Italy
{avola,cascio,cinque,fagioli,massaroni}@di.uniroma1.it
[2] Department of Mathematics, Computer Science and Physics, University of Udine,
Via delle Scienze 206, 33100 Udine, Italy
gianluca.foresti@uniud.it

Abstract. Recognizing different visual signatures of people across non-overlapping cameras is still an open problem of great interest for the computer vision community, especially due to its importance in automatic video surveillance on large-scale environments. A main aspect of this application field, known as person re-identification (re-id), is the feature extraction step used to define a robust appearance of a person. In this paper, a novel two-branch Convolutional Neural Network (CNN) architecture for person re-id in video sequences is proposed. A pre-trained branch, called Master, leads the learning phase of the other un-trained branch, called Rookie. Using this strategy, the Rookie network is able to learn complementary features with respect to those computed by the Master network, thus obtaining a more discriminative model. Extensive experiments on two popular challenging re-id datasets have shown increasing performance in terms of convergence speed as well as accuracy in comparison to standard models, thus providing an alternative and concrete contribution to the current re-id state-of-the-art.

Keywords: Person re-identification · Deep learning · Feature extraction

1 Introduction

The aim of the person re-id consists in comparing a person of interest, also called probe, to a gallery of candidates. Usually, the probe is acquired by a camera that is not overlapped with those used to make up the gallery. A ranking approach is finally used to identify the probe among the incorrect candidates. This application field is, moreover, complicated by several factors, such as camouflages, long-term re-id, similarity, and many others. Anyway, person re-id plays a key role in the modern computer vision, not only to support surveillance applications, but also in combination with other application fields, e.g., action recognition [4],

© Springer Nature Switzerland AG 2019
M. Vento and G. Percannella (Eds.): CAIP 2019, LNCS 11679, pp. 470–479, 2019.
https://doi.org/10.1007/978-3-030-29891-3_41

robotics [2], and vision-based rehabilitation [5], to obtain more smart and general purposes systems.

A main challenge for re-id methods regards the feature extraction step, especially due to appearance changes related to environmental and geometric variations caused by person movements among different camera viewpoints. Early works in the state-of-the-art used different strategies whose features were focused only on texture [6] or key-points [13, 19] to address the issues just reported. The achieved results have shown that individual types of features provide a too weak representation, which is not able to either maximize or minimize the inter-class and intra-class distances. To overcome this problem, more recent works make use of combination of features. In [15], for example, an Ensemble of Localized Features (ELF) is learned through the AdaBoost algorithm, thus obtaining a viewpoint invariant pedestrian recognition method. Instead, the similarity among different images of the same person is measured in [36] by the comparison of covariance descriptors obtained using colour feature, Gabor, and Local Binary Pattern (LBP) techniques. In [7], a set of complementary features representing people appearances, called Symmetry-Driven Accumulation of Local Features (SDALFs), is extracted to perform a symmetry-based description of the body. Finally, in [24], a novel representation of salient regions of a given person, called Saliency Weighted Histogram (SWH), is combined with a set of other visual features (i.e., color mean, key-point descriptor, and LBP) in a pairwise-based multiple metric learning framework.

Inspired by the good results obtained in many computer vision applications [3, 20, 28], several deep learning methods have been also proposed, in person re-id, to extrapolate robust features focusing especially on CNNs. A valid example is reported in [21], where a novel Filter Pairing Neural Network (FPNN) is proposed to learn features, handle misalignment, photometric and geometric transformations, as well as occlusions and background clutter. In [1], a deep convolutional architecture is proposed to learn both features and a corresponding similarity metric for re-id, capturing local relationships between the two input images based on their mid-level features. Adopting a multi-task learning framework based on CNNs, in [17] a two-stream strategy is applied to extract deep features using simultaneously both partial and full bodies. In the just discussed methods, networks are trained anew, making it difficult to reach the optimal convergence. Aware of this issue, we have noticed that by a deep Feature Fusion Network (FFN), reported in [33], hand-crafted features can lead CNNs in learning new robust and complementary features.

In this paper, extending the concept proposed in [33], we show how the training phase of a CNN, called Rookie, can be led by a second pre-trained CNN, called Master, on a known dataset for the re-id task, in order to get a more discriminative overall model. Differently from classical transfer learning techniques, where networks with similar structures are used, in this work the two branches can leverage different types of CNN-based networks (e.g., a DenseNet [18] could guide the training of an Xception [11] network). Finally, experiments on two benchmark re-id datasets show how the proposed model, based on Master-Rookie

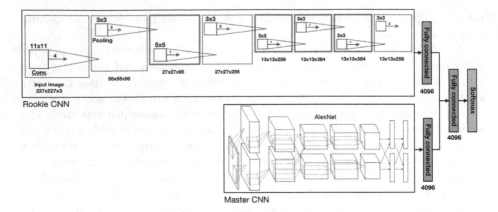

Fig. 1. The proposed two-branch CNN structure: bold squares are zero-padding applications to the image, red squares are convolution operations, finally, green squares are max-pooling operations. Top and bottom networks are Rookie and Master, respectively. (Color figure online)

training, provides good performance in terms of convergence speed and accuracy. The introduced model overcomes standard ones, thus demonstrating how our strategy can be extended to more complex architectures.

2   Network Architecture

The proposed network architecture is based on a two-branch CNN structure, as shown in Fig. 1. Although each branch can be based on any type of network, in this paper, to show the advantages provided by our strategy, an AlexNet [20] is used for the Master, while the Rookie is based on a simplified version of both AlexNet and ZE [35] networks. These CNNs are chosen as underlying structures because they have demonstrated great performances on the ImageNet [12] classification benchmark and, in addition, they are less computationally expensive with respect to the ResNet [16], VCG [29], and Google LeNet [31].

2.1   Rookie Network

Relying on the architecture of many popular networks, the Rookie CNN is designed as a single-path network that takes as input a square RGB image formed by 227×227 pixels. The network consists of five convolutional layers with ReLU [27] activation function and three pooling layers. The first two convolutional layers use a filter size of 11×11 and 5×5, respectively, while a reduced filter dimension (i.e., 3×3) is applied to the remaining layers. Excluding the first layer of convolution, which uses a stride of 4, all convolutional layers use a stride of 1 and, in addition, they apply a zero-padding operation.

All pooling layers perform a max-pooling by using a filter size of 3×3 and a stride of 2. In order to detect high frequency features with large responses, the biologically named lateral inhibition (i.e., the capacity of an excited neuron to subdue its neighbour increasing sensory perception) is applied after each pooling operation and it is implemented by using the following Local Response Normalization (LRN) [20]:

$$b^i_{x,y} = \frac{a^i_{x,y}}{(k + \alpha \sum_{j=\min(0,i-n/2)}^{\max(N,i+n/2)} (a^j_{x,y})^2)^\beta} \tag{1}$$

where $a^i_{x,y}$ is the neuron in the activation map in position (x, y) at the $i-th$ depth level of the output volume; $b^i_{x,y}$ is the new value to be computed for the neuron in position (x, y) of $i - th$ depth level; N is the total number of depth levels; n, k, α, β are hyper-parameters to be set (i.e., $n = 5, k = 1, \alpha = 0.0001, \beta = 0.75$) where n is the number of adjacent depth levels to be considered in the formula, k represents a bias, while the values α and β are a chosen constant scalar factor and exponent, respectively.

2.2 Merging of Master and Rookie Networks

Both network branches end in a fully connected layer, using a ReLU activation function. These layers outputs are concatenated and fed as input to another dense layer, effectively combining features learned from both Master and Rookie CNNs. Finally, a softmax function is applied to map all the features in a single vector, representing the classification, composed by the normalized probabilities associated to each identity label to which the probe can belong. During the training, the prediction obtained from this last layer is used to guide the Rookie network in learning the complementary and more discriminative features that lead to a highly robust re-id network. In fact, since the pre-trained parameters of the Master network are bound, the optimization algorithm, used to minimize the loss in the prediction, only optimizes the weights of the Rookie network layers, thus forcing it to calculate new features.

3   Experiments and Results

In this section the effectiveness on the person re-id task, for the introduced Master-Rookie CNNs structure, is shown by several tests performed on the most popular datasets designed for this application field: VIPeR [14] and CUHK01 [22]. We also report training details for the proposed model, using the Market1501 [37] dataset.

3.1 Datasets

The VIPeR dataset (Fig. 2a) consists of 632 pedestrian identity image pairs captured outdoors from two camera views with resolution of 128×64. The CUHK01 dataset (Fig. 2b) was collected by using two camera views in a university campus, and it contains 971 identities with two images per person in each view (i.e., four

Table 1. Most popular re-id public datasets properties.

Dataset	VIPeR [14]	CUHK01 [22]	Market1501 [37]
Release Year	2007	2012	2016
Nr. Identitites	632	971	1501
Nr. Cameras	2	2	6
Nr. Images	1264	3884	26051
Resolution	128 × 48	160 × 60	128 × 64

images per identity) with resolution of 160 × 60. Both datasets are challenging for the person re-id task due to occlusion, background clutters, illumination changes, pose and viewpoints variations. The Market1501 (Fig. 2c), one of the largest and most recent re-id dataset currently available, consists of 1501 person identities with resolution of 128 × 64, split into training and test sets and collected using six cameras in front of a supermarket in Tsinghua University. Each person was captured by at least two cameras. In Table 1 the main properties of the reported datasets are summarized.

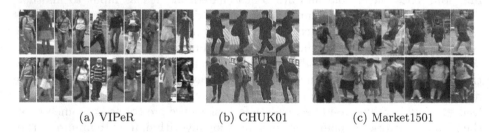

    (a) VIPeR   (b) CHUK01   (c) Market1501

Fig. 2. Example of images per identity contained in the: (a) VIPeR, (b) CHUK01, and (c) Market1501 datasets.

3.2 Training on Market1501 Dataset

The Master network was first individually pre-trained on Market1501, and the same dataset was then used to also train the Rookie network. The two CNNs take as input an image with 227 × 227 resolution whereas Market1501 images have a shape of 128 × 64, thus image preprocessing is required. Since the images are rectangular, simply resizing could introduce distortions, therefore we have chosen to crop the upper part of the image (i.e., keep a 64 × 64 portion) and then we performed the resizing. This partial re-id approach is able to handle the size difference and it represents also a more realistic challenge [38].

    At training time, mini-batch Stochastic Gradient Descent (SGD) with momentum [8] and a learning rate of 0.01 were used to speed up training convergence and minimize the update of weights close to a local minimum. For each batch, consisting of 64 training samples, the cross-entropy loss function was

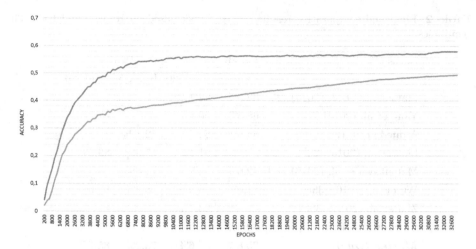

Fig. 3. Validation accuracy over the epochs, obtained during the training by our model (in blue) and AlexNet (in grey). Notice that, the proposed model uses less epochs to converge to the optimal value of accuracy with respect to the AlexNet. (Color figure online)

applied on predictions and the back propagation algorithm was used to update the weights. The Market1501 dataset contains 32668 annotated bounding boxes of 1501 identities, divided in train and validation set. These sets respectively count 12936 and 19732 images obtained from the aforementioned bounding boxes. On these collections, the Master network achieves a 48% validation accuracy score, estimated using a categorical accuracy in the training phase, whereas the proposed network, exploiting the Master-Rookie architecture, reaches up to 58.2%. The improvement offered by our solution also concerns the convergence speed. In fact, in Fig. 3 it can be noted how Master-Rookie architecture achieves an optimal validation accuracy faster than the basic model (i.e., the Master based on AlexNet), during the training phase.

3.3   Dropout

AlexNet is a network designed to classify one thousand object categories within 1.2 million images. The size of our Market1501 training set is too small with respect to the number of AlexNet parameters, therefore over-fitting [9] may occur. To prevent this outcome, the dropout technique [30] has been applied on the last fully connected layers of our proposed structure. The final choice of this technique instead of another approach, such as Batch Normalization [32], derives from empirical observations performed during preliminary network training.

3.4   Re-ID Task Results

To evaluate our proposed model, several tests were performed using the VIPeR and CUHK01 datasets. Both datasets were split into two equally sized subsets: a

Table 2. Final and comparative results on re-id task based on Rank-5 and Rank-20 accuracies.

Dataset	VIPeR		CUHK01	
	Rank-5	Rank-20	Rank-5	Rank-20
Matsukawa et al. (2014) [25]	62.0%	84.1 %	-	-
Yang et al. (2014) [34]	68.5%	90.4%	-	-
Ahmed et al. (2015) [1]	63.6%	84.5%	72.1 %	88.5%
Liao et al. (2015) [23]	-	91.1%	75.3%	89.5%
Matsukawa et al. (2016) [26]	72.0%	92%	71.8%	88.2%
Wu et al. (2016) [33]	81.0%	96.9%	78.4%	92.6%
Zhu et al. (2018) [39]	-	93.7%	-	-
Chen et al. (2018) [10]	80.0%	95.5%	91.2%	97.1%
Master (Our)	75.8%	88.6%	75.2%	85.5%
Master + Rookie (Our)	78.9%	93.7%	77.7%	90.1%

gallery, for identity matching, and a probe set, for testing purposes. Specifically, for the VIPeR dataset single images per identity were used in both subsets, while for the CUHK01, a gallery containing 3 images and a single probe per entry were used. In this step, the last softmax layer is not considered, because it is used only in the learning phase. In fact, after training, the remaining architecture is able to extrapolate the feature vector needed to perform the Cross-view Quadratic Discrimination Analysis (XQDA) [23], used to measure the distance between the probe and each gallery element.

Experiments were also conducted using only the pre-trained Master branch in order to show the advantages offered by our model compared to the standard AlexNet. All of the outcomes are summarized in Table 2, which shows how the proposed method outperforms most works present in literature, on the two considered datasets. Notice that by using a better performing Master and by designing a Rookie with more layers, the proposed methodology could most likely reach state-of-the-art accuracy. To conclude, the Master CNN features can indeed guide the Rookie in computing a new set of more discriminant features, without requiring the human effort as in [33], and thus obtaining a substantial improvement with respect to the performances of a single Master network.

4   Conclusions

In this paper, a novel deep learning architecture is proposed to show how the training phase of a CNN can be guided by a second pre-trained CNN based network, in order to learn new robust and complementary features for the re-id task. Experimental results, performed on two challenging datasets, highlight how our model overcomes standard ones, thus validating our idea. As future development, we are planning to extend the proposed training strategy to more complex architectures.

References

1. Ahmed, E., Jones, M., Marks, T.K.: An improved deep learning architecture for person re-identification. In: IEEE International Conference on Computer Vision and Pattern Recognition (CVPR), pp. 3908–3916 (2015)
2. Andreopoulos, A., Hasler, S., Wersing, H., Janssen, H., Tsotsos, J.K., Korner, E.: Active 3D object localization using a humanoid robot. IEEE Trans. Robot. **27**(1), 47–64 (2011)
3. Avola, D., Bernardi, M., Cinque, L., Foresti, G.L., Massaroni, C.: Exploiting recurrent neural networks and leap motion controller for the recognition of sign language and semaphoric hand gestures. IEEE Trans. Multimedia **21**(1), 234–245 (2019)
4. Avola, D., Bernardi, M., Foresti, G.L.: Fusing depth and colour information for human action recognition. Multimedia Tools Appl. **78**, 5919–5939 (2018)
5. Avola, D., Cinque, L., Foresti, G.L., Marini, M.R.: An interactive and low-cost full body rehabilitation framework based on 3D immersive serious games. J. Biomed. Inform. **89**, 81–100 (2019)
6. Bak, S., Corvee, E., Bremond, F., Thonnat, M.: Person re-identification using Haar-based and DCD-based signature. In: IEEE International Conference on Advanced Video and Signal Based Surveillance (AVSS), pp. 1–8 (2010)
7. Bazzani, L., Cristani, M., Murino, V.: Symmetry-driven accumulation of local features for human characterization and re-identification. Comput. Vis. Image Underst. **117**(2), 130–144 (2013)
8. Bottou, L.: Large-scale machine learning with stochastic gradient descent. In: International Symposium on Computational Statistics (COMPSTAT), pp. 177–186 (2010)
9. Caruana, R., Lawrence, S., Giles, L.: Overfitting in neural nets: backpropagation, conjugate gradient, and early stopping. In: International Conference on Neural Information Processing Systems (NIPS), pp. 381–387 (2000)
10. Chen, Y., Zhu, X., Zheng, W., Lai, J.: Person re-identification by camera correlation aware feature augmentation. IEEE Trans. Pattern Anal. Mach. Intell. **40**(2), 392–408 (2018)
11. Chollet, F.: Xception: deep learning with depthwise separable convolutions. In: 2017 IEEE Conference on Computer Vision and Pattern Recognition (CVPR), pp. 1800–1807 (2017)
12. Deng, J., Dong, W., Socher, R., Li, L., Li, K., Fei-Fei, L.: ImageNet: a large-scale hierarchical image database. In: IEEE International Conference on Computer Vision and Pattern Recognition (CVPR), pp. 248–255 (2009)
13. Gheissari, N., Sebastian, T.B., Hartley, R.: Person reidentification using spatiotemporal appearance. In: IEEE International Conference on Computer Vision and Pattern Recognition (CVPR), pp. 1528–1535 (2006)
14. Gray, D., Brennan, S., Tao, H.: Evaluating appearance models for recognition, reacquisition, and tracking. In: IEEE International Workshop on Performance Evaluation for Tracking and Surveillance (PETS), pp. 41–47 (2007)
15. Gray, D., Tao, H.: Viewpoint invariant pedestrian recognition with an ensemble of localized features. In: Forsyth, D., Torr, P., Zisserman, A. (eds.) ECCV 2008. LNCS, vol. 5302, pp. 262–275. Springer, Heidelberg (2008). https://doi.org/10.1007/978-3-540-88682-2_21

16. He, K., Zhang, X., Ren, S., Sun, J.: Deep residual learning for image recognition. In: IEEE International Conference on Computer Vision and Pattern Recognition (CVPR), pp. 770–778 (2016)
17. Hu, L., Hong, C., Zeng, Z., Wang, X.: Two-stream person re-identification with multi-task deep neural networks. Mach. Vis. Appl. **29**(6), 947–954 (2018)
18. Huang, G., Liu, Z., van der Maaten, L., Weinberger, K.Q.: Densely connected convolutional networks. In: 2017 IEEE Conference on Computer Vision and Pattern Recognition (CVPR), pp. 2261–2269 (2017)
19. Jüngling, K., Bodensteiner, C., Arens, M.: Person re-identification in multi-camera networks. In: IEEE International Conference on Computer Vision and Pattern Recognition WORKSHOPS (CVPRW), pp. 55–61 (2011)
20. Krizhevsky, A., Sutskever, I., Hinton, G.E.: ImageNet classification with deep convolutional neural networks. In: International Conference on Neural Information Processing Systems (NIPS), pp. 1097–1105 (2012)
21. Li, W., Zhao, R., Xiao, T., Wang, X.: DeepReID: deep filter pairing neural network for person re-identification. In: IEEE International Conference on Computer Vision and Pattern Recognition (CVPR), pp. 152–159 (2014)
22. Li, W., Zhao, R., Wang, X.: Human reidentification with transferred metric learning. In: Lee, K.M., Matsushita, Y., Rehg, J.M., Hu, Z. (eds.) ACCV 2012. LNCS, vol. 7724, pp. 31–44. Springer, Heidelberg (2013). https://doi.org/10.1007/978-3-642-37331-2_3
23. Liao, S., Hu, Y., Li, S.Z.: Person re-identification by local maximal occurrence representation and metric learning. In: IEEE Conference on Computer Vision and Pattern Recognition (CVPR), pp. 2197–2206 (2015)
24. Martinel, N., Micheloni, C., Foresti, G.L.: Saliency weighted features for person re-identification. In: Agapito, L., Bronstein, M.M., Rother, C. (eds.) ECCV 2014. LNCS, vol. 8927, pp. 191–208. Springer, Cham (2015). https://doi.org/10.1007/978-3-319-16199-0_14
25. Matsukawa, T., Okabe, T., Sato, Y.: Person re-identification via discriminative accumulation of local features. In: 2014 International Conference on Pattern Recognition (CVPR), pp. 3975–3980 (2014)
26. Matsukawa, T., Suzuki, E.: Person re-identification using CNN features learned from combination of attributes. In: International Conference on Pattern Recognition (ICPR), pp. 2428–2433 (2016)
27. Nair, V., Hinton, G.E.: Rectified linear units improve restricted Boltzmann machines. In: International Conference on International Conference on Machine Learning (ICML), pp. 807–814 (2010)
28. Nuzzi, C., Pasinetti, S., Lancini, M., Docchio, F., Sansoni, G.: Deep learning based machine vision: first steps towards a hand gesture recognition set up for collaborative robots. In: IEEE International Workshop on Metrology for Industry 4.0 and IoT (M4I), pp. 28–33 (2018)
29. Simonyan, K., Zisserman, A.: Very deep convolutional networks for large-scale image recognition. arXiv:1409.1556, pp. 1–14 (2014)
30. Srivastava, N., Hinton, G., Krizhevsky, A., Sutskever, I., Salakhutdinov, R.: Dropout: a simple way to prevent neural networks from overfitting. J. Mach. Learn. Res. **15**, 1929–1958 (2014)
31. Szegedy, C., et al.: Going deeper with convolutions. In: IEEE Conference on Computer Vision and Pattern Recognition (CVPR), pp. 1–9 (2015)
32. Szegedy, C., Vanhoucke, V., Ioffe, S., Shlens, J., Wojna, Z.: Rethinking the inception architecture for computer vision. In: 2016 IEEE Conference on Computer Vision and Pattern Recognition (CVPR), pp. 2818–2826 (2016)

33. Wu, S., Chen, Y.C., Li, X., Wu, A.C., You, J.J., Zheng, W.S.: An enhanced deep feature representation for person re-identification. In: IEEE Winter Conference on Applications of Computer Vision (WACV), pp. 1–8 (2016)
34. Yang, Y., Yang, J., Yan, J., Liao, S., Yi, D., Li, S.Z.: Salient color names for person re-identification. In: Fleet, D., Pajdla, T., Schiele, B., Tuytelaars, T. (eds.) ECCV 2014. LNCS, vol. 8689, pp. 536–551. Springer, Cham (2014). https://doi.org/10.1007/978-3-319-10590-1_35
35. Zeiler, M.D., Fergus, R.: Visualizing and understanding convolutional networks. In: Fleet, D., Pajdla, T., Schiele, B., Tuytelaars, T. (eds.) ECCV 2014. LNCS, vol. 8689, pp. 818–833. Springer, Cham (2014). https://doi.org/10.1007/978-3-319-10590-1_53
36. Zhang, Y., Li, S.: Gabor-LBP based region covariance descriptor for person re-identification. In: International Conference on Image and Graphics (ICIG), pp. 368–371 (2011)
37. Zheng, L., Shen, L., Tian, L., Wang, S., Wang, J., Tian, Q.: Scalable person re-identification: a benchmark. In: IEEE International Conference on Computer Vision (ICCV), pp. 1116–1124 (2015)
38. Zheng, W., Li, X., Xiang, T., Liao, S., Lai, J., Gong, S.: Partial person re-identification. In: IEEE International Conference on Computer Vision (ICCV), pp. 4678–4686 (2015)
39. Zhu, J., Zeng, H., Liao, S., Lei, Z., Cai, C., Zheng, L.: Deep hybrid similarity learning for person re-identification. IEEE Trans. Circ. Syst. Video Technol. **28**(11), 3183–3193 (2018)

Knee Osteoarthritis Detection Using Power Spectral Density: Data from the OsteoArthritis Initiative

Abdelbasset Brahim[1(✉)], Rabia Riad[2], and Rachid Jennane[3]

[1] IMT Atlantique, Brest, France
[2] Ibn Zohr University, Agadir, Morocco
abdelbasset.brahim@imt.atlantique.fr
[3] University of Orléans, I3MTO Laboratory, EA 4708, 45067, Orléans, France

Abstract. In this paper, an aided diagnosis method for OsteoArthritis (OA) disease using knee X-ray imaging and spectral analysis is presented. The proposed method is based on the Power Spectral Density (PSD) over different orientations of the image as a feature for the classification task. Then, independent component analysis (ICA) is used to select the relevant PSD coefficients for OA detection. Finally, a logistic regression classifier is used to classify 688 knee X-ray images obtained from the Osteoarthritis Initiative (OAI). The proposed diagnosis approach yields classification results up to 78.92% of accuracy (with 79.65% of sensitivity and 78.20% of specificity). Thus, it outperforms several other recently developed OA diagnosis systems.

Keywords: Power spectral density ·
Independent component analysis · Classification · OsteoArthritis

1 Introduction

OsteoArthritis (OA) is the most common chronic condition of the joints, causing pain and stiffness [1,2]. It is characterized by cartilage degradation and bone changes [3]. Thus, the detection of OA is relevant since earlier treatment could prevent the cartilage and bone destruction. It is challenging to diagnose OA at its early stage as it has been suggested that the first changes would occur in the subchondral bone [4] before the occurrence of joint space narrowing and osteophytes [5]. Knee OA detection consists of classifying a knee radiograph into healthy (CC) or OA [6]. The clinical grading of X-ray images is currently performed by experienced clinicians using several methods, such as the Kellgren-Lawrence (KL) score [6]. This approach is based on radiographic criteria by manually classifying the individual joints into one of five grades, with 0 representing normal and 4 being the severe OA [6]. The manual classification is time consuming, can be subjective and prone to error, since, the symptoms involved in OA classification are continuous.

© Springer Nature Switzerland AG 2019
M. Vento and G. Percannella (Eds.): CAIP 2019, LNCS 11679, pp. 480–487, 2019.
https://doi.org/10.1007/978-3-030-29891-3_42

Several approaches for the detection and analysis of OA using different knee images have been proposed in the literature [7–15]. Such approaches were employed to analyze texture and intensity changes in the bone of the knee. In [16], the authors developed a dissimilarity-based multiple classifier (DMC) system for the detection of OA. This system measures distances between TB texture images and generates a diverse ensemble of classifiers using prototype selection, bootstrapping of training set and heterogeneous classifiers. However, this proposed system is validated on few images (105 X-ray images: 68 CC and 37 OA). However, in [13], the authors proposed a new automatic method which is able to quantify the severity of knee OA from X-ray imaging using deep convolutional neural networks (CNN). An automatic method to extract the knee joint images was used. Their proposed segmentation method was based on using a linear support vector machine (SVM) with the sobel horizontal image gradients as features to detect the knee joints, as regions of interest. Their results were validated on a dataset of X-ray images from the Osteoarthritis Initiative (OAI) and were shown a sizable improvement.

In this paper, an aided diagnosis approach for knee OA detection, which is based on spectral analysis is proposed. Firstly, the frequency behavior of each image subject is studied. Thus, the PSD over different orientations of each image subject are computed and considered as features for the classification task to distinguish between normal knee (KL grade 0) and minimal OA (KL grade 2), which is, from a clinical point of view, the most challenging and interesting task. Then, in order to extract the most discriminative OA features in the frequency domain, the obtained features are combined with a feature extraction approach based on independent component analysis (ICA).

2   Materials and Methods

2.1   Osteoarthritis Initiative (OAI) Database

The X-ray knee images used in this paper were collected from the public dataset Osteoarthritis Initiative (OAI) [17,18], which is available for public access at "http://www.oai.ucsf.edu/". The OAI is a multi-centric, longitudinal, prospective observational study of knee OA. The OAI database contains bilateral fixed flexion knee radiographs of 4796 men and women followed since 2008. Their ages are between 45–79.

This work is focused on the early detection of knee OA, which is the most challenging. Therefore, only the radiographs with KL grade $= 0$ (considered as CC) and KL grade $= 2$ (considered as OA) are taken into consideration. In addition, only the computed radiography (CR) modality is considered, which is identified from the DICOM headers in order to avoid any digitalization artifacts. Thus, 688 knee radiographs were used in this study and to avoid any statistical bias of imbalanced dataset, the same number of knees was considered for both groups: 344 knees from CC subjects and 344 knees from OA subjects.

2.2   Regions of Interest (ROI)

Previous studies revealed that the most discriminating ROI were located under the medial compartment [9, 19, 20]. In this sense, a semi-automatic segmentation method was used [10] to extract the medial ROI of each image subject, with size 128×128 pixels. Figure 1 shows two samples from each class.

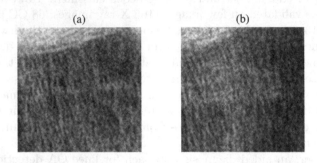

Fig. 1. The extracted Trabecular bone ROI for each class: (a) is from a CC subject and (b) is from an OA patient.

2.3   Power Spectral Density (PSD)

The Power Spectral Density (PSD) characterizes the signals in the frequency domain. The PSD corresponds to the square of the modulus of the Fourier Transform of the signal, usually computed using the Fast Fourier Transform (FFT). This estimate is called the periodogram. The periodogram estimate of the PSD of a signal $X_L(n)$ of length L is [21]:

$$\hat{P}(f) = \frac{1}{L \cdot F_s} \left| \sum_{n=0}^{L-1} X_L(n) \cdot e^{-j2\pi f n} \right|^2 \tag{1}$$

where F_s is the sampling frequency. In order to make the computation of the periodogram via an FFT algorithm more efficient, the actual computation of $\hat{P}(f)$ can be performed only at a finite number of frequency points. Most implementations of the periodogram method compute the N-point PSD estimate at the frequencies: $f_k = \frac{kF_s}{N}$, $k = 0, 1, \ldots, N - 1$. In our case $L = 128$ and $N = 64$ (to respect the Nyquist frequency limit).

2.4   Independent Component Analysis (ICA)

The Independent Component Analysis (ICA) [22–24] based feature extraction was used in order to extract the most significant PSD features from each ROI. ICA is a statistical technique that represents a multidimensional random vector as a linear combination of non-Gaussian random variables, called "independent components", to be as independent as possible. This approach is employed as a feature extraction strategy to avoid the small sample size problem [24]. Hence, using this feature extraction method, the first 20 components empirically chosen as they are the most discriminant, are retained and will be used for classification.

3 Results and Discussion

3.1 Spectral Analysis

The PSD is a useful tool to analyze images in the frequency domain, it displays the power of the variations as a function of frequency. In order to characterize the trabecular bone texture of the selected ROIs, the spectral analysis is used. For instance, due to the complexity of the trabecular bone structure, the mean periodogram of the increments of the lines (horizontal direction) presents two regimes with different slopes (Area 1 and Area 2 separated by a cut-off frequency f_c), as illustrated in Fig. 2. The f_c was chosen as the frequency corresponding to the maximum of the mean periodogram of each ROI. Thus, it could be interesting to study the discriminative ability of these areas and according to different orientations in the detection of knee OA.

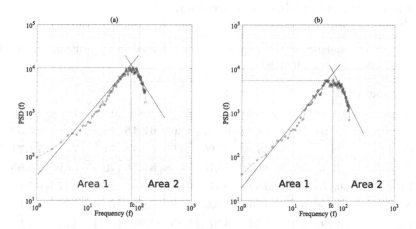

Fig. 2. The mean periodogram computed over the lines of an ROI from each class: (a) is from a CC subject and (b) is from an OA patient.

3.2 Quantitative Classification Performance of OA

The discriminative ability can be quantified by the measures of several statistics, such as the accuracy (Acc), sensitivity (Sens), specificity (Spec), positive and negative predicative values (PPV, NPV) and the values of Positive and Negative Likelihood (PL and NL) [25,26]. These classification performances were tested using logistic regression classifier [10] and the Leave-One-Out (LOO) cross validation strategy [27]. This classifier has a nice probabilistic interpretation, and its algorithm can be regularized to avoid overfitting.

Classification Using the Power Spectral Density as Features

The PSD is very often used as a feature for signal classification, such as EEG signals and Heart sound [28,29]. In this paper, it is used for the analysis of Knee X-Ray image for OA diagnosis.

As shown in Fig. 2, the mean periodogram of a ROI from each subject and N-point PSD in each area are different and changing from subject to another. For this reason, the slope of each region is used as a feature in the classification task. In Table 1, several statistical metrics are computed in three directions $\{0°, 0°, 90°\}$. The PSD at $0°$ orientation is computed over the increments of the lines of each image. The PSD at $90°$ orientation is calculated over the increments of the column of each image. However, The PSD at $45°$ orientation is computed over the increments of the lines of each image by using an oriented approach as in [30]. In this table, we can identify that the orientations $0°$ and $90°$ are the most discriminative for the early detection of knee OA. In addition, area 1 have a better discriminative ability when compared to area 2. This may be justified by the fact that area 1 is related to the high frequencies and thus reflects more the microtrabecular bone changes. However, taking into consideration area 1 and area 2 increases more the diagnostic accuracy.

Table 1. Several diagnostic accuracy measures achieved in the different orientation and using logistic regression classifier.

Orientation	$0°$			$45°$			$90°$		
Areas	1	2	$1+2$	1	2	$1+2$	1	2	$1+2$
Acc (%)	76.02	59.11	**77.76**	66.87	47.67	**67.15**	76.89	76.16	**77.33**
Sens (%)	74.71	75.58	**73.83**	47.96	25.87	**51.74**	74.13	74.42	**74.71**
Spec (%)	77.33	42.44	**81.69**	85.76	69.48	**82.56**	79.65	77.91	**79.95**
PPV	0.77	0.57	0.80	0.77	0.46	0.67	0.78	0.77	0.79
NPV	0.75	0.63	0.76	0.62	0.48	0.63	0.76	0.75	0.76
PL	3.29	1.31	4.03	3.37	0.85	2.96	3.64	3.37	3.72
NL	0.33	0.57	0.32	0.61	1.07	0.58	0.32	0.33	0.32

Classification Using Independent Component Analysis (ICA)

In the previous table, the results reveal that considering orientations $\{0°, 90°\}$ and the slopes of both areas are more relevant for distinguishing OA patients from CC subjects. Thus, it is meaningful to use the whole frequency response of each ROI for OA diagnosis. Hence, in order to extract the most significant PSD features of OA, the resulting PSDs in directions $\{0°, 90°\}$ are combined with ICA.

Table 2 shows the results of the proposed aided diagnosis approach. Our findings demonstrated that the extracted PSD over the increments of the lines and columns of each ROI could be more discriminating features for the early detection of OA. Moreover, there is a slight increase in the classification rates when using the combination of these resulting PSD among $\{0°, 90°\}$ orientations.

Table 2. Several diagnostic accuracy measures achieved by combining PSDs with ICA in the horizontal and vertical orientations and using logistic regression classifier.

Orientations	0°	90°	0° + 90°
Acc (%)	78.779	78.634	**78.924**
Sens (%)	79.942	82.849	**79.651**
Spec (%)	77.616	74.419	**78.198**
PPV	0.795	0.813	0.785
NPV	0.751	0.764	0.794
PL	3.869	3.881	3.653
NL	0.280	0.309	0.260

Comparison to Other Diagnosis Methods

The proposed aided diagnosis method was compared with several approaches for OA diagnosis from the literature. For instance, in [9], the authors developed an approach for the trabecular bone texture classification of 137 knee radiographs using a signature dissimilarity measure (SDM). The SDM system achieved 78.8% for the accuracy, 76.8% for the sensitivity and 80.9% for the specificity. In [13] and [15], their proposed computer-aided methods achieved accuracy values up to 77.2% and 72.61%, respectively. In this proposed aided diagnosis approach, the obtained classification accuracy is up to 78.92%. Besides that, the proposed method was validated on a large dataset (344 X-ray images of each population were used).

4 Conclusion

In this study, we propose a method for the early detection of OA. This approach is based on using the PSD combined with ICA to extract the relevant features of the disease in the frequency domain. Further spectral analysis of the different ROI proves the discriminative ability of the proposed method in the detection of knee OA. Moreover, the proposed texture approach yields a good classification results and could satisfy the clinical constraints of being highly efficient using large amount of data, contrary to several methods proposed in the literature.

Acknowledgments. The authors would like to thank the OAI study participants and clinic staff as well as the coordinating center at UCSF. The authors wish to thank the ANR for the financial support under the project ANR-12-TECS-0016-01.

References

1. Goldring, S.R., Goldring, M.B.: Clinical aspects, pathology and pathophysiology of osteoarthritis. J. Musculoskelet. Neuronal Interact. **6**(4), 376–378 (2006)
2. Sellam, J., Herrero-Beaumont, G., Berenbaum, F.: Osteoarthritis: pathogenesis, clinical aspects and diagnosis. In: EULAR Compendium on Rheumatic Diseases, pp. 444–463. BMJ Publishing Group LTD., Italy (2009)
3. Goldring, M.B., Goldring, S.R.: Articular cartilage and subchondral bone in the pathogenesis of osteoarthritis. Ann. N.Y. Acad. Sci. **1192**, 230–237 (2010)
4. Radin, E.L., Paul, I.L., Tolkoff, M.J.: Subchondral bone changes in patients with early degenerative joint disease. Arthritis Rheum. **13**(4), 400–405 (1970)
5. Wang, T., Wen, C.Y., Yan, C.H., Lu, W.W., Chiu, K.Y.: Spatial and temporal changes of subchondral bone proceed to microscopic articular cartilage degeneration in guinea pigs with spontaneous osteoarthritis. Osteoarthr. Cartil. **21**(4), 574–581 (2013)
6. Kellgren, J.H., Lawrence, J.S.: Radiologic assessment of osteoarthritis. Ann. Rheum. Dis. **16**, 494–501 (1957)
7. Wu, Y., Yang, R., Jia, S., Li, Z., Zhou, Z., Lou, T.: Computer-aided diagnosis of early knee osteoarthritis based on MRI T2 mapping. Biomed. Mater. Eng. **24**(6), 3379–3388 (2014)
8. Shamir, L., et al.: Knee X-ray image analysis method for automated detection of osteoarthritis. IEEE Trans. Biomed. Eng. **56**(2), 407–415 (2009)
9. Woloszynski, T., Podsiadlo, P., Stachowiak, G.W., Kurzynski, M.: A signature dissimilarity measure for trabecular bone texture in knee radiographs. Med. Phys. **37**(5), 2030–2042 (2010)
10. Janvier, T., et al.: Subchondral tibial bone texture analysis predicts knee osteoarthritis progression: data from the Osteoarthritis Initiative Tibial bone texture & knee OA progression. Osteoarthr. Cartil. **25**(2), 259–266 (2017)
11. Janvier, T., Jennane, R., Toumi, H., Lespessailles, E.: Subchondral tibial bone texture predicts the incidence of radiographic knee osteoarthritis: data from the osteoarthritis initiative. Osteoarthr. Cartil. **25**, 2047–2054 (2017)
12. Shamir, L., Ling, S.M., Scott, W., Hochbergk, M., Ferrucci, L., Goldberg, I.G.: Early detection of radiographic knee osteoarthritis using computer-aided analysis. Osteoarthr. Cartil. **17**, 1307–1312 (2009)
13. Antony, J., McGuinness, K., O'Connor, N.E., Moran, K.: Quantifying radiographic knee osteoarthritis severity using deep convolutional neural networks. In: 2016 23rd International Conference on Pattern Recognition (ICPR), pp. 1195–1200, December 2016
14. Stachowiak, G.W., Wolskin, M., Woloszynski, T., Podsiadlo, P.: Detection and prediction of osteoarthritis in knee and hand joints based on the X-ray image analysis. Biosurf. Biotribol. **2**, 162–172 (2016)
15. Kotti, M., Duffell, L.D., Faisal, A.A., McGregor, A.H.: Detecting knee osteoarthritis and its discriminating parameters using random forests. Med. Eng. Phys. **43**, 19–29 (2017)
16. Woloszynski, T., Podsiadlo, P., Stachowiak, G., Kurzynski, M.: A dissimilarity-based multiple classifier system for trabecular bone texture in detection and prediction of progression of knee osteoarthritis. Proc. Inst. Mech. Eng. H **226**(11), 887–894 (2012)
17. Lester, G.: Clinical research in OA-the NIH Osteoarthritis Initiative. Musculoskelet. Neuronal Interact. **8**(4), 313–314 (2008)

18. Eckstein, F., Wirth, W., Nevitt, M.C.: Recent advances in osteoarthritis imaging-the Osteoarthritis Initiative. Nat. Rev. Rheumatol. **8**, 622–630 (2012)
19. Woloszynski, T., Podsiadlo, P., Stachowiak, G., Kurzynski, M., Lohmander, L., Englund, M.: Prediction of progression of radiographic knee osteoarthritis using tibial trabecular bone texture. Arthritis Rheum. **64**(3), 688–695 (2012)
20. Hirvasniemi, J., et al.: Quantification of differences in bone texture from plain radiographs in knees with and without osteoarthritis. Osteoarthr. Cartil. **22**, 1724–1731 (2014)
21. Gonzalez, R.C., Woods, R.E.: Digital Image Processing, 3rd edn. Prentice-Hall, Inc., Upper Saddle River (2006)
22. Hyvärinen, A., Oja, E.: Independent component analysis: algorithms and applications. Neural Netw. **13**(4–5), 411–430 (2000)
23. Li, C.F., Yin, J.Y.: Variational bayesian independent component analysis-support vector machine for remote sensing classification. Comput. Electr. Eng. **39**(3), 717–726 (2013)
24. Khedher, L., Illán, I.A., Górriz, J.M., Ramírez, J., Brahim, A., Meyer-Baese, A.: Independent component analysis-support vector machine-based computer-aided diagnosis system for Alzheimer's with visual support. Int. J. Neural Syst. **27**(3), 1650050–1650068 (2017)
25. Brahim, A., Górriz, J., Ramírez, J., Khedher, L.: Intensity normalization of DaTSCAN SPECT imaging using a model-based clustering approach. Appl. Soft Comput. **37**, 234–244 (2015)
26. McGee, S.: Simplifying likelihood ratios. J. Gen. Intern. Med. **17**(8), 646–649 (2002)
27. Brahim, A., Górriz, J., Ramírez, J., Khedher, L., Salas-Gonzalez, D.: Comparison between different intensity normalization methods in 123 I-ioflupane imaging for the Automatic Detection of Parkinsonism. Plos One **10**(7), 1–20 (2015)
28. Naderi, M.A., Mahdavi-Nasab, H.: Analysis and classification of EEG signals using spectral analysis and recurrent neural networks. In: 2010 17th Iranian Conference of Biomedical Engineering (ICBME) (2010)
29. Kristomo, D., Hidayat, R., Soesanti, I., Kusjani, A.: Heart sound feature extraction and classification using autoregressive power spectral density (AR-PSD) and statistics features. AIP Conf. Proc. **1755**(1), 090007 (2016)
30. Houam, L., Hafiane, A., Boukrouche, A., Lespessailles, E., Jennane, R.: One dimensional local binary pattern for bone texture characterization. Pattern Anal. Appl. **17**, 179–193 (2014)

Object Instance Segmentation in Digital Terrain Models

Bashir Kazimi[✉], Frank Thiemann, and Monika Sester

Institute of Cartography and Geoinformatics, Leibniz University Hannover,
Hannover, Germany
{kazimi,thiemann,sester}@ikg.uni-hannover.de

Abstract. We use an object instance segmentation approach in deep learning to detect and outline objects in Digital Terrain Models (DTMs) derived from Airborne Laser Scanning (ALS) data. Object detection methods in computer vision have been extensively applied to RGB images, and gained excellent results. In this work, we use Mask R-CNN, a famous object detection model, to detect objects in archaeological sites by feeding the model with DTM data. Our experiments show successful application of the Mask R-CNN model, originally developed for image data, on DTM data.

Keywords: Instance segmentation · Digital terrain models · Deep learning

1 Introduction

Deep Learning approaches, and the use of Convolutional Neural Networks (CNNs) have gained a lot of popularity in many applications, specially in Computer Vision. Most of the advances in the field came after AlexNet [14] was created using CNNs and won the ImageNet Large Scale Visual Recognition Challenge [5] in 2012. Since then, CNNs are used for image classification, object localization, semantic and instance segmentation in images.

Since DTM data are represented in matrix form, as with RGB images, but only with a single channel, the same deep learning approaches used for RGB images could be applied on DTM data as well. In this research, our goal is to identify and locate objects of interest for archaeologists such as bomb craters, charcoal kilns, and barrows, among others. The data used is DTM, which is derived from airborne laser scanning (ALS) data acquired from the Harz Region in Lower Saxony, Germany.

DTM data can be leveraged by many methods in computer vision, such as classification, where the goal is to label a given rectangular matrix, part of the DTM, with an object class. It can also be used in object localization, where the task is to produce bounding box coordinates for possible objects in a given input matrix. Another method is semantic segmentation which outputs a class label

© Springer Nature Switzerland AG 2019
M. Vento and G. Percannella (Eds.): CAIP 2019, LNCS 11679, pp. 488–495, 2019.
https://doi.org/10.1007/978-3-030-29891-3_43

for each pixel. Finally, instance segmentation approaches give an outline for each object in the input matrix along with their class labels.

Our goal is to detect objects, and give the exact outline for each object in the region of interest. Therefore, we explore the use of Mask R-CNN [10], which gives the bounding box coordinates, as well as the outline of each instance in a given input image.

The rest of the paper is designed as follows. Section 2 outlines previous research in deep learning and computer vision methods, and their applications in image and DTM data. Section 3 gives an overview of our research, details of the deep learning model, and the data preprocessing methods. Section 4 includes details of experiments in this work. The results of the experiments and evaluation of the model are listed in Sect. 5, and finally, Sect. 6 summarizes this work, and gives hints on possible future tasks in this area.

2 Related Work

Convolutional Neural Networks (CNNs) are extensively used in image classification, and object recognition tasks. CNNs were first used for the task of document recognition [15], but earned their fame with the famous AlexNet model for image classification [14]. Several other CNN models emerged with improvements in performance over AlexNet, such as ZF-Net [26], GoogLeNet [23], VGGNet [22], and ResNet [11] for image classification. These models take an input image, and produce a single label for an object it may contain. An image may contain many objects, and it is sometimes required to identify and localize each object in the image. To serve this purpose, among others, R-CNN [8] was developed. R-CNN model first generates several candidate regions in the input image using selective search algorithm [24]. Each candidate region is then warped into a fixed size square image to be used by CNNs for feature vector extraction. Each feature vector is fed to a class-specific Support Vector Machines (SVM) for classification, and a regressor for bounding box generation.

R-CNN uses CNNs to extract features for each candidate region. It also uses a separate class-specific classifier, and a bounding regressor for each feature vector of the candidate regions. This is very time-consuming and hence, not applicable in real time. To speed up this process, Fast R-CNN [7] was proposed, which is an end-to-end algorithm combining the three models into one. The input image is directly fed to CNN for feature extraction, and the outputs of CNN are used by selective search to generate candidate regions. A Region of Interest (RoI) pooling layer is used to run on each candidate region and output a fixed-length feature vector. The output of RoI pooling layer is fed to a series of fully connected layers eventually leading to the output layers for classification, and bounding box generation.

Fast R-CNN speeds up detection compared to R-CNN by merging three separate models into one. However, it still uses selective search for candidate region generation. To resolve this, Region Proposal Networks (RPNs) [19] was created. RPNs replace the selective search in Fast R-CNN, and are faster to train, hence, the model as a whole is called Faster R-CNN. In this model, an image is given to a CNN for feature extraction. The feature maps given as output by the CNN are then used by RPN, which generates candidate regions, along with objectness score (probability that the region contains an object) and bounding coordinates for the object. RPN can be trained using the ground truth classes and bounding boxes for each region of interest. RoI pooling layer then uses the CNN feature maps to compute a fixed-length vector for each candidate region (using max pooling operation) with a positive objectness score, and finally a classifier and bounding box regressor are used to get the labels and the coordinates.

Objects come in many shapes, and a rectangular bounding box may not always be the best way to spot objects in a given image. Instance segmentation approaches give the exact outline of an object as a boolean mask. Mask R-CNN [10], which extends Faster R-CNN by adding a new branch to predict an object mask, is designed to output object bounding box coordinates, class labels, and segmentation masks. For image classification and object detection tasks, perfect alignment of pixels between the input and the output are not important as long as coarse spatial information is taken into account. However, for generating the exact outline of an object or the segmentation mask, it is necessary to have a better pixel-to-pixel correspondence between the input and the output. Thus, instead of the RoI pooling layer as in Fast and Faster R-CNN, Mask R-CNN implements RoIAlign. In RoI pooling, for each candidate region, features are selected from the CNN output feature map in order to further infer bounding boxes, and class labels. Each candidate region is divided into spatial bins, and the values in each bin are calculated by aggregating (max pooling) the feature values covered by the bins. This max pooling operation harms pixel-to-pixel alignment which is tolerable for classification and detection tasks, but not good for segmentation. RoIAlign uses bilinear interpolation from the neighboring points on the feature map, rather than max pooling. This results into a better pixel-to-pixel correspondence and gives better segmentation results.

The CNN used in the models explained previously are for extracting features from input images. Any famous CNN model trained on images could be used for this purpose. Famous CNN models used for this purpose are AlexNet [14], ZF-Net [26], VGG16 [22], ResNet [11], and FPN [16], among others.

Deep learning models have been successfully used for pattern recognition in DTM and other remote sensing data. Examples are classification [2–4,9,12,18, 20,21], and segmentation [17,25] of remote sensing data such as hyperspectral images, and ALS data, among others. In this research, we explore using Mask R-CNN for object instance segmentation in DTM data. Details of the model and necessary configurations are given in Sect. 3

3   Mask R-CNN for DTM

Mask R-CNN is a framework that takes an image and produces a rectangular bounding box, a class label for the object inside the bounding box, and a mask showing which pixels in the box belong to the object in the given image. It is an extension of Faster R-CNN which is in turn an extension to Fast R-CNN and R-CNN models. The first part of Mask R-CNN consists of a CNN model for feature extraction. The core feature extractor in Mask R-CNN is Feature Pyramid Network (FPN) [16] with ResNet-101 architecture [11]. FPN feature maps at different scales are given to RPN for candidate region generation. The regions with a positive objectness score by RPN are accompanied with bounding box offsets in different sizes. In Mask R-CNN, ROIAlign is used to crop or resize each bounding box from the feature maps in order to have a fixed input size to the classifier, and regressor in the final output layer. Additionally, the positive ROIs are fed to another CNN that generates binary masks for the object.

In this work, we are using Mask R-CNN for object detection and segmentation in DTMs. The input to the model is a raster with a spatial dimension of 256 × 256 where it is guaranteed to have an object at the center, and possibly objects in the other locations of the raster. The outputs are bounding box coordinates, a class label (one of bomb craters, charcoal kilns, or barrows), and binary masks representing pixels belonging to the detected object. The workflow for the model is illustrated in Fig. 1. We give more details of our experiments in Sect. 4 and evaluate the results in Sect. 5.

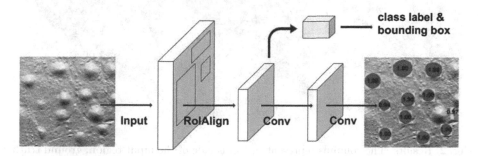

Fig. 1. Model workflow. The input is a DTM patch of size 256 × 256 pixels. The branch after the first convolutional layer outputs class label with confidence score, and bounding coordinates while the final branch produces instance mask. For visual purposes, the input illustrated here is a hillshade patch, rather than the original DTM patch used.

4   Experiments

In our experiments, we use DTM data, with a resolution of half a meter per pixel, derived from ALS point cloud acquired from Harz Region in Lower Saxony, Germany. The goal is to identify and locate objects of interest for archaeologists. Categories considered in our current research include bomb craters, charcoal kilns, and barrows. Using ArcGIS and knowledge about the region, known objects are labeled as circles for simplicity. To train Mask R-CNN, rasters with

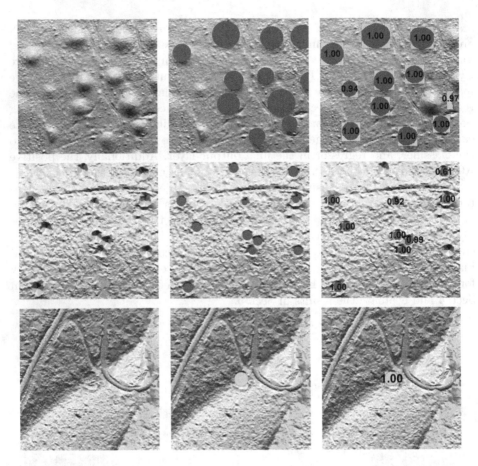

Fig. 2. Results. The columns represent raw hillshade of the input region, ground truth labels, and detection results, respectively. The rows represent results for barrows, bomb craters, and charcoal kilns, respectively. The numbers on the right column represent the confidence of the model in categorizing the detection.

a spatial dimension of 256 × 256 pixels are cropped from the DTM where it is guaranteed to include an object in the center, and possibly elsewhere in the raster, and the values are scaled between 0 and 1. For each labeled instance in the raster location, a binary mask and the corresponding label are generated to train the model with. Table 1 summarizes the statistics for the training and validation data for our experiments.

The model is trained with ResNet-FPN-101 backbone for 300 epochs with a batch size of 8 with and 64 anchors per image. 2000 region proposals are generated, and a threshold of 70% is used during non-maximum suppression for filtering the region proposals. After the region proposals are given to ROI objectness classifier, and ROI bounding box regressor, a threshold of 33% is used to filter the positive ROIs, i.e., one third of positive ROIs are used to train the

Table 1. Data statistics

Category	Number of examples	
	Training (80%)	Validation (20%)
Bomb craters	127	30
Charcoal kilns	854	190
Barrows	163	40

final category classifier and the mask predictor. The model is evaluated using average precision at an intersection over union above a certain threshold (AP @ IoU_{th}).

5   Results

The trained model explained in Sect. 4 is evaluated on validation set. We used a threshold of 50 and 75% for the IoU and calculated the mean average precision (mAP). The results are shown in Table 2.

Table 2. Mean Average Precision at IoU with thresholds of 50 and 75%.

mAP @ IoU = 50	mAP @ IoU = 75
81%	58%

To evaluate the model visually, examples are illustrated in Fig. 2. Even though the ground truth labels are circular for simplicity, and not all the true object instances are in perfectly circular shapes, the model is able to learn the true shape of the objects rather than memorizing the ground truth label or a circular shape. This is clearly visible in the first row of examples in Fig. 2. There are cases where the model fails to correctly identify objects as in the first row, the biggest barrow in the bottom right, and the bottom right bomb crater in the second row in Fig. 2. We assume this is due to the fact that the objects are in the corner of the given input, and the model does not have enough spatial information to detect some of the objects. On the positive side, there are examples that were not labeled while creating training and validation examples, but the trained model detects them nonetheless. An instance of this is shown in the first row in Fig. 2 where the model detects the barrow in the mid-left section of the input with a confidence score of 94%.

6   Conclusion

In this work, we successfully use Mask R-CNN, a famous instance segmentation approach for RGB images, and apply it to DTM data. The model is used for detecting bomb craters, charcoal kilns, and barrows in archaeological sites. Even though all objects were labeled with a circular shape for training the model, the model still somewhat learns the true shape of the objects. Results could be further improved with better ground truth labeling. Further work in this research direction includes addition of other objects of interest for archaeologists in the training data, and additional preprocessing and post-processing operations to use the model on bigger DTM patches, and not be constrained to the patch size during training and/or sliding window approach. Additionally, Mask R-CNN is an approach based on region proposals just like R-CNN, Fast and Faster R-CNN. The problem with these approaches are that the instance category is decided by the detected bounding box, and if two objects share the majority of their bounding boxes, the model cannot decide well which label to give to the boxes. If only a small part of the bounding box is shared, the pixels in that region are segmented to both objects resulting into multiple label for the same pixel. Finally, the number of region proposals generated by the model affects the number of instances in the detection. This could be either more than or less than the actual number of instances. To see how big of a problem these could be, another possible task is to use proposal-free detection methods such as [1,6,13] for DTM data and compare the results.

References

1. Brabandere, B.D., Neven, D., Gool, L.V.: Semantic instance segmentation with a discriminative loss function. CoRR abs/1708.02551 (2017). http://arxiv.org/abs/1708.02551
2. Castelluccio, M., Poggi, G., Sansone, C., Verdoliva, L.: Land use classification in remote sensing images by convolutional neural networks. CoRR abs/1508.00092 (2015). http://arxiv.org/abs/1508.00092
3. Chen, Y., Jiang, H., Li, C., Jia, X., Ghamisi, P.: Deep feature extraction and classification of hyperspectral images based on convolutional neural networks. IEEE Trans. Geosci. Remote. Sens. 54(10), 6232–6251 (2016)
4. Chen, Y., Lin, Z., Zhao, X., Wang, G., Gu, Y.: Deep learning-based classification of hyperspectral data. IEEE J. Sel. Top. Appl. Earth Obs. Remote. Sens. 7(6), 2094–2107 (2014)
5. Deng, J., Dong, W., Socher, R., Li, L.J., Li, K., Fei-Fei, L.: ImageNet: a large-scale hierarchical image database. In: IEEE Conference on Computer Vision and Pattern Recognition, CVPR 2009, pp. 248–255. IEEE (2009)
6. Fathi, A., Wojna, Z., Rathod, V., Wang, P., Song, H.O., Guadarrama, S., Murphy, K.P.: Semantic instance segmentation via deep metric learning. CoRR abs/1703.10277 (2017). http://arxiv.org/abs/1703.10277
7. Girshick, R.: Fast R-CNN. In: Proceedings of the IEEE International Conference on Computer Vision, pp. 1440–1448 (2015)
8. Girshick, R., Donahue, J., Darrell, T., Malik, J.: Rich feature hierarchies for accurate object detection and semantic segmentation. In: Proceedings of the IEEE Conference on Computer Vision and Pattern Recognition, pp. 580–587 (2014)
9. Hamraz, H., Jacobs, N.B., Contreras, M.A., Clark, C.H.: Deep learning for conifer/deciduous classification of airborne LiDAR 3D point clouds representing individual trees. arXiv preprint arXiv:1802.08872 (2018)

10. He, K., Gkioxari, G., Dollár, P., Girshick, R.: Mask R-CNN. In: 2017 IEEE International Conference on Computer Vision (ICCV), pp. 2980–2988. IEEE (2017)
11. He, K., Zhang, X., Ren, S., Sun, J.: Deep residual learning for image recognition. In: Proceedings of the IEEE Conference on Computer Vision and Pattern Recognition, pp. 770–778 (2016)
12. Kazimi, B., Thiemann, F., Malek, K., Sester, M., Khoshelham, K.: Deep learning for archaeological object detection in airborne laser scanning data (09 2018)
13. Kong, S., Fowlkes, C.C.: Recurrent pixel embedding for instance grouping. CoRR abs/1712.08273 (2017). http://arxiv.org/abs/1712.08273
14. Krizhevsky, A., Sutskever, I., Hinton, G.E.: ImageNet classification with deep convolutional neural networks. In: Advances in Neural Information Processing Systems, pp. 1097–1105 (2012)
15. LeCun, Y., Bottou, L., Bengio, Y., Haffner, P.: Gradient-based learning applied to document recognition. Proc. IEEE **86**(11), 2278–2324 (1998)
16. Lin, T.Y., Dollár, P., Girshick, R., He, K., Hariharan, B., Belongie, S.: Feature pyramid networks for object detection. In: Proceedings of the IEEE Conference on Computer Vision and Pattern Recognition, pp. 2117–2125 (2017)
17. Politz, F., Sester, M.: Exploring ALS and DIM data for semantic segmentation using CNNs. Int. Arch. Photogramm. Remote. Sens. Spat. Inf. Sci. ISPRS Arch. 42 (2018), Nr. 1 **42**(1), 347–354 (2018)
18. Politz, F., Kazimi, B., Sester, M.: Classification of laser scanning data using deep learning. In: 38th Scientific Technical Annual Meeting of the German Society for Photogrammetry, Remote Sensing and Geoinformation, vol. 27 (2018)
19. Ren, S., He, K., Girshick, R., Sun, J.: Faster R-CNN: towards real-time object detection with region proposal networks. In: Advances in Neural Information Processing Systems, pp. 91–99 (2015)
20. Rizaldy, A., Persello, C., Gevaert, C., Oude Elberink, S.: Fully convolutional networks for ground classification from LiDAR point clouds. ISPRS Ann. Photogramm. Remote. Sens. Spat. Inf. Sci. **4**(2), 231–238 (2018)
21. Rizaldy, A., Persello, C., Gevaert, C., Oude Elberink, S., Vosselman, G.: Ground and multi-class classification of airborne laser scanner point clouds using fully convolutional networks. Remote Sens. **10**(11), 1723 (2018)
22. Simonyan, K., Zisserman, A.: Very deep convolutional networks for large-scale image recognition. CoRR abs/1409.1556 (2014). http://arxiv.org/abs/1409.1556
23. Szegedy, C., et al.: Going deeper with convolutions. In: Proceedings of the IEEE Conference on Computer Vision and Pattern Recognition, pp. 1–9 (2015)
24. Uijlings, J.R.R., van de Sande, K.E.A., Gevers, T., Smeulders, A.W.M.: Selective search for object recognition. Int. J. Comput. Vis. **104**(2), 154–171 (2013). https://ivi.fnwi.uva.nl/isis/publications/2013/UijlingsIJCV2013
25. Yang, Z., Tan, B., Pei, H., Jiang, W.: Segmentation and multi-scale convolutional neural network-based classification of airborne laser scanner data. Sensors **18**(10), 3347 (2018)
26. Zeiler, M.D., Fergus, R.: Visualizing and understanding convolutional networks. In: Fleet, D., Pajdla, T., Schiele, B., Tuytelaars, T. (eds.) ECCV 2014. LNCS, vol. 8689, pp. 818–833. Springer, Cham (2014). https://doi.org/10.1007/978-3-319-10590-1_53

Improvement of Image Denoising Algorithms by Preserving the Edges

Ram Krishna Pandey$^{(\boxtimes)}$, Harpreet Singh, and A. G. Ramakrishnan

Department of Electrical Engineering, Indian Institute of Science, Bangalore, India
{ramp,agr}@iisc.ac.in, harpreet.singh.cse14@itbhu.ac.in

Abstract. Image restoration is one of the well-studied problems in low-level image processing tasks. Recently, deep learning based image restoration techniques have shown promising results and outperform most of the state of the art image denoising algorithms. Most of the deep learning based methods use mean square error as a loss function to obtain the denoised output. This work focuses on further improving the existing deep learning based image denoising techniques by preserving edges using Canny edge based loss function, and hence improving peak signal to noise ratio (PSNR) and structural similarity (SSIM) of the images while restoring the visual quality.

Keywords: Loss function · CNN · Denoising · Mean square error · Mean square Canny error · Edge preservation · PSNR · SSIM

1 Introduction

Image denoising deals with the task of obtaining a clean image x from a noisy observation y, given as $y = x + \eta$ where η is additive white Gaussian noise. It is one of the fundamental steps in solving many interesting and complicated image analysis and recognition tasks. Images are captured by different modalities that cause degradation, resulting in noisy versions. Image denoising is an ill-posed problem and hence does not possess a unique solution i.e a unique mapping between noisy and denoised image; hence, we are required to address this issue with a method that preserves perceptual quality and also the fine details of the denoised image. Denoising algorithms in the literature can be broadly classified into filtering [1,2], sparse coding [3,4], prior [5], low rank [7] and deep learning based algorithms [11,12]. The algorithms such as [1–3,5,7] achieve very good image restoration quality at the cost of high computational complexity during testing. Recent advancements in deep learning have resulted in elegant discriminative algorithms such as DnCNN [12] (specific noise level (DnCNN-S) and blind denoising (DnCNN-B)) that do not require an explicit prior information. Our main contribution lies in modifying the loss function in such a way that it improves the performance of any existing denosing algorithm using Mean Squared error (MSE) loss function. Our modified loss function has

M. Vento and G. Percannella (Eds.): CAIP 2019, LNCS 11679, pp. 496–506, 2019.
https://doi.org/10.1007/978-3-030-29891-3_44

resulted in consistent performance gain in terms of peak signal to noise (PSNR) and structural similarity (SSIM) over the existing state of the art algorithms (PSNR listed in Tables 1, 2, 3, 4, 5 and 6). Obviously, our modification does not increase computational time during testing.

2   Related Work

Because of their high representational power, Convolutional Neural Networks (CNN) have shown promising results in various image processing and computer vision tasks. In [8], the authors have shown that the CNN based architecture performs comparable or in some cases superior to the state of the art Markov random field (MRF) or wavelet based denoising algorithms, while avoiding the associated computational difficulty. In [9] a multi layer perceptron is trained to obtain noise-free images from noisy input images. In [10], the authors have combined the advantages of sparse coding and deep neural networks and have shown promising results on image denoising and inpainting tasks. Recent deep learning techniques such as TNRD [11,12] have achieved very good restoration quality. In [12], an architecture is developed using elegant techniques such as batch norm for faster training and mean square error (MSE) as the loss function. Recently proposed loss functions such as perceptual loss, adversarial loss, content loss [14,15] have shown good enhancement in terms of the perceptual quality of images. In this work, we are preserving one of the most important feature of an image, namely the edges, by penalizing the network if it tries to blur the edges. We have used various steps of the Canny operator to obtain the edges. However, these operations are performed during training only. Thus, while it involves a slight increase in the computational cost during training, there is no additional computational overhead during testing.

3   Loss Function

The discriminative learning algorithms use the loss function to quantify the performance of the model, given the Ground-truth results. The loss function gives the model the discriminatory power, which affects how the model makes predictions, given the input. The edge structure is an important characteristic of an image. Edges should not be blurred or smoothed out during the denoising process. In this work, to preserve the edges, we use a loss function, which is a weighted sum of the mean square loss and the edge-based loss computed between the Ground-truth image and the denoised image obtained from the model.

To compute the edge-based loss we need to compute the edge map for both normalized, Ground truth and denoised images. The edge map is generated using the four stages of Canny-edge detection [16] - preprocessing, gradient computation, non-maximum suppression and thresholding. In the preprocessing stage, we performed Gaussian blurring. We choose 1×5 Gaussian matrix for blurring initialized with standard normal distribution. Sobel operators are used for computing the gradient magnitude and direction. Non-maximum suppression is performed along the direction of the gradient to obtain the pixel, whose intensity is greater than its neighbors on both sides. For thresholding, the gradient values less than a set threshold are removed. We choose the value 2 as threshold since for this value the edge map quality was superior. We have avoided complete implementation of hysteresis thresholding, since it would be computationally very expensive during the training process. Given the Ground truth image as I_G, denoised image as I_D and our canny operator C, Canny edge loss is defined as

$$canny\_edge\_loss = ||C(I_G) - C(I_D)||^2 \tag{1}$$

$$square\_loss = ||I_G - I_D||^2 \tag{2}$$

$$Loss = \lambda \times mean\_square\_loss + (1 - \lambda) \times canny\_edge\_loss \tag{3}$$

where λ is the factor that controls the weight given to each type of loss in the final loss function. It can also be interpreted as a regularization factor between noise reduction and edge preservation. The complete implementation of Canny-edge detection steps has been done in Pytorch so as to use the GPU computation for edge map computation.

4   Experiments

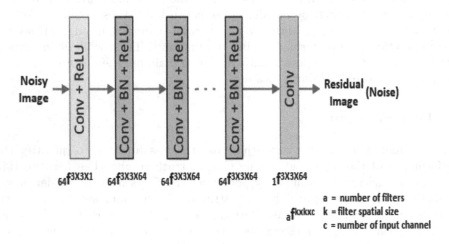

Fig. 1. DnCNN [12] architecture is trained with our loss function.

Figure 1 gives the architecture of DnCNN [12]. We have used this architecture (the best among most deep learning based architectures) for training with Canny edge map based loss function so that we can compare and report the performance improvement achieved by using our loss function.

4.1   Experimental Settings

We have trained the DnCNN model with our Canny-edge based loss function (Eq. 3) on the same dataset of grayscale images used in [12]. Thus, for training, Train400 and for testing, Berkely Images Segmentation Dataset (BSD68) and Set12 dataset are used. Also, to demonstrate the effectiveness of our loss function under identical conditions, we have used similar experimental settings as performed in [12]. For Non-Blind denoising, the patch size used is 40×40 with stride 10 and the batch size is 64. The depth of the network is 17. Separate models are trained for noise levels 15, 25, 50 using Canny edge based loss function given in Eq. 3 and these models are labeled as Ours-S, where noise level $\sigma = S$. The model Ours-S is used to report the results on test images which are generated by adding white Gaussian noise of noise level $\sigma = S$ to the Ground-truth images.

In the case of Blind denoising, we use the model similar to DnCNN-B [12]. The depth of the network used is 20 where 3 extra "Conv-Batch-Relu" units are added. The patch size used is 50×50 with a stride of 10 and the batch size is 64. We train a single model with noisy images generated by adding white Gaussian noise of σ chosen randomly in the range [5, 55] and by using our loss function (see Eq. 3). The results are reported on the test images generated by adding the white Gaussian noise with noise level $\sigma \in$ 15, 25, 50 to Ground-Truth test images. The value of λ is taken 0.8 for both non-blind and blind denoising since convergence is faster for this value and also training error turns out to be least. For values less than 0.8, the convergence rate was slower and for $\lambda > 0.8$ the convergence rate and training error was approximately similar.

4.2   Quantitative Evaluation

Tables 1 and 2 list the PSNR values of state-of-the-art image denoising methods and compare the results of our loss function based DnCNN model, Ours-S and Ours-B on BSD68 and Set12 datasets. Tables 3, 4, 5 and 6 list the PSNR and SSIM values of modified loss function based model and the original DnCNN models, the details of which are mentioned in the captions of the Tables. We have shown the results of using Canny edge based loss function with both DnCNN-S and DnCNN-B. The results are compared for three noise levels, 15, 25 and 50. It is to be noted that models trained using our Canny edge based loss function give better denoising performance than other approaches as reported in

Table 1. Comparison of our results (in terms of PSNR) with the state-of-the-art image denonising algorithms on BSD68 dataset. (We have trained the DnCNN and our model from scratch and use the models trained for same number of epochs for testing.)

Noise level	BM3D [2]	WNNM [7]	EPLL [5]	MLP [9]	CSF [6]	TNRD [11]	DnCNN-S [12]	DnCNN-B [12]	Ours-NB	Ours-B
$\sigma = 15$	31.07	31.37	31.21	-	31.24	31.73	31.736	31.604	**31.741**	**31.627**
$\sigma = 25$	28.57	28.83	28.68	28.96	28.74	28.92	29.239	29.1474	29.231	**29.167**
$\sigma = 50$	25.62	25.87	25.67	26.03	-	25.97	26.237	26.211	**26.241**	**26.227**

Table 2. Comparison of our results (in terms of PSNR) with the state-of-the-art image denonising algorithms on Set12 Dataset. (We have trained the DnCNN and our model from scratch and test them after the same number of epochs of training.)

Noise level	BM3D [2]	WNNM [7]	EPLL [5]	MLP [9]	CSF [6]	TNRD [11]	DnCNN-S [12]	DnCNN-B [12]	Ours-NB	Ours-B
$\sigma = 15$	32.372	32.696	32.138	-	32.318	32.502	32.867	32.71	**32.876**	**32.728**
$\sigma = 25$	29.969	30.257	29.692	30.027	29.837	30.055	30.448	30.349	30.446	**30.376**
$\sigma = 50$	26.722	27.052	26.471	26.783	-	26.812	27.19	27.154	27.187	**27.188**

Table 3. Comparison of results obtained from Ours-S with that of DnCNN-S [12] in terms of PSNR and SSIM on BSD68 dataset.

Noise level	DnCNN-S		Ours-S	
	PSNR	SSIM	PSNR	SSIM
$\sigma = 15$	31.736	0.9409	**31.741**	**0.9411**
$\sigma = 25$	29.239	0.902	29.231	0.901
$\sigma = 50$	26.237	0.826	**26.241**	**0.825**

Table 4. Comparison of results from Ours-S and DnCNN-S [12] on Set12 dataset in terms of PSNR and SSIM.

Noise level	DnCNN-S		Ours-S	
	PSNR	SSIM	PSNR	SSIM
$\sigma = 15$	32.867	0.954	**32.876**	**0.954**
$\sigma = 25$	30.448	0.93	30.446	0.929
$\sigma = 50$	27.19	0.877	**27.187**	**0.877**

Table 5. Blind model (explained in Sect. 4) results: Comparison of Ours-B results with those of DnCNN-B [12], on BSD68 dataset, in terms of PSNR and SSIM. (For testing, fixed values of σ 15, 25 and 50 are used to create noisy images.)

Noise level	DnCNN-B		Ours-B	
	PSNR	SSIM	PSNR	SSIM
$\sigma = 15$	31.604	0.938	**31.627**	**0.939**
$\sigma = 25$	29.1474	0.899	**29.167**	**0.899**
$\sigma = 50$	26.211	0.823	**26.227**	**0.824**

Table 6. Blind model results: our results compared with DnCNN [12] in terms of PSNR and SSIM on Set12. For testing, fixed values of σ of 15, 25 and 50 are used.)

Noise level	DnCNN-B		Ours-B	
	PSNR	SSIM	PSNR	SSIM
$\sigma = 15$	32.721	0.952	**32.728**	**0.953**
$\sigma = 25$	30.349	0.928	**30.376**	**0.928**
$\sigma = 50$	27.154	0.875	**27.188**	**0.877**

Tables 1 and 2. The modified DnCNN model gives much better performance with increased number of epochs. However, we have chosen to report the performance of DnCNN and Ours models which are trained for same number of epochs. With one or two exceptions, our proposed loss function based model gives better results in terms of PSNR and SSIM than the original model. As evident from the Tables, our model performs the best for blind denoising in every case. In blind denoising, the model is not trained for any specific noise level, but rather for noisy images with random level of noise between 5 and 55.

It is evident from Tables 5 and 6 that our proposed approach gives equal (in some cases) and better results in case of blind denoising where model is trained to test on any random noise level. In Tables 3 and 4 we observe the increase

| (a) Ground Truth | (b) Noisy | (c) DnCNN-S | (d) Ours-S |

| (e) Ground Truth | (f) Noisy | (g) DnCNN-S | (h) Ours-S |

| (i) Ground Truth | (j) Noisy | (k) DnCNN-S | (l) Ours-S |

Fig. 2. Qualitative comparison of the results of DnCNN-S [12] with Ours-S, on a sample image from Set12 dataset. First row: $\sigma = 15$; second row: $\sigma = 25$; third row: $\sigma = 50$.

in results is observed for noise level 15 and 50 but not for 25 which shows our proposed method is effective in removing noise of extreme noise levels effectively.

4.3   Qualitative Evaluation

Figures 2, 3, 4 and 5 show the perceptual quality of the images denoised by the DnCNN-S [12] and DnCNN-B [12] model and after modification with our loss function (Ours-S and Ours-B), for non-blind and blind cases, respectively (details mentioned in the caption of the Figures).

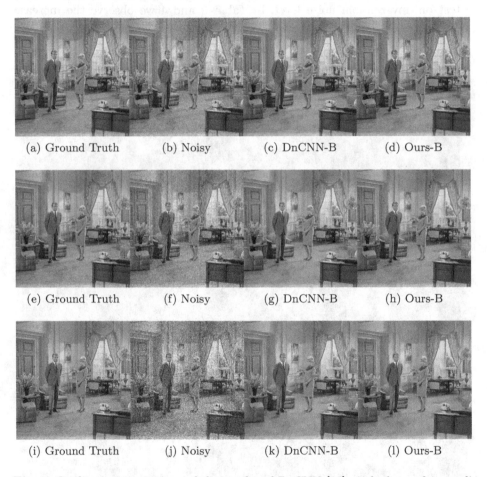

(a) Ground Truth   (b) Noisy   (c) DnCNN-B   (d) Ours-B

(e) Ground Truth   (f) Noisy   (g) DnCNN-B   (h) Ours-B

(i) Ground Truth   (j) Noisy   (k) DnCNN-B   (l) Ours-B

Fig. 3. Qualitative comparison of the results of DnCNN [12], with those after modification with our loss function, Ours-B on a sample image from Set12 dataset. Blind model (explained in Sect. 4): First row: $\sigma = 15$; second row: $\sigma = 25$; third row: $\sigma = 50$.

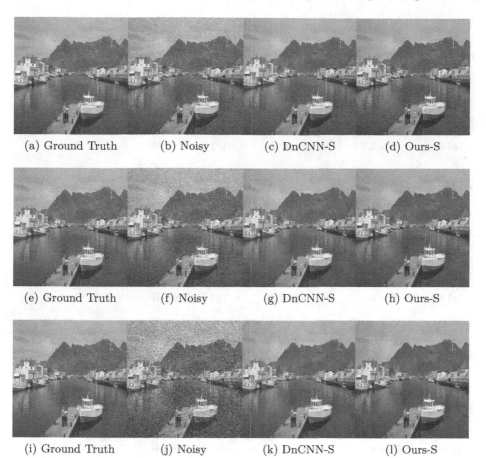

(a) Ground Truth   (b) Noisy   (c) DnCNN-S   (d) Ours-S

(e) Ground Truth   (f) Noisy   (g) DnCNN-S   (h) Ours-S

(i) Ground Truth   (j) Noisy   (k) DnCNN-S   (l) Ours-S

Fig. 4. Non Blind: First row $\sigma = 15$; second row $\sigma = 25$; third row $\sigma = 50$: Qualitative comparison of the results of DnCNN-S [12] with Ours-S (with modified loss function) from a sample image taken from BSD68 dataset

4.4   Discussion

The use of Canny-edge-based loss function ensures that the denoised output preserves the structure, thus improving the value of SSIM. Tables 1 and 2 compares the PSNR of some state-of-the-art image denoising methods with our canny-edge loss based models. Since our model performs better for each noise level for Blind Denoising, our model is best suited to tackle the noisy image with the random noise level. This is a major achievement for our model. Tables 3, 4, 5 and 6 compares the PSNR and SSIM of DnCNN [12] before and after the use of our loss function. Figures 2 and 3 shows the perceptual quality of sample images (from the set12 dataset) obtained from the original model and the model modified with our loss function for the noise level of 15, 25 and 50 (details are mentioned in the caption of Figures). Figures 3 and 5 shows the perceptual quality of sample

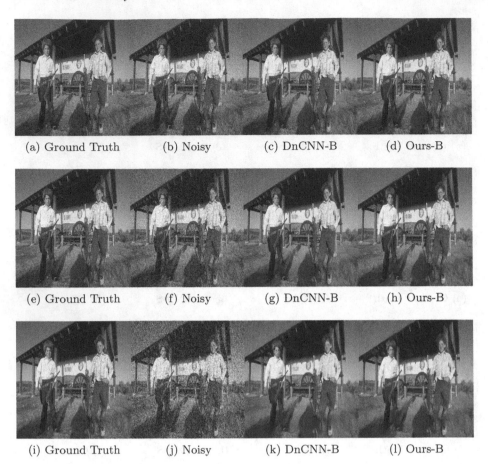

Fig. 5. Qualitative comparison of the results of DnCNN-B [12] with Ours-B, on a sample image from BSD68 dataset. Blind: 1st row: $\sigma = 15$; 2nd row: $\sigma = 25$; 3rd row: $\sigma = 50$.

images (from BSD68 dataset) obtained from the original model and the model modified with our loss function for the noise level of 15, 25 and 50 (details are mentioned in the caption of Figures).

5   Conclusion

In this work, we have shown that (i) the performance of DnCNN image denoising algorithm that uses loss function minimization such as MSE can be improved in terms of both PSNR and SSIM by performing a simple modification to the loss function i.e. using an edge-preserving loss function. (ii) Our loss function ensures the model learns while preserving the edges. (iii) Our models perform consistently better in terms PSNR and SSIM. In an earlier work, we have already shown that the addition of Canny edge based loss function improves the performance of super-resolution algorithms that use MSE loss function [13]. Thus, we expect that the addition of the proposed loss function will ensure performance gain to any existing algorithm using MSE. However, it is to be noted that it gives very good results in blind denoising case. This operation adds a marginal overhead in terms of computation during training, with no change in computational complexity during testing.

References

1. Buades, A., Coll, B., Morel, J.-M.: A non-local algorithm for image denoising. In: IEEE Computer Society Conference on Computer Vision and Pattern Recognition, CVPR 2005, vol. 2 (2005)
2. Dabov, K., et al.: Image restoration by sparse 3D transform-domain collaborative filtering. In: Image Processing: Algorithms and Systems VI, vol. 6812. International Society for Optics and Photonics (2008)
3. Elad, M., Aharon, M.: Image denoising via sparse and redundant representations over learned dictionaries. IEEE Trans. Image Process. **15**(12), 3736–3745 (2006)
4. Mairal, J., et al.: Non-local sparse models for image restoration. In: 12th IEEE International Conference on Computer Vision (2009)
5. Zoran, D., Weiss, Y.: From learning models of natural image patches to whole image restoration. In: International Conference on Computer Vision (ICCV). IEEE (2011)
6. Schmidt, U., Roth, S.: Shrinkage fields for effective image restoration. In: Proceedings of the IEEE Conference on Computer Vision and Pattern Recognition (2014)
7. Gu, S., et al.: Weighted nuclear norm minimization with application to image denoising. In: Proceedings of the IEEE Conference on Computer Vision and Pattern Recognition (2014)
8. Jain, V., Seung, S.: Natural image denoising with convolutional networks. In: Advances in Neural Information Processing Systems (2009)
9. Burger, H.C., Schuler, C.J., Harmeling, S.: Image denoising: can plain neural networks compete with BM3D? In: Computer Vision and Pattern Recognition (CVPR). IEEE (2012)
10. Xie, J., Xu, L., Chen. E.: Image denoising and inpainting with deep neural networks. In: Advances in Neural Information Processing Systems (2012)
11. Chen, Y., Pock, T.: Trainable nonlinear reaction diffusion: a flexible framework for fast and effective image restoration. IEEE Trans. Pattern Anal. Mach. Intell. **39**(6), 1256–1272 (2017)
12. Zhang, K., Zuo, W., Chen, Y., Meng, D., Zhang, L.: Beyond a Gaussian denoiser: residual learning of deep CNN for image denoising. IEEE Trans. Image Process. **26**(7), 3142–3155 (2017)
13. Pandey, R.K., Saha, N., Karmakar, S., Ramakrishnan, A.G.: MSCE: an edge-preserving robust loss function for improving super-resolution algorithms. In: Cheng, L., Leung, A.C.S., Ozawa, S. (eds.) ICONIP 2018. LNCS, vol. 11306, pp. 566–575. Springer, Cham (2018). https://doi.org/10.1007/978-3-030-04224-0_49
14. Ledig, C., et al.: Photo-realistic single image super-resolution using a generative adversarial network. In: Proceedings of IEEE Conference on Computer Vision and Pattern Recognition (2017)

15. Johnson, J., Alahi, A., Fei-Fei, L.: Perceptual losses for real-time style transfer and super-resolution. In: Leibe, B., Matas, J., Sebe, N., Welling, M. (eds.) ECCV 2016. LNCS, vol. 9906, pp. 694–711. Springer, Cham (2016). https://doi.org/10.1007/978-3-319-46475-6_43
16. Canny, J.F.: A computational approach to edge detection. IEEE Trans. Pattern Anal. Mach. Intell. **PAMI-8**, 679–698 (1986)

Fast Landmark Recognition in Photo Albums

Pierre Stefani[✉] and Cristina Oprean[✉]

Photobox, London, UK
{pierre.stefani,cristina.oprean}@photobox.com
http://www.photobox.com

Abstract. The performance of landmark recognition models has significantly improved following the introduction of dedicated CNN-based methods. Most existing algorithms rely on instance-level image retrieval techniques and this induces a scalability problem. Here, we tackle this landmark recognition as a classification task to achieve real-time processing. Our focus is on building an industrial architecture which provides an optimal trade-off between the execution time and performance. We first use a DELF model, which achieves state-of-the-art accuracy, to extract features. Second, we add VLAD layer to create fixed size features from the initial variable length DELF features. Third, the VLAD features are fed to a classifier which provides the final results. Finally, we include a light but powerful distractor handling post-processing step to avoid false positives. It is needed to cope with real datasets which include both landmark and non-landmark images. As an alternate pipeline, we test fine-tuning of different deep learning models to propose a simpler and faster model without the use of attention layers. The experiments show that our approaches have competitive performances while reducing the complexity of the recognition process.

Keywords: Image classification · Landmark recognition · Deep learning

1 Introduction

Photobox is a printing company selling personalized photo products (books, calendars, canvas, etc.). More than 3 millions photos are uploaded daily and can benefit from photo analysis in order to help product personalization. From detecting faces to describing image content, plenty of information can be extracted from pictures. Photo book creation is a time intensive task when done manually. Photobox customers are spending an average 5 h divided over 20 days to create a book. By analyzing photo content, we can help automating part of this experience (e.g. removing duplicate photos). A great share of photo book stories is about travels, including sightseeing. By recognizing landmarks in photos, we could help highlighting those important pictures in books.

© Springer Nature Switzerland AG 2019
M. Vento and G. Percannella (Eds.): CAIP 2019, LNCS 11679, pp. 507–518, 2019.
https://doi.org/10.1007/978-3-030-29891-3_45

It is thus important to include efficient landmark recognition tools. While an important research effort was dedicated to landmark recognition, several open questions remain in Photobox industrial context: variety of monuments, obstruction of monuments by people, hard categories (e.g. cathedrals), ambiguous monuments (e.g. Eiffel Tower in Paris and Las Vegas), processing time, ...

To design a fast, scalable landmark recognition pipeline for Photobox customer photos, we should first answer the following questions:

1. *Which landmarks appear most frequently in our customers' photos?* A study of tagged images in the Google Landmark Recognition Dataset showed that few landmarks were common between it and the most visited places by Photobox' customers. Most of the public datasets weren't depicting customers' usual touristic destinations, like Disneyland Paris or the Tower Bridge in London. A custom dataset was created to address the most interesting landmarks, company and customers wise. An analysis of the most frequented places by Photobox customers led to a selection of 263 places.

2. *What type of algorithm is more adapted?* We have investigated different existing landmark recognition methods. Most of them tackle the problem as a retrieval task while in our context, the problem is a classification one. Recent performing retrieval methods, such as DELF, include time-consuming steps like RANSAC [14]. To build a real-time landmark recognition system, we need to find a compromise between the processing time and the system's performance. For these reasons, we considered the landmark recognition problem directly as a classification task in a deep network.

3. *How to separate photos with landmarks from the others?* When the customers upload their photos on Photobox platforms, most of the photos don't contain landmarks. To avoid false positives, we should define a confidence score to make sure we only recognize known landmarks.

The objective of this work is to propose an industrial architecture for landmark recognition that makes a good compromise between the performance and execution time. We proposed two different approaches to tackle these questions and challenges. The first one is built around the DELF [14] feature extractor and combines different modules such as: VLAD [9] features, light geometric verification, contextual information (such as GPS and timestamps), etc. The second one uses ResNet [8] or VGG [22] based neural networks, fine-tuned iteratively on internal data that aims to make the compromise between the execution time and the accuracy. The experiments are carried out on public datasets to evaluate our models with the state of the art methods, but also on in-house datasets, built on internal data. At the end a discussion is led in order to highlight the advantages and inconveniences of each method. Some possible improvements are further introduced.

2   Related Works

Landmark recognition in computer vision has recently seen a spike in its applications, through progress in computer vision techniques, architectures, and hardware [1,13]. In order to identify an image that can be depicted in many different setups (angles, lightning, scales, obstruction), landmark recognition is often done through retrieval techniques. Historically, local descriptors were used to find and describe keypoints in an image [12,23] and were offering a compact and accurate image representation [9,15] that will later go through retrieval methods like nearest neighbour search. Among the first efficient local descriptors, we mention SIFT descriptors [12], where keypoints of an image were extracted from several scales of an image, and which were robust against orientation and scale invariance. Other local descriptors methods include BOFs (Bag of Features) representations [23]. Later works around this idea include the VLAD (Vector of Locally Aggregated Descriptors) [9], where descriptors are represented by their distance from the assigned visual words, and aggregated into a single vector.

Recent improvements in deep convolutional neural network architectures for image recognition [8,11,22,24], in computational power (GPUs) and in associated datasets [4], showed that such architectures performed well in describing images globally. CNNs can thus be viewed as feature extractors for retrieval [7,14] or classification tasks [6]. Region-based features obtained with CNNs are often aggregated to create global and compact descriptors. Babenko and Lempitsky introduced SPoC [2], a descriptor that associates each feature and its spatial coordinates with the sum pooling of the last layer's feature maps. Similarly, motivated by the performance of VLAD [9] descriptors, Arandjelovic et al. incorporated the VLAD computations into a trainable layer after the convolutions: NetVLAD [1]. Radenovic et al. introduced the MAC descriptors [20], a maximum over the feature maps. Gordo et al. used triplet loss [6] and a region aggregated descriptor, RMAC, to produce their compact image representation. Other improvements of these methods were made with GeM [21] descriptors, a generalized mean of the last convolutional layer feature maps.

A recent implementation outperformed state-of-the-art models [19]: the Deep Attentive Local Features model [14]. A fine-tuned ResNet [8] with the Landmarks Dataset [3] is used, and an attention step is performed to keep only the features relevant for landmark recognition. Part of our work was based on this pipeline, dedicated to landmark identification.

Despite having been around for several years, few datasets are available for the landmark recognition task. Most of the published works are tested on the Paris [16] and Oxford [17], two datasets for instance level retrieval evaluation, with few classes and queries. Recently, with deep learning techniques, two new datasets were published. In 2014, Babenko et al. built the Landmarks Dataset [3], with 672 classes and 213678 images, enabling many fine-tuning methods. In 2018, along with the DELF model [14], Noh et al. published the biggest dataset to date for landmark retrieval, with 15000 classes and more than 1 billion images [14].

3   Our Solution

In this section we describe the system used for our experiments. We start by describing the dataset that we create in order to be closer to customers needs. Then we detail the architecture that we consider for landmark classification. An overview of the system is shown in Fig. 1. It includes the attentive DEep Local Features methods introduced by Noh et al. [14], VLAD [9] for feature aggregation, a fully connected network for the prediction, and some post-processing steps.

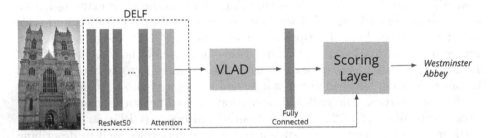

Fig. 1. Summary of the proposed model, combining DELF and VLAD with a classification layer for fast landmark recognition

3.1   Our Dataset

Publicly available datasets for landmark recognition didn't meet Photobox' needs: The Oxford [17] and Paris datasets [16] were too specific and the newly released Google Landmarks Dataset [14], with 15000 classes from very diverse and different landmarks, contains many places never visited by our customers. The dataset was also fairly unbalanced, with 3394 classes containing less than 5 images. We adopted a bottom-up approach and started by identifying with internal data the landmarks we wanted our model to detect. 263 landmarks were chosen this way. To add images for each class, we fetched data from the Google Landmarks Dataset [14], Paris [16] and Babenko [3] datasets. This allowed us to fill around half of the classes of our dataset. For the other half, we queried Flickr with personalized queries like "Place Vendome", "Vendome Column", "Vendome Selfie" (for Place Vendome related pictures). The retrieved images were then cleaned manually. In the end, our dataset consisted of 53000 images with 200 images per landmarks on average.

3.2   Our Method

Our solution uses DEep Local Features (DELF) [14] as basic representation. This choice is motivated by the fact that DELF achieves very competitive performance in recent evaluations of instance level landmark retrieval [19]. Our industrial context constrains us to process hundreds of photos in 3–4 s.

Since retrieval methods often take minutes to rank and compare input images with the whole database, we considered the problem as a classification task. A VLAD computation layer allows to obtain a fixed size representation of more compact features. Then a fully connected layer (FC) computes probabilities for our n classes. Additional steps were added, such as spatial verifications (SV), timestamps and GPS consistency, to remove false positives. In order to reduce more the execution time, we also considered a simpler and lighter pipeline, like in [21], with fine-tuned ResNet and VGG, GeM or MAC descriptors, and a fully connected layer for the prediction. However, we used a simple cross-entropy loss instead of a contrastive loss with siamese learning.

Attentive Deep Local Features [14]. For the feature extraction, the attentive DEep Local Features (DELF) model of Noh et al. was considered. First, to handle scale variations, input images are transformed into image pyramids using different image scales. Each scale will go through a fine-tuned ResNet50, and an attention layer will then score each features. The scoring process was learned for the landmark recognition task, and only the features with a high enough score are kept. In practice, the attention layer omits features related to skies, seas, roads, sometimes faces. But it also creates an output of varied size, making the use of standard classification algorithms complicated (Fig. 2).

Fig. 2. Visual examples of attention results on several landmarks.

Vector of Locally Aggregated Descriptors (VLAD) [9]. To create a fixed-size input for the classification task, we used VLAD, a method often used for instance level image recognition [1,9]. With VLAD, the image representation is done through a chosen number of k clusters. First, we learned a codebook of k clusters on 15000 images on our training dataset. During the inference phase, for an image I, the component of the first cluster, C_1 will be computed as follows:

$$C_1 = \sum_{x, \mathcal{C}(x)=c_1} dist(x, \tilde{c_1}) \tag{1}$$

where $\mathcal{C}(x) = c_1$ indicates the feature vector x assigned to cluster c_1, and $\tilde{c_1}$ is the centroid of cluster c_1. Square rooted normalization and L2 normalization are then performed. VLAD outputs a compact representation of our features. If we consider $k = 32$ clusters, and D the dimension of one deep feature, we were able to reduce the input features size from $N \times D = 12000$ (on average, $N = 300$

features are selected after the attention) to $k \times D = 1280$. This allows us to perform faster computations, while keeping most of the information. We observed good results even with few clusters for VLAD (e.g.: 24, 32). Images in the Fig. 3 were computed with 32 clusters and give good examples of the generalization power of VLAD: features describing similar elements in the landmarks are paired together, even for different landmarks.

Fig. 3. Visual examples of VLAD results on several landmarks. Features related to the same structures are assigned to the same VLAD clusters. 1 color per cluster, 32 clusters

Classification. Once VLAD features were extracted, we experimented several classification or retrieval methods. We implemented and tested two classification methods that showed the best results: one-vs-all SVMs and a fully connected (FC) layer with a Softmax function for the prediction. We also measured accuracy results of L2 nearest neighbour search as a retrieval method. Finally, we used our dataset to fine-tune popular deep learning networks like ResNet (50 & 101) and VGG 16 by performing GeM or MAC aggregation. The results obtained using these methods are presented in Sect. 4, Tables 2 and 4.

Additional Steps. To obtain a more robust model and to reduce the false positive rate, three light post-processing steps were added. First, a Scoring Step with spatial verification was implemented. Given the input image in inference, we fetch database images for the top-N outputs of the fully connected layer and compare the input image with each of these images. The comparison is performed using a simple k-NN with DELF features, for which we only keep features below a certain distance (hyperparameter threshold). Our final confidence score is the ratio of kept features in the input image. Usually, in instance-level image retrieval, this step is followed by stronger verification methods like RANSAC [5]. We didn't consider it since the computation time/added value trade-off wasn't good enough in our experiments. We also use the photo context to improve the results. When available, we verify if the predictions are consistent with the existent GPS information, and compute time clusters of the album in which a photo was uploaded. Predictions that are not consistent with the main location of our predictions for each time cluster are discarded.

4   Results and Evaluations

4.1   Evaluation Metrics

We run classification and retrieval experiments and use adapted metrics each
time. Accuracy is used for classification experiments, mAP for retrieval experiments. Finally, since our internal dataset includes distractors we evaluate performance on it using detection rate, accuracy, and false positive rates:

$$- \text{ detection rate: } \frac{\text{landmarks detected}}{\text{total landmarks}}$$
$$- \text{ accuracy: } \frac{\text{correct landmarks predicted}}{\text{landmarks detected}}$$
$$- \text{ false positive rate: } \frac{\text{distractors detected as landmarks}}{\text{total images}}$$

In our context, the detection rate is key, but we also expect to have a good
trade-off between accuracy of the predictions and the number of false positives.

4.2   Public and Internal Datasets

For our experiments we used two well-known public datasets for place recognition. The Oxford dataset [17] contains 5062 images, and the evaluation is
done on 55 queries, 5 for each of the eleven monuments included. Similarly,
the Paris Dataset [16] consists of 6412 photos, with 55 queries for 11 Parisian
landmarks for evaluation. In addition, 100k Flickr images were added to create the Oxford105k and Paris106k datasets [17]. We also evaluate ourselves on
the recently re-annotated Oxford and Paris datasets [19]. We only considered
Medium and Hard settings on the revisited datasets.

The internal Photobox dataset includes 263 landmarks. To evaluate the proposed methods on this task, we use two subsets as follows: (1) *easier dataset*:
13500 photos obtained with landmark names queries from Flickr, Bing and
Google which provide examples that are rather simple to classify and (2) *harder
dataset*: 1200 images retrieved from the same sources but with queries such as
'Venice tourists', 'Colosseum selfie' which provide harder examples. This second
subset also contains distractors (non-landmarks pictures). It is illustrated with
a few samples in Fig. 4.

Eiffel Tower   One World Trade Center Distractors (Places not belonging in
our classes)

Fig. 4. Examples of pictures in our test dataset

4.3 Results on Public Datasets

In Table 1, we present mAP results for public datasets. Here we evaluate the quality of the feature extraction pipeline which includes DELF and VLAD. We used Google Landmarks data to create the VLAD codebook. Features are then indexed and an L2-nearest neighbour search is performed. Closest images are then ranked based on their similarity to the query.

Table 1. mAP results on Oxford and Paris datasets. Dim is the dimension of the extracted features. † indicates results from the Revisited Oxford and Paris benchmarks [19]. * are results from the original paper

Model	Dim	Oxf5k	Oxf105k	ROxf-M	ROxf-H	Par6k	Par106k	RPar-M	Rpar-H
Ours	40	67	42,2	54,4	33,2	74,5	73,4	64,5	51,5
NetVLAD [1]	256	63,5*	-	37,1†	13,8†	73,5*	-	59,8†	35†
DELF [14]	40	83,8*	-	67,8†	43,1†	85*	-	76,9†	55,4†
ResNet-GeM [19]	2048	87,8*	84,6*	64,7†	38,5†	92,7*	86,9*	77,2†	56,3†

Our model provides reasonable performance but below state-of-the-art methods. This happens mainly because our pipeline was not built for retrieval. Classification algorithms for landmark recognition proved to be more effective with a small number of VLAD clusters. See Sect. 4.4 for more results on this.

4.4 Results on Internal Datasets

Results on Easier Dataset. We first present accuracy results on our first test subset, comprising 13500 images of the 263 landmarks handled by our models. All models were trained on the same training dataset. For DELF centered methods, we used their image preprocessing methods. Pictures are resized at $512 \times X$, and then rescaled at X different scales to form an image pyramid.

Tables 2 and 4 show the results obtained by the different models. For methods using VLAD for feature aggregation, we tested different codebook sizes: 16, 24, 32, 64 and 512. Codebooks were computed on the same 15000 images, from the training data. Then an L2-Search was performed with the Faiss [10] library, on 512 nearest neighbours. Spatial Verification (SV) was computed as described in Sect. 3.2. We also present inference time per image for all the methods tested. Experiments were performed on an Amazon instances, with a single Tesla K80 GPU.

Since the objective of this paper is to have an architecture that allows to have good performances with less computational cost, we also considered simpler architectures with a fine-tuned CNN for landmark recognition, and re-implemented ResNet and VGG architectures with MAC or GeM descriptors. We used the DELF-VLAD-FC model and restrictive thresholds to automatically label data fetched from Google, Bing, and Flickr and thus expand our

Table 2. Accuracy (%) for the easier internal subset (%) (13500 images) for DELF-centric methods and their execution time (per image).

Model	VLAD codebook size					Execution time (s)
	16	24	32	64	512	
DELF (7 scales) + VLAD + SVM	91	92	92,1	91,1	91,2	0,26
DELF (7 scales) + VLAD + L2-Search	48,7	49,4	49,3	54,1	62,4	0,18
DELF (7 scales) + VLAD + L2-Search + SV	73,1	77,2	72,7	82,7	84,1	0,24
DELF (7 scales) + VLAD + FC	93,1	94	**94,3**	92,9	91,8	0,18
DELF (Single Scale) + VLAD + FC	-	-	92,1	-	-	0,06

training dataset. The supplementary data included poorer quality images (faces, obstructed landmarks, ...) with potential errors. This dataset expansion was performed in three iterations:

1. First iteration was performed with a retrieved dataset of 33000 training images and 8220 'easier test' images.
2. For the second fine-tuning iteration, we added 17090 images, automatically labelled with the DELF-VLAD-FC pipeline and strong thresholds for landmark detection.
3. Finally, the third iteration added 2500 images in the less populated classes. Another fine-tuning operation was then performed.

Table 3 shows the results obtained on the easier internal dataset for each of the fine-tuning iteration.

Table 3. Accuracy (%) over iterations of the easier internal dataset

Model	Iteration I	Iteration II	Iteration III
DELF + VLAD + FC (ours)	93,2	93,9	94,3
ResNet50 + GeM (ours)	76,7	78,7	79,5
ResNet101 + GeM (ours)	77,4	80,3	80,9
VGG16 + GeM (ours)	81	83,6	85,8

These models showed promising results, especially with the GeM [21] pooling method, but not at the level of the DELF-VLAD-FC pipeline. As it can be observed in Table 4 the execution time for one photo is divided by a factor of almost 10.

Results on the Harder Test Dataset. Figure 5 shows examples obtained with the DELF-VLAD-FC pipeline (with 32 clusters for VLAD) on the harder test dataset described in Sect. 4.2. Table 5 summarizes accuracy, detection, and false positive rates achieved by four DELF-VLAD-FC pipelines with various

Table 4. Accuracy (%) on the easier internal subset which includes 13500 images for several fine-tuned models and their execution time (per image)

Model	Accuracy on the easier dataset	Execution time (s)
ResNet50 + GeM (ours)	79,8	0,020
ResNet50 + MAC (ours)	75,8	0,019
ResNet101 + GeM (ours)	80,9	0,024
ResNet50 + MAC (ours)	79	0,023
VGG16 + GeM (ours)	**85,8**	0,020
VGG16 + MAC (ours)	76,3	0,019

VLAD codebook sizes. We consider the VGG-GeM shared by Radenovic et al. in [18] that achieved state-of-the-art results [19]. Finally, we show results of our implementation of VGG with GeM pooling, fine-tuned on our data. Our DELF-VLAD-FC model showed better results compared to VGG models, especially when it cames to detecting monuments: landmarks were more often predicted with DELF methods, while fewer false positives were created. The best overall performance was achieved with 32 clusters for VLAD, and the following hyper-parameters for scoring: $0, 7$ as the upperbound distance allowed in the k-NN and 50% minimal percentage of features kept. With this, we were able to detect landmarks in $88, 4\%$ of the pictures, with an accuracy of $91, 2\%$. False positives were limited to $5, 2\%$. In practice, we are able to further reduce the number of false positives using the photo album context from 9% to 4% in our test experiments.

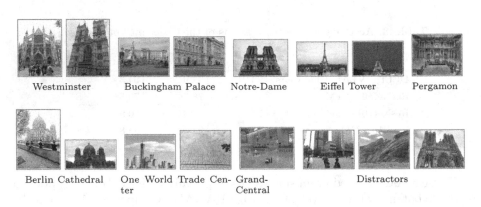

Westminster   Buckingham Palace   Notre-Dame   Eiffel Tower   Pergamon

Berlin Cathedral   One World Trade Center   Grand-Central   Distractors

Fig. 5. Examples of results on the hard dataset with accurate predictions in green. Second picture for One World Trade Center was labelled as The Shard in London. For distractors, first picture was wrongly classified as the Madison Square Garden. Predictions were rightly ignored for last two.

Table 5. Models performance on the hard dataset (1200 images)

	Detection rate	Accuracy rate	False positive rate
DELF-VLAD24-FC	88,3	90,6	5,2
DELF-VLAD32-FC	88,4	91,2	5,2
DELF-VLAD64-FC	87,5	90	5
DELF-VLAD512-FC	87,9	89,6	5,8
VGG-GeM [18]-FC	81,5	91,6	6,2
VGG-GeM-FC (ours)	81,3	80	8,9

5 Conclusion

In this paper, we present a new pipeline for fast landmark recognition, modeled
as a classification problem instead of an instance-level retrieval task. We used
deep attentive local features and combined them with VLAD to aggregate local
descriptors in fixed-size compact features that can be fed into a classifier. We
evaluate our method against state-of-the-art landmark recognition models using
public and internal datasets. Our model achieves good results and is particularly fit for Photobox' industrial environment. To answer question 1 from the
introduction we analyzed the customers' destinations and identified the most
frequented landmarks in order to focus the recognition model on them. As for
the second question, we are constrained with in an industrial environment and
we need to find a good balance between the execution time and performance.
We proposed two lightweight methods, one based on DELF+VLAD+FC and
one based on fine-tuned models with GeM. To answer question 3, related to
the separation of photos with landmarks from the others, we proposed a confidence score which improved considerably the landmark detection. Having a
simpler architecture, based only on a deep learning model, without any other
post-processing steps would further improve inference speed. Therefore future
work will focus on further fine-tuning experiments in which we would start from
models learned with thousands of landmarks to then specialize them for our
specific industrial context. By fine-tuning first on a large number of classes and
data we'll obtain more robust and generic features which can help on improving
the model's performance.

References

1. Arandjelovic, R., Gronát, P., Torii, A., Pajdla, T., Sivic, J.: NetVLAD: CNN architecture for weakly supervised place recognition. CoRR (2015)
2. Babenko, A., Lempitsky, V.S.: Aggregating deep convolutional features for image
   retrieval. CoRR (2015)
3. Babenko, A., Slesarev, A., Chigorin, A., Lempitsky, V.S.: Neural codes for image
   retrieval. CoRR (2014)

4. Deng, J., Dong, W., Socher, R., Li, L.J., Li, K., Fei-Fei, L.: ImageNet: a large-scale hierarchical image database. In: CVPR 2009 (2009)
5. Fischler, M.A., Bolles, R.C.: Random sample consensus: a paradigm for model fitting with applications to image analysis and automated cartography. Commun. ACM
6. Girshick, R.B., Donahue, J., Darrell, T., Malik, J.: Rich feature hierarchies for accurate object detection and semantic segmentation. CoRR (2013)
7. Gordo, A., Almazán, J., Revaud, J., Larlus, D.: Deep image retrieval: learning global representations for image search. CoRR (2016)
8. He, K., Zhang, X., Ren, S., Sun, J.: Deep residual learning for image recognition. CoRR (2015)
9. Jegou, H., Douze, M., Schmid, C., Pérez, P.: Aggregating local descriptors into a compact image representation. In: CVPR 2010 (2010)
10. Johnson, J., Douze, M., Jegou, H.: Billion-scale similarity search with GPUs. arXiv preprint arXiv:1702.08734 (2017)
11. Krizhevsky, A., Sutskever, I., Hinton, G.E.: ImageNet classification with deep convolutional neural networks. In: NIPS 2012 (2012)
12. Lowe, D.G.: Distinctive image features from scale-invariant keypoints. Int. J. Comput. Vis. **60**, 91–110 (2004)
13. Lowry, S., et al.: Visual place recognition: a survey. IEEE Trans. Robot. **32**, 1–19 (2016)
14. Noh, H., Araujo, A., Sim, J., Han, B.: Image retrieval with deep local features and attention-based keypoints. CoRR (2016)
15. Perronnin, F., Liu, Y., Sánchez, J., Poirier, H.: Large-scale image retrieval with compressed fisher vectors. In: CVPR 2010 (2010)
16. Philbin, J., Chum, O., Isard, M., Sivic, J., Zisserman, A.: Lost in quantization: improving particular object retrieval in large scale image databases. In: CVPR 2008 (2008)
17. Philbin, J., Chum, O., Isard, M., Sivic, J., Zisserman, A.: Object retrieval with large vocabularies and fast spatial matching. In: CVPR 2007 (2007)
18. Radenović, F., Tolias, G., Chum, O.: Fine-tuning CNN image retrieval with no human annotation. TPAMI **41**, 1655–1668 (2018)
19. Radenovic, F., Iscen, A., Tolias, G., Avrithis, Y.S., Chum, O.: Revisiting Oxford and Paris: large-scale image retrieval benchmarking. CoRR (2018)
20. Radenovic, F., Tolias, G., Chum, O.: CNN image retrieval learns from bow: unsupervised fine-tuning with hard examples. CoRR (2016)
21. Radenovic, F., Tolias, G., Chum, O.: Fine-tuning CNN image retrieval with no human annotation. CoRR (2017)
22. Simonyan, K., Zisserman, A.: Very deep convolutional networks for large-scale image recognition. CoRR (2014)
23. Sivic, J., Zisserman, A.: Video Google: a text retrieval approach to object matching in videos. In: Proceedings of Ninth ICCV (2003)
24. Szegedy, C., et al.: Going deeper with convolutions. In: CVPR 2015 (2015)

Fast and Robust Detection of Solar Modules in Electroluminescence Images

Mathis Hoffmann[1,2(✉)] [iD], Bernd Doll[2,3,4] [iD], Florian Talkenberg[5] [iD],
Christoph J. Brabec[2,3] [iD], Andreas K. Maier[1] [iD], and Vincent Christlein[1] [iD]

[1] Pattern Recognition Lab, Friedrich-Alexander-Universität Erlangen-Nürnberg,
Erlangen, Germany
mathis.hoffmann@fau.de
[2] Institute Materials for Electronics and Energy Technology,
Friedrich-Alexander-Universität Erlangen-Nürnberg, Erlangen, Germany
[3] Helmholtz-Institut Erlangen-Nürnberg, Erlangen, Germany
[4] Graduate School in Advanced Optical Technologies, Erlangen, Germany
[5] greateyes GmbH, Berlin, Germany

Abstract. Fast, non-destructive and on-site quality control tools, mainly high sensitive imaging techniques, are important to assess the reliability of photovoltaic plants. To minimize the risk of further damages and electrical yield losses, electroluminescence (EL) imaging is used to detect local defects in an early stage, which might cause future electric losses. For an automated defect recognition on EL measurements, a robust detection and rectification of modules, as well as an optional segmentation into cells is required. This paper introduces a method to detect solar modules and crossing points between solar cells in EL images. We only require 1-D image statistics for the detection, resulting in an approach that is computationally efficient. In addition, the method is able to detect the modules under perspective distortion and in scenarios, where multiple modules are visible in the image. We compare our method to the state of the art and show that it is superior in presence of perspective distortion while the performance on images, where the module is roughly coplanar to the detector, is similar to the reference method. Finally, we show that we greatly improve in terms of computational time in comparison to the reference method.

Keywords: Object detection · Automated inspection · EL imaging

1 Introduction

Over the last decade, photovoltaic (PV) energy has become an important factor in emission-free energy production. In 2016 for example, about 40 GW of PV capacity was installed in Germany, which amounts to nearly one fifth of the total installed electric capacity [3]. Not only in Germany, renewable electricity production has been transformed to a considerable business. It is expected, that by 2023 about one third of world wide electricity comes from renewable sources [14].

© Springer Nature Switzerland AG 2019
M. Vento and G. Percannella (Eds.): CAIP 2019, LNCS 11679, pp. 519–531, 2019.
https://doi.org/10.1007/978-3-030-29891-3_46

Fig. 1. Example EL image.

To ensure high performance of the installed modules, regular inspection by imaging and non-imaging methods is required. For on-site inspection, imaging methods are very useful to find out which modules are defect after signs of decreasing electricity generation have been detected. Typically, on-site inspection of solar modules is performed by infrared (IR) or electroluminescence (EL) imaging. This work focuses on EL imaging. However, it could be adapted to other modalities as well.

A solar module (see Fig. 1) consists of a varying number of solar cells that are placed onto a regular grid. Since cells on a module share a similar structure and cracks are usually spread out only within each cell, it is a natural algorithmic choice to perform detailed inspection on a per cell basis. To this end, an automatic detection of the module and crossing points between cells is required.

Our main contributions are as follows: We propose a method for the detection of solar modules and the crossing points between solar cells in the image. It works irrespective of the module's pose and position. Our method is based on 1-D image statistics, leading to a very fast approach. In addition, we show how this can be extended to situations, where multiple modules are visible in the image. Finally, we compare our method to the state of the art and show that the detection performance is comparable, while the computational time is lowered by a factor of 40.

The remainder of this work is organized a follows: In Sect. 2, we summarize the state of the art in object detection and specifically on the detection of solar modules. In Sects. 3 and 4, we introduce our method, which is eventually compare against the state of the art in Sect. 5.

2   Related Work

The detection of solar modules in an EL image is an object detection task. Traditionally, feature-based methods have been applied to solve the task of object detection. Especially, Haar wavelets have proven to be successful [10]. For an the efficient computation, Viola and Jones [13] made use of integral images, previously known as summed area tables [1]. Integral images are also an essential part of our method.

The detection of solar modules is related to the detection of checkerboard calibration patterns in the image, since both are planar objects with a regular structure. Recently, integral images have been used with a model-driven approach to robustly and accurately detect checkerboard calibration patterns in presence of blur and noise [8]. We will employ a similar model-driven approach that exploits the regular structure of the cells, but only uses 1-D image statistics. Similar techniques are applied by the document analysis community to detect text lines [9].

In the last years, convolutional neural networks (CNNs) have achieved superior performance in many computer vision tasks. For example, single-stage detectors like YOLO [11] yield good detection performance with a tolerable computational cost. Multi-stage object detectors, such as R-CNN [6], achieve even better results but come with an increased computational cost. In contrast to CNN-based approaches, the proposed method does not require any training data and is computationally very efficient.

There are not many preliminary works on the automated detection of solar modules. Vetter et al. [12] proposed an object detection pipeline that consists of several stacked filters followed by a Hough transform to detect solar modules in noisy infrared thermography measurements. Recently, Deitsch et al. [2] proposed a processing pipeline for solar modules that jointly detects the modules in an EL image, estimates the configuration (i. e., the number of rows and columns of cells), estimates the lens distortion and performs segmentation into rectified cell images. Their approach consists of a preprocessing step, where a multiscale vesselness filter [5] is used to extract ridges (separating lines between cells) and bus bars. Then, parabolic curves are fitted onto the result to obtain a parametric model of the module. Finally, the distortion is estimated and module corners are extracted. Since this is, to the best of our knowledge, the only method that automatically detects solar modules and cell crossing points in EL images, we use this as a reference method to assess the performance of our approach.

3   Detection of the Module

This work is supposed to be used for EL images of solar modules in different constellations. As shown in Fig. 6, modules might be imaged from different viewpoints. In addition, there might be more than one module visible in the image. In this work, we focus on cases, where one module is fully visible and others might be partially viewed, since this commonly happens, when EL images of modules mounted next to each other are captured in the field. However, this method can be easily adapted to robustly handle different situations. The only assumption we make is that the number of cells in a row and per column is known.

The detection of the module in the image and the localization of crossing points between solar cells is performed in two steps. First, the module is roughly located to obtain an initial guess of a rigid transformation between model and image coordinates. We describe the procedure in Sects. 3.1 and 3.2. Then, the resulting transform is used to predict coarse locations of crossing points. These locations are then refined as described in Sect. 4.

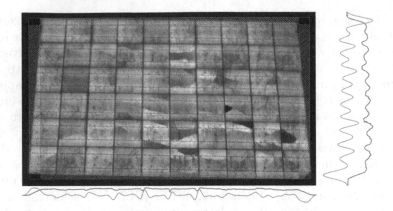

Fig. 2. Modules are located by integrating the image in x and y direction (blue lines). From the first derivative of this integration (orange lines), an inner and outer bounding box can be estimated (red boxes). The module corners can be found by considering the pixel sums within the marked subregions. (Color figure online)

3.1   Detection of a Single Module

We locate the module by considering 1-D images statistics obtained by summing the image in x and y direction. This is related, but not equal to the concept that is known as integral images [1,13]. Let I denote an EL image of a solar module. Throughout this work, we assume that images are column major, i.e., $I[x, y]$, where $x \in [1, w]$ and $y \in [1, h]$, denotes a single pixel in column y and row x. Then, the integration over rows is given by

$$I_{\Sigma x}[y] = \sum_{x=1}^{w} I[x, y]. \tag{1}$$

The sum over columns $I_{\Sigma y}$ is defined similarly. Figure 2 visualizes the statistics obtained by this summation (blue lines). Since the module is clearly separated from the background by the mean intensity, the location of the module in the image can be easily obtained from $I_{\Sigma x}$ and $I_{\Sigma y}$. However, we are merely interested in the absolute values of the mean intensities than in the change of the latter. Therefore, we consider the gradients $\nabla_\sigma I_{\Sigma x}$ and $\nabla_\sigma I_{\Sigma y}$, where σ denotes a Gaussian smoothing to suppress high frequencies. Since we are only interested in low frequent changes, we heuristically set $\sigma = 0.01 \cdot \max(w, h)$.

As shown in Fig. 2, a left edge of a module is characterized by a maximum in $\nabla_\sigma I_{\Sigma x}$ or $\nabla_\sigma I_{\Sigma y}$. Similarly, a right edge corresponds to a minimum. In addition, the skewness of the module with respect to the image's y axis corresponds to the width of the minimum and maximum peak in $\nabla_\sigma I_{\Sigma x}$, whereas the skewness of the module with respect to the x axis corresponds to the peak-widths in $\nabla_\sigma I_{\Sigma y}$.

Formally, let x_1 and x_2 denote the location of the maximum and minimum on $\nabla_\sigma I_{\Sigma x}$, and y_1 and y_2 denote the location of the maximum and minimum on $\nabla_\sigma I_{\Sigma y}$, respectively. Further, let x_{1-} and x_{1+} denote the pair of points where the peak corresponding to x_1 vanishes. We define two bounding boxes for the module (see Fig. 2) as follows: The outer bounding box is given by

$$B_1 = [b_{1,1}, b_{1,2}, b_{1,3}, b_{1,4}] = [(x_{1-}, y_{2+}), (x_{2+}, y_{2+}), (x_{2+}, y_{1-}), (x_{1-}, y_{1-})],$$
(2)

while the inner bounding box is given by

$$B_2 = [b_{2,1}, b_{2,2}, b_{2,3}, b_{2,4}] = [(x_{1+}, y_{2-}), (x_{2-}, y_{2-}), (x_{2-}, y_{1+}), (x_{1+}, y_{1+})].$$
(3)

With these bounding boxes, we obtain a first estimate of the module position. However, it is unclear if $b_{1,1}$ or $b_{2,1}$ corresponds to the left upper corner of the module. The same holds for $b_{1,2}$ versus $b_{2,2}$ and so on. This information is lost by the summation over the image. However, we can easily determine the exact pose of the module. To this end, we consider the sum over the sub-regions between the bounding boxes, cf. Fig. 2. This way, we can identify the four corners $\{b_1, \ldots, b_4\}$ of the module and obtain a rough estimate of the module position and pose. To simplify the detection of crossing points, we assume that the longer side of a non-square module always corresponds to the edges (b_1, b_2) and (b_3, b_4).

Fig. 3. Module detection with multiple modules.

3.2 Detection of Multiple Modules

In many on-site applications, multiple modules will be visible in an EL image (see Fig. 3). In these cases, the detection of a single maximum and minimum along each axis will not suffice. To account for this, we need to define, when a point in $\nabla_\sigma I_{\Sigma k}$, $k \in \{x, y\}$, will be considered a maximum/minimum. We compute the standard deviation σ_k of $\nabla_\sigma I_{\Sigma k}$ and consider every point a maximum, where $2\sigma_k < \nabla_\sigma I_{\Sigma k}$ and every point a minimum, where $-2\sigma_k > \nabla_\sigma I_{\Sigma k}$. Then, we apply non maximum/minimum suppression to obtain a single detection per maximum and minimum. As a result, we obtain a sequence of extrema per axis. Ideally, every minimum is directly followed by a maximum. However, due to false positives this is not always the case.

In this work, we focus on the case, where only one module is fully visible, whereas the others are partially occluded. Since we know that a module in the image corresponds to a maximum followed by a minimum, we can easily identify false positives. We group all maxima and minima that occur sequentially and only keep the one that corresponds to the largest or smallest value in $\nabla_\sigma I_{\Sigma k}$. Still, we might have multiple pairs of maxima followed by a minimum. We choose the one where the distance between minimum and maximum is maximal.

This is a very simple strategy that does not allow to detect more than one module. However, an extension to multiple modules is straightforward.

4   Detection of Cell Crossing Points

For the detection of cell crossing points, we assert that the module consists of N columns of cells and M rows, where a typical module configuration is $N = 10$ and $M = 6$. However, our approach is not limited to that configuration. Without loss of generality, we assume that $N \geq M$. With this information, we can define a simple model of the module. It consists of the corners and cell crossings on a regular grid, where the cell size is 1. By definition, the origin of the model coordinate system resides in the upper left corner with the y axis pointing downwards. Hence, every point in the model is given by

$$m_{i,j} = (i - 1, j - 1) \quad i \leq N, j \leq M. \tag{4}$$

From the module detection step, we roughly know the four corners $\{b_1, \ldots, b_4\}$ of the module that correspond to model points $\{m_{1,1}, m_{N,1}, m_{N,M}, m_{1,M}\}$. Here, we assume that the longer side of a non-square module always corresponds to edges (b_1, b_2) and (b_3, b_4), and that $N \geq M$. Note that this does not limit the approach regarding the orientation of the module since, for example, (b_1, b_2) can define a horizontal or vertical line in the image.

We aim to estimate a transform that converts model coordinates $m_{i,j}$ into image coordinates $x_{i,j}$, which is done by using a homography matrix H_0 that encodes the relation between model and image plane. With the four correspondences between the module edges in model and image plane, we estimate H_0 using the direct linear transform (DLT) [7]. Using H_0, we obtain an initial guess to the position of each crossing point by

$$\tilde{x}_{i,j} \approx H_0 \tilde{m}_{i,j}, \tag{5}$$

where the model point $m = (x, y)$ in cartesian coordinates is converted to its homogeneous representation by $\tilde{m} = (x, y, 1)$.

Now, we aim to refine this initial guess by a local search. To this end, we extract a rectified image patch of the local neighborhood around each initial guess (Sect. 4.1). Using the resulting image patches, we apply the detection of cell crossing points (Sect. 4.2). Finally, we detect outliers and re-estimate H_0 to minimize the reprojection error between detected cell crossing points and the corresponding model points (Sect. 4.3).

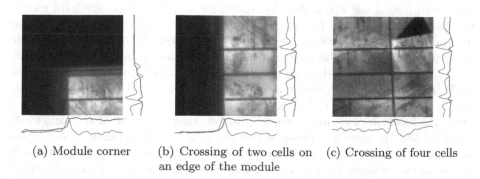

(a) Module corner   (b) Crossing of two cells on   (c) Crossing of four cells
an edge of the module

Fig. 4. Different types of crossings between cells (cf. Fig. 4b and c) as well as the corners of a module (cf. Fig. 4a) lead to different responses in the 1-D statistics. We show the accumulated intensities in blue and the gradient of that in orange. (Color figure online)

4.1 Extraction of Rectified Image Patches

For the local search, we consider only a small region around the initial guess. By means of the homography H_0, we have some prior knowledge about the position and pose of the module in the image. We take this into account by warping a region that corresponds to the size of approximately one cell. To this end, we create a regular grid of pixel coordinates. The size of the grid depends on the approximate size of a cell in the image, which is obtained by

$$\hat{r}_{i,j} = \|\hat{x}_{i,j} - \hat{x}_{i+1,j+1}\|_2, \tag{6}$$

where the approximation $\hat{x}$ is given by Equ. (5) and conversion from homogeneous $\tilde{x} = (x_1, x_2, x_3)^\mathsf{T}$ to inhomogeneous coordinates is $\hat{x} = \left(\frac{\tilde{x}_1}{\tilde{x}_3}, \frac{\tilde{x}_2}{\tilde{x}_3}\right)^\mathsf{T}$. Note that the approximation $\hat{r}_{i,j}$ is only valid in the vicinity of $\hat{x}_{i,j}$. The warping is then performed by mapping model coordinates into image coordinates using H_0 followed by sampling the image using bilinear interpolation. As a result, a rectified patch image $I_{i,j}$ is obtained that is coarsely centered at the true cell crossing point, see Fig. 4.

4.2 Cell Crossing Points Detection

The detection step for cell crossing points is very similar to the module detection step but with local image patches. It is carried out for every model point $m_{i,j}$ and image patch $I_{i,j}$ to find an estimate $x_{i,j}$ to the (unknown) true image location of $m_{i,j}$. To simplify notation, we drop the index throughout this section. We compute 1-D image statistics from I to obtain $I_{\Sigma x}$ and $I_{\Sigma y}$, as well as $\nabla_\sigma I_{\Sigma x}$ and $\nabla_\sigma I_{\Sigma y}$, as described in Sect. 3.1. The smoothing factor σ is set relative to the image size in the same way as for the module detection.

We find that there are different types of cell crossings that have differing intensity profiles, see Fig. 4. Another challenge is that busbars are hard to distinguish from the ridges (separating regions between cells) between cells, see for example Fig. 4c. Therefore, we cannot consider a single minimum/maximum. We proceed similar to the approach for the detection of multiple modules, cf. Sect. 3.2). We apply thresholding and non-maximum/non-minimum suppression on $\nabla_\sigma I_{\Sigma x}$ and $\nabla_\sigma I_{\Sigma y}$ to obtain a sequence of maxima and minima along each axis. The threshold is set to $1.5 \cdot \sigma_k$, where σ_k is the standard deviation of $\nabla_\sigma I_{\Sigma k}$. From the location of m in the model grid, we know the type of the target cell crossing. We distinguish between ridges and edges of the module. A cell crossing might consist of both. For example a crossing between two cells on the left border of the module, see Fig. 4b, consists of an edge on the x axis and a ridge on the y axis.

Detection of Ridges. A ridge is characterized by a minimum in $\nabla_\sigma I_{\Sigma k}$ followed by a maximum. As noted earlier, ridges are hard to distinguish from busbars. Luckily, solar cells are usually built symmetrically. Hence, given that image patches are roughly rectified and that the initial guess to the crossing point is not close to the border of the image patch, it is likely that we observe an even number of busbars. As a consequence, we simply use all minima that are directly followed by a maximum, order them by their position and take the middle. We expect to have an odd number of such sequences (an even number of busbars and the actual ridge we are interested in). In case this heuristic is not applicable, because we found an even number of such sequences, we simply drop this point. The correct position on the respective axis corresponds to the turning point of $\nabla_\sigma I_{\Sigma k}$.

Detection of Edges. For edges, we distinguish between left/top edges and bottom/right edges of the module. Left/top edges are characterized by a maximum, whereas bottom/right edges correspond to a minimum in $\nabla_\sigma I_{\Sigma k}$. In case of multiple extrema, we make a heuristic to choose the correct one. We assume that our initial guess is not far off. Therefore, we choose the maximum or minimum that is closest to the center of the patch.

4.3 Outlier Detection

We chose to apply a fast method to detect the crossing points by considering 1-D image statistics only. As a result, the detected crossing points contain a significant number of outliers. In addition, every detected crossing point exhibits some measurement error. Therefore, we need to identify outliers and find a robust estimate to H that minimizes the overall error. Since H has 8 degrees of freedom, only four point correspondences ($m_{i,j}$, $\hat{x}_{i,j}$) are required to obtain a unique solution. On the other hand, a typical module with 10 rows and 6 columns has 77 crossing points. Hence, even if the detection of crossing points failed in a significant number of cases, the number of point correspondences is typically much larger than 4. Therefore, this problem is well suited to be solved by Random Sample Consensus (RANSAC) [4]. We apply RANSAC to find those point correspondences that give the most consistent model. At every iteration t, we randomly sample four point correspondences and estimate H_t using the DLT. For the determination of the consensus set, we treat a point an outlier if the detected point $x_{i,j}$ and the estimated point $H_t \tilde{m}_{i,j}$ differ by more than 5% of the cell size.

The error of the model H_t is given by the following least-squares formulation

$$e_t = \frac{1}{NM} \sum_{i,j} \|\hat{x}_{i,j} - x_{i,j}\|_2^2, \tag{7}$$

where $\hat{x}$ is the current estimate by the model H in cartesian coordinates. Finally, we estimate H using all point correspondences from the consensus set to minimize e_t.

5 Experimental Results

We conduct a series of experiments to show that our approach is robust w. r. t. to the position and pose of the module in the image as well as to various degrees of distortion of the modules. In Sect. 5.1, we introduce the dataset that we use throughout our experiments. In Sect. 5.2, we quantitatively compare the results of our approach with our reference method [2]. In addition, we show that our method robustly handles cases, where multiple modules are visible in the image or the module is perspectively distorted. Finally, in Sect. 5.3, we compare the computation time of our approach to the state of the art.

5.1 Dataset

Deitsch et al. [2] propose a joint detection and segmentation approach for solar modules. In their evaluation, they use two datasets. They report their computational performance on a dataset that consists of 44 modules. We will refer to this dataset as DATAA and use it only for the performance evaluation, to obtain results that are easy to compare. In addition, they use a dataset that consists of 8 modules to evaluate their segmentation. We will refer to this data as DATAB, see Fig. 6b. The data is publicly available, which allows for a direct comparison of the two methods. However, since we do not apply a pixelwise segmentation, we could not use the segmentation masks they also provided. To this end, we manually added polygonal annotations, where each corner of the polygon corresponds to one of the corners of the module.

To assess the performance in different settings, we add two additional datasets. One of them consists of 10 images with multiple modules visible. We deem this setting important, since in on-site applications, it is difficult to measure only a single module. We will refer to this as DATAC. An example is shown in Fig. 6c. The other consists of 9 images, where the module has been gradually rotated around the y-axis with a step size of $10°$ starting at $0°$. We will refer to this as DATAD, see Fig. 6a. We manually added polygonal annotations to DATAC and DATAD, too.

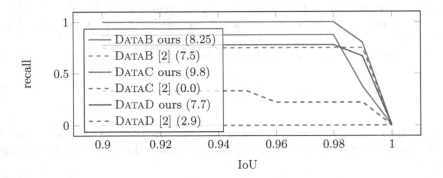

Fig. 5. Detection results on different datasets. We report the AUC in brackets.

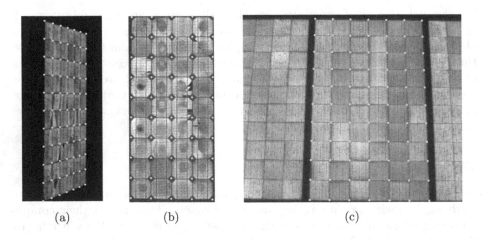

Fig. 6. Estimated model coordinates on different modules.

For the EL imaging procedure of DATAC and DATAD, two different silicon detector CCD cameras with an optical long pass filter have been used. For the different PV module tilting angles (DATAD), a Sensovation "coolSamba HR-320" was used, while for the outdoor PV string measurements a Greateyes "GE BI 2048 2048" was employed (DATAC).

5.2   Detection Results

We are interested in the number of modules that are detected correctly and how accurate the detection is. To assess the detection accuracy, we calculate the intersection over union (IoU) between ground truth polygon and detection. Additionally, we report the recall at different IoU-thresholds.

Figure 5 summarizes the detection results. We see that our method outperforms the reference method on the test dataset provided by Deitsch et al. [2] (DATAB) by a small margin. However, the results of the reference method are a little bit more accurate. This can be explained by the fact that they consider lens distortion, while our method only estimates a projective transformation between model and image coordinates. The experiments on DATAD assess the robustness of both methods with respect to rotations of the module. We clearly see that our method is considerably robust against rotations, while the reference method requires that the modules are roughly rectified. Finally, we determine the performance of our method, when multiple modules are visible in the image (DATAC). The reference method does not support this scenario. It turns out that our method gives very good results when an image shows multiple modules.

In Fig. 6, we visually show the module crossing points estimated using our method. For the rotated modules (DATAD), it turns out that the detection fails for 70° and 80° rotation. However, for 60° and less, we consistently achieve good results (see Fig. 6b). Finally, Fig. 6c reveals that the method also works on varying types of modules and in presence of severe degradation.

5.3   Computation Time

We determine the computational performance of our method on a workstation equipped with an Intel Xeon E5-1630 CPU running at 3.7 GHz. The method is implemented in Python3 using NumPy and only uses a single thread. We use the same 44 module images that Deitsch et al. [2] have used for their performance evaluation to obtain results that can be compared easily. On average, the 44 images are processed in 15 s, resulting in approximately 340 ms per module. This includes the initialization time of the interpreter and the time for loading the images. The average raw processing time of a single image is about 190 ms.

Deitsch et al. [2] report an overall processing time of 6 min for the 44 images using a multi-threaded implementation. Therefore, a single image amounts to 13.5 s on average. Hence, our method is about 40 times faster than the reference method. On the other hand, the reference method does not only detect the cell crossing points but also performs segmentation of the active cell area. In addition, they account for lens distortion as well. This partially justifies the performance difference.

6   Conclusion

In this work, we have presented a new approach to detect solar modules in EL images. It is based on 1-D image statistics and relates to object detection methods based on integral images. To this end, it can be implemented efficiently and we are confident, that a real-time processing of images is feasible. The experiments show that our method is superior in presence of perspective distortion while performing similarly well than state of the art on non-distorted EL images. Additionally, we show that it is able to deal with scenarios, where multiple modules are present in the image.

In future, the method could be extended to account for complex scenarios, where perspective distortion is strong. In these situations, the stability could be improved by a prior rectification of the module, e. g., using the Hough transform to detect the orientation of the module. Since point correspondences between the module and a virtual model of the latter are established, the proposed method could be extended to calibrate the parameters of a camera model, too. This would allow to take lens distortion into account and to extract undistorted cell images.

Acknowledgements. We gratefully acknowledge funding of the Federal Ministry for Economic Affairs and Energy (BMWi: Grant No. 0324286, iPV4.0) and the Erlangen Graduate School in Advanced Optical Technologies (SAOT) by the German Research Foundation (DFG) in the framework of the German excellence initiative.

References

1. Crow, F.C.: Summed-area tables for texture mapping. In: ACM SIGGRAPH Computer Graphics, pp. 207–212 (1984)
2. Deitsch, S., Buerhop-Lutz, C., Maier, A., Gallwitz, F., Riess, C.: Segmentation of photovoltaic module cells in electroluminescence images. arXiv preprint arXiv:1806.06530 [V2] (2018)
3. EU energy in figures - statistical pocketbook. European Commission (2018)
4. Fischler, M.A., Bolles, R.C.: Random sample consensus: a paradigm for model fitting with applications to image analysis and automated cartography. Commun. ACM **24**(6), 381–395 (1981)
5. Frangi, A.F., Niessen, W.J., Vincken, K.L., Viergever, M.A.: Multiscale vessel enhancement filtering. In: Wells, W.M., Colchester, A., Delp, S. (eds.) MICCAI 1998. LNCS, vol. 1496, pp. 130–137. Springer, Heidelberg (1998). https://doi.org/10.1007/BFb0056195
6. Girshick, R., Donahue, J., Darrell, T., Malik, J.: Rich feature hierarchies for accurate object detection and semantic segmentation. In: IEEE Conference on Computer Vision and Pattern Recognition, pp. 580–587 (2014)
7. Hartley, R., Zisserman, A.: Multiple View Geometry in Computer Vision. Cambridge University Press, Cambridge (2003)
8. Hoffmann, M., Ernst, A., Bergen, T., Hettenkofer, S., Garbas, J.U.: A robust chessboard detector for geometric camera calibration. In: International Conference on Computer Vision Theory and Applications, pp. 34–43 (2017)
9. Likforman-Sulem, L., Zahour, A., Taconet, B.: Text line segmentation of historical documents: a survey. Int. J. Doc. Anal. Recogn. (IJDAR) **9**(2–4), 123–138 (2007)
10. Papageorgiou, C.P., Oren, M., Poggio, T.: A general framework for object detection. In: International Conference on Computer Vision, vol. 6, pp. 555–562 (1998)
11. Redmon, J., Divvala, S., Girshick, R., Farhadi, A.: You only look once: unified, real-time object detection. In: IEEE Conference on Computer Vision and Pattern Recognition, pp. 779–788 (2016)

12. Vetter, A., Hepp, J., Brabec, C.J.: Automatized segmentation of photovoltaic modules in IR-images with extreme noise. Infrared Phys. Technol. **76**, 439–443 (2016)
13. Viola, P., Jones, M., et al.: Rapid object detection using a boosted cascade of simple features. In: IEEE Conference on Computer Vision and Pattern Recognition, vol. 1, pp. 511–518 (2001)
14. Zervos, A. (ed.): Renewables 2018. International Energy Agency (2018)

Large Field/Close-Up Image Classification: From Simple to Very Complex Features

Quyet-Tien Le[1,2]([⊠]), Patricia Ladret[1], Huu-Tuan Nguyen[2], and Alice Caplier[1]

[1] GIPSA Lab, Grenoble Alpes University, Saint Martin d'Heres Cedex, France
{quyet-tien.le,patricia.ladret,alice.caplier}@gipsa-lab.grenoble-inp.fr
[2] Vietnam Maritime University, Hai Phong, Vietnam
{tienlqcnt,huu-tuan.nguyen}@vimaru.edu.vn

Abstract. In this paper, the main contribution is to explore three different types of features including Exchangeable Image File (EXIF) features, handcrafted features and learned features in order to address the problem of large field/close up images classification with a Support Vector Machine (SVM) classifier. The impacts of every feature set on classification performances and computational complexities are investigated and compared to each other. Results prove that learned features are of course very efficient but with a computational cost that might be unreasonable. On the contrary, it appears that it is worthy to consider EXIF features when available because they represent a very good compromise between accuracy and computational cost.

Keywords: Image classification · Large field image · Close-up image ·
Handcrafted features · Exif features · Learned features ·
Feature evaluation · Feature selection · Support vector machine ·
Transfer learning

1 Introduction

Image classification has been studied for many years and the main idea is to use image features that are computed from image data either by hand [2,24] or via a learning algorithm [6,7] to separate images into different categories. The focused problem in this paper is large field/close-up image classification (image samples can be seen in Fig. 1). This classification can be used in many applications. By analyzing tourists' photos, it is possible to provide tourists with valuable information about places including beautiful panorama scenes (mountains, rivers, castles, ...) or local views (food, local specialty, exhibit, ...) [24]. This classification also helps understanding what attracts viewers' attention to improve aesthetic quality assessment [11].

Until now, there are few researches about this topic. In [26], Wang et al. propose a method using color coherence vector and color moments to classify

© Springer Nature Switzerland AG 2019
M. Vento and G. Percannella (Eds.): CAIP 2019, LNCS 11679, pp. 532–543, 2019.
https://doi.org/10.1007/978-3-030-29891-3_47

close-up and non close-up images. In another study, Zhuang et al. [27] divide an image into 256 parts. The number of edge points is counted in each part to build a 256 bin histogram. The 256 bin values and standard deviation of those values are the key features to classify close-up and distance view images. In [24], Tong et al. use features representing the distributions of high frequencies in the first classification stage, the spatial size and the conceptual size are used in the second one to classify distance/close-up view images. All features used in those classification methods are handcrafted features. The role of Exchangeable Image File (EXIF) features and learned features for that task is still a question.

Handcrafted features have been widely used for image classification [16]. Nowadays, deep learning approaches are the must for object classification [19]. At the same time, EXIF data has not been widely used for image classification. EXIF data are metadata (data information of data) and tags revealing photo information such as picture-taking time, picture-taking conditions [23]. Surprisingly, EXIF features have been only occasionally used in researches. In [9], Huang et al. use the manufacturer, camera model, date and time stamp and some other EXIF parameters as watermark information to protect image copyright. In [15], aperture, exposure value, ISO and picture-taking time are exploited to enhance region of interest detection. In [3,4], to classify in-door and out-door images, Boutell et al. present a method integrating image content and EXIF data consisting of exposure time, flash use and focal length.

In this study, the problem of large field/close-up image classification with Support Vector Machine (SVM) is considered. The performances of classification based on EXIF features, handcrafted features or learned features are compared in terms of accuracy and computational complexity. Handcrafted based feature method is considered as the reference for that study. In order to evaluate the influences of the different feature types fairly, SVM is chosen because of its simplicity. If complex classifiers are used, the accuracy of the classifications could be affected not only by input features but also by the suitability between the model structure and input features.

Experiments in this paper have been focused on 2 datasets[1]. First of all, the Flickr dataset including 800 large field images and 800 close-up images is used for experiments of large field/close-up image classification because for this database EXIF data are available which is not always the case. Another different database, the CUHKPQ dataset with 600 large field and 600 close-up images [22] without EXIF data is used only for the feature selection process among the handcrafted and learned features.

The paper is organized as follows. In Sect. 2, handcrafted features and learned features are defined and selected. EXIF features are described in Sect. 3. Section 4 presents experiments and results. Conclusions are drawn in the last part.

---

[1] The databases are available at "http://www.gipsa-lab.fr/~quyettien.le/projets_en. html" and "http://www.mediafire.com/file/58e8jui7547mam2/LargeFieldCloseup ImageDatabase.zip/file"

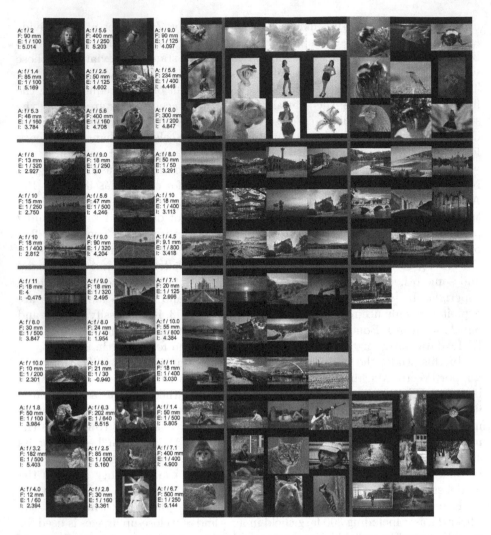

Fig. 1. The first, second, third and fourth rows (separated by the red lines) present the best close-up, large field image classifications (images being classified correctly and having the biggest distances to the hyper-plane) and the worst large field and close-up image classifications (images being classified incorrectly and having the biggest distances to the hyper-plane) based on the EXIF, handcrafted and learned features respectively. A: Aperture, F: Focal length. E: Exposure time, I: Illumination measure. (Color figure online)

2 Handcrafted and Learned Features

2.1 Handcrafted Features

The main goal of this part is to select among usual features computed from image data for large field/close-up image classification the most relevant ones.

Thus, a large handcrafted feature set is first built from common handcrafted features appearing in different researches [1,5,12,17,25]. Features consisting of color histogram, sharpness, hue, saturation, brightness, color saliency and contrast are computed for different regions including the whole image, regions of interest (regions attracting viewers' eyes), background regions and regions split by symmetry rules, landscape rule, rule of thirds (See Fig. 2) to define 2,003 handcrafted features.

Fig. 2. The two first left images present regions split by symmetry rules. The others show regions split by landscape rule and rule of third respectively.

2.2 Learned Features

Beside being handcrafted from images, features can also be learned from images by employing deep learning [14]. VGG16 [20] is a well-known deep convolutional neural network. It includes 3 main parts including convolutional layers, fully connected layers and a prediction layer. If the prediction layer is removed, that model can be considered as a feature extractor. From images of size 244×244, 4,096 features are learned by this model. Although those features have been learned for the task of classifying objects in images, they can be applied for different tasks [18] such as image quality assessment [10,21]. In this study, the VGG16 model without the prediction layer pre-trained on the ImageNet dataset for the task of classifying objects in images is considered to compute the learned features for the large field/close-up image classification on the corresponding database.

2.3 Feature Selection

Because those handcrafted and learned features have been primarily designed for a different task, the impact of each feature for the purpose of large field/close-up image classification is estimated by using the relief method [13]. CUHKPQ dataset is split into a training set and a testing set. Each set includes 300 large field (L) and 300 close-up (C) images. All features of each image in the training set are calculated and normalized to the range $[0, \ldots 1]$. The relevance of a given feature f for the classification is calculated as:

$$r(f) = dif(f, L, C) - dif(f, L, L) - dif(f, C, C) \tag{1}$$

$$dif(f, X, Y) = \frac{\sum_{i=1}^{\|X\|} \sum_{j=1}^{\|Y\|} (d(f, X_i, Y_j))}{\|X\| \times \|Y\|} \tag{2}$$

where $r(f)$ is a combination of the interclass and intraclass differences. The most relevant features are associated to the highest $r(f)$ values. $\| X \|$ is the number of images in set X. X_i is the ith image in the set X and $d(f, x, y)$ is the absolute difference between f values of the 2 images x and y.

After calculating and normalizing the relevance values to the range $[0, \ldots 1]$, a threshold needs to be determined to select the most relevant features for the classification. To do it, the features of the testing images are calculated. An algorithm inspired from the binary search algorithm is proposed to compute the threshold as:

Input:
- Feature set: $F = \{f_0, f_1, \ldots f_m\}$
- Relief set of F: $R = \{r_0, r_1, \ldots r_m\}$
- Training set S_1 and testing set S_2
Output: Threshold T
Algorithm:
- Set 2 thresholds: $T_1 = 0$, $T_2 = 1$
- For $i = 1$ to k (in this study k is set to 50)
   + For $j = 1$ to 2
     Use T_j as a threshold $F_T = \{f_x | r_x \geq T_j\}$)
     Use F_T, S_1, S_2 to train and test an SVM classifier.
     Gain testing accuracy A_j
     End of loop j
   + If $A_1 < A_2$
     $T_1 = T_1 + \frac{T_2 - T_1}{5}$
   + If $A_1 > A_2$
     $T_2 = T_2 - \frac{T_2 - T_1}{5}$
   + If $A_1 = A_2$
     $T_1 = T_1 + \frac{T_2 - T_1}{5}$
     $T_2 = T_2 - \frac{T_2 - T_1}{5}$
   End of loop i
- Return threshold $T = \frac{T_1 + T_2}{2}$

Applying the feature selection algorithm on the handcrafted and learned feature sets, 21 handcrafted features and 925 learned features are selected from the 2,003 handcrafted features and the 4,096 VGG16 features respectively.

3   EXIF Features

3.1   EXIF Feature Definition

In photography, camera tunnings are stored by digital cameras as EXIF data. 4 EXIF parameters and a combination of some of them are analyzed in this study.

Aperture. Aperture refers to the size of lens opening for light when a picture is captured. This parameter is stored as a *f-stops* such as $f/1.4$, $f/2$, $f/2.8$, ... in which *f-stops* $= \frac{f}{D}$ where f is the focal length and D is diameter of the entrance in a camera. A smaller *stops* value represents a wider aperture. The Depth Of Field (DOF) and brightness of pictures are affected by the aperture value.

Focal Length. Focal length exhibits the distance from the middle of the lens to the digital sensor and it also decides the angle of view in the picture. This parameter is measured in millimeters. A long focal length makes a narrow view and a wide scene is captured when using a short focal length.

Exposure Time. Exposure time represents the total time for light falling on the sensor of the camera during shooting. It is measured in seconds. In weak light conditions or to create some special effects, photographers use long exposure time. A short exposure time is regularly used when capturing moving objects like taking sport photos.

ISO. ISO describes the sensitivity level of the sensor in a camera. ISO parameter is measured with numbers such as 100, 200, 400, ... The lower ISO value represents the less sensitive mode of the sensor. The brightness of a photo decreases with the decrease of ISO.

Illumination Measure. Illumination measure refers to the light falling on a surface [8]. This feature is calculated as:

$$I_{measure} = \log_{10}(\frac{aperture^2}{exposure\ time}) + \log_{10}(\frac{250}{ISO}) \tag{3}$$

3.2 EXIF Feature Selection

In this subsection, the influence of EXIF features on large field/close-up image classification is investigated. At the first step, EXIF values of 400 large field and 400 close-up photos extracted from Flick dataset (the training set in the next experiments of large field/close-up image classification) are displayed in Fig. 3. It appears that the differences of EXIF parameters between close-up and large field images are significant in aperture, focal length, illumination measure and to a smaller extent in exposure time.

Unsurprisingly the aperture data is very significant to distinguish between close-up and large field images. Actually, a high aperture value is regularly chosen to highlight the objects by low DOF effect. In the other hand, because large field scenes are far from the camera, a small aperture value is set for capturing a large field photo to gain a deep DOF.

Focal length is the second discriminating feature. A large field scene is wide so photographers often use a short focal length to get the whole scene. In contrast, to focus on close-up objects, a longer focal length is regularly used to take close-up pictures.

Illumination measure and exposure time are also going to be considered for large field/close-up image classification. On the contrary, ISO feature is not relevant enough.

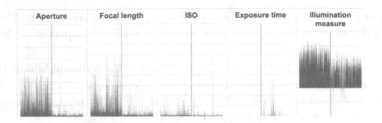

Fig. 3. EXIF values of 400 close-up images (the left side) and 400 large field images (the righ side).

Table 1. Overview of evaluation criteria.

Evaluation criteria	Formula
Overall accuracy	$A = \frac{TP+TN}{TP+FP+TN+FN}$
Balanced accuracy	$B = 0.5 \times \frac{TP}{TP+FP} + 0.5 \times \frac{TN}{TN+FN}$
Precision	$P = \frac{TP}{TP+FP}$
Recall	$R = \frac{TP}{TP+FN}$

4   Experiments

4.1   Dataset and Setup

Large field/close-up image classification is performed separately with EXIF, handcrafted and learned features. An SVM classifier is trained and tested to evaluate the classification performances for each feature set.

The experiments are performed on 1,600 images including 800 large field and 800 close-up images collected and categorized from Flickr website by our team. Half of the large field and close-up images are selected randomly to train the classifiers while the others are used to test. Each SVM classifier is applied with linear kernel, $C = 0.5, g = 1 \times 10^{-5}, e = 1.192 \times 10^{-7}$. Evaluation criteria in this study include overall Accuracy (A), Balanced accuracy (B), Precision (P) and Recall (R) where TP, TN, FP, FN are true positive, true negative, false positive and false negative respectively and they are expressed as a number of images (cf. Table 1).

4.2   Results and Discussions

Handcrafted Features. Table 2 shows the results of the classification based on the 21 handcrafted features. The reference classification rate using those handcrafted features is 0.873.

In order to prove the efficiency of the selected handcrafted features, the classification based on those features is compared with the classifications based on other handcrafted features including Wang's [26], Zhuang's [27] features. The results are given in Table 2. Despite using more features, the classifications with

Wang's (105 features) and Zhuang's (257 features) feature sets have lower accuracy at 0.774 and 0.854 respectively.

Table 2. Results for large field/close-up image classification based on the 21 selected handcrafted features compared with the classification based on other handcrafted features.

		Prediction	
		Close-up image	Large field image
Ground truth	Close-up image	TP = 349	FN = 51
	Large field image	FP = 51	TN = 349
Overall accuracy	**0.873**	Balanced accuracy	0.873
Precision	0.873	Recall	0.873
Overall accuracy of classifications based on other handcrafted feature sets			
Wang's features (105 features)			**0.774**
Zhuang's features (257 features)			**0.854**

Table 3. Results for large field/close-up image classification using the 4 selected EXIF features where TP, TN, FP FN are expressed as a number of images.

		Prediction	
		Close-up image	Large field image
Ground truth	Close-up image	TP = 348	FN = 52
	Large field image	FP = 46	TN = 354
Overall accuracy	0.878	Balanced accuracy	0.878
Precision	0.883	Recall	0.870

EXIF Features. The results of the classification based on the 4 selected EXIF features are presented in Table 3. Using a very small number of simple features, the classification accuracy 0.878 is impressive.

Learned Features. The results of classification with the 925 best features learned from VGG16 are shown in Table 4. Obviously, the classification with learned features has the highest overall accuracy (0.989) but the number of features is also the biggest (925 features) among the studied feature sets.

Comparisons. To start with, it appears that EXIF features are quite powerful for large filed/close-up image classification since the accuracy (0.878) is obtained with only 4 EXIF features. With handcrafted features, the number of features is higher (21 versus 4) while the classification accuracy is almost the

Table 4. Results for large field/close-up image classification based on the 925 selected VGG16 features.

		Prediction	
		Close-up image	Large field image
Ground truth	Close-up image	TP = 392	FN = 8
	Large field image	FP = 1	TN = 399
Overall accuracy	0.989	Balanced accuracy	0.989
Precision	0.997	Recall	0.980

same (0.873). Secondly, the classification with learned features has the highest accuracy (0.989). However the number of selected features is also the biggest (925 learned features against 21 handcrafted features and 4 EXIF features).

Table 5. Results for large field/close-up image classifications based on the 4 EXIF features, 21 handcrafted features, top 21 and top 4 most relevant learned features.

Feature set	TP	FP	TN	FN	A	B	P	R
EXIF features	348	46	354	52	0.878	0.878	0.883	0.870
4 learned features	389	9	391	11	0.975	0.975	0.977	0.973
Handcrafted features	349	51	349	51	0.873	0.873	0.873	0.873
21 learned features	391	6	394	9	0.981	0.981	0.985	0.978

In order to compare the role of those features, the classifications using the top 21 and top 4 most relevant learned features are performed and the results are shown in Table 5. It appears that the learned features are very efficient for large field/close-up image classification since with the same number of features as handcrafted features (21 features) the accuracy of the classification based on the 21 most relevant learned features is higher than that of the handcrafted features (0.981 versus 0.873). Similarly, with only 4 features as EXIF features, the accuracy of the classification based on the 4 best learned features is 0.975, a very high accuracy while the classification accuracy with EXIF features is 0.878.

Figure 1 shows the top 9 best classifications (images being classified correctly and having the biggest distances to the hyper-plane of the SVM classifiers) and the top 9 worst classifications (images being classified incorrectly and having the biggest distances to the hyper-plane) of each category. It appears that the feature sets are acting totally differently since there are no overlapping images between those results. The best classified close-up images using EXIF features are mostly low DOF images because of wide aperture values. Most of the best close-up images (7 of 9) have high apertures, high illumination measures and long exposure time ($A \geq 10$ and $I \geq 4.0$ and $E \geq \frac{1}{250}$) while no image of the best or worst large field photos and only one of the worst close-up images satisfies this condition. Additionally, 6 of the 9 best large field images have small focal lengths, short exposure time and illumination measures ranging from 2.75 to 3.418 ($F \leq 50$ *and* $E \leq \frac{1}{250}$ *and* $2.75 \leq I \leq 3.418$) while no image of the best close-up photos and only one of the worst large field images has EXIF data in those ranges. With handcrafted features the best classified close-up images almost have blank background because some features are handcrafted to estimate the number of background details of close-up images (those features cannot be used to classify blank background or blur background) so the classifier focuses on blank background. VGG16 being pre-trained on the ImageNet dataset for purpose of classifying objects in images, the extracted features have been designed to recognize objects very well. It explains why the top classified close-up images using those features are images with fish, bird, chicken, insect. Additionally, learned features seem to focus on the high frequency details in foreground of close-up images. In contrast, the differences between the best large field image classifications and the differences between the worst classifications are not clear. Last but not least, an experiment has been conducted on a PC equipped with an Intel Core i7-2670QM CPU 2.40 GHz and 11.9 GB memory to evaluate the feature computational time and classification time of EXIF, handcrafted and learned features. The feature computational time and classification time with 800 images are shown in Table 6. It is clear that EXIF features are the simplest ones when only one EXIF feature (illumination measure) needs to be computed and its feature computational time is only 1 ms. In contrast, the feature computational time of learned features is over 14 times higher than that of the handcrafted features (347,186 ms versus 23,994 ms). Additionally, it is impossible to compute a part of learned features. Thus, the feature computational time for the 21,925 or 4,096 learned features is the same. Although the time of SVM classification based on the computed feature sets is almost the same (3–4 ms) except the one of the 925 learned features (55 ms), the differences in the total classification time (the sum of the feature computational time and the time of SVM classification based on computed features) between those feature sets are significant. It points out that the classification based on EXIF features is very

Table 6. Feature computational time and classification time. In this table, the total classification time is the sum of the feature computational time and the time of SVM classification based on the computed features.

Feature set	Feature computational time (ms)	SVM classification time (ms)	Total classification time (ms)	Overall accuracy
4 EXIF features	1	3	4	0.878
21 handcrafted features	23,994	4	23,998	0.873
21 learned features	347,186	3	347,189	0.981
925 learned features	347,186	55	347,241	0.989

fast (only 4 ms). The classification based on handcrafted features is slower (24 s) while the classification with learned features is very slow (approximately 347 s) but the accuracy is not increasing in the same proportions so the question is: is the additional computational cost worthy regarding the gain in accuracy? The answer might depend on the considered application.

5   Conclusion

In this paper, large field/close-up image classification task is studied and 3 types of features are evaluated in terms of classification accuracy, complexity, running time. It appears that learned features are very powerful for that task, the accuracies of the classification reach 0.989 with 925 features and 0.975 with only 4 features learned from VGG16 although they are complex and it is not easy to understand them. EXIF features are quite efficient for large filed/close-up image classification since it is possible to obtain the same and quite good classification score by using 4 very simple EXIF features than by using 21 complex handcrafted features. EXIF features are simple, efficient but they are not always available.

References

1. Aydin, T.O., Smolic, A., Gross, M.: Automated aesthetic analysis of photographic images. IEEE Trans. Vis. Comput. Graph. **21**(1), 31–42 (2015)
2. Bosch, A., Zisserman, A., Munoz, X.: Image classification using random forests and ferns. In: 2007 IEEE 11th International Conference on Computer Vision, pp. 1–8, October 2007
3. Boutell, M., Luo, J.: Photo classification by integrating image content and camera metadata. In: Proceedings - International Conference on Pattern Recognition, vol. 4, pp. 901–904, January 2004
4. Boutell, M., Luo, J.: Beyond pixels: exploiting camera metadata for photo classification. Pattern Recogn. **38**(6), 935–946 (2005). Image Understanding for Photographs
5. Datta, R., Joshi, D., Li, J., Wang, J.Z.: Studying aesthetics in photographic images using a computational approach. In: Leonardis, A., Bischof, H., Pinz, A. (eds.) ECCV 2006. LNCS, vol. 3953, pp. 288–301. Springer, Heidelberg (2006). https://doi.org/10.1007/11744078_23
6. Guo, T., Dong, J., Li, H., Gao, Y.: Simple convolutional neural network on image classification. In: 2017 IEEE 2nd International Conference on Big Data Analysis, pp. 721–724, March 2017
7. He, S., Xu, C., Guo, T., Xu, C., Tao, D.: Reinforced multi-label image classification by exploring curriculum. In: The Thirty-Second AAAI Conference on Artificial Intelligence (2018)
8. Hiscocks, P.D., Syscomp, P.E.: Measuring luminance with a digital camera. In: Syscomp Electronic Design Limited 2011 (2011). http://www.atecorp.com/ATECorp/media/pdfs/data-sheets/Tektronix-J16_Application.pdf
9. Huang, H., Chen, Y., Chen, S.: Copyright protection for images with EXIF metadata. In: 2008 International Conference on Intelligent Information Hiding and Multimedia Signal Processing, pp. 239–242, August 2008

10. Jin, B., Segovia, M.V.O., Susstrunk, S.: Image aesthetic predictors based on weighted CNNs. In: Proceedings - International Conference on Image Processing, ICIP 2016, pp. 2291–2295 (2016)
11. Kao, Y., Huang, K., Maybank, S.: Hierarchical aesthetic quality assessment using deep convolutional neural networks. Signal Process. Image Communication **47**, 500–510 (2016)
12. Ke, Y., Tang, X., Jing, F.: The design of high-level features for photo quality assessment. In: Proceedings of the IEEE Computer Society Conference on Computer Vision and Pattern Recognition, vol. 1, pp. 419–426 (2006)
13. Kira, K., Rendell, L.A.: A practical approach to feature selection. In: Proceedings of the Ninth International Workshop on Machine Learning, pp. 249–256. ML92. Morgan Kaufmann Publishers Inc., San Francisco (1992)
14. Krizhevsky, A., Sutskever, I., Hinton, G.E.: Imagenet classification with deep convolutional neural networks. Commun. ACM **60**(6), 84–90 (2017)
15. Li, Z., Fan, J.: Exploit camera metadata for enhancing interesting region detection and photo retrieval. Multimedia Tools Appl. **46**(2–3), 207–233 (2010)
16. Lu, D., Weng, Q.: A survey of image classification methods and techniques for improving classification performance. Int. J. Remote Sens. **28**(5), 823–870 (2007)
17. Luo, Y., Tang, X.: Photo and video quality evaluation: focusing on the subject. In: Forsyth, D., Torr, P., Zisserman, A. (eds.) ECCV 2008. LNCS, vol. 5304, pp. 386–399. Springer, Heidelberg (2008). https://doi.org/10.1007/978-3-540-88690-7_29
18. Pan, S.J., Yang, Q.: A survey on transfer learning. IEEE Transactions on Knowledge and Data Engineering **22**(10), 1345–1359 (2010)
19. Rawat, W., Wang, Z.: Deep convolutional neural networks for image classification: a comprehensive review. Neural Comput. **29**(9), 2352–2449 (2017)
20. Simonyan, K., Zisserman, A.: Very deep convolutional networks for large-scale image recognition. In: 3rd International Conference on Learning Representations, ICLR 2015, San Diego, CA, USA, 7–9 May 2015. Conference Track Proceedings (2015)
21. Talebi, H., Milanfar, P.: NIMA: neural image assessment. IEEE Trans. Image Process. **27**, 3998–4011 (2018)
22. Tang, X., Luo, W., Wang, X.: Content-based photo quality assessment. IEEE Trans. Multimed. **15**(8), 1930–1943 (2013)
23. Technical Standardization Committee on AV & IT Storage Systems and Equipment: Exchangeable image file format for digital still cameras: Exif Version 2.2. Technical report JEITA CP-3451, April 2002
24. Tong, S., Loh, Y.P., Liang, X., Kumada, T.: Visual attention inspired distant view and close-up view classification. In: 2016 IEEE International Conference on Image Processing (ICIP), pp. 2787–2791, September 2016
25. Vailaya, A., Figueiredo, M.A., Jain, A.K., Zhang, H.: Content-based hierarchical classification of vacation images. In: Proceedings IEEE International Conference on Multimedia Computing and Systems, vol. 1, no. 2, pp. 518–523 (1999)
26. Wang, Y., Hu, B.G.: Hierarchical image classification using support vector machines. In: Asian Conference on Computer Vision, pp. 23–25 January 2002
27. Zhuang, C., Ma, Q., Liang, X., Yoshikawa, M.: Anaba: an obscure sightseeing spots discovering system. In: 2014 IEEE International Conference on Multimedia and Expo (ICME), pp. 1–6, July 2014

Enhancing Low Quality Face Image Matching by Neurovisually Inspired Deep Learning

Apurba Das(⊠) and Pallavi Saha(⊠)

TCS IoT Innovation Laboratory, Tata Consultancy Services, Banglore, India
{das.apurba,saha.pallavi}@tcs.com

Abstract. Computerized human face matching from low quality images is an active area of research in deformable pattern recognition especially in non-cooperative security, surveillance, authentication and multi-camera tracking. In low resolution and motion-blurry face images captured from surveillance cameras, it is challenging to get good match of faces and even extracting suitable feature vectors both in classical signal/image processing based and deep learning based approaches. In the current work, we have proposed a novel low quality face image matching algorithm in the light of a neuro-visually inspired method of figure-ground segregation (NFGS). The said framework is inspired by the non-linear interaction between the classical receptive field (CRF) and its non-classical extended surround, comprising of the non-linear mean increasing and decreasing sub-units. The current work demonstrates not only better detection of low quality face images in NFGS enabled deep learning framework, but also it prescribes an efficient way of low quality face image matching addressing low contrast, low resolution and motion blur which are prime responsible factors of making image low quality. The experimental results shows the effectiveness of proposed algorithm not only quantitatively but also qualitatively in terms of psycho-visual experiments and its statistical analysis outcome.

Keywords: Low quality face image matching · NFGS · ECRF · SIFT · FaceNet · ANOVA · Face recognition

1 Introduction

Object recognition is the most crucial and yet least understood aspect of psycho-visual perception. Translating the perception of recognition by human to a machine is even more challenging as imitating human vision system through computer is still an ongoing research. That's why even though it's difficult for machine to match faces from low quality images, it's not so difficult for human through the three level processing in primary visual cortex [1]. Researchers have been proposing different methods based on signal processing, image processing and machine/deep learning for quite sometime. Wang et al. [2] has provided an extensive study on the different methods to address various issues of

© Springer Nature Switzerland AG 2019
M. Vento and G. Percannella (Eds.): CAIP 2019, LNCS 11679, pp. 544–555, 2019.
https://doi.org/10.1007/978-3-030-29891-3_48

low-resolution face recognition segregating into large two categories as super-resolution for low resolution face recognition and tried to model a resolution-robust feature. Yang et al. [3] proposed a novel algorithm regarded as sparse low-rank component-based representation (SLCR) for face recognition in low quality images. Rudrani et al. [4], on the other hand, described the effectiveness of their proposed method by adjusting the degradation in the surveillance data achieved by partial restoration (using super-resolution, interpolation etc.) instead of designing a specific classifier space for that type of images. The extent of degradation has been estimated on the basis of the difference in the intensity histograms of face samples. Mohammad et al. [5] put forwarded an algorithm, Discriminant Correlation Analysis (DCA) to perform recognition in low quality face images. Both Karahan et al. [6] and Dodge et al. [7] have discussed the different types of degradation that can occur in an image (such as noise, blur and occlusion) in real time scenario and their impact on the performance of Deep Neural Networks based Face Recognition. Chellappa et al. [8] proposed a novel algorithm, Hyperface that performs concurrently face landmarks localization, pose and gender estimation using deep convolutional neural networks (CNN). Huang et al. [9] presented a novel method based on Binary Gradient Patterns for robust facial recognition. Zhou et al. [10] has shown that accuracy and performance is really poor when face recognition is tested with low quality images. Bosse et al. [11] presented a deep neural network based approach to assess the quality of image.

To the best of our knowledge this is the first time low quality face image matching is being addressed in complete binary framework inspired from neurovisual clues of human perception. In the current work we have demonstrated improvement in deep learning based detection of low quality face image categories into low resolution, low contrast, motion blurry. Further, the enhancement in low quality face image matching have been quantified with respect to state-of-art.

According to Marr [1], mid-level vision plays very important role in object feature understanding from intelligent figure-ground segregation. This work has improved and utilized the neuro-visually inspired figure ground segregation (NFGS) [12–14] for enabling deep neural network to detect low quality face image category and also improve face matching. It would be interesting to see the strength of efficient binary framework [14] in both classical image processing and deep learning based feature extraction from two-quantization-level face images whereas raw captured gray was not even accepted to be consumed by deep learning.

In the following sections, the detailed motivation, modeling of NFGS and methodologies to design/implement deep learning based classification and matching of low quality face images have been described. In Sect. 2, the fundamental idea of designing neuro-visually inspired figure ground segregation [12] have been discussed along with it's comparison with other state-of-art figure-ground segregation methods for low resolution face images. In Sect. 3, enhancement of classification accuracy have been discussed for different categories of low quality face images. Next, in Sect. 4, low quality face image matching have been demonstrated in proposed framework both using traditional image processing and deep learning based approach. A detailed psycho-visual survey has been conducted as depicted in Sect. 5 and effectiveness of the proposed algorithm has been supported qualitatively through statistical analysis. Finally, we concluded our findings with future direction of research in Sect. 6.

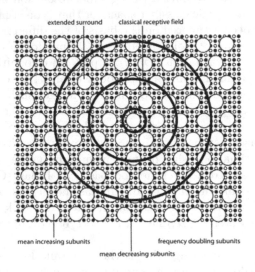

Fig. 1. The extra-classical receptive structure (adopted from Ghosh et al. [15]) demonstrating the extended surround region of the classical receptive field that itself contains a center and a surround.

2   Neuro-Visually Inspired Figure Ground Segregation (NFGS) for Low Quality Face Feature

Ever since the famous theory of Marr [1], psychologists and computer vision researchers are trying to model the entire mechanism of human vision mathematically. The objective is to imitate the technique of human vision computationally so that a machine can also perform the complex visual pattern recognition and pattern understanding tasks. An important step here comprises of finding the raw primal sketch of the image where zero-crossings are searched and the entire image is presented by two distinct levels. So, a perception based binarization is done over the image. Marr showed, Laplacian of Gaussian (LoG) [1] operator is equivalent to the lateral inhibition based center-surround receptive field model proposed by the physiologists, viz. the Difference of Gaussians (DoG) [16].

In addition to the classical ideas of center-surround receptive field, physiologists have also observed [17] that a number of cells lying outside the Classical Receptive Field (CRF) can modulate the behavior of that cell. Such modulation, termed as the extended/extra classical receptive field (ECRF), is known to elicit nonlinear responses as depicted in Fig. 1. Based on this idea of ECRF, Roy et al. proposed a neuro-visual model of figure ground segregation and has modeled in the form of a new digital mask [12, 14] as shown in Fig. 2.

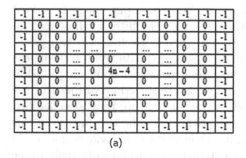

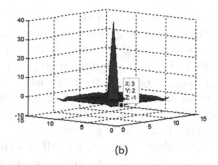

(a)   (b)

Fig. 2. (a) Tabular and (b) Graphical representation of ECRF kernel (size 11 × 11) [12, 14]

Algorithm 2.1: NFGS($inImg, kernelSize, numSeg$)

---

comment: $Output := I_{NFGSBIN}$ or $I_{NFGSMULTI}$

$Img_x := extrapolate(inImg, m = (kernelSize - 1)/2)$
$F := generateKernel(kernelSize)$
$I_{filt} := convolution(Img_x, F)$
$I_{NFGSBIN} := imgThresh(I_{filt}, 0)$
$grayVal[] := sortAscend(I_{filt})$
$span := numPix/numSeg$
$thresh[1] := 0$
for $i := 1 \ldots numSeg$
  do $\begin{cases} thresh[i+1] := grayVal[span * i] \\ grayLevI[i] := (i * 256)/numSeg - 1 \end{cases}$
for $r := 1 \ldots numRows$
  do $\begin{cases} \textbf{for } r := 1 \ldots numRows \\ \quad \textbf{do } \begin{cases} \textbf{if } (thresh[i-1] < I_{filt}[r, c] \leq thresh[i]) \\ \quad \textbf{then } I_{NFGSMULTI} := grayLevI[i] \end{cases} \end{cases}$

Here 'n' is the filter size ($n = 2m + 1 > 1, m \in Z+$). The numbers of zeros from the center to the periphery of the digital mask both along row and column is always 'm − 1'. Clearly, for its lowest value, i.e. 'm' = 1, the filter reduces to the finite difference approximation of the classical Laplacian mask. Each of the elements of the output of the convolved image is then binarized by thresholding at zero gray level. Das et al. have shown the effectiveness of face recognition [14] and detection [18] engine in NFGS based binary environment.

The following subsection would address the choice of relative size of NFGS filter kernels adaptively.

2.1   Algorithm of NFGS for Binary and Multi-level Segmentation

In order to maintain the size of the face image, first the input image is padded with nearest neighbors' extrapolation. After applying the filter to these extrapolated images if threshold is chosen to be zero then it results in a two grainblock, i.e. figure-ground segregated image, $I_{NFGSBIN}$. Multiple grain-blocks $(I_{NFGSMULTI})$, on the other hand, may also be formed with some simple additional steps on the filtered image. First the pixels are sorted according to their gray levels and then taking the gray level as the sole feature they are classified in equal number of groups as depicted in Algorithm 2.1. The reason behind this simple algorithm working well in forming multiple mid-level blocks is that when we are applying the filter to an image it extends the normal gray scale range of [0 to 255] to a very large range of [−30000 to +30000](approx) because of the derivative property of the filter (all differences are magnified). Naturally if now the pixels are equally grouped and assigned a gray value for each group an understandably more effective situation emerges for arriving at the grain-blocks, possibly because the dynamic range within which our visual system functions suits better the magnification obtained.

Figure 3 shows the effectiveness of NFGS over conventional figure-ground segregation methods demonstrating maximum information retrieval from input gray image even in binary. In this work, we will restrict our discussion only on 2 level segmentation to comply to maximum information retrieval from minimum data (one bit per pixel).

2.2   NFGS on Low Quality Face Images

The effectiveness of the proposed figure-ground segregation has been depicted in Fig. 4 where different kind of image quality issues have been addressed. We can

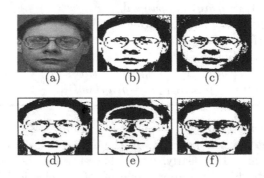

Fig. 3. Comparison of proposed NFGS algorithm with the state-of-art figure-ground segregation algorithms on face image: (a) Inout gray image, (b) Bay's algo, (c) Otsu's Algo, (d) K-means algo, (e) Region growing, (f) NFGS [14].

observe that for non-uniformly illuminated images, other binarization algorithm just sweeps of face features from one side, for low contrast image other algorithm fails to prevails any face feature whereas NFGS could maintain facial features for low resolution, shadowed, low contrast, and motion-blurry face images.

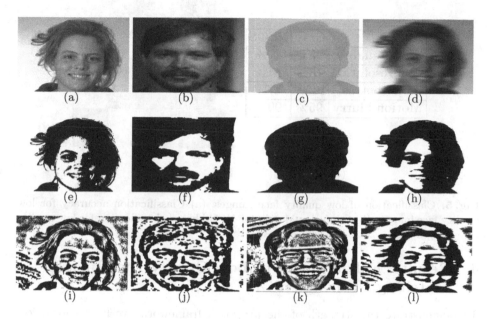

Fig. 4. Comparison of proposed NFGS algorithm with the state-of-art figure-ground segregation algorithms on low quality face images from FERET [19]: Column 1: One side shadowed, Column 2: Low resolution, Column 3: Low contrast, Column 4: Motion blurry; Row 1: Gray original, Row 2: Otsu's figure-ground-segregation, Row 3: NFGS based binarization

3   Low Quality Face Image Classification by Neuro-Visually Inspired Deep Learning

Primarily, we have used TensorFlow implementation of VGG16 [20] network for classifying different kinds of low quality face images with and without NFGS based pre-processing. We have used 290 training samples, 30 validation samples and 75 query samples for each class and trained the network for 500 epochs. We have considered 100×100 pixel size of face images and created motion blurry images by Gaussian kernels of size 1×3 with standard deviation 9 pixels. The low resolution images were created by 15% down-sampling the original images.

It was interesting to see that, we have achieved better classification accuracy than original gray images for low resolution and motion blurry images as depicted in Fig. 5(a). But there is an expected confusion between good quality and low contrast images in classification by our proposed framework. This is obvious as NFGS extracts underlying information in gray images such that there is no difference between good contrast and low contrast images. This has been also further demonstrated in the confusion matrix depicted in Fig. 5(b).

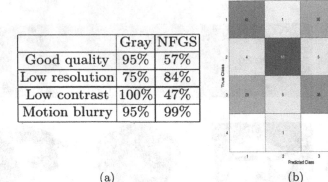

	Gray	NFGS
Good quality	95%	57%
Low resolution	75%	84%
Low contrast	100%	47%
Motion blurry	95%	99%

(a)   (b)

Fig. 5. Classification of low quality face images: (a) Classification accuracy for low quality face images, (b) Confusion Matrix for NFGS based classification for low quality face images

4   Results: Enhancement of Low Quality Face Image Matching Utilizing NFGS

To demonstrate the strength of the proposed framework, we have shown low quality face image matching by two following well-practiced ways: (a) Deep Learning based face matching [21] and (b) SIFT [22] based face matching. It was observed that for low resolution and motion blurry faces, FaceNet failed to extract the feature vector itself from original gray and color images whereas the same algorithm not only successfully extracted the feature vector, but also results expected face matching in proposed binary framework.

We used FaceNet [21] model for deep learning based low quality face matching and results have been depicted in Table 1 for our proposed model. We have created data-set of 500 good faces from FERET [19] binarized by our proposed algorithm for PIE varied faces followed by low quality degradation and NFGS based binarization as queries for the same 500 subjects. The recognition accuracy for 1st match has been depicted in Table 1.

Table 1. Low quality Face Image Matching Accuracy in proposed framework [19].

	Low resolution	Low contrast	Motion blurry	Non-uniformly shadowed
Accuracy	96.7%	98.2%	93.2%	95.2%

We have also re-validated the effectiveness of our algorithm by SIFT [22] based face matching as depicted in Fig. 6.

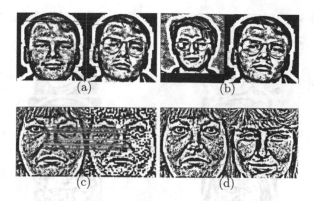

Fig. 6. SIFT [22] based face matching in proposed binary framework: (a) 20 points matching with same person, different expression, eye-glasses, (c) 40 points matching with low resolution face image of same person, (b) and (d) zero matching between different persons.

5   Psycho-Visual Experiment and Results

To validate the effectiveness of the proposed algorithm, a psycho-visual experimentation has been designed and performed in terms of a survey. The outcome of the survey has been finally analyzed through statistical significance measure. A simple GUI of 4×2 matrix was designed. The 1st column had 4 good quality, frontal face images of 4 random individuals binarized through NFGS. The $2^{n}d$ column has 5 randomly placed NFGS filtered face images with pose-illumination-expression (PIE) variation and 3 different low quality impacts: (a) low resolution, (b) low contrast, and (c) motion-blur.

In the survey phase, 100 subjects were identified randomly in two age groups (fifty subjects from age group <30 and fifty subjects from age group ≥30). The goal of the survey was to determine if the binary faces produced by the proposed system was recognizable by the subjects. The images were shuffled each time the survey was done. The subjects were asked to click on the best match according to his visual perception and allowed to add their confidence level also to each of the recognition between 0% to 100%. In the Table 2 we have weighted the confidence level to number of recognition and finally rounded off wherever required. Recognizing j^{th} face from i^{th} binary is represented as χ_{ij} in Table 2. In the table, only 3 instances have been shown (randomly chosen). The UI application used for the psycho-visual survey has been depicted in Fig. 7.

5.1   ANOVA: Validation Through Analysis of Psycho-Visual Survey

In statistics, analysis of variance (ANOVA) is a statistical model in which the observed variance in a particular variable is partitioned into components attributable to different sources of variation. One-way ANOVA finds out whether data from several groups have a common mean. That is, to determine whether

Fig. 7. Binary low quality face correspondence used for psycho-visual survey

Table 2. Psycho-visual survey report for low quality face maching in NFGS based binary environment

	χ_{11}	χ_{12}	χ_{13}	χ_{14}	χ_{15}	χ_{21}	χ_{22}	χ_{23}	χ_{24}	χ_{25}	χ_{31}	χ_{32}	χ_{33}	χ_{34}	χ_{35}
Age < 30 yrs	46	0	1	3	0	0	45	3	1	1	0	2	48	0	0
Age ≥ 30 yrs	43	0	0	7	0	0	48	2	0	0	1	2	44	2	1

the groups are actually different in the measured characteristic. From the Table 2 it's clear that most of the subjects could recognize persons from NFGS enabled low quality faces correctly. The box plot (Fig. 9) approves the fact.

Here, a balanced one-way ANOVA is performed for comparing the means of 15 columns of data in the 2-by-15 matrix X, as presented in Table 2 where each column represents an independent sample containing 2 mutually independent observations for the 2 predefined age groups. The function returns the p-value for the null hypothesis that all samples in X are drawn from the same population.

If the p-value is near zero, this casts doubt on the null hypothesis and suggests that at least one sample mean is significantly different from the other sample means. It is common to declare a result "statistically significant" if the p-value is less than 0.05. The ANOVA table (Fig. 8) has six columns: (1) the source of the variability, (2) Sum of Squares (SS) due to each source, (3) degrees of freedom (df) associated with each source, (4) Mean Squares (MS) for each source, which is the ratio SS/df, (5) F statistic, which is the ratio of the MS's, (6) p-value, which is derived from the cdf of F. The p-value decreases with increasing F. Table 2 clearly depicts that the proposed algorithm demonstrates face matching between correct pair of faces. The Figs. 8 and 9 confirms the significance of correct recognition $(\chi_{11}, \chi_{22}, \chi_{33})$ of face from low quality face queries, through the proposed algorithm.

```
One-way ANOVA Table:

Source of Variation    Sum of Squares    df   Empirical Var
******************************************************************
Between Groups             9592.0000     14        685.1429
Within Groups                30.0000     15          2.0000
----------------------------------------------------------------
Total                      9622.0000     29


Test Statistic f            342.5714
p-value                       0.0000
```

Fig. 8. ANOVA for the psycho-visual survey presented in Table 2

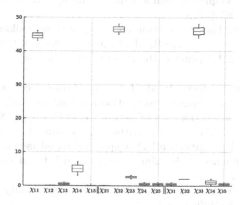

Fig. 9. Box plot for the ANOVA table presented in Fig. 8 for survey of Table 2

6 Conclusion

Face recognition from low quality images is an important research aspect in non-cooperative authentication and surveillance. In the current work, we have proposed a neuro-visually inspired algorithm of figure-ground segregation based on ECRF. The proposed framework has been shown itself efficient in handling different quality issues in face images like low resolution, low contrast, motion blur, non-uniform shadow. We have shown, the proposed framework has extracted maximum amount of information from face images even in said low quality degradation. The algorithm is generic in all the aforementioned degradation.

Experimental results have shown, better classification scores for most of the classes and interestingly significant confusion between low contrast and good quality images. This weakness of the obtained result of classification has been converted to strength on face matching and demonstrated excellent recognition accuracy in efficient binary framework proposed by us. The said quantitative results have been supported qualitatively by a psycho-visual experiment and statistical analysis of the same. We are working on recognized face tracking in live or offline videos utilizing the proposed framework which will be reported in near future with even more degree and combination of multiple kinds of image quality degradation.

References

1. Marr, D.: Vision: A Computational Investigation into the Human Representation and Processing of Visual Information, vol. 1 (1980). Proceedings of the Royal Society of London
2. Wang, Z., Miao, Z., Wu, Q.M.J., Wan, Y., Tang, Z.: Low-resolution face recognition: a review. Vis. Comput. **30**(4), 359–386 (2014)
3. Yang, S., Zhang, L., He, L., Wen, Y.: Sparse low-rank component-based representation for face recognition with low-quality images. IEEE Trans. Inf. Forensics Secur. **14**(1), 251–261 (2019)
4. Rudrani, S., Das, S.: Face recognition on low quality surveillance images, by compensating degradation. In: Kamel, M., Campilho, A. (eds.) ICIAR 2011. LNCS, vol. 6754, pp. 212–221. Springer, Heidelberg (2011). https://doi.org/10.1007/978-3-642-21596-4_22
5. Haghighat, M., Abdel-Mottaleb, M.: Lower resolution face recognition in surveillance systems using discriminant correlation analysis. In: 12th IEEE International Conference on Automatic Face and Gesture Recognition, pp. 912–917, June 2017
6. Karahan, S., Kilinc Yildirum, M., Kirtac, K., Rende, F.S., Butun, G., Ekenel, H.K.: How image degradations affect deep CNN-based face recognition? In: 2016 International Conference of the Biometrics Special Interest Group (BIOSIG), pp. 1–5, September 2016
7. Dodge, S.F., Karam, L.J.: Understanding how image quality affects deep neural networks. CoRR, abs/1604.04004 (2016)
8. Ranjan, R., Patel, V.M., Chellappa, R.: HyperFace: a deep multi-task learning framework for face detection, landmark localization, pose estimation, and gender recognition. IEEE Trans. Pattern Anal. Mach. Intell. **41**(1), 121–135 (2019)
9. Huang, W., Yin, H.: Robust face recognition with structural binary gradient patterns. Pattern Recogn. **68**, 126–140 (2017)
10. Zhou, Y., Liu, D., Huang, T.: Survey of face detection on low-quality images. In: 2018 13th IEEE International Conference on Automatic Face Gesture Recognition (FG 2018), pp. 769–773, May 2018
11. Bosse, S., Maniry, D., Müller, K., Wiegand, T., Samek, W.: Deep neural networks for no-reference and full-reference image quality assessment. IEEE Trans. Image Process. **27**(1), 206–219 (2018)
12. Ghosh, K., Roy, A.: Neuro-visually inspired figure-ground segregation. In: 2011 International Conference on Image Information Processing, pp. 1–6, November 2011

13. Das, A., Ajithkumar, N.: Engineering the perception of recognition through inter-active raw primal sketch by HNFGS and CNN-MRF. In: CVIP (2017)

14. Das, A., Ghosh, K.: Enhancing face matching in a suitable binary environment. In: 2011 International Conference on Image Information Processing, pp. 1–6, November 2011

15. Ghosh, K., Bhaumik, K., Sarkar, S.: Retinomorphic image processing. Prog. Brain Res. **168**, 175–91 (2007)

16. Rodieck, R.W., Stone, J.: Analysis of receptive fields of cat retinal ganglion cells. J. Neurophysiol. **27**(1), 833–849 (1965)

17. Ikeda, H., Wright, J.H.: Functional organization of the periphery effect in retinal ganglion cells. J. Vis. Res. **12**, 1857–1879 (1972)

18. Yesugade, S., Dave, P., Srivastava, S., Das, A.: Enhancing the performance of cooperative face detector by NFGS. In: Seventh International Conference on Digital Image Processing. SPIE (2015)

19. Face Recognition Technology (FERET) Database. https://www.nist.gov/programs-projects/face-recognition-technology-feret

20. Simonyan, K., Zisserman, A.: Very deep convolutional networks for large-scale image recognition. In: 3rd International Conference on Learning Representations, ICLR 2015, San Diego, CA, USA, 7–9 May 2015. Conference Track Proceedings (2015)

21. Schroff, F., Kalenichenko, D., Philbin, J.: FaceNet: a unified embedding for face recognition and clustering. CoRR, abs/1503.03832 (2015)

22. Lowe, D.G.: Distinctive image features from scale-invariant keypoints. Int. J. Comput. Vis. **60**(2), 91–110 (2004)

On the Computation of the Euler Characteristic of Binary Images in the Triangular Grid

Lidija Čomić and Andrija Blesić[(✉)]

Faculty of Technical Sciences, University of Novi Sad, Novi Sad, Serbia
{comic,andrija.blesic}@uns.ac.rs

Abstract. Apart from the widely used square grid, other regular grids (hexagonal and triangular) are gaining prominence in topological data analysis and image analysis/processing communities. One basic but important integer-valued topological descriptor of binary images in these grids is the Euler characteristic.

We extend two algorithms for the computation of the Euler characteristic from the square to the triangular grid, taking into account specific properties of the triangular grid. The first algorithm is based on simple cell counting, and the second is based on critical point approach. Both algorithms iterate over the grid vertices. We extend also their improvement based on reusing information common to the previous and the next vertex in the scan order. Our experiments show that the critical point based algorithms outperform the naive cell-counting ones, with the improved versions reducing the average runtime further.

Keywords: Digital topology · Image analysis · Euler characteristic · Triangular grid

1 Introduction

There are three regular tessellations of the plane, into regular squares, triangles and hexagons. The square grid has been extensively studied in the literature, with the other two regular grids receiving an increasing amount of attention in different frameworks, such as topology-preserving transformations [3,6,9,18], analytical [4,5] or computational [16,17] geometry, tomography [15], topological/combinatorial coordinate systems [8,14], distance transform [1], to name just a few.

The Euler characteristic, as one of the fundamental topological invariants, has been widely investigated in the square grid. We extend two algorithms [7] for the computation of the Euler characteristic, together with an improvement technique [19], from the square to the triangular grid. Both algorithms (and their improvements) iterate over the grid vertices. The first one is based on counting the cells (vertices, edges and triangles) in the cell complex Q associated with the

© Springer Nature Switzerland AG 2019
M. Vento and G. Percannella (Eds.): CAIP 2019, LNCS 11679, pp. 556–567, 2019.
https://doi.org/10.1007/978-3-030-29891-3_49

given image I; it examines all six triangles incident to the vertex. The second is based on tracking the changes in the value of the Euler characteristic of the level sets of the distance function from a specified line; it examines four incident triangles for each vertex. The improved versions store and reuse information on the triangles incident to the previous and the next vertex in the scan order; they examine four and three triangles, respectively. We provide a detailed experimental comparison of the proposed algorithms on a collection of synthetic images stored as matrices, which show that the second algorithm (and its improvement) outperforms the first (and its improvement), regardless of image density or size.

2 Preliminaries

We give some basic notions on the regular grids in 2D [3,10] and on the Euler characteristic of binary images in these grids [11].

2.1 Regular Grids in the Plane

There are three regular tessellations of the plane, into regular triangles, squares and hexagons, collectively called pixels. Two pixels are 1-adjacent (edge-adjacent) if they share an entire edge; they are (strictly) 0-adjacent (vertex-adjacent) if they share (only) a vertex.

A binary image I is a finite set of (black) pixels. The pixels in the complement I^c are white. The associated cell complex [12] is denoted by Q. It consists of all pixels in I and all their edges and vertices. (A k-cell is a homeomorphic image of a k-ball. A cell complex is a collection Q of cells that fit nicely together: the boundary of each cell in Q, and each non-empty intersection of two cells in Q, is composed of cells in Q). The number of k-cells in Q is denoted by c_k: c_2 is the number of pixels, c_1 is the number of edges and c_0 is the number of vertices in Q. A boundary edge (vertex) in Q is incident to at least one black and at least one white pixel.

Two black pixels p and q are 1-connected (0-connected) in I, if there is a sequence of black pixels, starting at p and ending in q, such that any two consecutive pixels in the sequence are 1-adjacent (0-adjacent). The 1-components (0-components) of I are maximal subsets of I with respect to the chosen connectedness. The number of 1-components (0-components) is denoted by c^1 (c^0). A hole is a finite connected component of the complement I^c of I. To maintain some similarity between the digital and continuous topology, components and holes are counted with opposite adjacencies. The number of holes with 1-adjacency (0-adjacency) for I and 0-adjacency (1-adjacency) for I^c is denoted by h^0 (h^1). For the image I illustrated in Fig. 1, $c^0 = 1$, $h^1 = 3$, $c^1 = 3$ and $h^0 = 1$.

2.2 The Euler Characteristic of 2D Binary Images

The Euler characteristic is one of the basic topological descriptors of images (objects or shapes). It can be computed:

Fig. 1. An image I, composed of black triangles, in the triangular grid.

– through the number of cells in the associated complex Q, or
– through the topological invariants (Betti numbers) of I.

In both cases, its value depends on the chosen adjacency relation. We denote $\chi^\alpha(I)$ the Euler characteristic of I with α-adjacency for black pixels and $(1-\alpha)$-adjacency for white ones, $\alpha = 0, 1$.

The Euler characteristic can be computed using only information from the black pixels. For an image I with 0-adjacency (and for its associated complex Q), the Euler characteristic is equal to the alternating sum of the number c_k of k-cells in Q, $k = 0, 1, 2$, i.e.,

$$\chi^0(I) = \chi^0(Q) = c_0 - c_1 + c_2. \tag{1}$$

For 1-adjacency, some vertices (at which the object is non-manifold), are counted more than once.

Alternatively, the Euler characteristic is equal to the number of connected components of I (its zeroth Betti number) minus the number of holes in I (the first Betti number), i.e., $\chi^\alpha(I) = c^\alpha - h^{1-\alpha}$. For the image in Fig. 1, $\chi^0(I) = -2$ and $\chi^1(I) = 2$.

3   Related Work

Many algorithms for the computation of the Euler characteristic in the square grid have been proposed. For brevity, we will only describe two algorithms [7], and an improvement of one of them [19], that we will extend to the triangular grid. These extensions take into account specific properties of the triangular grid.

The first algorithm [7] counts the numbers c_0 of vertices, c_1 of edges and c_2 of squares in Q. For 1-adjacency, the vertices at which Q is non-manifold (vertices incident to exactly two strictly 0-adjacent black and two strictly 0-adjacent white squares) are counted two times. The algorithm loops over the vertices, and for each one counts the vertex with appropriate multiplicity. The contribution of each incident edge and face to c_1 and c_2 is equal to $1/2$ and $1/4$, respectively (to prevent duplicating their contribution with other incident vertices).

The second algorithm [7] partitions the image through a set of parallel lines, such that each slab between two consecutive lines contains exactly one vertex in Q. The possible changes in the Euler characteristic between two slabs are of two types:

- a new local component is created in a slab, that did not exist in the previous one, increasing the number of components and thus increasing the Euler characteristic by one, or
- two local components from the previous slab are merged, decreasing the total number of components by 1, or increasing the total number of holes by 1; in both cases, the Euler characteristic is decreased by one.

The type of the topological change depends on the configuration of black and white squares around the vertex (and on the direction of the set of partitioning lines).

An improvement [19] on vertex classification of the second algorithm is based on storing and reusing information on the two squares shared by the previous and the current vertex. Thus, only the remaining two incident squares need to be examined to determine the configuration type at the current vertex.

4   The Proposed Algorithms

We describe the extension of the two algorithms, and their improvement, to the triangular grid.

4.1   Algorithm **Alg1** Based on Counting Cells

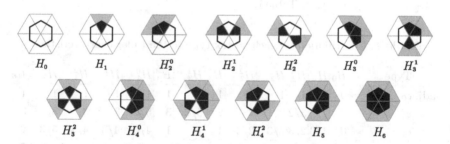

Fig. 2. The possible configurations of black and white triangles (up to rotation and symmetry) around a vertex in the triangular grid. Shaded triangles belong to the image I. The portions of edges and triangles that are counted with the central vertex of each configuration are in red and black, respectively. (Color figure online)

Our first algorithm **Alg1** adopts the definition of the Euler characteristic $\chi(I)$ as the alternating sum of the number of cells in the cell complex Q associated with the image I in the triangular grid. It extends the first algorithm by Gray [7] from the square to the triangular grid, taking into account an increased number of configurations and of non-manifold vertex types.

The vertex classes and their labels are illustrated in Fig. 2. Vertices of type H_0 and H_6 are (non-boundary) exterior and interior vertices, respectively. Other vertices are boundary vertices. They can be incident to one, two or three local 1-components of black (or white) triangles; they are called non-gap vertices (types H_1, H_2^0, H_3^0, H_4^0, and H_5), simple gaps (types H_2^1, H_2^2, H_3^1, H_4^1, and H_4^2) and double gaps (type H_3^2), respectively [2].

The algorithm counts the vertices in Q (the vertices not in H_0) as follows:

- For $\chi^0(I)$, each vertex in Q is counted once.
- For $\chi^1(I)$,
  - interior and non-gap vertices are counted once,
  - simple gaps are counted two times, and
  - double gaps are counted three times.

The algorithm iterates over the vertices in Q. The values c_0, c_1 and c_2 are initially set to 0.

- For each vertex v in Q, the number c_0 of vertices is increased as explained above.
- For each edge incident to v, the number c_1 is increased by $1/2$ (the same edge will be encountered once more, when its other endpoint is examined, and will again contribute $1/2$ to c_1).
- For each triangle incident to v, the number c_2 is increased by $1/3$ (the same triangle will contribute two more times to c_2, when its other two vertices are encountered by the algorithm).

We show the contribution of each configuration to the Euler characteristic, for both 0- and 1-adjacency, in Table 1.

Table 1. Contributions of each vertex type to the Euler characteristic.

	Type	H_0	H_1	H_2^0	H_2^1	H_2^2	H_3^0	H_3^1	H_3^2	H_4^0	H_4^1	H_4^2	H_5	H_6
0-adj.	c_0	0	1	1	1	1	1	1	1	1	1	1	1	1
	c_1	0	1	3/2	2	2	2	5/2	3	5/2	3	3	3	3
	c_2	0	1/3	2/3	2/3	2/3	1	1	1	4/3	4/3	4/3	5/3	2
	$c_0 - c_1 + c_2$	0	1/3	1/6	−1/3	−1/3	0	−1/2	−1	−1/6	−2/3	−2/3	−1/3	0
1-adj.	c_0	0	1	1	2	2	1	2	3	1	2	2	1	1
	c_1	0	1	3/2	2	2	2	5/2	3	5/2	3	3	3	3
	c_2	0	1/3	2/3	2/3	2/3	1	1	1	4/3	4/3	4/3	5/3	2
	$c_0 - c_1 + c_2$	0	1/3	1/6	2/3	2/3	0	1/2	1	−1/6	1/3	1/3	−1/3	0

Thus, if $|H_i^j|$ denotes the number of vertices of type H_i^j in I, then:

$$\chi^0(I) = \frac{|H_1|}{3} + \frac{|H_2^0|}{6} - \frac{|H_2^1|}{3} - \frac{|H_2^2|}{3} - \frac{|H_3^1|}{2} - |H_3^2| - \frac{|H_4^0|}{6} - \frac{2|H_4^1|}{3} - \frac{2|H_4^2|}{3} - \frac{|H_5|}{3},$$

and, similarly:

$$\chi^1(I) = \frac{|H_1|}{3} + \frac{|H_2^0|}{6} + \frac{2|H_2^1|}{3} + \frac{2|H_2^2|}{3} + \frac{|H_3^1|}{2} + |H_3^2| - \frac{|H_4^0|}{6} + \frac{|H_4^1|}{3} + \frac{|H_4^2|}{3} - \frac{|H_5|}{3}$$
$$= \chi^0(I) + |H_2^1| + |H_2^2| + |H_3^1| + 2|H_3^2| + |H_4^1| + |H_4^2|.$$

4.2 Algorithm **Alg2** Based on Critical Points

Our second algorithm **Alg2** is sweep-based: a sweep line (e.g., a line slightly tilted from the line $y = -x/\sqrt{3}$) is moving from the upper right direction, so that it meets the vertices in I one by one. The Euler characteristic of the swept part of I can only change at the boundary vertices: it increases at increasing vertices and decreases at decreasing ones. The change in the value of the Euler characteristic depends on the chosen adjacency and on the direction of the sweep line.

- At an increasing vertex a new local component is created, increasing the Euler characteristic by one.
- At a decreasing vertex, two local components (composed of black triangles incident to the vertex) merge, and thus either two global components merge, or one global component meets itself and forms a hole, in both cases decreasing the Euler characteristic by one.

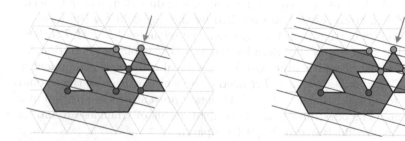

Fig. 3. Increasing (red) and decreasing (blue) vertices in the image I illustrated in Fig. 1, for (left) 0- and (right) 1-adjacency. (Color figure online)

Thus, to compute the Euler characteristic of a given image, it is sufficient to count the increasing and decreasing vertices and find their difference. For example, the image illustrated in Fig. 1 has two increasing and four decreasing vertices with respect to 0-adjacency, so $\chi^0(I) = 2 - 4 = -2$ (see Fig. 3 (left)). It has four increasing and two decreasing vertices with respect to 1-adjacency, so $\chi^1(I) = 4 - 2 = 2$ (see Fig. 3 (right)).

The increasing vertices of I for α-adjacency are the decreasing vertices of I^c for $(1 - \alpha)$-adjacency, with the opposite moving direction of the sweep line. This agrees with $\chi^\alpha(I) = 1 - \chi^{1-\alpha}(I^c)$ [13] (where 1 corresponds to the first vertex of the first white pixel in the finite subset of the grid containing I that is encountered by the sweep line).

We label the six triangles incident to a vertex v by their row (top or bottom) and column (left, middle or right) as TL, TM, TR, BL, BM, BR in the obvious manner. Using this notation, we describe the classification of the vertices for 0- and 1-adjacency separately. As opposed to the first algorithm, only four incident triangles determine the (increasing or decreasing) type of a given vertex.

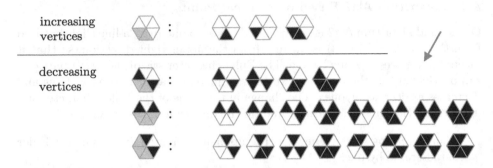

Fig. 4. Configurations of triangles incident to increasing and decreasing vertices with 0-adjacency. At least one of the gray triangles is black for increasing vertices (top part). Gray triangles can be black or white for decreasing vertices (bottom part).

0-Adjacency. An increasing vertex v (for the chosen direction) can only occur if all of its incident triangles that are reached by the line before v (its incident top triangles and its bottom right triangle, i.e., the triangles TL, TM, TR, BR) are white, and at least one of the triangles BL and BM is black. (The triangles TL and BR need to be white, otherwise no new local connected component is created at v. The triangles TM and TR need to be white, otherwise they would be 0-adjacent to a black triangle BL or BM, again preventing the creation of a new component.) The only three possible configurations of triangles around an increasing vertex are illustrated in Fig. 4 (top part).

For a decreasing vertex v, two local components of black triangles merge at v. Thus, at least one of the two incident triangles that are completely covered by the sweep line at the time v is reached (the triangles TM and TR) must be white, and at least one of TL and TM and at least one of TR and BR must be black. The possible configurations:

- triangles TL and BR are black, TM and TR are white,
- triangles TR and TL are black, TM is white,
- triangles TM and BR are black, TR is white,

are illustrated in Fig. 4 (bottom part). The color of the triangles BL and BM does not affect the classification of a vertex; the remaining four triangles completely determine its type.

1-Adjacency. The vertex classification for 1-adjacency is similar, and is described in Fig. 5.

4.3   Improvements **Alg1$^+$** and **Alg2$^+$**

We improve algorithms Alg1 and Alg2 by reusing and storing information on the color of the triangles incident to both the previous vertex v_P and the next vertex v_N in the scan order (see Fig. 6). There are two such triangles for Alg1, and one for each variant of Alg2.

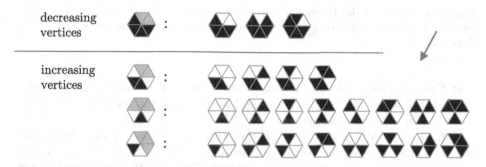

Fig. 5. Configurations of triangles incident to decreasing and increasing vertices with 1-adjacency. At least one of the gray triangles is white for decreasing vertices (top part). Gray triangles can be black or white for increasing vertices (bottom part).

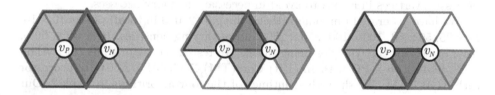

Fig. 6. Triangles incident to the previous vertex v_P (outlined in blue) and next vertex v_N (in green) in the scan order. The shared triangles (outlined in red) for the first algorithm (left), second algorithm with 0-adjacency (middle) and second algorithm with 1-adjacency (right). (Color figure online)

Thus, for each boundary vertex, the improved versions Alg1$^+$ and Alg2$^+$ of Alg1 and Alg2 access four and three new triangles, respectively. The reused triangles are updated with each processed vertex.

5   Implementation Results

Our algorithms take as input an image stored as a Boolean matrix $A_{m \times n}$ (with elements $a_{ij} \in \{T, F\}$), where T's encode black triangles and F's encode white ones. The elements a_{ij} with $i + j$ even (odd) correspond to $\triangle$ ($\triangledown$) triangles.

All algorithms iterate over grid vertices, represented by submatrices of size 2×3 such that the top and bottom triangles incident to the vertex are encoded by the first and second row of the submatrix, respectively (see Fig. 7). To ensure

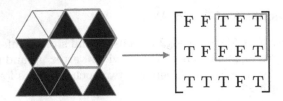

Fig. 7. An image in the triangular grid stored as a matrix of Boolean values. The triangles marked in red correspond to the six outlined elements in the matrix. (Color figure online)

that the triangles at the image border are processed correctly, the matrix is padded with a row of F's from above and from below, and with two columns of F's from the left and from the right.

All four algorithms first check if the vertex is an interior or exterior one, which, if true, implies the vertex can be skipped (only boundary vertices can influence the value of the Euler characteristic). They classify each boundary vertex v by evaluating appropriate Boolean functions on the relevant elements of the associated submatrix and they update the value of the Euler characteristic (initially set to zero) by the appropriate amount for each encountered configuration. The improved versions store the values of the triangles shared by two successive vertices in a row, to avoid unnecessary memory accesses.

We have generated random synthetic images (25000 in total) of size 10×10, 25×25, 50×50, 100×100, 250×250, and of varying densities, 10%, 30%, 50%, 70%, or 90% of the triangles being black. We tested our algorithms (in Python 3.6.8, 64-bit) on a PC with Intel(R) Core(TM) i7-6500U @2.50 GHz processor with 8 GB RAM. We show the runtimes of the four algorithms in Table 2. Our experiments show that, on the tested images:

- Alg2 is on average faster than Alg1 by three to five times,
- Alg2$^+$ is on average faster than Alg1$^+$ by two to four times,
- Alg1$^+$ is faster than Alg1 by 1.5 to 1.7 times,
- Alg2$^+$ is faster than Alg2 by 1.1 to 1.3 times,
- Alg1$^+$ is 2 to 3 times slower than Alg2, as it has to check more configurations for each boundary vertex.

The difference between the runtimes is higher for images of medium density, and the average execution time of all four algorithms achieves its maximum when black triangles comprise about 50% of the total number of triangles (see Fig. 8). This is because all algorithms first check if the six triangles incident to the current vertex are all black or all white, meaning that the largest number of boundary vertices are actually processed if the image is not mainly comprised of black or white pixels.

Table 2 shows the minimal, maximal (over all images and densities) and average execution time of all four algorithms, as well as the minimal, average and maximal number of boundary vertices that were processed (column bnd).

As expected, the chosen adjacency does not significantly influence the runtime of any algorithm.

All four algorithms would gain in speed if the boundary of the input image were given; then testing if the vertex is interior or exterior could be skipped.

6   Summary and Future Work

We proposed extensions of two algorithms, and their improved versions, for the computation of the Euler characteristic of a 2D binary image I from the square

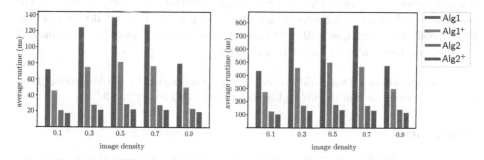

Fig. 8. Comparison of average runtimes for unimproved and improved algorithms with respect to image density. Images are with 0-adjacency, of size 100×100 (left) and 250×250 (right). Barplots for smaller images are similar up to scale.

Table 2. Minimal, average and maximal runtimes (in milliseconds) of all four algorithms, with regard to the size of the image, together with the average, minimal and maximal number of boundary vertices processed. Best times are in bold.

	0-adjacency				1-adjacency					
	Alg1	Alg1$^+$	Alg2	Alg2$^+$	Alg1	Alg1$^+$	Alg2	Alg2$^+$	bnd	Size
min	0.4	0.3	**0.1**	**0.1**	0.4	0.3	**0.1**	**0.1**	18	10×10
mean	1.5	0.9	0.4	**0.3**	1.4	0.9	**0.3**	**0.3**	48.4	
max	5.8	5.6	**1.6**	1.8	6.5	3.4	1.4	**1.2**	66	
min	4.2	2.7	1.3	**1.1**	4.0	2.6	**1.2**	**1.2**	136	25×25
mean	7.5	4.5	1.8	**1.4**	7.3	4.5	1.7	**1.6**	258.1	
max	20.9	24.7	20.2	**6.1**	17.0	11.0	8.2	**4.4**	343	
min	17.0	10.8	5.0	**4.2**	16.1	10.4	4.8	**4.5**	557	50×50
mean	27.9	16.9	6.6	**5.3**	27.5	16.8	6.5	**6.1**	974.4	
max	48.9	32.1	13.0	**10.8**	55.9	35.6	11.0	**11.9**	1290	
min	69.5	43.6	19.6	**16.2**	65.6	42.1	19.3	**18.1**	2288	100×100
mean	108.1	65.5	25.6	**20.42**	106.7	65.1	25.1	**23.8**	3782.8	
max	162.4	97.3	44.9	**37.2**	186.9	127.0	44.7	**48.3**	5006	
min	426.3	267.1	121.2	**100.7**	400.2	258.5	117.6	**110.9**	14521	250×250
mean	659.1	399.5	156.3	**123.8**	651.3	397.1	154.0	**145.2**	23215.5	
max	966.9	573.6	245.7	**153.0**	893.5	580.6	248.0	**227.9**	30681	

to the triangular grid. The extensions take into account specific properties of the triangular grid compared to the square grid: an increased number of pixels incident to each vertex, an increased number of non-manifold configurations around a vertex and the existence of two different types of triangles ($\triangle$ and $\triangledown$). The algorithms iterate over the grid vertices, and classify each boundary vertex (and its contribution to $\chi(I)$) based on the incident triangles (all six incident triangles for Alg1, only four incident triangles for Alg2). The improved versions execute faster by reusing some information, thus decreasing the number of triangle accesses from six to four for Alg1$^+$, and from four to three for Alg2$^+$.

Our algorithms could be further improved by skipping the test if the vertex is interior or exterior, and by processing only the boundary vertices (if the boundary of I is given, or needed for other purposes). This would be particularly beneficial for images with few boundary vertices compared to the number of non-boundary (interior and exterior) ones.

Acknowledgement. This work has been partially supported by the Ministry of Education and Science of the Republic of Serbia within the Project No. 34014.

References

1. Borgefors, G., Sanniti di Baja, G.: Skeletonizing the distance transform on the hexagonal grid. In: 9th International Conference on Pattern Recognition, ICPR, pp. 504–507 (1988)
2. Čomić, L.: Gaps and well-composed objects in the triangular grid. In: Marfil, R., Calderón, M., Díaz del Río, F., Real, P., Bandera, A. (eds.) CTIC 2019. LNCS, vol. 11382, pp. 54–67. Springer, Cham (2019). https://doi.org/10.1007/978-3-030-10828-1_5
3. Deutsch, E.S.: Thinning algorithms on rectangular, hexagonal, and triangular arrays. Commun. ACM **15**(9), 827–837 (1972)
4. Dutt, M., Andres, E., Largeteau-Skapin, G.: Characterization and generation of straight line segments on triangular cell grid. Pattern Recogn. Lett. **103**, 68–74 (2018)
5. Freeman, H.: Algorithm for generating a digital straight line on a triangular grid. IEEE Trans. Comput. **28**(2), 150–152 (1979)
6. Golay, M.J.E.: Hexagonal parallel pattern transformations. IEEE Trans. Comput. **18**(8), 733–740 (1969)
7. Gray, S.: Local properties of binary images in two dimensions. IEEE Trans. Comput. **20**, 551–561 (1971)
8. Her, I.: Geometric transformations on the hexagonal grid. IEEE Trans. Image Process. **4**(9), 1213–1222 (1995)
9. Kardos, P., Palágyi, K.: Topology preservation on the triangular grid. Ann. Math. Artif. Intell. **75**(1–2), 53–68 (2015)
10. Klette, R., Rosenfeld, A.: Digital Geometry: Geometric Methods for Digital Picture Analysis. Morgan Kaufmann Publishers, San Francisco (2004)
11. Kong, T.Y., Rosenfeld, A.: Digital topology: introduction and survey. Comput. Vis. Graph. Image Process. **48**(3), 357–393 (1989)
12. Kovalevsky, V.A.: Geometry of Locally Finite Spaces (Computer Agreeable Topology and Algorithms for Computer Imagery). Editing House Dr. Bärbel Kovalevski, Berlin (2008)

13. Morgenthaler, D.: Three-dimensional digital topology: the genus. Technical report TR-980, University of Maryland, College Park, MD 20742 (1980)
14. Nagy, B.: Cellular topology and topological coordinate systems on the hexagonal and on the triangular grids. Ann. Math. Artif. Intell. **75**(1–2), 117–134 (2015)
15. Nagy, B., Lukić, T.: Dense projection tomography on the triangular tiling. Fundam. Inform. **145**(2), 125–141 (2016)
16. Sarkar, A., Biswas, A., Dutt, M., Bhowmick, P., Bhattacharya, B.B.: A linear-time algorithm to compute the triangular hull of a digital object. Discrete Appl. Math. **216**, 408–423 (2017)
17. Sarkar, A., Biswas, A., Dutt, M., Mondal, S.: Finding shortest triangular path and its family inside a digital object. Fundam. Inform. **159**(3), 297–325 (2018)
18. Wiederhold, P., Morales, S.: Thinning on quadratic, triangular, and hexagonal cell complexes. In: Brimkov, V.E., Barneva, R.P., Hauptman, H.A. (eds.) IWCIA 2008. LNCS, vol. 4958, pp. 13–25. Springer, Heidelberg (2008). https://doi.org/10.1007/978-3-540-78275-9_2
19. Yao, B., et al.: An efficient strategy for bit-quad-based Euler number computing algorithm. IEICE Trans. Inf. Syst. **E97.D**(5), 1374–1378 (2014)

Feature GANs: A Model for Data Enhancement and Sample Balance of Foreign Object Detection in High Voltage Transmission Lines

Yimin Dou[1,2,3], Xiangru Yu[1,2,3], and Jinping Li[1,2,3]($\boxtimes$)

[1] School of Information Science and Engineering, University of Jinan,
Jinan 250022, China
ise_lijp@ujn.edu.cn
[2] Shandong Provincial Key Laboratory of Network Based Intelligent
Computing, University of Jinan, Jinan 250022, China
[3] Shandong College and University Key Laboratory of Information Processing
and Cognitive Computing in 13th Five-year, Jinan 250022, China

Abstract. The suspension of foreign objects on high-voltage transmission lines is extremely harmful to the safety of the line. If it is not handled in time, it will easily cause phase-to-phase short circuit of the transmission line and even cause forest fires. Foreign object suspension is a small probability event with fewer existing samples. To use CNN to perform target classification detection, there is a problem of insufficient sample or sample imbalance. Aiming at the above problems that often occur in engineering applications of CNN, we propose a data enhancement algorithm based on GANs. The main idea of this algorithm is: Firstly, the pre-training model is used to extract the feature map of sample, and GANs is used to learn the feature map directly. Then, the feature map generated by GANs and the original data are used to train the classification layer of the pre-training model, so as to achieve the purpose of data enhancement and balancing samples, and then enhance the classification ability of the model. The experimental results show that the classification performance of several classical CNN models can be improved significantly by using this method in the case of insufficient sample and sample imbalance.

Keywords: High voltage transmission line foreign object detection ·
Data enhancement · GANs · Migration learning

Foundation item: Supported by The National Natural Science Foundation of China (61701192); Shandong Provincial Key Research and Development Project (2017CXGC0810); Shandong Education Science Plan "Special Subject for Scientific Research of Educational Admission Examination" (ZK1337212B008).

M. Vento and G. Percannella (Eds.): CAIP 2019, LNCS 11679, pp. 568–580, 2019.
https://doi.org/10.1007/978-3-030-29891-3_50

1 Introduction

With the continuous development of economy and society, people rely more and more on electricity. High-voltage transmission line is the main artery of power transportation, so it is particularly important to ensure the safety of high-voltage transmission line. Foreign object suspension is an important problem affecting the safety of high voltage transmission lines, so it needs to be detected and processed.

In the detection of foreign objects in high-voltage transmission lines based on digital image processing technology, the description of foreign objects is a challenging problem, the main reason is the randomness of foreign object type and foreign object shape. The use of CNN (convolution neural network) for identification in engineering projects requires a large number of samples, but the probability of foreign objects hanging in high-voltage transmission lines is small, resulting in fewer valid samples to be obtained, which cannot meet the algorithm requirements. Figure 1 shows the hanging foreign object of the high-voltage transmission line and the number of positive and negative samples we collected.

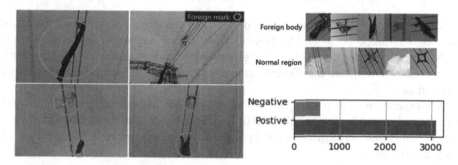

Fig. 1. High-voltage transmission line foreign object and the number of samples.

The negative sample is the foreign object labeled in Fig. 1, while the positive sample is the normal region, which can be any normal region in the sky. As shown in Fig. 1, there's a serious imbalance in the samples we've collected. If training is carried out directly, it will lead to over-fitting or even non-convergence.

In this paper, we propose a data enhancement method based on GANs (Generative Adversarial Nets) for the problem of insufficient or unbalanced samples that deep learning often occurs in practical engineering: Firstly the pre-training model takes the former n-layer network, migrating its weight to the target network, and randomly initializes other layers of the target network. Then extracts the image features using the n-layer pre-training network, and learns the extracted feature maps using GANs until the GANs converge. Finally, the stochastic initialization layer of target network is trained by using the feature maps generated by generator and the existing sample fusion.

As we all know, it is extremely difficult to train GANs with small samples and complex features [1, 2], and we use a good method to avoid this drawback of GANs. Because we know that many visual categories share some low-level concepts, such as edges, visual shapes, geometric changes, and the effects of light changes. And well-trained depth networks can extract these low-level concepts [3], which are represented as simpler feature maps, and feature maps remove redundant information. A large number of features are retained that are conducive to classification, and the amount of data is much smaller than the original. As shown in Fig. 2, in the VGG16 network, the amount of information in feature map is 1/6 of the original image, and simple features mean that we can better train GANs.

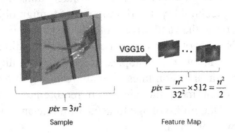

$$pix = \frac{n^2}{32^2} \times 512 = \frac{n^2}{2}$$

$$pix = 3n^2$$

Sample   Feature Map

Fig. 2. Comparison of the feature map and the original image.

Our main contributions are: (a) a new model combining GANs and migration learning was proposed to enable them to realize their respective advantages; (b) a GANs architecture (Feature GANs) for generating feature map was proposed; (c) improved CNN's frequent insufficient sample and sample imbalance in engineering applications.

We experimented with multiple CNN classic models, respectively, in foreign object datasets and in public datasets CIFAR10. Experimental results show that our method can maximize the performance of sample data and greatly improve the accuracy of CNN classification.

2   Related Work

More research has been made on the problems of insufficient sample and sample imbalance that often occur in CNN in engineering.

There are three main solutions to the problem of insufficient sample:

The first method is random oversampling, through rotation, translation, scaling and replication to increase the number of samples. This method has the advantage of relatively simple, but the drawback is that the resulting data features are sample, the resulting data is also limited. And most of the trained models still have the problem of overfitting [4, 5].

The second is fine tune. Fine tune method can solve the problem of insufficient data to some extent. But when the number of samples is much lower than the capacity of the model to fit the parameters (such as training a network with a full connection layer), it will still be overfitted, and fine tune cannot solve the sample imbalance [6].

Finally, transfer learning can solve the problem of insufficient sample, but it requires a strong relationship between source domain and target domain. There is few source domain relevant to our task. Transfer learning may not work as well [7, 8].

Data imbalance is a more common problem, which is often determined by the problem itself. In practical engineering applications, there is a certain imbalance in almost all the data, and there are three ways to solve such problems:

The first is sampling, which is divided into oversampling and under sampling. Oversampling is to copy multiple copies of minority class, or through the rotation translation and other affine transformation to increase the number of minority class samples. The under sampling is to remove some samples from the majority class, or only from the majority class to select part of the sample. The disadvantage of sampling is obvious, for some samples will appear repeatedly in the data set after oversampling, and the trained model will have overfitting, while the disadvantage of the under sampling is that the final training set loses data, and the model learns only part of the overall pattern [9].

The second is weighting, that is, when the category of minority class is divided incorrectly, the weight of the cost function is high, and the difficulty of this method lies in setting a reasonable weight. It is common practice to approximate the weighted loss value between each classification, but it is not necessarily effective, and it needs to be tested repeatedly in practical application.

Finally, data synthesis. SMOTE is a more common practice [9, 10], using minority class in the feature space similarity to generate a new sample. The sample $x_i \in S_{min}$ of the minority class randomly selects a sample point $\hat{x}$ from the K neighbor that belongs to the minority class to generate a new minority class of sample x_{new},

$$x_{new} = x_i + (\hat{x} - x_i) \times \delta \tag{1}$$

where δ is a random number, it subject to $\delta \in [0, 1]$, and SMOTE synthesizes a new sample for a previous sample, which brings some potential problems: On the one hand, it increases the possibility of overlap between classes and, on the other hand, generates samples that do not provide useful information [10]. The recent use of GANs synthetic data has also been used to solve the problem of insufficient or unbalanced samples [11]. But GANs without a lot of data and adequate training, it is difficult to get a better model on complex datasets, and often generating some useless samples, especially natural images.

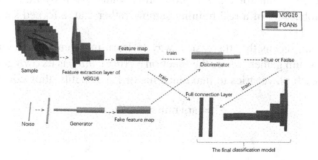

Fig. 3. Flow chart. As shown in the figure, we combine the FGANs generated feature maps with the feature maps of the original data to train the full connection layer of the CNN to improve the performance of the classifier.

DCGANs (Deep Convolutional Generative Adversarial Networks) proposed a more stable and easy to converge solution [2] while proving that GANs can generate high-quality natural images under the training of a large number of samples. Our samples are complex natural images, but the number is very limited and it is almost impossible to generate good images. But for a simple dataset like MNIST, even with a limited sample, GANs achieved good performance [12–14]. So our main idea is to represent complex natural image samples with simple semantic features, that is, to represent a complex dataset with a simple dataset, so that GANs can converge better.

3   Method and Model

We use a classic CNN model to extract feature maps for images, for ease of discussion, we used VGG16 in this section, and the model has been trained by ImageNet [15]. In addition, we propose a new GANs architecture to generate feature map, and the validity of it is proved by experiments. This new GANs architecture plays a key role in the entire process.

Figure 3 reflects the entire process. Next, we'll expand the methods that describe us separately.

We use the VGG16 as a feature extraction network, with the input sample size of $128 \times 128 \times 3$, and finally the feature map size is $4 \times 4 \times 512$. That is,

$$m = f(x)_{x \sim X} \tag{2}$$

where m represents the feature map we get, $f(\cdot)$ as a map function, that is, the feature extraction layer of VGG16, X is a foreign object sample.

Use M to represent a collection of all m, followed by M as a sample training GANs, here we review the fundamentals of GANs.

The generative confrontation network is a generative modeling method based on the differentiable generator network. It is based on a game theory scenario where the generator network must compete with the opponent. The generator network produces a sample $x = g(z; \; \theta(g))$. Its opponent discriminator network attempts to distinguish between samples extracted from the training data and samples extracted from the generator. The discriminator emits a probability value given by $d(x; \; \theta(d))$ indicating that x is the probability of a real training sample rather than a forged sample extracted from the model [1].

Formalization means that the easiest way to learn in a generative countermen sure network is zero-sum games, where the function $-v(\theta(g), \theta(d))$ is its own gain. During the study period, each player tries to maximize his or her benefits, thus converging on the

$$g^* = \arg\min_{g} \max_{d} v(g, d) \tag{3}$$

Where the default selection for v is

$$v(\theta^{(g)}, \theta^{(d)}) = E_{x \sim X} \log d(x) + E_{x \sim X} \log(1 - d(x)) \qquad (4)$$

This drives the discriminator to try to learn to classify samples correctly as true or falsified. At the same time, the generator tries to trick the classifier to convince it that the sample is true. When convergence, the generator's sample is indistinguishable from the actual data, and the discriminator's output is 1/2 everywhere, and then the discriminator can be discarded [1].

We propose a feature generative adversarial nets (FGANs), which is used to generate feature maps directly. And in order to obtain a more stable generation of samples, we followed DCGANs principles in designing this model [2]: (a) In order to obtain better sampling results, the discriminator does not use pooling layer, and using convolution kernel with a step length greater than 1 instead, so that it can learn how to reduce sampling; (b) Use of batch normalize; (c) Do not use the full connection layer; (d) The generator uses relu, and the discriminator uses leaky relu. After experiments and parameter adjustments, our GANs structure is shown in Fig. 4.

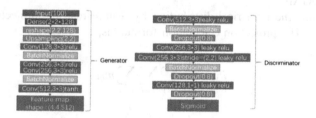

Fig. 4. Structure of FGANs.

In Fig. 4, the generator enters a normal distribution vector z with a length of 100, maps to a 512-dimensional vector through the full-connection layer. Then reshaped and once sampled, and after four convolution operations output a feature map with a size of $4 \times 4 \times 512$, the shape of this feature map is consistent with the shape of the feature map after VGG16 processing. The characteristics generated by this structure have been verified experimentally on our foreign object dataset, and the super parameters can be adjusted in practice in accordance with the principles described above.

The objective function is as follows,

$$\min_{G} \max_{D} V(D, G) = E_{m \sim M} \log d(m) + E_{m \sim M} \log(1 - d(m)) \qquad (5)$$

After the model converges, we get the generator G, by entering the G input noise z to obtain the generated sample, recorded as $\hat{m}$, will generate all the samples to do $\hat{M}$ and then the $\hat{M}$ and M mixed together to train the VGG16 full connection layer.

Next, the effectiveness of our method will be proved experimentally.

4   Experiment

The experiment was divided into five parts. In the first part, we verify that the numerical distribution of the generated features is consistent with the distribution of the real sample features, and the second part verifies that the semantic information of our generated features is similar to the semantic information of the real features, and the third part, we test the influence of FGANs and other algorithms on the classifier ROC (receiver operating characteristic) curve; We tested several CNN classic models to verify the extent to which our methods have increased them. Finally, we test and show the effect of our algorithm in the detection of foreign object of high voltage transmission lines in real environment.

4.1   Numerical Distribution of Generated Samples

We can't get an intuitive feeling about the features generated by FGANs. It is just some high-dimensional vectors. It can't be displayed on the screen like an image, and you can't get the color distribution, texture features, contour information and other information it represents. So we first verify the numerical distribution of the feature maps generated by FGANs.

We determine the numerical distribution by feature map the projection of x, y, z three directions. The projection calculation formula is,

$$P_x = \frac{1}{nw} \sum_{i=1}^{h} \sum_{j=1}^{c} \sum_{k=1}^{n} m_{ijk} \qquad (6)$$

$$P_y = \frac{1}{nh} \sum_{i=1}^{w} \sum_{j=1}^{c} \sum_{k=1}^{n} m_{ijk} \qquad (7)$$

$$P_z = \frac{1}{nc} \sum_{i=1}^{w} \sum_{j=1}^{h} \sum_{k=1}^{n} m_{ijk} \qquad (8)$$

where P_x, P_y, P_z is the projection of M in the x, y, z direction respectively, w, h, c is the width, height, number of channels of the feature map, n is the number of samples (Fig. 5).

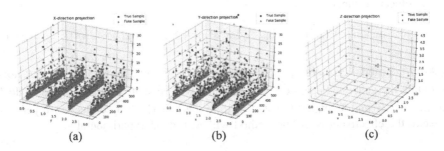

Fig. 5. Projection Scatter chart in three directions.

Firstly, the feature map of 500 real samples is extracted by VGG16, and then the FGANs is trained with the extracted features. And when the convergence is made, 500 generating samples are generated by entering different noise z into G, and finally we project the generation feature and the real feature onto the axis, and the projection diagram of three directions is obtained. Projection shows a consistent numerical distribution between features.

Through the above experiments, we show that our model has learned the low-level characteristics of real data [3], such as color distribution, edges, geometry and so on.

4.2   Generate Semantic Information of the Sample

In order to verify if the semantic information for the generated feature is correct, in this section we will use sufficient data training to obtain a classifier and use this classifier instead of the human eye to distinguish whether the features generated by FGANs are useful.

We prepare two kinds of sufficient samples A and B, and use VGG16 as the base net to train a binary classifier C (the weight of the fixed feature extraction layer). Then take a small number of samples in A and B to train FGANs, get two generators G_1, G_2, and finally we observe whether C can be a good distinction between G_1, G_2's generated samples $\hat{A}$ and $\hat{B}$, that is, whether the judgment $P(A|C)$ is equal to $P(\hat{A}|C)$ and $P(B|C)$ is equal to $P(\hat{B}|C)$.

Because the foreign object dataset is limited, we use the CIFAR-10 dataset here, which has a total of 60000 color images, with the size of 32×32. Divided into 10 categories. 6000 images per class, of which 5000 are used for training, and 1000 for testing [16]. We take the dog class and the truck class as A and B, respectively, and use bilinear interpolation to resize all of them to 128×128.

The sigmoid function is used to map the real number vector r obtained by the full connection layer to $\sigma(r)$, so that the probability range of both classes is between (0, 1).

The weight of the VGG16 feature extraction layer is fixed. A total of 10,000 training samples are used in A and B. The classifier is trained using Adam [17], and 2000 data is used for testing. Finally, 98.5% accuracy is obtained on the test set.

Next, we take 500 samples in each of A and B to train FGANs, and then get generators G_1, G_2, and then generate 500 data with G_1 and G_2 respectively, and send them to the fully connected layer to see if our classifier can distinguish the classification results. The results are shown in Fig. 6.

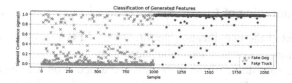

Fig. 6. Classification result of the classifier on the fake sample.

The first 500 data are the data of the generated dog, and the last 500 data is the data of the generated truck. In 1000 false data, the correct rate is 94.75%, which is only 3.75 percentage points lower than the real sample. That is, our experiment proves that the formula (9) is established.

$$\begin{cases} P(\hat{A}|C) \approx P(A|C) \\ P(\hat{B}|C) \approx P(B|C) \end{cases} \tag{9}$$

The above experiments show that our generating samples have semantic information similar to that of real samples and can be distinguished by the same classifier.

4.3   ROC Curve

The horizontal coordinates of the ROC (Receiver operating characteristic) curve plane are false positive rate (FPR), and the longitudinal coordinates are true positive rate (TPR). For a classifier, we can get a TPR and FPR point pairs based on their performance on the test sample. In this way, the classifier can be mapped to a point on the ROC plane. By adjusting the threshold of this classifier, we can get a curve that passes through (0, 0) and (1, 1), which is the ROC curve of this classifier [18].

In this experiment, we mainly tested the effect of FGANs on ROC curve and AUC value under the condition of unbalanced sample. The test model was VGG16, and the test dataset was foreign object dataset,, in which the real foreign object sample was 300, the non-foreign object sample was 3,000. We compared three methods that were often used to balance the sample, and the results are shown in the following Fig. 7.

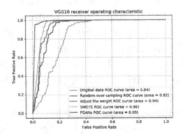

Fig. 7.   ROC curve.

4.4   FGANs Upgrading of Classic Networks

We separately tested the classification performance of FGANs on classical models in the case of insufficient samples and unbalanced samples.

To ensure the robustness of the algorithm, we tested it on a foreign object dataset and CIFAR-10 two different datasets, where we still take only two classes of the CIFAR10 datasets (dog and truck). The test model includes VGG16, VGG19, Resnet50 [19], Inceptionv3 [20], inceptionv4 [21] and Xception [22], where VGG16,

VGG19, Resnet50 contains a fully connected layer, while InceptionV3, inceptionV4, Xception use global Average pooling [23] instead of the full connection layer.

The experiment was conducted exactly according to the process in Fig. 3. We use Table 1 to simulate insufficient samples and sample imbalance.

Table 1. Contrast experimental parameters

Variable	Variable description
Insufficient sample, no use of FGANs	300 positive samples and 300 negative samples to train the model
Insufficient sample, using FGANs	300 positive samples and 300 negative samples, then 800 positive samples and 800 negative samples were generated with FGANs, and then trained. (A total of 1100 eigenvectors each)
The sample is uneven and does not use FGANs	2000 positive samples and 300 negative samples, of which the negative sample increased to 2000 after affine transformation
Sample imbalance, use FGANs	2000 positive samples and 300 negative samples, of which negative samples were increased to 2000 through FGANs

The test samples for our foreign object dataset were 600 (300 positive samples, 300 negative samples), and the CIFAR test sample was 2000 (1000 positive samples, 1000 negative samples). Finally, as a result of the experiment, the test data we obtained on two datasets are shown in the following Table 2.

Next, we analyze the performance of FGANs in different situations based on the table above. First of all, we can get a conclusion that in the case described in the table, FGANs has a certain improvement in the classification performance of CNN.

Table 2. Algorithm performance

Using FGANs?	Insufficient sample				Sample imbalance			
	FALSE		TRUE		FALSE		TRUE	
	Foreign	CIFAR	Foreign	CIFAR	Foreign	CIFAR	Foreign	CIFAR
VGG16	61.1%	92.3%	89.2%	93.1%	59.1%	72.5%	97.1%	98.4%
VGG19	57.3%	93.4%	83.1%	93.5%	60.5%	77.8%	97.4%	99.1%
Resnet50	59.2%	91.2%	79.3%	93.8%	59.5%	75.7%	96.9%	99.5%
InceptionV3	79.1%	92.6%	90.7%	94.1%	72.4%	88.1%	98.5%	99.3%
InceptionV4	75.5%	93.4%	92.2%	95.5%	75.2%	86.6%	98.5%	99.5%
Xception	83.3%	93.1%	92.1%	94.5%	72.2%	89.7%	99.1%	99.5%

FGANs performance is different for different datasets. The main reason is that CIFAR and ImageNet have similar domains, even small amounts of data can be transfered (Fig. 8).

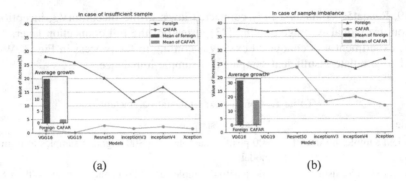

Fig. 8. The improvement of each model in the case of insufficient samples and unbalanced samples.

In the case of insufficient samples, the effect of FGANs on the full connection layer is better than the effect of global average pooling. And in the case of sample imbalance, our method is very obvious for the improvement of the two datasets. The full connection layer requires a mass of data to fit.

4.5 Effect of FGANs in Foreign Object Classification of High Voltage Transmission Lines

The classification accuracy we ended up with in the foreign object dataset was 97.1%. In foreign object detection, we use traditional selective search to obtain suspicious areas, and classify suspicious areas to determine whether they are foreign bodies. The following shows our use of FGANs before and after the test results.

It can be seen that before the use of FGANs, there are some false positives and false negatives. After the sample balance, false positives and false negatives are significantly reduced. The detection effect is significantly improved (Fig. 9).

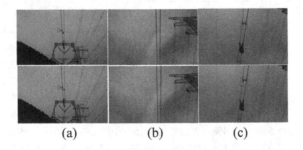

(a)   (b)   (c)

Fig. 9. Comparison of effects before and after using FGANs.

We selected three typical examples to reflect the effect of our algorithm in the real scene. In (a), because the use of a simple data enhancement algorithm caused the classifier to classify incorrectly, the wrong identification of the transmission line clip becomes a foreign object. resulting in the image of three false positives; (b) The misclassification of foreign bodies into non-foreign bodies, resulting in false negatives; (c) There were both false positives and false negatives and both false positives and false negatives were eliminated after the use of FGANs.

5 Conclusion

Insufficient sample and sample imbalance have been one of the bottlenecks restricting the development of deep learning. And in real applications such as foreign object detection of high-voltage transmission lines, it is not possible to collect large and balanced samples like datasets such as ImageNet or CIFAR. In order to solve this kind of problem, we propose the method of this paper.

We have shown that it can significantly improve CNN's ability to classify foreign object datasets and CIFAR datasets. In engineering application, it can effectively avoid the poor classification effect of classifier caused by insufficient number of samples or unbalanced sample type, so as to improve the detection efficiency significantly. Especially in the classification-based target detection application, it can effectively avoid false positives and false negatives due to the poor performance of the classifier.

References

1. Mirza, M., Osindero, S.: Conditional generative adversarial nets. Comput. Sci., 2672–2680 (2014)
2. Radford, A., Metz, L., Chintala, S.: Unsupervised representation learning with deep convolutional generative adversarial networks. arXiv:1511.06434 (2015)
3. Goodfellow, L., Bengio, Y., Courville, A.: Deep Learning, Chinese version, vol. 1, pp. 327–329. Posts & Telecom Press, Beijing (2017)
4. Abdi, L., Hashemi, S.: To combat multi-class imbalanced problems by means of over-sampling techniques. Soft. Comput. 19, 3369–3385 (2015)
5. Zhang, H., Wang, Z.: A normal distribution-based over-sampling approach to imbalanced data classification. In: Tang, J., King, I., Chen, L., Wang, J. (eds.) ADMA 2011. LNCS (LNAI), vol. 7120, pp. 83–96. Springer, Heidelberg (2011). https://doi.org/10.1007/978-3-642-25853-4_7
6. Yosinski, J., Clune, J., Bengio, Y., et al.: How transferable are features in deep neural networks? vol. 27, pp. 3320–3328 (2014)
7. Pan, S.J., Yang, Q.: A survey on transfer learning. IEEE Trans. Knowl. Data Eng. 22, 1345–1359 (2010)
8. Yin, X., et al.: CrossMine: efficient classification across multiple database relations. In: International Conference on Data Engineering. IEEE Computer Society (2004)
9. Chawla, N.V., Bowyer, K.W., Hall, L.O., Kegelmeyer, W.P.: SMOTE: synthetic minority over-sampling technique. JAIR 16, 321–357 (2002)
10. Han, H., Wang, W.-Y., Mao, B.-H.: Borderline-SMOTE: a new over-sampling method in imbalanced data sets learning. In: Huang, D.-S., Zhang, X.-P., Huang, G.-B. (eds.) ICIC 2005. LNCS, vol. 3644, pp. 878–887. Springer, Heidelberg (2005). https://doi.org/10.1007/11538059_91

11. Mariani, G., Scheidegger, F., Istrate, R., Bekas, C., Malossi, C.: BAGAN: data augmentation with balancing GAN. arXiv:1803.09655 (2018)
12. Arjovsky, M., Bottou, L.: Towards principled methods for training generative adversarial networks. In: NIPS 2016 Workshop on Adversarial Training. In review for ICLR (2017)
13. Salimans, T., Goodfellow, I., Zaremba, W., Cheung, V., Radford, A., Chen, X.: Improved techniques for training gans. In: NIPS (2016)
14. Gulrajani, I., Ahmed, F., Arjovsky, M., et al.: Improved training of wasserstein GANs. arXiv:1704.00028 (2017)
15. Simonyan, K., Zisserman, A.: Very deep convolutional networks for large-scale image recognition. arXiv:1409.1556 (2014)
16. Krizhevsky, A, Nair, V, Hinton, G: CAFAR-10 (2014). http://www.cs.toronto.edu/kriz/cifar.html
17. Kingma, D., Ba, J.: Adam: a method for stochastic optimization. arXiv:1412.6980v8 (2014)
18. Bradley, A.P.: The use of the area under the ROC curve in the evaluation of machine learning algorithms. Pattern Recognit. **30**, 1145–1159 (1997)
19. He, K., Zhang, X., Ren, S., et al.: Deep residual learning for image recognition, pp. 770–778 (2015)
20. Szegedy, C., Vanhoucke, V., Ioffe, S., et al.: Rethinking the inception architecture for computer vision. In: Computer Vision and Pattern Recognition, pp. 2818–2826 (2016)
21. Szegedy, C., Ioffe, S., Vanhoucke, V., et al.: Inception-v4, Inception-ResNet and the impact of residual connections on learning. arXiv:1602.07261 (2016)
22. Chollet, F.: Xception: deep learning with depthwise separable convolutions. arXiv:1610.02357 (2016)
23. Lin, M., Chen, Q., Yan, S.: Network in network. arXiv:1312.4400 (2013)

Embedded Prototype Subspace Classification: A Subspace Learning Framework

Anders Hast[(✉)], Mats Lind, and Ekta Vats

Division of Visual Information and Interaction, Department of Information Technology, Uppsala University, 751 05 Uppsala, Sweden
{anders.hast,mats.lind,ekta.vats}@it.uu.se

Abstract. Handwritten text recognition is a daunting task, due to complex characteristics of handwritten letters. Deep learning based methods have achieved significant advances in recognizing challenging handwritten texts because of its ability to learn and accurately classify intricate patterns. However, there are some limitations of deep learning, such as lack of well-defined mathematical model, black-box learning mechanism, etc., which pose challenges. This paper aims at going beyond the black-box learning and proposes a novel learning framework called as Embedded Prototype Subspace Classification, that is based on the well-known subspace method, to recognise handwritten letters in a fast and efficient manner. The effectiveness of the proposed framework is empirically evaluated on popular datasets using standard evaluation measures.

Keywords: Handwritten text · Subspaces · Deep learning · t-SNE

1 Introduction

Deep learning is gaining importance these days with remarkable advances in its research, where it enables machines to mirror the human brain using artificial neural networks [26]. In recent times, deep learning based methods have shown tremendous performance in handwritten text recognition [8,15,28]. This is due to availability of large scale of annotated data, GPU resources, efficient architectures (e.g. Convolutional Neural Networks (CNN), Recurrent Neural Networks (RNN), etc.) [8].

Although deep learning is considered as one of the major research areas required to advance handwritten text recognition, there are a few limitations and challenges that are to be addressed. Unlike a statistical model, that learns the data based on a concrete mathematical model, the learning process of a deep neural network can be regarded as a black-box. This is because it lacks a well-defined mathematical model, and the learning mechanism is not easy to comprehend as it is spread across the hidden units. Also, determining details about the deep learning architecture in regard with the training method, hyper-parameters, etc. is a challenge, with unfortunately no strong theory to guide.

© Springer Nature Switzerland AG 2019
M. Vento and G. Percannella (Eds.): CAIP 2019, LNCS 11679, pp. 581–592, 2019.
https://doi.org/10.1007/978-3-030-29891-3_51

In order to go beyond the black-box deep neural network, this paper introduces a novel learning framework called as Embedded Prototype Subspace Classification (EPSC), that is based on subspaces (or manifolds) for classification of handwritten letters. The proposed EPSC framework is intended to be both easy to comprehend and visualise, with mathematically well-defined components. This is inspired from the idea that subspaces can be regarded as neural nets (sometimes called associative memories) [12].

It is worth mentioning that, what we will refer to as *subspace learning*, using non-linear dimensionality reduction techniques (also known as embedding) has gained significant interest, with popular techniques such as Principal Component Analysis (PCA) [33], t-Distributed Stochastic Neighbor Embedding (t-SNE) [20], and Uniform Manifold Approximation and Projection (UMAP) [21], etc. The focus of this work is to further investigate the subspace learning techniques by understanding the theoretical foundations, and aim at achieving comparable performance to deep learning with a low computational cost. Hence, the proposed method will in most cases not beat the state of the art but come close enough to be an interesting alternative when speed is crucial.

This paper is organized as follows. Section 2 reviews the background literature on subspace methods. Section 3 presents the proposed EPSC framework for efficient subspace classification of handwritten letters. Note that first the learning is described where mathematically defined weights are obtained for a neural net, which is then used for classification. Section 4 demonstrates the efficacy of the proposed method on well-known datasets using standard evaluation measures. Section 5 concludes the paper.

2   Background

The subspace methods are statistical methods where each class is represented by a separate subspace. Subspace methods have gained a lot of attention in the decades before the millennium shift, and the interest of the research community is still growing with some paper published now and then in this area. The first application in pattern recognition was introduced by Watanabe et al. [31] in 1967, and further developed some years later [32]. Learning subspace methods were pioneered by Kohonen, Oja and other researchers, mainly in Finland [12–14,22]. In order to construct subspaces, a group of prototypes need to be chosen for each subspace, often referred to as manifold. These can be found by searching for the k nearest neighbors in feature space. Besides being a rather time consuming process, the main problem with this approach is to choose which ones to actually use.

The idea that will be expanded on here is to instead use t-SNE [20] to generate compact clusters of prototypes that are found by applying kernel density estimation (KDE) [1] and an inverse watershed transform (IWS) [24,30]. The IWS is simply the watershed transform used on an inverse image so that *valleys* between mountain tops are found in the image rather than watersheds, i.e. the *drainage divide*, which separates adjacent drainage basins. The mean shift

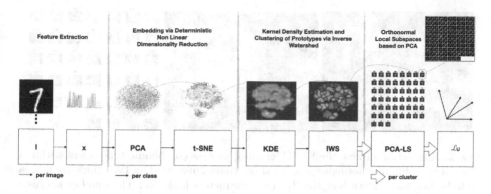

Fig. 1. Illustration of the EPSC learning framework that takes labeled images I belonging to different classes and compute features x. Subsequently, t-SNE is applied on each class by choosing the two first values from PCA instead of a random guess. KDE and IWS are used to find k clusters within each class, for which subspaces $\mathcal{L}_U$ are constructed. Figure best viewed in colors.

algorithm [4] could have been used to find clusters as well. However, since the aim was also to be able to visualise the clusters in an informative way, the KDE and IWS working in image space was chosen instead. In general, t-SNE helps in reducing the number of dimensions of a high dimensional data to two or three. It efficiently maintains a representation of similarities among features, such that similar features are represented as points closer to each other, and dissimilar points further from each other.

Furthermore, each compact cluster can be represented by a subspace, that are generated by PCA [33], unlike the Eigenface method [29] in which only one subspace (called eigenspace) is generated. Interestingly, by evaluating the norm of the projected vector rather than the residual, the result can be interpreted as a two layer neural network, where the weights are mathematically defined through PCA. The advantage is that the learning process can be easily visualised and the prototypes are chosen from the clusters. Hence, the subspace learning process is both well defined and easy to understand.

The trade-off between the computational cost and accuracy is often argued, where the state-of-the-art methods are most valued depending on their accuracy and precision rather than their time complexity. However, lack of strong expertise and computational resources (such as GPUs) limits the application of high-level methods (such as training a deep neural network using CNNs or RNNs) in real-world scenarios. Therefore, the main motivation behind this work is to develop methods with best attainable accuracy without compromising the computational cost. Ideally, the algorithm is desired to be able to complete the run in a few minutes, without the need of any additional computational resources, and still be able to achieve close to state-of-the-art accuracy.

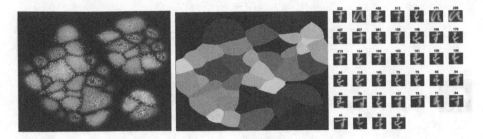

Fig. 2. Illustration of how the EPSC learning process can handle sub-classes within a class. Three different forms appear as three main clusters. The IWS finds each area and the heatmap shows how the different characters look like. The number suggests how many images are forming each heatmap. Figure best viewed in colors.

3   Embedded Prototype Subspace Classification

This section discusses the proposed subspace learning framework, called as Embedded Prototype Subspace Classification (EPSC). In general, subspace methods require that prototypes are found, i.e. features that are used as the base for each subspace. In the next step, PCA is used to construct the subspace. This is all needed for the learning phase. However, deciding the number of subspaces to use and finding the right prototypes among all features, is a tedious task. Quite recently t-SNE was proposed as a way to visualise features, and it is also a powerful tool for creating clusters. By using KDE and IWS it is rather straightforward to find clusters of similar features, and thereby also groups of prototypes from which subspaces are to be constructed. Figure 1 illustrates the main idea behind the EPSC learning framework, where it can be observed how PCA is used to find an initial start for t-SNE, instead of the random guess. In this way, the pipeline will be deterministic.

3.1   Clustering

By letting t-SNE find clusters within each class, it is also possible to distinguish between different appearances of each character, and hence find suitable prototypes within each sub-class. In Fig. 2, it is shown how three, rather different looking versions of a Hiragana character from the Kuzushiji-MNIST (K-MNIST) [2], are clustered into three major clusters. Within each cluster, sub-clusters are found and the IWS finds the borders between them. The heatmap shows the mean of the prototypes that are then used to create the subspaces.

3.2   Subspace Definition

Each object to be classified is represented as a vector $\mathbf{x}$ with m real-valued elements $\mathbf{x}_j = \{x_1, z_2 ... x_m\}, \in \mathbb{R}$, such that operations take place in a m-dimensional vector space $\mathbb{R}^m$. These vectors $\mathbf{x}$ can either be the result of pre-processing of the input images $\mathbf{I}$, such as feature extraction, or the gray-scale

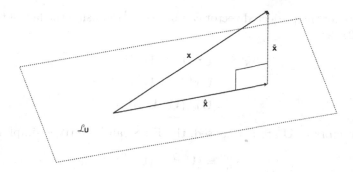

Fig. 3. Illustration of projecting the vector **x** into the subspace $\mathcal{L}_{\mathbf{U}_k}$. The norm of the projected vector $\hat{\mathbf{x}}$ tells how similar **x** is to the vectors used to construct the subspace.

images themselves. Any set of n linearly independent basis vectors $\{\mathbf{u}_1, \mathbf{u}_2, ...\mathbf{u}_n\}$, where $\mathbf{u}_i = \{w_{1,j}, w_{2,j}...w_{m,j}\}$, $w_{i,j} \in \mathbb{R}$, which can be combined into an $m \times n$ matrix $\mathbf{U} \in \mathbb{R}^{m \times n}$, span a subspace $\mathcal{L}_{\mathbf{U}}$

$$\mathcal{L}_{\mathbf{U}} = \{\mathbf{x}|\mathbf{x} = \sum_{i=1}^{n} \rho_i \mathbf{u}_i, \rho_i \in \mathbb{R}\} \tag{1}$$

where,

$$\rho_i = \mathbf{x}^T \mathbf{u}_i = \sum_{j=1}^{m} x_j w_{i,j} \tag{2}$$

While determining which class a vector **x** belongs to when projecting into each space $\mathcal{L}_{\mathbf{U}_k}$, one can either compute the norm of the residual $\tilde{\mathbf{x}}$ (refer to [16,22]), or the projected vector $\hat{\mathbf{x}}$ (refer to [17]), as depicted in Fig. 3. Alternatively, one could also compute the angle between the feature vector and the projected vector. In general, by projecting a vector on a subspace, the vector $\hat{\mathbf{x}}$ will be a reconstruction of the input vector using all vectors in the subspace.

Since one of the aforementioned methods is a function of the other, the final result is independent of the selected approach. However, while computing the projected vector, the computations can be easily visualised as a compact neural network, which renders the subspace method easy to understand. In general, the projected vector $\hat{\mathbf{x}}$ can be computed as

$$\hat{\mathbf{x}} = \sum_{i=1}^{n} (\mathbf{x}^T \mathbf{u}_i)\mathbf{u}_i \tag{3}$$

$$= \sum_{i=1}^{n} \rho_i \mathbf{u}_i \tag{4}$$

$$= \mathbf{U}^T \mathbf{U} x^T \tag{5}$$

The norm of the projected vector can be re-written using the law of transpose products [27] as:

$$||\hat{\mathbf{x}}||^2 = \mathbf{U}^T \mathbf{U} x^T \cdot \mathbf{U}^T \mathbf{U} x^T \tag{6}$$

$$= \mathbf{U} x^T \mathbf{U}^T \cdot \mathbf{U}^T \mathbf{U} x^T \tag{7}$$

$$= \mathbf{U} x^T (\mathbf{U} \cdot \mathbf{U}^T) \mathbf{U} x^T \tag{8}$$

Since the vectors in $\mathbf{U}$ are normalised, the Eq. 8 can be further simplified as,

$$||\hat{\mathbf{x}}||^2 = (\mathbf{U} x^T) \cdot (\mathbf{U} x^T) \tag{9}$$

$$= (\mathbf{U} x^T)^2 \tag{10}$$

$$= \sum_{i=1}^{n} \rho_i{}^2 \tag{11}$$

The derivation above follows from Oja and Kohonen [22] and Laaksonen [17]. As noted in [17,22], the subspace projection can be regarded as a neural network. However, they do not visualise it using the neuron metaphor, and therefore on investigating this further, we designed a neural net framework based on EPSC as in Fig. 4.

In the first stage, features x of length m are computed from the input images I of length s. Different feature extractors were tested and experimental analysis suggest the Histogram of Gradients (HoG) [5] produced better results. Significantly better results were obtained when a down-scaled version of the input image (1/4 in size) was added to the HoG feature vector. Nevertheless, the input image of length 784 was down-sized to length 340, which is down scaling to 43.37% of its original size.

Neurons compute the response ρ from weights w, using the quadratic response function $(\cdot)^2$, commonly referred to as an activation function. The response function is intended to be linear, unless in the final layer, and the mathematics of subspace defines it to be quadratic, since it is deduced from computing the norm as in Eq. 13. Also, it is suggested that the net does not perform well with other response functions. In the second layer, the weights w and the linear response function $(\cdot)$ are used. Here the response function is less important, and could potentially be replaced by other response functions. Finally, the $argmax$ is computed from the k similar nets using the same input features x, but with different weights w.

Furthermore, the output y is computed as $argmax\ \sigma_j, j = 1...k$, and suggests which subspace the feature is the most similar to. A look-up table is also necessary, since each subspace, created by t-SNE, belongs to different classes, i.e. has different labels.

The weights w in the final layer should be set to 1, according to the definition of the dot product. The results generated by using this weight and 24 vectors in the subspaces for projection are reported in Sect. 4.3. It is observed that using a fewer vectors gives more errors in the subspace reconstruction. On the other hand, using too many vectors help in generating a near perfect reconstruction,

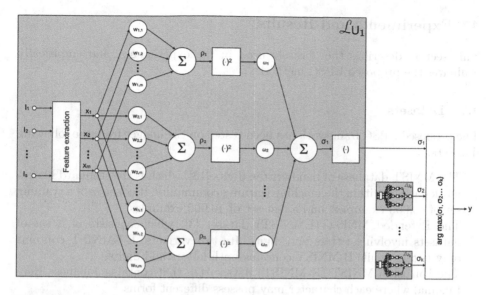

Fig. 4. Illustration of the neural net based on EPSC that is used for classification. In the first stage, features x of length m are computed from the input data I of length s. Neurons compute the response ρ from weights w, using the quadratic response function $(\cdot)^2$. In the second layer, the weights ω and the linear response function $(\cdot)$ are used. Finally, the $argmax$ is computed from the k similar nets with the same input features x, but different weights w.

making it impossible to suggest which subspace gives the strongest response. Therefore, it is reasonable to deduce that the initial vectors in the PCA are more important than the subsequent ones, and therefore different weights could be applied. A variant of EPSC, i.e. $EPCS^*$, is thus obtained, where 28 vectors were used and the weights were set to

$$\omega_i = 1 - \left(\frac{i+3}{50}\right)^2 \tag{12}$$

where i varies from 1 to n. This decaying function generated the best results for the MNIST dataset (further illustrated in Sect. 4.3), not excluding the possibility that other functions might generate comparable results. Moreover, other functions generate even better results for the other datasets, suggesting that these weight should be set by learning, rather than by a function. However, the advantage is that it is possible to make a prior good guess about what a good start value would look like.

Lastly, referring to Fig. 4, let σ be the response output function from every subspace projection $\mathcal{L}_\mathbf{U}$, then a closed-form solution of each σ is computed as a weighted sum, presented in the following equation:

$$\sigma = \sum_{i=1}^{n} \omega_i \rho_i{}^2 \tag{13}$$

4   Experiments and Results

This section describes the datasets used in the experiments, and empirically evaluates the proposed EPSC method.

4.1   Datasets

The proposed EPSC framework has been tested on the images from the following datasets:

- The MNIST database of handwritten digits [18], which is the standard benchmark dataset within the machine learning community. It consists of a training set of 60,000 examples, and a test set of 10,000 examples.
- The Extended MNIST (EMNIST) dataset [3], which consists of a set of datasets involving letters and digits. Its two variants, L-EMNIST contains only letters, while B-MNIST contains both letters and digits.
- The Kuzushiji-MNIST (K-MNIST) dataset [2], that contains Japanese Hentaigana, where each character may possess different forms.
- The Fashion MNIST (F-MNIST) [34] dataset, that contains miniature images of clothes and bags.

These datasets are popularly used in the research community, where all but F-MNIST and K-MNIST datasets contain handwritten digits and letters. They posses a similar format, that makes it easy to evaluate them on a variety of learning methods. However, even though the main focus of this work is on the classification of handwritten letters, it is worth investigating the performance of the proposed method on datasets such as F-MNIST (containing images of clothes and bags) and K-MNIST (containing signs) in order to highlight the importance of the EPSC method in diverse applications.

4.2   Hyperparameters Selection

Deep learning based methods often require several hyperparameters to be fine-tuned, which typically requires expert knowledge and the classification process is quite sensitive to the parameter settings [7]. Automatic hyperparameter optimisation has therefore become an important research field in itself [10,11]. In the proposed EPSC framework, we intend to use the default parameter settings of t-SNE, clustering method and PCA, and only one parameter was fine-tuned in embedding. This is to render the proposed framework to be simple and easy to understand. The fine-tuning of internal parameters and exploration of methods such as UMAP is desired as future work.

The main parameter that was fine-tuned is in the KDE algorithm, where the Silverman's rule of thumb [19] was used as the base level for computing the bandwidth h of the clustering,

$$h = \left(\frac{4\sigma^5}{3n} \right)^{1/5} \tag{14}$$

where σ is the standard deviation of n samples. h is computed as the optimal value from the distribution of points, and the experimental evaluations deem $0.5\,h$ to be the best value across the datasets. In the validation phase, the value of h can be varied in order to find the optimal setting.

Furthermore, PCA does not require additional parameters for constructing the subspaces. However, the selection of the number of vectors in the subspace is crucial. Experimental analysis suggest using 24 vectors for EPSC and 28 vectors for EPSC* for the MNIST dataset, where EPSC* uses the weights in Eq. 12. One might suspect that this is a value that depends on the size of the feature vectors, and perhaps even the features themselves. Nonetheless, this is also a value that can be optimised in a validation phase of the data in question.

4.3   Results

The experimental results are presented in Table 1. The proposed EPSC method, along with its variant EPSC* are compared to several popular learning methods using datasets that include MNIST, EMNIST, L-EMNIST, B-EMNIST, K-MNIST and F-MNIST. Note that we have compared our method with the method presented in the papers for different datasets. We do not claim to have done a complete comparison to all kinds of deep learning methods. Instead, the purpose is to show that the proposed method performs almost as good as the methods proposed in those papers. It can also be mentioned that a large number of classifiers such as Random Forrest, Linear SVC and Logistic Regression, etc, with non of them performing better than EPSC. Following are the learning methods of importance:

- Multilayer perceptron (MLP) and Convolutional Neural Network (CNN) by Rauber et al. [23].
- Keras CNN by Clanuwat et al. [2] that uses Keras Simple CNN Benchmark (the python deep learning library) and PreActResNet-18, which is a deep residual network [9].
- OPIUM [25] used by Cohen et al. [3], which is a kind of Extreme Learning Machine [6].
- MLP by Xiao and Rasul [34] for evaluating the MNIST and the F-MNIST datasets.

It is observed from Table 1 that the variant of the proposed EPSC method i.e. EPSC* achieves slightly better accuracy than EPSC. This suggests the possibility of adding learning via back propagation in the second layer, and even adding more layers. Nevertheless, with reference to all datasets used in the experiments, the proposed method is found to be most consistent and stable in performance. The main advantage of the proposed EPSC framework as conveyed in Table 1 is that it corresponds to a simple neural network, and still achieved comparable performance to sophisticated learning methods. Deep learning based methods require extensive training, however, the proposed EPSC method required only a single training phase via the t-SNE embedding, and the subsequent clustering and PCA. In total, the EPSC method completed the run in just 10 min on

Table 1. Evaluation results on popular datasets and comparison with other learning methods. Note that we have taken the results from each paper proposing these methods and therefore the table is not covering the use of all methods on all datasets.

Learning method	MNIST	EMNIST	L-EMNIST	B-EMNIST	K-MNIST	F-MNIST
Proposed EPSC	99.07%	99.15%	92.29%	85.37%	96.68%	87.31%
Proposed EPSC*	99.20%	**99.22%**	**92.40%**	**85.87%**	96.92%	**88.12%**
OPIUM [3]	-	96.22%	85.15%	78.02%	-	-
MLP [34]	97.20%	-	-	-	-	87.1 %
Keras CNN [2]	99.06%	-	-	-	95.12%	-
PreActResNet-18 [2]	99.56%	-	-	-	**97.82%**	-
MLP [23]	98.52%	-	-	-	-	-
CNN [23]	**99.62%**	-	-	-	-	-

a standard laptop for the MNIST dataset, unlike other learning methods that require several hours to run and intensive GPU resources. Therefore, a close to state-of-the-art accuracy is achieved by the proposed method in a fast and efficient manner, without the need of additional computational resources.

5   Conclusion

A novel learning framework for classification of handwritten letters is presented in this paper that is based on subspaces, with advantages such as easy to comprehend and visualise with mathematically well-defined components. The methodology is tested on well-known publicly available datasets. Preliminary experimental evaluation indicates that the proposed method achieved close to state-of-the-art performance by using subspace learning method, without the need of using exhaustive computational resources. Future work includes exploring and further investigating such methods by understanding the theoretical and mathematical foundations, and generating comparable performance to deep learning with a low computational cost. We intend to improve the accuracy further by adding more layers, and also improving the computational time of the method to a fraction of seconds for real-time processing.

References

1. Carbon, M., Hallin, M., Tat Tran, L.: Kernel density estimation for random fields: the l 1 theory. J. Nonparametric Stat. **6**(2–3), 157–170 (1996)
2. Clanuwat, T., Bober-Irizar, M., Kitamoto, A., Lamb, A., Yamamoto, K., Ha, D.: Deep learning for classical Japanese literature. CoRR abs/1812.01718 (2018). http://arxiv.org/abs/1812.01718
3. Cohen, G., Afshar, S., Tapson, J., van Schaik, A.: EMNIST: an extension of MNIST to handwritten letters. CoRR abs/1702.05373 (2017). http://arxiv.org/abs/1702.05373

4. Comaniciu, D., Meer, P.: Mean shift: a robust approach toward feature space analysis. IEEE Trans. Pattern Anal. Mach. Intell. **24**(5), 603–619 (2002). https://doi.org/10.1109/34.1000236
5. Dalal, N., Triggs, B.: Histograms of oriented gradients for human detection. In: 2005 IEEE Computer Society Conference on Computer Vision and Pattern Recognition (CVPR 2005), vol. 1, pp. 886–893, June 2005. https://doi.org/10.1109/CVPR.2005.177
6. Ding, S., Zhao, H., Zhang, Y., Xu, X., Nie, R.: Extreme learning machine: algorithm, theory and applications. Artif. Intell. Rev. **44**(1), 103–115 (2015). https://doi.org/10.1007/s10462-013-9405-z
7. Domhan, T., Springenberg, J.T., Hutter, F.: Speeding up automatic hyperparameter optimization of deep neural networks by extrapolation of learning curves. In: Proceedings of the 24th International Conference on Artificial Intelligence, IJCAI 2015, pp. 3460–3468. AAAI Press (2015). http://dl.acm.org/citation.cfm?id=2832581.2832731
8. Dutta, K., Krishnan, P., Mathew, M., Jawahar, C.: Improving CNN-RNN hybrid networks for handwriting recognition. In: 2018 16th International Conference on Frontiers in Handwriting Recognition (ICFHR), pp. 80–85. IEEE (2018)
9. He, K., Zhang, X., Ren, S., Sun, J.: Deep residual learning for image recognition. In: 2016 IEEE Conference on Computer Vision and Pattern Recognition (CVPR), pp. 770–778 (2016)
10. Ilievski, I., Akhtar, T., Feng, J., Shoemaker, C.: Efficient hyperparameter optimization for deep learning algorithms using deterministic RBF surrogates (2017). https://aaai.org/ocs/index.php/AAAI/AAAI17/paper/view/14312
11. Jamieson, K., Talwalkar, A.: Non-stochastic best arm identification and hyperparameter optimization. In: Gretton, A., Robert, C.C. (eds.) Proceedings of the 19th International Conference on Artificial Intelligence and Statistics. Proceedings of Machine Learning Research, vol. 51, pp. 240–248. PMLR, Cadiz, Spain, 09–11 May 2016. http://proceedings.mlr.press/v51/jamieson16.html
12. Kohonen, T., Lehtiö, P., Rovamo, J., Hyvärinen, J., Bry, K., Vainio, L.: A principle of neural associative memory. Neuroscience **2**(6), 1065–1076 (1977). https://doi.org/10.1016/0306-4522(77)90129-4. http://www.sciencedirect.com/science/article/pii/0306452277901294
13. Kohonen, T., Oja, E.: Fast adaptive formation of orthogonalizing filters and associative memory in recurrent networks of neuron-like elements. Biol. Cybern. **21**(2), 85–95 (1976). https://doi.org/10.1007/BF01259390
14. Kohonen, T., Reuhkala, E., Mäkisara, K., Vainio, L.: Associative recall of images. Biol. Cybern. **22**(3), 159–168 (1976). https://doi.org/10.1007/BF00365526
15. Krishnan, P., Dutta, K., Jawahar, C.: Word spotting and recognition using deep embedding. In: 2018 13th IAPR International Workshop on Document Analysis Systems (DAS), pp. 1–6. IEEE (2018)
16. Laaksonen, J., Aksela, M., Oja, E., Kangas, J.: Adaptive local subspace classifier in on-line recognition of handwritten characters. In: IJCNN 1999 International Joint Conference on Neural Networks. Proceedings (Cat. No. 99CH36339), vol. 4, pp. 2812–2815, July 1999. https://doi.org/10.1109/IJCNN.1999.833527
17. Laaksonen, J.: Subspace classifiers in recognition of handwritten digits, 07 May 1997. http://urn.fi/urn:nbn:fi:tkk-001249
18. LeCun, Y., Cortes, C., Burges, C.: Mnist handwritten digit database. AT&T Labs (2010). http://yann.lecun.com/exdb/mnist2

19. Läuter, H.: Silverman, B.W.: Density Estimation for Statistics and Data Analysis. Chapman & Hall, London, p. 175 (1986). £12.—. Biometrical Journal **30**(7), 876–877 (1988). https://doi.org/10.1002/bimj.4710300745

20. Maaten, L.v.d., Hinton, G.: Visualizing data using t-SNE. J. Mach. Learn. Res. **9**, 2579–2605 (2008)

21. McInnes, L., Healy, J.: UMAP: uniform manifold approximation and projection for dimension reduction. arXiv e-prints, February 2018

22. Oja, E., Kohonen, T.: The subspace learning algorithm as a formalism for pattern recognition and neural networks. In: IEEE 1988 International Conference on Neural Networks, vol. 1, pp. 277–284, July 1988. https://doi.org/10.1109/ICNN.1988.23858

23. Rauber, P.E., Fadel, S.G., Falcão, A.X., Telea, A.C.: Visualizing the hidden activity of artificial neural networks. IEEE Trans. Vis. Comput. Graph. **23**(1), 101–110 (2017). https://doi.org/10.1109/TVCG.2016.2598838

24. Roerdink, J.B., Meijster, A.: The watershed transform: definitions, algorithms and parallelization strategies. Fundam. Inf. **41**(1,2), 187–228 (2000). http://dl.acm.org/citation.cfm?id=2372488.2372495

25. van Schaik, A., Tapson, J.: Online and adaptive pseudoinverse solutions for ELM weights. Neurocomputing **149**(PA), 233–238 (2015). https://doi.org/10.1016/j.neucom.2014.01.071

26. Shapshak, P.: Artificial intelligence and brain. Bioinformation **14**(1), 38 (2018)

27. Shores, T.S.: Applied Linear Algebra and Matrix Analysis, p. 104. Springer Publisher, New York (2007). https://doi.org/10.1007/978-0-387-48947-6

28. Sudholt, S., Fink, G.A.: PHOCNET: a deep convolutional neural network for word spotting in handwritten documents. In: ICFHR, pp. 277–282. IEEE Computer Society (2016)

29. Turk, M., Pentland, A.: Eigenfaces for recognition. J. Cogn. Neurosci. **3**(1), 71–86 (1991). https://doi.org/10.1162/jocn.1991.3.1.71

30. Vincent, L., Soille, P.: Watersheds in digital spaces: an efficient algorithm based on immersion simulations. IEEE Trans. Pattern Anal. Mach. Intell. **13**(6), 583–598 (1991). https://doi.org/10.1109/34.87344

31. Watanabe, S., Pakvasa, N.: Subspace method in pattern recognition. In: 1st International Joint Conference on Pattern Recognition, Washington DC, pp. 25–32 (1973)

32. Watanabe, W., Lambert, P.F., Kulikowski, C.A., Buxto, J.L., Walker, R.: Evaluation and selection of variables in pattern recognition, vol. 2, pp. 91–122. Academic Press, New York (1967)

33. Wold, S., Esbensen, K., Geladi, P.: Principal component analysis. Chemom. Intell. Lab. Syst. **2**(1–3), 37–52 (1987)

34. Xiao, H., Rasul, K., Vollgraf, R.: Fashion-mnist: a novel image dataset for benchmarking machine learning algorithms. CoRR abs/1708.07747 (2017). http://arxiv.org/abs/1708.07747

Author Index

Printed in the United States
By Bookmasters